Human Cognition

R. Kim Guenther

Hamline University

PRENTICE HALL, Upper Saddle River, NJ 07458

Library of Congress Cataloging-in-Publication Data

GUENTHER, R. KIM.
    Human cognition/R. Kim Guenther.
        p.   cm.
    Includes bibliographical references and index.
    ISBN 0-13-140294-3
    1. Cognitive psychology.   2. Cognition.   I. Title.
BF311.G777   1998
    153—dc21   97-8651
                                                         CIP

Editorial Director: Nancy Roberts
Executive Editor: Bill Webber
Director of Production and Manufacturing: Barbara Kittle
Senior Managing Editor: Bonnie Biller
Production Editor: Randy Pettit
Editorial Assistant: Anita Castro
Manufacturing Manager: Nick Sklitsis
Prepress and Manufacturing Buyer: Tricia Kenny
Marketing Director: Gina Sluss
Marketing Manager: Mike Alread
Cover Design: Bruce Kenselaar
Cover Art: Tara Sosrowardoyo/Gamma Liason, Inc.

This book was set in 10/12 Palatino by Pub-Set
and printed and bound by R. R. Donnelly & Sons
The cover was printed by Phoenix

© 1998 by Prentice-Hall Inc.
Simon & Schuster/A Viacom Company
Upper Saddle River, New Jersey 07458

Printed in the United States of America
10   9   8   7   6   5   4   3   2   1

ISBN 0-13-140294-3

Prentice-Hall International (UK) Limited, *London*
Prentice-Hall of Australia Pty. Limited, *Sydney*
Prentice-Hall Canada Inc., *Toronto*
Prentice-Hall Hispanoamerica, S.A., *Mexico*
Prentice-Hall of India Private Limited, *New Delhi*
Prentice-Hall of Japan, Inc., *Tokyo*
Simon & Schuster Asia Pte. Ltd., *Singapore*
Editora Prentice-Hall do Brasil, Ltda., *Rio de Janeiro*

Contents

5   *Implicit and Semantic Memory*   157

6   *The Physiology of Learning and Remembering*   199

7   *Reasoning and Rationality*   232

9   *Individual Differences in Cognition*   313

Preface

"What a piece of work is man! How noble in reason!" Shakespeare's Hamlet may have been sarcastic in his description of humankind, but cognitive scientists are sincere in their appreciation of the wonder of human cognition. Even in the most mundane of activities, the express and admirable qualities of our mental faculties reveal themselves. A mother of two awakens from a dream of travel in a far-off land to the cries of her newborn infant and immediately perceives that her infant is hungry. Perhaps the awakening reminds her that her firstborn is now a walking, talking child of 4 who finally sleeps through the night without waking up. Perhaps she wonders how she can accommodate the demands of her second child and still get the sleep she needs to function effectively during the day. Maybe she will solicit the help of her husband, the baby's father, asking him to bring the baby to bed, to change the baby's diapers, and to return the baby to the crib.

This example illustrations the amazing capabilities of the human mind. Consciousness, perception, memory, reasoning, problem solving, and language are so much a part of our moment-to-moment lives that we easily overlook the intricate and impressive mental processes that make them possible. It is the cognitive scientist who seeks to explain how we accomplish such mental feats, using the techniques of science—controlled observation and hypothesis testing—to try to find the answers. And it is for writers of textbooks like this one to summarize the accomplishments of those cognitive scientists.

Customarily, textbook writers try to justify their work by demonstrating how their textbook is different from and an improvement on the textbooks that have come before. In this book I cover the same topics covered in most other books on the subject. But this book differs from others in several ways. The most important difference is that I focus on what I regard as the essential themes, issues, and controversies that inspire and shape the field of cognitive science. I hope to instill in you, the reader, an interest in cognitive psychology and a sense of the field's implications for the larger society. I do this by organizing each chapter around an important issue designed to explore the essential and enduring contrast between differing perspectives that inform cognitive scientists' thinking on the chapter's topic.

I'll illustrate what I mean with my chapter on memory. Most textbooks discussing memory describe a collection of models and experimental paradigms that have to do with storing and retrieving data located in a short- or a long-term memory. I try to step back from this morass of information about memory and ask what I think is a key question about memory: What is a good metaphor for how human memory works? Historically, the dominant answer is that memory is a storage system for keeping records of past experiences, and that remembering involves searching through and "reading" the memory records that are retrieved. In my chapter on memory I criticize this metaphor and suggest instead that memory is designed not to recapitulate the past but to anticipate the future. Memory is a constructive process. The human cognitive systems for perceiving, thinking, and acting change as a function of our experiences but do not keep a record-by-record account of those experiences. Remembering, according to the constructionist metaphor, is not reexperiencing the past but reconstructing a plausible version of the past based on current knowledge. I am able to discuss most of the important research on memory in the context of this contrast between the record-keeping and the constructionist perspectives and so integrate the memory research. A discussion of the constructionist model also enhances an appreciation of how a metaphor for memory has implications for evaluating eyewitness reporting, for understanding problem solving, and for devising educational practices.

In each chapter, then, I look for a theme that represents an interesting and ongoing debate about the essential nature of cognition, and organize the material around that theme. My hope is that each chapter reads as an independent, well-integrated essay. However, I extend themes across chapters. Constructionism, for example, makes its appearance in the chapter on perception (where a constructed view of perception is contrasted with direct perception) and in the chapters on memory, implicit and semantic memory, and the physiology of learning and remembering. In some cases I take a distinct point of view, as, for example, when I write in support of a constructionist model rather than a record-keeping model of memory. I think writing is more interesting and science more realistically portrayed when a scientific text is written with a point of view—provided, of course, that the point of view is warranted by the evidence.

Let me mention five other differences between my textbook and most others on the subject. First, I cover more adequately the neurophysiology of cognitive functions, although at a somewhat more simplified level than ordinarily would be the case in a neurophysiology textbook. In addition to the chapter on the physiology of learning and remembering, I cover the physiology of consciousness, perception, problem solving, individual differences, language, and cognitive development in the chapters in which those topics are discussed.

Second, I make extensive use of ecologically oriented research. For example, in the memory chapter I cite John Dean's Watergate testimony and an experiment in which participants in a seminar try to recollect who attended the last meeting, in order to make a point about what people ordinarily return from experiences. By focusing on research in natural contexts, I hope to make research ideas clearer and more interesting to students. At the same time, a more ecologically oriented approach reflects the field's increased emphasis on ecological validity.

Third, I highlight neural net models (also known as connectionist or parallel distributed processing models). Neural nets are models of an idealized brain, designed to simulate the brain's essential properties that are thought to give rise to mental phenomena. Neural net modeling has certainly become a dominant influence in the field in the last fifteen years. Neural nets are featured prominently in the introductory chapter, where you will find a beer-guzzling neural net, and in the chapter on the physiology of learning and remembering, where you will find a neural net that discriminates between the music of two fictional rock-and-roll bands. Neural nets also make brief appearances in the chapters on consciousness and on implicit and semantic memory. I also discuss some of the limitations of neural net approaches to human cognition.

Fourth, I include topics important to the field but usually covered minimally, if at all, in most other textbooks. These topics include the neural basis of consciousness, sleep and dreams, repression, individual differences in cognition, and the evolution of human language and cognitive capacity. The latter topic reflects another growing influence in the field—namely, the idea that many properties of human cognition are adaptive in a Darwinian sense.

Fifth, I end each chapter with a summary and set of recommended readings. My summaries are a bit longer than those in most other textbooks in order to help you better integrate and remember the material in the chapter. I tried to pick readings that would be interesting as well as informative. You will even find a couple of films and works of fiction among my recommendations. The book itself is summarized in the epilogue, where I review the essential themes discussed throughout the book.

Customarily, prefaces end with the author acknowledging those who helped with the book. I would like to thank the original acquisitions editor, Susan Brennan, for her faith in this project, and the editors who helped me see the book through to completion, Nicole Signoretti, Virginia Rubers, Ilene Kalish, and Randy Pettit. Ilene was especially helpful in the last frantic weeks before the manuscript was due, Virginia's copyediting greatly improved the prose, and Randy did a superb job in overseeing the final production of the textbook. I would also like to thank the following reviewers who read drafts of the manuscript and offered advice on how to improve it: Robert G. Crowder, Yale University; Susan Dutch, Westfield State College; Ira Fischler, University of Florida; Peter Gordon, University of North Carolina–Chapel Hill; David K. Hogberg, Albion College; Paul E. Jose, Loyola University of Chicago; F. Philip Rice, University of Maine; Edward S. Wood, University of Wisconsin, La Crosse. If you, the reviewers, manage to read it again, you will see that the book incorporates many of your suggestions. Most of all I thank my family—my wife Donna, who loves me and believes in me more than I do in myself; my son Jacob, who is my real creation; and my father Robert, who instilled in me a sense of love of and enthusiasm for education. God bless you all.

—*R. Kim Guenther*

1 *Introduction and Historical Overview*

What is human cognitive psychology? It is usually defined as an inquiry into how people acquire and use knowledge. The study of human cognition concerns itself with questions such as: What explains consciousness? How do we perceive the outside world? How do we remember our past? How do we learn and use concepts? How and how well do we reason and solve problems? What accounts for individual differences in intelligence? How do we acquire and use language? What enables children to become mentally competent adults?

In the modern world, the study of human cognition is a science. The essential assumption made by cognitive scientists is that cognitive phenomena, such as reasoning and remembering, are caused by orderly and self-regulating physical processes intrinsic to the arrangement of matter and energy in the brain. These are the same sorts of physical processes that underlie biology or physics. Adopting a scientific approach to human cognition means that the methods of science, such as hypothesis testing and controlled observation, may be usefully applied to the study of human mental life.

But the idea that mental processes reflect physical processes has only recently become widely accepted in our culture. A few centuries ago, Western culture took a radically different perspective on human cognition. To illustrate, consider how we understand dreams. Current theories explain dreaming as the result of activation of the cortex by the brain stem (Hobson, 1988). If we go back a few centuries to medieval Europe, however, we find that people thought that dreams had nothing to do with brain processes. Instead, even well-educated people had a supernatural explanation for dreams; they believed that dreams were prophetic warnings or messages from the gods. Unlike physical processes, supernatural phenomena are miraculous, unpredictable, and sometimes divinely inspired. The main topic of this introductory chapter is a discussion of the important events in our history that brought about the transition from the predominantly supernatural perspective that characterized the cosmology of medieval Europe to the natural perspective on human mental life that characterizes the cosmology of our modern culture. Much of what follows comes from Eiseley (1972), who provides a superb account of how Western culture came to view the world as natural.

SECTION 1: THE EMERGENCE
OF THE NATURAL PERSPECTIVE

THE WORLD BECOMES NATURAL

Part of the supernatural perspective of medieval Europe included the idea that humans have a unique place in the world of creation. According to this supernatural perspective, God created the world for humans, who are God's most important creation. Supposedly, we are made in God's image—not in the sense that we physically resemble God, who is, after all, a purely spiritual entity, but in the sense that we possess a free will. A rock rolling downhill or a bird flying south in the winter cannot be said to choose its action; but a person deciding to ignore another person's suffering, for example, is free to make that decision and so is responsible for it. One indication of the centrality of humans in the supernatural perspective was the strongly held belief that the earth is the center of the universe. If the universe exists for humans, if humans occupy a quasi-divine status that distinguishes them from the rest of the physical world, then it makes sense that all the other heavenly bodies ought to revolve around humanity's home place.

The year 1543 saw the beginning of the demise of the supernatural viewpoint. It was in that year that Nicolaus Copernicus (1473–1543), a Polish astronomer, published his remarkable thesis that the sun, not the earth, is the center of the solar system. His argument was based on the idea that one could more easily explain the motion of planets and the sun across the sky if one assumes that all planets revolve around the sun, except the moon, which revolves around the earth. Prior to Copernicus, astronomers had developed rather complicated models of the wandering motions of the planets in order to keep their worldview consistent with the notion that all planets revolved around the earth. The Copernican model provided a more parsimonious account of the solar system.

You can see the shattering implication of Copernicus's thesis, also called the heliocentric theory, for human centrality. The earth and the humans who live on the earth are not at the center of the universe, and so humans do not necessarily have some unique or quasi-divine status that sets them apart from the rest of the physical universe. About a century later, Galileo (1564–1642) championed the heliocentric theory and consequently ran into opposition from the Catholic Church, which threatened him with imprisonment. Galileo also observed that there were moons circling Jupiter and that our moon had mountains on it much like earth's mountains. His theories helped advance the notion that the earth's terrain and location in the cosmos are not unique. Isaac Newton (1642–1727) discovered the laws of motion, which he described with mathematical equations, and speculated about the cosmic machine. Newton, and others before him, notably Johann Kepler (1571–1630), imagined that the cosmos ran something like a giant clock that, once wound, was self-regulating and so could run itself without the need for divine intervention. James Hutton (1726–1797) applied Newtonian principles to the geology of the earth and concluded that natural forces, like erosion or the gradual uprising of land formations, shaped our world's landscape. The earth's present-day features have their origin in natural, not supernatural, forces. And so the physical, inorganic universe became natural, and humankind's place in that universe became ordinary.

LIFE BECOMES NATURAL

As the physical universe became natural, so too did the biological universe. By the 18th century, scientists understood the essential roles of the major body parts—for example, that the heart pumps blood, the intestines digest food, and the brain processes thoughts.

The 1800s saw an explosion of knowledge about biology and physiology. One of the outstanding scientists of the day was Hermann von Helmholtz (1821–1894), one of the founders of modern experimental physiological psychology. Helmholtz argued against a widely held view called **vitalism** that maintains that life requires the presence of a life force whose nature is not physical but spiritual. (Words in bold are defined in the text.) Without the life force, vitalists claimed, a creature would die. Contrary to vitalism, Helmholtz was able to demonstrate that food and oxygen consumption could account for all the energy an organism is able to expend. So there is no need to postulate the existence of a life force. Virtually no biologist today believes that an accounting of the nature of life requires any mysterious vital spirit (see Kahl, 1971, for selected writings of Helmholtz; also, Boring, 1950, and Hergenhahn, 1986, provide discussions of Helmholtz's contributions).

Arguably the most important biological insight of the 1800s was the theory of evolution proposed by people like Chevalier de Lamarck (1744–1829), Alfred Wallace (1823–1913), and Charles Darwin (1809–1892). The main claim of evolution is that the origin of any species is to be found in natural, evolutionary changes in predecessor species and not in divine miracles. The theory of evolution begins wih the observation that offspring of any species vary from one another and that only a small proportion of the offspring ever survive into adulthood. If a member of a species possesses an attribute that enhances its survivability (or, more accurately, its capacity to reproduce) then it is likely to reproduce more offspring than the member that does not possess that attribute. If the attribute is coded for in the genes, then it is likely to be passed on to the member's offspring, enhancing their capacity to reproduce as well. For example, a faster deer is more likely to survive and reproduce than a slower deer, and so is more likely to transmit the genetic basis for its superior speed to its offspring. Over time the species becomes more fleet-footed. **Mutations**, errors in genetic replication, also contribute to variability in a species. Typically, a mutation undermines survivability, but occasionally the mutation is beneficial to a member of a species and may be passed on to its offspring. After many generations, a portion of the population may become sufficiently dissimilar to the original species that a new species comes into existence.

The environment plays an important role in evolution. When the environment changes, then attributes that had been maladaptive can become adaptive. For example, when the climate cooled during the ice ages, animals with an abnormally thick coat, who in a warm climate would be likely to die off, could now outsurvive and therefore outreproduce their thin-coated kin and pass the thick-coated trait to their offspring.

As the doctrine of evolution developed, people realized that extinction of species plays an important role in the origin of a new species. Extinction opens up ecological niches into which new species can evolve to fit. For example, mammals remained mostly small, rodentlike creatures for about 100 million years until, about 65 million years ago, dinosaurs and other large reptiles became extinct. Mammals then evolved into a wide variety of forms, including the simians (monkeys and apes), which began to evolve about 35 million years ago. It is from apes that human species evolved, beginning about 5 to 7 million years ago. People in our culture were at first reluctant to believe in extinction. Perhaps they feared that if an animal species can become extinct, then so too could humans. Perhaps the purpose of the cosmos had nothing to do with the creation of humans.

The evolutionary doctrine has profound implications for understanding our nature. Human origins are not a consequence of divine intervention but of a natural process intrinsic to the nature of reproductive and developmental mechanisms and the interaction of living things with the physical environment. The evolutionary doctrine has made our species a part of the ordinary biological world.

Dualism or Materalism?—The Mind Becomes Natural

Over a period of several centuries, then, the physical and living worlds came to be perceived as governed by physical mechanisms that are orderly and self-regulating, but not spiritual, in their essential character. But can the same be said of our thought processes, feelings, and fantasies? Might it be the case that the rest of the biological world and even human bodies are governed by natural, physical processes, but human minds remain outside the natural realm? Probably the most famous advocate of this view, called **dualism**, was the French philosopher and scientist René Descartes (1596–1650). A translation of relevant works by Descartes may be found in Haldane and Rose (1931; see also Churchland, 1988; Flew, 1964; Gardner, 1985).

Dualism

The essential idea of dualism is that reality consists of two parts. One part is ordinary matter that occupies space and behaves according to physical laws. The brains and bodies of humans and other animals are made of matter and so may be regarded as physical mechanisms. The other part of reality consists of a radically different substance that does not obey ordinary physical laws and does not occupy space but, instead, has as its main feature the capacity to think. What we call the human mind is made of this nonspatial thinking substance. Thus, human mental phenomena are caused not by physical processes in the brain but by the autonomous actions of a nonmaterial, spiritual substance that has the capability of affecting the human brain. The brain is only the medium through which the thoughts of the mind affect the material world.

Some versions of dualism, like Descartes's version (also called **substance dualism**), claim that the mind-substance can exist independently of the body. Another version of dualism, sometimes called **property dualism**, claims that a complex brain brings into existence the mind, which then has emergent properties unlike those that characterize the physical world. According to property dualism, a mind cannot exist independently of a brain. All versions of dualism, though, make the important claims that the mind is fundamentally nonmaterial, does not obey physical laws, and can serve as the original cause of actions taken by the body.

Descartes provided several lines of evidence for dualism. He noted that when we observe the physical world we see matter in motion, but when we reflect on our thoughts we do not perceive brain tissue. Instead, we perceive ideas, images, and feelings. An especially compelling intuition we have about ourselves is that we can initiate action independently of bodily states or external stimuli. That is to say, it seems to us that we have free will, that the self is a first cause of the voluntary actions we take, that the self is an autonomous agent. For example, you would probably agree that it seems to you that you are free to continue to read this chapter, take a nap, or practice yodeling. Whatever you decide to do, it seems as though your mind does the choosing. Descartes believed that the apparent ability of the mind to initiate actions on its own, independently of the body, is the most important dissimilarity between the mind and physical processes. A physical process never really initiates action. There must always be an antecedent physical process that gives rise to it.

Descartes discussed other evidence in favor of dualism. He pointed out that while humans and other animals all possess brains, only humans use language or are capable of sophisticated reasoning. He noted that things in the physical world, like brains, are extended substances (i.e., have length, width, and depth). Extended substances can have their extended properties measured. The average human brain, for example, has a volume of about 1,400 cubic centimeters. Given such measurement, one can meaningfully calculate the volume of 100 brains, or the square root of the volume of a single brain. But mental processes are unextended and so cannot be similarly measured. Consider how meaningless is the notion of the square root of the volume of a creative thought. Descartes also suggested that it is possible to doubt the existence of anything in the physical world, including one's own body. Who has not had the thought that maybe everything in the world is only a product of one's own imagination? But because we have mental experiences, we cannot doubt our own existence. This is the meaning behind Descartes's famous pronouncement, "I think, therefore I am." The body's existence can be doubted but the mind's existence cannot be doubted, therefore the body and the mind must constitute different realms of reality. Descartes, a devout Christian, believed in life after death. Because the body certainly decays in death, what survives must be something nonphysical.

Dualistic views of the relationship between the mind and the body seem to provide a kind of loophole for the supernatural perspective on the human mind. The entire universe, even the human body, may be properly regarded as natural, but not the human mind, which is not part of the physical world and so not governed by natural law. Thus dualism denies the possibility of a cognitive science that is in any way analogous to the physical or biological sciences.

But a belief in dualism introduces a perplexing complication. It is obvious that events in the physical world can affect a person's mental state. A blow to the head can render a person unconscious, a stroke in the left cerebral hemisphere can render a person mute, alcohol ingestion can impair a person's judgment. How is it that a nonphysical substance like the mind can be affected by the physical world? One response a property dualist might make is to concede that the brain causes the nonphysical mind to come into existence; consequently, if the brain is degraded by damage, it would follow that the mind would be degraded as well. But there still remains the problem of how a nonphysical mind can affect the brain. For example, a woman who nurses her infant can initiate the let-down reflex—whereby the breast reflexively becomes engorged with milk—merely by thinking about her infant. If the mind is nonphysical, what gives it the capability of interacting with the physical world of neurons and muscles? This is the problem of mind–body interaction and it is one that Descartes and other dualists have never been able to solve to the philosophical community's satisfaction (Churchland, 1988).

In the centuries since Descartes, and especially in the 20th century, we have continued to learn more about how electrical and chemical processes taking place in the brain give rise to perceptions, language, dreams, emotions, and memories. We have studied carefully the victims of brain trauma and stroke to see where and how the brain damage exerts its crippling effect. We have models to explain how drugs like barbiturates and amphetamines alter neural functioning and so produce mood changes. Collectively, this evidence undermines the dualist position. Phenomena we label mental appear to be a consequence of physical events, so there seems no need to postulate the existence of a kind of ghostly mental entity to explain perception, or reasoning, or voluntary choice.

Evolution, a doctrine developed two centuries after the time of Descartes, proved to be another blow to the dualist position. If humans evolved from animals, and animals are part of the natural world, as Descartes conceded, then what accounts for the origin of an immaterial mind? The dualist could claim that a brain must reach a certain degree of complexity before a mind will inhabit it or before a nonphysical mind will emerge from it, but those claims amount to saying that brain complexity is the source of human mental phenomena.

Materialism

So dualism may not be a loophole for those who are committed to a supernatural perspective on the mind. Discoveries in the field of neurophysiology and the doctrine of evolution spawned a widespread rejection of dualism and a growing consensus favoring a view, called **materialism**, that argues that the mind is simply a label for the way the brain functions. The materialist sees no reason to claim that there is a separate realm of reality called the mental realm that stands apart from the physical realm; instead, there is only the physical brain whose function it is to do things we label mental. By way of analogy, we would not say that transportation is a spiritual entity that inhabits a physical contraption called an automobile; rather, transportation is the function provided by the mechanical operations of the automobile. Digestion serves as another analogy illustrating materialism. It is the function of the stomach to digest food; we need not postulate a digestive force that mystically interacts with stomachs in order to account for digestion. Materialism says that mind is to brain as digestion is to stomach or transportation is to automobile. It is worth noting that materialism is not a modern invention; in ancient times there were Greeks (for example, Epicurus, about 342 to 270 B.C.E.) and Romans (Lucretius, about 96 to 55 B.C.E.) who claimed that what we call mind reflects the actions of the body and nothing more. It is also worth noting that although materialism today enjoys widespread acceptance in the scientific community, dualism retains a greater popular acceptance.

If what we call mind, including consciousness, is merely a label for how the brain functions, then why is it that our introspections do not yield images of nerves firing, of organs secreting hormones, or of neurotransmitters migrating across synaptic clefts? Indeed, if you had not been told, you would not necessarily know that the brain has anything to do with mental phenomena. Many ancient Greeks, among them Aristotle (384 to 322 B.C.E.), believed that the center of feeling and reasoning was the heart, while the brain's function was to regulate body temperature. The materialist response to the introspection problem is that we possess no sensory apparatus to detect the neural properties of the brain. We have nothing analogous to an internal microscope that can be focused on bits and pieces of neural tissue. Consider that the temperature of air reflects the degree to which air molecules move; faster motion is perceived as warmer air. Yet when we experience hot or cold we do not perceive the movement of air molecules; still, that is what gives rise to the experience of temperature. We lack sensory apparatus to detect air molecule movement just as we lack sensory apparatus to detect brain processes. So, of course, our introspections do not contain any perception of those processes (Churchland, 1988).

SECTION 2: THE EMERGENCE OF COGNITIVE SCIENCE

Once the groundwork was laid for regarding the mind as a natural phenomenon, a science of cognition as a distinct and scientific enterprise emerged (see Boring, 1950, or Hergenhahn, 1986). The central tenet of cognitive science is that the mind reflects only the physical processes of the brain, so that the methods of hypothesis testing and experimentation that have proven fruitful in other sciences are useful for the study of human mental life as well. **Cognitive science**, which may be defined as the scientific study of mental processes, is really an umbrella term subsuming several allied approaches to the study of human mental life. In this and subsequent sections I will point out the various disciplines that constitute cognitive science.

COGNITIVE SCIENCE IN THE NINETEENTH CENTURY

Psychologists working in the 1800s became especially interested in developing a connection between neural and cognitive processes. Much of this work was (and still is) done in the area of perception. Helmholtz was the best-known scientist working on the physiology of perception. For example, he showed that pitch discrimination depends, in part, on which portion of the inner ear's basilar membrane is stimulated by the sound wave. A pitch of higher frequency stimulates the basilar membrane nearer the entryway to the inner ear and a pitch of lower frequency stimulates the membrane further away from the entry point.

Although most scientists studying human mental phenomena have come to accept that mental events reflect physiological processes, the emerging field of cognitive science did not focus exclusively on neurophysiology. Early experimental psychologists realized that it is possible to study mental phenomena without studying the brain.

Consider the topic of memory. We may ignore the physiological processes in the brain that make memory possible, yet still wonder about the nature of memory to which physiological processes give rise. Do we store all of our experiences, so that forgetting is due only to retrieval failure? If so, then we can characterize memory as a record-keeping system analogous to a library or videotape machine. If memory does not work this way, then what is a better way to characterize its functional properties? Note that we can explore this sort of issue, develop theories to explain the nature of memory, and run experiments designed to discriminate between theories, without worrying about the physiological basis for memory. At the same time, the development of a theory of the physiological basis for memory would require knowledge of the functional properties of memory. For example, a record-keeping model implies that there ought to be some segment of the brain that is dedicated to storing records of experience. If, instead, memory does not function like a record-keeping system, then there may not be any tissue in the brain that is specifically dedicated to storing experiences.

So the studies of functional properties and physiological processes of mental phenomena complement one another. Usually the label **cognitive psychology** is used for the study of the functional properties of human cognition while **cognitive neuroscience** is used for the study of the physiological underpinnings of cognitive phenomena. Cognitive psychology and cognitive neuroscience, then, are two of the most influential disciplines constituting cognitive science.

An example of 19th-century cognitive psychology is provided by the work of Franciscus Donders (1818 to 1889), who measured how quickly people could respond to a stimulus and used their reaction times to infer the speed of basic mental processes. In one of his experiments, he measured how fast a person could press a button after a single light was presented and compared that reaction time (called simple reaction time) to how fast a person could press a button to indicate which light in an array of several lights had been presented (called choice reaction time). Simple reaction time includes the time it takes to perceive the stimulus and to move the finger. Choice reaction time includes the time it takes to perceive the stimulus, to move the finger, and, in addition, to make a decision about which stimulus is present. Donders reasoned that the difference between simple and choice reaction time is a measure of the time needed to make a decision, a purely mental act (Donders, 1868). Donders's subtraction technique and modifications of that technique are still widely used in cognitive research.

Another example of 19th-century cognitive psychology is provided by the work of Hermann Ebbinghaus (1850 to 1909). In his most famous experiments, Ebbinghaus memorized lists of arbitrarily ordered words and syllables, and later tried to relearn the lists. The reduction in the number of trials needed to learn the list a second time was his measure of memory. Ebbinghaus varied the time between learning and relearning the list, the length of the list to be learned, the order of the syllables on the list, and so on, to see how each variation affected his memory (Ebbinghaus, 1885). Ebbinghaus was one of the first experimentalists to show that it is possible to quantify the functional properties of a mental process such as memory.

The Darwinian influence on early experimental psychology was reflected in an interest in individual differences in cognitive skill. As I mentioned earlier, evolution depends on variability among members of a species. In order for cognitive skills to evolve, individual members of human species must show cognitive variation, as indeed modern humans do. Some psychologists, notably Darwin's cousin Francis Galton (1822 to 1911), tried to determine the most meaningful way to characterize and measure cognitive differences. Galton thought that intelligence had to do with basic perceptual processes such as sensory acuity or reaction time needed to detect the presence of a stimulus. Examples of his tests included comparing bars to see which was longer, determining the highest audible pitch a person could hear, and responding as quickly as possible to an auditory stimulus. Galton noted that some mentally retarded people seem to have more trouble detecting differences in heat, cold, and pain than do people who are not retarded; these observations reinforced his theory (Galton, 1883). However, attempts to correlate measures of sensory acuity and reaction time to independent measures of intellectual ability, such as teachers' evaluations or academic grades, failed to show any reliable correlation (Wissler, 1901). Later, people interested in measuring cognitive differences developed more complex tests of cognition, such as sentence completion, reasoning tasks, and vocabulary. The first standardized IQ tests (Binet, 1911) were based on these more complex measures, which have been shown to predict academic performance reliably. Recently, cognitive psychologists have again begun to study simpler cognitive functions as the basis for individual differences in cognition (see Deary & Stough, 1996).

Perhaps the demise of the supernatural perspective and the triumph of the natural view of mind was completed by Sigmund Freud (1856 to 1939) and his psychodynamic psychology (Freud, 1953). For most of our culture's history, people we now label as emotionally disturbed or psychotic were thought to be possessed by demons. Freud, and others like Philippe Pinel (1745–1826) and Jean Charcot (1825 to 1893), made the case that even irrational, apparently bizarre behavior had natural underlying causes. Freud himself focused on early child rearing as the main source of emotional problems, while others, like Charcot, focused more on organic causes.

Freud also deepened our perspective on mental life. Freud believed that many of the essential motives regulating human behavior are unconsciously determined. He believed that slips of the tongue, free associations to word prompts, subtle signs of anxiety, difficulty in recollection of certain events, and dream content were manifestations of unconscious motives. Consider his treatment of dreams, which Freud believed reflect wish fulfillment, albeit in a symbolic form. As I mentioned before, in most cultures throughout history dreaming has been regarded as a supernatural phenomenon involving visits from God or foretellings of future events. Freud tried to show how events in daily life and unconscious motives like sexual desire fashioned all of a dream's images. By the early part of our century, then, even dreams and the thoughts of psychotics were regarded as natural phenomena.

COGNITIVE SCIENCE IN THE TWENTIETH CENTURY

The 20th century has witnessed the full flowering of cognitive science. An impressively large body of data and theoretical work has been compiled by cognitive psychologists working on functional descriptions of human cognitive phenomena. Experimental and statistical techniques have become more sophisticated as well. Today there is a vast wealth of information on how people perceive, remember, reason, solve problems, use language, and develop various cognitive skills over the life span. Furthermore, great advances have been made in our understanding of how different portions of the brain contribute to perception, the control of sleep and wakefulness, control over voluntary movements, memory, motives, emotions, and the use of language. Much of the progress in cognitive neuroscience has been due to the development of new technologies such as the electroencephalogram (EEG), recording of the electrical activity of single neurons, the deliberate destruction of small sections of the brains of animals, and the imaging of blood flow in the waking brain. Howard Gardner (1985), in his text *The Mind's New Science*, provides a highly recommended history of 20th-century developments in cognitive science.

Cognitive science greatly expanded its influence in the 20th century. **Cultural anthropologists** like Claude Levi-Strauss and Stephen Tyler began the study of the relationship between culture and mental processes as revealed in cultural metaphors, classification schemes, and folk stories (see Gardner, 1985).

Physical anthropologists like Louis Leakey (1903 to 1972), his wife Mary Leakey, and their son Richard, relying on new techniques like radioactive dating of fossils and artifacts, began to reconstruct in some detail how humans and human cognitive traits evolved from the more apelike species that lack many of our cognitive capabilities (Leakey & Lewin, 1977; Leakey, 1994).

Linguists, notably Noam Chomsky and Edward Sapir (1884 to 1939), began to develop detailed models of the grammars of the world's languages; models of how people learn, use, and understand language; and models of the relationship between grammar and the thought processes of the language user (see Gardner, 1985). Language is interesting in part because so much of the language we encounter or use is novel. Yet we ordinarily have no trouble understanding or using sentences we have never heard before. Linguists like Chomsky have tried to provide a way to explain this sort of routine creativity. Their claim is that the language learner is not learning specifically how to behave or respond to individual sentences but is instead learning the rules of the language, and basing the production and comprehension of sentences on the rules.

Developmental psychologists began to study how a child acquires cognitive skills. The 20th century's most influential developmental cognitive psychologist was Jean Piaget (1896 to 1980), who claimed that cognitive development proceeds through a series of distinct stages (Piaget, 1970). Piaget emphasized that children in different developmental stages have different ways of organizing their perceptions and reasoning about how the world works. Piaget was one of the first scientists to empirically test speculations about the thought processes of infants.

The invention of the programmable computer inspired another approach to cognitive science, usually called **artificial intelligence** or **AI**. The goal of AI is to write computer programs that accomplish goals that would seem to require human intelligence. In some cases, the programs are written to simulate human mental processes, such as solving a problem or retrieving a fact from memory. Computer simulations incorporate both the strengths and limitations of human mental processes. The attempt to simulate forces the cognitive scientist to be explicit about the nature of cognitive processes, because computer programs will not work unless every aspect of the process that the program simulates is made explicit. AI also helped shape a theoretical approach to cognitive psychology called information processing, discussed next.

SECTION 3: MIND AS MACHINE

An important characteristic of the materialistic view of the relationship between mind and body is the notion that mechanisms underlie mental phenomena. That is, the mind is like the actions of a machine. Not surprisingly, then, cognitive scientists have turned to machines for inspiration about how to characterize the mechanisms that enable a brain to think. In the 20th century, scientists have looked at information-transmitting devices such as telephones, televisions, and, especially, computers for such inspiration.

The study of information transmission systems has led to two ideas. The first is that it might really be possible to build machines, especially computerlike machines, that are able to think. Implications of this idea have been explored mostly in science fiction—in movies like *The Terminator* and *Blade Runner*, novels like Isaac Asimov's *I, Robot,* and Dan Simmons' *The Fall of Hyperion*, and short stories like Harlan Ellison's *I Have No Mouth and I Must Scream.*

The second idea inspired by information-transmitting machines is that human cognition has many of the properties of such machines. For example, humans take in information from the outside world, transform the information into neurological signals, and later base their behavior on the stored information. The idea that human thought processes are like the transmission of information in artificial devices is known as the **information processing** approach to human cognition.

INFORMATION PROCESSING

I illustrate the characteristics of information processing with a model I've concocted just for this book. The model is designed to determine from taste whether an alcoholic beverage is a regular American-style beer (e.g., Miller Beer), an ale, or a porter. Incidentally, in using a beer-drinking example, I don't mean to imply that all college students have some great interest in drinking beer. But some of you no doubt enjoy the occasional bottle of beer (I know I do), and, at any rate, the example lends itself nicely to an explication of information processing.

All beers are alcoholic beverages resulting from the fermentation of a malt, hops, and cereal brew. American beer has a bright, pale, golden color with a light-bodied and fresh flavor. Ale, which has a slightly higher alcoholic content, is a golden aromatic brew with a fuller, more complex taste and a more bitter flavor. Porter is a darker, creamier-foamed and more full-bodied beer that tastes "maltier" and sweeter than ale. The beer information processing model (portions of which are depicted in Figure 1-1) is supposed to simulate how real beer drinkers determine from taste alone the type of beer they are drinking. The model is admittedly oversimplified, as beer connoisseurs will no doubt realize.

Information Processing Claims

Information processing (described in more detail in Lachman, Lachman, & Butterfield, 1979) makes at least four claims that distinguish it from other possible approaches to the study of human cognition.

The first claim is that any cognitive process consists of the transmission of information through a series of stages in which the information is transformed, in order to achieve some goal such as deciding which beverage to serve at a dinner party. Information transformation takes the form of elaborating upon, simplifying, or converting the information into a new form. In the "beer" model, information about the gustatory contents of an alcoholic beverage is converted

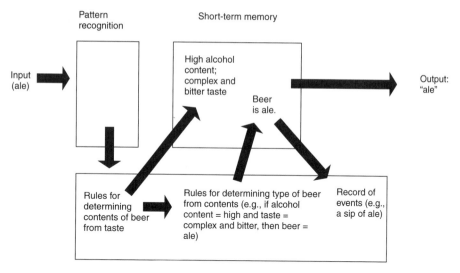

FIGURE 1–1   An information processing model that discriminates among three types of beer: American, ale, and porter. Only one of the rules for determining the type of beer from its contents is depicted. In this situation, the model is sipping an ale. Arrows indicate the flow of information transmission.

into the categorical membership of the beverage. This claim suggests that humans do not passively absorb information from the outside world, but actively transform the information in the service of some goal. A similar form of information transmission is observed in telephones, where acoustical energy is transformed into an electrical signal that preserves only about 25% of the information in the original acoustical signal. The transformation of an acoustical signal into an electrical signal enables the message to be sent over long distances.

A second claim of information processing is that higher mental processes, like reasoning or language, can be understood as the collective action of a set of very elementary operations. The intelligence of the system as a whole derives from the coordinated actions of elementary operations that themselves are not very intelligent. This is a point worth emphasizing. One cannot explain why a system is intelligent by evoking explanatory elements that already possess the intelligence one is trying to explain. For instance, reasoning cannot be explained by appealing to an internal reasoner. The question would remain, how does the internal reasoner accomplish reasoning? Instead, reasoning is explained by appealing to internal elements that have simple properties, like becoming activated or deactivated by certain stimuli, but that collectively function to reason.

Most information processing models favor elementary processes such as extracting elementary physical properties from a stimulus, placing information in a short-term memory, searching information held in short-term memory, activating information held in a long-term memory, storing new information in long-term memory, comparing one set of information to another set, and transforming information according to a list of rules. Similarly, the functioning of complex information-transmitting devices like computers can be understood as the coordinated actions of a set of simple components that include a memory, a central processing unit (described later), and so on. Researchers working within the information processing paradigm show an inclination toward measuring the speed with which various elementary operations are executed. The elemental components of the "beer" model include a pattern recognition component that extracts gustatory features from the beverage and activates knowledge about beer, a short-term memory that contains the features of the currently processed beverage, and a long-term memory that contains information about the properties of various kinds of beer.

A third claim of information processing is that human cognition has a limited capacity for storing and transmitting information, just as do telephones or computers, such that if the capacity is exceeded, information is lost. In most information processing models of human cognition, limited capacity arises because the short-term memory component is capable of holding only a few pieces of information at a time. Limited capacity is also reflected in the limits of the sensory systems for picking up information and in the limits of motor systems for executing responses. Long-term memory is usually assumed to have no capacity limits. The limited capacity of the "beer" model is reflected in the small number of pieces of information that can be held in its short-term memory and in the fact that only one information transformation command can be performed at a time.

The fourth claim of information processing is that there are especially apt analogies between human thought processes and **digital computers**. That is, of all the information processing devices, it is the digital computer that functions most like the human mind. The idea is that the essential components of a computer have their functional counterpart in human cognition. Digital computers have input and output devices; compilers that convert keyboard strikes into symbols; memories; a central processing unit (CPU) responsible for carrying out basic symbolic manipulations such as transferring a symbol from one memory location to another; and programs (software) that instruct the CPU on how to carry out the symbolic transformations. Symbol storage, symbol manipulation, and programmability are among the key features that distinguish conventional digital computers from other kinds of machines.

While human cognition is obviously accomplished using a very different hardware than that used by the digital computer, the claim is that the human cognitive system has components that function like the essential components that make up a computer system. Humans have sensory apparatus, such as taste buds, and motor apparatus such as speech musculature; perceptual systems that convert sensations into meaningful perceptions; memory; and various sets of internalized rule systems, such as the rules that underlie the grammar of language or provide the basis for categorizing alcoholic beverages.

The most important aspect of this claim is that humans, like computers, require for their intelligence the activation of rules that manipulate symbols. Rules, like computer programs, determine where symbols will be stored and how symbols will be transformed. The capacity for other elemental processes to coordinate their efforts in order to behave intelligently derives from the rules or programs that instruct them. Sometimes this claim is put into the form of the following analogy: The mind is to the brain as the software of the computer is to its hardware. In the beer information processing model, the ability of the model to classify the alcoholic beverage resides most essentially in its instructions that convert symbols that stand for gustatory properties into symbols that stand for alcoholic beverage categories (e.g., "if alcohol content = high and taste = complex and bitter, then beverage = ale").

Problems with the Computer Metaphor

Information processing dominated cognitive psychology in the 1950s, 1960s, and 1970s. And most cognitive psychologists continue to accept the information processing claims that mental processes are decomposable into elementary processes and that, in certain respects, mental processes, particularly those we associate with short-term memory, have a limited capacity. Many cognitive scientists, however, have begun to doubt the specific information processing claim that human thought processes have important similarities to conventional digital computers. A growing consensus is that the human mind is not at all like a digital computer—that the computer metaphor does not properly characterize how people learn, remember, reason, or experience awareness of an outside world (e.g., Graubard, 1988; Martindale, 1991; Searle, 1990).

Before discussing the problems with the computer metaphor of human cognition, I need to make a distinction between the functional properties of a digital computer system, on the one hand, and the computer programs that serve to simulate aspects of human cognition, on the other. As it turns out, computer programs can be used to simulate virtually any theory or model of virtually any phenomenon. One could write a program that simulates hurricane formation, for example. The program might take prevailing weather conditions as input and produce as output the size and ferocity of the hurricane that develops. But the model of hurricane formation simulated by a computer program has nothing in common with how a computer actually stores and manipulates symbols. The computer merely serves as a device for executing algorithms (step-by-step procedures), performing arithmetic operations, and displaying information in a convenient way.

Similarly, virtually any model of human cognition can be simulated by a computer program. But the model need not have anything in common with how the digital computer itself stores and manipulates symbols. For example, the various memories available to a computer allow it to store millions of symbols presented to it once, without forgetting a single symbol. Humans would forget most of the symbols. But the computer could be programmed so as to accept as input, say, a list of 30 words, and display on the screen the first 3 and the last 3 words along with a couple of words from the middle of the list. In this way the computer simulates the serial position effect, whereby people tend to remember the first and last few items on a list better than they do the items in the middle of the list (Murdock, 1962). Note that nothing intrinsic to the computer's own memory system creates a serial position effect. Still, it can be programmed to simulate that effect. The problems with the computer metaphor that I am about to explicate, then, pertain only to the functional properties of digital computers, and not to the use of computer programs to simulate models of human cognition.

Having made the distinction between the computer itself and simulations run on a computer, let me now list some of the reasons for doubting the digital computer metaphor—that is, for doubting that human cognitive processes are analogous to how a digital computer actually works.

One problem with the computer metaphor is that the nature of cognitive limitations in humans is quite different from the capacity limitations of a computer. The capacity of the computer is primarily determined by the speed of the CPU and the size of the computer's memory. Furthermore, a computer does not increase its capacity with practice. Should the user of the computer alter the hardware so as to speed up the performance of the CPU or expand the memory, then the computer will increase its capacity for any and all kinds of information it is able to process. Humans, on the other hand, can increase the amount of information they can process by practicing, but the increase in capacity does not generalize to other categories of information. For example, a person learning to drive a manual shift car can initially pay attention only to the driving. With practice, the person can drive, listen to the radio, fantasize about living in Tahiti, and carry on a conversation about alcoholism at the same time. But the increase in attentional capacity that comes from practicing driving the manual shift car does not generalize to flying an airplane or solving a crossword puzzle.

I want to be clear that information processing psychologists are certainly aware that practice results in a more efficient use of cognitive resources, and that the improvement is specific to the kind of task on which one practices. Models of information processing include a process called automatization whereby, with practice, a task that used to require a lot of attention and effort comes to require much less attention and effort (LaBerge & Samuels, 1974; Lachman, Lachman, & Butterfield, 1979). The point here is that automatization is not intrinsic to the workings of a digital computer, although the computer could be programmed to simulate automatization.

Another difficulty with the computer metaphor is that the way memory works in a computer is radically different from the way it works in humans. One of the essential differences is that the computer stores a faithful record of each its experiences, while humans change the way they understand the world as a function of having experiences but do not keep a record-by-record account of the experiences that give rise to those changes (see chapter 4: Memory). As a result, computers are good at providing accurate and detailed accounts of their input. People, on the other hand, usually forget the details of their experiences but are good at remembering the gist of past events.

Another problem with the computer analogy for human cognition has to do with the claim that thinking amounts to the judicious manipulation of symbols according to a program. In computers, the intelligence of the system derives from the program that instructs the computer how to store symbols in memory and how to transform various symbols into other symbols. However, if human thought consisted only of manipulating symbols in this way, then it would seem that people would never understand the meaning of the symbols (Searle, 1980, 1990). Symbols, as long as they are transformed only into other symbols, are bound to remain meaningless.

To illustrate the point, suppose I tell you that the symbol "pijiu" can be replaced with the symbols "jiu" and "shiliang." Does this transformation tell you what the symbol "pijiu" means? Obviously it does not (unless you know Chinese). In order for this or any symbol to become meaningful, it has to bring to mind an idea that itself is not symbolic. The idea of beer, for example, is distinct from the symbol that expresses it. Indeed, many different symbols can express the idea of beer, including "pijiu," which is the Chinese word for beer ("jiu" is Chinese for "alcoholic" and "shiliang" is Chinese for "beverage"). But the idea of beer, regardless of the symbol used to express it, includes the sensations associated with seeing and tasting beer. So it is clearly the case that something in addition to the symbol manipulation programs used by computers must underlie the derivation of meaning. Contrary to what is implied by the computer analogy, human thought is not essentially the manipulation of symbols, but the contemplation of ideas.

It is apparent, then, that the analogy that the mind bears the same relationship to the brain as does the computer's software to its hardware is wrong, or at least misleading. The computer has no way of knowing what the symbols it manipulates mean. Ideas are not evoked in the computer, but only in the human user of the computer who interprets the meaning of the symbols the computer manipulates. But nothing outside the brain of the human is required to enable the human to know the meaning of the symbols the human contemplates.

Neural Net Machines

If the mind is not like a digital computer, what kind of machine is it like? The 1980s saw a growing interest in trying to develop models of human cognition that embody the essential physiological processes that take place in the brain (Churchland, 1988; McClelland & Rumelhart, 1986a: Bechtel & Abrahamsen, 1991; Rumelhart & McClelland, 1986; Martindale, 1991; Churchland & Sejnowski, 1992). These more biologically realistic models are variously called **neural net models, connectionist models**, and **parallel distributed processing models**. The neural net label highlights the biological nature of the model, the connectionist label emphasizes that the model consists of elements that are connected to one another, and the parallel distributed processing label emphasizes that any given mental process involves the simultaneous activation of many elements. Because I am emphasizing the biological qualities of such models, I will use the "neural net" label.

Again, be clear that neural net models, like virtually all other models of all other phenomena, can be written in the form of a computer program and so simulated by the execution of the program. The point I am developing here is that a neural net model is a radically different view of human cognition than is a model based on an analogy to the way a conventional digital computer actually works.

A Beer-guzzling Neural Net

A typical neural net model consists of at least three layers of units, usually called **input units, output units, and hidden units** (see Figure 1-2). These units simulate neurons or groups of neurons in the brain. The input units often correspond to perceptual neurons that detect physical features of stimuli (e.g., the bitterness in beer), the output units correspond to motor neurons that control movements (e.g., drinking the beer), and the hidden units correspond to association neurons that intervene between perceptual and motor neurons. Sometimes the output units correspond to making a decision, such as deciding whether a face is male or female or whether a beer is an ale or porter. Like real neurons, the units of a neural net model transmit signals to one another. These signals cause other units to turn on or off. The rate at which units turn on and off is their *firing rate*. The

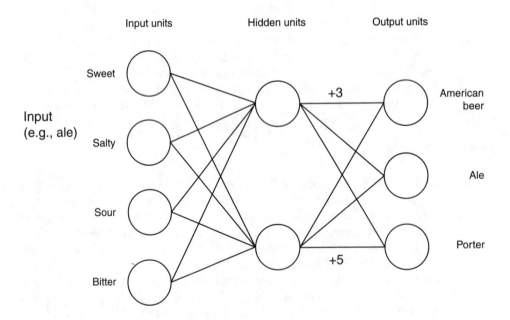

FIGURE 1–2   A neural net model that discriminates among three types of beer: American, ale, and porter. The units are the circles, the connections are the lines linking the circles. The strength of the connection is given by a number, where a higher number means a stronger connection. The figure depicts only the connection strengths between the upper hidden unit and the American beer output unit and between the lower hidden unit and the porter output unit.

firing rate of a unit simulates the rate at which real neurons send spikes of electrical impulses down their axons.

Like real neurons, the units of a neural net model are linked by excitatory or inhibitory connections that vary in strength. The strength of connections is meant to model the synaptic connections between real neurons. The more strongly two neurons are connected, the more readily one neuron can influence the firing rate of another neuron. Most neural net models have ways of modifying the strength of the connections depending on the nature of the stimuli and the feedback the model gets about its actions. In the brain, learning is thought to reflect changes in the strengths of the connections among neurons. More detail about the nature of learning and memory in brains and in the neural net models designed to simulate learning and memory is discussed in chapter 6 on the physiological basis of learning and memory.

Figure 1-2 illustrates a neural net model for determining whether an alcoholic beverage is American beer, ale, or porter. I intend for this model to stand in contrast to the information processing model discussed earlier. The neural net version of the "beer" model includes input units that detect the flavors of sweetness, saltiness, sourness, and bitterness. These units correspond to the taste receptors on the tongue and in the mouth. In real people, the taste of a substance depends on the overall pattern of activity among receptors that detect these four basic qualities of taste, as well as on the odor of the substance (see Carlson, 1994). The input units are connected to hidden units that in turn are connected to output units that control the responses "American beer," "ale," and "porter."

The way the model works is that it is first provided a profile of the gustatory properties of a sip of beer (e.g., mostly bitter, some sweet), which activates the input units. The input units in turn activate or inhibit the hidden units that in turn activate or inhibit the output units. Activation and inhibition are more likely to spread between units with stronger connections than between units with weaker connections. The output unit that fires at the highest rate will determine the response of the model to the beer. Should the response prove to be correct, the model will strengthen the connections that lead to the correct response. Should the response prove to be incorrect, the model will weaken the connections that lead to the response.

This particular beer-drinking model does not really need the hidden units in order to classify beer. In general, though, neural nets do require hidden units in order to be able to respond in a flexible way to the stimuli they detect. If there were only input and output units, then two very different inputs would always yield two different outputs. But people often respond the same way to different inputs. Too much or too little sleep both produce lethargy. A blue whale and a black bear are both mammals. A conscientious beer drinker might decide to drink beer only when feeling very thirsty or when at a party where other social drinkers are drinking. But the same beer drinker might decide never to drink beer if neither feeling thirsty nor attending a party (because there would be no pleasure to the drinking) and never to drink beer if both feeling thirsty and attending a party (because of the temptation to drink too much beer).

At any rate, given enough sips of beer, the neural net model is able to settle on a set of connections that serves to classify reliably and accurately the three categories of beer, even for brands of beer it encounters for the first time. That is, the model can generalize to new cases (no pun intended!). And don't worry about the model becoming intoxicated. It never actually sips beer but only "digests" descriptions of the gustatory properties of beer. A more interesting version of the beer model would, I suppose, simulate how alcohol consumption may cause inebriation.

So by implementing the essential properties of brains, namely those that govern the transmission of electrical pulses among neurons, neural net models attempt to simulate various aspects of human cognition. The extent to which these simulations resemble real human thought and behavior is the extent to which we understand the dynamic qualities of the brain that enable it to provide its cognitive functions. In other chapters I will show how neural net models explain various aspects of human cognition, such as how we remember and sometimes forget past events and why the capacity to process information is limited.

Differences between Neural Net and Information Processing Models of Human Cognition

Consider now some of the differences between neural net models and information processing models, especially information processing models that make use of the computer metaphor. A neural net model, like a real brain, has no program that controls what the model does, nor does it have a central processing unit (CPU) that carries out the symbol manipulations that constitute the program. Instead, the behavior of a neural net model depends on the current configuration of connections among its units and not on a set of explicit rules. To put it another way, symbols and rules are replaced by the overall pattern or configuration of connection strengths among a network of units.

The behavior of a neural net model, like that of a real brain, is not radically altered by the malfunctioning of one or a few units. That is because neural net models contain a large number of units acting to simulate the large number of neurons in the brain. Neural net models are said to degrade gracefully. On the other hand, the loss of the CPU or of one of the rules contained in a program of a computer would ordinarily be catastrophic for the computer system.

It is relatively easy to build a neural net model that learns from patterns of input and from feedback. For example, the neural net model that recognizes beer could start out with randomly selected connection strengths. If the model embodies a general learning algorithm, then it will eventually alter the strength of its connections so as to maximize the probability of correctly discriminating among various types of beers. Similarly, learning in real brains is largely a matter of changing the strength of connections among neurons. In a program that runs a computer, on the other hand, the programmer would need to know the basis of the discrimination before the system would ever work. Learning in a computer system ordinarily requires explicitly adding a new rule to the program. Real brains learn even without being told the explicit rule, as when children learn the grammar rules of their language.

Unlike the memory used in a computer, the memory in a neural net model does not entail storing records of experiences anywhere. Instead, memory is implicit in the current state of connections among units. Because these connections are always changing, memory for specific details of past experiences tends to be poor. Because strong connections between units reflect regularities present in the world, memory of the past tends to reflect the patterns or regularities in experience—that is, to reflect the gist of past experiences.

Probably the most important function of neural net models is that they illuminate the neural processes underlying the components that make up any information processing model. For example, the information processing model claims that there is a limited capacity for holding information in a state of awareness, and so postulates a short-term memory. But the information processing model does not reveal how the actions of neurons in a brain cause there to be a limited capacity for short term memory. The neural net approach more directly simulates the dynamics of the interactions among neurons that give rise to a short-term memory with limited capacity. A description of a neural net explanation of limited capacity is provided in chapter 2: Consciousness. The main point to be made here is that neural nets "unpack" or explain the underlying neural dynamics of the components of thought postulated by information processing models. Neural nets, to a greater extent than information processing, make explicit the materialistic claim that what we label mental reflects only physical processes taking place in the brain. It is largely for its materialistic implications that many, although by no means all, cognitive scientists have become enamored of neural nets. In other chapters of this book I will point out why some cognitive scientists and philosophers (e.g., Fodor & Pylyshyn, 1988) have expressed doubts about the value of neural net models as accounts of human cognitive phenomena.

SECTION 4: IS COGNITIVE PSYCHOLOGY NECESSARY?

THE BEHAVIORIST CHALLENGE

Materialism asserts that all cognitive processes, and the behavior based on them, derive from physiological mechanisms in the body and the external stimuli that impinge on the body. One implication some psychologists have drawn from materialism is the doctrine of **behaviorism**. The essential idea of behaviorism is that environmental stimuli control behavior, which increases in probability if reinforced. Well known behaviorists include John Watson (1878 to 1958) and B. F. Skinner (1904 to 1990). Behaviorists eschew explanations that make use of mentalistic constructs like "information manipulation," "memory," or "feelings."

Behaviorism makes two claims that are relevant to its disdain for cognitive psychology. The first claim is that there is no need to postulate complicated internal mental processes in order to predict or control human behavior. For example, a person may choose to drink iced tea rather than beer with a meal because the person is reinforced by friends and family for avoiding alcoholic beverages. The reinforcement contingencies account for the choice. There is no need to postulate a memory process or a reasoning process underlying the person's choice of the beverage. The mental process adds nothing to the prediction. Similarly, an English-speaking child places subjects before verbs in sentences because such behavior is reinforced directly by parents or indirectly by the successful communication of an intent or request. There is no need to postulate a process whereby the child activates rules of grammar in order to account for the child's tendency to produce grammatically acceptable sentences. Behaviorists do not deny that people have memories or other conscious experiences, but they claim that there is no point to developing models of these processes because they do not increase the ability to predict and control behavior.

The second claim made by behaviorism is that the cognitive psychologist's habit of using mental processes like recollecting the past or activating the rules of grammar to explain behavior invites a misleading implication. It would seem to suggest that mental processes exert a causal effect on the physical world (Skinner, 1990; see also Baum & Heath, 1992; Chiesa, 1992). But recollections of past events or rules of grammar are merely abstract descriptions of thoughts and behaviors. Only physical things, like external stimuli and neural activity, can cause behavior. To imply that recollections or rules cause behavior is to suggest a form of dualism, despite the avowed materialism of cognitive psychology.

THE COGNITIVE PSYCHOLOGIST'S RESPONSE TO THE BEHAVIORIST CHALLENGE

The cognitive psychologist's response to the behaviorist claims is based largely on what is called a mechanical view of causality. A mechanical view of causality specifies the mechanisms whereby stimuli force or compel behavior or outcomes. The mechanical approach usually details a chain of antecedent processes that bridge the gap between stimulus and response. The cognitive psychologist prefers the mechanical approach to causality because it seems a more satisfying and complete analysis of a phenomenon. Furthermore, and despite behaviorist claims to the contrary, the mechanical approach yields predictions in situations in which a purely behaviorist analysis fails to produce predictions.

Let me provide what I hope are a couple of compelling examples of the value of the cognitive psychologist's approach to explanation. The first example comes from research on the effect that parental responses to infant distress have on the subsequent development of the infants (e.g., Stroufe, 1979, 1983; Belsky & Cassidy, 1994). This research shows that infants who are reliably comforted by parents when in distress may initially appear more dependent on their parents, but as toddlers will actually become more autonomous than infants who are not reliably comforted by the parents. When confronted with a challenge, the comforted toddler will be more enthusiastic, persistent, and effective than the toddler who was not reliably comforted as an infant. It should be noted that the nature of parent–infant interactions is probably a function of the personalities of the parents and the intrinsic temperaments of the infants (Mangelsdorf, Gunnar, Kestenbaum, Lang, & Andreas, 1990).

From a purely behaviorist perspective, this pattern of results appears inexplicable. Based only on reinforcement contingencies, one would predict that the infant who regularly receives the reinforcement of comfort when crying would actually become more "clingy" and dependent than the infant who does not receive such reinforcement. Instead, what seems to happen is that the comforted infant learns to internalize a model of a safe and secure world (Belsky & Cassidy, 1994; Belsky, Spritz, & Crnic, 1996). Based on this "secure" model, the toddler is able to explore and confront the world without an excessive need to cling to the parents. The unreliably comforted infant, on the other hand, learns to internalize a model of an insecure, hostile world. Based on this "insecure" model, the toddler will be less able to explore and confront challenges it encounters and instead will cling to the parents. The point is that the internalized model, acquired from interactions with the parents, is a necessary part of the causal chain that controls the toddler's behavior. Without a mechanism in which the child internalizes a model which then produces behavior, there is no easy way to explain how past reinforcement histories lead to future behavior. The notion of the internalized model serves to bridge the causal gap between the original stimulus (interactions with parents) and the future response (the toddler's attempts to act autonomously).

Now for the second example. Have you ever had the experience of trying too hard to fall asleep? The attempt to fall asleep sometimes has the paradoxical effect of keeping us awake. Indeed, there are many situations in which high motivation to accomplish one behavior produces the opposite behavior (Wegner, 1994). We try to concentrate, or relax, or appear humble, and we find instead that our attention wanders, our mood becomes more anxious, or we come off as braggarts. What explains such irony? Why doesn't the stimulus always produce the intended consequences?

A recent theory of behavior and thought control (Wegner, 1994) postulates that motivating stimuli are processed by a mental system that does two things. First, the mental system searches for mental contents consistent with implementing the intention. Second, the mental system monitors the situation by comparing mental processes and behaviors with mental contents inconsistent with the intention. To concentrate on a lecture, for instance, one must activate a mental program that keeps attention fixed on the lecture and one must recognize when attention wanders to something other than the lecture. An important and reasonable assumption of the model is that the first process, finding the mental contents necessary to achieve the goal, is more effortful than the monitoring process. Under conditions when mental capacity is overloaded, then, only the monitoring process that activates mental contents inconsistent with the intention will work properly. The result is irony. If you are worried about final exams, you might find your attention drifting all the more readily from a lecture on neuro-transmitters to the sarcastic whisperings of a hostile classmate.

As an example of one of many experiments on ironic effects, consider an experiment by Wegner, Ansfield, & Bowser (reported in Wegner, 1994). They gave their subjects a cassette tape to listen to when falling asleep. For some sub-jects, the tape narrator began by strongly encouraging subjects to fall asleep as fast as possible, while for other subjects the narrator provided no such encour-agement. For some subjects, the tape continued with restful New Age music while for others it continued with more complex music, specifically a medley of John Philip Sousa marches. For subjects presented with the restful music, which presumably imposed a low mental load, those encouraged to fall asleep quickly did in fact fall asleep more quickly than subjects not so encouraged. The stimu-lus to motivate sleep had the intended effect, as the behaviorist would have it. But among subjects presented with the more challenging music, which presum-ably imposed a high mental load, the subjects who were encouraged to fall asleep actually took longer to fall asleep than those who were not so encour-aged. The stimulus to motivate sleep had the opposite (ironic) effect, contrary to the predictions of any straightforward behaviorist account. Here, then, is another nice example of how the successful prediction of the effect of a stimu-lus on behavior requires postulating an intervening mental process.

In general, then, the cognitive psychologist points out, and has been point-ing out for some time (e.g., Craik, 1943; Hebb, 1949), that many behaviors can be understood only if one examines the processes that intervene between stim-ulus and response. The causal mechanisms underlying human behavior are often rather complicated; they entail a chain of events whereby external stimuli are internally processed before a behavioral response emerges. To be consistent with materialism, it must be noted that such mechanisms reflect neural processes. But one can certainly discuss the functional properties of intervening processes without necessarily providing their underlying physiological basis.

SUMMARY AND SPECULATIONS

In summary, events of the last few centuries have produced a radical change in our cosmology. Where once the universe seemed supernatural, created for humans who lived at its center, it is now seen as a natural universe in which humans and human mental processes are explained by the same physical processes that govern the behavior of the rest of the biological and even inani-mate world. Copernicus and Galileo taught us that the sun and not the earth is the center of our solar system; Newton taught us that the physical world can be described by mathematical equations and so must be a rational, self-regulating mechanism; Darwin taught us that human origins are due to natural evolution-ary processes that govern the origin of all species of life; Freud taught us that even apparently crazy behavior has a natural, comprehensible explanation; and the many neuroscientists and cognitive psychologists working in the last 100 years have shown us something of how the mind functions and of how neuropsychological processes may account for these mental functions. Our mind has become natural. Dualistic views that separate mind and brain into two different categories of phenomena represent a challenge to the natural view of mind, but evolution and neuroscience would seem to refute dualism.

That the mind is natural means that we are not only in the universe, but of the universe. It means that something physical and only something physical gives rise to mental experiences like memories, feelings, and creative thoughts. It means that the methods of experimentation can help us discover the causes of mental phenomena. Such an insight suggests the possibility that human cognition might resemble the functioning of a machine, in particular a digital computer. But whatever kind of physical device our minds may be like, the conventional digital computer does not seem to be such a device. The computer metaphor turns out to be a misleading one in terms of how the human mind operates. Cognitive scientists are now trying to build models of machines, based on neural net principles, that are designed to work like real brains.

Materialism means that only physical processes underlie mental phenomena. In materialism there is a place for the cognitive neuroscientist who studies the neural processes that underlie cognition and there is a place for the behaviorist who studies environmental influences on behavior. Is there a place, though, for the cognitive psychologist who develops models of cognitive processes without stipulating the underlying physical mechanisms? Behaviorists like Skinner say no, the cognitive psychologist confuses description with explanation. The cognitive psychologist's response is that cognitive models reflect the complex causal chains that often intervene between stimulus and response, and that such causal chains are necessary to explain people's behavior. I will briefly take up the issue of behaviorism again in chapter 11: Cognitive Development.

Now that the naturalized view of mind has matured into a full-fledged science, we might ask if this science of cognition has been a source for technological and social progress as the physical and biological sciences have been. I think the answer is yes. Consider, first of all, many of the important changes made in our educational systems in the last few decades. We see changes in schools that reflect what we have learned about cognitive development, the mechanisms underlying learning, and individual differences in intelligence (e.g., Glaser, 1984; Glaser & Bassok, 1989; Mayer, 1987; Bruer, 1993).

Consider other examples of cognitive progress. We know more about how to treat depression, language disorders, and memory disorders than we did even a few decades ago (e.g., Brewin, 1988). We know better how to design complex and imposing technological environments, like computer work stations, in such a way that a person can easily perceive information, learn new information, or remember previously learned information (e.g., Wickens, 1984).

Finally, we see evidence of cognitive progress in the development of machine intelligence. Neural net models that are based on neurophysiological principles are beginning to be used to develop the architecture for more intelligent machines. Such machines may be able to help people solve complex problems, like the effects of human activity on climate, that are difficult to solve using ordinary computers.

Critics of cognitive science have suggested that likening the mind to a mechanism suggests a metaphor that is dehumanizing. In particular, they say, it promotes the view that people lack free will, that people can be treated as if they were machines. But cognitive science celebrates our humanity. Cognitive science delights in and is intrigued by those properties that make our species distinctive, namely our cognitive talents. And cognitive science increases the possibility that we can learn to solve many problems that undermine the quality of our lives—problems like mental retardation, dyslexia, and psychopathology.

What of free will? If our minds reflect only electrical/chemical events in the brain, then is not our behavior finally determined by those processes? Why, then, does it seem to us that we have control over our actions in a way that is independent of factors that affect the brain? For example, a person may resist yielding to a temptation to steal money even though the person is economically desperate and is unlikely to get caught. Let me attempt to reconcile the dilemma between our apparent free will and the implication of cognitive science that all of our thought and behavior is determined by physical processes in the brain, which is itself affected by outside stimuli.

Consider that many factors can influence any thought or behavior. For example, a person might be offered two jobs and choose the one that pays the most money. But the choice of job is not absolutely determined by the money. The person might have turned down the higher-paying job. Pay influences the choice, but so do many other factors, such as the nature of the work, the prestige of the work, the location of the work, and even factors about which we, as observers, are unaware. Because thoughts and behaviors are nearly always influenced by many factors interacting in complex ways, any person's behavior will not be completely determined by the particular factors we are able to observe. There will always be factors, such as the effect of some long past traumatic experience, that we are unable to observe and measure.

Furthermore, our human ability to reflect increases considerably the number of factors that may exert influence on our behavior. For example, a person might reflect on society's ecological problems and decide to turn down a job with a company that pollutes the atmosphere. Or the person might reflect on the inevitability of death and decide to take a job with more free time. In brief, the evolution of reflective thought has dramatically increased the number of factors that determine our actions and thoughts to the point that, as individuals reflecting on the reasons for our own actions or as scientists trying to predict the actions of others, we can never be aware of all the relevant factors. So our actions are at best only partially correlated to the few factors we can measure (Lewontin, Rose, & Kamin, 1984).

The interesting implication is that there is no functional difference between the claim that we possess free will and the claim that our behavior is completely determined by the combined influence of many factors, but we cannot know about or measure all the factors that determine our behavior. In this sense, cognitive science has verified our intuition that we are free. We are free of the undue influence of any one or two factors and instead are free to be influenced by any of a large number of factors, some of which cannot influence other creatures.

Our behavior, unlike that of other animals, can be affected by the knowledge of our mortality, our commitment to a value system, and our understanding of our cognitive nature.

RECOMMENDED READINGS

Eiseley's (1972) *The Firmament of Time* is a vivid and original discussion of how humans in the last few centuries have changed their vision of nature. Gardner's (1985) *The Mind's New Science* provides an excellent history of cognitive science and a discussion of some of the persistent debates within the field of cognitive science. Churchland's (1988) *Matter and Consciousness* is an accessible discussion of various philosophical approaches to the mind–brain relationship. Churchland also provides a very clear description of neural net models. Chomsky's (1959) review of Skinner's (1957) *Verbal Behavior* provides what is regarded as one of the most devastating critiques of behaviorism, in an essay in which Chomsky not only criticizes but even ridicules the behaviorist approach to language acquisition.

2 *Consciousness*

A few years ago an acquaintance of mine suffered a massive stroke in his right cerebral hemisphere, and consequently he now exhibits what is called visual neglect. He often seems to be unaware of the environment on the left side of his visual field. Shortly after the stroke, he claimed that his phone book was defective because his daughter's phone number was no longer listed in it. In fact, the phone number was listed in the left-most column of one of the pages.

My acquaintance's stroke disturbed the nature of his **consciousness**, the subject of this chapter. I will use the concept of consciousness in two ways. Consciousness can refer to the subjective experience of being aware, as when a person is aware of the sights and sounds and smells that make up the outside world and of the feelings, thoughts, and sensations that make up mental experiences. Call this **conscious awareness**. Consciousness can also refer to reflective thought, as when a person examines motives, recollects past experiences, searches for solutions to problems, or infers reasons for observed regularities in nature. Call this **reflective consciousness**. Presumably one has to be aware of information in order to reflect upon it, although one may be aware without engaging in reflection.

Consciousness, in either of its senses, has contents; we are conscious of something. We may be aware of the sweet smell of a rose or remember attending the Rose Bowl football game. The contents of consciousness are subjective; they are available only to the person having the conscious experience and are not directly observable by anyone else. The contents of our thoughts are usually about something other than themselves; they are said to have **intentionality** (not to be confused with "intentional,"). For example, if I experience the taste of beer or think about the importance of moderation in drinking beer, those thoughts refer to a substance that exists outside of my thoughts about it.

Furthermore, the contents of consciousness are typically about the outcomes or products of mental processes and not about the means by which such processes are accomplished (Nisbett & Wilson, 1977). I notice that beer tastes bitter without having any conscious access to the workings of my perceptual system that perceives the bitterness. I remember attending the 1996 Rose Bowl football game in which Northwestern University lost to the University of Southern California (darn it!), without having any sense of how I am able to recollect that experience.

Consciousness has a unitary character. Any given person is aware of being a single, unified self, despite ongoing changes in thoughts, experiences, and memories. And that self is separate from other selves and from the rest of the external world. One's thoughts and dreams and pains are one's own.

Among writers on the topic of consciousness, there is considerable difference of opinion on what a theory of consciousness ought to explain (see, for example, Dennett, 1991; Edelman, 1992). The approach I will take is to establish first the materialist theme that consciousness, in both its awareness and self-reflective senses, is a function provided by neurophysiological processes taking place in the brain. A theory of consciousness based on materialism seeks to explain how neurophysiological processes give rise to the phenomenological character of consciousness. Materialism tries to answer the question of what happens in the brain to cause people to have subjective experiences and to be capable of reflecting on the self. Materialism stands in contrast to dualism, which maintains that consciousness reflects the actions of an immaterial mind-stuff that happens to interact with the brain but is not itself a physical process.

I will then extend the materialism theme into a discussion of two features of conscious experience. One feature has to do with states of consciousness. Daily we pass through nondreaming sleep, dreaming sleep, and wakefulness. In my discussion I will focus on the nature of dreaming and on the physiological basis of the experiential characteristics of the dream state. The other feature of consciousness I discuss has to do with the limitations on awareness and reflection. At any given moment we are aware of, or use, only a small percentage of all the possible information that might make up a conscious experience. What physiological processes underlie such limitations?

Finally, I will conclude the chapter with a discussion of the purpose of consciousness. What advantage does consciousness confer upon cognitive processes? Could we function as well if we had no subjective awareness of a self and of an outside world or if we were unable to self-reflect?

SECTION 1: MATERIALISM AND THE PHYSIOLOGICAL BASIS OF CONSCIOUSNESS

I begin the discussion of consciousness by trying to make a case for the materialistic explanation of consciousness. The current view is that consciousness reflects processes taking place in several areas of the brain or among several neural circuits which themselves may be represented in several areas of the brain (Dennett, 1991). Each of these processes is functionally simpler than, say, feeling melancholy while listening to music or remembering last night's dinner conversation. And each process contributes a different aspect to the phenomenological experience of consciousness.

DISSOCIATIONS AND THE DISTRIBUTED NATURE OF CONSCIOUSNESS

Consciousness depends on the brain. The human brain consists of tens of billions of neurons and tens of billions of support cells that function largely to nourish and support the neurons (see Carlson, 1994, for a general discussion of neurons). The neurons are unique in that only they carry an electrical impulse and communicate with other neurons. As discussed more in chapter 6: The Physiology of Learning and Remembering, neurons communicate by releasing chemicals called neurotransmitters from the end of the axon of one neuron to the dendrite of another neuron.

The brain is not an undifferentiated mass of neurons. There are a variety of structures into which neurons are differentiated. The grossest level of neural organization separates the brain into the base, the midsection, and the cerebral hemispheres, which are connected by the corpus callosum (the cerebral cortex of the brain is pictured in Figure 2-1). The base includes the medulla, responsible for regulating basic anatomical functions such as breathing; the locus coeruleus and pons, responsible for controlling the sleep–wake cycle; and the cerebellum, responsible for coordinating movement. The midsection of the brain includes the limbic system, made up of a collection of structures including the hypothalamus and hippocampus, which controls motives, emotions, and memory consolidation. The outer portions of the brain are made up of the cerebral cortex, which is divided into four pairs of lobes: the frontal, temporal, occipital, and parietal lobes. The frontal lobes control planning, motor movement, and the grammatical aspects of language; the temporal lobes control audition and the semantic aspects of language; the occipital lobes control vision; and the parietal lobes control somatosensory functions, such as touch.

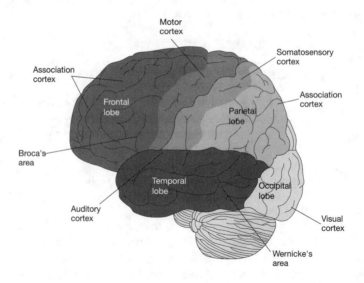

FIGURE 2–1 The four lobes of the cerebral cortex.

A particularly revealing source of information about the brain's role in consciousness is provided by the phenomenon of **dissociation** (Farthing, 1992). The dissociation phenomenon is characterized by an individual who in some respects reacts to a stimulus like a conscious person but claims to have no awareness of the stimulus or is unable to reflect on the experience. The study of dissociations provides at least some clues as to how certain brain processes produce consciousness.

Blindsight

One example of dissociation is **blindsight**. Damage to visual cortex, particularly the striate cortex located in the posterior occipital lobe, usually results in blindness in the visual field processed by the damaged tissue. If secondary visual cortex is relatively unimpaired, however, the patient may be able to respond to visual stimuli even though he or she has no subjective experience of seeing the visual stimuli (Weiskrantz, 1990, 1995; Zihl, Tretter, & Singer, 1980). For example, Weiskrantz (Weiskrantz, 1980, 1986; see Farthing, 1992, or Weiskrantz, 1995, for a discussion of similar cases) tested a man who had a tumor removed from his right visual cortex and as a result was blind in most of his left visual field. If flashes of light or lines were presented to his left visual field, he claimed no awareness of them. Yet after some coaxing to get him to try, the patient was able to locate accurately the position of flashes of light or the orientation of lines even though he continued to insist that he could not see the flashes or lines. The accuracy depended on using a forced choice procedure in which the patient had to choose from among a limited number of responses (e.g., vertical or horizontal) and was forbidden to say "I don't know."

Apparently it is an intact secondary visual cortex and the connections it receives from the superior colliculus (protrusions on top of the midbrain) and from the dorsal lateral geniculate nucleus (part of the thalamus) that enables blindsight patients to process accurately some visual information (Carlson, 1994). Secondary visual cortex (discussed more in chapter 3: Visual Perception) is found in the occipital, temporal, and parietal lobes. The conscious experience of seeing, however, requires that both primary and secondary visual cortex function properly. The blindsight phenomenon suggests that it must be the collective activity of these centers that gives rise to visual consciousness.

Neglect

Another example of dissociation is **neglect** (see Farthing, 1992; Robertson, 1994). Patients (like my acquaintance mentioned at the beginning of the chapter) with extensive damage to the right parietal lobe will sometimes ignore all information on the left side of their body and ignore visual information in their left visual field. Right-field neglect caused by left hemisphere damage is much rarer. Some patients with the neglect syndrome will fail to groom the left side of their bodies, or will draw only the right side of a scene, or will eat only the food on the right side of the plate.

Patients with neglect may or may not be blind in their left visual fields. Some patients will report seeing objects on their left side but mistakenly locate them on the right side. The left-side neglect will persist even when patients are free to move their heads and eyes. In one study of visual neglect, Marshall and Halligan (1988) simultaneously presented two drawings of a house to a neglect patient. The drawings were aligned one above the other and were identical except that in one there were flames coming out of the left side of the house. The patient reported that the drawings were identical. She did not notice the flames. But when asked in which house she would prefer to live, she reliably chose the house that was not burning.

Amnesia

Another kind of dissociation is **anterograde amnesia**, discussed more fully in chapter 6: The Physiology of Learning and Remembering. Anterograde amnesia occurs when the left and right hippocampus, a part of the limbic system, is damaged. Patients with this syndrome can remember events prior to the onset of the syndrome, have normal short-term memory spans, but have trouble remembering any event subsequent to the onset. Such patients cannot easily learn new names, will read the same magazine articles over and over without remembering having read them before, and have trouble remembering lists of words presented to them by researchers.

Curiously, an amnesic patient can learn new skills, such as tracing patterns when the pattern and pencil can only be seen in a mirror, nearly as well as normal people. Yet the amnesic patient has no memory for practicing the skill (Schacter, McAndrews, & Moscovitch, 1988). Experiences change the way various cognitive functions are performed, but without an intact hippocampus those experiences cannot be consciously recollected.

Split Brains

Another kind of dissociation is observed in patients with a severed corpus callosum, the major band of fibers that connects the two cerebral hemispheres. Usually the severing is done by a surgeon in order to prevent the spread of epileptic seizures. The two cerebral hemispheres are differentially specialized in humans (see Springer & Deutsch, 1993). In most people, the left cerebral hemisphere plays a dominant role in language (especially the grammatical aspects of language) and other sequential operations. The right cerebral hemisphere plays a dominant role in visual-spatial tasks, such as face recognition, and in other tasks that involve processing information presented simultaneously. In the ordinary case, both hemispheres work together. In the split-brain patient, however, it is difficult for the brain to transfer information from one hemisphere to another. Such patients sometimes exhibit a dissociation between awareness and information processing.

In one investigation of split-brain patients (Gazzaniga, 1970), the patients were briefly presented pictures of common objects, like spoons and keys, to either their left or right visual field. The presentation time was set to less than 150 milliseconds, making it nearly impossible for the patients to move their eyes in time to change the picture's visual field. When the picture was presented to the right visual field, the patients were able to name the objects in the pictures, because information in the right visual field is sent directly to the left cerebral cortex, which controls most aspects of language. But when the pictures were presented to the left visual field, the patients usually claimed they saw nothing at all. Yet they were able to reach with their left hand under a screen that hid several objects from view, and identify from among the objects the one that had been presented in the picture. The right hemisphere was able to process the visual information in the picture and direct the left hand to identify tactilely the object depicted in the picture. But the information could not be transferred to the left hemisphere, where it would have engaged the language system. Similar results have been found by Levy, Trevarthen, and Sperry (1972) and Sperry, Zaidel, and Zaidel (1979).

Sleepwalking

An intriguing example of a dissociation is sleepwalking (**somnambulism**), fairly common in young children but not unheard of in adults (Anch, Browman, Mitler, & Walsh, 1988). About 20% of all children sleepwalk at least once. Typically, sleepwalkers are in a deep stage of sleep (stages 3 or 4, described below) and not in the Rapid Eye Movement (REM) stage of sleep. During sleepwalking a person is able to negotiate the environment and perform activities such as eating or dressing. Injuries are common, however. Sometimes sleepwalkers will stumble down stairs or walk into traffic. If awakened during an episode of somnambulism, the person is disoriented. There is generally no recall of the episode the next morning.

There are a few disturbing cases of individuals who have murdered in their sleep but claim no awareness of their heinous actions (see Cartwright & Lamberg, 1992, for a discussion of some of these cases). On May 24, 1987, Kenneth Parks, in debt and fired for embezzling $32,000 from his employer, fell asleep and then drove 14 miles to his in-laws' house, where he murdered his mother-in-law by stabbing her to death with her kitchen knife. He also stabbed his father-in-law. Parks awoke and, appalled at what he had done, called the police. Parks claimed that he had no awareness of committing the assault and murder, that he must have been sleepwalking. Certainly he had nothing to gain financially by murdering his in-laws, who had little money and no life insurance. Parks had a history of sleepwalking, as did other members of his family. A jury acquitted Parks, believing his story that he was asleep when he committed the murder and therefore not responsible for it.

As far as I know, there is no good physiological model to account for the dissociation between perceptual–motor processing and conscious awareness observed in sleepwalking. A sleepwalker who walks down a flight of stairs and makes a roast beef sandwich on rye while asleep would seem to be seeing the environment and performing actions to appropriately modify the environment in a purposeful way. Yet the sleepwalker is unaware of the environment and the self's interactions with it. It is clear that the EEG, a measure of the gross electrical activity of the outer portions of the cerebral cortex, is quite different in the deep stages of sleep—the stages in which sleepwalking usually occurs—than in REM or the waking state. The gist of the difference is that the EEG of a waking, alert person is highly irregular and of low amplitude whereas the EEG of the deep stages of sleep is more regular and of higher amplitude (more detail concerning EEG in sleep is described below). In some sense, presumably, the cerebral cortex is not functioning the same way in the deep stages of sleep as it does during the waking state.

Regulatory Malfunctions

The frontal lobes of the cerebral cortex seem to have what may be described as a regulating and planning function (see Goldman-Rakic, 1987a, for a more complete overview of frontal lobe function). The frontal lobes play an especially important role in reflective thought. Patients with frontal lobe damage sometimes have difficulty in organizing their behaviors (Luria, 1973), in focusing on relevant and ignoring irrelevant information (Squire, 1987), and in delaying a response when the task requires delay (Goldman-Rakic, 1987a; Luria, 1973). Depending on the exact location and extent of the damage, patients with frontal lobe brain damage may become less emotional, less assertive, less spontaneous, prone to behave in socially inappropriate ways, or unable to carry out verbal requests made by others (Stuss & Benson, 1986). Damage to the prefrontal lobe sometimes produces a condition in which patients still feel pain but claim that the pain does not bother them—the emotional component of pain is lost. Frontal lobes are also thought to play a role in using strategies to reconstruct past events. For example, a patient with frontal lobe damage may have trouble reconstructing the temporal order of past events even when the events are familiar to the patient (Squire, 1987). The frontal lobes may function as a component of "working" memory that helps sustain the activation of neurons involved in processing perceptual and symbolic information that may then be used to plan ahead and make decisions (Goldman-Rakic, 1992). I discuss working memory later in this chapter.

Note that consciousness itself cannot be said to reside in the frontal lobes. Patients who have experienced damage to their frontal lobes still are aware of stimuli, but show various kinds of impairments in the planning and regulation of behavior. It is also noteworthy that humans have proportionally more frontal lobe cortex than other animals. Presumably it is the additional frontal cortex that enables humans to excel at planning and at reflecting on the reasons for things. The frontal lobes play an important role in planning and reflecting because they receive a lot of input from other brain centers whose function involves perception of external stimuli, perceptual imagination, and manipulation of symbols (Goldman-Rakic, 1992; Jones & Powell, 1970). Frontal lobes, then, are well suited for integrating information on which planning and regulation of behavior is based.

IMPLICATIONS OF DISSOCIATIONS

What do dissociations tell us about consciousness? First, brain damage (and, in some cases, ordinary sleep) can interfere with consciousness but leave intact the ability to detect and respond to stimuli. As the materialist claims, consciousness is a function provided by the actions of physical processes taking place in the brain.

Second, consciousness depends on the recruitment of several brain centers working together. No one center controls all of consciousness. That is, there is no seat of consciousness, no single site where consciousness "takes place" (Dennett, 1991). If there were a single center for consciousness, then we would expect to see brain damage that undermines all of consciousness but leaves intact the capability of responding to all aspects of the outside world. In fact, dissociations are selective. They interfere with only one aspect of consciousness, such as the ability to be aware of visual information or recollect past experience. In the case of sleepwalking, where all of consciousness does seem dissociated from perceptual–motor processing, neural activity across the entire cerebral cortex, and not just in one small portion of the cortex, is quite different from the neural activity associated with waking consciousness. Furthermore, areas of the brain that when damaged lead to dissociation cannot by themselves produce a conscious experience. For example, an intact primary visual cortex may be necessary for a conscious visual experience, but vision also requires a functioning retina, optic nerve, and secondary visual cortex in order to produce normal visual consciousness.

Third, dissociations suggest that not all neural centers are equal in their contribution to the conscious character of experience. Many kinds of brain damage can cause blindness without blindsight. Damage to the right parietal lobe can cause visual and spatial deficits without causing neglect. Many kinds of brain damage can perturb memory without eliminating the conscious recollection of past events. What do the neural centers that underlie dissociations have in common that set them apart from the neural centers that do not? The answer to this question might go a long way toward telling us exactly how brain processes make consciousness possible, rather than just where in the brain those processes take place.

One suggestion, made by Michael Gazzaniga, is that consciousness requires the activation of language centers, or, more generally, the left hemisphere centers involved in interpreting experiences (Gazzaniga, 1985; 1988). Perhaps, then, consciousness is undermined when connections between language centers and other areas of the brain are damaged. The research on split-brain patients seems consistent with this idea. Split-brain patients will claim to be unaware of information processed only in their right hemisphere. And perhaps phenomena like blindsight can be explained as a disturbance in the connection between language centers and visual centers. If the damage is such that the visual system can still function, then the visual system will still be able to detect light, but not send information to the language centers in order to produce the conscious experience of seeing. Similarly, perhaps damage to the hippocampus makes it difficult for the brain to connect the language centers to other areas of the brain involved in recollecting an experience. Consequently, patients with bilateral hippocampal damage have no conscious recollections of the past subsequent to the damage. But other areas of their brain retain the ability to learn.

However, not all the evidence supports the model that consciousness requires intact connections between the language centers and other areas of the brain. For one thing, split-brain patients are able to report conscious awareness for some types of information presented only to their right hemisphere. One split-brain patient was presented pictures of faces to his left visual field (right hemisphere) and asked to indicate whether he recognized the faces and whether the faces were emotionally positive or negative. One of the pictures was of Hitler; the rest were of unfamiliar people. The patient recognized that Hitler's face was familiar but did not initially know the name. Furthermore, the patient indicated that the picture of Hitler was emotionally negative. This happened despite the fact that the connections between the visual centers of the patient's right hemisphere and his language centers in the left hemisphere were severed surgically (Sperry et al., 1979).

Another problem with Gazzaniga's model is that extensive damage to language centers can sometimes render a person mute, yet the person remains aware and is able to regulate behavior and plan ahead. Damage to the frontal lobes, on the other hand, can interfere with regulating and planning but leave language skills intact. It may be more reasonable to claim that connections to language centers are important to the reflective sense of consciousness, especially when those reflections are verbal in nature. The activation of language centers may not, however, be necessary for consciousness in the sense of awareness.

SECTION 2: DREAMING AS A STATE OF CONSCIOUSNESS

Human consciousness can be described in terms of states or levels of awareness. Daily, we pass through at least three distinct states of consciousness: the waking state, the nondreaming sleep state, and the dreaming state. The character of awareness and reflective thought is different depending on the conscious state. This section will focus on the dreaming state.

A TYPICAL NIGHT OF SLEEP

Let me begin by describing a typical night's sleep in an adult human (see Hobson, 1988; Carlson, 1994). Sleep usually lasts about 7 to 8 hours and is sometimes interrupted by brief periods of being awake, although many people sleep through the night without waking up. A night of sleep typically cycles through five stages of sleep, distinguished by electroencephalogram (EEG—an indirect

Awake, Relaxed

Stage I: Drowsy

Stage II: Light Sleep

Stage III: Deep Sleep

Stage IV: Very Deep Sleep

REM Sleep

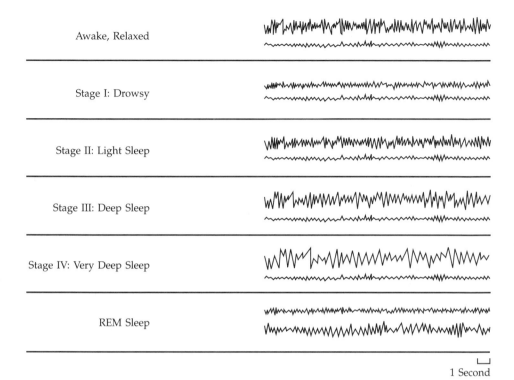

1 Second

FIGURE 2–2   An EEG recording of the stages of sleep. From *Psychology* by Fernald, Dodge, © 1994. Reprinted by permission of Prentice-Hall, Inc., Upper Saddle River, NJ.

measure of the gross electrical activity of the cerebral cortex); electro-oculogram (EOG—a measure that detects eye movements); electromyogram (EMG—a measure that detects muscle contraction); and other physiological measures. Some of the physiological correlates of the stages of sleep are depicted in Figure 2-2.

The first stage, called **stage 1**, occurs on falling asleep. The EEG of stage 1 sleep is usually of lower amplitude than waking EEG, although it otherwise resembles waking EEG. Often people will report brief but vivid dreams, or **hypnogogic hallucinations** as they are called. Such hallucinations are often described as bizarre continuations of fantasies entertained by the person just before falling asleep.

Within about 10 minutes or so, people usually enter **stage 2** sleep, characterized by an EEG containing K complexes (sharp rises and falls in EEG) and sawtooth rhythms. The EEG of stage 2 usually has a slower frequency and a greater amplitude than the EEG of stage 1. It takes a somewhat more intense stimulus to awaken a person from stage 2 than from stage 1 sleep. The skeletal muscles of the body are generally relaxed but toned (in a state of partial contraction). Bodily movement, as when a person turns over, is common during stage 2.

After about 15 to 20 minutes of stage 2, people enter **stage 3** followed by **stage 4** sleep, the deep stages of sleep. The EEG of deep sleep is characterized by slow waves of high amplitude, called **delta rhythm**. If the amount of delta wave in the EEG is less than about 50%, the sleeper is in stage 3. Once the percentage of delta wave in the EEG reaches at least 50%, the sleeper is in stage 4. Delta waves may reflect the simultaneous firing of many cortical neurons. Such synchronized firing indicates that the cortex is not receiving much information from perceptual centers or other parts of the brain. In contrast, the EEG of an awake person is desynchronized; many different inputs are causing the cortical neurons to fire in complex ways. The preponderance of delta waves in deep sleep indicates that the cerebral cortex is not doing much information processing although the existence of sleepwalking, which usually occurs during deep sleep, suggests that the brain does retain some ability to process external information. Less blood flows to the cerebral cortex during the deep stages of sleep than during other sleeping and waking states. It usually takes a very intense stimulus to awaken a person from deep sleep. Note, though, that people can be awakened from deep sleep. We are never completely cut off from the outside world.

Following deep sleep, people usually cycle back through stage 2 sleep and then enter the **rapid eye movement (REM)** stage of sleep, usually about 90 minutes after first falling asleep. REM is characterized by bursts of rapid horizontal and vertical movements of the eyes and by a desynchronized EEG reminiscent of a waking EEG. REM is sometimes referred to as paradoxical sleep because the EEG and other metabolic functions, like heart rate and respiration rate, resemble those of an awake person. Blood flow to the cerebral cortex increases during REM.

As you probably know, people awakened from REM will almost always report that they were dreaming. Dreaming is less likely to occur in other stages of sleep, although sometimes people awakened from non-REM stages of sleep will report that they were dreaming. Usually, the cognitions associated with non-REM stages lack the storylike quality and the wide range of images, sounds, and emotions that make up a dream. One of the most reliable distinctions between REM and non-REM cognitions seems to be the length of the dream report, with longer dreams associated with REM (Antrobus, 1991). Much of the cerebral cortex receives sustained activation during REM-stage sleep, consistent with the observation that dreams take place during REM. The cerebral cortex is never completely inactive, though, so there is always the possibility of significant cognitions during non-REM sleep.

Other physiological correlates of REM include penile erections in males, increased vaginal blood flow in females, increased variability of heart rate and respiration rate, and a loss of skeletal muscle tone. The lack of muscle tone prevents the dreamer from moving around too much during dreaming. Yet the motor cortex of the brain is quite active during REM, giving rise, presumably, to the sense that one is moving during the dream.

After spending about 10 to 15 minutes in the first bout of REM, people typically descend through stage 2 into the deep stages of sleep again and then ascend through stage 2 back into REM. Over the course of a night, people usually cycle through all of the stages (except for stage 1) of sleep about 4 to 6 times. A typical young adult spends about 5% in stage 1, 48% in stage 2, 23% in stages 3 and 4, and 24% in REM. However, the percentage of time people spend in the deep stages of sleep decreases while the percentage of time they spend in REM increases over the course of a night's sleep. By the last cycle, people may spend only a minute or two in deep sleep but spend 45 minutes or so in REM.

As the amount of time spent in REM increases over the course of the night, so too do the fanciful and bizarre elements of the typical REM dream. Based on the reports of subjects awakened after several REM bouts, the dreams at the end of a night's sleep tend to be longer, more bizarre, and less reflective of the previous day's events than the dreams from the beginning of a night's sleep (Cartwright, 1977; Kondo, Antrobus, & Fein, 1989). **Lucid dreams**, defined as dreams in which the dreamer is aware that she or he is dreaming, are also more common in the later bouts of REM (LaBerge, 1985). Still, there is often a continuity among the dreams of a single night of sleep. When naive judges are given transcripts of dream reports from a single subject, the judges reliably rate the dreams from the same night to be more similar than the dreams from two different nights. Apparently, the similarity of the dreams across a single night comes from the recurrence of an important object, person, or emotional state. The actual story that unfolds in each dream is not repeated across a night's dreams (Cipolli, Baroncini, Fagioli, & Fumai, 1987).

There is considerable variability among people with respect to how long they sleep, how many times they wake up, and the exact percentage of time spent in each stage of sleep (Webb, 1975). Furthermore, the exact pattern of stages may differ from person to person and from night to night within the same person's sleep. For example, some people may go back and forth between stage 2 and the deep stages several times before entering REM, while other people may enter REM after every pass through stage 4. What people have in common is the cyclic nature of a night's sleep, especially the tendency to drift in and out of REM and the deep stages several times a night, the tendency for the length of REM to increase and the length of deep-stage sleep to decrease over the night, and the physiological characteristics of each stage. It is worth noting that virtually everyone dreams several times a night, even though many people remember very few of their dreams.

THE FUNCTION OF REM SLEEP

One theory of the function of sleep claims that sleep helps the body and the brain restore themselves, perhaps by increasing protein synthesis and replenishing the neurotransmitters used to communicate among neurons. Another, conceivably complementary theory is that sleep enforces the conservation of energy in warm blooded animals (i.e., mammals and birds), who use a lot of energy to maintain body temperature (see Anch, Browman, Mitler, & Walsh, 1988; Hobson, 1988; or Empson, 1993, for a discussion of theories of sleep function).

REM-stage sleep, however, presents a paradox. Why is the brain so active during REM, especially if the function of sleep is to restore neurotransmitters or conserve energy? Dreams are often too bizarre and poorly remembered to serve the function of useful reflective thought. Yet REM presumably has some function. Almost all mammalian species display REM sleep. Many neural centers in the brain stem control the cycling in and out of REM over the course of a night. When people are selectively deprived of REM sleep for several nights, they display a greater percentage of REM when allowed to sleep normally (Dement, 1960; Agnew, Webb, & Williams, 1967). **REM rebound**, as it is called, suggests that people need to make up REM that is lost from sleep. What, then, is the function of REM sleep? There are at least two theoretical perspectives on REM function.

Learning and REM

One theoretical perspective is that REM-stage sleep plays a role in learning (I discuss learning in more detail in chapter 6: The Physiology of Learning and Remembering). As a consequence of intense stimulation of cortical and other brain tissue, an animal or person may benefit from, or assimilate better, the previous day's experiences (see McGrath & Cohen, 1978; Smith, 1993; Winson, 1990). The claim is not that the content of a dream necessarily provides information that might be useful in learning from a previous day's experiences. After all, people do not necessarily dream of the experiences they need to remember nor do they remember very many of their dreams. Rather, the claim is that the activity of stimulating the brain will help consolidate experiences, regardless of the actual dream content.

One bit of supporting evidence for a learning function for REM comes from the observation that human infants spend about 8 of their typically 16 hours of sleep in REM (50%) whereas adults spend about 2 of their 8 hours of sleep in REM (24%). Presumably, infants are learning information at a greater rate than adults.

Other research has demonstrated a correlation between how much a person learns and how much time that person spends in REM (Lewin & Gombosh, 1973; Paul & Dittrichoria, 1975). For example, among students learning a foreign language, those who were making more rapid progress at learning the new language also tended to show a greater increase in the percentage of time they spent in REM (de Konoick, Lorrain, Christ, & Proulx, 1989). Research on animals reveals the same correlation between degree of learning and amount by which REM increases (e.g., Portell, Marti, Segura, & Morgado, 1989; Smith, 1996.). There have also been failures to observe a correlation between amount of learning and amount of REM (e.g., Castaldo, Krynicki, & Goldstein, 1974), but usually such failures are observed when the information the subjects are asked to learn is simple or trivial, like lists of words (McGrath & Cohen, 1978).

Some experiments on REM deprivation also seem consistent with a learning function for REM. A subject can be deprived of REM by being awakened immediately on entering REM. Typically such subjects will still spend appreciable amounts of time in the other stages of sleep, because REM usually comes at the end of each cycle and not at the beginning. The procedure selectively interferes with REM but not the other stages of sleep. Researchers who study the effects of REM deprivation always include a control group that is either randomly awakened in the course of a night or selectively deprived of another stage of sleep, usually stage 4. The performance of the REM-deprived group is then compared with the performance of the control group.

Some REM deprivation experiments suggest that when people are deprived of REM they have trouble remembering complex information, like stories, taught to them just prior to the REM deprivation (Empson & Clarke, 1970; Tilley & Empson, 1978; Smith, 1993; see McGrath & Cohen, 1978, or Smith, 1993, for a review). REM deprivation has little effect on the retention of simple information, like lists of words (Castaldo et al., 1974; Chernik, 1972). Sometimes experimenters find no effects of REM deprivation on memory and cognition (e.g., Chernik, 1972).

An example of an REM deprivation experiment comes from Karni, Tanne, Rubenstein, Barton, Askenasy, and Sagi (1994). Their subjects first began to learn a visual discrimination task and then had either a normal night of sleep, their non-REM sleep disrupted, or their REM sleep disrupted. The disruption of REM resulted in a lack of improvement on the visual discrimination task, as compared with the other conditions, in which the subjects did improve on the task. Important to the interpretation of the experiment was the finding that REM disruption had no effect on the performance of another perceptual task learned before the disruption. So REM disruption undermined the learning of a new task but not the capacity to perform already-learned tasks.

Among the many variants of the hypothesis that REM aids in consolidating memory (see Moffitt, Kramer, & Hoffman, 1993) is the idea that REM helps the sleeper better assimilate emotional experiences. Consistent with this proposal is an experiment in which subjects were presented a stressful movie (depicting a gruesome circumcision rite performed with stone knives by a remote South Pacific tribal group) (ouch!), just before going to sleep and again the next day. The subjects who were not REM deprived showed less of a stress reaction to the second viewing of the film than did the subjects who were REM deprived (Greenberg, Pillard, & Pearlman, 1972). Incidentally, subjects who are not REM deprived rarely dream directly of the events in the stressful movies (see Arkin & Antrobus, 1978), but nevertheless seem to display reduced stress-reactions to such movies when allowed to dream.

The physiological basis for how REM-stage sleep enhances learning is unclear. One suggestion (Winson, 1990) is that REM activates the hippocampus, which is a brain structure important to consolidating memory. As I discuss in chapter 6: The Physiology of Learning and Remembering, the hippocampus seems to help strengthen the connections among neurons that underlie the conscious recollection of all past events. Pavlides and Winson (1989) have shown that for rats, the neurons in the hippocampus that represent locations encountered when the rat explores its environment while awake also become activated during REM sleep. Presumably, the activation of the hippocampus during REM helps the animal to remember how to navigate its environment, and, perhaps, the human to remember the previous day's events. One problem with Winson's idea, though, is that it would seem to predict that dreams would ordinarily be memorable. After all, dreaming frequently occurs in REM when the hippocampus is supposedly activated. Yet unless people wake up during or right after a dream, their dreams are usually forgotten.

Priming and REM

A second theoretical perspective on REM function is that REM serves to periodically activate the brain in preparation for waking up. The idea is that prolonged sleep makes the brain so sluggish that it must occasionally be charged up, thereby enabling the person or animal to orient quickly to the environment on awakening. The priming would include periodic activation during REM sleep of the perceptual, thought, and emotional systems of the brain (Antrobus, 1993). Without this sort of priming, a person or animal would take too long to orient to the environment, or possibly might even go into coma (Vertes, 1986; Snyder, 1966). The main evidence consistent with the priming function for REM is that people and animals spend more time in REM near the end of the sleep period, close to the time when awakening is most probable, rather than near the beginning of the sleep period.

One intriguing additional piece of evidence for a priming function of REM comes from observations of dolphins, who sleep one brain hemisphere at a time and do not display REM sleep (Mukhametov, 1988). Because the sleep pattern of dolphins permits an alternating half of the brain to remain alert and active during sleep, the dolphin would have no additional need to prime the brain, as would other mammals for whom the hemispheres sleep simultaneously.

Other evidence consistent with a priming function for REM is the observation that people find it much easier to orient to the environment if they are awakened during REM than during the deep stages of sleep. Subjects have longer reaction times in their responses to stimuli and make more errors on a vigilance task when awakened from the deep stages than when awakened from REM (Scott, 1969, Jeannaret & Webb, 1963).

Finally, the priming hypothesis explains why the person or animal cycles in and out of REM several times over the course of a period of sleep. It is as if the cycling process ensures that the brain is regularly primed in case it is required to wake up and orient to the environment at any point during the sleep period. It may even be the case that an infant would die if the periodic priming provided by REM did not occur. There is some evidence that one of the causes of sudden infant death syndrome (SIDS) may be a lack of adequate REM sleep. Infants whose siblings have died of SIDS tend to have longer intervals between REM than does the average infant (see Vertes, 1986).

Still, the priming idea does not explain all the salient facts about dreams. Why are the contents of a dream often related, albeit in a fanciful and sometimes bizarre way, to a person's waking concerns and experiences? Why does the percentage of REM increase when a person is learning a new skill like a foreign language? Why does REM deprivation cause REM rebound?

As you have no doubt noticed, neither explanation of dream function elegantly explains all the salient facts. It is possible, of course, that REM and the dreams that accompany REM have several functions, including a learning and priming function. Or perhaps the essential function of REM is still unknown.

EXPLAINING THE CONTENTS AND CHARACTERISTICS OF DREAMS

The learning and priming theories of REM function suggest that REM and the dreams that accompany REM are general activities that benefit person or animal. They are examples of theories of dream *function*. It does not matter what specific dreams a person has in order for REM to help consolidate memory or to prime the brain in preparation for waking. But these theories do not explain the specific contents or characteristics of dreams. Why did I dream last night about playing volleyball with an eraser, rather than, say, about finding money in a suitcase? Why do I sometimes dream that I am being chased but am unable to move? Why do I have dreams that juxtapose people, events, and settings that never happen in real life? Why do my dreams usually seem real to me at the time?

Dreams as Extensions of Waking Concerns

One of the simplest ideas about the contents of dreams is that dreams are merely an extension of daily thoughts reflecting daily concerns. And certainly to some extent this idea is true. For example, Breger, Hunter, and Lane (1971) discuss the case of a railroad worker awaiting surgery to remove a vascular blockage in his leg. The worker dreamed of trying to unclog a railroad switch jammed with rust and sand. Van de Castle (1971) found that pregnant women were more likely to report dreams of babies, motherhood, and anxiety related to childbirth than were other women. Van der Kolk, Blitz, Burr, Sherry, and Hartmann (1984) found that many Vietnam combat veterans who suffer from posttraumatic stress report recurring nightmares representing traumatic events from the war.

While many dreams reflect waking concerns, not all dreams do. Often dreams depict events that never occurred or have unusually bizarre characteristics. And even when dreams directly or indirectly reflect waking life, there remains the question of why the dream involves one rather than some other event from waking life.

Freud's Theory of Dreams

Sigmund Freud provided a theory of dreams that departs from the simple view that dreams merely reflect the events and concerns of waking life. Briefly, Freud argued that a person's thoughts and behaviors are controlled in part by instinctual urges like the urge to mate, to eat, and to attack. Collectively these instinctual urges are called the **id**. Freud claimed that the id is an unconscious mechanism upon which a person would not ordinarily be able to reflect, but that the id exerts on the psyche a kind of pressure that can be relieved by satisfying the urge. Freud also thought that the urges of the id could be partially relieved by fantasies and dreams. So the urge to mate may be satisfied by actually mating, by fantasizing about mating, or by dreaming about mating. It is the **ego's** job to satisfy the urges of the id, within the restrictions imposed by the environment and by the **superego**, the moral aspect of the mind.

Thus, dreams, according to Freud, represent the fulfillment of the wishes of the id. Usually dreams are fashioned from waking thoughts (the "day residue"), but sometimes they make use of symbols that the ego uses to disguise the id's motives. So a dream about a train passing through a tunnel might symbolize the desire of the id for sexual intercourse. The purpose of this indirect way of expressing urges is to prevent the dreamer from becoming too anxious about the dream and thereby waking up.

To illustrate how Freud analyzed dreams, consider one of the examples he discussed in his masterpiece *The Interpretation of Dreams* (Freud, 1900/1953). One of his clients had a dream in which she was trying to prepare a dinner for several friends. In the dream the woman was unable to purchase what she needed in order to give the party and consequently had to abandon her wish. At what Freud called the "manifest," level, the dream admittedly seemed the opposite of wish fulfillment. Indeed, many dreams seem to be ridden with frustration, anxiety, or fear. However, Freud claimed that at the "latent," level, even negative dreams, like the dream of this patient, are wish fulfillments of one kind or another. The way Freud interpreted the patient's dinner party dream began with his observation that the patient had recently expressed concern that her husband was becoming interested in another woman. She claimed that her husband usually preferred women whose physique might be described as voluptuous. Freud interpreted the patient's dinner party dream as an unconscious wish to starve her rival and so make the rival less appealing to her husband.

Unfortunately, it is difficult to prove that dream content reflects some psychological need like wish fulfillment. The major difficulty is that most dreams are subject to alternative interpretations. For example, maybe Freud's female client had the dinner party dream because she was feeling insecure in her role as wife and so dreamed that a dinner party for which she was responsible was a disaster. As another example, if one has a dream that one's father died, maybe the dream represents a desire to restore a relationship with the father, or an unconscious hostility towards the father, or a fear of losing the father, or a fear of death of self symbolically represented by the father, or a regret about some past misunderstanding concerning the father, or any of a number of other possibilities. What evidence would prove one interpretation is the correct one?

There is evidence that supports Freud's theory that at least some dreams represent wish fulfillment. For example, one experiment (Hauri, 1970) required subjects to study for 6 hours on one day and to exercise for 6 hours on another day. After each day, subjects were awakened during REM and asked to report the contents of their dreams. Consistent with the idea that dreams represent wish fulfillment, subjects dreamed less about physical activity after exercising for 6 hours and dreamed less about problem solving after 6 hours of studying. Presumably, 6 hours of an activity leaves a person no longer wishing to engage in that activity. Note that if dreams merely reflect the events of the recent past, then it should have been the case that subjects would have dreamed more about exercise after exercising for 6 hours and more about problem solving after studying for 6 hours. Another example comes from the dreams that survivors of Nazi concentration camps remember having while living in the camps. They remember dreaming frequently of food, family, home, and sex (Susulowska, 1983). Be clear that the evidence that some dreams may represent wish fulfillment does not prove that all dreams represent wish fulfillment.

ACTIVATION-SYNTHESIS AND THE PHYSIOLOGICAL BASIS OF DREAM CONTENT

Freud was a materialist who believed that dreaming involves physiological mechanisms; however, his theory of wish fulfillment does not lend itself to developing physiological models. A very different approach to explaining the nature of dreams that is more physiologically based is Hobson's (1988) **activation-synthesis theory** and related proposals (Antrobus 1991). The gist of activation-synthesis theory is that the brain stem initiates the activation of the sensory, motor, and emotional areas of the cerebral cortex, which, in turn, produces the raw imagery for dreams. The cortex, especially the frontal lobes, responds to this activation as it would respond to information originating from outside the brain—namely, by trying to interpret, or synthesize, the raw imagery generated by the brain stem. The result of such a synthesis is the storylike quality of the dream.

The reason dreams involve a wide range of seemingly real sensations like sights, sounds, movements, and feelings is that the areas of the cortex involved in waking perception, movement, and feeling are activated by the brain stem, which is programmed to cycle in and out of REM several times a night. To some extent, there is a haphazard quality to this activation, due to the widespread and diffuse nature of the connections between the brain stem and cerebral cortex. In contrast to Freud's theory, then, unconscious wishes are not likely to be the event that triggers the onset of dreams.

The sense that the dream is really happening may be a consequence of the fact the cortex interprets the imagery activated by the brain stem as it would interpret external stimuli. Furthermore, the dreamer, unlike the awake fantasizer, cannot compare the imagined sensations with what is happening in the outside world and so verify that the sensations are only imaginary. Dreams, unlike most waking fantasies, probably seem involuntary because they are regularly triggered by the brain stem, regardless of what ideas or images the sleeper is entertaining at the time of the activation. The images are generated without the usual conscious decision-making process that controls most waking fantasies.

As I suggested above, the narrative quality of many dreams may reflect the involvement of the frontal lobes, which seem to play a role in organizing and integrating thoughts and behaviors to achieve some goal. It is known that damage to the frontal lobes can sometimes interfere with a person's ability to understand the point or theme in a story. Since the frontal lobes function to plan and regulate a wide range of actions and events, it is unlikely that dreams would only be about wish fulfillment.

Recent events and concerns are often reflected in dreams, probably because the connections among neurons that represent recent events are likely to be stronger than the connections among neurons representing less recent events. When dreams seem to be about events, people, and settings from the more distant past, they rarely are depictions of actual events. Instead, they imaginatively embellish upon some well-established patterns from one's life (also reflected in strong connections among neurons).

Why are dreams sometimes bizarre? One reason might be that the brain stem subjects the cortex to a more diffuse activation than the activation caused by external stimuli. Consequently, systems of neurons that in waking life would not be simultaneously activated are so activated during sleep. Freud thought that dreams are frequently bizarre in order to disguise the true intent of the id. Activation-synthesis theory, on the other hand, claims that bizarreness merely reflects the partially unsuccessful struggle of the cerebral cortex to interpret the ongoing barrage of images activated by the brain stem. For example, if a system of neurons representing a college classroom and a system of neurons representing a clown happen to be activated by the brain stem at the same time, the cortex may synthesize those images in a dream in which a clown is delivering a lecture in a classroom. Bizarreness is expected in longer dreams because longer dreams bring more unrelated images, which are therefore even more difficult to synthesize consistently.

Furthermore, waking thought is to some extent under the control of immediate perception. If you are talking to a friend, for example, the perception of the friend and the nature of the conversation is going to control the contents of your thoughts, giving them a coherent structure. But during a dream there is no outside world to provide structure and feedback; consequently, the flow of thought and the association of perceptions is less constrained than in ordinary waking thought. In fact, people who are awake but are in a quiet, dark room with no task demands placed on them will come to have fantasies as bizarre as their dreams (Antrobus, 1991).

Why do dreams sometimes seem to be metaphorical or symbolic? Hobson claims that dreams are, in fact, usually transparent. They usually depict the ordinary and obvious concerns and experiences of the dreamer. If the dreamer dreams of a train tunnel, it is because the cortex interpreted an image as a train tunnel. Had a dream image been interpreted as a sexual act, then the image would have likely been more explicitly sexual. Still, it does seem that dreams are sometimes metaphorical. What might be the physiological basis of metaphor in dreams?

One possibility is based on how waking experiences have strengthened the connections among neurons. Consider again the trainman awaiting surgery for vascular obstruction. He dreamed of repairing railroad track but not directly of surgery. A reason may be that the neural system representing his concept of repair, activated by a concern about the surgery, was strongly connected to a neural system representing fixing railroad tracks. Because the trainman was not familiar with surgery, there were no connections to represent a surgical operation. Consequently, the trainman did not directly dream about the surgery. Again, note that this sort of analysis of the metaphorical quality of dreams stands in contrast to the more Freudian idea that dreams are metaphorical so as to disguise their true nature and thereby protect the sleeper from anxiety.

SECTION 3: CONSCIOUSNESS IS LIMITED

One of the most salient characteristics of consciousness is that it is limited. That is, we are aware of or can reflect on only a small amount of information at any one time. What accounts for the limitations of consciousness?

In trying to answer this question, I will discuss two manifestations of the limitations of consciousness. One is **selective attention**, which has to do with a limit to how much information in the outside world we can take in, or pay close attention to, at any given moment. The other is **short-term memory**, which has to do with how much information, especially new information, we can keep in mind at any given moment.

SELECTIVE ATTENTION

Our capacity for paying attention to the external environment is limited. Suppose there are three conversations simultaneously going on around you. In one conversation people are talking about tax reform, in another they are talking about whether R.E.M. or the Rolling Stones are the better musicians, and in a third they are talking about transformational grammar. You might be able to follow and later remember something about one of these conversations, the one you pay attention to, but you won't be able to follow or remember much about the other two conversations. Why not? Why is attention selective?

Filter Models of Selective Attention

One explanation for why attention is selective is called the **filter** (or **bottleneck**) **model of attention** (Broadbent, 1958). The general idea of the filter model is that the processing of information passes through three basic stages. In the first stage all sensory stimuli are analyzed for their gross physical attributes (such as intensity and location), in the second stage the stimuli are analyzed for their meaning, and in the third stage the interpretations given to stimuli are placed into a permanent or long-term memory (LTM).

The model, depicted in Figure 2-3, claims that between the first and second stages of analysis there is a filter that screens out much of the information before it is processed for meaning. What information passes through the filter depends on what a person's goals are. For example, if a person's goal is to pay attention to the conversation on music taking place among a group of people on the person's left side, and ignore a conversation on transformational grammar taking place among a group of people on the person's right side, then auditory stimuli will be analyzed for their gross physical attributes and only the sounds coming from the left side will be allowed to pass through the filter to be analyzed for meaning. Sounds coming from the right side will be filtered out and so never analyzed for meaning.

The strongest support for the filter model comes from **dichotic listening experiments** in which subjects hear one verbal message played to their right ear and another verbal message simultaneously played to their left ear. In the typical dichotic listening experiment (Cherry, 1953; Moray, 1959), subjects are instructed to repeat aloud (or, as it is usually put, to "shadow") what they hear in one ear and ignore the message played in the other ear. The experimental

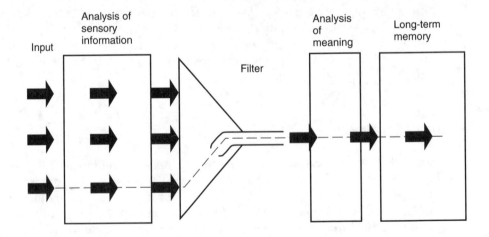

FIGURE 2–3 Filter model of attention. The dotted line highlights the channel of information that makes it through the filter.

arrangement simulates listening to one person in a room where several people are talking.

The major findings from dichotic listening experiments are as follows. First, subjects find it easy to shadow one message without experiencing much interference from the ignored message. Second, subjects are also good at shadowing a message even when both messages are played to one ear, as long as there is some discernible physical difference between the acoustical properties of the two messages (e.g., one message is spoken by a woman and the other message is spoken by a man). Third, if later asked about the ignored message, subjects will remember the physical characteristics of the ignored message, such as whether it was spoken by a male or a female, but not remember much about the semantic content of the ignored message, such as whether it was a lecture on transformational grammar or popular music. Of course, subjects will remember both the physical and the semantic features of the shadowed message.

Other research has revealed problems with the filter model, however. The main problem is that people are often aware of the presence of extremely important information in a channel of information that is supposedly filtered out. In dichotic listening experiments in which a subject's own name was presented in the ignored message, about one third of the subjects noticed and remembered the mention of their name later on (Moray, 1959; Wood & Cowan, 1995). But according to the filter model, the name should have been filtered out and never processed for meaning. So how did some of the subjects know that it was their name played in the ignored message?

Limited Resource Model

Kahneman (1973) and others (see Martindale, 1991; Ashcraft, 1994) have suggested that a better way to think about the selective nature of attention is to suppose that cognitive systems, such as the visual system, have only a **limited amount of cognitive "resources" or "energy"** for activating stored knowledge and cognitive skills. That is, only a portion of any given cognitive system can be active at any given moment.

The idea, then, is that any cognitive processes must receive some amount of activation that exceeds a threshold in order for that process to be effective. If the activation is below the threshold, then that particular process will not function or will function inefficiently. Attention, in the sense I am using it here, is the phenomenological consequence of activating cognitive processes, especially perceptual processes, to their threshold. Because there is a limit to how much of the cognitive system can be activated at any one time, our phenomenological experience is that we are aware of only a limited portion of our environment at any given moment.

According to this limited resource model of selective attention, the available resources are sufficient only for activating perceptual and other cognitive processes necessary to pay attention to one channel of information at a time. So processing two different messages for their meaning is difficult, not because a filter screens out one of the messages, but because there are not enough resources to activate the processes required to pay attention to two messages. The model also claims that different cognitive operations require different amounts of the limited pool of activation to work efficiently. Processing for meaning, for instance, ordinarily uses more cognitive resources than processing for gross physical characteristics. Identifying one's own name or any other very familiar stimulus uses fewer cognitive resources than identifying less familiar stimuli like income tax concepts. Thus subjects in a dichotic listening experiment may recognize their name in an ignored message because the tiny proportion of cognitive resources not committed to processing the shadowed message is enough to carry out the task of identifying a very familiar stimulus.

An important modification of resource models of attention is the idea that people possess several independent pools of resources. One pool may be dedicated to processing verbal information, another may be dedicated to processing visual information, another may be dedicated to motor processing, and so on. Such a proposal was motivated by the observation that people can carry out several lines of information processing simultaneously (such as reading and listening to music) without much interference between them, as long as the types of information are dissimilar (Hellige, 1990; Svenko, Jerneic, & Kulenovic, 1983; Wickens, 1984; Dawson & Schell, 1983).

Attention and Perception

In the case of paying attention to stimuli in the outside world, probably the most important of the activated cognitive systems are the perceptual ones (discussed in the next chapter)whereby the nature of external stimuli is ascertained (e.g., determining that a visual stimulus is a human face). Paying attention may also involve other cognitive processes, such as those underlying memory and reasoning. Paying attention to a conversation on popular music, for example, might include remembering that "Losing My Religion" was an R.E.M. hit song.

The connection between attention and perceptual processes has been developed in an influential model of attention and perception proposed by Anne Treisman (1988). Her model consists of two stages. The first stage is called **preattentive processing** and has to do with the simple perceptual operation of detecting the presence of a particular stimulus. According to Treisman, this simple preattentive process requires relatively few resources. It is relatively easy to pay attention to a stimulus if all one has to do is detect whether the stimulus is present. For example, it is easy to find a child's red toy truck in the playroom if none of the other toys are trucks. One need then pay attention only to whether a toy has the shape of a truck.

The second stage is called **focused attentive processing** and has to do with the more complex operation of determining whether some combination of stimuli are present. In order to pay attention to the combination, one must use more resources. For example, it is harder to find the child's red toy truck in the playroom if there are other toy trucks and other red toys. Now one must use the more resource-demanding focused attentive processes in order to find the stimulus that has the combination of redness and truckness. Things get really tough if there are lots of red toy trucks in the playroom and the child absolutely will not get dressed until you find for her the red toy truck that Uncle Carl bought last summer!

A nice experimental example illustrating the differential resource requirements of preattentive and focused attentive perceptual processes comes from Treisman and Gelade (1980). In this experiment, subjects searched for the letter *T* in an array of *I*s and *Y*s. Subjects found the *T* relatively quickly. In this array, none of the distractors contained the horizontal line of the *T*, so subjects could look for just the horizontal line when searching for *T*. Preattentive processing was all it took to find the horizontal line and therefore the letter *T* in the array. In another condition of the experiment the subjects looked for the *T* in an array of *I*s and *Z*s. Now it took the subjects relatively longer to find the *T*. The second array contained distractors that possessed the horizontal line (*Z*) or the vertical line (*I*), so the subjects had to look for a stimulus that was a combination of the vertical line and the horizontal line. That required focused attentive processing that takes more resources and so a longer time to accomplish. Moreover, when Treisman and Gelade increased the number of letters in the array, subjects looking for *T* were slowed down much more when they had to pay attention to a combination of features (i.e., the distractors were *I*s and *Z*s) than when they had to pay attention to only a particular feature (i.e., the distractors were *I*s and *Y*s).

SHORT-TERM MEMORY

Another manifestation of the limitations of consciousness is the phenomenon of **short-term memory (STM)**, which has to do with limitations on how much information we can use or keep in mind at any given moment. To illustrate, suppose I asked you to read and then repeat back verbatim from memory this sentence: "Call me Ishmael." No problem, right? Now read and try to repeat back from memory this sentence: "Some years ago—never mind how long precisely—having little or no money in my purse, and nothing particular to interest me on shore, I thought I would sail about a little and see the watery part of the world." It's getting harder. And of course there is no chance that you would be able to repeat back from memory the first 10 pages (much less the entire novel) of Herman Melville's *Moby Dick*. Well, why not? Why is human short-term memory so limited?

Older Models of Short-Term Memory

A model of short-term memory (STM) that was influential 20 or 30 years ago was the model developed by Atkinson and Shiffrin (1968). This model, which may generically be called a **duplex model** (Klatzky, 1980), proposes that STM is a kind of memory system that is distinct from another kind of memory system, usually called **long-term memory (LTM)**. The STM system can store only a few items; that is, it has a limited storage space, and can ordinarily keep those items in the short-term store for only a few seconds. Certain activities, in particular rehearsal (repeating information to oneself), can prolong the duration the information is held in STM. LTM, on the other hand, is supposed to have a virtually unlimited capacity that can store information for decades. Certain activities, again rehearsal being the predominant one, can cause information to be transferred from STM to LTM. If a person does not engage in those activities, information in STM will not enter LTM and so will be lost.

Evidence for the duplex model of STM comes from several kinds of experiments (see Klatzky, 1980, for a review). One kind of experiment asks subjects to repeat back, in order, a series of rapidly presented symbols, such as digits. Most subjects can recall the symbols perfectly, as long as there are no more than about 7 symbols (Miller, 1956). Recall becomes error-ridden when subjects are asked to recall more than about 7 or so unrelated symbols. This sort of experimental demonstration is known as **memory span**. Measures of memory other than verbatim recall, such as recognition, yield slightly different estimates of memory span (see Stern, 1985). Although memory for newly encountered information is ordinarily limited to only a few items, people can remember very large amounts of information from their past. That is, LTM has a much larger storage capacity than does STM.

One well-known fact about memory span is that the number of symbols that can be remembered depends on the relationships among the symbols. If subjects are able to perceive a relationship between adjacent symbols in the set, they may understand the related symbols as one chunk of information. A subject may have a memory span of 7 letters for unrelated letters like "NQZWSD" but have a memory span of 21 letters if each set of three letters is a simple word (e.g., "cat"). However, subjects are likely to remember only about seven 3-letter words. As another example, a subject may remember 5 unrelated digits but remember 20 digits if each set of 4 digits stands for a meaningful year (e.g., 1066, 1492, 1776, 1984, 2001) (see Stern, 1985).

Another characteristic of STM, but not LTM, is that information is held in STM for only a short period of time. The classic experiment on the transient nature of STM was done by Peterson and Peterson (1959). On each of a series of trials, Peterson and Peterson required their subjects to remember three unrelated letters (e.g., XRZ), for a varying amount of time. The experiment prevented the subjects from mentally rehearsing (repeating the letters to oneself) by requiring them to count backwards by threes from some arbitrarily selected number (e.g., 657). Then the subjects were required to recall the three letters. On the first few trials, subjects recalled most of the letters, even after rather long delays. But after a few trials, delays began to have a dramatic effect on recall. After only a 5 second delay, subjects remembered only about 50% of the letters. After a 15 second delay, subjects recalled only about 10% of the letters. Note that LTM does not seem to have the transient property that gives STM its name. People can accurately recall some information about at least a few events that occurred years and even decades in their past.

Evidence for the duplex model of STM is also provided by the **serial position effect in recall**. The serial position effect refers to the finding that when subjects are given a list of words (or other symbols) to remember and are later allowed to recall the list in any order, they will remember the first few words on the list and the last few words on the list better than the words in the middle of the list (Murdock, 1962). The advantage for the first few words is called the **primacy effect**, while the advantage for the last few words is called the **recency effect**.

The usual explanation is that the primacy effect reflects the fact that the first few words are better rehearsed and so are more likely to enter LTM than are words in the middle and end of the list. Consistent with the LTM explanation of the primacy effect is the finding that if words are presented very fast, and thereby less likely to be rehearsed, the primacy effect is diminished (Murdock, 1962). The recency effect reflects the fact that the last few words are still in STM. Consistent with the STM interpretation is the finding that if recall is delayed for 30 seconds by requiring subjects to perform mental arithmetic, then the recency effect disappears (Postman & Phillips, 1965). Note that speed of presentation and delay have different effects on recall, consistent with the idea that STM and LTM are separate memory systems. In the next section I will discuss more recent work that challenges the STM explanation of the recency effect in recall of lists.

The Demise of the Duplex Model of Short-Term Memory

There are a number of experiments that led to the demise of the duplex model of STM (nicely summarized by Anderson, 1995). One influential line of research was initiated by Craik and Lockhart (1972) and is usually called **levels or depth of processing**. I discuss this research again in the memory chapter. The gist of this research is that people ordinarily remember information better if they process that information for meaning than if they process it for its superficial characteristics or if they passively rehearse the information. For example, Parkin (1984) found that subjects who made judgments about the meaning of words on a list recalled more of the words than did subjects who made judgments about the number of vowels in each word. Sporer (1991) showed that subjects more accurately recognized whether they had been presented photographs of faces if they had previously judged each face for how honest it appeared rather than for the sex of the face.

The main point to be made here is that the degree to which information is initially learned is one of the important determinants of memory. When information is processed more deeply, it is ordinarily better recalled (there is a qualification to this conclusion, discussed in the chapter on memory). There is no need, then, to postulate a short-term memory in order to explain the remembering and forgetting of newly encountered information. Furthermore, and contrary to the duplex model, frequency of rehearsal per se does not reliably predict how well information is remembered later on. Glenberg, Smith, and Green (1977) fooled subjects into believing that they were to remember four-digit numbers. After the presentation of each four-digit number, subjects were required to rehearse a word for 2, 6, or 18 seconds. When given a surprise recall test for the words, the number of seconds of rehearsal did not matter to recall (although it did matter to how well subjects could recognize whether the word had been rehearsed).

What about the recency effect in recall, which suggests that information at the end of the list is held in STM? It turns out that there is legitimate reason to doubt the STM explanation of the recency effect. When there is a substantial delay (e.g., 20 seconds) between the presentation of each and every item on the list, during which subjects are distracted from rehearsing, the subjects are still more likely to recall the last few items on the list than they are to recall the items in the middle of the list (see Greene, 1986). The delays should have eliminated from short-term memory all of the items, yet the recency effect persists. It may be that the final items on a list are better remembered because they are temporally distinctive and therefore more salient than are the items in the middle of the list (Glenberg & Swanson, 1986). Even after much longer delays between the presentation and recollection of information, information that is distinctive is better remembered (see chapter 4: Memory).

What about the fact that people tend to forget recently presented information rather rapidly? This tendency may be described as **negatively accelerated forgetting**. The longer the delay between the presentation of information and the attempt to remember it, the more the forgetting. The rate at which information is forgotten, however, is greater at first and less later on—forgetting is negatively accelerating. It turns out that this tendency is observed even when measuring retention after delays ranging from seconds to weeks (e.g., Wickelgren, 1975; see Wixted & Ebbesen, 1991). The very rapid forgetting observed in some short-term memory experiments (e.g., Peterson & Peterson, 1959) is largely due to the fact that the information is so poorly learned in the first place. When information is better learned, then the rate of forgetting tends to slow down. But the same negatively accelerated forgetting is observed (Anderson & Schooler, 1991). So there is no need to postulate a separate short-term memory system to account for the rapid forgetting of (some) recently presented information. What matters to the rate of forgetting is how well the information is initially learned.

Newer Models of Short-Term Memory

More current models of STM do away with the idea that there are two distinct memory systems with different properties. Instead, according to these newer models (see Schneider, 1993), there are complex cognitive systems, portions of which are activated at any given moment in order to accomplish some given task. Some cognitive scientists prefer to call this newer model **working memory**, rather than short-term memory. I will use the working memory label to stand for a model of short-term memory. The short-term memory label will stand for the collection of phenomena surrounding the retention of recently presented new information.

The basic idea of what may be called a generic working memory model is similar to the limited resources model of selective attention. At any given moment, environmental stimuli interact with ongoing brain processes and so activate various portions of the memory and cognitive systems. For example, consider a person who wants to dial the phone number of WaitnLate Airline and finds the 7-digit number for the airline in a personal phone book. The environment will activate the brain processes underlying the perception of the seven numbers, the recollection that the number must be preceded by 1-800, and the motor programs for dialing numbers. Crucial to all of this is that something enables all of these processes to remain active long enough to complete the task of dialing WaitnLate. Enter working memory.

I want to be clear that working memory does not constitute a separate memory where only a little information is stored for only a short period of time. Rather, working memory is a collection of skills or processes, like any other cognitive process, such as perceiving, remembering, reasoning, and executing movements. The main function of the collection of skills that constitute working memory is that it prolongs the activation of other cognitive processes. Working memory is not a special place or a separate memory system where things are temporarily stored. Rather, it is an operation that stimulates other operations until the task at hand is completed.

Why is it difficult to remember more than about seven new items of information or to remember new information more than a few seconds? The working memory model makes use of the same sort of limited resources idea that was used to explain selective attention. Indeed, one of the strengths of the working memory model is that it claims that selective attention and a limited short-term memory are manifestations of the same process—limited cognitive resources. The idea is that the working memory operation itself draws on the limited pool of resources available to the cognitive system as a whole. And some of those resources are also used by the other cognitive operations that the working memory operation seeks to prolong. So the working memory operation can draw on only so many resources before the pool of resources is drained dry. If a task requires too much information or too many procedures to accomplish (e.g., rehearsing the 87-word sentence that is the fourth sentence of Melville's *Moby Dick*), then the working memory operation will not be able to keep all the relevant elements active and so forgetting will occur.

Furthermore, task demands are likely to activate ever-changing cognitive operations and data, requiring that the working memory operation stop sustaining the activation of one set of operations and begin sustaining the activation of a different set of operations. Consider the person who is rehearsing WaitnLate's phone number in anticipation of dialing the airline in order to get flight information and is interrupted by a friend who wants to know whether

her R.E.M. CD has been returned. The phone number rehearsal operation must give way to the retrieving CD information operation. As a result, the phone number rehearsal operation will lose enough of its activation that the person is at risk of forgetting the phone number. If the person also lost her friend's R.E.M. CD, she is really in trouble. At any rate, she cannot sustain the activation of the phone number very long before task demands will require some other cognitive operation's activation to be sustained. The consequence is that recently encountered information tends to be quickly forgotten.

Some of the findings that embarrassed the duplex model are not problematic for the working memory model. Consider the levels of processing research. What matters to memory is how new information (e.g., a person's face) is processed (e.g., for honesty or for sex), and not how long it is rehearsed. Working memory models posit the sustaining of the activation of cognitive processes. If the processes so activated lead to longer term retention, then new information will be remembered better than if the activated processes are less suitable for longer term retention.

Retrieval of Recently Encountered Information

The idea that short-term memory may be conceived of as a working memory that functions to prolong activation is supported by research on the rate at which people can retrieve an item from a short list of recently presented items. A paradigm for studying the rate of retrieval from short-term memory was first developed by Saul Sternberg (1966, 1969).

Sternberg required subjects to memorize a short list of unrelated digits (e.g., 3 and 7). The size of the to-be-remembered set of digits was always less than the usual memory span of about 7 items. Subjects were then given a single number, called a probe, and had to decide if the probe was in the set. To illustrate, suppose subjects were given 3 and 7 to memorize and then were given 7 as a probe. They would respond "yes" (by pressing a button). But if the subjects were given 5 as a probe, they would respond "no" (by pressing another button).

Sternberg varied the size of the set, sometimes asking subjects to memorize only one digit, sometimes two digits, sometimes three digits, and so on. He found that the bigger the size of the to-be-remembered set, the longer it took subjects to respond to a single probe. For example, subjects would take about 40 milliseconds longer to respond "yes" to the digit 7 if they had been required to remember the set 3, 7, 8 than if they had been required to remember the set 3 and 7. Similarly, subjects would take about 40 milliseconds longer to respond "no" to 2 if the memorized set had been 3, 7, 8 than if the set had been 3 and 7. Each new digit placed in the memorized set adds about 40 to 50 milliseconds to the decision time about a single probe. Many similar experiments have also found that response time to probes increases as the memory set size increases (see Ashcraft, 1994). Figure 2-4 shows a typical subject's reaction times, but only for the "yes" responses. The results are about the same for the "no" responses.

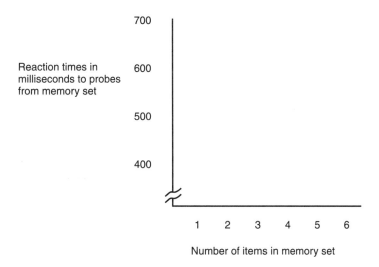

Reaction times in
milliseconds to probes
from memory set

Number of items in memory set

FIGURE 2–4   Typical results from experiments (e.g., Sternberg, 1966) on retrieving items from a set of to-be-remembered items. The response times are for the probes requiring a positive response.

Sternberg interpreted such results as indicating that subjects search through their STM one digit at a time, that is **serially**, as opposed to accessing all digits at the same time, that is, **in parallel**. If the search process were a parallel one, Sternberg reasoned, then the addition of each digit to the memorized set would not slow down subjects' responses to a single probe.

More recently, some cognitive psychologists have interpreted Sternberg's results using the working memory concept of a limited capacity for sustaining activation (Baddeley & Ecob, 1973; Martindale, 1991). The explanation is that the more items that must keep active, the less activation there is for any one item in the set, and so the longer it takes to make the judgment about any item.

The working memory model's explanation of retrieval predicts that subjects should be able to respond most quickly to a probe that is the last item in the memorized set, because that item will likely retain more activation than the first few items in the set. Critically important to the prediction is that the probe be presented immediately after the memorized set is presented. The serial search model originally proposed by Sternberg predicts, instead, that subjects should respond most slowly to a probe that is the last item in the set, because it will be the last one searched. Most of the results support the working memory model's explanation (see Wickelgren, 1977). For example, subjects given 8 as a probe immediately after studying the memory set would more quickly respond "yes" if the memory set were 3, 7, 2, 8 than if it were 3, 8, 7, 2.

Baddeley's Tripartite Working Memory

Of what does the working memory operation consist? Baddeley (1986, 1992) has one of the more influential versions of a working memory model. Baddeley claims that there are at least three components to working memory. These are the articulatory loop, the visuospatial sketchpad, and the central executive. Collectively, these three components work together to keep relevant information and cognitive processes activated until a task is completed or a new task is begun.

The **articulatory loop** is a kind of internal speech mechanism that functions to rehearse verbal information. An example of evidence for the articulatory loop is that the rate at which people can read a list of words is directly related to the number of words they can immediately recall from the list (see Cowan, 1994). For example, people take longer to read and have a harder time remembering "Czechoslovakia, Somaliland, Nicaragua, Afghanistan, Yugoslavia" than to read and remember "Chad, Burma, Greece, Cuba, Malta." Baddeley, Thomson, and Buchanan (1975) found that subjects could remember an average of 2.80 out of 5 words from the longer-word list but 4.17 out of 5 from the shorter-word list. More shorter-length words than longer-length words can be cycled through the articulatory loop in any given amount of time, so each of the shorter-length words will more likely have a level of activation above the threshold necessary for them to be in mind when the subject tries to recall the words.

Incidentally, the advantage for short words is eliminated when there is a long delay between the presentations of each and every word on the list (see Cowan, 1994). Such delays tend to equalize the amount of time for cycling the short and long words through the articulatory loop, so recall is now as good with long words as with short words.

The second component of Baddeley's working memory model is the **visuospatial sketchpad**, which functions to rehearse visual images, such as the image of a person's face. Baddeley claims that the visuospatial sketchpad is independent of the articulatory loop. In a famous study (famous in cognitive psychology circles, anyway), Baddeley and Hitch (1974) required subjects to rehearse digits and to make judgments about the spatial arrangement of letters. The tasks were done simultaneously. In the spatial task, subjects saw two letters (e.g., *AB*) and had to decide if a sentence describing the relationship between the two letters (e.g., "*A* follows *B*") was true or false. The intriguing finding was that the number of digits the subjects were required to rehearse did not affect their performance on the spatial task. The subjects performed the spatial task at about the same speed and with the same number of errors when rehearsing as many as 8 digits as when rehearsing only 1 digit. That is, increasing the amount of activation necessary to use the articulatory loop to rehearse the numbers did not affect the activation of the visuospatial sketchpad necessary to hold in mind the spatial relationship between the letters.

The third component of Baddeley's working memory model is the **central executive**. This may be regarded as a skill or process that makes decisions about which other component of working memory must be activated in order to accomplish a task. For example, a primarily visual task would require the activation of the visuospatial sketchpad but not the articulatory loop. The central executive presumably functions to decide when activation of one set of operations should cease and activation of another set of operations begin, in response to task demands.

In one intriguing line of research, Baddeley (1992) has provided evidence that one of the deficits associated with Alzheimer's disease may be an ineffective central executive. In one experiment, patients with Alzheimer's disease, as well as young and elderly normal subjects, were required to perform a visual tracking task and a verbal memory span task. At first, the subjects performed each task separately. The difficulty of each task was then adjusted so that Alzheimer patients were making the same proportion of errors on the tasks as were the younger and elderly control subjects. Subjects were then required to perform the two tasks simultaneously. Normal elderly patients were only slightly impaired by the requirement to perform both tasks simultaneously; moreover, their degree of impairment was the same as that of the younger subjects. But Alzheimer patients showed a marked impairment in the simultaneous condition, suggesting that they lost much of their ability to coordinate their cognitive resources, a function of the proposed central executive.

Brain Location of Short-Term Memory

The essential idea of a working memory model, then, is that short-term retention reflects the sustained activation of any of a large number of cognitive processes. Working memory is not a particular place in the brain that stores recently encountered information, as the old duplex model of short-term memory would have it. Instead, according to a working memory model, the phenomenological experience of having information in short-term memory potentially involves activity taking place in many locations throughout the brain. In fact, studies of brain activity suggest that a sustained neural activation, correlated with performance on a short-term memory task, is observed in many locations of the brain. These locations include temporal cortex, parietal cortex, and prefrontal cortex (see Schneider, 1993).

One example of the research on sustained neural activity comes from Funahashi, Bruce, and Goldman-Rakic (1989). They measured neural activity in monkeys' prefrontal cortex while the monkeys were engaged in a short-term memory task. The task required the monkey to fixate a central stimulus while a peripheral cue from one of eight locations was presented briefly. The monkey had to remain fixated on the central stimulus for 1.5 to 6 seconds after the cue blinked off. The monkey then directed its fixation to the peripheral cue and got a reward. To get the reward, though, the monkey had to remember the location of the cue for up to 6 seconds. The neurons in the prefrontal cortex responded longer when the delay was longer. Furthermore, if the activity of the neurons decayed during the delay interval, the monkey was more likely to make an error.

Goldman-Rakic (1992) has argued that the frontal lobes, in particular, play a role in prolonging or inhibiting activity in other parts of the brain. Goldman-Rakic bases this argument on animal studies like that just described and on brain lesion studies that show that lesions in the monkey's prefrontal cortex undermine its performance on short-term memory tasks. The frontal lobes are particularly well-suited for this function because of their connections with motor and sensory cortex located in other lobes of the brain. Perhaps, then, the frontal lobes play the role of something like Baddeley's central executive control process.

THE EFFECTS OF PRACTICE ON ATTENTION AND SHORT-TERM MEMORY

In the previous sections I discussed two manifestations of the limitations to consciousness: selective attention and short-term memory (STM). The currently influential models of selective attention and STM have in common that they postulate activation processes that possess certain limitations. Only so much can be activated before the pool of resources for such activation is entirely consumed. Processing a message for meaning, for example, uses so many of the cognitive resources for activating cognitive processes that ignored messages are poorly remembered. Rehearsing longer words, for example, uses more resources than rehearsing shorter words, so memory span is greater if the words are shorter.

A simple and obvious fact about any cognitive process is that it becomes more efficient with practice. For example, when you first learned to drive a manual shift car, you needed to devote all of your attention to the task of driving and shifting the gear stick. You would not try to learn to manipulate the stick while driving in heavy traffic. Having to attend to the traffic and concentrate on shifting would cause you to feel overwhelmed with information. With enough practice, though, you could easily shift gears, navigate the car through heavy traffic, listen to the R.E.M. song on the radio, converse with your friend, and fantasize about whale-hunting off Tahiti. Practice seems to reduce the effort—the cognitive resources—necessary to accomplish tasks.

Research confirms and clarifies these intuitions. Consider selective attention. Neisser and his colleagues (Hirst, Spelke, Reaves, Caharack, & Neisser, 1980) have done experiments that show that ordinary people can learn in about 100 or so hours to read a story and simultaneously take dictation on sentences unrelated to the story, without either task suffering. Initially the subjects are overwhelmed by the amount of information they must process, but eventually they seem to be able to hold in consciousness both sets of information. Treisman and her colleagues (Treisman, Vieira, & Hayes, 1992) have shown that when subjects are given extensive practice looking for target stimuli that are composed of a combination of features (e.g., searching for something that is both blue and X-shaped), they can locate those targets as fast as they can a single-feature target (e.g., something that is simply blue). Recall that without extensive practice, subjects typically locate the single-feature targets faster than they do the multifeatured targets (Treisman, 1988).

Now consider short-term memory. In one well-known experiment, a subject was able, after about 190 hours of practice, to increase his memory span for digits from 7 to about 80 digits (Ericsson, Chase, & Faloon, 1980). In another study, Neisser (1964) presented subjects list of letters 50 lines long and required them to find some target letter that was buried somewhere in the list. He measured how long it took subjects to find the target. Like Sternberg (1966), Neisser varied the number of target letters that subjects had to search for in the list. In some cases subjects had to search the list to see if any one of 10 target letters was somewhere on the list. Unlike Sternberg, Neisser let the subjects practice extensively on any given set of targets. That is, the set of targets remained constant for many trials. Neisser found that when target sets were well practiced, subjects' search time was as fast when they had 10 targets to search for as when they had only 1 target. With practice it was as easy for subjects to keep in mind 10 target letters as it was for them to keep in mind only 1 target letter. In yet another study, De Groot (1965, 1966) asked master and novice chess players to study a chessboard for 5 seconds. The pieces, arranged as they would be in a real game of chess, were then removed and the subject had to reconstruct their positions. The masters (who certainly had much more practice playing chess) were able to reconstruct the positions of about 20 pieces whereas the novices could reconstruct only about 4 or 5 pieces.

An important characteristic of practice is that practice affects only the operations or activities on which one practices; the effects do not generalize to operations or activities that are dissimilar. For example, practicing driving a manual shift car will not generalize to flying an airplane. Practicing memorizing digits to increase memory span will not generalize to an increased memory span for words (Ericsson et al., 1980). Master chess players do not have superior short-term retention for chess pieces if the chess pieces are randomly arranged on a chessboard (Chase & Simon, 1973). Random arrangements of chess pieces make the task dissimilar to real chess.

How does the limited resource concept underlying the current selective attention and working memory models account for the effects of practice? The usual explanation is that, with practice, a particular cognitive operation, like taking dictation or controlling a manual shift car, draws on progressively fewer cognitive resources until the operation is said to be **automatic** (Hasher & Zacks, 1979; LaBerge & Samuels, 1974; Shiffrin & Schneider, 1977). An automatized operation uses almost no cognitive resources (the operation feels effortless) and does not occupy conscious awareness (attention is directed instead toward other tasks).

The construct of limited capacity still leaves unanswered the deeper question about why the processes that prolong or sustain activation produce limits in how much a person can keep in mind at any given moment. What is going on in the brain that leads to limitations in cognitive resources for unpracticed operations and to the automatization of those operations after extended practice?

PHYSIOLOGICAL BASIS OF LIMITED RESOURCES

An attempt to enhance the explanatory power of the limited resources construct, and the models of selective attention and working memory based on limited resources, comes from an approach to cognition called **neural net modeling**. The neural net approach, discussed in several chapters in this textbook, makes the claim that the essential properties of a brain that enable it to provide cognitive functions are to be found in the strength of excitatory and inhibitory connections among neurons that fire at variable rates. Experiences can change the strengths of the connections. Neural net models simulate these critical properties of brains. How might a neural net model simulate the limited capacity of consciousness? To put it another way, what are the essential properties of the brain that give rise to limitations in the pool of resources that sustain selective attention and short-term memory?

In this section I present a simplified version of a neural net model designed to simulate memory span (the model is depicted in Figure 2-5). It is based on more complicated models discussed by Grossberg (1978, 1980) and by Martindale (1991; see also Schneider, 1993). The neural net model for explaining memory span can also be generalized to other situations that reveal the limited capacity of consciousness and the effects of practice on consciousness. The model contains units that detect letters and a unit that represents the whole list

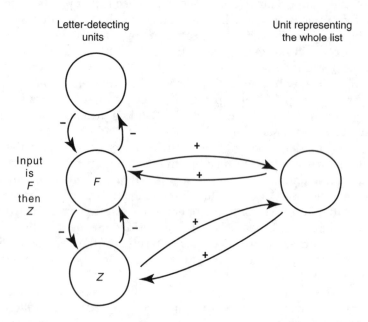

FIGURE 2–5   A neural net that simulates memory span for a series of unrelated letters that include "F" and "Z". The circles represent units; the lines represent connections that may be excitatory (+) or inhibitory (−).

of letters. Units are connected to one another either by excitatory or inhibitory connections.

Suppose the model is presented as a series of unrelated letters, such as *R F Z M Y K X J B P*. Let's see what happens when the letter *F* is presented. The presentation of *F* activates the letter-detecting unit for *F*. This unit is part of a module of units that functions to perceive letters. Units in neural net models represent the actions of neurons or groups of neurons. The model claims that the unit that detects *F* will tend to inhibit other letter-detecting units. In real brains, it is common for neurons within a layer to inhibit one another. Such **lateral inhibition** helps sharpen distinctions among perceived objects. In this way, if *F* is detected, the system does not mistakenly activate other letter-detecting units, like those that detect *E* or *L*.

The unit that detects *F* will also increase the activation of the higher order unit that represents the idea of a list of letters. The activation of the higher order unit will in turn feed activation back to the *F*-detecting unit. That is, the letter will be rehearsed in anticipation of recalling it. **Excitatory feedback** between layers of neurons is common in real brains; such feedback helps the system prepare for new stimuli. In this case, the feedback may reflect activation received from another module of units that functions to sustain the activity of the letter perception module. This other module corresponds to a rehearsal mechanism, such as Baddeley's articulatory loop.

Now consider what happens when the next letter, Z, is presented. The presentation of Z activates the Z-detecting unit, which inhibits the activation of other letter-detecting units, including the unit that detects *F*, and increases the activation of the unit representing the list. Again the list unit will feed excitatory activation back, this time to both the *F*- and the Z-detecting units. At this point the activation that the *F*-detecting unit received from the presence of the letter *F* and continues to get from the feedback will be greater than the inhibition the *F*-detecting unit receives from the Z-detecting unit. As long as the activation of a unit is maintained at a higher than usual level, the unit continues to be a part of the model's immediate memory. However, as more letters are presented, the feedback activation must be spread out over more letter-detecting units, diminishing the amount the *F*-detecting unit receives. Meanwhile, the activation that the *F*-detecting unit got from the original presentation of the letter *F* will dissipate. As more letters are presented, the lateral inhibition the *F*-detecting unit receives from other letter-detecting units will continue to increase, eventually canceling out any lingering activation the *F*-detecting unit had been receiving. Eventually, the *F*-detecting unit will no longer have sufficient activation to keep it above the threshold necessary to remember it. It happens that it takes about 7 letters before the inhibition cancels out the activation. The result is that the model (and the typical person whose short-term memory it simulates) can keep only about 7 letters in mind before the model begins to forget some of the letters.

With practice, people would be able to increase their memory span for randomly ordered letters. How might this happen? In neural net models, experiences change the strength of connections among units (see Chapter 6: The

Physiology of Learning and Remembering). The connections between units that detect the letters *C*, *A*, and *T*, for example, would have become strongly connected to a single higher order unit that represents the word CAT. In a memory span experiment that uses CAT as one of the stimuli, the higher order unit at the word level will be activated by the letters *C*, *A*, and *T* and by the feedback from an even higher order unit that represents words on a list. The word-detecting unit for CAT will not be laterally inhibited by other letter-detecting units, which are in a different layer. The CAT unit will be laterally inhibited by the activation of other *word*-detecting units, as other words from the list are presented. So the span of memory for words will be about 7 words. But for three-letter words, the span will be about 21 letters.

If a subject spends scores of hours in a memory span experiment that involves the presentation of randomly ordered letters, the subject will eventually see repetitions of letter combinations. For many of these letter combinations the subject might invent a meaning (e.g., FRD means friday). In the neural net model simulating this, connections between the units that detect random letter combinations and units that represent words will be strengthened. Subsequent presentation of the random letter combinations will then result in activation of units at the word layer in the hierarchy. Lateral inhibition at this layer will limit the subject to remembering about 7 or so words. However, the number of randomly ordered letters the neural net model will be able to remember will be considerably greater than 7, because most words consist of more than one letter. In this way the model (and the real person) who learns to treat random three-letter combinations as meaningful words will increase the memory span for letters from about 7 to about 21 letters.

In neural net models, then, the pool of resources available to accomplish a cognitive operation is represented as excitatory and inhibitory connections among layers of units arranged in a hierarchy. Experiences change the configuration of connections, so that the apparent size of the pool of resources can change, but only for well-practiced operations. The pool is limited because units at the same layer in a hierarchy tend to laterally inhibit one another, because the activation received by any one unit from a transmitting unit lessens when the transmitting unit transmits activation to several other units, and because activation dissipates with time.

SECTION 4: THE FUNCTION OF CONSCIOUSNESS

Up to this point I have focused on the nature of consciousness—in particular, the physiological basis for consciousness, the cycle of states of consciousness, and the limitations of consciousness as reflected in selective attention and short-term memory. But why is there consciousness at all? And what important function does consciousness serve? How are humans better off having the capability of being aware of themselves and an outside world, and of reflecting on the contents of awareness? And why are the putative advantages of consciousness served by conscious processes that are limited in their capacity for holding or processing information?

CONSCIOUSNESS AS CONTROL

Jacoby (Jacoby, Lindsay, & Toth, 1992) suggests that the main function of conscious processes—particularly those I refer to as reflective processes—is to enable a person to render control over the environment, in order to accomplish a goal. Control is evidenced when unexpected forces in the world perturb behavior designed to achieve some goal, yet the goal is nevertheless obtained.

The idea of control can be illustrated with a simple example. A person may drive to work the same way every day, always turning left onto University Avenue. If one day the driver becomes aware that a flood has washed out University, then the driver may choose not to turn left on University but to turn right in order to take an alternate route to work. The ability to make that adjustment in driving illustrates control over the route environment. Unconscious information processing, on the other hand, is not as likely to allow a person to control the environment. If the hypothetical driver had not paid attention to the flood, for example, then the driver would have made the usual left-hand turn onto University Avenue and would have been stopped by the flood.

What might be the physiological basis of conscious control? Conscious control might be thought of as a feedback mechanism that appropriately dampens or enhances the activation of a network of neurons. Perhaps conscious mechanisms are needed to temporarily inhibit otherwise strong connections among neurons, and/or to temporarily excite otherwise weak connections among neurons, in order to respond to unexpected situations (see Roberts, Hager, & Heron, 1994). Note that inhibiting operations are critical to the control function of consciousness. When conscious control processes are not engaged, then the flow of activation across already-established connections will determine a person's response to a stimulus. The person deliberating on how to get to work when a flood washes out University Avenue, for example, may inhibit the strong connections among neurons representing University Avenue and a left turn and excite the weak connections among neurons representing University Avenue and a right turn. The person who fails to pay attention to the flood, for example, will not make the temporary adjustments in strength of connections among neurons representing University Avenue, left turning, and right turning. The person's driving behavior will then be guided only by the spread of activation over the established connections (see Klinger & Greenwald, 1995), which means that the person will turn left into the flood.

A variety of research is consistent with a control function for consciousness (e.g., Neely, 1977; Posner & Snyder, 1975; Schneider & Shiffrin, 1977; Klinger & Greenwald, 1995). One example comes from Engle, Conway, Tuholski, & Shisler (1995; see also Roberts, Hager, & Heron, 1994). They presented subjects with a pair of partially superimposed letters; one letter was red and the other was green. The subjects were instructed to name the red letter and ignore the green letter. The perception of the green letter had to be inhibited. In some cases, the green letter of one trial became the red letter of the very next trial (which the subjects then had to name). Because the perception of that letter had been inhibited on the first trial, it took subjects longer to name the letter when it appeared as a red letter on the next trial. It took longer than if the letter had not been the green letter on the previous trial. This tendency may be called the inhibition effect.

Some subjects were required to perform the letter-naming task while also memorizing a short list of words. The more words they had to remember, the less was the inhibition effect. The explanation is that if the control function of consciousness is occupied with rehearsing words, there is not as much opportunity to inhibit the perception of the green letter. Should that green letter appear as a red letter on the next trial, it will then be more readily named than if its perception had been inhibited on the previous trial.

A fascinating implication of the control function of consciousness is revealed in research on racial and gender stereotypes (e.g., Devine, 1989; see Greenwald & Banaji, 1995). For instance, Gaertner and McLaughlin (1983) presented subjects with pairs of letter strings for which subjects had to decide whether both strings were English words. Subjects of European descent (i.e., whites) responded faster to pairs in which the first word was "white" and the second word connoted a positive trait (e.g., white–smart) than when the first word was "black" and the second word was positive (e.g., black–smart). The results were the same for subjects who scored low as for those who scored high on a direct, standardized self-report measure of racial prejudice.

A possible explanation begins with the observation that everybody knows the racial stereotypes, even though many recognize that the stereotypes are almost always false (Devine, 1989). Unprejudiced people may be able to exert conscious control over racial stereotypes by inhibiting the effects on thought processes of the stereotypical knowledge. Under conditions in which even unprejudiced people are unable to inhibit such knowledge (as when subjects are forced to respond quickly), the racial stereotypes influence their thought processes. Perhaps that is why when an unprejudiced person becomes angry towards a person from another racial group, the angered person may sometimes blurt out disturbingly prejudiced epithets. Perhaps anger undermines the capacity of consciousness for dampening certain categories of knowledge.

The notion that consciousness functions to control the environment by temporarily activating weak connections or inhibiting strong connections suggests why it is important for consciousness to be limited in its capacity. The appropriate activation and inhibition necessary to achieve control requires that the activation or inhibition be directed specifically at certain connections, and not be allowed to spread to irrelevant connections. A driver who must dampen the strong tendency to turn left on University and activate an otherwise weak tendency to turn right must activate a cognitive process that takes knowledge of the consequences of floods and of compensatory driving techniques and uses that knowledge to make appropriate adjustments to driving behavior. If consciousness were not limited in capacity, then activation and inhibition would spread to irrelevant cognitive processes. The cognitive system would be overwhelmed by irrelevant and even contradictory knowledge. Presumably in such a chaotic cognitive environment, no control over unexpected perturbations in the external environment would be possible.

THE PUZZLE OF CONSCIOUSNESS

Cognitive neuroscientists have at least some understanding of the physiological sites and mechanisms associated with conscious experiences, and are even able to supply some preliminary accounts of how the brain gives rise to perception, memory, self-reflection, dreams, attention, and the limited capacity short-term memory (Carlson, 1994; Edelman, 1992). These are the problems that depend on objective measures of performance that are thought to reveal something of the character or nature of consciousness. Chalmers (1995) argues that such problems within the study of the brain's role in consciousness are the relatively easy ones to solve. But the hard problem is why it is that some brain processes are accompanied by a subjective, phenomenological experience. And cognitive neuroscience lacks completely an explanation of how the brain makes possible the subjective sense of being aware (Chalmers, 1995). This is the sense of consciousness I labeled conscious awareness. Neurophysiology may explain, for example, how the brain discriminates the color red from the color blue, but it cannot explain why the act of processing color information is accompanied by the subjective experience of seeing red. Why is a person also aware of seeing red when discriminating red from blue? Could not an unconscious automaton also discriminate among colors?

To see the argument, suppose that you learn that memory for recently presented information is associated with sustained neural activity across layers of neurons. If you also learn that neurons within a single layer are connected to one another by inhibitory connections, then it is apparent that only a few units of a layer can sustain activation at the same time. It is apparent, then, that the system must have a limited capacity for simultaneously processing information. So one aspect of consciousness, namely its limited capacity, is putatively accounted for by brain processes.

But the awareness quality of consciousness, the subjective experience itself, is not apparent from models of brain processes. The notions of sustained activation and lateral inhibition do not explain why one is aware of the information for which processing is limited. The same activation–inhibition model could be used to describe the performance of the cyborg "brain" of an unconscious Terminator. It, too, might have a limited capacity for processing information, but it wouldn't be aware of the information it processes. Now if the exact same neurophysiological model serves as an account of a conscious human and of an unconscious automaton, then the model has no explanation for the existence of conscious awareness. Be clear here that my point is not that it is impossible to make a conscious machine (I don't know if that is possible) but that neurophysiological theories do not reveal how it is that the human brain gives rise to conscious experiences.

Now it does not necessarily follow from this argument that materialism is wrong and dualism is right. Indeed, the materialist argument is bolstered by the study of physiology, especially the study of dissociation phenomena. We know from the phenomenon of blindsight that neurons in the primary visual cortex are essential to the phenomenological experience of seeing; we know from the phenomenon of amnesia that neurons in and around the hippocampus are essential to the phenomenological experience of remembering the past.

Clearly, then, it is the function of some neurons in the brain to provide the subjective experience that we label conscious awareness. But how it is that neurons make possible the subjective experience of being aware remains maddeningly elusive. Presumably, and astonishingly, it is the variable rates of firing among populations of neurons that give rise to conscious awareness. Certainly, no single neuron can be said to be conscious of anything. But how it is that variable rates of neural firing (or any other physiological activity) cause conscious awareness is not at all understood. Maybe, as Nagel (1974) has suggested, physiological explanations have limits. And one of those limits may be that we can never get from physiological mechanisms a deep understanding of exactly how those physiological mechanisms create the phenomenological experience of being aware of ourselves and the world we inhabit. At any rate, we do not yet have such a physiological explanation for conscious awareness. Chalmers's "hard" question remains unanswered.

SUMMARY AND CONCLUSIONS

In this chapter I developed the materialist theme that consciousness is a label we give to one of the functions of the brain. As a result of a number of simple physiological processes taking place in various places in the brain, the brain enables a person to be aware of a self and an outside world and to reflect upon the contents of awareness. Materialism is contrasted with dualism, which claims that consciousness requires that an ethereal, incorporeal mind interact with the brain but remain independent of the brain.

In the first section I discussed how consciousness is distributed in the brain. I noted that certain kinds of brain damage cause a dissociation between information processing and consciousness. Examples are blindsight and visual neglect. Such observations strongly reinforce the materialist contention that consciousness depends on the activity of neural processes widely distributed about the brain. Dissociations also provide clues as to how the brain makes possible at least the self-reflective aspect of consciousness. Gazzaniga suggests that connections between language centers and other neural systems may enable self-reflective capacity. What remains elusive, unfortunately, is how brain processes produce the sense of subjective awareness.

An important aspect of conscious experience is that consciousness passes through a daily sleep–wake cycle. I reviewed in section 2 the stages of sleep. I also reviewed the learning and priming theories of the function of REM sleep and the Freudian and activation-synthesis theories of the characteristics of dreams. The activation-synthesis theory helps illuminate the brain processes that give rise to many of the common characteristics of dreaming, including the narrative and sometimes bizarre quality of many dreams.

In the third section I examined another important aspect of consciousness, namely that it is selective or limited. One manifestation of that selectivity is selective attention. I reviewed two models of selective attention: the filter model and the limited resources model. The filter model supposes that only one of several channels of information is selected for complete processing; the other channels are filtered out. The downfall of the filter model is its inability to explain how subjects could notice important messages in the channel of information they were supposedly filtering out. The limited resource model accounts for selective attention by supposing that there is a limited pool of cognitive resources available for accomplishing cognitive tasks. One influential model of selective attention is Treisman's model, which distinguishes between preattentive processing, which uses few cognitive resources, and focused attention, which uses many cognitive resources.

Another manifestation of the limits of consciousness is short-term memory. I reviewed the duplex model of short-term memory and some of the problems with that model. More current models of short-term memory, called working memory models, postulate that short-term memory reflects the sustained activation of various cognitive processes. Such processes must be sustained in order to complete a task. The operation of sustaining cognitive processes is itself a collection of processes or skills. Baddeley argues that working memory includes an articulatory loop, a visuospatial sketchpad, and a central executive. As in the newer models of selective attention, the working memory model posits limitations in the pool of resources required by working memory to sustain activation of cognitive processes.

The problem with the limited resources construct, though, is that it provides neither the physiological basis for limited capacity nor any deep explanation of why practiced tasks no longer draw upon the limited pool of resources but instead are accomplished automatically. More recently, some cognitive scientists have turned to neural net models, which incorporate the essential properties of neural communication thought to underlie human cognition. I discussed one example of a neural net model that explains the basis for a memory span of only about seven items and explains how practice increases the apparent size of the memory span.

In the fourth section I turned to the function of consciousness. Jacoby has suggested that the main function of a conscious mode of cognitive processing is to provide control over the environment. A physiologically based way to think about conscious control is that it entails activation of weakly connected neural units and inhibition of strongly connected neural units.

I concluded my discussion of the function of consciousness by making a distinction between the relatively easy problems of consciousness and the one incredibly hard problem. The easy problems are the ones having to do with explaining how the brain makes possible objective performance taken to be revealing of the nature of consciousness. There are physiological models explaining color perception, dreams, short-term memory, and so on. But the hard problem is explaining why it is that the brain processes that underlie perception, dreaming, short-term memory, and so on happen to be accompanied by a conscious, subjective experience. Why does the sense of consciousness I labeled "conscious awareness" exist?

Now we do know that certain neurons in the brain are responsible for the subjective character of consciousness. We know this because destruction of certain neurons undermines the subjective sense of conscious awareness. But why it is that a normally functioning brain gives rise to consciousness is not known. In my opinion, the supreme challenge for cognitive science is to find the answer to the hard problem of consciousness.

RECOMMENDED READINGS

Two good examples of materialist explanations of consciousness, in well-received books written for the lay public, are Dennett's (1991) *Consciousness Explained* and Edelman's (1992) *Bright Air, Brilliant Fire*. Hobson's (1988) *The Dreaming Brain* compares and contrasts his activation-synthesis theory of dreaming to the Freudian wish fulfillment theory. Miller's (1956) *Psychological Review* article on the magical number seven (plus or minus two) remains an entertaining and thought-provoking essay on the limitations of perception and short-term memory. Chalmers's (1995) *Scientific American* article on consciousness discusses the easy and hard questions of human consciousness and even tries to provide a new approach to consciousness that circumvents the hard question.

3 *Visual Perception*

Examine Figure 3-1 and see which line appears longer, (A) or (B). The fact that line (A) appears longer than line (B), even though the two lines are of identical length, constitutes the well-known Muller-Lyer illusion. The illusion is a consequence of the cognitive processes that underlie **perception**, the topic of this chapter. In this chapter I will focus almost exclusively on visual perception, although many of the themes and theories I discuss also pertain to perception in the other sensory modalities. The main question I will ask about visual perception is this: Do we perceive the world as it really is, or does our perceptual process actually modify and even distort reality in some way?

Before I try to answer this question, let me explain what we mean by perception. Perception can be defined as the process by which we arrive at an interpretation of sensory experiences. The interpretive process provides meaning to stimuli; it makes sense of the sensations we experience. A visual sensation might be interpreted as a mustache, an auditory sensation might be interpreted as the word *nuance*, a tactile sensation might be interpreted as a cold liquid. The notion of interpretation used here is not meant to be taken as a conscious deliberation on facts and data. Rather, the rendering of an interpretation by the processes we label perception ordinarily lies outside of conscious awareness. We are unaware of the action of computing an interpretation of our sensations but are aware of the output of those computations. One simply sees line (A) as longer than line (B). One is not initially aware of seeing lines of indeterminate relative length nor of thought processes that are used to determine which line is longer.

A theory of perception, then, seeks to explain how we apprehend stimuli registered by our sensory organs. The development of a theory of perception is

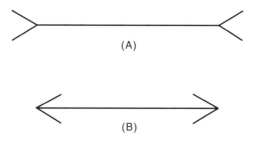

(A)

(B)

FIGURE 3–1   The Müller-Lyer illusion.

hampered by the lack of introspective evidence to bring to bear on the problem of perception. Indeed, the unconscious nature of the perceptual act makes it difficult for people to appreciate what a theory of perception aims to accomplish. It may seem that the meanings we attach to our sensations are just there, that they don't require the activation of any process that needs explaining. But, of course, some kind of process must produce the interpretations we have of the stimulus world. Perception is not magic.

PERSPECTIVES ON PERCEPTION: DIRECT OR CONSTRUCTED?

The main theme I will use to integrate the research and theoretical approaches to visual perception is a contrast between two perspectives (see Gardner, 1985; Best, 1995). One perspective is called **direct perception**, or sometimes **ecological perception**. Its main proponent in the 20th century was James J. Gibson (1904 to 1980) (Gibson, 1950, 1966, 1979), whose work has been carried on by Michael Turvey and Robert Shaw (e.g., Turvey, Shaw, Reed, & Mace, 1981), among others.

The main claim of direct or ecological perception is that the perceptual process ordinarily creates an accurate interpretation of reality, and does so with minimal cognitive computational effort. To elaborate, perception is viewed as a rather passive process by which the perceptual system functions primarily to pick up, or detect, the attributes of objects and events. Implicit in the direct perception approach is that the information in the external stimulus that gives rise to sensations is adequate to accomplish accurate perception. Direct perception does not claim that perceptual errors or distortions are never made. Rather, perceptual errors are attributed to incomplete data in the stimulus or to factors, like stress, that might cause a breakdown in the perceptual process. The term "direct perception" reflects the notion that the world is perceived without much intervening analysis. The term "ecological" reflects the idea that the study of perception ought to focus on the nature of the stimulus world in which one moves and with which one interacts.

Direct perceptionists point out that the features of the physical stimulus that a brain picks up depend on the needs and capabilities of the organism. Gibson referred to the relevant features as **affordances** (Gibson, 1979). An affordance is a combination of properties that provides meaning and/or the possibility for action. For example, horizontal surfaces that are also solid afford support, while an aperture or gap in an enclosure affords entry and exit. Gibson's idea was that the perceptual system extracts affordances from the stimulus, based on the uses to which the stimulus is put. These uses cause the perceptual system to attend to certain aspects of stimuli and ignore other aspects. A person looking for a tool to pound a nail into a board will attend to the solid and flat-surface features of a hammer. A person looking for a tool to extract a nail from a board will attend to the solid and claw-like features of a hammer.

In contrast to direct or ecological perception is the perspective usually called **constructed perception**, also known as **constructivist** or **computational perception**. Constructed perception was implicit in the work of Hermann

Helmholtz in the 19th century (Helmholtz 1866/1962) and dominates the theories of most perceptual psychologists of the middle and late 20th century (e.g., Marr, 1982; Ittelson & Cantril, 1954; Ullman, 1980; see Best, 1995). The main claim of constructed perception is that the perceptual system works to modify the sensory input in order to compute an interpretation of reality. That is, the sensory input is "spruced up," or elaborated on, by the act of perceiving. Helmholtz referred to this computation as unconscious inference, to highlight the computational character of perception and to clarify that we are ordinarily unaware of the computations that give rise to our perceptions. Perception is conceived of as an active process that makes use of sources of information that lie both inside and outside of the sensation itself. The outside source of information usually consists of expectations and knowledge that have been built up from previous acts of perception.

Implicit in constructionism is the idea that the stimulus world is often not adequate, in and of itself, to accomplish perception. Many stimulus elements are ambiguous and therefore require a cognitive machinery that adds information to (and sometimes subtracts from) the stimulus. The result is that some perceptual inaccuracies are attributed, not to breakdowns in the system or to incomplete data, but to processes intrinsic to ordinary perception. Our perceptual system is designed in such a way that it is bound to perceive inaccurately in some cases.

To illustrate the difference between the two perspectives on perception, consider a hypothetical example of how we perceive objects. The example is meant to evoke the environment in which our species evolved. Imagine our ancient *Homo sapiens* ancestors struggling to survive on the Serengeti Plain of Africa. Suppose that way off in the distance an object moves, and one of our ancestors, Ogg, interprets what he sees as a lion.

According to direct perception, Ogg's visual system detects the visual attributes, such a particular body shape and stalking movement, that lions have in common. The visual sensation created by light reflecting off the moving object contains some of these lion attributes, so Ogg perceives a lion moving among the bushes. Ogg pays special attention to the lion's motion, because Ogg is concerned about avoiding danger. And lions afford danger. From the point of view of direct perception, no further mental computational processes need be postulated in order to explain his perceptual experience. In general, the stimulus provides all the information necessary to perceiving its identity; the human perceptual system merely "picks up" this information. To understand Ogg's perception of the lion, then, one must study the ecology of the environment in which people interact with lions.

The account offered by the constructed perception perspective does not dispute anything in the direct perception account. But constructionism maintains that there must be more to Ogg's perception of the object as a lion than the mere detection of lion attributes in the visual sensation. To get a sense of the additional explanatory apparatus proposed by constructionism, suppose Ogg had just been told by his sister Ugg (and who knows what names were in vogue on the Serengeti Plain 50,000 years ago?) that she heard that there was a dangerous lion in the area. The expectation of seeing a lion created in Ogg's mind by the rumor may contribute to Ogg's interpretation of the moving object as a lion. According to constructionism, perceptual analysis of sensations makes use of expectations as well as of the information in the actual sensation. For Ogg, the expectation might mean that his perceptual system does not have to analyze the visual sensation quite so thoroughly in order to arrive at the interpretation of the visual sensation as a lion. The quick perceptual analysis permitted by the expectation of seeing a lion might save Ogg's life. Ogg can escape before the lion gets too close and devours him.

The expectation might also mean that certain ambiguous aspects of Ogg's visual sensation, such as a movement pattern that could describe either lions or the less dangerous hyena, might be given the unambiguous interpretation of "lion" movements. It is even possible that Ogg's expectation of encountering a lion might distort his perception of the moving object, causing him to misperceive a hyena as a lion. He might run away from the animal needlessly. Of course, constructed perception is not committed to the idea that our perceptions of the world are routinely distorted or wrong, for then it would be hard to explain the survival of our species. The lion would have eaten the Oggs and Uggs who had error-ridden perceptual systems. But constructionism does claim that some distortions and errors are a natural consequence of a soundly operating perceptual system, and not due only to breakdowns in that system. Note that Ogg's misperception of a hyena as a lion reflects the natural tendency of the perceptual system to combine expectations and sensory data into a coherent interpretation of the sensation. From the perspective of constructionism, the trade-off is the gain of more efficient perceptual processing at the cost of making the occasional error in object identification.

In the following sections of this chapter I will discuss and contrast the direct and constructionist views of visual perception. My sense is that most cognitive scientists working today respect the direct perception perspective, but are themselves constructionists who believe that some additional cognitive machinery is necessary to account for perception. This chapter will reflect that consensus.

In the first section I provide an overview of the visual system of the brain. In the next two sections I discuss depth perception (How does Ogg know how far away that lion is?) and object perception (How does Ogg know what the object is?). Finally, I discuss visual imagination (What enables Ogg to imagine seeing a lion in, say, a dream?).

SECTION 1: THE PHYSIOLOGY OF VISION

VISUAL PROCESSING BY THE EYE

Visible light constitutes a narrow range of electromagnetic radiation that also includes gamma rays, X-rays, and radio waves. Light can be conceptualized as waves whose wavelengths are between 380 and 760 nanometers. Variations in wavelength correspond to light's perceived hue. Light with shorter wavelength tends toward blue; light with longer wavelength tends toward red. Most light contains a mixture of wavelengths that blend together, although one wavelength may dominate. Variations in the height of the waves correspond to variations in brightness. Higher waves are perceived as brighter. Light can also be conceptualized as particles of electromagnetic energy called photons. Variations in the energy level of photons are perceived as variations in hue. Blue is associated with more energetic photons; red is associated with less energetic photons. Variations in the density of photons in a stream of photons are perceived as variations in brightness. The higher the density of photons in the stream, the brighter is the light.

The perceptual processing of light begins in the retina, which contains the **photoreceptors** that convert the energy of light into neural impulses, although these impulses do not take the form of the action potentials of most other neurons (see Carlson, 1994; Goldstein, 1996; or Sekuler & Blake, 1994, for a general discussion of the physiology of vision). The photoreceptors include about 6 million cones, responsible for color vision, and about 120 million rods, responsible for black and white vision in dim light.

Within the retina, the photoreceptor cells pass signals to a network of cells called collector cells, which in turn pass signals to **ganglion cells**. Since there are about 126 million photoreceptor cells and only about 1 million ganglion cells, the ganglion cells must be condensing the raw images registered by the receptor cells. Visual perception begins in the eye.

Ganglion cells, like all cells in the primary visual system, are said to have **receptive fields**. The receptive field of a cell refers to a portion of the retina, and therefore a portion of the visual field, such that light falling on that portion affects the activity of the cell. When light falls outside the receptive field of the cell, the cell is not affected. The receptive fields of ganglion cells vary in size but usually have a circular shape.

Knowledge of the receptive fields of ganglion cells (and of other cells in the visual system) comes from the **single-cell recording paradigm**. In this paradigm a microelectrode is placed into a single neural cell of an animal (cats are often used) and light from one of a set of different patterns emanating from some portion of the immobilized animal's visual field is projected onto a corresponding portion of the animal's retina.

About half of all ganglion cells have an on-center, off-surround receptive field. This means that when light strikes the center of the receptive field, the ganglion cell increases its rate of firing to a rate greater than its baseline rate of firing (neurons are rarely completely inactive). When light strikes the periphery of the receptive field, the cell decreases its firing to a rate below the baseline level. When light falls completely outside the receptive field, the ganglion cell maintains its baseline rate of firing. The other half of the ganglion cells have off-center, on-surround receptive fields. These cells increase their rate of firing when light strikes the periphery of the receptive field and decrease their rate of firing when light strikes the center of the receptive field.

The nature of the on–off arrangement in the receptive field means that ganglion cells are most active when there is a light–dark boundary, an edge, in the light striking the receptive field. To see why, suppose light illuminated the entire receptive field of an on-center ganglion cell. Then the cell would be excited by the light in the center of its receptive field but inhibited by the light in the periphery of its receptive field. The net result would be only a slight change to the activity of the cell. If, instead, the light illuminated the center of the receptive field but not the periphery, as would happen in the case of an edge, then the ganglion cell would show a large increase in activity.

SENSORY MEMORY

In the course of processing visual information, the visual system maintains the sensation for a brief amount of time, about 250 milliseconds, even after the stimulus that gave rise to the sensation is gone. The persisting visual sensation, a kind of **sensory memory**, is called **iconic memory** (also known as the *icon*). Nearly all of the information present in the light will be held in iconic memory, even if the amount exceeds the capacity of short-term memory.

The classic research on iconic memory was conducted by George Sperling (1960). In some of his experiments, subjects were presented an array of letters and digits, four symbols in each of three rows. The array was presented for only 50 milliseconds. In one condition, called the **whole report procedure**, subjects had to report all of the symbols in the array. Subjects were able to report accurately only about 4 or 5 of the symbols, and so were remembering about 40% of the 12-symbol array.

In another condition, called the **partial report procedure**, subjects were presented a tone to indicate which row of the array they had to report. A high tone meant report the upper row, a middle tone meant report the middle row, and a low tone meant report the lower row. The tone was presented just after the array disappeared. Subjects in the partial report procedure could accurately report all or nearly all of the symbols in a row (about 90% of the symbols on average). Because subjects could not know in advance which row they would be asked to report, the inference is that subjects had some transient memory of at least 90% of all of the symbols. If a delay was introduced between the disappearance of the array and the presentation of the tone, then the percentage of symbols from the array that subjects were able to report declined from around 90% to around 40%. Most estimates are that whole and partial report performance becomes equivalent after about a 250 millisecond delay (van der Heijden, 1981).

The explanation Sperling offered was that the visual sensation persists in the form of a high-capacity iconic memory for about a quarter of a second. When subjects have to report all of the symbols in the array, the icon has faded away before the report can be completed. So subjects report only about 4 or 5 symbols. When subjects have to report only one row of the array, they can report most of the symbols in the row before the icon fades. Presumably, then, the icon contains essentially all of the visual information in the visual sensation.

Researchers debate the physiological basis for the icon, as well as the icon's function in ordinary vision. Some researchers argue that the icon reflects the persistence of neural activity in the retina (Sakitt, 1975), while others claim that the icon is located more centrally (Di Lollo & Hogben, 1987). One conceivable function is that the icon enables visual sensations to appear stable despite movements of the eyes (Irwin, Zacks, & Brown, 1990) although some theorists argue that the icon plays no important role in perception (Haber, 1983). Incidentally, there has also been research on other sensory memories, notably the echoic sensory memory for auditory sensations (e.g., Darwin, Turvey, & Crowder, 1972).

VISUAL PROCESSING IN PRIMARY VISUAL CORTEX

The axons of most of the ganglion cells go to the **lateral geniculate nucleus (LGN)** of the thalamus. On the way, at the optic chiasm, the ganglion axons whose receptive fields are in the nasal portion of the retina cross over to the opposite hemisphere of the brain while the ganglion axons whose receptive fields are in the temporal portion of the retina remain on the same side of the brain. The axons of the LGN cells terminate in the occipital lobe of the cortex, also called the visual cortex (see Figure 2-1). The cortical region that contains the neurons at which the LGN axons terminate is known variously as area 17, area V1, or **primary visual cortex**. I will use the "primary visual cortex" label.

The pioneering studies of David Hubel and Torsten Wiesel (Hubel & Wiesel, 1977, 1979) have illuminated the role of cortical cells in visual perception. In their work, for which they won the Nobel Prize, Hubel and Wiesel recorded the activity of individual neurons of cat brain while displaying various patterns of light to selected portions of the cats' retina. Hubel and Wiesel found that, as with ganglion and LGN cells, the receptive fields of primary visual cortex are especially sensitive to edges of objects and respond only to the illumination of a very restricted portion of the retina.

An important difference between ganglion cells and the cells of the primary visual cortex is that the cortical cells do not simply respond to light, but to certain features of light. While Hubel and Wiesel suggested that neurons in primary visual cortex detected lines and edges, the current thinking (see Carlson, 1994) is that most of the neurons in the primary visual cortex respond to particular **spatial frequencies**. Spatial frequency has to do with the rate of change of intensity of light within some spatial region (as opposed to the frequency of light waves, which has to do with color). The higher the spatial frequency, the more frequent is the change of illumination within some given spatial region. Some neurons are more responsive to light with high spatial frequency, some are more responsive to light with low spatial frequency, and so on.

Any given visual scene can be considered as a complex of different spatial frequencies. For instance, large objects tend to have low spatial frequency, while small objects—and the detailed features of large objects—tend to have high spatial frequency. So the neurons responsive to low spatial frequencies contribute more to the analysis of gross features of larger objects whereas the neurons responsive to high frequency contribute more to the analysis of details.

Most neurons in primary visual cortex also vary with respect to the orientation of the light to which they are responsive. Some neurons are maximally responsive to grids of light oriented 45 degrees to the horizontal, others to grids of light oriented 35 degrees to the horizontal, and so on. As a grid of light is rotated away from the preferred orientation, the neuron becomes increasingly less responsive to the grid. Some neurons in primary visual cortex are maximally responsive to grids of light moving in a direction perpendicular to their preferred orientation.

Many neurons within the primary cortex are innervated by LGN cells from both sides of the brain. They are, then, binocular, with receptive fields in both eyes. Most **binocular neurons** respond most vigorously when the preferred grid of light is in a slightly displaced location within one eye's receptive field relative to its location within the other eye's receptive field. The displacement is called **disparity**. Disparity is a consequence of the separation of the two eyes, each of which receives light emanating from a given source at a slightly different angle. Cortical neurons, then, vary with respect to the degree of disparity that maximally activates the neuron. Some neurons respond most vigorously when the disparity is great, others when the disparity is slight, and so on. Disparity, as we shall see in the next section, is an important cue for determining the distance between an object and the viewer.

Primary visual cortex consists of about 2,500 modules containing about 150,000 neurons per module. All the neurons within a single module have receptive fields in approximately the same location on the retina. Within the module, the full range of spatial frequencies, orientations, and disparities is represented. In addition, there are collections of neurons that are sensitive to particular colors (some are responsive to red, some to blue, and so on) and to textures (some neurons respond to rougher surfaces, some to smoother surfaces, and so on). The overall pattern of firing of neurons within a module represents the spatial frequency, orientation, disparity, movement, color, and texture of the light falling on a particular region of the retina. The gross arrangement of modules across the primary cortex follows a **retinotopic organization**, which means that adjacent modules have adjacent receptive fields on the retina.

VISUAL PERCEPTION IN SECONDARY VISUAL CORTEX

It is probably fair to say that the ganglion cells, the LGN cells, and the neurons of primary visual cortex function to provide a kind of low-level or preliminary perceptual analysis of a visual stimulus. They function to detect spatial frequencies, orientations, movement, disparity, color, and texture in particular regions in the visual field. But this information must be somehow integrated in order to arrive at the meaning of the pattern of light striking the retina. How is this higher level perceptual analysis performed in the brain?

A lot of visual processing takes place in areas of the cortex that lie outside the primary visual cortex of the occipital lobe. These other areas are widely distributed throughout the cerebral cortex, and are often labeled **secondary visual cortex**. Evidence suggests that it is in secondary visual cortex that higher visual perception takes place.

A rather gross characterization of the difference between primary and secondary visual cortex goes something like this. In any given module of neurons of primary cortex, a variety of information (spatial frequency, orientation, color, and so on) about light is provided, but it is provided only for light striking one small portion of the retina. In secondary visual cortex, any given module (or circuit) of neurons seems to be dedicated to only one particular perceptual function. One module is dedicated to processing color, another to processing movement, another to processing form, and so on. But any given secondary module processes light from all receptive fields of the retina. That is, within any given secondary module, only one kind of information about the light is provided, but it is provided for light that strikes anywhere on the retina. Presumably, then, the secondary modules engage in a kind of integrative processing whereby comparisons and contrast can be made about some category of information across the entire visual field. It should be noted, though, that modules in secondary visual cortex are not as well defined anatomically as they are in primary visual cortex.

The claim that the modules or circuits of neurons of secondary visual cortex are dedicated to processing only one kind of information about light is supported by single-cell recording and selective ablation (surgical removal) studies of nonhuman primates, by the visual deficits observed in brain-damaged humans, and by PET scanning and other brain imaging techniques used on humans without brain damage (Carlson, 1994).

Damage to the primary visual cortex, if widespread, will produce blindness. Damage to selected portions of the primary visual cortex will produce blindness in a restricted portion of the visual field. Damage to a restricted portion of secondary visual cortex, however, will produce a loss of a specific visual function (e.g., color perception) in all portions of the visual field. For instance, damage to area MT can selectively undermine motion perception (Zihl, Von Cramon, & Mai, 1983) whereas damage to area V4 can selectively undermine color vision (Rizzo, Naurot, Blake, & Damasio, 1992). PET techniques reinforce these interpretations (e.g., Zeki et al., 1991; Lu et al., 1991).

Areas of cortex located in the inferior temporal lobe, as well as areas in the occipital lobe outside of primary visual cortex, constitute a module or circuit of neurons important in form perception (e.g., determining that the pattern of light constitutes a circle or truck or lion). For instance, based on single-cell recording in temporal lobes in a monkey, we have learned that there are neurons that respond best to three-dimensional objects (or photographs of them), such as a tiger's head, rather than to simple stimuli, such as grids or lines (see Tanaka, 1992, for a review of such studies). These cells appear to process whole objects, not specific features. Incidentally, it is unlikely that any given cell functions as a "tiger's face analyzer" or in general detects such complex objects. Rather, it is more likely the case that a pattern of activity within form modules constitutes the recognition of a complex object.

Damage to secondary visual cortex in humans can result in a deficit known as **visual agnosia**. Visual agnosia refers to a difficulty in identifying visual stimuli, even though vision itself is intact and the person retains normal intellectual capacity. A patient suffering from visual agnosia might not be able to identify a wristwatch by sight, but be able to identify it if allowed to hold it (Warrington & James, 1988). In some cases, patients may have little difficulty discriminating among visual stimuli on the basis of size, color, or brightness, yet have enormous difficulty discriminating on the basis of shape (Carlson, 1994). PET scans reveal different, although partially overlapping, neural circuits involved in each of these discriminations (Corbetta, Miezin, Doobmeyer, Shulman & Petersen, 1991).

MYSTERIES

What is not yet well understood is exactly how the arrangement of primary and secondary visual cortex finally leads to evoking a meaningful interpretation of a visual scene. Consider two examples of the limitations of our knowledge of the physiology of visual perception.

Binding

One limitation to our understanding of the physiology of perception has to do with solving what is known as the **binding problem**. Suppose I see a red sphere and recognize it as an apple. One portion of visual cortex processes the red color, and another portion processes the spherical shape. Yet my perception integrates, or binds, these features into a single unified object, the apple. In particular, I do not experience a sensation of red that is separate from my sensation of sphere. The question is, what explains the binding?

One proposed solution to the binding problem is that anatomically disparate areas of the visual cortex become bound when the rate of firing among relevant neurons is synchronized to a particular frequency. There is some evidence from single-cell recording that when separate groups of visual neurons oscillate in phase at around 40 cycles per second (called Hertz or Hz), the functions that the disparate groups serve will be bound into a single unified percept (Gray & Singer, 1989; Crick & Koch, 1990). So if the neurons that represent the color red and the neurons that represent the spherical form are all firing at 40 Hz, the result is the perception of a single thing that is simultaneously red and spherical (i.e., an apple).

There is a lot more research that needs to be done, though, before we can have any confidence in the 40 Hz synchronization solution to the binding problem. Consider, does the 40 Hz rate hold up in all cases where visual features are perceived as bound? What is so special about 40 Hz anyway? Why not 80 Hz or 255 Hz? Does the same synchronization model work in other areas of perception, as, for example, when I feel a substance that is both liquid and cold? And why doesn't synchronization bind together all the features of all visual objects within a scene? I can simultaneously perceive a red apple next to a yellow banana, and so bind red to sphere and yellow to oblong, but I do not bind the yellow to the sphere nor the red to the oblong nor all to each other and so experience a kind of unified apple-banana. Yet, presumably, the red and yellow and sphere and oblong neurons are all firing away at 40 Hz.

The synchronization model is complicated by research that suggests that, under some circumstances, binding is undermined (e.g., Treisman & Schmidt, 1982; see Prinzmetal, 1995). In a typical study, subjects are simultaneously presented several objects and a sequence of rapidly displayed numbers. The subjects' primary task is to report the numbers. Their secondary task is to report on the color and shape of the objects. In this rather challenging situation, subjects often make illusory conjunctions. For instance, on being shown a red X next to a green Y, subjects may sometimes erroneously report seeing a red Y. Such errors, incidentally, reinforce the idea that color and form are handled by two different subsystems in the brain.

Ordinarily, in the world outside of the research laboratory, people do not make illusory conjunctions. If you attend to a blue automobile next to a brown garage, you are not going to perceive a blue garage. Ogg is not likely to perceive the redness of the rock in front of the lion as part of the lion. Perhaps illusionary correlations tend to occur because the perceived locations of features are sometimes in error (Prinzmetal, 1995; Ashby, Prinzmetal, Ivry, & Maddox, 1996). In the ordinary day-to-day world, objects tend to be organized in such a way as to constrain how the perceptual system locates and binds their features.

Gestalt psychology describes some of the principles by which the perceptual system correctly integrates features (Prinzmetal, 1995). The main tenet of the Gestalt approach to perception is that there is a tendency for human perception to impose certain types of organization on sensations, and that these organizing tendencies are based on grouping and segregation of forms (Wertheimer, 1923/1958; see Pomerantz & Kubovy, 1986). Among the **Gestalt principles**, illustrated in Figure 3-2, are the principles of **proximity** (the tendency to group items that are close together), **similarity** (the tendency to group items that are similar in form), **closure** (the tendency to unite neighboring contours), and **good continuation** (the tendency to form a line). Although Gestalt principles describe a basis for predicting what stimuli will be bound, they do not illuminate the physiological basis by which the brain achieves binding.

Externalization in Visual Perception

Another limitation to our understanding of the physiology of vision (and to perception in general) is the phenomenon of **externalization** (Prinz, 1992). Visual and auditory perception have in common that the sources that give rise to the perceptions are perceived to be located in the outside world. That is, the sensations of sight and sound are externalized. If I were to wave a knife in your face, you would perceive the silver color of its blade as a part of an object that lies outside your body. In particular, you would not experience the blade's color as being in your retina. On the other hand, if I should stab your leg with that knife

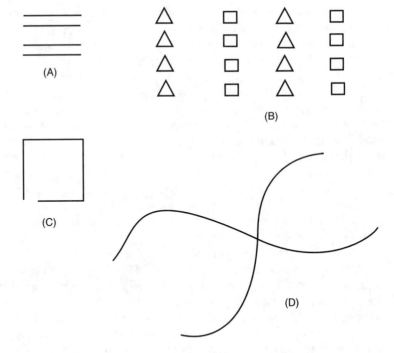

FIGURE 3–2   The Gestalt principles of (A) proximity, (B) similarity, (C) closure, (D) good continuation.

(and of course I would never do such a thing, I just want to conjure up a graphic image), you would perceive the pain as in your leg, and not as in an externally located object. By and large, kinesthetic sensations like pain, pressure, taste, and temperature are located in the body whereas sight and sound sensations are located in the outside world. Indeed, it may be that we would have no awareness of an outside world at all unless we externalized certain of our sensations.

Why is it that we externalize sights and sounds but not other sensations? Somehow the brain must construct an outside world based on its perceptions of visual and auditory stimuli; the external nature of the stimuli is not available in the sensation itself. Exactly how the brain accomplishes externalization of certain of its sensations is not understood (Sekuler & Blake, 1994).

The binding and especially the externalization problems emphasize the complexity and sophistication of the neural processes underlying perception. The higher level problem of binding together and externalizing features of the visual scene demonstrates that the brain must perform computations on the sensations it receives. Consistent with constructed perception, the brain does not merely pick up the binding or the external locus, which are not in the sensation itself. The brain somehow deduces their existence from the actions of poorly understood integrative mechanisms.

SECTION 2: DEPTH PERCEPTION

When we see the world we see objects that possess length, width, and depth. The dimension of depth is particularly intriguing because the visual sensation as extracted by the retina of the eyes contains only the dimensions of length and width. How is it, then, that we so readily perceive the third dimension of depth?

THE INVARIANTS OF DEPTH

Monocular Cues for Depth

In fact, the two-dimensional image of light on the retina does include information about depth. The various kinds of information available in the retinal image are called depth (or distance) cues. One set of cues are called **monocular cues**; these are available to a single eye. Monocular cues can only provide relative depth information—that is, whether one object is closer or farther away than some other object. Monocular cues include, but are not limited to, interposition, size, textual gradient, aerial perspective, horizon, linear perspective, shadows, motion parallax, and optical flow patterns (see Sekuler & Blake, 1994; or Goldstein, 1996, for a discussion).

Consider, again, our friend Ogg, who must determine the distance between himself and the lion. What cues enable Ogg to keep a safe distance? **Interposition** is one cue. If a tree obscures part of the lion, then the tree is closer to Ogg than is the lion. **Relative size** also provides a depth cue. The bigger the image of the lion on Ogg's retina, the closer must be the lion. As objects recede in the distance, the distance between the textural elements on the object's surface will appear closer together. The degree of separation in the **textual gradient** of the lion's body surface, then, is another monocular depth cue for Ogg. **Aerial perspective** refers to the fact that light scatters as it moves through the atmosphere. More distant lions appear hazier than do nearby lions. The height of an object in comparison to the **horizon line** is another cue for depth. If the head of the lion appears below the horizon line, the lion is relatively far away. If its head is above the horizon, run for your life, Ogg!

There are other monocular cues for depth. One is **linear perspective**. Parallel lines, like the edges of a road, appear closer together as the lines recede into the distance. **Shadowing** is another cue. If an object has a surface that recedes from the observer, light shining from above the object will cast a shadow on the lower portion of the surface. If an object has a surface that extends toward the observer, the light will cast a shadow on the upper portion of the surface.

When an object or the observer is in motion, the sensation of light from the object also moves across the retina at some rate. The closer the object, the more rapidly its image moves across the retina. **Motion parallax**, as this cue is called,

FIGURE 3–3   The optical flow pattern as seen by a pilot approaching a runway. Arrow length indicates the rate at which the visual scene flows by the pilot.

also informs the observer of the object's distance, provided the observer or object is on the move.

Gibson was especially interested in the role motion plays in perception (Gibson, 1966, 1979; see Best, 1995). He noted that as we move toward an object, visual information seems to emerge from the point toward which we are moving. The rate at which this information flows toward us is slow for objects far away, but gets faster as we get closer to the object. A pilot landing an airplane and directing attention toward the point of contact with the runway will perceive the bottom of the runway stretch out at an ever faster rate as the plane approaches the runway. The top of the runway will also stretch, but the rate of stretching will slow down as the plane approaches the runway. This pattern of a changing visual array is referred to as the **optical flow pattern** (see Figure 3-3), an example of what Gibson called a higher-order invariant. A higher-order invariant is a complicated, abstract constancy of the environment that Gibson claimed the perceiver picks up or attends to in order to determine the distance of objects.

Binocular Cues for Depth

Other cues for depth are available only when both eyes are used together to perceive the object (again, see Sekuler & Blake, 1994, or Goldstein, 1996). Two **binocular cues** are **oculomotor cues** and **stereopsis cues**.

As Ogg tries to achieve maximum visual acuity of the lion, he will move his eyes in such a way as to focus the image on the foveas of both retinas. If the lion is close, Ogg will rotate his eyes toward one another; that is, his eyes will converge. If the lion is far away, Ogg will rotate his eyes away from each other; that is, his eyes will diverge. Different degrees of convergence and divergence are reflected in the type and degree of muscular tension in the oculomotor muscles that control eye rotation. Oculomotor cues, then, are a source of information about the distance between observer and object.

Because the two eyes see objects from slightly different angles, due to the approximately 65 millimeter lateral separation between the eyes, the image of objects on the two retinas will be laterally displaced. To illustrate how this displacement provides information about depth, suppose Ogg is looking at the lion lying near a tree. There will be some separation between the image of the lion and the image of the tree on both of Ogg's retinas. Because Ogg's eyes see the lion and tree from slightly different angles, the distance between the retinal images of the lion and the tree will be different for the two eyes. If one object, say the lion, is much closer to Ogg than the tree, then the degree of difference in the distance between the two images on each retina will be large. If the lion and the tree are about the same distance from Ogg, then the degree of difference will be quite small. The difference in the distance between two images on the retina is the **retinal disparity**. Note that retinal disparity provides information only about the distance between two objects, and not directly about the distance between either object and the perceiver.

Retinal disparity also enables the perceiver to tell which of the two objects is the closer. Let's say Ogg fixates directly on a lion that is in front of a tree. The tree will appear to the left of the lion in Ogg's left eye, and will appear to the right of the lion in Ogg's right eye. This situation is described as uncrossed disparity, and it tells Ogg that the lion is closer than the tree. Now let's say Ogg fixates directly on a lion that is behind a tree. In this case, the tree will appear to the right of the lion in Ogg's left eye and will appear to the left of the lion in Ogg's right eye. Now the disparity is crossed, and it tells Ogg that the tree is closer than the lion.

The ability to make use of binocular retinal disparity in order to perceive depth is called **stereopsis**. Stereopsis is remarkably keen. Using binocular disparity information, people are able to tell which of two objects located about 1 meter away is closer when the difference in distance is as small as 1 millimeter. In this case, the resulting disparity between the views of the two eyes is less than about .0004 millimeters, a distance actually smaller than a single visual receptor on the retina.

The various monocular and binocular cues for depth suggest that, consistent with direct perception, depth perception is essentially a matter of detecting the cues that are present in ordinary visual and oculomotor sensations. The direct perceptionist would argue that the brain needs only to detect such cues in order to produce the perceptual experience of seeing depth in two-dimensional retinal images. No further explanatory apparatus is required to account for depth perception.

In contrast, constructionism argues that more explanation is required. In particular, according to constructionism, cognitive functions that themselves are not directly involved in detecting depth cues play a role in the brain's perception of depth. It is to the constructionist argument that I now turn the discussion.

THE CONSTRUCTION OF DEPTH: THE INFLUENCE OF CULTURE
ON DEPTH PERCEPTION

Again, the main claim of the constructionist approach to perception is that the cognitive systems responsible for perception add information to sensations, thereby making it possible that what is perceived is not the same as what is actually present in the world. Evidence for inherent perceptual errors comes from visual illusions, which are persistent and reliable errors of visual perception. A classic example of a visual illusion, and one that provides an argument for constructionism (Best, 1995), is the **Müller-Lyer illusion** that opened this chapter.

Although there is some debate as to the explanation for the Müller-Lyer illusion, the most popular theory is usually called **depth theory** (Gregory, 1970; see Coren & Girgus, 1978, or Goldstein, 1996, for a discussion of depth theory and other theories of the illusion). According to depth theory, the arrowheads on the ends of the lines are perceived as angles formed by connecting right-angled surfaces (see Figure 3-4). When the arrowheads point outward, the two surfaces are seen as slanted toward the observer and so relatively close. When the arrowheads point in, the surfaces are seen as slanted away from the observer and so relatively farther away. Yet both lines connecting their two surfaces cast images of the same length on the retina. The only way objects at different perceived distances can cast images of the same length on the retina is if one of the objects is in fact longer than the other. Hence, we see the line with the arrowheads pointing in as the longer line, due to the unconscious inference that it is farther away.

Note the idea of an unconscious inference in which two separate pieces of information, retinal size and perceived depth, are used to calculate the length of the lines. There are other illusions that seem to involve similar unconscious cal-

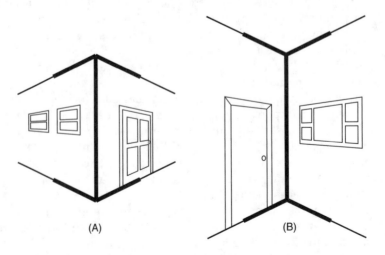

(A)   (B)

FIGURE 3–4   The Müller-Lyer illusion could arise from implied depth information.

culations, including the moon illusion, in which the full moon looks larger on the horizon than when it is high in the sky. The usual explanation of the moon illusion (see Goldstein, 1996) is that the moon on the horizon appears farther away than the moon high in the sky because all other objects on the horizon will appear between the viewer and the moon. Yet the moon has an equal size on the retina in both locations. The unconscious inference is that the horizon moon that is implicitly assumed to be farther way, yet has the same retinal size, must therefore be larger.

The perception of an illusion can be affected by cultural experiences. The Müller-Lyer illusion, for instance, seems to depend on experience with right-angled surfaces. Such surfaces are rare in nature but do characterize the artifacts of modern human societies. Research suggests that people from cultures that lack right-angled artifacts do not experience the Müller-Lyer illusion, or other similar illusions, to the same degree as do people from more modern cultures (Deregowski, 1972; Rivers, 1905; Segall, Campbell, & Herskovits, 1966; Stewart, 1973).

Age is another factor that seems to play a role in the perception of the Müller-Lyer illusion (and similar illusions). The effect of the illusion seems to decline with age among people from modern cultures (Segall, Campbell, & Herskovits, 1966; Wagner, 1977). The decline with age may seem paradoxical, given that the experience with cultural artifacts that supposedly underlies the illusion presumably increases with age. Research by Wagner (1977) may resolve the apparent paradox. Wagner found that when the illusion was embedded in a picture, the effect of the illusion did increase with age among formally educated urbanites but declined with age among people from rural backgrounds. Embedding the illusion in a context may activate the artifactual information that underlies the interpretation of the depth and length of the lines. Educated urbanites, more than rural people, increase their knowledge of the relevant artifacts as they age, and so are more affected by the illusion when that artifactual knowledge is made salient.

The main point made by studies of the effect of culture and age on the perception of the Müller-Lyer illusion is that culturally dependent experiences play a role in the perception of depth. The perceiver combines cultural knowledge with the actual visual data in the picture of the two lines to arrive at a perceptual interpretation of the visual input. The intrusion of knowledge based on experience with artifacts into the depth perception process is a good example of how perceptions are constructed, and are not directly experienced.

Indeed, the mere prevalence of visual illusions is usually taken as evidence for some form of constructed perception (Best, 1995; Goldstein, 1996). The idea that people unconsciously calculate size or depth from several pieces of information (e.g., length as a function of retinal size and perceived depth) and so perceive an illusion (e.g., the Müller-Lyer illusion) is consistent with the constructed perception view that ordinary perception entails computations and can sometimes produce perceptual errors, even when the perceptual system is functioning normally. However, Gibson himself had little use for visual illusions, arguing that motion usually removes the ambiguity in the illusion. Still, human visual perception functions whether the viewer and object are motionless or are in motion. And the Müller-Lyer illusion in particular persists even when one moves while looking at the illusion.

SECTION 3: PATTERN RECOGNITION

The visual system does more than locate things in a three-dimensional space; it also identifies objects (e.g., lions) and events (e.g., Ogg running away from the lion). The identification of objects and events is usually called **pattern recognition**. Pattern recognition must involve what I earlier called low-level perception (e.g., the detection of the degree of orientation of a grid of light on some portion of the retinal field) and high-level perception (e.g., associating an ensemble of spatial frequencies, orientations, movements, and colors with the idea of a hungry lion). In this section I will focus on the higher level processes underlying the recognition of patterns.

THE DIRECT PERCEPTION APPROACH TO PATTERN RECOGNITION

The essential claim of direct perception is that patterns, like a lion or the pouncing of a lion, are recognized because the perceiver picks up from the ambient light the invariant properties associated with objects and the movement of objects. All the information necessary to recognize patterns is available in the light—that is, in the external world. The perceiver does not need to process such information to any degree.

To get a sense of how direct or ecological perceptualists' study pattern recognition, consider two examples. The first is how people perceive the degree of aging in a face. Shaw and Pittenger (1977; also Pittenger & Shaw, 1975) noted that as the human head ages it is affected by gravity, muscular change, growth, and so on. Such changes may be labeled **strain**. Shaw and Pittenger applied the strain transformation to a series of pairs of profiles and asked subjects to judge which profile appeared older (examples of profiles illustrating strain are shown in Figure 3-5). The profile subjected to the greater degree of strain was reliably picked as the older profile. Degree of strain, then, is a kind of invariant, in this case a rather abstract or higher order invariant, that people use to perceive age.

Another example has to do with the perception of movement. Johansson (1973) attached light bulbs to a model's shoulders, elbows, wrists, hips, knees, and ankles. The model was photographed in the dark so that only the lights were visible. Subjects perceived the lights as a meaningless random group. However, the model was also videotaped in the dark while engaging in various activities, such as walking or climbing. From the movements of the lights alone, the subjects were able to identify the type of activity in which the

FIGURE 3–5   A set of faces to illustrate strain.

model was engaged and even whether the model was male or female (Koslowski & Cutting, 1977). The relationship of the lights in motion provides the observer with enough information to perceive the pattern of motion and the sex of the model.

Both of these examples illustrate the research strategy of direct perceptionists. The main goal is to determine the properties of light associated with a meaningful interpretation. The assumption is that light contains all the information necessary to determine its meaning. The perceiver does not need to elaborate on the stimulus nor to deconstruct the stimulus on the way to analyzing its meaning.

MODELS OF PATTERN RECOGNITION

Approaches to pattern recognition from within mainstream cognitive psychology have followed a different strategy than that of direct perception. Most of the mainstream approaches have focused much more on what is happening inside a person to make pattern recognition possible. To varying degrees, such approaches are more consistent with constructed perception, which postulates a significant role for internal processes in an account of pattern recognition (Goldstein, 1996). These hypothesized internal processes typically deconstruct the stimulus and compare the deconstructed version to internal representations of the class of stimuli into which a given stimulus in categorized.

A challenge to any model of pattern recognition is to explain how people are able to recognize novel variations of familiar patterns. We can (usually) recognize the letters and words in handwriting that we have never before encountered, a new species as belonging to the cat family, or a new car as a type of sports car. Similarly, we can recognize familiar objects when we see them in unfamiliar orientations, such as an upside-down lion seen from the head end, or when we see only part of an object, such as the back end of a lion sticking out from some tall grass. Indeed, this is the essential difficulty in explaining pattern recognition—how do we readily identify objects, given the multitude of sensations associated with any given object? Pattern recognition, even of novel variations of familiar patterns, is usually quite fast—less than one tenth of a second (Intraub, 1981)—and usually error free.

Feature Models of Pattern Recognition

One kind of model of pattern recognition is called a **feature model**. The idea behind a feature model is that the brain acquires from repeated exposures to objects an ensemble of attributes, or features, that most exemplars of any given object have in common. The identification of any object, like a lion, amounts to extracting features from any given sensation and matching those features to lists of previously acquired features. Irrelevant variations among exemplars are either ignored, or the variation itself is taken as one of the attributes of the pattern (Homa, 1978). The extraction process is a kind of deconstruction of the stimulus; the ensemble of attributes is a kind of representation to which the deconstructed stimulus is compared. Feature models typically have a hierarchical character in which low-level features, like edges, are first extracted from the sensation and then combined into higher level features, like legs. The higher level features are compared to lists of higher level features associated with objects, such as chairs, in order to determine the category of object into which to place the sensation.

Feature models make the essential prediction that distinguishing between two objects should be difficult to the extent that objects share features. Research supporting this prediction comes from experiments on the speed and accuracy with which people can identify the letters of the alphabet (e.g., Gibson, 1969; Kinney, Marsetta, & Showman, 1966). The typical result is that subjects take longer and make more errors distinguishing between two letters that share features (e.g., F and E) than between two letters that do not share features (e.g., F and O).

Research by Neisser (1964) is illustrative. In his study, subjects searched for a target letter in an array of letters. The letters that were not the target letter might be called the distractors. Suppose the target letter was Z. If the distractors were composed of some of the features of the target letter, as would be the case for distractors such as X and H, subjects took longer to find the target letter and made more errors than if the distractors were composed of features that are dissimilar to the ones found in the target, as would be the case for distractors such as O and S.

The straightforward explanation of Neisser's experiment is that object identification first requires the extraction of features from the stimulus. These features are compared with a list of features stored in memory. If a subject is looking for Z but encounters O, then the comparison process produces no match between the features of the stimulus O and the stored target list of features. So it is easy to reject the O as an example of a Z. If a subject encounters X, then the comparison process yields matches between some of the stimulus's features and the target features, making it more difficult to reject the X as a Z.

Geons

There are a number of different kinds of feature models that differ according to the types of lower level features that are extracted from a sensation, the types of higher level features into which the lower level features are combined, and the means by which features are combined (see Goldstein, 1996, for a discussion). A currently influential version of a feature model is **Recognition-by-Components** (Biederman, 1987, 1995).

The Recognition-by-Components model conceives of feature analysis as a hierarchical process in which lower level features, such as lines, vertexes, cusps, and edges, are first detected from the stimulus. These features, in turn, activate a small subset of a couple of dozen primitive volumes, called **geons** (for "geometrical ions"). In a sense, geons are to objects as letters of the alphabet are to words. Examples of geons are provided in Figure 3-6. The lower level features also activate the spatial relationships among geons. Relationships are critical to the identity of the object. For instance, a simple pail and simple cup are composed of the same two geons, but the spatial relationship between the two geons is different in a cup than in a pail (see Figure 3-6). The geons and their relationships are compared with memory record of the ensemble of geons and relationships associated with a class of objects. A match between the geon ensemble in a stimulus and the geon ensemble associated with a category constitutes the identification of the stimulus.

In the model, the geons are composed of a subset of only a few lower level features consisting of edges, cusps, and vertexes. So there are only a few lower level features and a few possible relationships among the lower level features associated with any given geon. Furthermore, only a subset of the lower level features associated with a particular geon needs to be visible in order for the viewer to identify the geon. In this way, it is easy to see how geons can be identified when visually degraded (e.g., partially covered by another object). In turn, there are only a few geons and relationships among geons associated with any

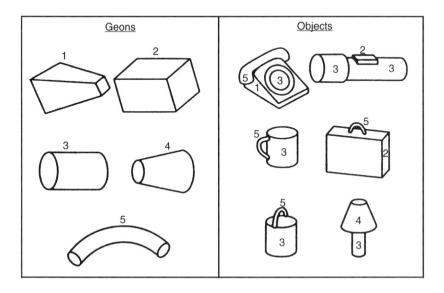

FIGURE 3–6   (Left) Five geons. (Right) Only two or three geons are required to uniquely specify an object. The relations among the geons matter, as illustrated by the pail and cup. From *Visual Cognition: An Invitation to Cognitive Science*, Volume 2, by Stephen Kosslyn and Daniel Osherson. Copyright © 1995, The MIT Press, Cambridge, MA. Reprinted with permission.

given object. Yet the possibility of activating a subset of up to 3 to 4 geons bearing any of several relationships to one another from a population of about 24 geons permits tens of thousands of distinct geon ensembles. It is easy, then, for the geon system to identify any of tens of thousands of objects and to do so quickly and without error. Thus the model explains the extraordinarily high speed at which objects are identified. And because geons are easily discriminable from one another regardless of their orientations, distortions, or degree of visual degradation, a geon-based model of pattern recognition can readily identify novel variations of familiar objects.

You may wonder why we can't do away with geons, and just claim that the identification of cusps, vertexes, and edges can be compared with a list of such lower level features associated with a class of objects. Why propose that the perceptual system must identify geons (or any higher level feature) before it can identify objects? As Biederman (1995) notes, it is possible to degrade an image of an object in two complementary ways such that there is absolutely no overlap among the lower level features that make up the degraded images (see Figure 3-7). Everywhere that there are vertexes, cusps, or edges in one image there is a gap in the other image. As long as the degradation does not render the geons unidentifiable, however, the objects depicted in the two degraded images can be readily identified as the same object. Their identity is established by the identity of their geons, not by the identity of the lower level features.

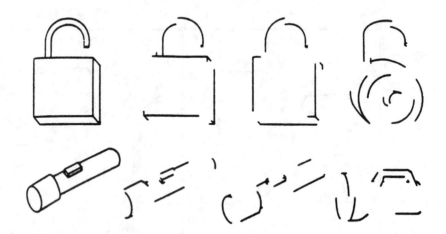

FIGURE 3–7   Complementary-feature images. From an original intact image on the left, two complementary images in the middle two columns were formed by deleting every other vertex and edge from each part so that each image had 50% of its contour. When superimposed, the two complements comprise the original image with no overlap in contour. Note that these two images are readily identifiable. In the right-most column is an image from another complementary pair; this image is difficult to identify. From *Visual Cognition: An Invitation to Cognitive Science*, Volume 2, by Stephen Kosslyn and Daniel Osherson. Copyright © 1995, The MIT Press, Cambridge, MA. Reprinted with permission.

Of course, merely to demonstrate that the objects of the world are decomposable into geons does not constitute proof that people actually make use of geons when they identify objects. Luckily, there is more direct evidence for geon-based feature models of pattern recognition (see Biederman, 1995). For example, Biederman (1987) deleted some lower level feature information from an object in one of two ways (illustrated in Figure 3-7). In the first way, the deletion rendered geons unidentifiable, in the second way the deletion left the geons identifiable. Even though the equivalent amount of information was deleted in the two cases, objects were much more difficult to recognize when the deletion undermined the identifiability of the geons.

Biederman's geon-based feature model also predicts that recognition should be faster for objects made up of more geons, because there will be more combinations of geons that can trigger recognition. An elephant, for example, can be described by 5 geons, whereas a lamp can be described by 2 geons. As predicted, subjects recognized the objects with more geons faster than the objects with fewer geons (Biederman, 1987).

Prototype Models of Pattern Recognition

A somewhat different model of pattern recognition is based on the idea that new sensations are compared to idealized representations of a class of objects or events (Posner & Keele, 1968; Edelman, 1995). The idealization is called a **prototype**. Prototypes depict the visual characteristics of the most typical members of the class or are like averages of all the class members. For example, for most Americans, the prototype of bird would resemble a robin more than an ostrich. Prototypes are abstractions and need not resemble exactly any single member of the class. The prototypical bird, for example, may not look exactly like any real bird. Prototypes are ordinarily acquired from repeated exposure to exemplars of a class, although some prototypes may be innate.

The prototype model depicts the identification of a sensation as computing a set of quasi-distance relationships between the sensation and the prototypes. The quasi-distance relationship represents the similarity between the sensation and the prototype. The sensation is judged a member of the class that has the shortest quasi-distance (i.e., the most similarity) between its prototype and the sensation.

As with feature models, prototype models assume that perception requires that sensations (e.g., a particular lion) be compared to internalized representations of classes of objects (e.g., the prototype of a lion). In the feature model, the representation is a feature list, created from processes that deconstruct exemplars of a class into essential features, usually arranged in a hierarchy. In the prototype model, the representation is a well-organized idealized version of the class, created from processes that compute a kind of mathematical average of a set of exemplars of a class. The prototype representation makes more explicit the relationships and global characteristics of a class of objects. Note that both types of models require a fair amount of computation for pattern recognition to occur. In feature models, such as the geon model, the pattern recognition system processes hierarchies of features. In prototype models, the pattern recognition system computes a similarity relationship between the sensation and prototypes.

An essential prediction of prototype models is that pattern recognition should ordinarily be fast and accurate to the extent that the new sensation overlaps with the prototype. Research supports this prediction (e.g., Franks & Bransford, 1971; Reed, 1972). Posner and Keele (1968) conducted the classic prototype experiment. In one condition of their experiment, Posner and Keele created three random dot patterns that served as prototypes for the creation of other stimuli used in the experiment. Each of the dots of each prototype was moved according to an algorithm that changed each dot's location slightly. The more often this relocation algorithm was applied to the dots, the more distorted was the original pattern of dots. The fewer the distortions, the greater the similarity between the dot pattern and the original prototype from which the pattern was created.

Subjects were presented four distortions of each prototype until the subjects could reliably categorize the distortions into the three categories defined by the prototypes. However, the subjects did not actually see the prototypes nor were they told that the stimuli they were categorizing were made from three prototypes. Later, subjects were given old (previously classified) distortions, novel distortions, and the actual prototypes to categorize. Subjects correctly classified the old distortions in 87% of the cases but classified the novel distortions in only 75% of the cases. The intriguing finding was that subjects correctly classified the prototypes as well as they classified the old distortions, despite the fact that the prototypes were also novel. Furthermore, the more a novel distortion resembled the prototype, the more accurately it was categorized.

It should be noted that there is some debate on whether one needs to postulate prototype formation to account for such results. Some models (Brooks, 1978; Medin & Schaffer, 1978; Nosofsky, 1991) suggest that new sensations are compared to previously categorized patterns retrieved from memory. New patterns are classified into the same category as the retrieved example most similar to the new pattern. In particular, these models postulate no prototype formation. Prototypical patterns are readily classified because they are likely to be quite similar to most retrieved patterns from within a class. Still, an explicit memory of particular patterns is not required to produce the superior classification of prototypes. Adult amnesics have trouble remembering specific instances of a category, yet can remember the category's prototype as well as normal control subjects can (Cohen in McClelland & Rumelhart, 1986b).

Average Is Beautiful

An interesting extension of the concept of visual prototypes comes from research investigating the features of the human face that make a face seem physically attractive. It turns out that faces that are closest to the prototypical face are perceived as attractive (Langlois & Roggman, 1990; Langlois, Roggman, & Musselman, 1994; Rhodes & Tremewan, 1996). Prototypical faces can be artificially created by first taking a group of black-and-white photographs of various faces of one sex, then digitizing the photographs so that each digit represents a degree of grayness, and finally finding the mathematical average of the digits at the same relative location on the face. Research shows that people judge such faces as attractive—more attractive than the individual faces that yielded the prototypes. Be clear that the prototypical face is not average in the sense of commonplace, but in the sense of the arithmetic mean.

You might think that standards of physical attractiveness are learned from exposure to popular media and vary widely from culture to culture. However, very young infants prefer looking at faces that adults find attractive (Langlois et al., 1987). Furthermore, standards of facial attractiveness are similar across cultures (e.g., McArthur & Berry, 1987; see Langlois, Roggman, & Musselman, 1994). Perhaps this apparently innate preference for prototypical faces reflects a biological mechanism by which evolution ensures that infants direct their attention to the most human face–like objects in the environment (Johnson & Morton, 1991).

THE EFFECT OF CONTEXT ON PATTERN RECOGNITION

Research on perception demonstrates a powerful influence of context on the identification of objects and events. Context refers to stimuli that are encountered before or after the to-be-identified stimulus within the stimulus stream or to expectations people have about the stimuli they are likely to encounter. Context effects are also known as **top-down processes**, which are distinguished from **bottom-up processes** that make use only of information in the visual sensation.

One line of research on context asks subjects to identify letters (e.g., Reicher, 1969; Johnston & McClelland, 1973). In one example (Wheeler, 1970), subjects were very briefly shown either a word (e.g., WORK) or a letter (e.g., K). They were then presented the originally displayed stimulus and a distractor stimulus and had to decide which had been displayed. In the case of words, subjects would see a stimulus pair in which only one letter was different between each word (e.g., WORD and WORK). In the case of letters, subjects would see the pair of letters that in the word condition had served to distinguish between the word and the distractor (e.g., D and K).

The main finding was that subjects were faster and more accurate when the stimuli were words than when they were letters, despite the fact that there were more elements to process in the case of words. But the presence of the other letters within the word served to enhance the processing of any given letter within the word.

Context effects in visual perception are not limited to linguistic stimuli. For example, the identification of a common object, like a fork, is faster when the fork is in a scene depicting a kitchen than when the same fork is in a scene in which the objects comprising a kitchen are randomly rearranged (Biederman, Rabinowitz, Glass, & Stacy, 1974). Similarly, Palmer (1975) demonstrated that an object like a fork was more rapidly recognized when it was in its natural context, such as a kitchen, than when in an unusual context, such as an office. These experiments are nice demonstrations of how knowledge (e.g., kitchen knowledge) that lies outside the sensation itself (e.g., the visual sensation of the fork) influences the perception of the sensation.

The effect of context is also established by research on ambiguous objects. One well-known example of an ambiguous object is the ambiguous figure that can be interpreted as either a young woman or an old woman (illustrated in Figure 3-8). Usually people will find that their perception of the figure fluctuates between the young and old woman interpretation, but that their first impression is of an old woman. If, however, people are shown an unambiguous figure of a young woman and then are shown the ambiguous figure, they are much more likely to perceive the ambiguous figure as a young woman (Leeper, 1935). Apparently, though, this effect occurs only if subjects actually see the unambiguous young woman first. If subjects are merely told to expect to see a young woman and are then shown the unambiguous figure, they still tend to see the old woman first.

So I guess my example of Ugg telling Ogg about the lion and so influencing Ogg's interpretation of an ambiguous object does not work as a good illustration of the research on context effects. Maybe a better hypothetical example would be that if Ogg had just seen a lion, he would be prone to interpret a subsequently encountered ambiguous stimulus as a lion. Then again, maybe my original example wasn't so bad. Rock and Mitchener (1992) found that if subjects were merely told that they would find that their perception of the figure would alternate between old and young woman, the subjects in fact perceived more fluctuations than did subjects not so forewarned. Furthermore, adult subjects who were unaware that an ambiguous figure was reversible perceived only one interpretation of the figure (Rock, Hall, & Davis, 1994). Without the expectation that the figure is ambiguous, subjects failed to see the ambiguity.

FIGURE 3–8   The young woman/old woman ambiguous figure.

While ambiguous figures like the young–old woman figure are contrived, visually ambiguous patterns are common in day-to-day life. From a distance, an object moving down the highway might be a car, truck, or van. From a brief glance at a printed page, the information actually picked up might be consistent with the word JUNK or HUNK. A group of lights moving across the night sky might be an airplane or, for people who have read too many Kurt Vonnegut novels, a flying saucer from the planet Tralfamadore. An everyday example of how expectations influence the interpretations given to ambiguous stimuli comes from research comparing police officers to ordinary civilians (Clifford & Bull, 1978). Both the officers and the civilians were shown films of street scenes and had to look for the presence of certain types of people (e.g., an elderly man) and for crimes of theft. The two groups did not differ in their detection of the types of people. However, the police officers were more likely to interpret an event as a theft than were the civilians. Now, the depictions of the events were identical for both groups. So information in the depictions themselves could not have been the source of the difference between the police officers and the civilians. Presumably, police officers, more than civilians, have the expectation that people are prone to steal. It is presumably this expectation that biased how the officers interpreted the ambiguous scenes.

Although this chapter is on visual perception, I think it is important to point out that context effects in perception are not limited to the visual modality. Many experiments have demonstrated context effects in the perception of sounds, for example. One of the classic demonstrations comes from a study by Warren (1970; see also Samuel, 1981, 1987). Warren presented subjects sentences auditorially in which one phoneme in one word was replaced with a coughing sound of the same intensity. Phonemes are the simplest sounds that make a difference to the meaning of a word. The word *rough*, for example, consists of three phonemes; the /r/ sound, the /u/ sound, and the /f/ sound. An example of one of the stimuli in Warren's experiment was a sentence containing the word *legislature* with the /s/ replaced by a cough. Subjects were supposed to identify where in the sentence the cough occurred. Surprisingly, subjects were not accurate in identifying the location of the cough. Instead, subjects typically heard the full word (e.g., *legislature* with the /s/), and heard the cough in the background. They were not aware that the phoneme (e.g., /s/) was missing. It was as if knowledge of a word like *legislature* was used by the perceptual process to restore the missing phoneme to the sound stream. Hence, the name of the effect is **phonemic restoration**.

Note that when a perceptual system restores to *legislature* the missing /s/, it has no /s/ in the sound wave to identify. The perceived /s/ must come from knowledge obtained from previous encounters with *legislature*, knowledge that becomes activated by the perception of other information in the speech sound wave. Indeed, Samuel (1990) demonstrated that phonemic restoration is more likely in a real word than in a pseudoword. For example, if the /o/ phoneme was masked, subjects were more likely to restore it when the word was *progress* than when it was *crogress*.

The experimental demonstration of phonemic restoration may seem contrived, but in fact it is similar to what happens in day-to-day speech. It is commonplace for ordinary speech to be replete with coughs, slurs, clips, and so on, that effectively remove phonemes, syllables, and even whole words from the sound wave. If an experimenter records ordinary speech, and then plays back only the portion of the tape associated with a single word, listeners can accurately identify only about 50% of the words (Pollack & Pickett, 1963). We need the information provided by at least one or two other words in a phrase or sentence in order to identify reliably any given word from ordinary conversation.

My favorite example of real-world phonemic (or maybe whole-word) restoration is the perception many people have of the lyrics in the Kingsmen's version of the classic rock song "Louie Louie." Many people swear they hear lyrics that contain rather sexually explicit content. As it turns out, the song contains no explicit sexual content, but the singer manages to slur the words and sing in a sexually suggestive tone of voice in such a way as to inspire the sexually explicit interpretation.

HOW DIRECT IS PATTERN RECOGNITION?

Recall that the theme integrating this chapter is the contrast between direct or ecological perception on the one hand, and constructed or computed perception on the other. The idea that there are discoverable visual features of patterns that enable them to be reliably recognized is consistent with the more general claim of direct perception that the visual environment supplies all the information necessary for fast and accurate perception. All the brain has to do is direct attention to that information and it will be picked up. In some cases, the invariant features associated with the identification of objects are rather abstract, as in the example of the degree of strain associated with the age of a profile.

However, most prevailing models of pattern recognition propose a fair bit of computational complexity in the detecting and processing of visual information in the environment. Such complexity is more consistent with constructed perception (Goldstein, 1996; Marr, 1982). Feature models propose a deconstruction of a sensation into features that are processed by a hierarchical analysis in which objects are represented as hierarchies of features. Prototype models propose that acts of perception result in the creation of an internal idealized representation of a class of objects, and that subsequent acts of perception involve comparing new sensations to the internal representation. Direct perception tends to eschew internalized representations. Prototype models, then, are also more consistent with constructed approaches to perception (Best, 1995).

What's more, prototype formation is usually regarded as a general cognitive process not unique to perception (Best, 1995). For example, prototypes have been used as a way of representing the meaning of concepts (e.g., Rosch, 1973; see chapter 5: Implicit and Semantic Memory) and the nature of personality (Buss & Craik, 1983; Cantor & Mischel, 1977; Rothbart & Lewis, 1988). For instance, Rothbart and Lewis (1988) had subjects read about hypothetical fraternity members who varied in the degree to which they resembled prototypical fraternity members. The hypothetical members were also described as voting for either Ronald Reagan or Walter Mondale in the 1984 presidential election. Subjects were required to estimate the degree of political liberalism of the fraternity as a whole. The more prototypical the hypothetical fraternity member, the more that member's vote influenced the liberalism judgment. The fraternity was seen as more liberal if the prototypical member voted for Mondale than if the nonprototypical member voted for Mondale; similarly, the fraternity was seen as more conservative if the prototypical member voted for Reagan than if the nonprototypical member voted for Reagan.

The main point is that the use of general cognitive processes in perception imparts a kind of intelligence to the perceptual process (Dretske, 1995), consistent with constructed perception. Direct perception, on the other hand, claims that the external stimulus supplies enough information: perception does not need to draw on the general cognitive skills underlying the kind of intelligence by which people generally understand the nature of the world.

The effect of context (i.e., top-down processing) on pattern recognition is also usually taken as evidence for a constructed approach to perception (Galotti, 1994; Goldstein, 1996). Context includes expectations, such as the expectation that police have concerning the prevalence of crime, that lie outside the visual information stream, yet contribute to the perception of that stream. Still, a diehard direct perceptionist might argue that most context effects do not seriously challenge direct perception. As an anonymous reviewer of my textbook pointed out, the lion in the zoo is not the same as the lion in the bush.

The notion of affordances, important to the direct perception approach, has also been criticized (Ullman, 1980; Fodor & Pylyshyn, 1981; see Gardner, 1985). If a person perceives some particular property in an object, the Gibsonian can say that the object affords that property. A rock can be a weapon because it is hurlable. A rock can be a decoration because it is colorful. The problem, though, is that there is no explanation, within the Gibsonian account, for how a person comes to perceive a particular affordance. What enables the warrior to see the hurlable affordance and the artist to see the colorful affordance in the same rock? Something inside the person must direct the perceptual process to the appropriate aspects of the rock to enable the rock to be perceived as a weapon or decoration. Affordances are not entirely in the stimulus but must reflect a contribution of past learning and current expectations the person brings to the perception of the stimulus.

SECTION 4: IMAGINED PERCEPTIONS

The previous sections have focused on how people process visual sensations in order to interpret them. But people are capable of having perceptual-like experiences in the absence of any sensory information. One might call these imagined or quasi-perceptual experiences. People can imagine the sight of their mother's face, the sound of an electrical guitar, or the taste of chocolate. Our dreams and fantasies are replete with such quasi-perceptual experiences. In this section I will focus on visual imagination. The two main points I will make are: (1) that visual imagination simulates ordinary visual perception and (2) that the products of visual imagination—the visual images—are constructed from several sources of knowledge.

A few words about terminology. People who study visual imagination often invoke the word *image* to stand for the imagined visual scene. This language is potentially misleading (see Shepard, 1984). The notion of an image would seem to imply that there is some object inside the head that some internal person perceives. It is as if the researchers are claiming that there is a little person, a **homunculus**, inside the head that views a little picture inside the head. But the postulation of a homunculus leaves unexplained how the homunculus imagines visual scenes. And it is an explanation of how visual imagination works that is the goal of the research.

To avoid the misleading implication of the word *image* in the context of visual imagination, one might talk only of the process of imagining a visual scene and never about the image that is imagined. Still, I prefer to use the terminology of the visual image, but I merely mean it to stand for the process whereby a person has the subjective experience of imagining a visual scene in the absence of actually viewing the visual scene. The advantage of using *visual image* is in saving words, as the previous sentence demonstrates.

VISUAL IMAGINATION SIMULATES VISUAL PERCEPTION

The other night I had a dream in which I was able to dunk a basketball over the head of Michael Jordan. Michael Jordan, for those of you who don't know, is a phenomenally talented basketball player, one of the best ever to play the game. I, on the other hand, am not. In my dream, Mr. Jordan looked like himself, the basketball was round, the movements of the players on the court resembled those of real players. The giveaway that it was a dream was that I was playing with these guys and actually dunking the basketball.

Clearly, though, the visual aspects of my dream simulated the essential qualities of real visual perception. The visual scene was three-dimensional, objects possessed only one form at any given moment in time, movement of objects required that they pass through points in space, I was able to see only one side of an object at any given moment in time, and so on. My dream was not of a two-dimensional scene in which the basketball was simultaneously round and square, seen simultaneously from the front and back, moving instantaneously from my hand to the basket.

A variety of research on visual imagination has not only verified the intuition that the visual imagination is capable of simulating the visual world but has demonstrated the rather surprising degree to which visual imagination is constrained by the ecological properties of the visual world. I say "surprising" because there does not seem to be any obvious reason why visual imagination couldn't be free to conjure up any old image it wants, including images that violate ecological laws (e.g., the simultaneously round and square basketball). Even when the visual imagination conjures up images that are unlike anything encountered in the real world, like a basketball that expands into a house, the altered reality of the visual imagination usually continues to obey ecological laws.

Mental Rotation

Probably the best-known example of the ecological nature of visual imagination comes from the **mental rotation** experiments originally designed by Roger Shepard (who first conceived of the experiment in a dream he had while falling asleep). In the typical mental rotation experiment (e.g., Cooper & Shepard, 1973), subjects are presented a visual stimulus in any of a number of orientations and must judge whether the stimulus is identical to or mirror-reversed from some target stimulus. For instance, subjects might be given the letter *R* in its ordinary upright position, and in other positions rotated some number of degrees from upright. Furthermore, the letter might be in its standard form or mirror-reversed. The response measure is how long it takes subjects to decide whether the *R* is standard or mirror-reversed. Figure 3-9 depicts a typical subject's response times in experiments like Cooper and Shepard (1973).

The main finding is that the more degrees of orientation the stimulus is rotated from the horizontal, the longer it takes subjects to decide whether the stimulus is standard or mirror-reversed. Indeed, reaction time in such a situation is strictly linear. This finding is quite robust, as many experiments using

Standard letter	R	↷	ꓤ
Mirror-reversed letter	Я	↶	ꓤ
Degrees of rotation	0	45	90
Typical reaction time (in milliseconds)	580	650	720

FIGURE 3–9 Typical reaction times in mental rotation experiments (e.g., Cooper and Shepard, 1973) in which subjects decide whether a letter is standard or mirror-reversed.

many types of visual materials have found it (e.g., Shepard & Metzerl 1971; Jordan & Huntsman, 1990; Desrocher, Smith, & Taylor, 1995). The explanation given by Shepard and others is that subjects mentally rotate the stimulus until it is in its upright position, and then mentally compare the rotated stimulus to the target. The more degrees through which the stimulus must be rotated to become upright, the longer the response time. Note that the rotation is imagined; the stimulus the subjects confront does not move. Thus the experiments are known as mental rotation experiments (although the mental rotation is inferred).

What is noteworthy is that subjects do not seem to imagine the stimulus jumping instantaneously from one orientation to the upright orientation, even though it would be to their advantage to do so, because then they would be able to respond faster. Were subjects able to imagine the instantaneous movement to the upright orientation, reaction time would not be a linear function of degrees of rotation. Instead, the subjects seem to imagine the stimulus traveling through all the points in space between its actual orientation and its imagined upright orientation. In the real world of movement, objects must travel through all the points in space between locations. That is, objects cannot move without travel-ing through space (the wormholes of science fiction notwithstanding). The main point is that imagined movement also requires that the object move through space. The more space through which the object's movement must be imagined, the longer it takes the subject to respond in the experiment.

Imagined Size

Real objects and real pictures of objects vary in size. There can be large or small pictures of lions, and real lions can be close or far away. Ordinarily, it is easier to see details in larger visual realizations of objects than in smaller visual real-izations of the same objects. That lions possess whiskers, for example, is easier to determine from a large picture of a lion than from a small picture. What hap-pens when one imagines seeing objects? Do visual images of objects possess size? Is it easier to "see" the details in a large image than in a small image?

Evidence that visual imagination simulates size comes from some inge-nious experiments conducted by Stephen Kosslyn (1975), one of the best-known researchers in the area of visual imagination (for a treatise describing his research, see Kosslyn, 1983). He wanted subjects to vary the size of their visual images of animals and then to use their images to answer questions about prop-erties of the animals. To accomplish this, Kosslyn had subjects image various tar-get animals (e.g., mouse, cat, kangaroo) next to a referent animal. For one group of subjects the referent animal was always an elephant, for the other group the referent animal was always a fly. Subjects had to answer questions concerning visually realizable properties of the target animals (but not the referent animals). Examples of questions were "Does a mouse have a beak?" and "Does a rabbit have an eyebrow?"

Kosslyn reasoned that an image constructed next to the referent fly would be bigger than an image next to the referent elephant. His assumption was that people have a limited visual ``space'' in which they can conjure up visual images. If that space is mostly used up by the image of the elephant, then there is little space left over for constructing an image of the target animal. If the space is barely used by the image of the fly, then there is a lot of space left over for constructing an image of the target animal.

Kosslyn found that subjects took about .2 seconds longer to answer questions about the target animals when they were imaged next to an elephant than when they were imaged next to a fly. To be sure that the results were due to image size and not some other property of imagined flies and elephants, Kosslyn asked one group of subjects to image the targets next to a very tiny elephant and another group to image the targets next to a gigantic fly. Here he found that people were faster at making judgments about the targets when they were imaged next to the tiny elephant than when next to the large fly. Kosslyn's interpretation of the results was that visually imagined objects possess the attribute of size, just as do real objects. Therefore, larger images have the properties of larger visual realizations of actual objects; namely, that it is easier to see the details in larger objects (i.e., in larger pictures of such objects or when the objects are closer). Again, the larger point is that visual images simulate the ecological properties of real visual perception. Visual images are constrained by ecological laws.

Reaction Time on Demand?

A criticism of the imagery research has been that subjects merely respond in order to satisfy the expectations of the experimenter; the formation of images has nothing to do with the results (e.g., Intons-Peterson, 1983). That is, the results may be due to **demand characteristics** implicit in imagery research. So a subject who takes longer to see whiskers in a cat next to an elephant than in a cat next to a fly is, according to this complaint, deliberately slowing down the reaction time in order to perform as the subject thinks the experimenter demands the subject perform.

I don't think the demand characteristic complaint is justified, however. An example of research contradicting the demand characteristic explanation of the imagery experiments is based on a finding that images simulate distance. Experiments have demonstrated that if subjects are asked first to imagine a previously encountered map containing several landmarks (e.g., a hut, a tree), then to fixate on one landmark (e.g., the hut) on the imagined map, and then to scan the imagined map to see if it contains another landmark (e.g., the tree), reaction time is slower the farther apart the landmarks are on the map (Kosslyn, Ball, & Reiser, 1978). The explanation based on the imagery hypothesis, on the idea that images preserve the ecological properties of real perception, is that the imagined scene simulates distance.

To test to see if the results were due instead to demand characteristics, Goldstein, Hinrichs, and Richman (1985) explicitly told some subjects that the time to scan a long distance in an imagined scene would be faster than to scan a short distance in the same scene. Even still, these subjects were slower to scan the longer distance. Furthermore, naive subjects who were not asked to form images were poor at predicting the results of imagery scanning experiments (Denis & Carfantan, 1985). So it does not appear that the results of imagery experiments are due to subjects' giving in to demand characteristics.

The Causal Role of Images in Cognition

There is a long-standing debate over whether the visual image is necessary to explain any observable behavior (see Gardner, 1985, for a discussion). Even people who are diehard cognitive scientists and who firmly believe that internal mental states play a causal role in behavior are not necessarily convinced that mental images play such a role. It could be that the subjective experience of imagining a visual scene is merely an **epiphenomenon**—something that occurs as a byproduct of thought, but is of no causal consequence (Pylyshyn, 1973). Instead, all cognitive processes might be accomplished in a completely image-less mode of thought. By way of analogy, green is the color of the chemical that enables plants to photosynthesize, but the color itself plays no role in photo-synthesis. Maybe images are to cognition as green is to photosynthesis. Alternatively, images may play a causal role in cognition. It may be that the acti-vation of the visual image constitutes a cognitive process with different proper-ties than those of other cognitive processing modes.

I believe images do have a causal role to perform in cognition. Images may help bring to conscious awareness knowledge that is only implicit. Indeed, a number of innovators have claimed that they became aware of a solution to an important problem through the visual imagery of a dream. It was apparently in a dream that a gynecologist discovered how to tie a surgical knot deep in the pelvis with one hand; that Otto Loewi devised the experiment that led to the discovery of the chemical basis of neural transmission; that Elias Howe discov-ered the crucial insight necessary for perfecting the sewing machine; and, as I mentioned earlier, that Roger Shepard designed his mental rotation experiment (see Shepard, 1984).

Imagery might also help people prepare for future actions. There is research, for instance, that shows that people can benefit as much from imagin-ing that they are practicing a skill as from literally practicing the skill (e.g., Ziegler, 1987). In one example of such research (Predebon & Docker, 1992), expe-rienced basketball players who only imagined that they were practicing shoot-ing free throws improved their free-throw performance more than did experienced players who engaged in real practice and more than experienced players who did not practice at all.

Another possible function of imagery is to enhance memory for verbal information (see Paivio, 1971). Bower and Winzenz (1970) had subjects study a list of concrete word pairs (e.g., pencil–clock) and later recall the second word (e.g., clock) of each pair given the first word (e.g., pencil) as a cue. Some sub-jects were instructed to repeat silently to themselves the word pairs as they stud-ied them; other subjects were instructed to generate a mental image in which the words interacted (e.g., a pencil functioning as the big hand on a clock face). Subjects in the verbal repetition condition remembered only 5.2 out of 15 words whereas subjects in the interactive imagery condition remembered 12.7 words out of 15.

Interactive imagery is also a useful way to learn a foreign language (Atkinson & Raugh, 1975; Kasper & Glass, 1988). The idea is to imagine a visual scene in which a native-language word is seen interacting with a second native-language word that phonetically resembles the foreign-language translation. For English speakers learning Spanish, you can remember that the Spanish word *rodilla* means *knee* by imaging a cowboy with protruding knees riding a horse in a rodeo (*rodeo* sounds like *rodilla*).

The generation of an image may affect memory, but the effect need not always be beneficial. Consider a study by Dobson and Marham (1993). They presented subjects with a film of a crime and then a series of written descriptions of the crime that included details not shown in the film. Later, subjects were given descriptions of the details and had to judge whether the details had originally been presented to them in the film or in writing. The subjects who claimed to have vivid visual images had more trouble recalling the source of the information—they often claimed they saw the detail in the film when in fact they read about it in the verbal description—than did the subjects who claimed that their images were not as vivid. A reasonable explanation of this study is that the good imagers created a vivid visual image of the written descriptions. Because the images seemed similar to the experience of viewing the film, the vivid imagers confused the written descriptions with the film. In chapter 4: Memory, I also discuss the effects of imagery on memory and the difficulties people sometimes have in recalling the source of information.

NEUROPHYSIOLOGY OF VISUAL IMAGINATION

Visual imagination simulates the ecological properties of the visual world. That is, it models visual perception; it is constrained by the properties of the visual system and of the visual ecology the system is designed to interpret. For instance, imagined objects take longer to move through greater than through shorter distances, and the visual properties of larger imagined objects are easier to discern than are the visual properties of smaller images. Yet the visual imagination involves no light, no real objects, and no retinal activity. Why, then, is the visual imagination constrained by the properties of real visual perception?

The answer is that the essential experience of visual imagination seems to entail the activation of the same cerebral centers involved in real sight (Farah, 1988; Kosslyn, 1994). The main difference between real seeing and imagined seeing may be that real seeing also invokes the activation of the peripheral components (e.g., the retina) of the visual system. Imagined seeing may also involve brain centers important in the initiation of thought and behavior.

One line of evidence comes from brain damage. Individuals whose visual systems become damaged will sometimes suffer losses to both visual perception and visual imagination. For instance, brain-damaged patients who have trouble perceiving differences in color also have trouble forming visual images that include color (Beauvois & Saillant, 1985; Damasio, Yamada, Damasio, Corbett, & McKee, 1980). Patients with left-field neglect, usually caused by damage to the right parietal lobe, also neglect the left half of their visual images (Bisiach, Luzzatti, & Perani, 1979). Left-field neglect in imagery was demonstrated by having the patients examine pairs of bloblike pictures that moved behind occluding surfaces. The patients had more trouble judging whether the blobs were the same or different when the occlusion was on their left side than when the occlusion was on their right side. Farah, Soso, and Dasheiff (1992) studied a patient who had half of her occipital lobe near primary visual cortex removed for medical reasons and subsequently revealed in tests of visual imagery that the horizontal angles subtended by objects in her images shrank by about one half.

Another line of evidence that visual imagery and visual perception use the same neural centers comes from studies of intact brains. In a typical study, Goldenberg et al. (1988) found that the visual cortex (located in the occipital lobe) showed increased blood flow when subjects responded to questions whose answer required visual imagination (e.g., "The green of pine trees is darker than the green of grass. Correct or incorrect?"). In contrast, the occipital lobes did not show increased blood flow when subjects responded to questions that involved minimal visual imagery (e.g., "Columbus named the natives of America Indians because he believed he was in India. Correct or incorrect?").

The Construction of Visual Images from Knowledge

The main theme of this chapter is a contrast between direct or ecological perception, on the one hand, and constructed perception, on the other. Consistent with the direct perception approach, imagined perception reflects the constraints imposed by the ecology of the visual world. In this section I wish to describe some research consistent with a constructionist view of imagined perception. As with real perception, imagined perceptions are constructed from the visual knowledge in the imaged scene and from knowledge that lies outside the scene itself.

One line of evidence for the constructionist claim is the finding that it is difficult for people to generate images that accurately contain all the visual details possessed by objects in real visual scenes. Consider—can you draw the head side of a penny? In fact, people have trouble remembering which way Lincoln faces on a penny, despite having looked at the face of a penny thousands of times (Nickerson & Adams, 1979; see also Madigan & Rouse, 1974). The difficulty with remembering the orientation of Lincoln on the penny probably reflects a lack of nonvisual knowledge concerning Lincoln's orientation. It simply does not matter to most of us which way Lincoln faces (although it might matter to an official of the U.S. Treasury Department should some incredibly stupid criminal decide to flood the economy with counterfeit pennies). Without the nonvisual knowledge to support the generation of the image, the image remains imprecise.

Another line of evidence that imagery incorporates nonvisual knowledge is provided by Norman, Rumelhart, and the LNR Research Group (1975). They asked 15 people who lived in a married-student dormitory to draw the floor plan of the dorm apartment. Despite having lived in the apartments for months and even years, about half of the students made an error in their drawings of the balcony. They thought that the balcony was constructed flush with the exterior of the building when, in fact, the balcony protruded in the normal way from the building. Most of the other details of the floor plan, such as the location of the sink in the kitchen, were drawn accurately. The probable reason for the balcony error was that there were brick walls located on both sides of the balcony. Most of the time a brick wall functions to separate a room from the out-of-doors. Presumably it was knowledge of the normal function of brick walls that was used to reconstruct, inaccurately in this case, the location of the balcony relative to the bedroom. In other words, knowledge that was itself nonvisual was used to generate a visual image.

Another example demonstrating the role of nonvisual information in imagery comes from an experiment in which people were queried about their knowledge of geography. For instance, subjects were asked whether Reno, Nevada, is east or west of San Diego, California. Most people responded that Reno is east of San Diego, when, in fact, it is west of San Diego (Stevens & Coupe, 1978). Now, these subjects had surely looked at maps of the United States many times. Yet their image of the map misplaced Reno east of San Diego. Everyone knows that California is west of Nevada, but most people forget that California actually slants in a westwardly direction as one travels from south to north.

Another geography example. Moar and Bower (1983) studied people who had lived for five or more years in Cambridge, England. The researchers had their subjects estimate the angles formed by the intersections of Cambridge streets that formed triangles. The subjects tended to estimate that the angles were closer to 90 degrees than was really the case. For instance, three streets that formed a triangle had angles of 67, 63, and 50 degrees. The subjects estimated these angles to be 84, 78, and 88 degrees. One explanation is that most street angles are closer to 90 degrees. This knowledge of intersections may have caused subjects to distort their estimates towards 90 degrees. The Moar and Bower study and the Stevens and Coupe study (see Matlin, 1994, for even more studies) make the point that, as constructed perception would have it, our mental maps are not a perfect representation of our spatial environment but are contaminated, as it were, by other kinds of knowledge we possess.

SUMMARY AND CONCLUSIONS

I began this chapter by asking whether people perceive physical reality as it is or whether people sometimes misperceive reality. I recast the question as a debate between direct perception (also known as ecological perception) and constructed perception. Direct perception claims that people readily and accurately detect the invariants available in the physical stimulus that supply all the information necessary for perception. Mistakes in perception are attributable to performance lapses. Constructed perception emphasizes computational processes that intervene between the detection of a physical stimulus, such as light, and the interpretation given to the stimulus. In particular, these intervening computations may simplify or spruce up the stimulus. Usually the alterations are done on the basis of knowledge acquired from previous acts of perception. The intrusion, as it were, of "extra-sensory" knowledge into the perceptual process means that perception does at times distort reality. That is, mistakes in perception are occasionally attributable to processes intrinsic to ordinary perception and not only to performance lapses.

With the debate between direct and constructed perception as an integrating theme, I discussed the physiology of visual perception, visual depth perception, visual pattern recognition, and imagined visual perception. I suggested throughout my survey of visual perceptual theory and research that the prevailing perspective is generally more consistent with constructed perception than with direct perception.

What we know and what we don't know about the physiology of visual perception is consistent with the constructed perspective. The visual system performs an amazingly complex analysis of light. In the primary visual cortex, located in the occipital lobes, modules of neurons process spatial frequency, orientation, movement, disparity, color, and texture information for light falling on some restricted portion of the retina. Information from primary visual cortex is sent to secondary visual cortex, located in many areas of the brain. Modules and circuits of secondary visual cortex typically perform only one kind of analysis of light (e.g., movement) but do so for light falling anywhere on the retina. Secondary visual cortex seems to perform the integrative functions necessary to recognize basic forms (e.g., whether the light constitutes a square or a circular pattern).

What remains mysterious is how the visual cortex binds elements of visual perception into a unified perception (e.g., binds the red color and the spherical form into a unified perception of an apple) and why visual perceptions (as well as auditory perceptions) are externalized while somatosensory perceptions are internalized. Notice, though, that however these processes are accomplished, the binding of visual properties and the externalization of visual perceptions are not in the light striking the retina, as the direct perceptionist would have it, but are imposed on perception by the brain. Binding and externalization represent constructions of the visual world, and not purely objective descriptions of the visual information in the light.

In section 2 I discussed depth perception. A challenge for any theory of visual perception is to explain how we see depth, given that the image falling on the retina is only two-dimensional. The direct perceptionist says we should look for information in the two-dimensional retinal image of an object that informs the perceiver of the distance of the object. That information includes monocular cues, such as relative size, interposition, and motion parallax. Gibson was especially interested in the depth cues present in the ambient light while the perceiver is in motion. Depth is also provided by binocular cues, which involve oculomotor sensations and stereopsis. Stereopsis is based on retinal disparity and is a particularly informative cue for depth.

But the perception of depth does not rely only on the information in the light reflecting off objects. Cultural knowledge plays a role. This was illustrated by cultural differences in the perception of the Müller-Lyer illusion (and similar illusions), which apparently reflects knowledge of right-angled surfaces common to Western culture. In cultures where there are few right-angled surfaces, people do not experience the illusion to the same degree as do Western people. The evidence that cultural knowledge influences perception—indeed, in the case of an illusion, renders an inaccurate interpretation of reality—is usually taken as arguing for the constructed approach to perception.

Another challenge for theories of perception is to explain how we reliably identify objects, such as cursive Ls and hungry lions, given that any kind of object comes in a potentially limitless number of forms and orientations. As I discussed in section 3, the direct perception account looks to the stimulus to see what sorts of invariants are associated with similarly perceived objects and events. Strain is an example of an invariant associated with the perception of age in a human profile.

The constructed perception account focuses on the internal processes that give rise to pattern recognition. One influential feature model postulates that the brain extracts any of a few dozen types of lines, edges, vertexes, and so on, from a visual sensation and identifies these low-level features as belonging to any one or several of a possible two dozen geons. A geon is a higher level feature resembling a simple volume. The type and arrangement among geons is then compared to stored representations of the geon complex associated with a given category of object. Virtually any object can be described as an arrangement of three or fewer geons. This scheme explains how the process of visually identifying objects is fast and accurate, and how it handles novel variations of familiar patterns.

Another model, called the prototype model, claims that pattern recognition entails comparing a sensation to an idealized, quasi-average representation of a class of objects. Generally, pattern recognition is more accurate to the extent that a sensation matches the prototype. In one example of an extension of the prototype model of perception, research has shown that prototypical faces are perceived as attractive.

Constructed perception claims that the brain routinely uses "extra-sensory" information to accomplish object identification. Evidence consistent with constructionism comes from the effects of context and expectations on the identification of objects. Light reflecting off a fork is more readily perceived as a fork in the context of a kitchen than in the context of an office. Letters are more rapidly identified in the context of words than when isolated, despite the fact that the visual system must process more information in the case of words. Police more frequently identify a pattern of human interactions as theft than do ordinary civilians. In another example, the mere expectation that a figure is ambiguous increases the tendency for the interpretation of the actual figure to fluctuate between an old woman and a young woman.

Perception is intriguing in part because it is possible to have a quasi-perceptual experience in the absence of a physical sensation. In section 4 I explored the topic of visual imagery as an example of a quasi-perceptual experience.

Visual images simulate real visual experiences in the sense that images "obey" the ecological principles of real visual perception. In real visual perception, objects have size, they can take only one form at a time, they move through space, and so on. The same is true of visual images. Shepard's classic work on mental rotation demonstrated the ecological nature of imagery. When subjects must compare a visual stimulus to a target, and the stimulus is rotated, the time it takes to make the comparison increases linearly with the degree of rotation. The interpretation is that subjects mentally rotate the stimulus back to its upright position in order to make the comparison with the target. The more space through which the image must rotate, the longer the reaction time. Imagery simulates real visual perception because the act of visual imagination activates many of the same neural areas also activated in real visual perception.

What purpose, if any, does imagery serve? I suggested that imagery may aid in enabling us to engage in a sort of dress rehearsal for future events. As evidence, people are able to benefit from mental practice, such as imaging that they are shooting free throws. Interactive imagery may also aid in making information more memorable. In fact, interactive imagery has been used to help students learn a foreign language.

As the constructionist approach to perception would have it, visual imagination is affected by nonvisual knowledge. Mental images of maps, for example, have Reno east of San Diego. These errors reflect the intrusion of misleading geographical knowledge into the image. Imagined perceptions, like real perceptions, are constructions of reality that use a variety of kinds of knowledge to interpret sensations.

RECOMMENDED READINGS

Goldstein's (1996) *Sensation and Perception* is one of the best textbooks on the subject of perception. In this book, Goldstein covers virtually every topic on perception in every sensory modality. Gardner's (1985) excellent history of cognitive science (*The Mind's New Science*) includes a chapter discussing the dispute between the direct perception and computational perception schools as well as a chapter on whether visual imagery plays a causal role in thought or is merely an epiphenomenon. The intellectually hardy among you might try reading Marr's (1982) *Vision*, generally regarded as one of the most influential books on visual perception theory, and J. J. Gibson's (1979) *The Ecological Approach to Visual Perception*, one of several treatises by the main thinker behind direct perception. Hubel and Wiesel's (1979) *Scientific American* article provides an accessible overview of their Nobel Prize–winning work on receptive fields in the visual cortex. Biederman (1995) discusses general issues in visual pattern recognition and his own Recognition-by-Components theory in particular. Kosslyn's (1975) study on imagined flies and elephants remains one of my favorite works on the topic of imagery. R. Shepard, of mental rotation fame, has an important essay on visual imagery in his 1984 *Psychological Review* article. In his review Shepard also gives examples of creativity in dreams.

4 Memory

Donald Thompson, a noted expert on memory and a frequent expert witness in legal cases involving eyewitness memories, became a suspect in a case himself when he was found to match a rape victim's description of her rapist. Luckily, Thompson had an airtight alibi—he had been doing an interview on live television, where he was discussing how people can improve their memory for faces. He was cleared when it became apparent that the victim had been watching Thompson on television just prior to the rape and so had confused him with her memory of the actual rapist (this case is described in Schacter, 1996). Indeed, a number of cases have been reported in which eyewitnesses to crimes provided erroneous identifications of perpetrators after they encountered the accused outside the context of the crime (Read, Tollestrup, Hammersley, McFadzen, & Christensen, 1990; Ross, Ceci, Dunning, & Toglia, 1994). Why do people make such mistakes? What accounts for the fallibility of human memory?

In this chapter I will provide an overview of what cognitive psychologists have learned about memory, including how we learn new information, how we recollect previous experiences, and why we sometimes forget important information. I will focus on *explicit memory*, sometimes called *episodic memory*, which is our conscious recollection of personal experiences. In other chapters I will discuss the unconscious influence of past experiences on current thought and behavior and the physiological basis for memory and forgetting.

SECTION 1: PERSPECTIVES ON MEMORY

RECORD-KEEPING VERSUS CONSTRUCTIONIST ACCOUNTS OF MEMORY

I will begin the discussion with the question: What is the principle function of human memory? One possible answer is that memory functions to preserve the past—that it is designed to retain records of previous experiences. Such a perspective has lead to an approach to memory I will label the **record-keeping** approach.

The essential idea of any record-keeping theory is that memory acts as a kind of storage bin in which records of experiences are placed, much as books might be placed in a library. The record keeping theory is really a family of theories that have in common the following principles: (1) Each experience adds a new record of the experience to the storage bin; consequently the number of records expands over time. Similarly, the number of books stored in a library increases over time. The records actually stored may be more accurately described as interpretations of experiences. (2) Remembering involves searching through a network of memory locations for some particular record, as one might search for a particular book in a library. Once found, the target memory record is "read" or in some sense reexperienced. The search need not be done haphazardly, since the memory records may be connected or organized in such a way as to improve the efficiency of the search. Libraries, for example, organize books by subject matter in order to make finding the books easier. (3) Forgetting is primarily due to search failure caused by the interfering effect of the presence of lots of memory records, just as in a library the huge number of books stored there makes finding any one book difficult. Some versions of the record-keeping theory claim that no memory record is ever really lost. All records of past experiences are potentially recoverable.

The metaphor of record keeping is compelling for several reasons. The word *memory* implies a preserving of the past; we sometimes have vivid and accurate recollections of the past, and nearly all of the artificial memory systems we know about, such as libraries, videotapes, and computers, are record-keeping systems designed to preserve information. Indeed, it is difficult to imagine any other basis for memory. Nevertheless, I will argue in this and other chapters that the record-keeping approach to human memory is a misleading one (Schacter, 1996). Human memory works according to a different set of principles.

An alternative to the record-keeping approach may be called a **constructionist** approach to memory. I first introduced the notion of constructionism in chapter 3: Visual Perception, where I discussed how knowledge from sources outside of the stimulus stream affects the perception of the stimulus. A similar notion plays a role in a constructionist account of memory.

The constructionist account begins with the important insight that human memory is not designed primarily to preserve the past, but to anticipate the future (Morris, 1988). Most constructionist theories are characterized by these principles: (1) Each new experience causes changes in the various cognitive systems that perceive, interpret, respond emotionally, and act on the environment, but no record-by-record account of the experiences that gave rise to those changes is stored anywhere. That is, memory reflects how the cognitive systems have adapted to the environment. Usually this adaptation takes the form of noting regularities in experiences and basing future responses on these regularities. The cognitive systems are also sensitive to unexpected exceptions to the regularities ordinarily observed. (2) Recollection of the past involves a reconstruction of past experiences based on information in the current environment and on the way cognitive processing is currently accomplished. Remembering is a process more akin to fantasizing or planning for the future than searching for and then "reading" memory records, or in any sense reexperiencing the past. The past does not force itself on a passive individual; instead, the individual actively creates some plausible account of her or his past. (3) Forgetting is not due to the presence of other memory records but to the continuous adaptive changes made to the various cognitive systems in response to events.

Let me distinguish between the record-keeping and constructionist approaches with a simple example. Suppose an individual—let's call him Jim— witnessed a robbery in a convenience store. Let's say that the burglar was wearing a black sweatshirt and black jeans, stole money from the cash register, and stole a radio that was lying on the counter. Suppose that after the burglar fled, Jim heard a customer claim that the burglar stole a camera. Later on, when questioned by the police and when testifying in a court of law, Jim must try to recollect as accurately as possible the details of the crime. For example, Jim might be asked: "What was the burglar wearing?" or "What did the burglar steal?"

Any record-keeping theory claims that witnessing the crime caused Jim to store a new record (or records) in his memory system. When later asked to recollect the crime, Jim must first search through his memory records until he finds the record representing the crime, and then try to "read" its contents. If Jim correctly answers questions about the crime, it is because he was able to locate the relevant memory record. If Jim forgets, it is because the presence of so many other memory records made it difficult for him to find the appropriate memory record or because he was unable to access all the details stored in the record.

According to constructionist theories, no record-by-record account of past events is maintained in a storage system. Instead, the cognitive systems for interpreting and acting on experiences change as a function of the event. For example, as a result of the crime experience, Jim might learn to avoid convenience stores and to distrust men who wear black clothes. Jim's cognitive systems function to anticipate possible future events. When Jim is asked questions about the crime, he has no memory records to "read." Instead, he uses the knowledge currently available in his cognitive systems to derive a plausible rendition of the past event. For example, he may use his newly acquired distrust of men in black clothes to deduce that the burglar must have worn black clothes. If Jim forgets, it is because his reconstruction of the past event was inaccurate. For example, he may remember something about a camera, and so reconstruct that he saw the burglar steal a camera when, in fact, the burglar stole a radio.

The main organizing theme of this chapter, then, is the contrast between record-keeping and constructionist accounts of memory. A number of cognitive scientists have noted that this contrast is fundamental to understanding approaches to memory (e.g., Neisser, 1967; Bransford, McCarrell, Franks, & Nitsch, 1977; Rosenfield, 1988; Howes, 1990). Still, probably no contemporary theory of memory entirely embodies the record-keeping theory. Even contemporary theories that may be characterized as predominantly record keeping also make use of constructionist principles (see Bahrick, 1984; or Hall, 1990). For example, a theory based primarily on record-keeping may claim that people resort to reconstructing the past when they fail to find a relevant memory record. So the record-keeping theory discussed in this chapter serves mainly as a basis of contrast to help make clear how memory does not work. Examples of contemporary theories that primarily (but not exclusively) embody record-keeping principles can be found in Anderson (1983), Anderson and Milson

(1989), Atkinson and Shiffrin (1968), Penfield (1969), and Raaijmakers and Shiffrin (1981). Approaches to memory that may be characterized as predominantly constructionist can be found in Bartlett (1932); Bransford et al. (1977); Loftus (1980, 1982); Neisser (1967, 1984), and Schacter (1996). Constructionist approaches to memory are also implicit in neural net (also known as connectionist or parallel distributed processing) models of memory (e.g., Rumelhart, Hinton & Williams, 1986; Grossberg & Stone, 1986; see Collins & Hay, 1994, for a summary). Neural net memory models are discussed in chapter 6 in the section on the physiology of memory. Raaijmakers and Shiffrin (1992) provide a technical description of various contemporary memory models, while Bolles (1988) provides a nontechnical overview of a constructionist approach to memory written by someone outside the field.

HISTORICAL SUPPORT FOR RECORD-KEEPING THEORIES OF MEMORY

Although I will champion the constructionist theory in this chapter, historically it has been record-keeping metaphors that have dominated thinking about memory (Roediger, 1980). The ancient Greek philosopher Plato, in the Theaetetus dialogue, likened memory to a wax tablet on which experiences leave an impression and likened the process of recollection to trying to capture birds in an aviary. We may not always be able to capture the one we seek. Saint Augustine (A.D. 354–430), an important Christian theologian, and John Locke (1631–1704), a British empiricist famous for his claim that there are no innate ideas, both characterized memory as a storehouse containing records of the past. More recently, cognitive psychologists have used libraries (e.g., Broadbent, 1971), keysort cards (e.g., Brown & McNeill, 1966), tape recorders (e.g., Posner & Warren, 1972), stores (e.g., Atkinson & Shiffrin, 1968), and file systems (e.g., Anderson & Milson, 1989) as metaphors for memory.

The modern era of memory research is usually said to have begun with the publication of Hermann Ebbinghaus's *Uber das Gedachtnis* (*On Memory*) in 1885 (Ebbinghaus, 1885; Hoffman, Bringmann, Bamberg, & Klein, 1986). Ebbinghaus presented himself lists of arbitrarily ordered words or syllables (but not nonsense syllables, as is often claimed) and counted the number of recitations it took him to recall the list perfectly. In some experiments he later attempted to relearn those lists; the reduction in the number of trials to learn the list the second time constituted another, more indirect, measure of memory.

From years of doing these experiments, Ebbinghaus established several important principles of memory. One principle, sometimes known as the Ebbinghaus forgetting curve, is that most forgetting takes place within the first few hours and days of learning (see Figure 4-1). After a few days, the rate at which information is lost from memory is very slow and gradual. He also showed that as the number of syllables on a list increased, the number of trials to learn the list increased exponentially. A list of 36 items took him 50 times the number of repetitions to learn as a list of 7 items. Ebbinghaus did not just study arbitrarily ordered lists; he also tried to memorize more meaningful information,

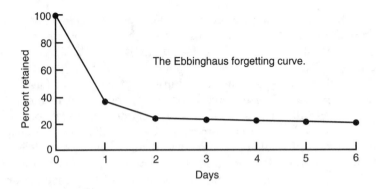

FIGURE 4–1   The Ebbinghaus forgetting curve.

specifically various sections of the poem *Don Juan*. He found that he needed only one tenth as many recitations to memorize the poem as he needed to memorize the equivalent number of arbitrarily ordered syllables. Meaningful information is easier to memorize.

Ebbinghaus did not spend much time on developing theories about the nature of memory. His primary concern was to demonstrate that human memory is an orderly and measurable phenomenon that can be described with the same precision as biological phenomena. Still, Ebbinghaus's main legacy is his emphasis on memorization of lists of stimuli. Such an emphasis suggests that memory's most important function is to preserve detailed records of past events. Psychologists continue to use experimental methodologies that require subjects to memorize lists of stimuli, such as unrelated words or sentences. Sometimes psychologists make use of Ebbinghaus's relearning paradigm to test memory; more commonly, researchers use **free recall** tests (e.g., "Write down all the words on the lists"), **cued recall** tests (e.g., "What word was paired with *duck* on the list?"), or **recognition** tests (e.g., "Did the word *duck* appear on the list?").

Another development that encouraged the use of record keeping theories of memory was the invention of the digital computer. Many memory theorists, especially those enamored of the information processing approach to human cognition, have perceived an analogy between how a computer stores information and human memory (e.g., Anderson, 1976, 1983; Winnograd, 1976). Computers store each piece of information by placing records of that information into separate locations, each of which has an address. The memory system in a computer is distinct from the central processing unit (CPU) that actually carries out the manipulation of information. Computers retrieve information either by scanning through the set of locations until the information is found or by going to the address of the memory location and accessing what is stored there. To some theorists, the computer's memory system seems a better metaphor for memory than do passive systems, like libraries. The programs that instruct computers can manipulate and transform stored information, just as we seem to do when we answer questions about and draw inferences from past experiences.

HISTORICAL SUPPORT FOR CONSTRUCTIONIST THEORIES OF MEMORY

Although record-keeping metaphors have dominated the history of memory research, there has been a constructionist countertradition. As Brewer (1984) noted, a constructionist conception of memory was the prevalent continental European view in the 1800s (Ebbinghaus notwithstanding). Sigmund Freud also held to a constructionist approach, writing frequently of how people falsify and remodel their past experiences in the course of trying to recollect them (Freud, 1900/1953; see Erdelyi, 1990). The constructionist approach to memory was introduced to Anglo-American psychology by Frederic Charles Bartlett in his 1932 book *Remembering*. Bartlett was also one of the first to establish a research program investigating the experimental implications of constructionism.

Bartlett's ideas about memory are illustrated in his most famous memory experiments, in which he presented his English subjects an English translation of a Native American folk story called "The War of the Ghosts." The subjects were required to recall the story in as much detail as possible at various time intervals after the story was originally presented to them. The story and one subject's recollection of it are presented in Figure 4-2.

"The War of the Ghosts" seems odd to people raised in Western cultures. It includes unfamiliar names, it seems to be missing some critical transitions, and it is based on a ghost cosmology not shared by educated Western people. Bartlett found that his subjects' recollections of the story were incomplete and often distorted. The subjects had trouble remembering the unusual proper names, they invented plausible transitions and, most important, they altered the facts about the ghosts. In fact, many subjects failed to remember anything at all about ghosts. Bartlett claimed that the subjects used their Western cultural knowledge of the nature of stories and other pertinent information to imaginatively reconstruct the story. When relevant cultural knowledge was missing or inappropriate to understanding a story from another culture, the Western subjects' memories were transformed to make their recollections more consistent with their own cultural knowledge. Bartlett's (1932) experiments on memory led him to conclude that remembering is a form of **reconstruction** in which various sources of knowledge are used to infer past experiences.

Another historically influential event in the development of the constructionist tradition was the publication of Ulric Neisser's *Cognitive Psychology* in 1967. In this book Neisser discussed his opposition to the idea that past experiences are somehow preserved and later reactivated when remembered. Instead, Neisser claimed that remembering is like problem solving, a matter of taking existing knowledge and memories of previous reconstructions to create a plausible rendition of some particular past event. Neisser used the analogy of recon-

The War of the Ghosts

One night two young men from Egulac went down to the river to hunt seals, and while they were there it became foggy and calm. Then they heard warcries, and they thought: "Maybe this is a war party." They escaped to the shore, and hid behind a log. Now canoes came up, and they heard the noise of paddles, and saw one canoe coming up to them. There were five men in the canoe, and they said:

"What do you think? We wish to take you along. We are going up the river to make war on the people."

One of the young men said: "I have no arrows."

"Arrows are in the canoe," they said.

"I will not go along. I might be killed. My relatives do not know where I have gone. But you," he said, turning to the other, "may go with them."

So one of the young men went, but the other returned home.

And the warriors went on up the river to a town on the other side of Kalama. The people came down to the water, and they began to fight, and many were killed. But presently the young man heard one of the warriors say: "Quick, let us go home: that Indian has been hit." Now he thought: "Oh, they are ghosts." He did not feel sick, but they said he had been shot.

So the canoes went back to Egulac, and the young man went ashore to his house, and made a fire. And he told everybody and said: "Behold I accompanied the ghosts, and we went to fight. Many of our fellows were killed, and many of those who attacked us were killed. They said I was hit, and I did not feel sick."

He told it all, and then he became quiet. When the sun rose he fell down. Something black came out of his mouth. His face became contorted. The people jumped up and cried.

He was dead.

Subject's Reproduction

Two youths were standing by a river about to start seal-catching, when a boat appeared with five men in it. They were all armed for war.

The youths were at first frightened, but they were asked by the men to come and help them fight some enemies on the other bank. One youth said he could not come as his relations would be anxious about him; the other said he would go, and entered the boat.

In the evening he returned to his hut, and told his friends that he had been in a battle. A great many had been slain, and he had been wounded by an arrow; he had not felt any pain, he said. They told him that he must have been fighting in a battle of ghosts. Then he remembered that it had been queer and he became very excited.

In the morning, however, he became ill, and his friends gathered round; he fell down and his face became very pale. Then he writhed and shrieked and his friends were filled with terror. At last he became calm. Something hard and black came out of his mouth, and he lay contorted and dead.

FIGURE 4–2   The text of "The War of the Ghosts" and one subject's reproduction of it. From Bartlett, 1932.

structing a complete dinosaur skeleton from a few bone fragments and knowledge of anatomy. He suggested that "executive routines" guide the process of gathering and interpreting evidence upon which a reconstruction of the past is based. Neisser thought that executive routines were strategies acquired through experience.

Another source of inspiration for a constructionist approach to memory comes from research on the neurophysiology of memory and cognition (see Squire, 1987; Carlson, 1994). Such research (discussed more fully in chapter 6: The Physiology of Learning and Remembering) has revealed that there is no single place in the brain where past experiences are stored. That is, there does not seem to be anything that corresponds to a storage bin in the brain. Instead, memory reflects changes to neurons involved in perception, language, feeling, movement, and so on. Because each new experience results in altering the strengths of connections among neurons, the brain is constantly "tuning" itself in response to experiences. But it has no neural tissue dedicated only to storing a record of each experience.

SECTION 2: RETAINING EXPERIENCES IN MEMORY

What is it that is retained in our cognitive system as a result of having experiences? The essential idea of a record-keeping theory is that a record of each experience is put into a kind of storage bin. Such records may take a variety of forms, including abstract descriptions or interpretations of events (see Anderson, 1983), lists of items and contextual information (see Raaijmakers & Shiffrin, 1981) or images of the perceptual qualities of events (see Paivio, 1971).

In contrast, the essential idea of a constructionist approach is that the various cognitive systems (e.g., the visual system, the language system) are changed by experiences, but no record-by-record accounts of the experiences are stored anywhere. Instead, the cognitive system is designed to extract the unchanging elements or patterns from experience and to note deviations from enduring patterns.

A CONSTRUCTIONIST ACCOUNT OF RETENTION

To get a somewhat more precise sense of how a constructionist theory explains what is retained from experience, consider this simple example: remembering what you ate for dinner last Thursday night. Research on the effects of diet on health frequently relies on people's memory of what they have eaten. Is memory for food consumption reliable?

In general, research suggests that accurate recall of food items consumed declines to about 55% a week after the consumption (DeAngelis, 1988). The longer the retention interval, the poorer the memory for specific food items consumed (Smith, Jobe, & Mingay, 1991). Over time, people rely more on their generic knowledge of their own dieting behaviors than on a precise memory of any given meal (Smith et al., 1991). In some cases, knowledge of one's own dieting may distort memory. In one study, women on a low-fat diet remembered fewer of the snack items they had eaten the day before than did women on normal or high-fat diets (Fries, Green, & Bowen, 1995). People also tend to underestimate in their memories how much food they have eaten (Fries et al., 1995).

The constructionist account of memory for past meals would go something like the following (see Figure 4-3). You have in your cognitive system concepts and ideas about food and food consumption. These include concepts such as iced tea, spaghetti, and entrees as well as ideas such as that snack foods are high in fat content and desserts are served at the end of a meal. The constructionist theory emphasizes that experiences change the strengths of the connections among these ideas and concepts (more details about this process are to be found in chapter 6: The Physiology of Learning and Remembering).

To illustrate, suppose that on one night you have spaghetti for an entree and iced tea for a beverage, on the second night you have lamb chops and iced tea, and on the third night you have fried chicken and iced tea. On each night,

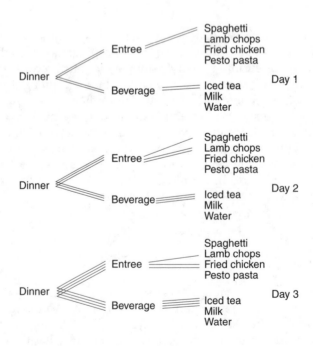

FIGURE 4–3 Depiction of a constructionist account of memory for three dinners. The more lines that connect one concept to another, the more likely the connections between those concepts will be remembered.

then, the connections between the ideas of dinner and entree, between the ideas of dinner and beverage, and between the ideas of beverage and iced tea will all be strengthened. These strong connections represent the enduring pattern in the dinner event. On the other hand, your cognitive system will not consistently strengthen the connection between the idea of an entree and the ideas that represent any particular entree (e.g., spaghetti), because the entrees change nightly. For instance, on the second night the connection between entree and lamb chops will be strengthened while the previously established connection between entree and spaghetti will weaken.

If you are later asked what you had for dinner on the first night, the strong connections between the dinner and entree ideas, between the dinner and beverage ideas, and between the beverage and iced tea ideas mean that you will reconstruct that you had some kind of an entree and iced tea. The connections between the idea of entree and any particular entree, such as spaghetti, will be relatively weak; consequently you will not be able to reconstruct as reliably which entree you had the first night. Instead, you may reconstruct only that you had an entree. Note that these reconstructions are accomplished without retrieving an actual record of each night's dinner. Other facts about food consumption may also influence your memory. If you are on a low-fat diet, for example, you may use your knowledge of fat content to deduce that you did not eat potato chips with your meal. In a later section of this chapter I will discuss in more detail how ideas and beliefs affect recollection. Although my example is greatly simplified, it at least illustrates how the cognitive system extracts the invariants of dinner experiences and uses them to form a plausible reconstruction of past dinner experiences.

Constructionist theory, then, predicts that people will not be able to remember very well the constantly changing details of events, such as the particular entree for any given dinner. Similarly, people might not be able to remember very well such things as what color shirt they wore on any given night out on the town or exactly where in the lot they parked their car on any given excursion to the beach. But it should be easy for people to remember the **invariants** or enduring patterns of events, such as always drinking a beverage with dinner, always wearing a casual shirt to the night club, or always parking in the cheaper lot at the beach.

Record-keeping theories, like constructionist theories, would also predict that accurate memory for any one event is likely to decline as more records are stored (see, for example, Anderson, 1976). But without embellishment, record-keeping theories have no ready way to explain why memory should be strong for the enduring patterns of experience. At the very least, a record-keeping theory would have to postulate the existence of another cognitive mechanism designed only to extract patterns from experiences. That is, it is not a natural consequence of keeping records that enduring patterns are extracted from those records. The advantage of constructionist theory is that it postulates that the creation of memories and the extraction of patterns from experience are accomplished by the same mechanism; namely, the altering of connection strengths among the concepts and ideas that constitute knowledge.

EVIDENCE FOR THE CONSTRUCTIONIST ACCOUNT OF RETENTION

Empirical Evidence That Memory Preserves Patterns but Not Details of Experiences

A nice example of the principle that memory preserves the enduring patterns and themes but not the changing elements in events comes from the testimony of John Dean, a key figure in the Watergate scandal of the early 1970s (Neisser, 1981). John Dean had been President Nixon's attorney and testified against him in a highly publicized Senate hearing on the Watergate break-in. Dean tried to recollect the details of meetings, including who participated, what was said, and when the meeting took place. Dean's memory seemed quite remarkable (and damaging to Nixon); he was able to supply many details that other members of Nixon's administration claimed to be unable to recall.

It was discovered later that all meetings in the Oval Office had been tape recorded, so that many of Dean's recollections could be compared with the actual transcripts of those meetings. It turns out that Dean was often inaccurate about details of the meetings but was accurate in his recollection of the general tenor of a number of the meetings; namely, that Nixon and other high-ranking members of his administration knew about the Watergate break-in and tried to cover it up. What distinguished Dean's testimony from that of the others was that Dean decided to tell the truth about the coverup. Dean's memory was not especially accurate about those elements that were always changing, like the details of conversations or which participants were at particular meetings, but his memory was quite accurate about the sorts of topics and issues that endured across many meetings.

Many memory experiments also make the point that our memories permit easier recall of enduring patterns than of details of specific experiences (e.g., Bartlett, 1932; Bransford & Franks, 1971; Thorndyke & Hayes-Roth, 1979). For example, participants in a weekly seminar on math were asked to recall the names of the other participants who had attended the last meeting of the seminar (Freeman, Romney, & Freeman, 1987). The subjects were not able to recall very accurately; about half of their responses were errors. The errors were revealing, however. Sometimes subjects mistakenly excluded someone who had attended the last meeting, but usually the excluded person had not regularly attended the seminar. And sometimes subjects mistakenly included someone who had missed the last meeting, but usually the included person had attended most of the other meetings. The errors suggest that the subjects had extracted the general pattern of attendance from their experiences in the seminar and had used that pattern, reasonably enough, to reconstruct who had attended the last meeting.

Memory for patterns is also reflected in the tendency for people to remember the gist but not the details of their experiences. Research has shown that subjects will forget the exact wording of any given sentence in a passage after reading only a few more sentences, but will usually be able to remember the meaning of the sentence (Sachs, 1967; for similar results with pictures, see

Gernsbacher, 1985). Research has also shown that after studying a text or a set of pictures, people will tend to believe mistakenly that a sentence or picture was explicitly in the set of information they studied, when, in fact, it was only implied by the information (e.g., Bransford, Barclay, & Franks, 1972; Harris & Monaco, 1978; Maki, 1989; Sulin & Dooling, 1974; Thorndyke, 1976). For example, if a passage describes an event in which a long-haired customer sat in a barber's chair and later left the barbershop with short hair, a subject who had read that passage may mistakenly believe that the passage also contained a sentence describing the barber cutting the man's hair. The reason for the mistake is that the implicit information is likely to be consistent with the passage's essential themes, which would form the basis of the reconstruction of the details of the passage.

That memory is better for the patterns or invariants than for the ever-changing details of experiences is what enables memory to be adaptive, to anticipate the future. It is the invariants of experience that we are likely to encounter in future events, so a cognitive system that readily notices such patterns will be better prepared to respond to new experiences.

Good memory for the patterns or invariants of experience stands in contrast to our extremely poor memory for the details of the majority of experiences. Consider—can you describe in detail what you were doing around 3:00 P.M. on May 15th two years ago? Do you remember what the topic of conversation was when you first met your next-door neighbor? Or what your boss was wearing when you first met him or her? Or the first 10 sentences of this chapter? You see the point. What is especially remarkable about our memories is the almost complete lack of detail they provide about the majority of our past experiences! And it is easy to demonstrate experimentally that people do not remember very much about long-past experiences. For example, people have trouble remembering their infant-rearing practices, such as whether they fed their infants on demand (Robbins, 1963), their formerly held opinions on important political issues, such as whether they supported busing to equalize education (Goethals & Reckman, 1973); whether they voted in any given election (Parry & Crossley, 1950); and what they had to eat for dinner six weeks ago (Smith et al., 1991).

Accurate Memory

A possible objection to the constructionist theory is the observation that people can sometimes remember past events accurately. A record-keeping theory of memory claims that accurate memory occurs when a person successfully locates a memory record. How can the constructionist theory account for accurate recollections? And, one might also object, what about people who have extraordinarily accurate memories, who seem to have a memory system that works like a videotape machine?

Constructionist theory implies that there are three circumstances in which memory is likely to be accurate. First, as I have already discussed, constructionist theory predicts that repetitious events, like always having iced tea with dinner, should be well remembered, because they promote the creation of strong connections among elements. A high probability, therefore, exists that at least some of the relevant connections created by the repetitive event will remain stable over time and so permit the accurate reconstruction of that event. Research shows that information that is repeated is more easily remembered than information that is presented only once (e.g., Jacoby, 1978; Greeno, 1964). To be fair, record-keeping theories also predict that repetition improves memory, because repetition would increase the number of records of that event, making any one record easier to find.

Second, constructionist theory predicts that recent events, such as what one ate for breakfast this morning, should be well remembered, because the strength of the connections among elements representing recent events would not yet be weakened by subsequent events. Researchers since Ebbinghaus have observed that recently experienced events are usually the easiest to remember (Ebbinghaus, 1885; Wickelgren, 1972).

Record-keeping theories need a modification to predict that recent events are better remembered. The modification is that recent events are stored in a more accessible manner or location. One way to visualize that is to imagine that events are stored in a push-down stack (Anderson & Bower, 1973). Recent events are first placed at the top of the stack but are gradually pushed further down into the stack by the continuous storage of even more recent events. The retrieval mechanism would begin its search at the top of the stack.

Third, constructionist theory predicts that unusual or distinctive events should be well remembered because they promote the creation of connections among elements that would not likely be reconfigured by future events. Consider an unusual event such as becoming nauseated after eating lamb chops. The connection between the feeling of nausea and the idea of lamb chops is not likely to be diminished by subsequent dinner experiences, because lamb chops would not ordinarily become associated with other ill feelings nor would nausea become associated with other entrees. Any subsequent activation of the lamb chops idea, then, is also likely to activate the feeling of nausea, permitting accurate memory for that experience of nausea.

Record-keeping theories could also predict that distinctive events are better remembered. One way to do so is to imagine that events are stored in locations that reflect the attributes of the event. Memories of happy experiences might be stored in one place, memories of car repair experiences might be stored in another place, and so on. A distinctive event has a collection of attributes that is different from other events and so would be stored in an uncluttered place in the memory system. It is easier to find a memory record in an uncluttered space than in a cluttered space, just as it would be easier to find *The Joy of Nausea* in a library that had only one book on the topic of nausea than in a library that carried hundreds of books on nausea.

That distinctive events are readily remembered has been well established by research (see Schmidt, 1991, for a review). In one experiment that required subjects to recall words from a list, the subjects were better able to remember that an animal name appeared on the list if the animal name was embedded in a list of names of countries than if the same animal name was embedded in a list of other animal names (Schmidt, 1985). This finding is an example of the **Von Restorff effect,** after the psychologist who first discovered it (Von Restorff, 1933). In another experiment, subjects were given photographs of human faces and were asked to judge the distinctiveness of each face. When later asked to recognize which faces they had previously studied, the subjects more accurately recognized the faces they rated as distinctive than the faces they rated as common (Cohen & Carr, 1975). At least some research shows that events associated with strong emotions, which are presumably distinctive, are better remembered than emotionally more neutral events (e.g., Waters & Leeper, 1936; Holmes, 1972).

Best-selling books on how to improve memory (e.g., Lorayne and Lucas, 1974) encourage the use of bizarre imagery to improve the memorability of verbal information, such as names of people. Bizarre images presumably make information more distinctive. But does the use of bizarre imagery really improve memory? The answer seems to be a qualified yes.

The standard experimental paradigm investigating the role of imagery in memory requires subjects to memorize word pairs (e.g., CHICKEN–CIGAR) by making various kinds of images of the words. The results have shown that when people create bizarre images to connect the words (e.g., a chicken smoking a cigar), they will later recall more of the words than when they create common images (e.g., a chicken pecking a cigar) to connect the words (for a review, see Einstein, McDaniel, & Lackey, 1989). However, the advantage of bizarre over common images usually occurs only when the same person is required to make bizarre images for some of the words on the to-be-remembered list and ordinary images for the rest of the words on the list. When subjects are required to make bizarre images for all the words on the list, then the individual images are not as distinctive, and there is no longer an advantage of bizarre images over common images. Research also suggests that the superiority of the bizarre image technique is greater if the memory test is done days after studying the list (Webber & Marshall, 1978). When the delay between forming the images and recalling the words is only a few minutes, memory for the words is at least as good using the common image technique.

That distinctive events are memorable is also revealed in memory for real-life experiences. Erickson and Jemison (1991) had students record one event from their lives each day for 12 weeks, and 5 months later take several memory tests on the events. They found that the more memorable events tended to be the distinctive ones—that is, the ones rated atypical, infrequent, or surprising. They also found that positive events were more memorable, possibly because positive events are likely to be thought about and discussed frequently.

When we have accurate memories of long-past events, these events are almost always remarkable—that is, distinctive—in some way. For example, I vividly remember a championship Little League baseball game in which I got five hits and scored the winning run (a newspaper account verifies that my memory is accurate). However, about all I remember from the many other Little League games in which I played is that I was good at throwing and catching but not so good at hitting.

Psychologists have studied memory of remarkable experiences by asking people what they were doing on the occasion of some historically significant event like the assassination of John F. Kennedy (Brown & Kulik, 1977; Pillemer, 1984). Usually people can describe what they were doing in great detail, although ordinarily the psychologist is unable to check the accuracy of the person's account. Memory for a remarkable event, sometimes called a **flashbulb memory**, is vivid (McCloskey, Wible, & Cohen, 1988) because the event is distinctive and because people talk about and think about the event much more frequently than about other, more mundane, experiences.

It should be noted, though, that memory for what one was doing at the time of a historically significant event is frequently wrong (McCloskey et al., 1988; Neisser & Harsch, 1991). For example, Neisser and Harsch (1991) asked students on the day after the Challenger disaster how they heard about the disaster and asked them again 3 years later. On the test conducted 3 years after the disaster, one third of the subjects gave inaccurate accounts, although they were confident that their accounts were accurate.

Brain Stimulation and Accurate Memory

Sometimes memory researchers cite data that seem to indicate, as the record-keeping theory would have it, that human memory does contain records of nearly all past experiences, although it might ordinarily be hard to retrieve most of those records. Some of the most compelling data comes from the research of a brain surgeon named Wilder Penfield, who removed small portions of cortical tissue in order to prevent the spread of seizures in epileptic patients (Penfield & Jasper, 1954; Penfield & Perot, 1963). Ordinarily such patients are awake during the operation, because the cortex is impervious to pain. Penfield needed to electrically stimulate various portions of the cerebral cortex, in order to locate accurately the epileptic site. When he did so, some of the patients described vivid recollections of mostly trivial past experiences. Penfield reasoned that the cortex must therefore keep a record of all past experiences and that forgetting must be due to retrieval failure.

After Penfield began to publish his findings, some psychologists questioned his interpretations (Loftus & Loftus, 1980; Squire, 1987). First of all, only about 3% of Penfield's patients ever reported remembering past experiences in response to electrical stimulation. Furthermore, for those patients who did, the evidence suggested that they were not accurately recalling an actual experience but unintentionally fabricating one. One patient, for example, reported having a memory of playing at a lumberyard, but it turned out the patient had never been to the lumberyard. Another patient claimed to remember being born.

Recognition and Accurate Memory

Another kind of data sometimes cited to support the claim that the brain stores records of virtually all experiences, any one of which is potentially retrievable, comes from research on recognition memory. In some recognition experiments, subjects are shown thousands of detailed pictures, such as magazine advertisements, and weeks to months later are given a recognition test in which they must discriminate the OLD pictures from NEW ones (e.g., Standing, 1973). In one of these experiments, subjects' recognition accuracy was 87% after one week (Shepard, 1967), while in another experiment recognition accuracy was 63% after a year (chance performance would be 50%) (Standing, Conezio, & Haber, 1970).

However, it also possible to design such experiments so that a person's recognition accuracy is not much better than chance, only minutes after viewing pictures (Goldstein & Chance, 1970). Critical to performance in recognition experiments is the similarity between the OLD stimuli and the NEW stimuli used as foils (Dale & Baddeley, 1962; Pezdek et al. 1988). When OLD and NEW pictures closely resemble one another, recognition accuracy is poor. But when the OLD and NEW pictures are dissimilar, subjects need not remember very much about a set of pictures to distinguish between OLD and NEW ones. Note that pictures of advertisements used in the high-accuracy memory experiments are relatively dissimilar from one another.

Still, the high percentage of correct responses in some recognition experiments does make the important point that we have much better memory for our experiences than we might ordinarily think. How good our memory seems to be for any given event depends critically on how we are tested. As I will discuss later, performance is usually better on recognition than on recall tests and is better the more cues there are in the environment to prompt memory. But it would be a mistake to assume that if a more sensitive test improves memory scores, then all experiences must be stored in, and therefore potentially retrievable from, memory.

Autobiographical Memory

Another kind of finding sometimes used to support the notion that nearly all experiences are potentially retrievable comes from individuals who have for years kept records of details of important autobiographical experiences and later tried to recall some of those details (Linton, 1978; R. T. White, 1982, 1989). These individuals seem to remember something about nearly all the events they recorded.

Typical of this research is a study done by Willem Wagenaar (Wagenaar, 1986). Each day for six years Wagenaar selected an event or two and recorded what happened, who he was with when it happened, the date it happened, and where it happened. He tested his memory for an event by reading some details about the event (e.g., "I went to a church in Milano") and trying to recall other details (e.g., "I went to see Leonardo da Vinci's *Last Supper* on September 10, 1983"). He found that even years afterwards he was able to recall at least one detail of about 80% of the events he recorded.

Does his research contradict the constructionist theory that predicts forgetting of most events? I think not. First of all, Wagenaar deliberately selected salient, distinctive events to record; he avoided mundane events. The constructionist theory predicts good memory for distinctive events. It is interesting to note that after about one year, Wagenaar was able to recall accurately slightly less than 50% of the details of even these distinctive events. Furthermore, Wagenaar had no way to control for talking or thinking about the events later on; consequently, many of these events were likely recycled many times through his cognitive systems. Also, he was often able to make plausible guesses about what happened. For example, given the cue "I went to a church in Milano" he may have been able to guess the approximate date by just remembering that his trip to Italy took place during the first two weeks of September in 1983. Finally, Wagenaar had no "foils"—events that could plausibly have happened to him but did not—to see if he could accurately discriminate between real events and foils. In fact, research demonstrates that people have a hard time distinguishing between actually experienced events and plausible foils in their recollections about important autobiographical experiences (Barclay & Wellman, 1986).

In short, research on autobiographical memory does not prove that we have accurate and detailed memory for nearly all of our experiences. It suggests that we can remember, or at least infer, some of the details of our most distinctive experiences.

"Photographic" Memory?

But what about individuals who seem to have something akin to a photographic or videotape memory in which all experiences are accurately remembered? Wouldn't the existence of these people contradict the constructionist approach to memory? Incidentally, I do not intend for the notion of photographic memory to imply that the individual has only an especially good memory for visual information. Instead, "photographic" is meant to be a metaphor for extraordinary memory for all kinds of information.

A few extensive investigations of such rarely encountered individuals have been carried out. Probably the best-known memory expert was S. V. Shereshevskii, usually referred to as S. S grew up around the turn of the century in Latvia and was a Moscow newspaper reporter when his editor noticed his exceptional memory. The editor recommended that S have his memory evaluated at the local university; there he met Aleksandr Luria, a great Russian psychologist.

Luria studied S over a period of about 30 years (Luria, 1968). Luria verified that S's memory was quite extraordinary. For example, S was able to repeat back a series of 70 randomly selected numbers in order after hearing them only once. As another example, he was able to recall lists of arbitrary and randomly ordered words 15 years after Luria presented the words to him. S claimed that he formed vivid and detailed images of every stimulus he was asked to remember and often associated the images with images of familiar locations, like Gorky Street in Moscow. He would later retrieve the words from memory by taking a mental "walk," noticing the images associated with the landmarks. This **mnemonic technique** (i.e., a strategy for memorizing) is called the **method of loci**, and can be used effectively by anyone trying to memorize a list of stimuli (Groninger, 1971). Techniques like the method of loci improve memory for several reasons, one of which is that they help make information more distinctive.

S made use of other mnemonic techniques, as well. He seemed to have the exceedingly rare ability, known as **synesthesia**, to conjure up vivid images of light, color, taste, and touch in association with almost any sound. These images also helped him remember new information. For a time, S found work as a memory expert on stage. People would call out words or numbers for him to remember and he would try to recall them exactly. Interestingly, though, S sometimes needed to develop new mnemonic techniques to overcome occasional errors in memory and so improve his act. For example, he had difficulty remembering names and faces. If S had a photographic memory, he would have been able to memorize accurately any kind of information presented to him. His extraordinary memory, then, was not a result of possessing anything analogous to a photographic mind, but was rather a result of having an appropriate mnemonic strategy. Tragically, S ended his life in a Russian asylum for the mentally ill.

Some people, called **eidetic imagers**, seem to have an extraordinary ability to remember visual details of pictures. Eidetic imagers report that, after viewing a picture, they see an image of the picture localized in front of them and that the visual details disappear part by part. While they remember many more visual details of a picture than would the ordinary person, often the accuracy of their reports is far from perfect (Haber & Haber, 1988; see Searleman & Herrmann, 1994).

The all-time champion eidetic imager was an artist known as Elizabeth. Her most remarkable achievement had to do with superimposing two random-dot patterns to see a three-dimensional image. In one experiment (Stromeyer & Psotka, 1970), she was first presented with a 10,000-random-dot pattern to her right eye for 1 minute. The first pattern was then removed for 10 seconds and a second 10,000-random-dot pattern was presented to her left eye. She was instructed to superimpose her memory of the image of the first pattern onto the second. The patterns were designed so that when superimposed and examined through both eyes, a three-dimensional figure (e.g., a square floating in space) would appear. It was impossible to determine the three-dimensional image from either pattern alone, however. Elizabeth was able to superimpose a memory of the first pattern onto the second pattern and thus accurately identify the three-dimensional image. In fact, in one case, she was able to hold a 1,000,000-random-dot pattern in memory for 4 hours and then superimpose her memory of that pattern onto a second 1,000,000-random-dot pattern to identify successfully the three-dimensional image! It is possible to see the three-dimensional figure in the superimposed patterns even when one of the patterns is significantly blurred, although the blurring will also make the edges of the three-dimensional image more rounded. So Elizabeth need not have remembered the exact position of all of the dots to accomplish seeing the three-dimensional figure, although she claimed that the edges of her three-dimensional image were sharp and not rounded.

No one else has yet been found who can come close to Elizabeth's visual memory; indeed, some people are skeptical of her feats (see Searleman & Herrmann, 1994). As far as I know, Elizabeth was not tested for memory of anything other than visual information. It remains unclear, then, whether she had an outstanding all-purpose memory or an extraordinary memory for only visual information.

Another remarkable memorizer is Rajan Mahadevan, who has a phenomenal memory for numbers. He is able to recite the first 31,811 digits of pi from memory (I'm lucky if I can remember the first four digits!). In a series of experiments comparing his memory to that of college students, Rajan Mahadevan dramatically outperformed the students on any memory test involving numbers (Thompson, Cowan, Frieman, Mahadevan, & Vogel, 1991). For example, he recalled 43 randomly ordered digits presented to him once, while the college students recalled an average of only about 7 digits. Rajan Mahadevan claims that he does not use imagery to help him remember numbers but instead uses a rather vaguely described mnemonic system whereby numbers are associated with numerical locations in a series. It does not seem that he has anything analogous to a videotape or photographic memory, however. His recall for nonnumerical information, such as word lists or meaningful stories, was about equal to that of the average college student. For example, he recalled an average of about 41 ideas from several previously read Native American folk tales similar to "The War of the Ghosts," while the college students recalled about 47 ideas on average from the same stories.

A reasonable conclusion, then, is that individuals like *S* and Rajan Mahadevan make use of mnemonic devices that others could use to help make information more memorable (Ericsson & Polson, 1988; Hunt & Love, 1972). While the memorizing skill of these mnemonists can seem phenomenal, it is clear that their memories do not work like a videotape recorder; otherwise they would be able to remember the details of any and all of their experiences. Instead, their memory is good for classes of information in which they are experts (Elizabeth was a skilled artist) or for which they have learned mnemonic memorizing strategies. The Hollywood version of the person with a "photographic" mind probably does not exist.

THE ASSIMILATION PRINCIPLE

Making information distinctive or associating information with distinctive images and ideas can promote better memory of that information. Such techniques may be called learning strategies. What other learning strategies help make information memorable? Another useful learning strategy is based on the principle that memory for an event will be improved to the extent that the event can be assimilated into something that already exists in memory (Stein & Bransford, 1979; Stein, Littlefield, Bransford, & Persampieri, 1984). This principle is called the **assimilation principle**.

Assimilation means that new information is incorporated into relevant pre-existing knowledge useful for interpreting the new information. For example, a passage describing the nature of electricity would be more memorable if the passage reminded readers of their knowledge of rivers. The passage would not be as memorable if it did not remind readers of relevant knowledge, nor would it be as memorable if it reminded readers of irrelevant knowledge, such as their knowledge of baseball. The constructionist theory explains the assimilation principle this way: When new information is assimilated into relevant preexisting knowledge, there is widespread activation of the cognitive system for interpreting an event and an increase in the number and strength of the connections among elements of that cognitive system. Reconstruction of the event is improved to the extent that strong connections among elements in that cognitive system can be found.

Experimental Support for Assimilation

A variety of research supports the assimilation principle. One kind of support comes from experiments that show that people remember more new information if that information is within their area of expertise than if the new information is outside their area of expertise (Bellezza & Buck, 1988; Chiesi, Spilich, & Voss, 1979; Morris, 1988). For instance, experienced bartenders remember better than do novices their customers' drink orders (Beach, 1988). Football experts can remember more about descriptions of fictitious football games than nonexperts (Bellezza and Buck, 1988). Chess experts will remember the positions of chess pieces on a chessboard better than chess novices, provided the pieces are arranged in a way consistent with the rules of chess. If the chess pieces are randomly arranged, however, the chess expert can remember their locations no better than the novice (Chase & Simon, 1973).

Sometimes when people must learn new material, like the material in this textbook, they have a hard time figuring out what general patterns or principles are implied by the material and so are unable to associate the material with the appropriate elements in their cognitive systems. Any aids that help people find such principles in the material will improve memory. If subjects are required to memorize a list of words, they will remember more of them if the words in the list are grouped according to categories, like animal names, than if the words are presented in a random order (Bower, Clark, Lesgold, & Winzenz, 1969; Mandler, 1979). Subjects given titles that clarify the meaning of otherwise obscure pictures or passages remember more than subjects not given titles (Bransford & Johnson, 1972). When subjects read technical or scientific passages, the subjects first given guides to help them associate the information with familiar ideas (e.g., electrical current is like a river) or help them see the relationships among key ideas in the text will later be able to recall more of the text than subjects not first given the guides (Dean & Kulhavy, 1981; Brooks & Dansereau, 1983; Lorch & Lorch, 1985). Most of the advantage for subjects receiving the guides is in remembering the conceptual information and not the technical detail (Mayer, 1980; Mayer & Bromage, 1980).

Levels of Processing and the Assimilation Principle

Another manifestation of the assimilation principle is found in investigations of what is usually called **levels of processing** (Craik & Lockhart, 1972; Koriat & Melkman, 1987). This research establishes that when people think about the meaning of information, they remember more of it than when they think about the physical properties or when they merely try to rote memorize the information. Elaborating on the meaning is a more effective learning strategy than is rote memorizing.

In one example of research on levels of processing, subjects studied a list of words by making judgments about each word, and later recalled the words. Subjects recalled more words for which they had been asked to judge "How pleasant is the word?" than words for which they had been asked to judge "Does the word contain the letter *e*?" (Hyde & Jenkins, 1975; Parkin, 1984). Subjects who studied a list of words by elaborating each word into complete sentences (called elaborative rehearsal) later recalled more of the words than subjects who only rote memorized the words (called maintenance rehearsal) (Bjork, 1975; Bobrow & Bower, 1969).

The advantage of processing for meaning is not limited to verbal information. Subjects were better at recognizing pictures of faces if they previously thought about whether each face seemed friendly than if they previously thought about whether each face had a big nose (Smith & Winograd, 1978) and if they assessed faces for honesty rather than for the sex of the face (Sporer, 1991). In general, thinking about the meaning of a stimulus or elaborating on the stimulus is likely to permit the stimulus to be assimilated by a greater portion of a cognitive system, and so create more possibilities for reconstructing a memory of the stimulus later on. Elaboration may also help make information more distinctive (Craik & Lockhart, 1986; Winnograd, 1981).

Processing the meaning of a stimulus improves memory only when that processing connects the stimulus to relevant knowledge. For instance, asking a person whether a shirt is a type of clothing enhances memory for the word *shirt*, as opposed to the case where the person is asked whether the word *shirt* contains more vowels than consonants. However, asking a person whether a shirt is a type of insect does not promote very good memory for *shirt* (Craik & Tulving, 1975). In the latter case, answering the question does not encourage the person to connect *shirt* with knowledge of shirts (see Schacter, 1996).

Recall that in chapter 2: Consciousness I discussed the levels of processing research in which that research was used to challenge the duplex model of short-term memory (see Klatzky, 1980). I hinted that there is an important qualification to the general finding that thinking deeply about information promotes better memory than does thinking in a shallow manner about the information. The qualification is that it depends on how memory is tested. If the memory testing procedure matches the manner in which information is originally learned, then memory for that information is better than if there is a mismatch.

An example comes from a study by Morris, Bransford, and Franks (1977). Subjects were required to decide for each of a group of words whether the word could have a particular semantic property (e.g., "Does a train have a silver engine?") or whether the word rhymes with another word (e.g., "Does *train* rhyme with *rain*?"). The semantic task was the "deep" task and the rhyming task was the "shallow" task. Later, some subjects were given a standard recognition task in which they had to pick out the target word from a list of distractors. Subjects who had made the semantic judgment did better on the recognition task than did subjects who had made the rhyming judgment. But other subjects were given a very different test of memory in which they had to pick out from a list of words which word rhymed with one of the words previously studied. Now it was the subjects who had originally made the rhyming judgments who did better. This finding, usually called **transfer appropriate processing**, is discussed again later in this chapter.

INDIVIDUAL DIFFERENCES IN MEMORY

Why does one person have a better memory than another person? Record-keeping theories, especially those that liken human memory to the memories of computers or libraries, imply that there is an all-purpose memory system for storing every kind of experience. According to the record-keeping theory, the reason some people have better memories than others is that some people have more efficient mechanisms for storing or retrieving records. Even Plato talked about some people having a purer kind of wax tablet for storing experiences.

Constructionist theories, on the other hand, imply that there is no all-purpose memory system. Memory is instead a byproduct of changes to the various components of cognition that underlie perception, language, emotions, and so on. From the perspective of the constructionist approach, there are no storage and retrieval mechanisms whose efficiency varies from person to person. Instead, people vary with respect to how much they know about various domains of knowledge. According to constructionist theory, the main reason some people have better memories than others is that some people have more expertise in the domain of knowledge sampled by the test of memory. For example, a baseball expert can use the knowledge that runners on second base often score after a single to reconstruct that the home team scored a run in the previous inning. However, baseball knowledge would not help the baseball expert remember, say, a passage about climate in South America.

The constructionist theory claims, then, that the best predictor of how well a person remembers new information in some domain, such as baseball, is how much knowledge the person already possesses about that domain. General intellectual skills, especially skill at memorizing lists of information unrelated to the domain, should not predict individual differences in memory for information within some domain. If, instead, memory is an all-purpose system, it would follow that performance on tests of memory and on general intellectual skills would readily predict memory for new information.

The research supports the constructionist theory's explanation of individual differences in memory. Good memory for information within some domain is primarily a function of expertise in that domain and not a function of any general intellectual skill. Schneider, Korkel, and Weinert (1987) and Walker (1987) found that subjects who scored low on a test of general aptitude but happened to know a lot about baseball recalled more facts about a fictitious baseball game than did subjects who scored high on the general aptitude test but knew very little about baseball, and recalled as many facts as did high-aptitude subjects who knew a lot about baseball. Kuhara-Kojima and Hatano (1991) found that knowledge about music, but not performance on a test of memory for unrelated words, predicted how many new facts subjects recalled from a passage about music.

Merely possessing domain knowledge does not guarantee better memory for new information in that domain, however. DeMarie-Dreblow (1991) taught people about birds but found that the newly acquired bird knowledge did not help subjects recall a list of bird names any better than subjects not given the knowledge about birds. The knowledge has to be well-learned, and people need practice using the knowledge in the context of reconstructing a memory for the new information (Pressley & Van Meter, 1994).

For instance, Pressley and Brewster (1990) taught their Canadian subjects new facts about Canadian provinces. Some subjects were given prior knowledge in the form of pictures of some prominent setting in the province. By itself, this prior knowledge did not help subjects remember the new facts all that much better than the subjects not given the prior knowledge. Other subjects were given imagery instructions for which the subjects were to imagine the fact occurring in a setting unique to the province referred to by the new fact. Imagery instructions also did not help subjects all that much. However, subjects given both the prior knowledge and the imagery instructions did recall substantially more new facts than did subjects who did not have both the prior knowledge and the techniques (i.e., imagery) for using that knowledge to learn and remember new information.

The better predictor of memory for novel information, then, is a person's degree of expertise in that domain (provided the person knows how to use the knowledge for learning and remembering) and not the person's general intellectual level or memorizing ability for unrelated information. The main practical implication is that people develop good memory, not to the extent that they become better memorizers, but to the extent that they develop expertise in domains for which it is important to remember details accurately.

By way of summarizing this section, let me suggest how a student can make use of the material I have discussed. Suppose you must study this chapter on memory in preparation for an exam, and so are required to learn a lot of factual details. What can you do to make the chapter more memorable? Just repeatedly reading the facts will not in itself enhance your memory for this chapter very much. Instead, you must first look for the themes and patterns that serve to organize the material presented in the chapter. For example, the chapter presents two points of view about memory, the record-keeping theory and the constructionist theory, and argues that the constructionist theory is superior. You must then try to understand these themes by relating them to what you already know. You might note that the record-keeping theory is similar to how books are stored in and retrieved from a library. You should then attempt to figure out for each piece of information how it makes a distinctive contribution to the thesis. You might ask what unique insight each experiment makes concerning the predictions of the constructionist theory. Finally, and to anticipate the next section, you should practice studying the material in a way similar to the way you are going to be tested. If you know that the test will be an essay test, then write out answers to essay questions. Remember, human memory is designed to anticipate the future, not recapitulate the past.

SECTION 3: RECOLLECTING THE PAST

So far I have focused on how cognitive systems change as a result of experiences. Now I wish to change the focus to the cognitive processes responsible for recollecting a past event. What is a good model of recollection?

RECORD-KEEPING AND CONSTRUCTIONIST MODELS OF RECOLLECTING THE PAST

The record-keeping approach claims that recollecting the past means searching through a storehouse of records of past events until the target record is retrieved. Finding or "reading" the memory record is like reexperiencing the past event. The search process is thought to be guided by information in the current environment that acts as a sort of address for the location of the target record. The search through the records need not be haphazard, because the records may be organized, much the way books in a library are organized by content.

The constructionist approach to memory claims that recollecting the past is essentially a process of reconstructing the past from information in the current environment and from the connections serving the various cognitive systems. Recollection typically involves making plausible guesses about what probably happened. Recollection is an active process, akin to fantasizing or speculating about the future, whereby people recreate or infer their past rather than reexperience it. Another way to put it is that people learn reconstruction strategies that enable them to deduce past events. Loftus (1982) provides a discussion of some of the various types of reconstruction strategies.

To illustrate, suppose a person returns to the scene of a car accident and tries to recall the details of the accident, which occurred several days earlier. Returning to the intersection is likely to activate the same elements of the cognitive system involved in originally perceiving the accident; consequently some perceptual details necessary to reconstruct the accident will become available (e.g., cars move quickly through the intersection). Thoughts about a car accident may also activate knowledge of how cars work (e.g., brakes often squeak when a driver tries to stop a rapidly moving vehicle). Such knowledge may then become a basis for reconstructing the accident. Information that was provided to the person after the accident occurred may also be activated and inserted into the reconstruction of the accident (e.g., a friend at the scene of the accident later claimed to have seen a van cut in front of the car). The confluence of activated elements constitutes the memory of the accident (e.g., a van cut in front of a fast-moving car, which tried to stop, causing its brakes to squeal). The memory may appear to the person to be vivid and accurate, yet some details may be in error (e.g., perhaps the van never cut in front of the car).

RECONSTRUCTING THE PAST

An important implication of reconstruction is that when people try to recollect a past event, what they will remember about that event will depend on what they currently know or believe to be true about their lives. Errors in recollecting events will not be haphazard, but will instead reflect knowledge and beliefs. So researchers interested in demonstrating reconstruction often vary a person's current knowledge and show that the person's recollection of some past event will be distorted as a consequence (Dooling & Christiaansen, 1977; Hanawalt & Demarest, 1939; Snyder & Uranowitz, 1978; Spiro, 1977).

A nice demonstration of reconstruction is provided by Spiro (1977). In his experiment, subjects read a passage about a couple, Bob and Margie, who were engaged to be married. Bob was reluctant to tell Margie that he did not want to have children, but, by the end of the story, finally confronted Margie with his wishes. In one version of the story, Margie told Bob that she wanted children very badly. Afterwards, the subjects were told either that Bob and Margie are now happily married or that the engagement had been broken off. Days to weeks later, subjects returned and tried to recall the details of the story. Subjects who were told that the engagement had been broken off tended to recall accurately that Bob and Margie disagreed sharply about having children. In some cases they even exaggerated the disagreement. But the subjects told that Bob and Margie were now happily married tended to recall that the disagreement was much less severe than was actually depicted in the story. And the longer the time between reading the story and recalling it, the more likely these subjects distorted the story so as to resolve the inconsistency between the disagreement and the subsequent marriage. Furthermore, subjects who incorrectly recalled minimal disagreement between Bob and Margie were every bit as confident of their mistaken recollections as they were of their accurate recollections about other aspects of the story.

These results make sense if we assume that subjects did not activate a memory record of the story, but instead used their belief that successful engagements require agreement about whether to have children, in order to reconstruct the story. If Bob and Margie are still married, then it would have seemed that any disagreement about children must not have been very serious.

An intriguing implication of a reconstructionist approach to memory is that it ought to be possible to create false memories—that is, memories of events that never happened. Some researchers have suggested that some memories of sexual abuse are actually false memories created by psychotherapeutic practices that encourage clients to interpret certain psychological symptoms as evidence of past abuse. I review evidence for the creation of false memories of disturbing experiences, such as abuse, in a discussion of repression in the next chapter.

Eyewitness Memory and Reconstruction

Reconstruction has been studied extensively in the context of eyewitness memory. A variety of research has shown that eyewitnesses tend to distort their memories of crimes and accidents based on information they receive after the crime or accident.

For example, eyewitness memory research demonstrates what is called **photo bias**. In one experiment on photo bias, subjects were first shown a film of a crime and were later presented photographs of suspects. Later still the subjects were required to pick the actual perpetrator out of a lineup. What happened was that subjects tend to be biased towards identifying as the perpetrator any suspect whose photograph they had recently seen, even when the person was innocent of the crime (Brown, Deffenbacher, & Sturgill, 1977). Apparently, when the subjects viewed the lineup, they recognized that they had seen one of the suspects before, and erroneously assumed that it must be because the suspect was the criminal.

Elizabeth Loftus, one of the most influential advocates of a reconstructionst approach to memory, has conducted a variety of experiments in which subjects are shown a film of an accident and are later asked questions about the film (Loftus, 1979; Loftus, Miller, & Burns, 1978; Loftus & Loftus, 1980; Loftus & Palmer, 1974). In one experiment, she asked one group of subjects leading questions like "Did another car pass the red Datsun while it was stopped at the stop sign?" when, in fact, the Datsun was stopped at a yield sign. (This particular experiment was conducted before Datsun changed its name to Nissan.) When questioned again about the film, these subjects were much more likely to claim they saw the Datsun stop at a stop sign than another group of subjects not initially asked the misleading question. In some cases, memory was tested by showing subjects two slides, a slide of a Datsun stopped at a stop sign and a slide of the Datsun stopped at a yield sign. Most of the misled subjects selected the slide displaying a stop sign, even when the misled subjects were offered a substantial reward ($25) for remembering accurately. Incidentally, this experimental paradigm usually contains a whole set of questions about various details of the accident or crime. I am illustrating the paradigm with only one of the questions that might be used. At any rate, the subjects were presumably using the information implied by the question to reconstruct the details of the accident. If the question falsely implied that the car stopped at a stop sign, then subjects reconstructed a stop sign in their recollections of the accident.

Exactly what would such a reconstruction be based on? One possibility is that mentioning a stop sign effectively erased or somehow undermined the connection between the accident and the yield sign and replaced it with a connection between the accident and the stop sign (Loftus & Loftus, 1980). There is another possibility, though. Maybe subjects do remember that the film contained, say, a yield sign and that the subsequent question mentioned a stop sign. But when given the choice between a yield and stop sign, the subjects figure that the experimenter wants them to say that they saw a stop sign in the film (otherwise, why would the experimenter ask the question?). In other words, maybe subjects' memories are just fine in this paradigm; maybe they are just responding to the demands characteristic of the experiment; maybe this research is not supportive of a construction approach to memory (McCloskey & Zaragoza, 1985).

To see if the question about the stop sign really erased the information about the yield sign (or, more generally, if misinformation erases previously acquired information), McCloskey and Zaragoza (1985) devised a somewhat different experimental paradigm (this paradigm, the Loftus paradigm, and a couple of other paradigms that I discuss below are all illustrated in Figure 4-4). Subjects first saw a film that contained details like the yield sign, and then read a text that contained misinformation, such as a description of a stop sign, and then were asked to decide if the original film contained a yield sign or, say, a caution sign. Again, the actual paradigm includes several pieces of information, and not just information about traffic signs. If the misinformation really wiped

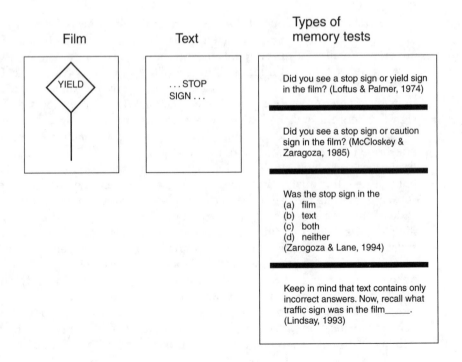

FIGURE 4–4 Experimental paradigms to investigate the impact of misleading information on eyewitness memory.

out memory of the yield sign, subjects should be just as likely to choose the yield sign as to choose the caution sign. Instead, subjects overwhelmingly selected the correct alternative, the yield sign in this case.

So does this mean that the misinformation has no effect on eyewitness memory at all? No. In other research (see Lindsay, 1993), subjects were first shown a film (or slide show) of a crime or accident, then read a text that contained some misleading information, and then were asked of each piece of information whether the information was presented in the film, in the text, in both places, or in neither place. The memory test in this case (see Figure 4-4) asks subjects the source of the information. The idea is to see whether source memory is worse for a detail in the film when there is misinformation in the text than when there is not misinformation in the text.

The main finding is that **source memory** tends to be good (i.e., subjects correctly remember that the stop sign was in the text and not in the film) when it is easy for subjects to discriminate between the experience of seeing the film and reading the text (e.g., Zaragoza & Lane, 1994; see Lindsay, 1993). One way to make the discrimination easy is to present the film on one day, wait until the next day to present the text, and then immediately follow the text with the memory test. Source memory tends to be poor (i.e., subjects think that the stop sign was in the film) when it is hard for subjects to discriminate between the experience of seeing the film and the experience of reading the text. For example, a way to make the discrimination hard is to present the text right after the film, ask subjects to visualize the text, and present the memory test the next day. Source memory also tends to be poor if the misleading suggestions contained in the text are repeated several times rather than presented in the text only once (Zaragoza & Mitchell, 1996).

One other paradigm (see Figure 4-4) that suggests that memory really is affected by subsequently presented misinformation comes from Lindsay (1990; also Weingardt, Loftus, & Lindsay, 1995; see Lindsay, 1993). Again, say that subjects see a yield sign in the film and later read a text about a stop sign. The description of a stop sign is misinformation. Now subjects are correctly informed that the text did not contain any correct answers to a subsequent memory test. In the memory test, subjects are asked to report details about the traffic sign, and subjects know that the correct answer comes from the film and not from the text. When it is hard to discriminate between the film and text experiences, subjects are likely to recall incorrectly details from the text, such as that the traffic sign was a stop sign. Such incorrect recall occurs less often when subjects are asked to recall details from the film about which no misinformation was given in the text. Here the demand characteristics of the experiment unambiguously push subjects to recall only the information in the film, yet they frequently recall inaccurately the information in the text.

I went through these experimental paradigms in some detail because I want you to see exactly how researchers refine their paradigms in response to alternative interpretations of findings. In this case, we can say that misinformation is likely to affect recollection when it is relatively difficult for people to discriminate between the misinformation event and the to-be-remembered event

(Lindsay, 1993). So, for example, our hypothetical Jim—mentioned at the beginning of this chapter—might be prone to remember incorrectly that the thief stole a camera (when, in fact, he saw the thief steal a radio) because he heard someone at the crime scene tell the police that the thief stole a camera. But Jim would be far less likely to remember incorrectly that the thief stole a camera if he heard someone talking about a missing camera the day after the theft and in a different physical setting than where the theft took place.

Loftus (1986) estimates that thousands of people in the United States are wrongfully convicted each year, and that many of these wrongful convictions are due to inaccurate eyewitness testimony. Juries deliberating the fate of people accused of crimes need to be made aware of the fallibility of human memory and the ease with which details of the past can be inaccurately recollected.

Hypnosis and Memory

Sometimes it is supposed that hypnosis can help people better recollect crimes and accidents. As it turns out, psychologists debate whether hypnosis is a distinctive state of waking consciousness that is different from ordinary wakefulness or is merely an occasion in which some people are unusually motivated to carry out the requests of the hypnotist (see Farthing, 1992). Whatever the exact nature of hypnosis, certainly it is commonly believed that hypnosis promotes such accurate recall of the past that nearly all events must be stored in memory. The reality, though, is that when hypnosis is used to help eyewitnesses recollect a crime, accident, or any past event, hypnotized people do not remember details any more accurately than do nonhypnotized people. Hypnotized people, though, may be more confident about their recollections than nonhypnotized people (Buckhout, Eugenio, Licitia, Oliver, & Kramer, 1981; Krass, Kinoshita, & McConkey, 1989). Furthermore, hypnotized eyewitnesses are influenced by misleading questions even more than are nonhypnotized people.

Putnam (1979) presented subjects a videotape of a car accident and later hypnotized some subjects. When asked a misleading question like "Did you see the license plate number on the car?" some hypnotized subjects claimed to remember the numbers on the license plate when, in fact, the license plate was not visible in the film. Note that by using the phrase "the license plate," the question implies that the license plate was visible. Some of the hypnotized subjects presumably used the misleading implication in the question to reconstruct a number for the license plate. The subjects who were not hypnotized were less likely to fall for the misleading questions.

Hypnosis has also been used to attempt age regression, in which hypnotized adults may claim that they are really reliving some experience from childhood. But investigations reveal that the recollected details are often inaccurate (Nash, 1987). In one case, an adult who was hypnotically age-regressed remembered inaccurately a first-grade teacher's name. In another case, an adult who was hypnotically regressed to age 6 was asked to draw a picture. While the picture the adult produced looked childlike, it did not resemble the subject's own drawings made at age 6. Instead, the drawing reflected an adult's conception of a childish drawing, but not real children's drawings.

In brief, hypnosis, which is supposed to help people relive past experiences, does not really work. The research on hypnosis and memory is consistent with the idea that records of past experiences are not routinely maintained in memory, but must be reconstructed.

The Influence of Beliefs on Memory

The idea that recollecting is reconstructing suggests that we reconstruct a memory of our past from our current beliefs and what we believe to be true about human personality in general (Ross, 1989). One idea that people have about personality is that beliefs remain rather stable over time. As a result, people tend to remember that their past beliefs were similar to their currently held beliefs, even when their beliefs have, in fact, changed over time. Let me provide a few experimental demonstrations.

In one study (Goethals & Reckman, 1973; see also Markus, 1986), high school students filled out a survey asking them for their opinion on various topics, including forced busing. About two weeks later, students met with a respected high school senior who presented a carefully crafted and well-rehearsed argument to the students about busing that was the opposite of the students' own opinion. For example, students who were opposed to forced busing heard a counterargument in favor of forced busing. Following the counterargument, students were again asked their opinion on busing, and were also asked to try to recall how they had filled out the survey two weeks earlier. The instructions emphasized the importance of accurate recall.

The counterarguments were effective; students tended to reverse their opinion about busing after hearing the counterargument. The result, consistent with reconstruction, was that the students tended to remember that they originally filled out the survey question about busing in a way consistent with their newly formed opinion and inconsistent with the way they actually had originally answered the busing question. For example, the students who were originally opposed to forced busing but heard a persuasive argument in favor of forced busing tended to remember that they had been in favor of forced busing all along. It was as if the students examined their current belief about busing, assumed that attitudes remain stable over the short period of two weeks, and so reconstructed that they must have held their current attitude two weeks earlier.

Galotti (1995) studied the criteria students use when selecting a college. Galotti asked students to recall the criteria that they had listed in a previously filled-out questionnaire assessing the basis on which they decided where to go to college. Galotti also asked the students to describe the ideal criteria that they thought, in retrospect, they ought to have used. The questionnaires had been filled out 8 to 20 months earlier. Subjects recalled about half of the criteria they had used when originally making the decision about where to go to college. But the overlap between what they recalled and the ideal criteria was substantially greater than the overlap between what they recalled and the criteria they had actually used. It was as if subjects used their current sense of the ideal decision criteria to reconstruct a memory of the criteria they used when originally making the college decision.

Many people, at least in our culture, believe that a woman's mood is likely to become more negative just before and during menstruation. It turns out, though, that this belief may be false. Based on diary studies, there seems to be no reliable correlation between a woman's mood and her menstrual cycle, at least when large numbers of women are studied (see Ross, 1989). The idea of reconstruction suggests that women may use this belief about mood and menstruation to remember inaccurately that their mood had been worse during a previous menstruation phase than during an intermenstrual phase of the cycle.

Evidence consistent with the reconstruction hypothesis is provided by Ross (1989). He reports a study in which a group of women was asked to keep detailed diaries in which they recorded various life events and daily moods. The women were not told that the study focused on the menstrual cycle. At one point in the experiment, the women were asked to recall their mood from a day two weeks earlier. The women were supplied the date and day of the week and a small portion of their diary entries, including an entry that indicated whether they were menstruating. For one group, the to-be-recalled day was during the menstruation phase of their cycle, while for the other group the to-be-recalled day was during the intermenstrual phase. The actual diary entries for the to-be-recalled days indicated that the women's mood was no worse on average during the menstrual phase than during the intermenstrual phase. Yet the women tended to recall that their mood was worse on the menstrual day. Moreover, the more the women believed in a correlation between menstruation and mood (as assessed by an attitude survey), the more likely they were to exaggerate how negative their mood was on the day when they were menstruating.

CONFIDENCE AND ACCURACY

As I suggested earlier, record-keeping theories of human memory may concede that recollection of the past often involves reconstruction. The record-keeping theory could claim that a person resorts to reconstruction when the retrieval process fails to locate the necessary record. The constructionist theory claims instead that people use a reconstruction strategy every time they reflect on the past.

The record-keeping theory implies that people should be able to tell the difference between when they are able to read a record that accurately preserves the details of the past event, and when they are unable to locate the record and so must resort to making guesses about the past. People would presumably have more confidence in their memory for a past event if they are reading the record than if they are only reconstructing it. Therefore, according to the record-keeping theory, people's confidence in the accuracy of their memory for a past event should be reliably greater when the event is remembered accurately than when an event is remembered inaccurately.

The constructionist theory, on the other hand, claims that all recollection is reconstruction. Constructionist theory suggests that confidence and accuracy may sometimes be related, particularly when people have developed learning and reconstruction strategies for which they have been provided feedback as to how well those strategies work. In such cases, people may use their knowledge about how well a strategy has worked in the past to predict accurately how well it will work in the future. However, constructionist theory predicts that confidence will not be strongly related to accuracy when people have had no opportunity to develop adequate learning and reconstructive strategies, or when there is misleading information that fools people into thinking that they have accurately reconstructed an event. In these latter two situations, people may be as confident in the accuracy of an incorrectly reconstructed event as they are of a correctly reconstructed event.

Consistent with the predictions of constructionist theory, a variety of experiments have demonstrated that the correlation between confidence and accuracy is typically quite low, especially in situations where eyewitnesses to crimes and accidents must recollect details of those crimes and accidents (Wells & Murray, 1984; Donders, Schooler, & Loftus, 1987; Smith, Kassin, & Ellsworth, 1989). Presumably most people have not had much practice developing learning and reconstruction strategies for eyewitness information, and therefore have not learned when such strategies produce accurate recollections (see Perfect, Watson, & Wagstaff, 1993).

On the other hand, the correlation between confidence and accuracy is reliably higher in situations where people have had such practice. For example, the correlation between confidence and accuracy is moderately high when subjects are asked to answer general knowledge questions, such as "Who wrote *The Mill on the Floss*?" (e.g., Hart, 1967; Perfect et al. 1993; see Nelson, 1988 for review). Presumably most people have learned how good they are at answering general knowledge questions (Perfect et al., 1993). The correlation between confidence and accuracy is also moderately high when subjects are asked to answer questions about short texts they have recently read (e.g., Stephenson, 1984; Stephenson, Clark, & Wade, 1986). In this case, experience in academic settings has presumably taught most people how good they are at answering questions about texts.

Record-keeping theories of memory would predict that any variable that decreases memory accuracy should also decrease confidence in the accuracy of the memory. Contrary to the recorded-keeping prediction, Chandler (1994) reported a series of studies in which accuracy was decreased but confidence increased. Chandler had subjects study nature pictures, such as pictures of lakes. Later, subjects were required to determine which of two related pictures (e.g., two different lakes) had been previously displayed and to indicate their confidence in their recognition judgment. When the subjects had also studied a third related picture (e.g., a third lake), their recognition performance declined but their confidence in their selection increased (compared to the case when there was no third picture). The constructionist explanation is that subjects become more familiar with the general theme (e.g., scenic lakes) of the pictures as they study more of the related pictures. Both alternatives on the recognition test fit the theme, making discrimination between them difficult, so recognition memory performance declines. But because the selected picture fits the theme, confidence in the selection is high.

Also consistent with constructionist theory is the finding that people become confident of inaccurate recollections when those recollections are reconstructed from misleading information supplied to them by an experimenter (e.g., Davis & Schiffman, 1985; Spiro, 1977). Consider a study by Ryan and Geiselman (1991). They presented subjects a film of a robbery and a week later had them read a summary description of the film. For some of the subjects the summary included a misleading detail, such as "The police car is at a brown house" (in fact, the house in the film was white). The subjects then answered questions about the film (e.g., "What was the color of the house?"). The interesting finding was that subjects who were biased by the incorrect detail, and therefore gave the wrong answer (e.g., "The house was brown"), were more confident of their wrong answer than were the subjects who were not given the misleading detail and so usually gave the correct answer (e.g., "The house was white").

People may become confident of their inaccurate memories when some inaccurately remembered piece of information is nevertheless consistent with the gist of some previously presented information. For instance, Roediger and McDermott (1995; see also Deese, 1959) presented subjects list of words (e.g., *bed*, *rest*, *awake*) for which every word on a list was related to a target word (e.g., *sleep*) not presented on the list. Later, on tests of recall and recognition, subjects remembered that the target words (e.g., *sleep*) were on the list about as often and with about the same confidence as they remembered the words that were actually presented on the lists. Moreover, the greater the number of related words presented on the list, the more likely subjects were to recall or recognize the target word not presented on the list (Robinson & Roediger, 1997). Presumably, the tendency to think of the target word when studying the list created a false memory for that target word that seemed as real to subjects as their memories of actually presented words.

THE OVERLAP PRINCIPLE

The fact that memory makes use of reconstruction strategies, such as relying on one's current beliefs to deduce past beliefs, means that remembering is often inaccurate. But recollections of the past are not inevitably inaccurate. The study of memory has established that memory of an event is more accurate when the environment at the time of recollection resembles the environment of the originally experienced event (Begg & White, 1985; Guthrie, 1959; Tulving, 1983; Tulving & Thomson, 1973). This principle may be called the **overlap principle**—people's memory for a past event improves to the extent that the elements of the recollection environment overlap with the elements of the past event. By environment, I mean a person's cognitive and emotional state, as well as the person's physical environment. The overlap principle also goes by the name of **encoding**

specificity, to emphasize that how an event is processed or "encoded" will determine what kinds of cues will later be effective at promoting memory for the event (Tulving & Thomson, 1973).

Experimental Evidence for the Overlap Principle

A good experimental demonstration of the overlap principle comes from research designed to help eyewitnesses more accurately remember crimes and accidents. Courts of law place strong emphasis on eyewitness accounts when assessing responsibility and punishment. Yet people often have a hard time remembering important details of crimes and accidents they have witnessed, a point I used earlier to illustrate the concept of reconstruction in memory. A variety of research suggests that eyewitness memory improves if the context surrounding the event is reinstated (see Geiselman, 1988).

Cutler and Penrod (1988; see also Geiselman, Fisher, MacKinnon, & Holland, 1985) had subjects view a videotape of a robbery and a few days later pick out the robber from a lineup. Some subjects were given photographs (not containing the robber) taken from the scene of the crime, or were asked to think back through the events from beginning to end while imagining the robbery. These subjects tended to identify the robber more accurately than subjects not given any context-reinstating cues.

Other experiments have demonstrated that memory for an event is more accurate if retrieval takes place in the same physical environment as the one where the event originally occurred (e.g., Canas & Nelson, 1986; see Smith, 1988 for a review). In one of my favorite studies, subjects who learned a list of words while scuba diving later recalled more of the words if the recall test took place while the subjects were again scuba diving than if the recall test took place on land (Godden & Baddeley, 1975).

It should be noted, though, that the overlap of physical environments is probably an important determinant of memory when the to-be-learned information can be associated with the physical environment (Baddeley, 1982; Fernandez & Glenberg, 1985). An eyewitness may be more likely to remember the events of an accident, such as a car crashing into a tree, if the eyewitness recollects at the scene of the accident, than if the eyewitness recollects in the police station. The tree at the crash site is associated with the accident, so that seeing the tree is likely to activate information that may be used to reconstruct the accident. On the other hand, it is probably not as important that a student take an exam in the same room where he or she studied for the exam (Saufley, Otaka, & Bavaresco, 1985) since academic information would not ordinarily be associated with the physical elements of a room. Much more important is that the student understand the academic material, organize the material, and make the details contained within the material distinctive.

One demonstration that the overlap principle depends more on the similarity of cognitive processing than on similarity of physical stimuli comes from research on mood. The usual finding is that subjects induced to feel elated or depressed will more likely and quickly recall past events experienced in the same mood, than those experienced in a different mood (Snyder & White, 1982; Teasdale & Fogarty, 1979; see Blaney, 1986, for a review). In experiments conducted by Eich (1995), subjects were placed in a setting (e.g., a laboratory) and then responded to a list of 16 words designed to prompt memories of past experiences. The subjects' mood was also measured. Later, subjects were placed in either the same physical setting or a different setting, and were induced to feel either happy or sad. Mood was induced by having subjects listen to either joyful musical pieces while entertaining elating thoughts or melancholy musical pieces while entertaining depressing thoughts. The subjects then had to recall the 16 prompt words and the events the prompts elicited. Recall was better when the mood at the time of recall matched the mood experienced when the prompt words were first presented. Overlap in physical setting, on the other hand, did not matter to recall.

Problem Solving and the Overlap Principle

Another interesting demonstration that the overlap principle is based on similarity in the way events are processed, and not on the mere presence of overlapping stimulus cues, comes from research on problem solving. A seemingly perplexing finding of this research is that people often fail to remember facts that would help them solve a problem (Perfetto, Bransford, & Franks, 1983; Weisberg, Dicamillo, & Phillips, 1978). To illustrate with a hypothetical example, suppose a student in a psychology class learned the fact that, paradoxically, ignoring a young child who is whining and crying promotes the development of a dependent personality. On an examination, the student remembers this information and so correctly answers questions based on it. Yet when the student becomes a parent and encounters the whining of the child, the parent chooses to ignore the child, in the mistaken belief that the child will thereby become more independent.

Why does the parent fail to remember and make use of the relevant information previously learned in school? The answer is that trying to solve problems is unlikely to engage the portion of the cognitive system used to memorize facts, so the memorized facts play no role in the attempt to arrive at a solution. Perhaps if the parent had practiced solving child-rearing problems in school, rather than only memorizing facts about child rearing, the parent would have been more likely to transfer the information to real problems.

My hypothetical example about child rearing was inspired by experiments conducted by Adams et al. (1988); Perfetto et al. (1983); Lockhart, Lamon, and Glick (1988), and Needham and Begg (1991), among others. In one of these experiments (Perfetto et al., 1983), one group of subjects read a list of sentences that included sentences like "A minister marries several people a week" while a control group of subjects did not read the sentences. Both groups of subjects were then asked to solve brain teasers like "How can it be that a man can marry several women a week, never get divorced, yet break no law?" Note that the sentences the first group read were designed to help them solve the problems presented later on. Surprisingly, the subjects who first read the helpful sentences were no more likely to solve the brain teasers than the control subjects.

What would it take to get the subjects to make use of previously studied information to solve a new problem? Adams et, al. (1988) and Lockhart et al. (1988) presented groups of subjects with sentences like this: "The man married ten people each week" and, 5 seconds after each sentence, gave the subjects a clue to help solve the puzzle suggested by the sentence—for example "a minister." Note that the subjects were not memorizing the sentences but instead approaching each sentence as a kind of miniature problem for which they were quickly given the solution. Subjects asked to approach the sentences as a set of problems were later on better at solving the brain teasers than either the subjects who first only memorized the sentences or the control subjects who never read any sentences. When the experiment ensured that the information processing activity required by the brain teaser matched the information processing activity required by the original presentation of the sentences, the subjects were able to make use of the sentences to help them solve the brain teasers.

These findings are examples of transfer appropriate processing (discussed earlier in the chapter), and are a manifestation of the overlap principle. If the kind of cognitive processing taking place in the testing environment resembles that taking place in the original learning environment, then what is learned will likely transfer to the test. Other experiments demonstrating transfer appropriate processing can be found in Blaxton (1989); in Glass, Krejci, and Goldman (1989); and in the Morris, Bransford, and Franks (1977) study I discussed in the "levels of processing" section earlier in this chapter. The obvious educational implication of transfer appropriate processing is that if schools want to increase the odds that what students learn in school will help them solve problems later in life, then schools should engage students in solving problems that resemble those encountered outside of school. Students who demonstrate on examinations that they remember the material are not necessarily going to be able to use the material to solve problems they encounter later on. I discuss problem solving at greater length in chapter 8: Problem Solving (where else?).

Recognition Versus Recall

Another demonstration of the overlap principle is the finding that, under most circumstances, people can recognize more accurately than they can recall a past event (McDougall, 1904). A recognition test usually supplies more information about the original event than does a recall test, because the correct answer to any memory question is contained in the recognition test. For example, subjects asked to recall as many names as they could remember from their high school class that graduated 47 years earlier recalled on average only about 20 names (about 30% of the class), but accurately recognized about 45 names (about 65% of the class) (Bahrick, Bahrick, & Wittlinger, 1975).

It is possible, however, to devise situations for which people can recall what they are unable to recognize (Watkins & Tulving, 1975; see Klatzky, 1980, for a review). Such situations are characterized by a recall testing environment that more closely resembles the original learning environment than does the recognition testing environment.

In one experiment demonstrating recall without recognition (Nilsson, Law, & Tulving, 1988), subjects were presented a list of famous names (e.g., George Washington) in the context of descriptive phrases (e.g., "He was the first in a long line but the only one on horseback—George Washington"). Seven days later the subjects were given a recognition test in which a set of famous names was presented. This set contained the previously studied names as well as foils (e.g., Charles Darwin). Subjects had to indicate which names they had studied a week earlier. Then subjects were given the descriptive phrases and had to recall the famous names (e.g., "He was the first in a long line but the only one on horseback—?"). Subjects were often able to recall famous names that they did not recognize.

SECTION 4: FORGETTING

Forgetting past experiences, if not in their entirety, at least in most of their detail, seems the rule. Why do we so easily forget most of our past? Certainly, if we fail to pay attention to certain information contained in an event then we are unlikely to remember that information later on. Or if we are not motivated to try to remember an event, or are not given enough information to enable us to be sure what it is we are supposed to remember, then we are not likely to remember the event.

INTERFERENCE

Another important reason for forgetting, besides those mentioned above, is that one's memory for any given event from one's past is undermined by the occurrence of other events. When memory for an event is undermined by events that precede it, the result is called **proactive interference**. When memory for an event is undermined by events that follow it, the result is called **retroactive interference**.

A variety of experimental paradigms have been used to demonstrate interference (see Klatzky, 1980, or Watkins, 1979, for a review). The classic demonstration of retroactive interference comes from Jenkins and Dallenbach (1924). In their experiment, subjects were first presented a list of nonsense syllables, then spent the following 8 hours either asleep or awake, and then tried to recall the nonsense syllables. The subjects who remained awake, and so experienced more interfering events, recalled fewer syllables than did the subjects who went to sleep. This experiment is not the ideal demonstration of retroactive interference, though, because the subjects who experienced less interference also experienced a night of sleep. Maybe people are more motivated or less fatigued after sleeping, and so perform better on memory tests.

An example of a better controlled experiment demonstrating interference is provided by Kalbaugh and Walls (1973; also see Barnes & Underwood, 1959; McGeoch, 1942; Melton & Irwin, 1940). They required their eighth-grade subjects to study a critical passage describing the essential biographical details of a fictional character. Some subjects read no other passages while other subjects read

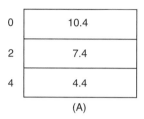

Number of items recalled
from critical biography

Number of biographies read before reading critical biography (proactive interference)		
0	10.4	
2	7.4	
4	4.4	

(A)

Number of items recalled
from critical biography

Number of biographies read after reading critical biography (retroactive interference)		
0	7.1	
2	4.9	
4	3.7	

(B)

FIGURE 4–5   Proactive and retroactive interference. Based on Kalbaugh and Walls, 1973.

either two or four other biographical passages. The additional passages were presented either before the critical passage or after the critical passage. As summarized in Figure 4-5, the experiment demonstrated both retroactive and proactive interference. The subjects who read additional passages, whether presented before or after the critical passage, recalled less about the critical passage than subjects who read only the critical passage. The more additional passages the subjects read, the poorer was their recall of the critical passage.

Another way in which interference is demonstrated is in experiments that measure how fast people can decide whether a fact about a concept was on a previously memorized list of facts. Interference in this paradigm takes the form of an increased response latency to facts whose concepts are found in lots of other facts on the list. In one such experiment, subjects memorized sentences that described a professional in some location (e.g., "The lawyer was in the park"). The number of facts about any one professional or about any one location varied. Subjects might memorize two facts about a lawyer (e.g., "The lawyer was in the park," "The lawyer was at the beach") and one fact about a doctor (e.g., "The doctor was in the park") and might memorize two facts that involved parks and one fact that involved beaches. The typical result (illustrated in Figure 4-6 for "true" responses) is that the more facts associated with a character or

Number of facts about a location

1	2	3
1.169	1.196	1.248

Reaction time, in seconds, to respond "true"

Number of facts about a profession

1	2	3
1.144	1.202	1.267

Reaction time, in seconds, to respond "true"

FIGURE 4–6   The more facts about a professional or location, the longer the response time to verify the fact. Based on Anderson, 1974.

with a location, the longer it takes to decide if the fact is true or false (Anderson, 1974, 1976). Sometimes this finding is known as the **fan effect**. The more facts that "fan off" a concept, the longer it takes to verify whether any given fact about the concept was previously memorized.

EXPLAINING INTERFERENCE

The record-keeping theory has an easy explanation for interference. People search memory records by first finding in memory a target element, such as a character's profession. People then scan through the set of facts associated with the target element until the desired fact is found, or until the search is exhausted. The more associations to be searched, or the longer or more effort it takes to find the desired fact, the more likely the fact will not be found. It is as if all of the associations, facts, and lists of facts stored in memory compete with the target information for the attention of the search process (Anderson, 1976, 1983; McGeoch, 1942; Postman, Stark, & Fraser, 1968).

The ease with which a record-keeping theory explains interference in memory experiments is one of the most compelling sources of evidence for it. But the explanation leads to a paradox (Smith, Adams, & Schoor, 1978). As we go through life, the number of associations with elements in our memory should continually increase. It follows, then, that over time we should become increasingly inefficient at finding information stored in our memory. Becoming an expert would be especially difficult, because the expert learns many facts about a set of concepts. Experts, then, would be expected to have an ever-increasing difficulty in remembering information in their area of expertise. Obviously this does not happen. The record-keeping theory's explanation for interference observed in many memorization experiments cannot easily explain the obvious facts that an adult's memory skill remains stable over time and that experts get better, and not worse, at remembering information in their area of expertise.

The difficulty that the record-keeping theory of memory has with explaining everyday observations about memory reminds us that explanations must have **ecological validity**. That is, theories of memory should explain how memory works in the actual environment in which we use our memory. Some memory theorists, notably Ulric Neisser (Neisser, 1978), have argued that a lot of memory research does not look at memory in realistic settings and so may not be ecologically valid. Neisser has urged the cognitive psychological community to make more use of experimental paradigms that resemble real-life situations. I have tried to include a fair number of such experiments in this chapter. Some memory theorists, however, have complained that experiments that have resembled real-life situations have not really uncovered any new principle of memory (Banaji & Crowder, 1989; see articles in the January 1991 issue of the *American Psychologist*). Perhaps, though, the contrast between the results of list memorization experiments and the everyday observations that memory is stable over time and that experts have good memory constitutes a compelling example of the importance of conducting ecologically valid research.

The constructionist theory is able to explain both the decline in memory performance exhibited in the memorization experiments and the lack of decline in memory observed in ordinary day-to-day situations or in experts. Memorization of related lists of words should generally present difficulties because the same elements would be used repeatedly to understand each new list. A subject who must memorize two lists of state-city associations, for example, would find that the connections among the cognitive elements used to understand and recollect the first list would be reconfigured when the second list was studied, thereby undermining memory for the details of the first list. Memorization, therefore, should be poorer or slower if a person has to memorize several related lists than if a person has to memorize unrelated lists. Furthermore, the repeated use of similar lists would make accurate and detailed reconstruction of any one list difficult.

The stability in an adult's memory skill occurs because the elements used to understand experiences do not expand in number as a result of having many experiences. Only the connections among elements change with experience. Experts become good at remembering information in their area of expertise because the portions of their cognitive system that support the expertise will have many enduring patterns of connections to represent and reconstruct that information. For example, an expert on climate may be able to remember that Seattle has a milder winter than Denver by activating the general principle that oceans moderate climate. Much of what is involved in becoming an expert is understanding the general principles that a body of information entails.

One of the important predictions of the constructionist account of interference is that interference is not inevitable. Interference is expected when there is no effective learning strategy for extracting the patterns that integrate increasingly larger bodies of information. If such patterns can be extracted and used to reconstruct the information, then increasing the amount of information should not produce interference. Research confirms this prediction.

In one experiment, Jones and Anderson (1987) required subjects to memorize varying numbers of facts about hypothetical characters. In some cases, the facts were all related by a common theme. For example, subjects might learn that John has a rifle, John is a hunter, and John is in the forest. In other cases the facts were unrelated—for example: Jerry has a rifle, Jerry is a researcher, and Jerry is at the beach. As in other experiments investigating the fan effect, the subjects were then asked to verify whether particular facts were true (e.g., "John has a rifle") or false (e.g., "John is a researcher"). When the facts were unrelated, the usual fan effect was observed. Subjects took longer to verify facts about a character when there were six unrelated facts about that character to memorize than when there was only one fact to memorize. But when the facts were related by a common theme, the fan effect was greatly reduced. When the facts were related by a theme, subjects took about as long to verify facts about a character when there were six related facts to memorize about that character as when there was only one fact to memorize. Similar results have been obtained by Radvansky and Zacks (1991) and by Smith, Adams, and Schorr (1978). The constructionist explanation is that when the facts are related by a theme, that theme can be used to reconstruct whether a fact fits the theme and so must be true, or does not fit the theme, and so must be false.

The constructionist theory of memory also implies that interference depends on what kind of information subjects are asked to remember. If subjects in list-memorizing experiments were asked to remember the general pattern of information in the lists, rather than the unique details of each list, then presenting subjects with several lists should promote better memory of the general pattern, even while undermining memory for the unique details of each list.

Evidence consistent with the constructionist prediction is provided by Reder and Ross (1983). They required subjects to memorize a varying number of facts about hypothetical characters. Later, some subjects were required to indicate whether a particular fact was explicitly on the memorized list, while other subjects were asked to indicate whether a particular fact was similar to (implied by) other facts on the list. For example, subjects might learn three facts about Marvin: Marvin skied down the slope, Marvin waited in the lift line, and Marvin waxed his skis. The usual fan effect was observed if the memory test required subjects to judge whether a particular fact was explicitly on the list (e.g., Marvin waited in the lift line). The greater the number of memorized facts about a character, the longer to verify whether any given fact about the character was on the list. The opposite of the usual fan effect was observed if the test required that subjects decide whether a fact was implied by other facts on the list (e.g., Marvin adjusted his skis). The greater the number of facts about a character, the faster subjects could verify whether a fact was similar to one of the memorized facts. The constructionist explanation is that the similarity judgment allowed subjects to compare a fact to the pattern or theme extracted from the memorized facts. The more facts there were to memorize, the more likely that such patterns would be extracted.

Another demonstration that increasing the amount of information can improve memory for patterns but undermine memory for details comes from an experiment by Bower (1974). Bower required his subjects to learn a critical passage describing the biography of a hypothetical character. The basic form of the biography described the time and place of birth, the occupation of the character's father, the way the father died, and so on. Subjects then studied some additional passages. For some subjects, the additional passages were biographies similar in form but different in detail from the critical passage. For other subjects, the additional passages were unrelated to the critical passage in form and in detail. Later, all subjects had to recall the same critical passage. Bower found that subjects who studied the related passages recalled fewer details of the critical passage (e.g., the father was a servant) but more of the general pattern of the passage (e.g., the passage described the father's occupation) than did subjects who studied unrelated passages.

Students often feel overwhelmed by the amount of material they must learn for an exam. Perhaps it would hearten them to learn that interference for newly acquired information is not inevitable. If students can relate each piece of information to a common theme, then interference is not likely to occur. The student should be able to remember large sets of information as well as small sets. Similarly, if the examination tests for general principles rather than specific details, then again interference is not inevitable. The more information one must learn, the more likely the general principles can be extracted from the information.

SUMMARY AND CONCLUSIONS

In the first section of this chapter, I introduced two competing types of theories of memory. One is the record-keeping theory, which argues that memory is a system for storing records of past events, that recollection is searching through and reading the records, and that forgetting is caused primarily by the distracting presence of many memory records. The second is the constructionist theory, which argues that memory reflects changes to the cognitive systems used to interpret events, that recollection is reconstructing the past, and that forgetting is caused primarily by the continuous changes each new experience makes to the cognitive systems that interpret and act on stimuli. Few contemporary theories of memory embody all the features of record-keeping theories, although some contemporary theories, especially those that use computers as metaphors for memory, seem closer in spirit to the record-keeping than to the constructionist theory. Certainly the record-keeping theory has dominated the history of memory research and seems to reflect the ordinary person's view of memory (Loftus & Loftus, 1980).

I have argued that the evidence overall supports the constructionist theory over the record-keeping theory. In the second section, I discussed how experiences are retained in memory. Evidence consistent with constructionist theory is that memory is good for invariants or patterns that endure across many experiences, but is poor for the details of specific experiences. Usually people remember the details of a particular experience because those details are unusual or distinctive in some way. Even people with very remarkable memory for details, such as Luria's *S*, make use of mnemonic devices and learning strategies that help them make information more distinctive.

The constructionist approach claims that memory reflects the strength of connections among elements of the cognitive systems used to perceive, think about, and act on events. Such connections undergo continuous reconfiguration in response to experiences. In a sense, memory is only a byproduct of connections among the components of various cognitive systems. There is no separate memory system in which information is "stored." Consistent with the idea of memory as a byproduct is the assimilation principle: How well people remember new information about a topic depends on how much they already know about that topic. Also consistent is the observation that individual differences in memory are largely attributable to expertise in the relevant domain of knowledge. General intellectual skill, or skill at memorizing, does not seem to predict memory for new information from some domain of knowledge as well as does expertise in that domain.

Especially telling for the constructionist theory is that conscious recollection of the past depends on current knowledge and on recollection strategies. As I discussed in the third section, a person's recollections of the past are often distorted by misleading questions or general knowledge. For example, eyewitnesses to crimes and accidents sometimes mistakenly remember details, like a car going through a stop sign, that they never observed. Usually such mistakes are made when someone or some process implies that the details were a part of the crime or accident. Especially difficult for the record-keeping theory is the finding that people are often as confident of inaccurate as of accurate reconstructions of past events.

Although forgetting is common, people certainly are able to reconstruct accurately some of their past experiences. Memory is more accurate when there is considerable similarity between the retrieval and original learning environment, a phenomenon called the overlap (also called the encoding specificity) principle. The constructionist theory explains the overlap principle by claiming that memory is improved when the retrieval environment activates the same portions of the cognitive system used to interpret the original environment. For instance, people are more likely to use information previously learned in one environment to solve a new problem if the original environment also required them to use that information to solve problems.

The most important principle of forgetting, called interference, is that the more information a person must memorize, the more likely the person will be unable to remember or will be slower at remembering any given piece of information. As I discussed in the fourth section, the record-keeping theory suggests that interference is primarily due to the distracting effects of other memory records, which increase in number as the amount of information to be remembered increases. But the record-keeping theory implies a paradox: Adults should show a gradual decline in their memory as they learn more about various topics. Experts should have especially poor memory in their domains of expertise. Yet neither of these propositions is true.

The constructionist theory predicts interference when no distinctive patterns enable the person to reconstruct information, as is likely to happen in list memorization experiments. Because the constructionist theory claims that no memory records are kept, an adult's memory remains stable over time. Because experts learn to find patterns in and to develop reconstruction strategies for their domain of expertise, experts have a good memory for that domain. The constructionist theory correctly predicts that interference usually observed in list learning experiments is eliminated if the memorized facts can be integrated by a common theme, or if the memory test requires people to remember the patterns rather than the details contained within the memorized material.

Although constructionist accounts of memory are currently influential (see Schacter, 1996), some cognitive psychologists continue to support record-keeping theories (see Hall, 1990). One might argue that, with suitable modifications, the record-keeping theory can explain the data I claimed support the constructionist theory. For example, a record-keeping theory could include a pattern recognition system that either stores descriptions of patterns or examines memory records to find patterns in events. Consequently, patterns of experiences would be readily remembered. A record-keeping theory could posit that reconstruction strategies are used when a sought-after memory record is not located.

It is true that such modifications would make the record-keeping theory work more like real human memory. Note, though, that the proposed modifications have the effect of making the record-keeping theory more like the constructionist theory. Furthermore, the modifications are not intrinsic to, or a natural consequence of, the central idea that memory is a matter of storing records of experiences. There is nothing about putting a record of an experience someplace in a storage bin that inevitably leads to extracting a pattern. There is nothing about reading memory records that leads to making plausible guesses about what happened in the past. These modifications are just tacked on, because without them the system does not resemble human memory. To put it another way, the record-keeping theory so modified lacks theoretical elegance.

In contrast, consider that the central idea of the constructionist theory, that the cognitive systems change the strength of their connections in response to events, does lead naturally to how human memory actually works. Remembering patterns, but not details, is a natural consequence of such a system, because the invariants in experiences strengthen already existing connections. No pattern recognition system has to be added on. Reconstruction happens because no records of past experiences are ever "read" or "reexperienced"; rather, past events must be inferred from the current state of connections. And, as you will see in chapter 6, a constructionist theory of memory more closely reflects what is known about the neurophysiology of learning and remembering.

RECOMMENDED READINGS

Schacter's (1996) *Searching for Memory* is an outstanding book in which the author skillfully weaves theory, experimentation, real-life issues, and contemporary art in an exciting discussion of the current state of memory research. Neisser's historically important (1967) *Cognitive Psychology* includes a chapter on why memory is reconstructive and not reproductive; and his (1981) article in the journal *Cognition* discusses the theoretical implications of John Dean's memory of the Watergate coverup. Raaijmakers and Shiffrin (1992) provide a rigorous discussion of several theories of memory, including theories I label record keeping. Almost any study by Loftus, an enthusiastic advocate of constructionist approaches to memory, is informative and entertaining—try Loftus, Miller, and Burns (1978); Loftus (1979); or Weingardt, Loftus, and Lindsay (1995). Ross (1989) discusses several memory experiments, including the menstruation–mood experiment, in a review article assessing the implications of constructed memory for social attitudes and behaviors. J. Anderson's (1974, 1976) fan effect experiments remain elegant approaches to the study of memory by a talented scientist who happens to favor the record-keeping perspective.

5 *Implicit and Semantic Memory*

In the early 1970s former Beatle George Harrison released a hit song entitled "My Sweet Lord." Unfortunately, the melody was nearly identical to "He's So Fine," released in 1962 by The Chiffons. In a lawsuit brought against him, Harrison admitted that he had heard "He's So Fine," but denied that he had intentionally used its melody when writing "My Sweet Lord." Harrison lost the case, in which the trial judge held that Harrison had unintentionally copied from his unconscious memory the melody of "He's So Fine" while composing "My Sweet Lord" (this case is described in Schacter, 1996).

As George Harrison learned, memories can affect us even when we are unaware of the past events exerting the influence. Such unconscious memory is the subject of this chapter. The Harrison plagiarism case is an example of one kind of unconscious memory. A tragic, and controversial, example of another kind of unconscious memory is that of a woman who finds that she is frightened of her uncle, but has no memory of the abuse she received from him when she was a child. A commonplace kind of influence of the past is knowledge of facts and word meanings. People know, for example, that the Beatles were a famous rock-and-roll band and that uncles are male, but do not usually remember the experiences in which this knowledge was first acquired.

The purpose of this chapter is to discuss how cognitive psychologists have studied the unconscious influence of past experiences on current perceptions, thoughts, and behaviors. In the first section I will discuss some of the experimental paradigms and theoretical interpretations of the experimental evidence that demonstrate an unconscious influence of past events on current information processing. In the second section I will take up the issue of repression—the controversial claim that human memory is designed by nature to resist allowing any memory of deeply disturbing experiences, such as child abuse, from becoming accessible to consciousness. In the third section I will discuss what it means to know the meaning of a concept, such as the concept of an uncle, and how such concepts are processed when a person is asked questions about them.

The prevailing theme of this chapter is the continuation of the constructionist approach to memory introduced in the previous chapter. The constructionist approach will be extended to account for similarities and differences between conscious and unconscious memory.

SECTION 1: IMPLICIT MEMORY

TERMINOLOGY

The study of unconscious influences of the past is not new (e.g., Leibniz, 1916, originally published in 1704; Maine de Biran, 1929, originally published in 1804; Korsakoff, 1889; Bergson, 1911; Freud, 1957, originally published in 1915; see Schacter, 1987). However, most of the research in this area has been done in the last 15 years. Consequently, cognitive psychologists are still grappling with terminology issues. What I referred to as the unconscious influence of some particular past event, such as George Harrison composing a melody without an accompanying conscious awareness that he had already learned the melody from a previously released song, is usually called **implicit memory**. What I described as the influence of knowledge, such as knowing that uncles are male, is usually called **semantic memory**. Semantic memory can be thought of as a form of implicit memory, because most of the time we use knowledge without remembering the occasions on which we acquired that knowledge. Be clear that what is unconscious about semantic memory is the memory for the experiences in which we acquired the knowledge. Of the knowledge itself we are ordinarily aware. When contrasted with implicit memory, the conscious recollection of the past, as in remembering seeing the Beatles perform on the *Ed Sullivan Show* (am I dating myself?), is usually called **explicit memory**. When contrasted with semantic memory, the conscious recollection of the past is usually called **episodic memory**. To simplify, I will use the explicit label only to refer to conscious recollection.

Memory tasks that depend on explicit memory are called **direct memory** tasks; examples are recall and recognition. Performance on recognition and recall tasks ordinarily requires that subjects think about some specific past experience. An example of a direct memory task is a recognition experiment in which subjects are first presented a list of unrelated words, are later presented another list that includes words presented earlier, and then are asked to indicate which words on the second list were also on the first list. Performance on direct memory tasks can sometimes be "contaminated" by implicit memory, however. For example, when asked to recognize which words were on a previously presented list, subjects might use a general sense that a word is easy to perceive in order to deduce that the word must have been on the list.

Tasks that depend on implicit memory are called **indirect memory** tasks. Performance on an indirect memory task does not require that subjects actually remember a particular past experience to perform the task. An example of an indirect memory task is an experiment in which subjects are asked to study a list of unrelated words and are later briefly presented some of the same words, as well as some new words. The subjects must try to read all of the words out loud as quickly as possible. The task is made difficult because the words are presented very briefly. Subjects would not need to remember which words were on the original list in order to read them. The influence of implicit memory would be reflected in faster response times to words that had been on the original list. Another example of an indirect memory task would be if subjects were asked whether ducks are mammals or birds. Again, subjects need not remember any occasion on which they learned the meaning of the word "duck," although those occasions obviously enabled them to know that ducks are birds. Performance on indirect memory tasks can sometimes be "contaminated" by explicit memory. For example, subjects may remember that a particular word was on a previously studied list and use that memory as a basis for identifying a briefly presented word.

DEMONSTRATIONS OF IMPLICIT MEMORY

How is it demonstrated that people are unconsciously influenced by past events? One line of evidence comes from patients who have suffered bilateral damage to the hippocampal regions of the limbic systems of their brains. This evidence is discussed further in chapter 6: The Physiology of Learning and Remembering. Usually these patients have difficulty recollecting experiences subsequent to the damage. They typically report that they have no conscious awareness of the experiences. Yet amnesic patients will continue to be influenced by the experiences they cannot consciously recollect. For example, they can learn new perceptual-motor skills (Corkin, 1968), can learn to solve new conceptual problems such as the Tower of Hanoi problem, which involves stacking rings according to certain rules (Cohen, Eichenbaum, Deacedo, & Corkin, 1985), and are influenced by recently presented words when asked to complete word fragments, such as *def*, with complete words (e.g., *define*) (Graf, Squire, & Mandler, 1984). In fact, amnesics' performance on these indirect memory tasks is nearly as good as that of subjects who are not brain damaged.

Implicit memory can also be demonstrated in ordinary people who have not suffered brain damage. The usual experimental paradigm is to give subjects stimuli to study and later administer to them a direct memory test and an indirect memory test. Evidence for the unconscious influence of the past comes from demonstrating that factors which affect performance on direct memory tasks do not affect performance on indirect memory tasks. Incidentally, the idea that people without brain damage have implicit memory for some piece of information does not necessarily mean that they can never have an explicit memory for that same piece of information. Implicit memory in ordinary people simply means that they have no conscious recollection of the information on some particular occasion in which that information nevertheless influences their thoughts or behavior.

Let me illustrate implicit memory in people without brain damage with an experiment by Tulving, Schacter, and Stark (1982). They first presented subjects a list of words to study. Later, they gave them a recognition test (e.g., "Was *fascism* on the list?") and a task in which they had to complete a fragment of a word with a whole word (e.g., *f__c_ sm*). Some but not all of the words that completed the fragments had been presented on the original list. Note that the recognition test is direct because it requires subjects to think about what words appeared on the list, and the word fragment task is indirect because subjects need not think about the words on the list in order to complete the fragments.

The results showed that subjects were much better at figuring out what word completed a fragment if the word had been on the previously studied list than if it had not. The independence between the indirect and direct tasks was demonstrated in two ways. First, recognition performance was poorer if the recognition test was given 7 days after the list was presented than if the recognition test was given only 1 hour after the list was presented. But the tendency to be more accurate on the word fragment task if the word had been on the list did not decline after 7 days. Even as the subjects' conscious memory for the words eroded over time, their performance on the word fragment task was still influenced by the words. Second, the probability that subjects successfully completed a word fragment was the same for words they thought had been on the list as for words they thought had not been on the list. That is, words from the list influenced performance on the word fragment task even when the subjects did not remember that the words were on the list.

Other studies investigating differential effects of implicit and explicit memory may be found in Jacoby and Witherspoon (1982); Graf and Mandler (1984); Jacoby and Dallas (1981); Smith, MacLeod, Bain, and Hoppe (1989); and Blaxton (1989) (see Schacter 1987, 1990 for reviews). The direct memory tasks used in these sorts of investigations are usually recognition, free recall, or cued recall. The indirect memory tasks usually involve measures of perceptual processing. Besides **word fragment completion** and **perceptual identification**, indirect memory tasks include **word stem completion** (e.g., *def___*), **lexical decision tasks** (e.g., "Is *hot* a word?"), and demonstrations of **priming**, as when the presentation of a word facilitates the lexical decision made about a subsequently presented word (e.g., the presentation of *cold* reduces the time it takes to decide that *hot* is a word). Sometimes indirect memory tasks do not involve perceptual processing. For example, a test of general knowledge may serve as an indirect memory test if the answers make use of previously presented information (e.g., "What is a synonym for *frigid*?").

WHAT UNDERLIES THE EXPLICIT–IMPLICIT MEMORY DISTINCTION— A CONSTRUCTIONIST ACCOUNT

What is the difference between consciously remembering a past event and being affected by a past event *without* consciously remembering it? In the previous chapter on memory I championed a perspective on memory called **constructionism**. The general idea of constructionism is that there is no memory system in which records of the past are stored. Rather, there are changes made to various cognitive systems (e.g., visual perceptual processing, language processing) as a consequence of experiences, and there are reconstruction strategies that use the current states of the various systems to deduce some past event. In this chapter I wish to expand a bit on the constructionist perspective so as to account for the explicit–implicit memory distinction. The account discussed here embodies several related proposals, including those of Weber and Murdock (1989), Masson (1989), MacLeod and Bassili (1989), Graf and Mandler (1984), and Squire (1992).

I will illustrate the account with a fictional example. Suppose an engineer meets a physicist named Laura Light at a wine-tasting party where Dr. Light discusses her opposition to the Big Bang theory. Let's see what happens to the engineer's various cognitive systems (e.g., visual perceptual system, language system) that enable her to have an explicit and implicit memory of the wine-tasting party.

As a consequence of her attending the party, some of the engineer's cognitive systems will become activated and altered so as to accommodate any new information acquired at the party. Accommodation means that the cognitive system changes so as to represent the new information. Her visual system will accommodate the physicist's face and the party setting; her language system will accommodate the physicist's name; her conceptual system dedicated to understanding the meaning of *physicist* will accommodate the new knowledge (for her) that some theoretical physicists are women; her conceptual system processing cosmology will accommodate the idea that the Big Bang theory is not accepted by all practicing physicists; her gustatory system will accommodate the taste of an especially bold red wine; and so on.

The key embellishment on the constructionist perspective I wish to make here is the idea that a conscious recollection of the event requires the creation of connections among the accommodations made by some of these various systems and the activation of such connections when recollecting. So, in order to have an explicit memory of the wine-tasting party, our hypothetical engineer would need to make connections among the various cognitive systems that represent the physicist's face and name, the party setting, the wine tasting, the knowledge that some physicists are women, and so on. The activation of this distributed set of accommodations within these various systems constitutes having a conscious recollection of the wine-tasting party. Note that the connections necessary to have such a conscious memory of the specific event are distributed about the cognitive systems and that such connections serve to represent a context—that is, a time and place for the event.

Often the formation of distributed connections reflects the use of a learning strategy, such as embellishing on the meaning of words; or a reconstruction strategy, such as using one's current beliefs about child rearing to deduce past child-rearing practices. Such strategies help establish and exploit the distributed connections necessary to have an explicit memory. If such strategies are not employed, then the necessary distributed connections may not be made or not exploited. Maybe the engineer would not make use of the strategy of connecting the discussion of the Big Bang with what she already knows about cosmology (especially if she knows little about cosmology) or maybe she would later fail to attempt to search for connections between her knowledge of cosmology and wine-tasting experiences to reconstruct the party event. In either case, she might have no explicit memory for the party. Certainly the engineer would not remember the party if she only had a sense that some physicists are women or that red wines are bolder than white wines.

She may, however, have any of several kinds of implicit memory of the party. The accommodations made by any one of the various cognitive systems activated during the party could serve as the basis for an implicit memory. For example, months after the party she might sample a bold red wine and so activate the gustatory system that had accommodated to the bold taste. Consequently, she may find that she now likes the taste of bold red wines, yet not remember the wine-tasting party at which she acquired her fondness. Similarly, she may know that the Big Bang theory is not uncritically accepted by all physicists or find that "Laura" comes more readily to mind when thinking of names for a female child, but not remember the wine-tasting party where she had the experience that gave rise to such implicit memories.

In a nutshell, then, an implicit memory reflects accommodations made by some particular cognitive system. Explicit memory reflects accommodations made by several cognitive systems as well as the connections that associate these various cognitive systems, thereby establishing a setting or context. In the chapter that follows, on the physiology of learning and memory, I will discuss the physiological underpinnings of the explicit–implicit memory distinction outlined here. There I will explain what happens in the brain when cognitive systems accommodate experiences and when distributed connections among disparate systems are formed.

Factors That Affect Explicit but Not Implicit Memory

Let me now discuss some of the experimental investigations of implicit memory in light of the constructionist account of explicit–implicit memory distinction. Some of these investigations establish that there are factors that affect explicit but not implicit memory.

Consider research conducted by Jacoby, Woloshyn, and Kelley (1989). In one of their experiments, subjects first read a list of people's names, some of which were of moderately famous people (e.g., Minnie Pearl) and some of which were names that were not of famous people but sounded as though they could be famous (e.g., Valerie Marsh). Half of the subjects also had to listen simultaneously to numbers and indicate when those numbers contained a run of three odd numbers. The point of the number task was to siphon some attention away from reading names. Later, all subjects were given a second list of people's names, some of which had been on the previously presented list. Half of the subjects had to decide for each name whether it had been on the first list (a recognition test of explicit memory) while the other half of the subjects had to decide if the name was that of a famous person (a fame-judging test of implicit memory).

There were two important results, illustrated in Figure 5-1. First, on the fame-judging task, there was a greater tendency to judge a nonfamous name as famous if the name had been presented on the first list than if it had not been

Probability of deciding that a nonfamous name was famous

	Old names	New names
Full attention	.25	.13
Divided attention	.25	.14

(A)

Probability of responding that a nonfamous name
was on the first list (recognition)

	Old names	New names
Full attention	.60	.05
Divided attention	.39	.13

(B)

FIGURE 5–1   Results of fame-judging and recognition task. Based on Jacoby, Woloshyn, and Kelley (1989).

presented on the first list. Presumably the familiarity of a first-list nonfamous name led subjects to deduce that the name must be famous. So if you want your Warholian 15 minutes of fame, make sure that people read your name in the context of a list of semi-celebrities.

The other main result was that the subjects required to perform the additional task of listening to numbers while reading the first list of names did not do as well on the subsequent recognition test as subjects who only had to read the names. When the subjects' attention was divided between listening to numbers and reading names, explicit memory for the names suffered. However, dividing subjects' attention had no effect on the fame-judging results. The subjects who had to listen to the digits while reading the names were just as likely to judge the nonfamous names as famous as were subjects who did not have to listen to digits. A generalization is that dividing people's attention during an event undermines explicit but not implicit memory of that event.

How might the constructionist account of the explicit–implicit memory distinction explain the results of Jacoby et al. (1989)? A simple explanation is that dividing subjects' attention between reading names and listening to digits makes it difficult for those subjects to associate the names with other aspects of the experimental event, such as the visual appearance of the experimental laboratory. Consequently, subjects are less likely to create connections between the language system that processes the names and other cognitive systems that might process the experimental setting. Such subjects will do worse on a direct memory test than will subjects whose attention was not divided. Still, even when attention is divided, subjects will activate the language system that will accommodate the new names. Later, the language system will again be activated when making the fame-judgment. The accommodations the language system made to first-list names will mean that subjects will experience those names as familiar, and hence famous. And that sense of familiarity will be about as great for the subjects whose attention was divided as for subjects whose attention was undivided. So performance on the indirect test of memory will be unaffected by the attention-dividing task.

There are other factors that affect explicit memory much more than implicit memory. For example, elderly people tend to perform worse than younger people on direct memory tests but as well as younger people on indirect memory tests (Mitchell, 1989; Howard, Fry, & Brune, 1991; Light & LaVoie, 1993; see Graf, 1990). For instance, Isingrini, Vazou, and Leroy (1995) required subjects to learn a list of words (e.g., *blimp*) that were members of taxonomic categories (e.g., vehicles). Later, subjects were given the category name and were instructed to provide a list of examples. Evidence for implicit memory was that the subjects were more likely to include an example if it had appeared earlier on the list. The tendency to include previously studied examples was as great among elderly subjects (whose age was over 75 years) as among younger adults (in the 20-to-35-year age range). The experiment also required subjects to recall the words from the list given the category name as a cue. The younger subjects recalled almost twice as many words from the list as did the elderly subjects. A possible explanation for why explicit but not implicit memory declines with age is that elderly people are not as motivated to use learning and reconstruction strategies that might form or exploit the distributed connections necessary for good explicit memory.

Another factor that differentially affects explicit and implicit memory has to do with processing for meaning. Elaborating on the meaning of verbal information tends to improve the recall and recognition of the verbal information more than it enhances performance on indirect memory tests, at least in most studies (see Richardson-Klavehn & Bjork, 1988, or Brown & Mitchell, 1994). For instance, Schacter and Graf (1986) presented subjects a list of words and required some subjects to elaborate the words into sentences. Those subjects recalled more of the words than did subjects who did not elaborate the words into sentences. However, the two groups of subjects did not differ very much in their performance on a perceptual identification task based on the words. The perceptual identification task required identifying words from brief presentations of the words. In general, perceptual identification was better for words that had been previously studied. It did not matter, however, whether the previously studied words had been elaborated into sentences. So elaboration improved performance on the direct memory task but not on the indirect task. Presumably, elaboration on meaning helps connect perceptual and conceptual systems, thereby creating more of the distributed connections serving explicit memory.

Hamann (1996) found similar results in blind subjects who studied Braille words. The subjects studied one list of Braille words under a semantic study condition in which they thought about how much they liked each word. They studied the other list of Braille words under a physical study condition in which they examined whether the same vowels were presented in successive words. Later, subjects were given Braille word stems and for some stems had to recall which word, if any, had been completed with that stem on the previously studied list (direct recall task) or had to provide the first English word that came to mind (indirect word-stem completion task). Subjects recalled more words if they had studied the words under the semantic condition than under the physical condition. But the tendency to complete a word stem with a word from the previously studied list was the same regardless of whether the words had been studied under the semantic or physical condition.

Factors Undermining Implicit but Not Explicit Memory

Are there any factors that affect implicit memory more than explicit memory? Yes. Implicit memory is weakened more than explicit memory when the memory test is given in a different stimulus modality (e.g., visual) than the modality of the originally presented information.

Consider a study by Craik, Moscovitch, and McDowd (1994). Subjects first studied words that were presented either visually or auditorially. Later, subjects were given a direct and indirect memory task, both in a visual mode. The direct task was a recognition test in which subjects were visually presented a second list of words, some of which were from the first list. Subjects had to say whether any given word was or was not on the first list. Note that for some of the words on the recognition test, the modality had switched from auditory in the study phase to visual in the test phase. For other words, the modality remained visual in both the study and test phases of the experiment. Craik et al. (1994) used several different kinds of indirect tests; one was word-fragment completion (e.g., _z_n_). Subjects were better at completing the fragments if they had studied the correct word (e.g., *ozone*) on the first list than if they had not. Again note that for some of the words used to complete the fragments, the modality had switched from auditory to visual while for other words used in the word fragment test the modality was visual in both phases of the experiment.

The main finding was that changing the modality from auditory during the study phase to visual in the test phase undermined performance on the indirect memory test (e.g., the word fragment completion) compared with the case where the modality had been visual in both the study and test phases. In one experiment, subjects successfully completed a visually presented word fragment with a word from the first list 52% of the time when the study list was also visually presented, but only 44% of the time when the study list was auditorially presented. Changing modality had no effect on recognition performance, however. In one experiment, subjects correctly recognized a visually presented word 70% of the time regardless of whether the word had been originally presented visually or auditorially. In a nutshell, changing stimulus modality undermined implicit but not explicit memory. Other research is also consistent with the conclusion that stimulus modality shifts undermine implicit memory more than explicit memory (e.g., Schacter & Graf, 1989; see MacLeod & Bassili, 1989).

And how might the constructionist account of the implicit-explicit memory distinction explain the negative impact of changing stimulus modality on implicit memory? The idea is that implicit memory reflects the use of a cognitive system that has accommodated some new information. If subjects study visually presented words, a visual word perception system would accommodate the words. If subjects study auditorially presented words, an auditory word perception system accommodates the words. The word fragment task relies heavily on the word perception system. When the modality shifts from auditory to visual, then the subjects would activate the wrong word perception system and so not do as well on the word fragment completion task.

Explicit memory, on the other hand, relies on distributed connections among several systems; some of these connections serve to establish a setting for the event. For instance, connections would be formed among the word perceptual system, the word meaning system, the experimental setting perceptual system, and so on. Even when the modality of word presentation shifts from auditory to visual, most of these connections would remain in place when the subject tries to remember which words were on the list. Consequently, explicit memory for the word list does not suffer very much from the modality shift.

SECTION 2: REPRESSION AND MEMORY FOR DISTURBING EXPERIENCES

For many people, the kind of implicit memory that is most intriguing, and disturbing, is that which seems to accompany profoundly distressing experiences, such as being sexually abused. Clinical psychologists and psychiatrists have often made the claim that people tend to have amnesia for such distressing experiences. Yet the experiences continue to exert an effect on a person's feelings and behavior, as when, for example, a woman abused as a young girl by her uncle has trouble maintaining healthy relationships with men. Historically, most of the research on the impact of disturbing experiences on memory has been used to evaluate Freud's theory of repression.

REPRESSION

Freud (1957, originally published in 1915) claimed that there is a tendency for people to have amnesia for disturbing events, and that the cause of the amnesia is **repression**. The degree and nature of the amnesia is different from ordinary forgetting. Freud described repression as a defense mechanism that tends to prevent the conscious recollection of experiences associated with a great deal of anxiety. A person does not simply avoid thinking about the anxiety-provoking experiences, but is unable to recollect the experience even under conditions when other experiences would be remembered. Repression may also involve an avoidance of thinking about disturbing ideas, impulses, and fantasies (Bowers & Farvolden, 1996). Repression supposedly evolved in species capable of self-reflection, in order to protect conscious mechanisms from becoming incapacitated by depression and anxiety. Freud claimed that the repressor is unaware that he or she is preventing the retrieval of the experience, but that a person's feelings and behavior could still be influenced by the experience. Some repressed experiences supposedly manifest themselves in disturbing dreams and fantasies, in anxiety-laden thoughts, and in dysfunctional behaviors, although repression may be important in maintaining a healthy optimism. Freud emphasized that the kind of experience likely to be repressed is one in which there is a conflict between motives, such as between an unconscious wish and a moral injunction. If the anxiety associated with a repressed experience is reduced, Freud claimed, the memory may then enter consciousness and, eventually, the disturbing thoughts and neuroses may diminish (Freud, 1915/1957; Brenner, 1957; Geisler, 1986). The elimination of the amnesia is sometimes called the **lifting of repression**.

Clinical and Forensic Evidence for Repression

Most of the evidence for repression comes from numerous clinical reports of clients who present some emotional symptoms, such as fear of mature relationships with the opposite gender, and in the course of therapy start to remember a disturbing event for which they previously had amnesia. The lifting of amnesia is sometimes associated with, though not necessarily the cause of, improvement the emotional problem. Examples of relevant clinical cases may be found in Weiner (1988); Stern (1988); Fagerstrom (1980); Herman and Schatzow (1987); Rieker and Carmen (1986); and Williams (1987). Typical is Rieker and Carmen (1986), who described a woman who entered psychotherapy because of sexual problems and in therapy recovered previously forgotten memories of being sexually abused by her father as a child. Williams (1987) described a case of a male patient who entered psychotherapy for depression and insomnia and during therapy recovered a memory of being molested by a servant.

A belief in repression is held not only by many psychotherapists, especially psychoanalysts (Erdelyi & Goldberg, 1979), but by a number of legal scholars (e.g., Lamm, 1991; see Loftus, 1993). In a landmark case (described in Loftus, 1993), George Franklin's daughter Eileen Franklin-Lipsker, as an adult in her 20s, began to recover memories of her father murdering an 8-year-old girl, Susan Kay Nason. The murder had occurred some 20 years earlier on September 22, 1969, in the Bay area of California. Eileen claimed that her first memory of the incident occurred when her own daughter asked her a question like "Isn't that right, mommy?" at which time Eileen suddenly recalled Susie Nason and the look of betrayal in her eyes. As more memory fragments returned, Eileen developed a detailed memory of her father sexually abusing and murdering Susie in the back of a van. The memory included a number of accurately recollected details, such as a damaged silver ring on Susie's finger. On November 30, 1990, a jury, impressed by Eileen's testimony, found Franklin guilty of the murder. It was apparently the first time an American citizen had been tried and convicted of murder based on a memory that had been repressed.

Despite the beliefs of many psychotherapists and their patients, it is not clear that the clinical and legal cases constitute convincing evidence for repression (Loftus & Ketcham, 1994). First of all, in most cases there is no evidence, aside from the memory, that the supposedly repressed event ever occurred (the Franklin murder case is an exception). Perhaps the event never really happened. The clinical setting and the theoretical orientation of the clinician may even subtly bias memory in such a way that the client occasionally reconstructs a disturbing event that never occurred—a point on which I will elaborate later. Second, it is generally never proven that the client was really unable to remember the event during the time when it was supposedly repressed. Perhaps the client has recollected the experience before (but now does not remember having done so) or perhaps the occasion for remembering the experience has not presented itself for a very long time. Third, it is not usually proven that the client has more difficulty remembering the anxiety-provoking event than any other event. Recollections of the vast majority of past events, especially events from decades earlier in a person's life, are mistake-ridden and incomplete. Most past events cannot be recollected at all (see chapter 4: Memory). Perhaps, then, experiences associated with anxiety are remembered no better or worse than any other experience. For example, one study found that of 1,500 people who had been discharged from a hospital within the previous year, about one fourth did not remember the hospitalization (see Loftus, 1993). The experience of being hospitalized is no doubt distressing, but is not likely to be repressed, since it rarely involves a moral conflict. Fourth, it is difficult to prove that a supposedly repressed event is the cause of some current problem or neurosis, like difficulty maintaining healthy adult relationships. Perhaps the cause of the current problem has nothing to do with the disturbing event.

Assessing the Clinical and Forensic Evidence for Repression

Many people who claim to be victims of childhood sexual abuse also claim to have had long-term amnesia for the abuse (see Loftus, 1993). Recently there has been renewed interest in a controversy over whether such claims reflect repression of the abuse or the reconstruction of a false memory of an abusive experience (see Loftus & Ketcham, 1994). Be clear that the issue here is not whether some children are abused; we know that a tragically large number of children are abused. According to one report there are about 150,000 cases of child sexual abuse documented each year in the United States (Trickett & Putnam, 1993), although the magnitude of the problem is debated (see Loftus, 1993). The issue is whether a memory of abuse is likely to be accurate in the case where the person claims that a long-term amnesia for the abuse has been lifted.

An important clinical study done by Herman and Schatzow (1987) addresses the issue of accuracy of supposedly repressed memories of abuse. They worked with a group of 53 women who claimed to have been sexually abused. Thirty-three of these women initially displayed some degree of amnesia for the abuse. The women were more likely to have amnesia for the abuse if it occurred before adolescence than if it occurred during or after adolescence. Consistent with repression, amnesia was more likely when the abuse was extremely violent than when it was only mildly violent. Just prior to or during the course of therapy these 33 women began to remember the abusive experiences. Almost three quarters of the women claimed to have obtained corroborating evidence of the abuse from other sources, thereby validating their memories. Most of the women who did not find corroborating evidence of abuse in fact made no effort to corroborate their memories.

Unfortunately, though, Herman and Schatzow's published paper only discussed four cases of corroboration, and in only two of these did the women have severe amnesia for the abuse. Of these two, only one reported corroborating evidence (a dead brother's diary that described the brother's abuse of the client). And even in this case, as well as in the others in which there were claims of corroboration, there was no independent verification that the alleged victims actually found the corroborating evidence. Apparently, the psychotherapists simply took the women's word for it that the corroborating evidence was obtained (Wakefield & Underwager, 1992). Furthermore, and assuming that the supposedly repressed abuse really happened in at least some cases, there was no way of verifying that these women were really unable to remember the abuse even on occasions when they would be expected to recall it, and that their memory of the abusive experience was poorer than their memory for other childhood experiences.

What about the Franklin case, in which Franklin's daughter Eileen recovered a memory of her father murdering Susie Nason 20 years earlier? Eileen accurately recollected a number of details about the crime, thereby making her previously repressed memory seem accurate. Still, media reports from the time period of the murder contained the same details, so perhaps Eileen was remembering details that she had read and not directly observed. Also, Eileen's recovered memory of the murder changed over time. For example, she first told the police that she remembered that the van trip began in the late morning or early afternoon. Later on, however, and after presumably being reminded that Susie was not reported missing until after school let out, Eileen claimed to remember that the van trip took place in the late afternoon. At least some portions of her memory of the murder, then, were not accurate. Eileen also told prosecutors that she remembered her father raping and murdering an 18-year-old teenager named Veronica Cascio in 1976. Yet George Franklin was at a union meeting at the time of the Cascio murder; furthermore, DNA tests were inconsistent with Franklin's involvment in the rape. In 1995 a higher court overturned Franklin's conviction in the Susie Nason case. In July of 1996 George Franklin was released from prison and is unlikely to be tried again.

False Memories of Abuse?

Is it likely that a person would unintentionally fabricate an abusive experience? You may remember from the last chapter that people can sometimes be quite confident of the accuracy of false memories. Does that tendency generalize to even abusive experience?

Spanos, Menary, Gabora, DuBreuil, and Dewhirst (1991) demonstrated fabrications of abuse in a remarkable set of experiments investigating memory for past-life experiences. In the experiments, hypnotized subjects were asked to regress to a previous life and to report on experiences from that life. Most of the subjects really believed that they were able to life regress, and most were able to describe an experience from their previous life. The researchers first demonstrated that their subjects were not in fact regressing to past lives. The subjects were not able to accurately report historical information that they should have known had they really lived the past life. For example, the subjects were unable to identify the leader of their country and were unable to determine whether their country was at war at the time of the life regression experience. In a subsequent experiment, half of the subjects were led to believe that child abuse was much more common in times past than it is today. When these subjects were hypnotically induced to life regress, they reported many more memories of abuse in their previous lives than did the control group that was life regressed without being provided the additional information about abuse. Clearly, the subjects who were provided the bogus information about the history of child abuse were using that information to fabricate abuse in imagined past lives.

In 1988 Paul Ingram, of Olympia, Washington, was arrested for child abuse, based on the accusations of two of his adult daughters, who claimed that Ingram began raping them as young children. The children also accused their father, mother, and several other people of participating in a Satan-worshiping cult that involved ritual child abuse and the ritual murder of 25 babies. The daughters maintained that they had been repressing the abuse. Ingram initially denied the accusations but after a time began to confess to the crimes. He maintained that he had been repressing the perpetration of the crimes. A riveting and disturbing account of the Ingram case can be found in Wright (1994). Paul Ingram was the first, and as far as I know, the only person ever to have admitted to being a member of a satanic cult that practices child abuse. A number of people have claimed to have recovered memories of being victimized by satanic cults, but there is no evidence at all (apart from these supposedly recovered memories) for a covert, highly organized, transgenerational satanic cult involved in bizarre and heinous ritualistic abuse and murder of children. At least no evidence until Ingram confessed.

Typically, Ingram would at first not remember any specific allegation, but after making a concerted effort, would come up with a detailed recollection. Richard Ofshe, a social psychologist hired by the prosecution to interview Ingram, decided to test the credibility of Ingram's "confessions." Ofshe made up and described to Ingram a story in which Ingram's children accused him of forcing them to have sex in front of him. Within several hours, Ingram developed a vivid memory for the event, which he described in graphic detail in a three-page "confession." Yet this particular abusive event never happened; it was invented by Ofshe. Ingram went on to claim that this "memory" was as real to him as the other memories surrounding the abuse. Because he confessed to the crimes, Ingram was sent to prison. Since being sent to prison, Ingram has recanted his confession and appealed his sentence. Despite the demonstration that Ingram was susceptible to false memories and that he had been intensely pressured by the police and a minister to recognize that he was "in denial," and despite a complete lack of physical evidence for the crimes for which Ingram was accused, his appeal has so far been denied. I mention this tragic case here to demonstrate that an apparently normal person can concoct a false memory of a very disturbing experience—in this case the memory of being an abuser of one's own children.

There is other evidence that distressing experiences can be unintentionally fabricated. Loftus and Coan (in Loftus, 1993) solicited the help of family members of subjects to induce in those subjects false memories of being lost as a child. For example, the brother of one subject convinced his brother, Chris, that Chris had been lost in a shopping mall when he was years 5 old. Chris was asked by the experimenters to try to remember that event. After some effort, Chris recalled in great detail the experience of being lost in the mall, and claimed that his memory was reasonably clear and vivid. Yet the event never happened. Abhold (in Loftus, 1993) interviewed people who had attended a high school football game in which a player went into cardiac arrest (the football player was subsequently revived). Six years later the subjects were interviewed. More than one fourth of the subjects were persuaded that they had seen blood on the player's jersey, after receiving a false suggestion from the experimenter to that effect. Pynoos and Nader (1989) studied elementary school children who survived a sniper attack on their school that killed one child and injured 13 others. In recalling the event, children who had not been at school at the time of the attack tended to remember themselves as being closer to the school than was, in fact, the case. For example, one boy, who was away on vacation, inaccurately recalled that he had been on his way to school during the attack and had heard the shots.

None of the evidence I just discussed proves that claims of previously repressed abuse are inevitably false. But the evidence does suggest that people are sometimes going to recollect abusive experiences that never happened, and so report the "memories" as a lifting of repression. One situation where false memories of abuse may tend to surface is the psychotherapeutic experience (Ganaway, 1989). In psychotherapy some patients undergo an extensive analysis of their emotional problems and family history in a context in which stories of child sexual abuse abound and where repression is widely accepted as valid, and with therapists who believe that anybody who often feels powerless and ashamed was probably abused (Bass & Davis, 1988). Furthermore, some therapists actively encourage their clients to interpret various clinical symptoms (e.g., a troubling dream) as evidence of repressed childhood abuse (e.g., Olio, 1989; see Ganaway, 1989). Support groups for people who survived incest may promote the development of false memories of abuse in group members who initially have no memory for abuse (see Nathan, 1992; Ellis, 1992). The result is that many people are being falsely accused of sexual abuse, and even going to prison, based only on allegations of people who claim to have previously repressed the abuse. Again, this is not to say that the sexual abuse of children is exceedingly rare; tragically, it is more prevalent than some people realize. Nor does the likelihood that some allegations of abuse reflect false memories mean that all allegations of abuse reflect false memories.

EXPERIMENTAL INVESTIGATIONS OF REPRESSION

There are certainly many people who sincerely claim to have repressed and then recovered memories of childhood abuse and other morally troubling experiences. As I have discussed, however, these cases cannot be said to constitute convincing evidence for repression. A convincing case that people have more difficulty remembering distressing experiences than remembering neutral experiences would require a carefully controlled experiment. Obviously, though, an experimenter cannot deliberately involve subjects in disturbing experiences to see whether those subjects repress the experiences. Cognitive psychologists have tried to develop a number of experimental paradigms to simulate situations in which repression is expected, without subjecting people to emotional or physical harm.

Experiments Purporting to Demonstrate Repression

One example is a paradigm in which two groups of subjects are asked to remember the same set of data, but one group learns to associate a mild form of anxiety with the data (see Holmes, 1974, for a review). Typical of the paradigm is Zeller (1950), who asked subjects to learn a list of pairs of nonsense words (e.g., DAX–JER). Subjects then engaged in a psychomotor task for which half the subjects were told that they failed (regardless of their performance) while the other half were told that they performed successfully. The assumption was that the embarrassment over failure would generalize to the whole experiment, so subjects in the "failure" group would be prone to repress their experience. As predicted by the repression hypothesis, the "failure" subjects recalled fewer nonsense words when tested a week later than did the "success" subjects.

Both groups of subjects then engaged in the psychomotor task a second time, and now all subjects were told they were successful (regardless of their actual performance). When asked to recall the nonsense syllables a second time, the recall performance of the original "failure" group improved so as to equal that of the original "success" group. Presumably the "failure" subjects now had less anxiety about their performance, so their repression lifted and the memory of the syllables entered conscious awareness.

The results of the Zeller (1950) experiment, and of others like it (Merrill, 1954; Flavell, 1955; Penn, 1964), would seem to be consistent with the repression hypothesis. The experimenters used anxiety that mildly threatened the subjects, verified the accuracy of the subjects' memory, provided an occasion for subjects to recollect the relevant information, and found that when information is associated with anxiety it is less memorable than when the same information is not associated with anxiety. Furthermore, the experimenters showed that memory for the information associated with anxiety improves when the anxiety is reduced at the time the information is retrieved.

Still, there are problems with this sort of experimental paradigm. First, the paradigm does not provide any demonstration of an implicit memory for the failure. Second, and perhaps more critically, there are alternative interpretations of the results of these experiments (Holmes, 1990). It may be that the embarrassment some subjects experience in these experiments is all too memorable— so memorable, in fact, that it draws the subjects' attention away from the processing activities needed to recall the information. That is, the results may be due to competition between thinking about embarrassment and trying to recollect the information, rather than due to repression (Holmes, 1974). Note that the **competition hypothesis** is exactly the opposite of the repression hypothesis.

Consistent with the competition hypothesis, but inconsistent with repression, is research that shows that subjects in the "negative experience" condition of repression experiments claim to think more about the experiment than subjects in the "positive experience" condition (D'Zurilla, 1965). Also supporting the competition hypothesis is an experiment by Holmes (1972), who asked subjects to think of the first word that came to mind for each of several stimulus words. Subjects were told that their responses indicated either a pathological personality, an unusually well-balanced and talented personality, or a normal personality. The personality feedback was, of course, dependent on the group to which subjects were randomly assigned, and not on subjects' actual responses to the words. Later, all subjects had to recall the stimulus words. Consistent with the competition hypothesis but not with repression, the subjects who were told that their responses were abnormal and the subjects who were told that their responses were unusually positive both recalled fewer words than the subjects given neutral feedback. Presumably, both the very positive and very negative feedback produced a strong emotion that interfered with the subjects' attempts to recall the words. The repression hypothesis would predict poorer recall only in the negative feedback condition. When the subjects were told that the feedback was bogus, subjects in both the negative and positive feedback condition then recalled as many words as did the control group.

A recent suggestion is that repression takes the form of difficulty in remembering the source of the memory (Kunzendorf & Morgan, 1994). People abused as children, for example, might remember something about abuse, but not be sure if the abuse was only imagined, happened to someone else, or really happened to them.

Kunzendorf and Morgan (1994) tested the **source amnesia hypothesis** of repression in a three-part experiment in which subjects had to solve difficult anagrams. Prior to the first part some subjects were told that failure on the task meant that the subjects were not very intelligent. Presumably for those subjects, failure was made stressful. In the first part of the experiment the subjects worked on 12 anagrams. For each anagram a clue word related to the anagram was projected on a screen in front of the subjects (e.g., a clue for the anagram HTLEAENP might be "animal"). In the second part, the subjects again worked on anagrams but the clue words were presented auditorially, and the subjects were instructed to imagine that the clues appeared on the screen. In the third part, the subjects were given clue words that had been visually displayed, clue words that had been auditorially presented, and new words. Subjects had to indicate for each word whether they saw the word on the screen, only imagined seeing the word of the screen, or were not presented the word as a clue at all.

The main result was that, consistent with source amnesia, the subjects for whom failure was made stressful were more likely to misremember the visually presented clues as only imagined clues. However, the experimental paradigm did not test to see if reducing the stress resulted in a lifting of repression (i.e., in an improved memory for source).

Another recent suggestion is that a tendency to repress is actually a personality trait that varies quite a bit among people (Weinberger, Schwartz, & Davidson, 1979; Davis, 1987). It may be that only some people are prone to repress disturbing experiences. Myers and Brewin (1995; see also Holtgraves & Hall, 1995, for a similar experiment) used paper-and-pencil tests to distinguish repressors from nonrepressors. Both groups were asked to recall a fictional story containing positive and negative information about mothers and fathers. An example of positive information from the story was "my father would buy the toys and games I asked for" and an example of negative information was "my father always said I was stupid doing this." The repressors were less likely to recall the negative material than were the nonrepressors. There was no difference between repressors and nonrepressors in their recall of the positive material. Again, though, the experiment lacked a condition in which repression was lifted; furthermore, the validity of paper-and-pencil tests supposedly identifying repressors is disputed (Holmes, 1990).

Repression and Implicit Memory

An important claim of the repression hypothesis is that the repressed experience continues to influence a person's thoughts, feelings, and behaviors, even though the distressing experience cannot be consciously remembered. Indeed, the reason I include repression in this chapter is that it supposedly manifests itself more often as an implicit memory. Clinical evidence suggests that adolescent and adult victims of child abuse, whether they repress the abuse or not, often display lowered self-esteem, feelings of not being able to control events, attention problems, inappropriate sexual behavior, and aggressiveness, among other problems (Trickett & Putnam, 1993). However, it is not always clear if the problems are caused by the abuse or by other factors (e.g., a bad marriage). For that matter, it is not clear in any particular case whether a person claiming a recovered memory of abuse is unintentionally fabricating the abuse, in order, perhaps, to account for the psychological problems. Still, the experimental evidence on implicit memory discussed in the previous section makes it clear that experiences of which one has no conscious awareness do influence thoughts, feelings, and behaviors. So the implicit memory claim of the repression hypothesis can be said to have some experimental support.

More direct support for an implicit memory associated with distressing information comes from Blum and Barbour (1979). They first required subjects to practice solving anagrams (e.g., CLKI) to a set of target words such as LICK. Later, subjects had to learn associations between the target words and pictures known as "Blacky" pictures. Blacky pictures depict a young dog named Blacky engaging in various activities, some of which symbolically suggest morally troubling themes like masturbation or incest. Subjects might associate the word LICK with a picture of Blacky licking himself (herself). Some subjects were told to remember the association because Blacky was licking his (her) sexual organs, while other subjects were told to remember the association because Blacky was a mature puppy who has finally learned how to take care of fleas. In one case, then, the word LICK suggested a morally threatening theme but in the other case LICK suggested a positive theme. Finally, subjects were required to once again solve anagrams for words, some of which were made from the target words associated with the Blacky pictures. Performance on the anagram test presumably reflected the unconscious influence of the Blacky pictures on the words used to make the anagrams.

Consistent with repression, subjects who associated a target word with a troubling theme took longer to solve the anagram after learning the association than before learning the association, and took longer than subjects who associated the same target word with a positive theme. For example, subjects who made the embarrassing association between LICK and a Blacky picture took longer to solve the anagram (CLKI). Because subjects were faster on anagrams that had positive associations, the competition hypothesis discussed earlier cannot explain the results. Furthermore, when all subjects were queried about what they thought was the purpose of the experiment, only one subject mentioned repression.

It should be noted, though, that this pattern of results applied to only about two thirds of the subjects who participated in the experiment. The subjects to whom these results applied were generally slower to solve anagrams, including filler anagrams that were not associated with Blacky pictures. The authors speculated that the subjects may have been slow because they were engaged in the kind of processing necessary to defend against anxiety associated with some of the pictures. It should also be noted that this experiment did not assess whether subjects demonstrated a difficulty in explicitly remembering words associated with embarrassing themes.

Experimental Evidence That Contradicts Repression

There is experimental evidence that directly contradicts the repression hypothesis. Some research has found that positive material is not remembered better than disturbing material (Menzies, 1936; Thompson, 1985). Other research suggests that people identified as repressors by paper-and-pencil tests supposedly measuring the tendency to repress may be induced to remember dismal memories even more accurately than nonrepressors. House (1975) presented to subjects a list of statements, some of which were disturbing (e.g., "Frank slit a neighbor girl's throat with a butcher knife"). The results were that male repressors who were told to pay close attention to the threatening statements actually recalled more disturbing statements than did the nonrepressors. The experiment suggests that at least male repressors may be willing to report morally threatening experiences if it is clear to them that it is socially desirable to do so.

Also in apparent contradiction to the repression hypothesis are findings from research on eyewitness memory for emotionally disturbing accidents and crimes. Most of the research on eyewitness memory has focused on explicit memory. Although the results of this research are not always consistent, the typical finding is that eyewitnesses to violent events tend to have very good memory for the details specifically related to the violence, but poor memory for the details that are peripheral to the violence (reviewed by Christianson, 1992). An eyewitness to a murder committed by one of two robbers, for example, may have better than average memory for the weapon used by the robber who committed the murder but poorer than average memory for the weapon carried by the other robber.

To illustrate, Christianson and Loftus (1991) presented subjects a series of slides in which the emotionally disturbing quality of one critical slide was varied. In the critical slide, some subjects saw a woman riding a bicycle, while other subjects saw the same woman lying injured on the street near the bicycle. In both versions a car was seen in the background. Subjects who saw the injured woman remembered more details about the woman (such as the color of her coat) but fewer details about the car than did subjects who saw the neutral version of the slide. In another study, Christianson and Hubinette (1993) interviewed victims of and eyewitnesses to real armed robberies. Both the victims and the eyewitnesses remembered well the details of the actual robbery (e.g., type of clothing of the robber) but had more trouble remembering peripheral details (e.g., the characteristics of the other people who witnessed the crime). In general, and again contrary to the repression hypothesis, the victims had better memory of the robbery than the eyewitnesses (see also Yuille & Cutshall, 1986).

Conclusions About Repression

I have subjected the repression hypothesis to rather strict standards, for two reasons. First, the hypothesis makes a startling claim: namely, that experiences that are distinctive and often recurring—experiences that the bulk of the literature on memory suggests ought to be well remembered—tend to be forgotten, if those experiences are disturbing or morally threatening. But the repressed experience, according to this hypothesis, still exerts an unconscious, or implicit, effect on people's thoughts, feelings, and behaviors. The experiences are not necessarily forgotten forever; the repression may lift and the memory for the disturbing events may return. Second, there are important legal implications of repression. At least 19 states, beginning with the state of Washington in 1989, have suspended statutes of limitations in cases where victims claim repression. Many jurors seem to accept uncritically the idea that people routinely repress distressing experiences.

It is extremely important, then, to evaluate carefully the evidence for repression. Unfortunately, there does not seem to be unequivocal evidence for repression. Clinical observations are suspect, mainly because the clinical setting is one in which clinicians are trained to be accepting of their clients. Consequently, the accuracy of supposedly repressed experiences is almost never verified. The one exception (Herman & Schatzow, 1987) failed to provide independent evidence of the corroborations obtained by some of the sexually abused patients. Furthermore, clinical studies have never demonstrated that clients who claim to have repressed an event were in fact any less likely to recollect that event than to recollect any other event from their past. After all, forgetting of the past is the rule.

The experimental evidence is also problematic. Many studies that would seem to be consistent with repression (e.g., Zeller, 1950) can be explained by the competition hypothesis (Holmes, 1990). Some experiments do provide unequivocal evidence that, under some circumstances, people can unintentionally fabricate a disturbing experience that in fact never happened. This evidence strongly suggests that juries should not uncritically accept eyewitness testimony of recovered memories of heinous crimes, such as abuse, especially when the testimony is based on memories recovered in psychotherapeutic settings conducted by therapists who are prone to interpret any of a wide range of problems as evidence of childhood sexual abuse. Finally, a number of studies, notably those on eyewitness memory, directly contradict repression. People seem to be able to remember quite accurately the details of violent crimes to which they were witness or of which they were victims (Christianson, 1992).

I would not wish to conclude this section by saying that repression does not exist. Proponents of repression may legitimately point out that the lack of independent verification of most clinical cases does not mean that previously repressed memories are therefore false. And because some people may unintentionally fabricate memories of sexual abuse does not mean that all people claiming to have recovered such memories are fabricating them.

The experimental literature may not be compelling because it is exceedingly difficult to study in a laboratory the kinds of experiences people are likely to repress over the periods of time in which repression is likely to emerge. The eyewitness research may not be so damaging to the repression hypothesis if one assumes that repression is likely only when people are unable to avoid the distressing circumstances. People can (or at least perceive that they can) take action to minimize being a victim of a violent crime, but children may not be able to avoid abuse. Consistent with this possibility are the results of Gershuny and Burrows (1990). They presented college students either a story about a violent automobile accident or a story about death from cancer and later asked them questions about the story. The subjects recalled fewer negative details from the story about the (unavoidable) terminal illness than from the story about the (avoidable) automobile accident. Still, though, even this study cannot be said to prove repression, given the absence of a demonstration that the amnesia for the details of the terminal illness story could be lifted.

Let me conclude this section on a hypothetical note. Suppose unequivocal evidence for repression is forthcoming. Would such evidence undermine the constructionist theory of memory I have been advocating in this textbook? The repression hypothesis would seem to imply that records of past dismal experiences lie dormant in memory, only to be awakened should the anxiety associated with the experience be lifted. However, I think that repression could be explained by a constructionist approach to memory. Difficulty in recollecting an abusive experience with an uncle, for example, may reflect a reconstruction strategy based on the premise that family members are trustworthy. From such a premise it would be difficult to infer that an uncle was abusive. Difficulty in remembering an abusive experience might also reflect a reconstruction strategy in which a person begins to remember a disturbing event but then deliberately short-circuits the recollection. As such short-circuiting becomes habitual, there will remain no conscious memory for the event (Bowers & Farvolden, 1996). Should the abuse victim acquire new information relevant to the abuse (such as that abused people often have disturbing dreams and very low self-esteem), then that new information may serve as a basis for a reconstruction strategy that permits the abuse to be accurately recollected. A point in favor of the constructionist approach is that the same reconstruction strategies that would enable the memory for the abuse to be lifted would also underlie the reconstruction of a false memory for abuse. In fact, according to the constructionist approach and to a lot of experimental evidence, it would be difficult for a person to distinguish reliably between accurately recollected and fabricated memories of abuse.

SECTION 3: SEMANTIC MEMORY

Another way the past exerts an unconscious influence on the present goes by the name of **semantic memory**. Semantic memory refers to a person's world knowledge, and includes such things as the meaning of words (e.g., *uncle* means the brother of one's father or mother), knowledge about human motives (e.g., most people seek approval from others), knowledge about physical processes (e.g., objects fall towards the surface of the earth), and so on. We use this knowledge all the time as we comprehend experiences or reflect back on past experiences. As in the case of other kinds of implicit memory, we ordinarily do not think about the exact moments in our past when we acquired this knowledge, yet the knowledge affects how we currently think and act. In most cases we are unable to remember the occasions on which we acquired semantic information.

Semantic memory, like other forms of implicit memory, may be contrasted with explicit memory. Semantic memory refers to knowledge that is ordinarily acquired over an extended period of time and is shared by other people, while explicit memory refers to events that happen at particular times and places, usually to only one person. For example, my knowledge that three strikes constitutes an out in baseball is part of my semantic memory, while my recollection of getting five hits in a championship Little League baseball game is part of my explicit memory.

Just as cognitive psychologists have devised indirect memory tests to study implicit memory, they have devised semantic tasks to study semantic memory. A typical kind of semantic task is to present subjects with simple statements like "a canary is a bird" or "a truck in a flower," and ask them to verify whether the statement is true or false. From the reaction times to such simple statements, cognitive scientists can infer what it means to have knowledge and how the knowledge is activated and used. As with other indirect memory tests, semantic tasks do not require subjects to remember past events.

In this section I will focus on one aspect of semantic memory—namely, the knowledge we have of the meanings of single words. I refer to this knowledge as knowledge of **concepts**. Examples include the concept of bird, of truck, and of love. Most concepts may also be thought of as categories. There are usually numerous instances or manifestations of any one concept. For example, there are many types of birds and many instances in which someone feels love. I will try to answer two questions about concepts. First, what is the nature of a concept; that is, what does it mean to know the meaning of a concept? Second, how are concepts processed when a person is posed questions about the meanings of words, especially questions in which people must decide if some entity (e.g., robin) is an instance of a concept (e.g., bird)? Again, I remind the reader that the sense in which semantic memory for concepts is implicit or unconscious is that people ordinarily do not remember the experiences in which they acquired knowledge about concepts. Certainly, though, people are conscious of the conceptual knowledge itself.

WHAT IS THE NATURE OF A CONCEPT?

A long-standing philosophical tradition claims that any concept is composed of a concatenation of a set of primitive **semantic features**, just as the various kinds of matter are composed of atoms. A semantic feature is at once conceptually simpler than a whole concept and is contained in many other concepts. In this way, a very large number of concepts can be formed from a relatively small set of semantic features. For example, the semantic features that make up the concept of "bird" include "living," "lays eggs," and "has feathers." Each of these features represents a conceptually simple aspect of the bird concept, and each is found in many other concepts. The idea of living, for example, seems an intuitively simple component of meaning. The distinction between living and nonliving is a basic one among the objects of the world, and is one made by all cultures. At the same time, many concepts (e.g., trees, bees, chimpanzees) contain the feature of living. The claim is that people learn from experience the elementary components that concepts have in common, and learn how any one concept is a concatenation of those elementary components. Again, an analogy is that of scientists discovering the 92 essential atoms that make up all forms of matter, and the particular arrangement of a subset of atoms that underlies any particular piece of matter.

The idea that concepts consist of concatenations of semantic features is attractive for several reasons. First, the idea makes use of an essential strategy of science: that of breaking down or reducing a complex phenomenon into simpler, more elementary components. The bewildering number and variety of concepts can be reduced to the concatenation of a much smaller and simpler set of elementary features of meaning. Second, the feature approach readily accounts for some essential intuitions about similarities and differences among concepts. For example, birds are similar to bats because both fly, but are different because only birds have feathers and lay eggs. Third, the linguistic behavior of children suggests that they acquire concepts feature by feature (Clark, 1973). For example, a young child may call a cat a "doggie." It is as if the child understands only some of the features of dog (e.g., animal, four-legged) but not the features that would enable the child to distinguish dogs from cats (e.g., dogs but not cats bark). Fourth, evidence suggests that some people who suffer damage to the temporal lobes of the brain will behave as if they have lost a few semantic features, and so will have trouble accessing the precisely correct word label for concepts that make use of those features. Such a patient presented a picture of a dog may only be able to describe the picture by saying "it is an animal," and may have no idea of the size or typical behavior of the animal in the picture (Damasio & Damasio, 1992).

The Classical Approach to Concepts

One example of an approach to concepts that makes use of semantic features is known as the **classical approach to meaning**. The classical approach, which can be traced back as far as Aristotle, claims that the semantic features that compose a concept are the necessary and sufficient features that define the concept. These are the features that enable a person to decide reliably whether any particular instance is an example of a concept. In a sense, the classical approach claims that the concept that comes to mind when a person encounters or intends to use a word is analogous to a dictionary definition. The concept of a bird, for example, would consist of an animal that lays eggs and has feathers. These are the features that are necessary and sufficient to say whether any given entity (e.g., robin, bat) is a bird. The concept of truck would consist of the essential features of a means of transportation with wheels used to move heavy objects.

There are at least two problems with the classical approach, however. First, for many concepts, there are no defining features that all instances possess. Ludwig Wittgenstein (1889 to 1951), an Austrian philosopher, provided what has become a famous example to illustrate this point: the concept of a game (Wittgenstein, 1953). He noted that there is simply no single feature that all games have in common. Most games have winners and losers, but not all (e.g., ring around the rosie); and most games involve at least two people, but not all (e.g., solitaire). Some games are played on a board (e.g., Monopoly) but some are not (e.g., tennis), and some are played with a ball (e.g., baseball) but some are not (e.g., bridge).

Instead of defining features, games have what is called a **family resemblance**, analogous to how members of a family of people share physical traits, even though no one trait is necessarily shared by all members of the family. Similarly, any given type of game shares features with many but not all other types of games. No single type of game has all the features possessed by all the other games, nor is any one feature shared by all types of games. And the same notion applies to many other concepts as well. Consider the concepts of love, of evil, or of democracy. The instances that make up these concepts have a family resemblance. They share some features, but do not possess some set of necessary and sufficient features.

A second reason to doubt the classical approach to concepts is based on semantic experiments that assess people's understanding of concepts. Concepts such as bird, game, dog, and so on, have some members that seem typical of the category, and some that seem atypical (Mervis, Catlin, & Rosch, 1976). Typical members share properties with many other members of the category, while atypical members share fewer properties with other members of the category (Rosch & Mervis, 1975). That is, the family resemblance is stronger in typical than in atypical instances. For example, a canary is a fairly typical bird because, like most other birds, it flies, lives in trees, and has feathers. An ostrich is not typical of the bird category because ostriches do not fly or live in trees, although they do have feathers. A hammer is a typical tool because, like most other tools, it is an instrument used or worked by hand with a handle for holding. An anvil is not as typical, because it lacks a handle.

In semantic tasks in which subjects must decide if a statement is true (e.g., "a canary is a bird") or false (e.g., "a hammer is a bird"), subjects are reliably faster at responding "true" to statements about typical members of categories (e.g., "a canary is a bird" or "a hammer is a tool") than to statements about atypical members (e.g., "an ostrich is a bird" or "an anvil is a tool") (Rosch, 1975; Rips, Shoben, & Smith, 1973; Smith, Shoben, & Rips, 1974; see Chang, 1986). This finding is called the **typicality effect**. The problem the classical approach has with the typicality effect is that any definition of a concept, like bird, is bound to apply as well to atypical instances as to typical instances. Both canaries and ostriches, for example, fit the dictionary definition of a bird (an animal with wings and feathers). Yet people are able to decide more rapidly that canaries are birds, so people must not be accessing anything like a mental dictionary to make that decision.

The Prototype Approach to Concepts

As an alternative to the classical approach, modern psychologists (e.g., Lakoff, 1987; Rosch, 1973) have developed an approach to meaning usually called the **prototype approach**. I first discussed prototypes in chapter 3: Visual Perception. The main premise of the prototype approach is that a concept is understood as a set of semantic features, such that some of the features are more probable and other features are less probable in the various instances of the concept. To put it another way, when people have a concept in mind, they have something like a typical instance, or prototype, of the concept in mind. When people think about birds, for example, they think of the typical bird that flies, lays eggs, has feathers, and lives in trees. These are the features that are highly probable in various types of birds, although some of the probable features (e.g., flying) are not a part of the dictionary definition of bird.

Prototype theory explains why some instances seem to be better or more typical of a category, and so are categorized more quickly in semantic experiments. The typical instances, like canaries, are more similar to the prototype, while the atypical instances, like ostrich, are less similar to the prototype. Furthermore, the atypical instances of a concept may be as similar to the prototype of another concept as they are to the prototype of the concept in which they are usually placed. A bat—an atypical mammal—has some of the features of the prototypical mammal (e.g., bears live young) but also has some of the features of the prototypical bird (e.g., flies, lives in trees). This explains why there often seem to be fuzzy boundaries between concepts, like the boundary between the concepts of mammal and bird (Lakoff, 1987). The bat lies in the fuzz between mammal and bird.

HOW ARE CONCEPTS PROCESSED?

The prototype approach to meaning has been the inspiration for the development of several psychological models of how people respond to semantic tasks in which they must decide if statements like "a bat is a mammal" are true or false. I will first discuss a model usually called the feature comparison model of semantic memory.

The Feature Comparison Model

The **feature comparison model** was first developed by Smith, Shoben, and Rips (1974) and later modified by McCloskey and Glucksberg (1979). The feature comparison model embodies the prototype approach to meaning. According to the model, all concepts may be described as a list of symbols that represent the semantic features that describe the properties of the concept. The features are not the features described by the classical approach, but are the features described by the prototype approach; namely, those features that are associated with the typical instances of a concept.

The feature comparison model focuses on the strategies used in semantic memory experiments by subjects who must decide whether an exemplar (e.g., canary) is a member of a larger category (e.g., bird). The strategy comprises two rules. The first rule is that if a feature associated with the exemplar is found that is also associated with the category, then that constitutes positive evidence that the exemplar is a member of the category. For example, the fact that canaries and birds both fly is positive evidence that canaries are birds. The second rule is that if a feature associated with the exemplar is found that is not associated with the category, then that constitutes negative evidence. For example, the fact that trucks have wheels but wheels are not associated with the bird category constitutes negative evidence that trucks are birds. Subjects respond "true" once enough positive evidence accumulates and respond "false" once enough negative evidence accumulates. These rules can be described as a **heuristic**. They constitute a strategy that usually, but not inevitably, results in a correct conclusion.

The feature comparison model predicts the typicality effect because the features associated with typical exemplars of a category should overlap a good deal with the features associated with the category. For example, nearly all the features associated with canary will overlap with the features associated with bird, because canaries are typical birds. Both canaries and birds have feathers, live in trees, fly, and so on. So subjects can respond "true" very quickly to statements like "a canary is a bird," because for the typical examples positive evidence will accumulate very quickly. On the other hand, the features associated with atypical exemplars, such as ostrich, do not overlap very much with the features associated with categories, such as bird. Most birds, but not ostriches, fly and live in trees. So for statements like "an ostrich is a bird," positive evidence will not accumulate as quickly, and the statement will take longer to verify.

The feature comparison model also explains another commonly observed finding called the **false relatedness effect** (see Chang, 1986). The false relatedness effect refers to the observation that subjects respond "false" to an incorrect statement faster when the exemplar is unrelated to the category than when the exemplar is somewhat related to the category (Collins & Quillian, 1970, 1972; Rips et al., 1973; Holyoak & Glass, 1975; Lorch, 1978). For example, a subject is likely to respond "false" more quickly to a statement like "a truck is a bird" than to a statement like "a tiger is a bird." While neither is true, the concept of tiger has some features in common with the concept of bird (both are living), while the concept of truck has virtually no features in common with the concept of bird.

The explanation of the false relatedness effect, according to the feature comparison model, goes like this. When two concepts are unrelated (e.g., truck and bird), there is no overlap between their features. Consequently, none of the features associated with the exemplar will match the features associated with the category, and negative evidence will accumulate very quickly. So subjects respond "false" very quickly to statements like "a truck is a bird." When two concepts are partially related (e.g., tiger and bird), there is a small amount of overlap between their features. Consequently, a few of the features associated with the exemplar will match the features associated with the category, and negative evidence will accumulate more slowly. So subjects respond "false" more slowly to statements like "a tiger is a bird."

The feature comparison model explains another commonly observed finding called the **levels effect**. The levels effect is based on the fact that many concepts are part of a hierarchy in which one concept subsumes another. Examples include animal-bird-canary, clothing-pants-Levis, vehicle-car-sedan, tool-screwdriver-Phillips screwdriver, and fruit-apple-McIntosh apple. Some concepts are more superordinate (e.g., vehicle) while others are more subordinate (e.g., sedan). In between are concepts of an intermediate level of abstraction (e.g., car); these are called **basic-level concepts**.

Rosch, Mervis, Gray, Johnson, and Boyes-Braem (1976) did a series of studies that demonstrated that basic-level concepts are ordinarily the most useful, and are the most likely to come to mind. For example, Rosch et al. noted that basic-level names (e.g., "car," "sofa," "dog") tend to be acquired by children before superordinate names (e.g., "vehicle," "furniture," "animal") or subordinate names (e.g., "sedan," "rocking chair," "poodle"). Rosch et al. found that adult subjects were more likely to name a picture with its basic-level name (e.g., "car") than with its subordinate name (e.g., "sedan") or its superordinate name (e.g., "vehicle"). When asked to list attributes shared by the exemplars of concepts, the adult subjects listed only a few attributes shared by exemplars of superordinate concepts, such as vehicle, but listed many attributes shared by exemplars of basic-level concepts, such as car. The number of attributes shared by exemplars of subordinate concepts, such as sedan, was not appreciably greater than the number shared by exemplars of the basic-level concept. Other research, measuring reaction time, has shown that subjects are faster at deciding that a picture is an example of a basic-level concept, such as apple, than that it is an example of a superordinate concept, such as fruit (Smith, Balzano, & Walker, 1978).

To understand how the feature comparison model explains the levels effect, consider the Smith et al. (1978) experiment. According to the feature comparison model, the picture is converted into a list of semantic features that are compared to the equivalent list of features associated with the word. In the case where the words refer to superordinate concepts, such as fruit, any given word has relatively few features to represent its meaning. Consequently, when comparing the feature list associated with pictures to the feature list associated with the superordinate words, positive evidence does not accumulate very fast, and reaction time is slowed down. In the case where the words refer to basic-level concepts, such as apple, any given word has relatively more features to represent its meaning. The concept of apple, for example, is bound to have more features than the concept of fruit, because an apple is a fruit, but has additional properties (e.g., red) not shared by all other fruit. Consequently, when the feature list associated with pictures is compared to the feature list associated with the basic-level words, positive evidence accumulates relatively fast, and reaction time is speeded up.

The reason that people prefer to think at the basic level, according to the feature comparison model, is that basic-level categories are the most useful for predicting the features of any member of the category (Corter & Gluck, 1992; Rosch et al., 1976; but see Jones, 1983). For example, all apples are round, have short stems, and grow on trees. At the same time, many of these features are not shared by exemplars from other basic-level concepts. Many other kinds of fruit, such as bananas, melons, and oranges, have different features than do apples. For example, a banana, unlike an apple, is yellow, elongated, and has an inedible peel. Basic-level labels are thus informative—they imply a long list of features; and they are discriminating—the features so implied are minimally shared by other basic-level labels. Superordinate labels, such as "fruit" and "furniture," do not imply a long list of features, and so are not as informative. There are fewer features associated with fruit than with apple, for example. Subordinate labels, such as "McIntosh apple" or "rocking chair," are informative but are not very discriminating, because the features associated with a subordinate concept overlap with the features associated with the other concepts at the subordinate level. McIntosh apples, for example, share many features with Delicious apples. Phillips screwdrivers share many features with slot tip screwdrivers.

With suitable modifications, the feature comparison model also explains an important insight about the levels effect: as people become experts in some domain of knowledge, they tend to think more at the subordinate level than at the basic level (Rosch et al., 1976). A car expert thinks in terms of sports cars, sedans, recreational vehicles, and so on. A dog expert thinks in terms of poodles, Doberman pinschers, collies, and so on. The simple explanation is that experts acquire more features that discriminate among subordinate-level concepts. For example, the car expert, through encounters with many different types of cars, learns that four doors characterize sedans but not sports cars. In fact, research shows that experts can provide more features that are unique to subordinate concept labels, such as "flute" or "violin," than can nonexperts (Palmer, Jones, Hennessy, Unze, & Pick, 1989; Rosch et al., 1976; Tanaka & Taylor, 1991).

The Spreading Activation Model

Another example of a model of semantic memory goes by the name of the **spreading activation model** (Collins & Quillian, 1969; Collins & Loftus, 1975). Like the feature comparison model, the spreading activation model assumes that concepts are represented as a set of semantic features. In the spreading activation model, concepts and their features are depicted as a network of connections among **nodes** through which activation spreads. The nodes are symbols that represent features and concepts, while the connections are symbols that represent various types of relationships between a concept and a feature, or between two concepts. The model claims that when a concept is accessed, it will become "excited" and so spread activation to other concepts and features to which it is connected in the network. These other concepts and features will then also become excited, making them temporarily more accessible than they would have been if they had not become excited. The spread of activation through the network of nodes is assumed to be temporary; it will tend to dissipate after only a few seconds.

Figure 5-2 illustrates a tiny portion of a network that includes nodes that represent the concepts of canary and bird, and the feature that represents flying. The canary concept is connected to the bird concept by a category relationship and to the flying feature by a property relationship. The flying feature is also connected to the bird concept by a property relationship. Like the feature comparison model, the spreading activation model assumes that the features con-

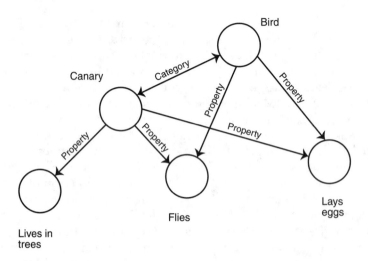

FIGURE 5–2   A portion of a semantic network.

nected to a concept are the typical features (e.g., birds fly), and are not restricted to features that would appear in a dictionary definition of the concept (flying is not part of the dictionary definition of bird).

The spreading activation model borrows the activation construct from neurophysiology. In real brains, the activation of a neuron increases (or, in the case of inhibitory connections, decreases) the firing rate of other neurons to which it is connected. The spreading activation model in effect translates the feature comparison model into a quasi-neurophysiological model. Because the spreading activation model subsumes the feature comparison strategy, it can account for the typicality, false relatedness, and levels effects observed in semantic memory research. I will illustrate only how the spreading activation model accounts for the typicality effect.

Suppose a subject encounters the statement "a canary is a bird." The words *canary* and *bird* cause the nodes that represent the concepts of canary and bird to become excited. Their excitement spreads activation to other nodes to which they are connected. Activation is likely to spread from canary to the features that represent flying, living in trees, possessing feathers, and yellow. Those features will then become excited. Because most of these features are also connected to the concept of bird, the activation of the features will in turn spread activation to the concept of bird. Activation is also likely to spread from bird to the features that represent flying, living in trees, and possessing feathers, which in turn will spread activation back to canary. When activation converges from two directions on a node, that node reaches a higher level of excitement in a shorter period of time, and so spreads even more activation to other nodes. In other words, there will quickly be established a number of highly activated connections linking the highly excited nodes of canary and bird to one another, providing the subject with ample data that a canary is a bird. The decision process will therefore be fast.

Now suppose a subject encounters the statement "an ostrich is a bird." In this case, activation is likely to spread from ostrich to the features that represent possessing feathers, but not to the features that represent flying or living in trees. Activation is also likely to spread from bird to the features that represent flying, living in trees, and possessing feathers. But the features of flying and living in trees will not be activated from both directions, nor will the bird node receive much activation from the ostrich node. In other words, there will not be as many highly activated connections linking ostrich to bird, nor will the nodes representing ostrich and bird be as excited. As a result, the decision process will take longer.

In addition to the typicality, semantic relatedness, and levels effect, the spreading activation model accounts for an effect called the **semantic priming effect**. The semantic priming effect is that subjects can make a decision about a concept more readily if they have just made a decision about a semantically related concept than if they have just made a decision about a semantically unrelated concept. For example, subjects are faster at deciding that a canary is a bird if they had just decided on the previous trial that an eagle is a bird than if they had just decided that a car is a vehicle (Loftus & Loftus, 1974; Guenther, Klatzky, & Putnam, 1980). Subjects are also faster at deciding that a letter string is a meaningful word if the word is preceded by a semantically related word (e.g., Meyer & Schvaneveldt, 1971; Moss, Ostrin, Tyler, & Marslen-Wilson, 1995). For example, subjects are faster at deciding that *milk* is a word if it is preceded by *cow* than if it is preceded by *pig*.

The spreading activation model accounts for the semantic priming effect by assuming that the first statement spreads activation to the semantic features that will be used to process the second statement, when the second statement refers to related concepts. The activation of flying and laying eggs that occurs when subjects encounter "an eagle is a bird" will persist for a short while, and so make those features more accessible. Should subjects then encounter "a canary is a bird," the features necessary to respond "true" will be more readily available, and the decision process will be relatively fast.

New Developments in Semantic Memory

Neural Nets and Distributed Accounts of Semantic Memory

The feature comparison and the spreading activation models of semantic memory are both examples of a type of model sometimes called **symbol systems** (Best, 1995; Bechtel & Abrahamsen, 1991). A symbol system model describes knowledge as a set of symbols that stand for features and the relationships between features. Spreading activation models are quasi-physiological, but are still composed of symbols. In a symbol system model of bird knowledge, the symbol for bird is connected to the symbol for feathers by the symbol for property. The symbol for canary is connected to the symbol for bird by the symbol for category membership. The symbol system model is reminiscent of data bases used by computers for storing information. The heuristic of accumulating positive and negative evidence from a search of features is reminiscent of a simple computer program for retrieving and using data from a data base.

There are at least a couple of problems with symbol system models. One problem is that the symbols into which knowledge decomposes are themselves without meaning. That is, any given symbol is connected only to other symbols which, in turn, are connected to other symbols, and so on. It takes something outside the model to understand what the symbols mean. A second problem is that the symbol system model is unrevealing of the physiological basis of understanding concepts.

More recently, some cognitive scientists have used neural net models to simulate semantic memory (Masson, 1995; Hinton & Shallice, 1991; Sharkey, 1990). Neural nets do away with symbols and instead represent a concept as a set of connections of varying degrees of strength among sets of neural-like units. These neural-like units include units that detect features of physical stimuli, control behavior, and intervene between stimuli and behavior (so-called hidden units).

In neural net models, no one unit or connection means anything, any more than a single neuron or synaptic connection represents a concept like bird or a semantic feature like living. Instead, the units are rather primitive entities that merely increase or decrease their rate of firing in response to activation. Knowledge of any given concept is distributed—it involves many connections among many units. Moreover, many of the same units are used to represent different concepts; the concepts are distinguished from one another by the particular set of connections among the units that represent the concepts. Accessing a given piece of knowledge, like the meaning of *cow*, in a neural net amounts to creating a distinct pattern of activation among the set of units. Furthermore, the pattern of activation that represents some piece of knowledge is typically anchored to units that detect stimuli and control responses. In this sense, the firing pattern among units is not entirely symbolic. Neural nets are discussed in several chapters in this text, especially in the introductory chapter and in chapter 6: The Physiology of Learning and Remembering.

Neural net models retain and even refine the idea from spreading activation models that accessing knowledge involves a flow of activation in a network. As such, neural net models make predictions similar to spreading activation models. Consider semantic priming, as when subjects more quickly judge that a canary is living if they had just made that judgment of a robin than if they had just made that judgment of a tree. According to a neural net model of semantic memory, the pattern of activation among units created by processing "robin" will resemble the pattern of activation created by processing "canary" (Masson, 1995). Hence, judgments about the canary concept will be faster.

In some cases, neural net models predict semantic priming effects that are different from those predicted by the spreading activation model discussed before (Collins & Loftus, 1975). Masson (1995) presented subjects with stimuli that included pairs of words. On some trials the first word was semantically related to the second word (e.g., *cow—milk*) while on other trials the first word was unrelated to the second (e.g., *tree—milk*). The words were presented successively, and not simultaneously. Subjects had to name the second word. The stimuli also included a neutral row of eight lowercase *x*s displayed between the first and second word (so the subject actually saw, for example, *cow—xxxxxxxx—milk*). A semantic priming effect was observed. Subjects were faster at naming the second word (e.g., *milk*) if it was preceded by the related word (e.g., *cow*) than if it was preceded by an unrelated word (e.g., *tree*). Masson's results are presented in Figure 5-3.

According to the neural net model, the encounter with *cow* creates a pattern of activation among the units representing meaning that resembles the pattern associated with *milk*, making *milk* easier to name. The row of *x*s would not interfere with the semantic priming effect because the *x*s lack meaning. Consequently, the processing of the intervening row of *x*s would not perturb the conceptual portion of the neural net.

The novel aspect of the experiment was that on some trials a semantically unrelated word was presented between the first and second related pairs of words, instead of the neutral row of *x*s (e.g., the subjects saw *cow—truck—milk*). The unrelated intervening word severely reduced the semantic priming effect on word naming. Subjects were not much faster at naming *milk* having first seen *cow* when there was an intervening unrelated word (e.g., *truck*) in the stimulus set. Other research has also found a reduction in semantic priming when unrelated words intervene between two related words (e.g., Sharkey & Sharkey, 1992; see Masson, 1995, for a discussion of such studies and a resolution of some inconsistencies observed among studies).

The neural net model's explanation of Masson's (1995) results is that the unrelated word (e.g., *truck*) sets up a pattern of activation among units that represent meaning that is quite different from either the pattern established by the

	Relationship between words	
Intervening stimulus	Related in meaning (e.g., *cow—milk*)	Unrelated in meaning (e.g., *tree—milk*)
Neutral (i.e., xxxxxxxx)	517.6	530.2
Unrelated (e.g., truck)	544.7	548.0

Response times (in milliseconds) to name the second word (e.g., milk)

FIGURE 5–3   Results of Masson's (1995) word naming experiment.

first word (e.g., *cow*) or the to-be-named word (e.g., *milk*). The pattern created by *truck* perturbs the pattern established by *cow*, thereby undermining the benefit of having recently processed *cow*.

The nifty thing about Masson's (1995) experiment is that the Collins and Loftus (1975) model actually predicts that there would still be a substantial semantic priming effect even when the intervening word is unrelated. That is because in the spreading activation model, a concept's meaning is not distributed about a network but is instead localized in a symbolic node. In the case of seeing *cow—truck—milk*, the excitation of the cow node would be expected to spread activation to the milk node, while the excitation of the truck node would be expected to spread activation to nodes like the car node. Car and truck nodes are not directly connected to cow and milk nodes, so the activation that *milk* receives from cow should not be lost just because *truck* and its semantically related nodes are also activated. In fact, though, the presentation of the unrelated *truck* does reduce the priming effect of *cow* on naming *milk*.

In the neural net account, the meaning of cow, milk, truck, and car are distributed about networks that share units. The processing of any concept is likely to spread activation among at least some of the units shared by even unrelated concepts. What mainly distinguishes the concepts in neural nets is the overall pattern of activation among units. That is why neural nets predict the reduction of semantic priming when an unrelated word intervenes. So score one for neural net models.

Another advantage of neural net models is that they help us understand the effects of brain damage on cognitive processing. Again, symbol system approaches, such as the feature comparison model discussed before, are unrevealing of the physiological underpinnings of semantic memory.

In the case of semantic memory, several kinds of semantic impairment have been reported (reviewed in Farah & McClelland, 1991). Bilateral temporal lobe brain damage can sometimes impair knowledge of living things while leaving knowledge of nonliving things relatively well preserved. Large left hemisphere strokes can sometimes impair knowledge of nonliving things while leaving knowledge of living things preserved.

Farah and McClelland (1991) have developed a neural net model to account for these impairments. Their model simulated how the brain learns to name objects. The model was given a picture of any of several living and nonliving objects as input and produced as output the name of the object. The model eventually learned to name correctly the whole set of pictures. Their model contains several populations of units, including one that represents visual information and one that represents functional information. The distinction between visual and functional units was motivated by the claim that living things are understood, at least by most lay people, primarily in terms of their visual appearance. Canaries are yellow, whales are big, elephants have trunks that stick out of their faces. Nonliving things, on the other hand, are understood primarily in terms of their function. Large beanbags and stools are both chairs because they enable sitting. Cars and blimps are vehicles because they enable transportation.

Anyway, Farah and McClelland damaged their neural net model by destroying some of the connections among units. Damage to the visual units primarily undermined performance on the living objects, whereas damage to the functional units primarily undermined performance on nonliving objects. Their neural net model thus simulated what happens to real brain-damaged patients (see also Hinton & Shallice, 1991, for another example of a neural net simulation of brain damage).

Concepts as Implicit Theories

The classical and prototype approaches to the meaning of concepts, and the feature comparison and spreading activation models based on the prototype approach, all assume that concepts are composed of a set of semantic features. The concept of a bird, for example, is embodied in a set of features such as lays eggs, flies, and is living. The semantic feature viewpoint extends the idea of atoms to the phenomenon of concepts.

But is an atomistic approach appropriate for concepts? A number of philosophers (e.g., Quine, 1977; Putnam, 1975) and cognitive psychologists (e.g., Murphy & Medin, 1985; Keil, 1989; Barsalou, 1989) have recently argued that the semantic feature approach is misleading—that the analogy to atoms is misconceived. In place of features, these people propose that concepts are like **implicit theories**, or mental models, that people have about each concept. The concept of a bird, for example, is actually a theory that serves to integrate and explain the features associated with birds. It is not just that birds have feathers, but that feathers contribute to the ability of the bird to fly. The notion of implicit theories does not ignore the fact that concepts have features. Rather, the notion claims that meaning does not essentially reside in the features, but resides in the underlying theory that explains the relevance of the features.

The analogy appropriate for concepts, then, is not the atoms of matter, but the theories scientists use to account for observations. However, the implicit theories people use to understand concepts are not necessarily the precise, well-integrated, and empirically verified theories constructed by scientists. Indeed, implicit theories may not even be accurate. They are explanations that simplify reality, remain consistent with other knowledge, describe relationships between concepts, and form a basis for predicting future events (Murphy & Medin, 1985). Implicit theories may be idiosyncratic, and are usually difficult to articulate.

One reason to doubt the feature approach to meaning is that it is not apparent which of the many potentially available features should be used when one brings to mind a concept. Depending on the context, the concept of bird can suggest eggs, pets, communication over long distances, food, feathers for a hat, or a symbol of freedom. Another problem with features is that there seems to be no principled way to distinguish concepts from the features into which concepts decompose. Why should bird be a concept, but living a feature? Could not the concept of birdness be regarded as a feature of something else (e.g., a bat), could not the feature of living be broken down into more features (e.g., breathes, reproduces)? In the world of matter and energy, there is a limited and discoverable number of naturally occurring atoms (92, to be exact). Is there any comparable limit to the number of features one could posit?

Another kind of problem emerges when we consider how people compare concepts in order to decide if one concept is a member of another concept's category. We know that a canary is a bird but a truck is not a bird. From the perspective of features, we know this because the features of canaries overlap with the features of birds, but the features of trucks do not overlap with the features of birds. In fact, though, there is an unlimited number of features shared by truck and bird. Both are smaller than the Empire State Building, both exist in the modern world, both are to be found in the city of St. Paul, both weigh more than an ounce, both are opaque to light, and so on. Indeed, any two concepts have an arbitrarily large number of features in common (see Medin, Goldstone, & Gentner, 1993). So it is not clear how feature overlap can be a reliable heuristic for determining whether one concept is a member of another concept's category.

Implicit theories can explain why some of the potentially infinite number of features come to mind in any particular context. To borrow an example from Murphy and Medin (1985), consider that both coal and money are flammable, but ordinarily one only thinks of flammable in the context of coal. An implicit theory of coal is likely to describe its role as a fuel, and so focus on its flammable property, while an implicit theory of money is likely to describe its role in economics, and so not focus on its flammable property.

The claim that implicit theory advocates make is that the features that are regarded as relevant reflect implicit theories that underlie the meaning of the concept. To illustrate, Medin and Shoben (1988) asked subjects to judge which pair of concepts is more similar for a large number of pairs. For example, subjects judged the similarity of white hair and gray hair, of gray hair and black hair, of white clouds and gray clouds, and of gray clouds and black clouds. Note that the features on which the concepts varied were the same for hair and clouds. Yet the subjects judged that white hair and gray hair are more similar than white clouds and gray clouds, but that gray clouds and black clouds are more similar than gray hair and black hair. The authors claim that this finding is due to the fact that most people have an implicit theory to explain the similarity of gray and white hair—namely, that both reflect aging. Black hair would not have aged yet. The implicit theory relevant to clouds has to do with the weather conditions reflected in clouds. Gray clouds and black clouds are associated with stormy conditions and so are judged more similar than either is to white clouds, which are associated with calm conditions.

More evidence for the importance of implicit theories in assessing similarity comes from Rips (1989) and Smith and Sloman (1994). These researchers presented college students with sparse descriptions of objects, such as "a circular object with a 3 inch diameter." The students were asked whether the object was more similar to a quarter or to a pizza; most chose a quarter. Other students were asked whether the object was more likely to be a quarter or a pizza; now most chose pizza. Implicit theories of coins and pizzas explain the results. Most pizzas are much larger than 3 inches in diameter, but a quarter is only slightly smaller than 3 inches. Still, pizzas can be of virtually any size, but coins must be of a highly standardized and consistent size (in the case of quarters, about one inch in diameter) in order to function as currency.

From the perspective of implicit theories, it would be expected that different cultures would have different implicit theories, and so would categorize the world in different ways. For example, in the biblical book of Leviticus, dietary rules describe "clean" and "unclean" animals (this and the subsequent example come from Murphy & Medin, 1985). Clean animals include gazelles, frogs, most fish, and grasshoppers; unclean animals include camels, ostriches, crocodiles, and eels. What features do camels, ostriches, crocodiles, and eels have in common that make them unclean? Apparently the Middle Eastern culture at the time believed that there should be a kind of harmony between habitat, locomotion, and biological structure (Douglas, 1966). Creatures that violated the harmony were unclean. Ostriches have wings but do not fly. Crocodiles have front appendages that resemble hands, yet walk on all four limbs.

As another example of cultural differences, the Karam of New Guinea do not consider a cassowary (an ostrichlike animal) a bird. Apparently, this is the case because the cassowary plays a special role in Karam thought concerning the relationship between the forest and cultivated land (Bulmer, 1967). Other birds do not play this role.

Some of the research that provides the empirical justification for an implicit theory approach to concepts investigates the imaginative use of concepts. One example comes from the research of Keil (1989), who compared the imaginations of children to those of adults. Keil posed to children and adults a series of hypothetical alterations of a concept, in order to see at what point the subjects believed the concept was changed into another concept. To illustrate, consider a raccoon. Suppose the fur of the raccoon is dyed so that it is black with a white stripe down its back. Is it still a raccoon, or is it now a skunk? Suppose a smelly sac is implanted into the raccoon and it is taught to spray the contents of the sac at its enemies. Now has it changed into a skunk? Keil found that children older than about 8 were reluctant to believe that these superficial changes actually transformed the raccoon into a skunk. Younger children, on the other hand, were prone to believe that such changes transformed the raccoon into a skunk. Older children and adults have acquired a theory of animals. A raccoon is a raccoon by virtue of its DNA, or by virtue of having raccoon parents. Until children acquire such theories, they rely more on superficial features to make judgments about category membership.

In another study of the imaginative use of concepts, Ward (1994) asked college students to imagine animals that might live on a planet somewhere else in the galaxy. Subjects drew pictures and wrote descriptions of their imagined extraterrestrial animals. The main finding was that the imagined animals had many of the features of typical earth animals. Now, subjects could have described creatures without heads or creatures composed of interacting flotsam and jetsam, but in fact they described creatures that were bilaterally symmetrical and with the same types of sensory receptors and appendages as those of terrestrial animals. That subjects were relying on a kind of implicit theory of terrestrial animals was further supported by the finding that the subjects' extraterrestrial creatures possessed the same correlations among features as exhibited in terrestrial animals. For instance, when told that the extraterrestrial creature had wings, subjects were likely to create an animal with wings and feathers.

SUMMARY AND CONCLUSIONS

This chapter explored the unconscious influence of past experiences on current thought and behavior, an influence usually called implicit memory. I used several examples to illustrate the various unconscious ways that the past influences the present: an intuition that a melody that comes to mind is pleasing in the absence of any memory of having previously heard the melody, a fear of an uncle in the absence of any memory of sexual abuse, and the knowledge that ducks are birds in the absence of any memory for the experiences through which this knowledge was obtained. All of these forms of implicit memory may be contrasted with explicit memory, such as remembering that the Beatles appeared on the *Ed Sullivan Show* in the 1960s.

Although the idea of implicit memory has been around for a long time, most of the research has been done in the last 15 years. The usual way cognitive psychologists demonstrate implicit memory is to find a dissociation between performance on a direct memory task, such as recognition, and performance on an indirect memory task, such as word fragment completion. Unlike direct memory tasks, indirect tasks do not require that subjects actually recollect some particular event or recently presented information.

In section 1, I outlined how a constructionist theory of memory accounts for the difference between explicit and implicit memory. Simply put, explicit memory entails the successful use of a reconstruction strategy that enables a person to deduce from the strength of connections distributed among various cognitive systems what happened at some place and time in the past. The connections serve to establish a setting or context for some event. Implicit memory draws only on the accommodations made by some particular cognitive system. I then discussed some of the research consistent with this account. Aging and divided attention undermine explicit memory but not implicit memory. Elaborating on meaning enhances explicit memory more than implicit memory, whereas changing stimulus modality undermines implicit memory more than explicit memory.

In section 2 I discussed a controversial and tragic form of implicit memory; the phenomenon in which people claim to have amnesia for a disturbing experience, such as being abused, but seem nevertheless to be affected by the experience. For example, an abuse victim who claims having had amnesia for the abusive experience may display clinical symptoms such as fear of entering into mature adult relationships. The effects of amnesia for disturbing experiences may not always be negative, however. One might be incapacitated by dwelling too much on negative experiences. Freud's account of amnesia of disturbing experiences was that people unconsciously defend against the anxiety that accompanies disturbing experiences by repressing them. Much of the research on amnesia for disturbing experiences has taken seriously the repression hypothesis.

Most of the evidence for repression comes from clinical cases in which clients have apparently repressed a traumatic experience but in the course of therapy begin to remember the experience and at the same time overcome its presumed consequences. Indeed, some of these cases have formed the basis of lawsuits against parents and alterations of the statutes of limitations in 19 states. A number of people who have denied any wrongdoing are nevertheless serving time in prison based on the testimony of people (often their own children) who claim to have recovered memories of abuse that took place decades earlier. Unfortunately, it is difficult to prove from clinical cases whether the supposedly repressed experience ever happened, although Herman and Schatzow provide some evidence that most women who initially claimed to have amnesia for sexual abuse were in fact victims of abuse. Furthermore, it remains likely that at least some people who believe they remember a past abusive experience are instead unintentionally fabricating the experience. In fact, a number of experiments have demonstrated conclusively that people can sometimes be deceived into believing sincerely in a traumatic event that never actually occurred.

Despite the ethical constraints, a number of highly imaginative studies have attempted to design well-controlled experiments in order to find empirical evidence for repression. Some of these experiments have found that when information is associated with a mild form of anxiety, it is not remembered as well as when the information is not associated with the anxiety. However, there are alternative interpretations for such findings. For example, it could be that an all-too-vivid memory for the negative quality of the experiment competes with the subject's attempt to reconstruct the information. The implicit memory literature does at least render plausible the claim of the repression hypothesis that distressing experiences, such as child abuse, may have an unconscious effect on thoughts, feelings, and behaviors.

Some research, notably on eyewitness memory for disturbing crimes and accidents, would seem to contradict repression. It seems that eyewitnesses tend to have good explicit memory for the central details of violent events, but poor explicit memory for the details peripheral to the violence.

I concluded the section on repression by suggesting that we as yet have no convincing, unequivocal evidence for repression, despite the claims of many psychotherapists and their patients. I tried to make clear that repression may be a viable hypothesis, but that cognitive psychologists and psychotherapists need to develop better paradigms for studying and validating repression.

In section 3 I discussed semantic memory, a label for world knowledge, such as the knowledge that uncles are male or canaries are birds. Semantic memory may be regarded as a form of implicit memory because people ordinarily do not remember the occasions on which they acquired the knowledge. I focused on semantic memory for the concepts that underlie the meanings of words. Cognitive psychologists usually study semantic memory by presenting subjects with simple statements like "a canary is a bird" or "a robin is a fish" and timing how long it takes subjects to respond "true" or "false."

I first presented a semantic feature approach to concepts. According to the notion of semantic features, any one of the many concepts we know may be decomposed into a few semantic features, just as molecules of matter may be decomposed into atoms. The bird concept, for example, may be decomposed into the features of living, laying eggs, and having feathers. The assumption is that there are fewer features than concepts, and that features are semantically simpler than the concepts whose meaning they describe. One version of a semantic feature approach to concepts is called the classical approach. According to the classical approach, a concept contains only its necessary and sufficient features (e.g., a bird is a living creature that lays eggs and has feathers). The problem with the classical approach is that the instances that make up many concepts (e.g., love, game) have no set of features in common. Another problem is that the classical approach cannot account for the typicality effect observed in semantic memory experiments. The typicality effect is that subjects are faster at making decisions about typical members of categories (e.g., "a canary is a bird") than about atypical members (e.g., "an ostrich is a bird").

An alternative way to think about the semantic features of concepts is called the prototype approach. The prototype approach assumes that concepts are made up of their characteristic features. These are the features observed in most, but not necessarily all, instances of the concept. According to prototype theory, a bird would be decomposed into features such as flies and lives in trees, because most birds fly and live in trees.

The prototype approach has inspired several models of how people answer questions (e.g., "Is a canary a bird?") posed to them in semantic memory experiments. The feature comparison model describes a strategy in which the list of characteristic features associated with the potential exemplar (e.g., "canary") is compared with the list of characteristic features associated with the larger category (e.g., "bird"). When a feature from one list is found on the other list, positive evidence accrues; when a feature from one list is not found on the other list, negative evidence accrues.

The spreading activation model translates the feature comparison model into a quasi-neurological model in which questions excite concepts that then spread activation to other concepts and features with which they are connected in a network. Response times in semantic memory experiments depend on how quickly features and concepts are excited by the spread of activation through the network. The next chapter will greatly expand the discussion of the neurophysiological underpinnings of implicit and explicit memory.

Both the feature comparison model and the spreading activation model can account for the typicality effect. Both models can also account for two other effects, the false relatedness effect and the levels effect. False relatedness means that subjects are faster at judging that a statement is false when the concepts are unrelated (e.g., "a canary is a vehicle") than when the concepts are related (e.g., "a canary is a mammal"). The levels effect means that people are more facile with concepts situated in intermediate levels of a hierarchy (the basic level) of concepts. In addition, the spreading activation model accounts for the semantic priming effect whereby subjects are faster at judging that an exemplar is a member of a category if on the previous trial they made the judgment about concepts related to the category.

I concluded the chapter with a discussion of some newer approaches to semantic memory. One new approach is to simulate semantic memory with neural net models that depict concepts as patterns of connections among a large population of input, hidden, and output units. Neural net models may be contrasted with the symbol system approach implicit in the feature comparison and spreading activation models. In neural nets, no one unit stands for or symbolizes a concept; rather the concept is represented by a distributed set of connections. The activation of a concept by a query is represented by a pattern of activation throughout the network of connections, which vary in type (excitatory and inhibitory) and strength. Neural net models can account for some semantic priming effects not readily accounted for by symbol systems. Furthermore, neural net models can readily simulate the effects of brain damage on semantic memory.

Another new approach to semantic memory eschews semantic features in favor of implicit theories. According to the implicit theory approach, concepts are understood by reference to an implicit theory that explains why the concepts have the features they do. An implicit theory of the concept bird would focus on the DNA of birds that enables them to fly. An advantage of the implicit theory approach is that it avoids the difficulty that concepts may have an unlimited number of semantic features, depending on the context in which the concept is used. Some research suggests that people compare concepts based on implicit theories and not on features per se, and that, by age 8, most people understand concepts according to implicit theories and not superficial features. To use an example from Putnam (1975), people know that painting brass with the color of gold does not turn brass into gold. Rather, changing brass into gold would require altering the molecular structure of brass. Gold's characteristic yellow color is given to it by virtue of its molecular structure. Implicit theories will reappear in chapter 11, on cognitive development. First, however, the discussion of memory continues in the next chapter, the physiological basis of implicit and explicit memory.

RECOMMENDED READINGS

Schacter's (1996) *Searching for Memory* provides an extensive and beautifully written discussion of implicit (as well as explicit) memory. Schacter is one of the world's leading experts on implicit memory. Bowers and Farvolden (1996) have a recent review article in which they discuss how Freud came to understand repression; modern theories of repression; and the controversy surrounding the reality of repression. Loftus (1993) describes research relevant to repression and false memories. She elaborates on her skepticism concerning the reality of repression in a coauthored book, *The Myth of Repressed Memory* by Loftus and Ketcham (1994). Spanos's fascinating and creative research on past-life regression (Spanos et al, 1991) is must reading for those interested in the false memory issue. Wright's book on the Paul Ingram case, *Remembering Satan* (1994), is one of the most compelling and disturbing case studies on the repression issue. The book makes clear the devastating impact on families and whole communities that false accusation of abuse can have. Chang (1986) reviews previous research on semantic memory, the heyday for which was back in the 1970s. Best's *Cognitive Psychology* (1995), one of my competitors in the field of cognitive textbooks, has a nice chapter comparing symbol system approaches to neural net approaches. For an articulate and interesting introduction to the implicit theory approach to semantic memory, try Murphy and Medin (1985).

6 *The Physiology of Learning and Remembering*

In the 1950s a patient known as H. M. suffered from debilitating temporal lobe seizures. The surgeon, William B. Scoville, removed the medial portion of both of H. M.'s temporal lobes and so reduced the disturbing effects of the seizures. Unfortunately, the surgery also caused a devastating memory deficit. H. M. lost the ability to form explicit memories. For example, he could never remember interacting with members of the hospital staff, even though he saw them every day. Yet H. M. had a clear memory for events prior to the operation, such as what job he held; retained good use of language; and continued to score in the bright-normal range on IQ tests. And he retained the capacity to acquire implicit memories, such as learning new perceptual-motor skills.

The purpose of this chapter is to discuss the physiology of learning and remembering—the physical changes that occur to neurons that enable us to profit from experiences and consciously remember those experiences. The main theme is that learning and remembering reflect changes in the strengths of connections among neurons involved in perception, language, and so on. There is no discrete place in the brain dedicated specifically to learning and memory. In a sense, this chapter provides the physiological basis for the constructionist theory of memory developed in previous chapters. Much of what we have learned about the physiology of learning and remembering comes from tragic cases like that of H. M. Perhaps the knowledge humanity gains from the misfortunes of these patients and the potential for using this knowledge to repair brain damage will mean that they will not have suffered in vain.

NEURAL TRANSMISSION

Before developing the main theme of this chapter, I need to provide some background on neural transmission. The brain consists of tens of billions of **neurons** and tens of billions of support cells that function largely to nourish and support the neurons (see Carlson, 1994). The neurons are unique in that only they carry an electrochemical impulse and communicate with other cells. Most neurons receive thousands of inputs from other neurons and send thousands of outputs to other neurons. In some cases a neuron can send outputs back to a neuron from which it receives inputs, and in some cases will send outputs to itself.

A typical neuron consists of a main cell body (or **soma**) that contains the nucleus, a long slender tube called an **axon** that sends signals to other neurons, and **dendrites** that receive signals from other neurons. The dendrites resemble the branches of a tree. A neuron in its resting state has more negatively charged ions inside its axon than outside; that is, the resting electrical charge of the axonal membrane is negative (typically about –70 mV). The cell fires when positive ions enter the cell causing the voltage to become more positive. Once a threshold value is reached the cell conducts an electrical signal down the axonal membrane toward the terminal end of the axon. Neurons are rarely inactive; they usually propagate electrical impulses (fire) dozens of times per second (and sometimes as often as 500 times per second) at what is called a base rate.

As illustrated in Figure 6-1, neurons are separated by tiny gaps called **synapses**; the gap itself is called the synaptic cleft and is typically about 200 angstroms wide (one angstrom is one ten-millionth of a millimeter). The vast majority of neurons communicate with other neurons through the medium of **neurotransmitters** that are released from small vesicles at the end of the neuron's axon. When the signal reaches the terminal buttons of the axon, calcium ions enter the terminal buttons, activate protein molecules which then propel neurotransmitter-containing vesicles to the presynaptic membrane, where they burst open and spill their neurotransmitter into the synaptic cleft. The axonal

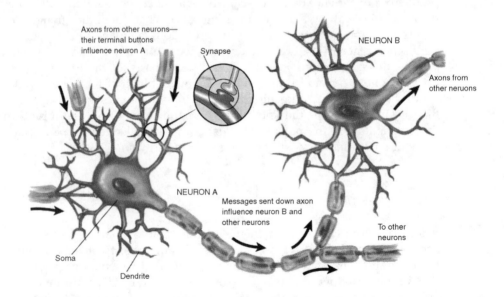

FIGURE 6–1   An overview of the synaptic connections between neurons. From Noel R. Carlson (1994), *Physiology of Behavior*, 5E. Allyn and Bacon.

membrane that releases the neurotransmitter is called the **presynaptic membrane**. The neurotransmitter diffuses across the synaptic cleft and attaches to receptor sites located on the dendrites of the next neuron. The process usually takes less than 1 millisecond. The dendritic membrane to which the neurotransmitter attaches is usually called the **postsynaptic membrane**. Communication at any one synapse is usually one way—from the pre- to the postsynaptic membrane. For the sake of clarity I'll call the neuron releasing the neurotransmitter the **presynaptic** or **transmitting neuron** and the neuron receiving the neurotransmitter the **postsynaptic** or **receiving neuron**.

Neurotransmitters have their effect on the receiving neuron by altering the postsynaptic membrane's permeability. When the action of the neurotransmitter is excitatory, then electrical potential difference between the inside and outside of the postsynaptic membrane is reduced—the inside becomes more positive—and the receiving neuron is moved closer to the state at which it fires. If enough neurotransmitter attaches to the postsynaptic membrane then the receiving neuron will fire. The postsynaptic neuron will receive the requisite amount of neurotransmitter if a few transmitting neurons fire at appreciable rates for an extended period of time (**temporal summation of neurotransmitter**) or if lots of transmitting neurons simultaneously send neurotransmitter to the receiving neuron (**spatial summation of neurotransmitter**).

In many cases the neurotransmitter has an inhibitory effect. In inhibition, the action of the neurotransmitter is to increase the difference in electrical potential between the inside and outside of the postsynaptic membrane—the inside becomes more negative—and so move the receiving neuron farther away from the state at which it will fire. Spatial and temporal summation of neurotransmitter acting to inhibit will decrease the firing rate of the receiving neuron. Currently, most neuroscientists believe that what is informative to the brain is whether a neuron is firing either faster or slower than its base rate. That is, information is primarily carried by changes to the firing rates of neurons.

To complete the story of neural communication, there are also processes by which neurotransmitters are removed from the synapse. Enzymes residing in the postsynaptic membrane may enter the synaptic cleft and break down the neurotransmitters into inactive parts. In some cases the action of the presynaptic membrane pumps neurotransmitters out of the synaptic cleft and back into the transmitting neuron. Thus a neurotransmitter's effect on a receiving neuron is only temporary. Unless the transmitting neurons continue to pump more than the average amount of neurotransmitter into the synapse, the receiving neuron will return to its base rate of firing.

The number of neurons and the gross pattern of connections among neurons are for the most part established by developmental processes taking place in the womb and first few months of life. After that time no new neurons grow. In fact, there is dramatic cell loss just before birth. So experiences do not increase the number of neurons or make any dramatic changes in which neurons any given neuron is connected to. Instead, as I discuss in the next section, experiences seem to influence the strengths of connections among neurons.

SECTION 1: THE PHYSIOLOGY OF LEARNING

Learning usually entails the formation of associations among elements whereas remembering reflects accessing those associations. The fact that associations are at the core of learning and memory (Fanselow, 1993) is revealed in various learning paradigms (Lieberman, 1990).

Classical conditioning, first studied systematically by Pavlov (1927), involves an association between an initially impotent stimulus (e.g., a bell) that does not elicit a target behavior (e.g., salivation) and a potent stimulus (e.g., food) that does elicit the target behavior. The pairing of the stimuli will eventually turn the impotent stimulus into a potent stimulus (e.g., the bell elicits salivation). An example of classical conditioning in humans is consumers finding that an automobile becomes more attractive when it is advertised with an attractive model.

Association is at the core of **instrumental conditioning** as well. Instrumental conditioning typically involves an association between a behavior (e.g., pressing on a bar) and a stimulus (e.g., a bright light) that signals that the behavior will lead to a reward (e.g., a morsel of food). Examples of instrumental conditioning in humans are employees going to work during weekdays in order to obtain money, and inmates studying school subjects in order to get extra privileges.

Some instances of learning do not involve associating behaviors to stimuli but instead entail associations among mental elements. In **conceptual learning**, new concepts are often associated with old concepts. An example is a student learning about electricity by associating the idea of the flow of electrons to the idea of the flow of water in a river. Recollections of past events involve associations among ideas, feelings, images, and so on. An example is an old ballplayer recalling a championship game in which images of getting the winning hit are associated with images of the baseball stadium, feelings of elation, and knowledge of baseball.

What is the physiological basis of the associations that lie at the core of learning and memory? That is, what happens in the brain to make it possible to learn from experience? One might imagine any of a number of physiological mechanisms for learning. Maybe learning involves growing new neurons, or altering the chemical composition of regions of the brain, or increasing the rate at which neural signals are conducted. In fact, the current view is that experiences **change the strength of the connections between neurons**, and that such connections form the basis of remembering the experience later on (Carlson, 1994). Donald Hebb was one of the first modern psychologists to propose that learning entails the alteration of the synapse so as to increase or decrease the connection strength between neurons (Hebb, 1949).

LONG-TERM POTENTIATION

One physiological paradigm for learning that has received a lot of interest in recent years is known as **long-term potentiation**. Long-term potentiation refers to a long-term increase in the excitability of a receiving neuron to a particular synaptic input from a transmitting neuron caused by high frequency activity of that transmitting neuron (Carlson, 1994). In effect, the synaptic connection between the transmitting neuron and the receiving neuron increases in strength. As a result, it will subsequently take a lower rate of firing in the transmitting neuron to initiate an increase in the firing rate of the receiving neuron. Many researchers (e.g., Fanselow, 1993) believe that long-term potentiation is a primary mechanism—perhaps *the* primary mechanism—whereby the brain establishes the associations that lie at the core of learning.

Experimental Evidence for Long-Term Potentiation

The primary experimental evidence for long-term potentiation comes from the study of the **hippocampus**, a section of the limbic system of the brain located just underneath the temporal lobes. Most of the research has been done on rodent hippocampi, which are sometimes removed prior to the study. If preserved properly, a rat's hippocampal tissue can maintain neural activity for several days in vitro. In animals, at least, the hippocampus seems to play a role in learning about spatial arrangements. Rats with intact hippocampi can learn to navigate their environment, especially in order to locate food. This skill is lost if the hippocampus is bilaterally removed (Olson & Samuelson, 1976). The hippocampus intrigues memory researchers because in human and nonhuman mammals it plays a unique role in the recollection of the past, as I discuss in a subsequent section of this chapter.

Several lines of evidence support the long-term potentiation mechanism. Lomo (1966, 1971) and Bliss and Lomo (1973) studied the neurons in the rat's entorhinal cortex (a region of cerebral cortex close to the hippocampus), which sends axons to the dendrites of granule cells in the dentate gyrus, a part of the hippocampus (see Figure 6-2). The granule cells in turn send axons to other parts of the hippocampus. When an axon of the entorhinal cortex is artificially stimulated by just one pulse of electrical current, the receiving neuron in the dentate gyrus will respond by temporarily increasing its rate of firing. This can be observed through single-cell recording of neurons in the dentate gyrus. The experimenters stimulated neurons in the entorhinal cortex with hundreds of pulses per second. A few minutes after receiving this intense electrical stimulation, the activation of the entorhinal cortex by only a single pulse then caused the neurons of the dentate gyrus to increase the intensity of firing by about 250%, compared with the firing rate before the intense stimulation. Dramatically increasing the firing rate of the axons of the entorhinal cortex, then, causes the dendrites of the dentate gyrus to become more receptive to future firings of the transmitting neurons in the entorhinal cortex.

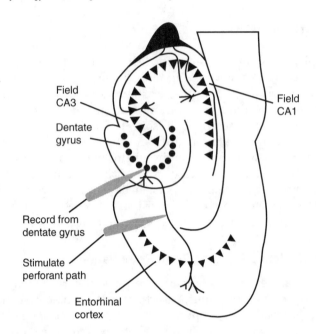

Field
CA3

Dentate
gyrus

Field
CA1

Record from
dentate gyrus

Stimulate
perforant path

Entorhinal
cortex

FIGURE 6–2   The procedure for producing long-term potentiation in the hippocampus. From Noel R. Carlson (1994), *Physiology of Behavior*, 5E. Allyn and Bacon.

Research on long-term potentiation has uncovered many cases where a receiving neuron will become more sensitive to neurotransmitter only when two different transmitting neurons fire in some particular pattern. For example, in some cases a receiving neuron will increase its sensitivity to neurotransmitter only when two transmitting neurons simultaneously increase their firing rates. Another example is that of a receiving neuron increasing its sensitivity to neurotransmitter only when one transmitting neuron fires 200 milliseconds before a second transmitting neuron. If both transmitting neurons fire at the same time or if the delay between the increased firing rates of the two transmitting neurons is longer than 2 seconds, then the receiving neuron will not show much increase in sensitivity to neurotransmitter (Larson & Lynch, 1986).

Current research suggests that one of the important neurotransmitters responsible for long-term potentiation in the hippocampus is the excitatory neurotransmitter called **glutamate**, and one of the important receptors to which glutamate binds is called an **NMDA** (short for **n-methyl-d-asparate**) **receptor** (see Cotman, Monaghan, & Ganong, 1988; Fanselow, 1993; or Carlson, 1994, for a summary of NMDA receptors and their role in long-term potentiation). The most compelling evidence for the role of NMDA receptors in long-term potentiation comes from studies with drugs that block NMDA receptors. One such drug is AP5. Research establishes that when the drug is injected into the hippocampus the result is that long-term potentiation is impaired (e.g., Brown, Ganong, Kairiss, Keenan, & Kelso, 1989; Davis, Butcher, & Morris, 1992). It is also known that the amount of AP5 necessary to impair long-term potentiation parallels the dose necessary to impair learning (e.g., Morris, Anderson, Lynch, & Baudry, 1986; see Fanselow, 1993). That learning is impaired when long-term potentiation is also impaired increases our confidence that the long-term potentiation mechanism underlies learning. For example, rats injected with AP5 (and similar NMDA blockers) do not learn to suppress activity when placed in a chamber where they have been shocked, as will ordinary rats (e.g., Kim, Fanselow, DeCola, & Landeira-Fernandez, 1992; Young, Fanselow, & Bohenek, 1992; other examples of learning becoming undermined when NMDA blockers are used include Staubli, Thibault, DiLorenzo, & Lynch, 1989; and Robinson, Crooks, Shinkman, & Gallagher, 1989). However, the interpretation that NMDA receptors mediate long-term potentiation has been disputed (Keith & Rudy, 1990; but see Fanselow, 1993).

The Synaptic Basis for Long-Term Potentiation

What structural changes occur at the synapse to enable long-term potentiation? Two of the more likely mechanisms are: (1) an increase in the sensitivity of the postsynaptic membrane to neurotransmitter and (2) an increase in the amount of neurotransmitter released by the presynaptic membrane. These are illustrated in Figure 6-3. Evidence suggests that the brain uses both of these mechanisms.

Currently, there is some consensus that the long-term potentiation mediated by NMDA receptors (and possibly by other receptor types) is initiated in the postsynaptic neurons by the entry of calcium ions (Carlson, 1994). Apparently the calcium ions activate several calcium-dependent enzymes called **protein kinases**. These enzymes in turn have various affects on the postsynaptic membrane, including that of increasing the number and sensitivity of glutamate receptors in the postsynaptic membrane. That is, the postsynaptic membrane acquires more receptive sites to which neurotransmitter can bind (Lynch, Muller, Seubert, & Larson, 1988; Desmond & Levy, 1988). Geinisman, de Toledo-Morrell, and Morrell (1991) found that long-term potentiation in the hippocampus increased the number of synapses with more than one receptive site and more than one region containing a postsynaptic thickening. The increase in receptor sites means that during future transmissions more neurotransmitter can bind to the postsynaptic membrane and less neurotransmitter is left wasted in the synaptic cleft. Injecting the hippocampus with the drug EGTA, which makes calcium insoluble, prevents neurons from becoming potentiated by intense stimuli (Lynch, Larson, Kelso, Barrionuevo, & Schottler, 1984).

Apparently the postsynaptic membrane retains this increased sensitivity for as long as several days or even weeks. However, the postsynaptic membrane will eventually lose its increased sensitivity in the absence of any more intense stimulation of its transmitting neurons. Neurophysiologists have speculated that the postsynaptic membrane eventually alters its structure in such a way as to lose its extra receptor surface area (McNaughton, 1989).

More recently, evidence has been obtained that suggests another synaptic basis for long-term potentiation. It may be that stimulation of the postsynaptic membrane causes the postsynaptic membrane to send a "retrograde messen-

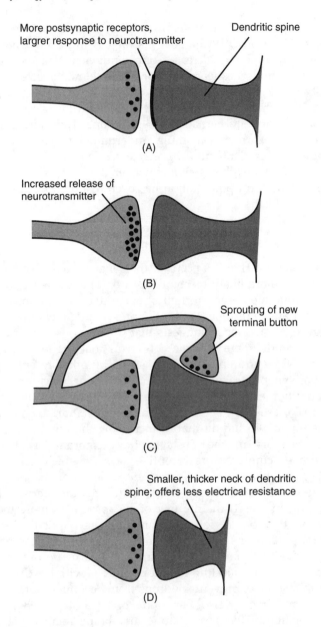

More postsynaptic receptors,
largrer response to neurotransmitter

Dendritic spine

(A)

Increased release of
neurotransmitter

(B)

Sprouting of new
terminal button

(C)

Smaller, thicker neck of dendritic
spine; offers less electrical resistance

(D)

FIGURE 6–3   Hypothetical changes that could account for the synaptic strengthening
produced by long-term potentiation. From Noel R. Carlson (1994), *Physiology of
Behavior*, 5E. Allyn and Bacon.

ger" back to the presynaptic membrane that subsequently transforms the presynaptic membrane in such a way that it will release more neurotransmitter per
firing (Carlson, 1994). There is evidence that in some hippocampal areas displaying long-term potentiation, the presynaptic neuron releases more glutamate

neurotransmitter than before the potentiation took place (Dolphin, Errington, & Bliss, 1982; see Lynch & Baudry, 1991; Siegelbaum & Kandel, 1991). Note that the idea of a retrograde messenger runs counter to the usual case that transmission in the synapse goes in one direction, from presynaptic to postsynaptic membrane. Nitric oxide has been identified as a possible retrograde messenger (see Kandel & Hawkins, 1992). Inhibiting the synthesis of nitric oxide in the postsynaptic membrane prevents long-term potentiation (Haley, Wilcox, & Chapman, 1992).

The long-term potentiation mechanism is not limited to the hippocampal system using glutamate and NMDA receptors. It is a learning mechanism that is likely used in disparate neurological sites that may use any of several neurotransmitters.

Evidence that long-term potentiation takes place in tissue outside the hippocampus can be found in Berger (1984); Iriki, Pavlides, Keller, and Asanuma (1989); and Abraham, Corballis, and White (1991). For example, research done on young chicks has established areas in the chick's cortex that are altered as a function of imprinting and making visual distinctions between tasteful and distasteful objects. If these regions are examined at high magnification under an electron microscope, it can be observed that the number of neurotransmitter-containing vesicles in the presynaptic membrane increases relative to regions not involved in the learning (Horn, 1985). As another example, high-frequency stimulation of individual cells in the motor cortex of cats resulted in long-term potentiation of neurons to which they were connected (Kimura, Caria, Melis, & Asanuma, 1994).

Research indicates that glutamate is not the only neurotransmitter involved in long-term potentiation (Carlson, 1994). For example, acetylcholine and norepinephrine have been shown to facilitate long-term potentiation in hippocampal tissue (Burgard & Sarvey, 1990; Markram & Segal, 1990; Dahl & Sarvey, 1989). Furthermore, long-term potentiation has also been established in visual cortex that does not involve NMDA receptors (Aroniadou & Teyler, 1991; see Carlson, 1994, and Fanselow, 1993, for other examples).

NEURAL RESPONSES TO EXPERIENCE

Demonstrations of long-term potentiation generally involve experimenters artificially stimulating a neuron. What about learning from ordinary experience—does experience produce the same kinds of synaptic changes observed in demonstrations of long-term potentiation? The answer appears to be yes. When the brains of animals that have been reared in enriched (i.e., highly stimulating) environments are compared with the brains of animals reared in impoverished environments, the neurons in the "enriched" brains have more synapses, different distributions of presynaptic vesicles (which contain neurotransmitter), altered shapes and sizes of synapses and synaptic contact zones, and greater amounts of dendritic branching (Weiler, Hawrylak, & Greenough, 1995). Such neural changes would impact the strength of connections between neurons and so reflect the increased amount of learning presumably experienced by the animals in the more stimulating environment.

For example, young rats placed in a cage with lots of toys and other objects can be compared with rats reared in a visually dull cage. When the brains of the animals are later dissected, the visual cortex of the visually enriched animals typically contains about 10% more branching of the dendrites than does the visual cortex of the visually impoverished animals. Furthermore, there are more synapses on the neurons and thicker dendritic spines (Greenough, 1975; Sirevaag & Greenough, 1987). Experiences can induce rather rapid changes in neural structure. Wallace, Kilman, Withers, and Greenough (1992) found that the neurons in the visual cortex of rats housed for only four days in a stimulating environment had substantially longer dendrites and more dendritic branching than did the neurons of rats housed in a duller environment.

The ability to grow more extensive dendritic branches is not limited to the young. Even adult animals placed in enriched environments for a period of weeks will grow more dendritic branches than control adult animals. Studies of human brains suggest that at least some portions of the brain—for example, the hippocampal cortex—show more extensive dendritic branching in elderly adults (average age of death 79.6 years) than in middle-aged adults (average age of death 51.2 years). Interestingly, elderly adults (average age of death 76 years) diagnosed with senile dementia had less extensive dendritic branching than the middle-aged adults (Buell & Coleman, 1978). Dementia is, in part, characterized by memory impairment.

It is important to demonstrate that neural changes, such as increased dendritic growth, observed in the environmentally enriched animals occurs only in the relevant cortex (e.g., visual cortex for animals raised in a visually enriched environment) and nowhere else in the brain; otherwise, the neural changes might not be due to learning but to improved health or motivation of animals reared in a more interesting environment. Accordingly, research has shown that if rats are given only unilateral exposure to a visually interesting environment, only the dendrites of neurons activated by the exposed eye increase their density (Chang & Greenough, 1982). Other experiments have varied the amount of motor stimulation, olfactory stimulation, and social stimulation in the environments of rats and demonstrated an increase in the dendritic branching in the relevant areas of the brain (see Greenough & Bailey, 1988).

NEURAL BASIS OF FORGETTING

The evidence from physiology suggests that a change in the strength of connections between neurons is typically temporary; over time a strong connection can become weaker or a weak connection can become stronger (Carlson, 1994). The alteration of the strengths among neural connections previously established by learning is a basis of forgetting.

Recall that long-term potentiation is not permanent. There is also evidence that when some of the synapses of a receiving neuron are made more sensitive to neurotransmitter released by the transmitting neurons, the other synapses of the receiving neuron become less sensitive to that neurotransmitter (Abraham & Goddard, 1983; Levy & Steward, 1979). If the postsynaptic neuron is artificially stimulated without a corresponding stimulation of the presynaptic membrane, then any previously established long-term potentiation between the neurons is diminished (Stanton & Sejnowski, 1989).

Also providing a basis for forgetting is the phenomenon of **long-term depression**. Long-term depression refers to a reduction in the activity of the receiving neuron caused by low-frequency activity in the transmitting neuron. For example, Dudek and Bear (1992) demonstrated that stimulating the neural inputs to neurons in the hippocampus at a rate above 10 Hz caused an increase in the sensitivity of those neurons to subsequent input activity (long-term potentiation) but at a rate below 10 Hz caused those neurons to be less sensitive to subsequent input activity (long-term depression). Stanton and Sejnowski (1989) demonstrated that in some hippocampal neurons, long-term potentiation occurred when a weak input was simultaneously paired with a strong input. However, if the two inputs were stimulated at different times, then long-term depression occurred. Long-term depression has also been demonstrated in the motor cortex of cats (Sil'kis, Rapoport, Veber, & Gushchin, 1994). It should be noted that while long-term depression could account for a weakening of connections previously established by learning (i.e., forgetting), it could also reflect a kind of learning. Often, learning takes the form of weakening one thought or response while strengthening another thought or response. An example is learning that sharks do not lay eggs, as do other fish, but bear their young live, as do most mammals.

The changing of connection strengths strongly suggests that the brain does not keep a detailed record of each of its experiences. Instead, it constantly erases records of its past by altering the strength of connections among neurons. This does not mean that people have no memory for past events; obviously they do. It means that accurate memory for the details of some past event requires that the connections representing the event not be changed or reconfigured. As I discussed in previous chapters, if an event is recent then the connections will not yet be altered. If an event is thought about repeatedly, then its configuration of connection strengths will be maintained and possibly represented in several locations in the brain. If an event is distinctive, then the precise connections involved in representing the event are unlikely to be reconfigured, since similar events that would do so do not occur. Finally, many events may be reconstructible from the current configuration of connection strengths, even though the connections that originally represented the event have been altered.

It might seem that it would be advantageous to have a brain that did keep records of all experiences. However, such a hypothetical brain would presumably need neurons dedicated only to storing experiences. Until such neurons were activated by experience, they would contribute nothing to mental function but would nevertheless require energy to survive. Certainly there is no evidence for blocks of inactive neurons that could serve as repositories of memory records. Instead, nearly all neurons are connected to thousands of other neurons through direct and indirect connections and are firing at appreciable rates nearly all the time. At any rate, if there were inactive neurons waiting to be connected by experience, we would run into a big problem when those neurons finally all became "activated"—we would no longer be able to store new experiences. Yet many elderly people are capable of learning new skills and recollecting recently occurring events.

SECTION 2: THE PHYSIOLOGY OF MEMORY

Recall from previous chapters that a conscious recollection of the past (explicit memory) involves reconstructing past events based on the current state of the cognitive system and on information in the environment. Recall, too, that past events can affect current thought and behavior even if one has no memory for the events (implicit memory). This section will examine the physiological basis for explicit and implicit memory.

THE PHYSIOLOGY OF EXPLICIT MEMORY

What is the physiological basis of consciously remembering a past experience? Suppose you attend a wine-tasting party at an art museum (maybe the same wine-tasting party attended by Dr. Laura Light, who so impressed the engineer in the previous chapter), meet a guy named Jim, and get into an argument with him over the plausibility of the science fiction movie *Total Recall* in which the main character has memories of a trip to Mars implanted in his brain. Naturally, you argue against the film's plausibility. In order to recollect this experience consciously, you would need to associate wine tasting, the physical setting of the museum, Jim's name, Jim's facial features, the plot of *Total Recall*, and the debate. Merely thinking about the taste of wine or the name "Jim" would not, in and of itself, constitute having a memory about the party. As I discussed in the previous chapter, we can say that a conscious recollection of the past entails accessing a distributed set of associations among several different cognitive systems, such as the systems underlying taste, vision, and language. We would expect, then, that the physiological basis for explicit memory lies in the integrated activity of a variety of distinct neural centers, each making a separate contribution to the phenomenological character of the memory.

I will first discuss some of the evidence that different neural centers make different contributions to a conscious recollection, and then discuss where and how in the brain these disparate centers are integrated so as to produce the sense of remembering a specific past event.

The Distributed Nature of Memory

Historically, physiological psychologists have debated whether memory (or any cognitive process) is localized to one particular area of the brain or is distributed about the brain (Gardner, 1985). Some record-keeping models, especially those that take seriously the idea of computers as metaphors for memory, would suggest a localized view; there ought to be a place in the brain that functions like the memory chip of the computer. Constructionist models of memory suggest a distributed view of memory. If memory represents changes to how we interpret and act on experiences, then the places where memory is located in the brain would be the same as the places where the brain functions to enable perception, language, movement, and so on.

The neurological evidence supports the constructionist prediction: Memory is not "located" in one area of the brain but is distributed about many areas of the brain. However, each area of the brain makes a different contribution to the conscious experience of remembering. That is, there is no brain area specifically dedicated to memory; memory does not exist as a separate system in the brain. In this respect, memory is not like visual perception or language, for which anatomically distinct neural systems exist. Instead, memory is a byproduct of changes in connection strengths among areas of the brain dedicated to perception, language, action, and so on.

The main source of evidence for the distributed account of memory distribution comes from studying brain damage caused by strokes, diseases, or missile penetration. Such damage often selectively interferes with one cognitive process, and with the memory associated with that process, but leaves intact other cognitive processes and the memories associated with those other cognitive processes.

The frontal lobe seems to have a planning and regulatory function; its contribution to memory therefore seems to be to implement the strategies that underlie making new information more memorable and the strategies for reconstructing the past. Damasio, Graff-Radford, Eslinger, Damasio, and Kassell (1985) found that patients with damage to the basal forebrain (much of which is located in the frontal lobes) sometimes produce wild fabrications of past events from their own lives, which seem to combine details from newspapers, TV shows, and other irrelevant sources. Yet such patients can recognize words or objects from lists presented to them in memory experiments nearly as well as control groups of ordinary people. Janowsky, Shimamura, and Squire (1989) found that patients with frontal lobe lesions had a difficult time predicting whether they would be able to recognize words they were unable to recall from a previously presented list of words. A control group of amnesic patients with damage in the hippocampus area but not in the frontal lobes, on the other hand, had a harder time recalling words but were better than the frontal lobe patients at predicting whether they would be able to recognize words they couldn't recall. Presumably, the ability to predict how well one can recognize words that one could not recall reflects the planning function of the frontal lobe.

Frontal lobe damage has also been shown to interfere with memory for the temporal order of events. In experiments done by Shimamura, Janowsky, and Squire (1990), patients with frontal lobe damage were compared with control groups who experienced damage in the temporal lobes. All subjects were presented lists of words or photographs of paintings and from time to time were shown a pair and had to decide which of two words or which of two photographs was presented more recently. Compared with the control groups, the frontal lobe patients had difficulties with the recency task, but did well with a task in which they had only to recognize whether they had seen a given word or a given photograph on the list. Skill at reconstructing when an event took place is thought to reflect, in part, a strategy by which people assume that the more detail they can recall about an event, the more recent the event must be (Brown, Rips, & Shevell, 1985). If frontal lobe damage undermines the use of reconstruction strategies, then it follows that frontal lobe patients will have difficulty making temporal judgments.

Occipital and temporal lobe cortex play a role in visual perception; brain damage to those areas will undermine visual perception. The damage will also interfere with visual memory. In some cases individuals with this type of brain damage will have difficulty in recognizing faces or common objects by sight alone, although they may recognize objects from touch. Yet such individuals are not blind. This deficit is called **apperceptive visual agnosia**. Such individuals will also have difficulty in learning to recognize the shape of new objects or faces but usually continue to be able to read (Carlson, 1994). Yet their memory for nonvisual information, such as facts, will not be impaired. Apperceptive visual agnosia is usually associated with damage to the medial portion of the occipital and posterior temporal cortex. Other patients may exhibit a slightly different problem; they may be able to perceive an object, as evidenced by retaining the ability to draw a picture of an object, but not be able to recall the name for the object. Similarly, they may have trouble learning new object–name associations. This deficit is called **associative visual agnosia**, the anatomical basis of which has not been established (see Carlson, 1994).

One more example of the distributed nature of memory. The left posterior frontal lobe and the left temporal lobe control the use and comprehension of language. Damage to those areas will produce **aphasia**, disorder in the use of language. Aphasic patients also have difficulty remembering verbal information, but have less difficulty remembering nonverbal information (Cermak & Moreines, 1976; Cermak & Tarlow, 1978; DeRenzi & Nichelli, 1975).

The distributed nature of memory makes it unlikely that people will ever be able to take a memory pill that will induce in them memories of past experiences or enable them to suddenly acquire a skill such as speaking a foreign language. The chemical in the pill would have to migrate to a variety of locations and alter the strength of connections among just the right neurons in each of those locations. If the chemical altered the connections among the wrong neurons or failed to affect the appropriate neurons, the memory would not be induced. No reasonable mechanism has been proposed whereby a chemical could pick out sets of neurons and control the specific rates of firing for each neuron or the connection strengths between specific neurons. Instead, chemicals seem to have a more general effect; they seem to affect whole populations of neurons.

It may some day be possible, though, to take medication that will improve learning and memory in general. A variety of chemicals are known to have a widespread effect on the firing rate of large numbers of neurons. These chemicals include stimulants, depressants, hallucinogens, hormones, and a class of chemicals called neuromodulators that are released from within the brain. Unlike neurotransmitter, these chemicals do not transmit signals from one neuron to another but affect the activity of many anatomically separated neurons. But their presence in the brain may modulate learning (see Graham, 1990).

For example, when a person is in a highly emotional state, the hormones released may increase the activity of a large batch of neurons, making it more likely that processes like long-term potentiation will take place. As a result, people may be more likely to remember an association (like the connection between a name and a face) when they are in a highly emotional state than when they are in an emotionally neutral state (see Blaney, 1986). Injection of modulating drugs may improve the ability to learn new facts and skills in general, although it may not transmit any specific skills. There is interest in developing such drugs to help the elderly, some of whom have memory problems. Some research suggests that drugs that enhance the action of acetylcholine (a neurotransmitter) improve memory in people (Davis et al., 1978) whereas drugs that block the action of acetylcholine undermine memory in people (Drachman, 1978). However, acetylcholine-enhancing therapies have not helped Alzheimer's patients overcome their memory difficulties (Graham, 1990).

Integrating the Disparate Neural Centers: The Role of the Hippocampus

In order for a conscious recollection of a past event to take place, it is critical that there be some integration of, or association among, the disparate areas of the brain that make unique contributions to a conscious recollection. If one is to remember the wine-tasting party where the debate with Jim took place, the relevant neural systems of the perceptual, linguistic, and frontal lobe cortex must become activated in a coordinated or associated fashion. As I discussed before, if only one of these neural systems were activated but not somehow associated to other systems, then one might only have a sense that red wines are bolder than whites or that Jim is an ignoramus about the physiology of memory. It is only when such musings become integrated that one has the sense of remembering a particular event, such as debating memory with Jim at the wine-tasting party. Another way to put this is that the integration creates a context, a time and place, that gives one's musings the character of a memory of some specific event from one's past.

Recall that in the previous chapter on implicit memory I suggested that the essential difference between explicit and implicit memory was that explicit memory included distributed connections among cognitive systems that established a context. Physiological research suggests that it is the hippocampus, studied extensively in the work on long-term potentiation, that plays the major role in forming the connections among neurons from disparate places in the brain (Squire, 1992). The hippocampus is located in the temporal lobe and has major connections to many parts of the cerebral cortex and subcortical regions of the brain.

The main evidence for the role of the hippocampus in explicit memory comes from people who suffer **bilateral hippocampal damage**, usually due to strokes, viral attacks, or the unfortunate side effects of surgery. Probably the best-known example of hippocampal damage is the tragic case of H. M. (discussed at the beginning of the chapter) who, before the role of the hippocampus in memory was established, underwent bilateral removal of temporal areas of the brain that included the hippocampus (Milner, 1970; Milner, Corkin, & Teuber, 1968). As discussed before, he has a hard time consciously recollecting any event subsequent to the damage to his hippocampi, although his memory for events preceding the damage remains about normal. That is to say, H. M. suffers from **anterograde amnesia**. The amnesia extends to all sensory modalities. For example, he can hear the same joke over and over and find it funny every time; he does not remember previous recitations of the joke. He can be introduced repeatedly to a person and never remember having met them before. He has trouble navigating around the neighborhood in which he now lives because he moved there after the operation. He watches the news on television every night. Yet he has almost no memory for newsworthy events since 1953, the year in which the operation took place. But H. M.'s short-term memory seems about normal. For example, he can retain a new fact as long as he is able to rehearse it. But as soon as he is distracted, the fact is forgotten. H. M. is aware of his amnesia.

Anterograde amnesia in humans can also be caused by damage to brain centers outside the hippocampal area, although such damage may indirectly affect the functioning of the hippocampus. For example, thiamine (vitamin B1) deficiency undermines the brain's ability to metabolize glucose and so leads to shrinkage and death of neurons throughout the brain, especially in the thalamus and mammillary bodies. The resulting deficiency, known as **Korsakoff's syndrome**, includes anterograde amnesia as well as **retrograde amnesia** (poor memory for events just prior to the onset of the syndrome) (see Carlson, 1994). Thiamine deficiency is almost always caused by severe and prolonged alcoholism. As another example, Alzheimer's disease results in the degeneration of cerebral cortex as well as the hippocampus. The symptoms usually begin with minor forgetfulness but gradually progress to severe anterograde and retrograde amnesia. Also associated with Alzheimer's disease is confusion, hallucinations, depression, and disturbances to basic bodily functions (see Kalat, 1992).

The evidence seems pretty clear that the hippocampus plays a role only in the conscious recollection of the past—that is, in explicit memory—but plays no role in the unconscious influence of the past—that is, in implicit memory. (In the context of the physiology of memory, explicit memory is often called **declarative memory**, whereas implicit memory is often called **procedural memory**.) Patients with hippocampal damage are still able to learn new skills or make new perceptual distinctions. For example, H. M. learned the skill of drawing while watching his hand in a mirror at about the same rate as someone without amnesia (Milner, 1962, 1970). Other research has compared anterograde amnesics with control groups and found no difference between them in how quickly they learn to solve complex problems like the Tower of Hanoi problem, which involves stacking rings according to certain rules (Cohen and Corkin, 1981). Amnesics and control groups improve at the same rate when they practice rotary pursuit tasks (Cohen, 1984) and tasks that require reproducing complex patterns (Musen & Treisman, 1990). But the amnesics typically have no conscious recollection of experiences in which such skills were learned (see Squire, 1987, 1992).

Amnesics can become classically conditioned. For example, amnesics and control groups can both learn to blink their eyes in response to a signal, when, over a series of trials, the signal reliably anticipates a puff of air blown into the eyes (Daum, Channon, & Canavar, 1989). Again, though, the amnesics usually have no conscious memory of the series of trials in which signals preceded puffs of air.

Amnesics can learn to become primed by verbal stimuli. For example, if amnesics and control subjects are presented a list of words that contains raspberry, the probability doubles for both groups that the same word will be given as a response to stimuli such as "think of examples of fruit." But the amnesics are much less likely than the control subjects to remember that the word raspberry was on the previously studied list (Graf, Squire, & Mandler, 1984). Schacter, Church, and Treadwell (1994) presented amnesics and control subjects a list of spoken words. Later, subjects were given two tasks involving making judgments about words, some of which were on the original list. In the first task, the subjects had to identify words spoken against a background of white noise (an implicit priming task). White noise is a sound containing a blend of all audible frequencies. In the second task, they had to determine for each of a set of words spoken without background white noise whether it had been presented earlier in the experiment (an explicit recognition task). Amnesics performed like the control subjects on the implicit task—both groups more readily identified in the white noise the words that had been presented earlier. However, the amnesics performed much worse on the recognition task.

How does the Hippocampus Produce an Explicit Memory?

The evidence suggests that destruction of the hippocampus undermines explicit but not implicit memory. In some sense, then, the hippocampus functions to bind together elements of various cognitive systems, giving those bound elements the character of a memory of some specific event (Eichenbaum & Bunsey, 1995). By what means does the hippocampus perform its binding function?

First of all, it is important to understand that the hippocampus is not the site of memory; rather, the information needed to reconstruct past events involves neural activity in various disparate sites in the brain. Memory is neuroanatomically distributed. We know this because the destruction of the hippocampus does not eliminate memory for events that occurred prior to several years before the damage (Squire, 1992). So the role of the hippocampus in explicit memory must be a temporary one.

Let me sketch out for you what I think is one reasonable model of how and why the hippocampus plays a role in memory (based on Mishkin & Appenzeller, 1987; Squire, 1992; Halgren, 1984; McNaughton & Nadel, 1990; and McClelland & Rumelhart, 1986b). The basic idea is that the hippocampus serves to prolong the activity of neurons that connect disparate cognitive systems, and so enhance the strength of the connections those neurons serve.

I will illustrate the model by using it to explain the results of an experiment by Johnson, Kim, and Risse (1985). The experimenters presented amnesics and control subjects without amnesia a set of novel melodies. Later, the subjects were presented the same set of melodies, as well as a new set of novel melodies. In a test of preference, both groups tended to find more aesthetically pleasing the melodies that were previously played to them. In fact, it is a common finding that people prefer things that are familiar. Note that the familiarity effect, an example of implicit memory, was observed in the amnesics. Unlike the normal subjects, however, the amnesics were usually unable to remember where they had heard the melodies that they perceived as pleasing—namely, in the experimental laboratory setting. The amnesics had poor explicit memory for the melodies.

The model to explain these results begins by noting that listening to a novel melody played in a laboratory setting activates neurons dedicated to vision, audition, emotion, and so on. The activation of these disparate systems of neurons, in turn, causes three things to happen.

First, the neurons within each system alter the strength of their connections in ways that accommodate the experience. For example, the connections among some of the neurons that underlie perceiving a melody become strengthened (and in some cases maybe weakened), resulting in a configuration of connections that makes the melody more pleasing to the person the next time it is encountered.

Second, activation spreads along neural pathways that serve to connect different systems, but are not contained within the systems. I label these neural pathways "between system" pathways. For example, activation spreads along a pathway of neurons that connects the neurons that perceive the melody to the neurons that perceive the appearance of the laboratory setting. Many of the neurons that make up "between system" pathways happen to be located near the hippocampus. This activation is experienced as an integration of the diverse elements that make up any experience (e.g., the melody is played in the lab).

Third, the activation stimulates the hippocampus, which, in turn, serves to prolong or modulate the activity of the neurons that make up the "between system" pathways. The effect of this modulation is a form of long-term potentiation. The additional stimulation given by the hippocampus enhances the strengthening of the connections among the neurons representing "between system" pathways in the extrahippocampal sites (McClelland Rumelhart, 1986b). Without this modulation, the changes necessary to permit sufficiently strong associations among the disparate systems of the brain would not occur, and the person would have no explicit memory of ever hearing a melody in the lab.

The activation of the hippocampus would not have much effect on the connections among neurons that lie in anatomically more distant sites, such as the sites that serve to process sensory information, language, and so on. Damage to the hippocampus would not, therefore, undermine implicit memory, which depends only on the connections among neurons that lie within a single system, such as the auditory system for processing melodies.

The principle evidence for the model just outlined has already been discussed; namely, the destruction of the hippocampus undermines explicit memory for events subsequent to the damage but does not undermine implicit memory or explicit memory for events that occurred years prior to the damage. Another observation that supports the model of the hippocampus as a modulator of "between system" neural pathways has to do with the anatomical location of the hippocampus (see Carlson, 1994). The hippocampus is part of the limbic system, which is important in emotional processing. It has connections to the basal forebrain, which plays a role in sleep; to the diencephalon, which includes the thalamus (a major relay center to the cerebral cortex) and the hypothalamus (important in motivation); and to the brain stem which also plays a role in sleep and alertness. The hippocampus also connects, via its entorhinal cortex, to all major sensory areas and association areas of the cerebral cortex. The consequence of its strategic location is that it is anatomically close to the kinds of neural pathways that are likely to connect the various anatomically disparate sites that are involved in processing various aspects of an event.

A clue as to how the hippocampus affects explicit memory also comes from the phenomenon of **retrograde amnesia**, a commonly observed component of the amnesic syndrome (Squire, 1992). Retrograde amnesia, which sometimes accompanies damage to the hippocampus (and other areas of the brain), is characterized by a temporally graded amnesia for events prior to the damage-inducing trauma. This means that when amnesics are compared with control subjects, the amnesics have relatively more difficulty remembering the events just prior to the trauma than remembering the events from the more distant past. For events that occurred just a few years before the damage, amnesics remember less about those events than do control subjects asked to remember events that occurred an equivalent amount of time in their past. For example, Squire, Haist, and Shimamura (1989) tested amnesics with hippocampal damage on their recall of public events that occurred between 1950 and 1985. The amnesic patients had poorer recall than the control subjects for public events as far back as 15 years before the onset of the amnesia.

Hippocampal damage does not always produce demonstrable retrograde amnesia, however. Squire (1992) claims that if the damage is limited to the CA1 region of the hippocampus, then the retrograde amnesia is limited to about a year before the onset of the amnesia. Retrograde amnesia can also accompany electroconvulsive shock and blows to the head (Squire, Slater, & Chace, 1975; Zubin & Barrera, 1941). Sometimes events "lost" to retrograde amnesia are later recovered; usually it is the events from the more distant past that are recovered first.

The phenomenon of retrograde amnesia suggests that the process by which the hippocampus affects the connections serving explicit memory occurs over an extended period of time. That is, the effect of the hippocampus on "between system" neurons is not to change immediately the strength of their connections, but to introduce gradual changes in those connections. The idea of a gradual process is usually labeled the **consolidation** of memory. Consolidation may reflect a variety of processes, including the initial exposure of receptive sites on the postsynaptic membrane (which may happen within seconds of appropriate stimulation from the hippocampus), the gradual bending of dendritic spines (which may take minutes to days), and the growth of new dendritic spines (which may take days to years) (see Graham, 1990). If the hippocampus is damaged before these changes are completed, explicit memory suffers.

The model I have described is not the only viable model of the role of the hippocampal system in memory. Another model, proposed by Gluck and Myers (1995; see Eichenbaum & Bunsey, 1995, for a similar model), has the hippocampal system forming a set of connections among its neurons that serve to associate stimulus elements. In effect, the hippocampus becomes a place where the brain temporarily stores a representation of the environment, complete with its contextual elements. The hippocampal system transfers this information to various cortical sites so as to enable them to better accommodate new information and to form the necessary connections for an integrated or bound representation of the context. In this model, the hippocampus serves as a kind of short-term memory and influences the formation of both implicit and explicit memories. Usually, however, implicit memory formation does not depend much on the influence of the hippocampus. That is why implicit memory is usually intact even after hippocampal destruction. However, electrical or chemical disruption of the hippocampus is known to undermine some new learning, such as simple conditioning (Solomon, Solomon, Van der Schaaf, & Perry, 1983). Presumably, then, the normal activity of the hippocampus does help cortical sites make the neural changes necessary for forming at least some new implicit memories.

THE PHYSIOLOGY OF IMPLICIT MEMORY

Implicit memory refers to the unconscious effect of past experiences on current perceptions, thoughts, and feelings. The research makes it clear that the hippocampus is not usually important to the establishment of implicit memory. As I just   discussed, damage to the hippocampus will ordinarily leave patients with the ability to learn new perceptual motor skills, to become classically conditioned to signals that precede puffs of air, to respond like ordinary people to verbal primes, and so on (see Squire, 1992).

The anatomical structures underlying the various forms of implicit memory are diverse. A different set of structures are likely to underlie each of the many possible kinds of implicit memory. The main evidence for such diversity is that brain damage can selectively impair one kind of implicit memory, without affecting other kinds of implicit memory (e.g., Butters, Heindel, & Salmon, 1990; see Squire, 1992). For example, damage to the neostriatum (a part of the basal ganglia that helps control movement) impairs skill learning (Heindel, Butters, & Salmon, 1988; Wang, Aigner, & Mishkin, 1990); damage to the amygdala (a part of the limbic system important in emotional behavior) impairs emotional conditioning (Davis, 1986; LeDoux, 1987); and damage to primary visual cortex impairs the formation of priming effects in visual perception (Squire et al., in Squire, 1992).

A good example of the specificity of brain damage's effect on implicit memory comes from Gabrieli, Fleischman, Keane, Reminger, and Morrell (1995), who studied a patient with a lesion in the right occipital lobe. The patient has normal explicit memory, as measured by the recall and recognition of words, and normal conceptual implicit memory, as measured by the increased tendency to select as an exemplar of a conceptual category (e.g., "musical instrument") a word (e.g., *banjo*) previously presented on a list. But the patient displayed an impaired implicit memory for visual priming, as evidenced by a lack of an ability to recognize very briefly presented words more readily if they were previously presented on a list.

Similarly, Butters, Heindel, and Salmon (1990) studied patients with Alzheimer's and Huntington's disease and found that patients in the early stages of Alzheimer's disease showed deficits in word fragment effects—they did not tend to complete a word fragment with a word they had recently seen on a list. But they were able to improve on a perceptual-motor task. Patients in the early stages of Huntington's disease, on the other hand, showed little improvement from practice on the perceptual-motor task, but did exhibit the word fragment effect. Alzheimer's disease initially damages the temporal cortex, important in language processing, and Huntington's disease initially damages the basal ganglia, important in motor performance.

SECTION 3: NEURAL NET MODELS OF LEARNING AND MEMORY

The idea that memory for past events reflects changes in connection strengths among neurons (i.e., long-term potentiation) and that the neurons necessary for a memory are widely distributed in the brain may seem a long way from learning how to distinguish between bluegrass and country music or remembering your high school prom. Indeed, one might wonder whether it takes only changes in the strengths of connections among disparate groups of neurons to produce learning and memory, or whether other mechanisms are also required. One way to pose the question is to ask whether it is possible to build an artificial memory system, based primarily on changing connections among neural-like units, to see whether it displays some of the properties of human learning and memory.

A ROCK-AND-ROLL EXAMPLE OF A NEURAL NET MODEL

As I've discussed in several other chapters, especially in the introductory chapter, the last decade has seen an increasing interest in the development of artificial systems designed to simulate neural properties (see McClelland & Rumelhart, 1986a; Rumelhart & McClelland, 1986; Bechtel & Abrahamsen, 1991; Churchland & Sejnowski, 1992). These artificial systems are usually called connectionist, parallel distributed processing, or **neural net models**. Neural net models embody what we currently believe to be true about the physiological basis of learning. So if neural net models actually learn and remember as do humans, then we have validating evidence for the proposed physiological mechanisms, such as long-term potentiation.

Here I will discuss another example of a neural net model in order to illustrate how neural nets learn (the model is illustrated in Figure 6-4). This model is designed to simulate how a musically naive college student might learn to discriminate between the music of two (fictional) rock-and-roll bands. The first band, Pavlov's Dog, favors heavy metal. Its music is usually (but not always) characterized by loud electrical guitar sounds accompanied by angry vocals. The band's music is often played over the public-address system in the school's weight room. The second band, Kartesian Kats, favors an easy listening style. Its music usually (but not always) features acoustical guitar accompanied by poetic lyrics. This band's music is often played in the school's elevator. The music of both of the bands is played in the student union and occasionaly in the dining hall. The goal of the neural net model is to take as input a description of a song (e.g., "very loud electrical guitar, mostly angry lyrics, played in the student union"), without the name of the band that performs the song, and to produce as output the name of the band that performed the song. While the model may initially make incorrect decisions, the expectation is that, from many descriptions of songs played by the two bands, the model will learn to identify reliably which band is performing any given song. In fact, the model should get to the point where it is able to make this discrimination for songs it has not "heard" before.

As with many neural net models, this music neural net model has three layers of units, where units correspond to neurons or groups of neurons. The first layer consists of **input units** that detect various kinds of physical stimuli. Input units correspond to perceptual neurons. In the example, some input units detect whether the sounds are made by an electric or acoustic guitar, other input units detect whether the lyrics are angry or lyrical, and others detect whether the setting is the weight room, the elevator, the student union, or the dining hall. The third layer of units consists of **output units** that correspond to neurons in the linguistic and motor cortex. When an output unit fires, it directs the system to respond in some way. In the example, the output units direct the system to respond either "Pavlov's Dog" or "Kartesian Kats." Situated in between the input and output units is a layer of **hidden units**; these correspond to neurons in the association cortex. Hidden units are connected to input units and output

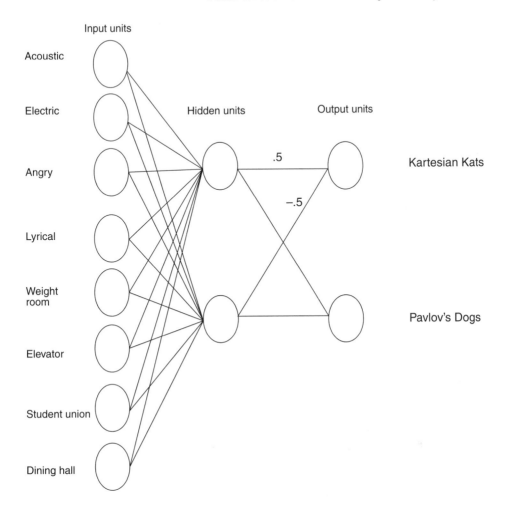

FIGURE 6–4   A neural net that learns to discriminate the music of two fictional rock-and-roll bands, Pavlov's Dog and Kartesian Kats. The figure provides weights of connections only for the connections to the Kartesian Kats output unit.

neurons. Any one unit may be connected to several other units, simulating the fact that in the brain, neurons are connected to many other neurons.

As in other neural net models, the units of this rock-and-roll neural net are linked by connections of varying strength, sometimes indicated on a graph as a numeric weight. The connections are excitatory or inhibitory, indicated graphically with a plus or minus sign. The rate at which any given unit fires depends on the amount of activation and inhibition it receives from other units. In the case of input units, the amount of activation reflects the nature and intensity of the stimulus input.

To illustrate, suppose the "Kartesian Kats" output unit has two hidden units connected to it. Suppose the weight of the connection between the first hidden unit and the output unit is .5 and suppose the first hidden unit fires at the rate of .9 (90% of the maximum rate at which the unit can fire). Then the activation it sends to the output unit will equal the firing rate multiplied by the connection strength; that is, .5 × .9 = .45. Suppose the weight of the connection between the second hidden unit and the same output unit is −.5 and suppose the second hidden unit fires at the rate of .1 (10% of its maximum rate). Then the amount of activation strength it sends to the output unit is −.5 × .1 = −.05. Note that this second hidden unit is actually inhibiting the output unit. The net activation the output unit receives from the two hidden units will equal .45 − .05 = .40.

The output unit representing the "Kartesian Kats" response will therefore fire at a rate that is some function of .40. Usually the rate at which any given unit fires is based on some nonlinear function of the activation it receives from all connecting units. An example of a nonlinear function is that a unit does not fire until it receives some threshold of net activation. Such nonlinear functions are biologically realistic and are required of neural net models if they are to simulate learning about complex stimulus patterns (see Bechtel & Abrahamsen, 1991). In this case let's say that the nonlinear function is such that the "Kartesian Kats" output unit receiving a net activation of .40 fires at a rate of .60 (60% of its maximum rate). And let's say that the output unit representing "Pavlov's Dog" fires at a rate of .25 (25% of its maximum rate). The system therefore responds that the band is the Kartesian Kats. The greater the difference between the firing rate of the two output units, the greater the "confidence" the model has in its decision. Ideally, the correct output unit should fire at a rate of 1 (100%) while the incorrect output unit should fire at a rate of 0 (0%).

HOW NEURAL NET MODELS LEARN AND REMEMBER

Back Propagation, Teachers, and Learning

The neural net model must have some way of changing the connection weights as a function of experience, just as experiences change the strengths of the connections between real neurons. That is, neural net models must be able to simulate learning from experience. One commonly used learning mechanism that accomplishes the adjustment of connection strengths is called the **back propagation** learning mechanism (see Bechtel & Abrahamsen, 1991, for a more complete description of back propagation). Back propagation requires the addition of another component to the neural net model. The label I give to this additional component is the **teacher**.

The teacher has three functions. First, it records whether the response of the model was correct or incorrect, and uses that feedback to judge how the output units should have fired so as to have produced a correct response. Second, it examines the firing rates of the hidden and input units to see which units were most responsible for the response. Third, it adjusts the weights of the connections among the units so that the responses will be more accurate in the future.

To illustrate (refer to Figure 6-5), let's see what happens as the model listens to a song, "Leather Nuns," which is angry in tone, makes use of both electric and acoustic guitars, and is heard in the weight room. Let's suppose that the connections among the units are weighted such that, in this case, the output unit for "Kartesian Kats" responds at 60% and the output unit for "Pavlov's Dog" responds at 25%. The model is wrong; the song was performed by Pavlov's Dog. The teacher first determines that the "Kartesian Kats" output unit should have fired at a rate of 0% whereas the "Pavlov's Dog" output unit should have fired at a rate of 100%. The teacher then examines the connections of the hidden units to the output unit that represents "Kartesian Kats," and adjusts the connection weights appropriately. The excitatory connections that were most responsible for activating the "Kartesian Kats" output unit are weakened the most, while the inhibitory connections that inhibited the activation of the "Kartesian Kats" output unit are strengthened. The teacher also increases the strength of the excitatory connections that activated the "Pavlov's Dog" output unit and decreases the strength of the inhibitory connections that inhibited the activation of the "Pavlov's Dog" output unit. The teacher then examines the connections between the input units and the hidden units and adjusts those connection weights so as to increase the odds that the appropriate hidden units will be activated and so lead to a correct response. In this way, if "Leather Nuns" is ever played again, the model would be more likely to make the correct response of "Pavlov's Dog."

The teacher also makes changes to the weights of connections when the system makes a correct response. Usually those changes involve increasing the strength of excitatory connections to the output unit that made the correct

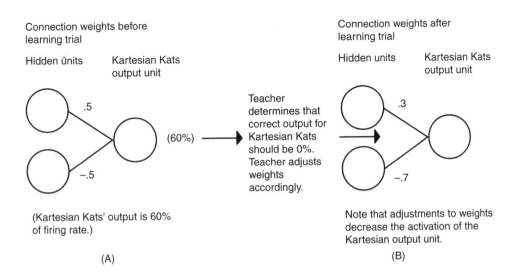

Connection weights before
learning trial

Hidden units   Kartesian Kats
                      output unit

.5

(60%)

(Kartesian Kats' output is 60%
of firing rate.)

(A)

Teacher
determines that
correct output for
Kartesian Kats
should be 0%.
Teacher adjusts
weights
accordingly.

−.5

Connection weights after
learning trial

Hidden units   Kartesian Kats
                      output unit

.3

−.7

Note that adjustments to weights
decrease the activation of the
Kartesian output unit.

(B)

FIGURE 6–5 Adjustment of weights of connections in a portion of a neural net.

response, decreasing the inhibition to the output unit that made the correct response, decreasing the excitatory connections to the output unit that represents the incorrect response, and increasing the inhibition to the output unit that represents the incorrect response.

The description I have supplied of the back propagation learning mechanism is, believe it or not, rather overly simplified and incomplete. Furthermore, I dispensed with the rather complicated equations that compute weight adjustments. The reader interested in seeing these equations and in learning more about back propagation is referred to Bechtel and Abrahamsen (1991) or to Hinton (1992). Still, the description should give you some sense of how the learning scheme works. Note that the adjustments are made first on the connections between hidden units and output units and then on the connections between input units and hidden units. That is, the adjustments are back propagated through the system. Furthermore, the relative size of the adjustment of any given connection reflects its relative contribution to the error. Connections that made a strong contribution to the error are adjusted more than connections that made a weaker contribution to the error. The absolute size of an adjustment is never great, in any case, in order that the model not be too overly influenced by the latest song it has heard. Adjustments are almost always rather small.

Interestingly enough, if such a neural net model, with the teacher mechanism implementing the back propagation rule, is given many descriptions of songs, it will eventually reach a set of connection weights that reliably produce correct output. The neural net model will even be able to identify the performer of songs to which it had not been exposed. Thus the model simulates the student learning the musical style of the two bands. Neural net models using this sort of learning algorithm have learned to produce the phonemes of English given letters as input (Rosenberg & Sejnowski, 1987), to judge the orientations and curvatures of physical objects displayed in pictures (Lehky & Sejnowski, 1988), and to simulate the hippocampus's role in classical conditioning (Gluck & Myers, 1995).

Neural Net Models and Human Memory

There are a number of ways in which the neural net model that discriminates between Pavlov's Dog and Kartesian Kats provides a realistic simulation of human memory. First of all, the model learns the discrimination without being told explicitly how the musical styles of the bands differ. Indeed, for many skills we learn, it is difficult to express the rules or basis for the skill. As I mentioned in another chapter, the grammar of language is one such skill. A neural net model can always learn to discriminate among categories as long as the categories are in principle discriminable and the input units are able to perceive physical features relevant to the discrimination.

Second, neural net models are good at extracting the canonical or prototypical pattern from a set of instances (see McClelland & Rumelhart, 1986a). The pattern is represented as the strongest set of connections in the network of units. Similarly, real people are good at remembering the enduring patterns of their experiences, such as remembering that Uncle Freddy usually likes to discuss dream analysis at family gatherings (see the research discussed in chapter 4: Memory). The pattern enables people to recognize novel variations of familiar patterns. A child who has finally learned to distinguish male and female faces, for example, will be able to make the gender distinction for any new face that comes along. Similarly, the music neural net model is able to accurately classify new songs that it has never before encountered.

A manifestation of pattern extraction is the finding that people more efficiently categorize the typical members of a category than the atypical members (Posner & Keele, 1968; Hartley & Homa, 1981). For example, people are more likely to correctly recognize that a painting is a Picasso if the painting is typical of Picasso's style (e.g., his 1906–07 cubist piece *Les Demoiselles d'Avignon*) than if it is atypical (e.g., his 1922 classical piece *Mother and Child*). Prototypes were also discussed in the chapters on perception and on implicit and semantic memory. Neural net models can easily simulate this sort of finding. The musical neural net model would be better at judging the identity of a song that is more typical of a band than a song that is atypical. The prototypical examples are those with features that occur in most of the other examples, that fit the pattern. A prototypical performance of Pavlov's Dog includes loud electrical guitars accompanying angry lyrics. In the network of connections, these features will be represented by the strongest connections between input units that detect the features and the output unit for "Pavlov's Dog." Should a new song include the typical features, then a great deal of activation is likely to spread to the output unit for "Pavlov's Dog." But should Pavlov's Dog perform an atypical song (perhaps with kinder, gentler lyrics), less activation is likely to spread to the output unit for "Pavlov's Dog."

Third, just as real people do, the neural net model sometimes remembers a complete episode from partial information. Listening to the melody of one of Pavlov's Dog's songs ("Ruff Ruff") may evoke a memory of the lyrics ("We don't want no doggie biscuits . . ."). The basis for the neural net model's simulation of this "filling in the missing details" quality of explicit memory lies in the flow of activation among the units. Stimulation of some of the units in the network will spread activation to the other units. For example, the sound of an electric guitar may stimulate hidden units that in turn feed back to the input unit that detects angry lyrics. The activation of the "angry lyric" input unit simulates recollecting that the band expresses anger, given only the stimulus of an electric guitar.

Fourth, the model does not keep any record of each stimulus it sees; rather, it merely reconfigure the weights of the connections among units in response to feedback. Thus the model need not grow in size as it encounters new stimuli and so it never runs out of "storage space." Rather, memory is a byproduct of the current configuration of connections among units. This simulates the important property of human memory discussed at great length in the previous chapters—memory is not a system for keeping records of each event but a constructionist system that changes in response to events.

Fifth, because a neural net model does not keep records of its experiences, it will tend to forget the details of most experiences, because each new experience causes a reconfiguring of the weights of the connections among units. Real people also have trouble remembering the details of the vast majority of their experiences, many of which are forgotten in their entirety. Just as do real people, the model would be able to remember well the details of recent experiences, because no subsequent events would yet have occurred to cause the connection weights to change.

Sixth, the neural net model's memory will be better for unusual events than for ordinary ones. Again, as discussed in previous chapters, good memory for the unusual characterizes the recollections of real people. To see how connectionism simulates this property of memory, suppose that last Thursday a Kartesian Kats song ("Soft, with Whiskers") was played in the dining hall, rather than in the usual setting of the elevator or student union. This unusual experience would produce an increase in the weights of connections among the units representing "Kartesian Kats" and the dining hall setting. If the dining hall setting is presented later on, the strength between those units will permit the model to reconstruct accurately that it heard a Kartesian Kats song in the dining hall last Thursday. On the other hand, the student union is a setting in which the songs of both bands are frequently heard. So the connections between the student union setting units and the "Pavlov's Dog" unit and the connection between the student union setting units and the "Kartesian Kats" unit are both rather strong. Suppose that last Thursday a Kartesian Kats song happened to have been played in the student union. If the student union setting is presented, the existence of the two strong sets of connections will mean that the model will not be as accurate in its reconstruction of which band's music it heard played last Thursday.

PROBLEMS WITH NEURAL NET MODELS

Many researchers are excited by neural net models; still, neural nets are not without problems or limitations. A potentially serious difficulty is that many neural net models simulate learning by using the back propagation rule in which a teacher examines connection weights to see which contributed the most to success or failure and then makes appropriate adjustments in the strength of those connections. The problem is that the teacher scheme is not biologically plausible (Churchland, 1988). The teacher component works according to principles that have nothing to do with the activation and inhibition of units; rather, it uses mathematical equations to calculate the strengths of connections, and it makes changes to those connections without the participation of the units. The teacher does not represent any known or even hypothesized physical process— it lies outside the network of units that comprise the model of the brain. But the whole premise of a neural net simulation is that cognitive phenomena are a consequence of the activity among neural-like units. To be consistent with this premise, then, any learning scheme must reflect the activity of units and nothing more.

Happily, some neural net modelers have developed learning schemes that do not require a teacher. Instead, appropriate changes to the strengths of connections are accomplished entirely within the network of units and are based only on the firing rates of units. An example of such a learning scheme is **competitive learning** (see Hinton, 1992). In this scheme, each hidden unit is connected to lots of input units. Each hidden unit, though, has a different pattern of connective weights with the input units. Hidden units also have inhibitory connections to other hidden units and feedback connections to input units. Given any stimulus, one of the hidden units will fire more than the others: this hidden unit is said to win the competition. The winning hidden unit will increase the strength of its connection to the most active input units and decrease the strength of its connection to the least active input units. At the same time, the winning hidden unit will inhibit the firing of other hidden units and so deny to them any opportunity to alter their connections with input units. For example, if the input units that detect the sounds of an electrical guitar and that detect the sound of angry lyrics are strongly activated by a Pavlov's Dog song, the winning hidden unit will increase its connections with those input units. In this way the model begins to learn that Pavlov's Dog likes to perform angry songs accompanied by electrical guitars.

Another concern about neural net models is that much of the strategic and reconstructive character of human memory has not been simulated by neural net models. Recall that people use a variety of strategies and draw on knowledge from a variety of domains to help them make an ongoing event memorable or to reconstruct a past event. For example, deliberately associating an event to what one already knows (the assimilation principle discussed in the memory chapter) makes new information memorable. Very few current neural net models attempt to simulate these learning and reconstructive strategies. Indeed, it would be difficult to simulate the complexity and range of a person's strategies using current neural net models, given that most neural net models are simply too small to represent anything more than a very tiny fraction of a person's knowledge. Furthermore, very little is currently known about how the brain comes to acquire and use sophisticated strategies and make choices about which strategy to use in any given situation.

A property of neural net models is that they seem to learn all kinds of knowledge and skill in fundamentally the same way. Yet a great deal of work in the study of human cognition suggests that children acquire different domains of knowledge and skill in fundamentally different ways (see chapter 11: Cognitive Development). For instance, children may make use of inborn tacit knowledge of the general properties of language to acquire language. Linguistic tacit knowledge would have no influence on the acquisition of other skills, such as abstract reasoning (Pinker, 1994). Generally, most neural net approaches to human cognition have failed to specify how learning might be different in various knowledge domains and how inborn tacit knowledge might influence learning (see Pinker & Prince, 1988, or Fodor & Pylyshyn, 1988, for critiques of neural nets that raise issues along these lines).

Finally, it may be noted that real brains have more than three types of neurons and have many more neurons than any neural net model has units. Furthermore, neurons do more than just fire at different rates (they also secrete neurotransmitters, alter their connections with support cells, and so on). In other words, real brains are capable of learning a wider range of information and exhibiting more complex behavior than can be simulated by any neural net model.

Still, the observation that neural net models can simulate some of the salient properties of learning and memory suggests that real brains do learn and remember by changing connections among neurons. Successful simulations also increase our confidence in the constructionist view of memory put forth in this and the previous chapter.

It is worth noting that the claim that learning and memory involve changes in connections among neurons might be radically misleading, despite recent research on long-term potentiation and despite the success of neural net models. Among a number of alternative possibilities, it may be that the mechanisms that are critical to learning and memory involve interactions among large-scale structures of neurons (see Edelman, 1992). An example of a large-scale structure would be a set of thousands of neurons from the same neural module involved in processing motion in the visual input. The nature of interactions among such large-scale structures may not resemble the interactions between individual neurons. To be utterly speculative, it may be that the action of one structure of neurons is to produce neuromodulating chemicals (e.g., hormones) that selectively affect the production of neuromodulating chemicals in other structures of neurons. A neuromodulator, unlike a neurotransmitter, influences the behavior of groups of neurons located at sites relatively distant from the neuron secreting the neuromodulator. Important aspects of memory may then be represented, not by the strengths of connections among neurons, but by the patterns of neuromodulator synthesis. And, of course, there may be many other possibilities. The main point here is that theories of the physiology of learning and memory may some day be quite different from current approaches. In my judgment, more work needs to be done to see how large-scale structures of neurons behave, and to simulate learning and memory in more complex and realistic environments than are currently used by neural net modelers.

SUMMARY AND CONCLUSIONS

This chapter has continued the theme developed in the memory chapters. Human memory is not a record-keeping system in which a record-by-record account of experience is stored in some kind of storage system. Instead, memory reflects an extraction from experience of the regularities and patterns that are used to reconstruct past events. The contribution of this chapter was to provide the physiological basis of learning and remembering.

In the first section, I noted that the essential claim of modern physiological psychology is that learning reflects changes to the strengths of connections among neurons. From the study of the hippocampus in rats and other creatures, we have observed that the postsynaptic membrane becomes more receptive to neurotransmitter when it is activated by a pattern of excitation from its transmitting neurons. This mechanism, called long-term potentiation, appears to reflect anatomical changes to the postsynaptic membrane that result in the exposure of more receptive sites. It is also possible that long-term potentiation reflects the influence of a retrograde messenger that transforms the presynaptic membrane in such a way that it can release more neurotransmitter per firing. Long-term potentiation can support more complex kinds of learning, such as learning that a painter prefers to paint disturbing scenes in bold styles and display the paintings in obscure art galleries. Research has also shown that experiences can affect the connectivity of neurons. For example, enriched visual experiences may increase the branches of dendrites on neurons in visual cortex, making those neurons more receptive to the activity of their presynaptic neurons.

A variety of evidence was discussed to show that the brain constantly reconfigures the strengths of neural connections, in some cases weakening previously strengthened connections. Such reconfiguration provides a mechanism for forgetting and reinforces the constructionist idea that the brain does not keep records of experience.

In the second section I discussed the physiological basis of remembering the past. As a constructionist view of memory would have it, there is no place in the brain where memories are stored; rather, memory is distributed throughout the cognitive systems that perceive, reflect, and act on experiences. The main evidence for a distributed view of memory comes from brain damage. For example, damage to the frontal lobes undermines strategic processes, like reconstructing when an event took place, while leaving intact the determination of whether an event took place. Damage to the posterior and temporal lobes can undermine verbal memory but leave nonverbal memory intact.

In order for someone to have a memory of some specific event, it is necessary that the disparate elements that make up the event be integrated, or bound. Merely accessing one's knowledge that a painter likes to paint in bold strokes, for example, does not constitute remembering seeing a painting in a particular art gallery. The evidence suggests that the hippocampus performs the integrating function so essential to explicit memory. Bilateral damage to the hippocampus produces anterograde amnesia—the unfortunate victim no longer has conscious memory for events subsequent to the damage. However, bilateral damage to the hippocampus does not usually undermine implicit memory. Patients retain a normal ability to learn new motor skills, to become sensitized to previously encountered stimuli, and to respond in new ways to stimuli associated with noxious events. But such patients have no conscious memory of the experiences that enabled such learning to take place.

I sketched out one popular explanation of how the hippocampus may play a role in explicit but not implicit memory. The gist of the explanation, admittedly speculative, is that the hippocampus modulates the formation of connections among neurons from anatomically and functionally different sites in the brain. It is connections among such disparate groups of neurons that are essential for the integration necessary for explicit memory. These neurons must lie outside the hippocampus, since the bilateral destruction of the hippocampus does not usually undermine memory for events that took place years before the damage. The main reason that it is the hippocampus and not some other portion of the brain that performs integration is because the hippocampus is strategically located at a kind of neural crossroads, and so is close to neurons that connect to most other regions of the brain.

Implicit memory involves changes of connections among neurons within some discrete neural system. Different neural systems permit different kinds of implicit memory. The main evidence comes from patients with localized brain damage; typically, such damage undermines some cognitive skill and the implicit memory associated with that skill. Damage to the occipital lobe, for example, can undermine visual perception and a kind of implicit memory called visual priming. But the same damage can leave intact explicit memory and other kinds of implicit memory.

In the third and final section of the chapter I discussed neural net models of learning and memory. I suggested that neural net models could be understood as plausibility studies. If what underlies learning and memory is essentially the reconfiguration of the strengths of connections among neurons, then a system that simulates such a reconfiguration should display the same kind of memory possessed by real people. I illustrated neural net models with a simple model designed to learn the differences in the musical styles of two fictional rock-and-roll bands, Pavlov's Dog and Kartesian Kats. The model used the back propagation learning algorithm whereby a "teacher" alters the strengths of connections among units so as to reduce the likelihood of making errors. In this way the model eventually learns to identify reliably the performer of songs.

Neural net models seem to simulate reasonably well many of the salient properties of learning and memory. Like people, neural net models learn to classify without being explicitly told the basis of the classification; base the classifications on recurring patterns and so are readily able to correctly classify novel stimuli; do not keep a record of each individual experience and so forget most experiences; can remember some distinctive experiences; and can reconstruct an experience from a few cues. Neural net models are not without limitations; for example, most do not simulate the complexity of the reconstruction strategies people routinely employ. Furthermore, many neural net models employ what I called "teachers," which are mechanisms that perform an examination of the weights of connections and then change the weights so as to maximize accuracy of performance. Such teachers are used to implement the back propagation rule for adjusting weights of connections. But teachers are not themselves a part of the network of units; their adjustments to weights are not caused by the firing of the units. In other words, teachers have the exceedingly undesirable property that they do not simulate the activity of neurons. Happily, there are weight adjustment mechanisms, such as competitive learning, that reflect only the activity of units, and so are biologically plausible.

I spent a fair amount of time describing neural net models because I think that it is critical that we be sure that prevailing physiological theories of learning and memory be capable of accounting for the various facets of human memory. The successes of neural net models increase our confidence in mechanisms like long-term potentiation, thought to underlie learning.

Many people are also enamored of neural net modeling because they believe that neural net models are an important breakthrough in artificial intelligence, and so may revolutionize the construction of intelligence machines. Unlike conventional artificial intelligence based on information processing, neural net models learn from experience in a manner analogous to how humans learn. Perhaps neural net models will someday enable us to build the intelligent robots and androids of science fiction, like the "good guy" cyborg in the film *Terminator 2: Judgment Day* who was programmed by a neural net processor to learn about humans from experience. At any rate, if such devices are ever actually built, we can expect our culture to be radically revolutionized, as we and our institutions confront the presence of intelligent machines that learn and remember as real people do.

RECOMMENDED READINGS

If you have been reading my recommendations, it won't surprise you to learn that I again recommend Schacter's (1996) *Searching for Memory* as a beautifully written and current overview of the field of memory. Schacter includes chapters on the physiology of learning and memory, as does Carlson (1994), in an excellent introductory book (*Physiology of Behavior*) on the broader topic of physiological psychology. Fanselow (1993) has a review article on long-term potentiation and the importance of NMDA receptors to the development of long-term potentiation. Kandel and Hawkins (1992) have a *Scientific American* article on the physiology of learning. In the same *Scientific American* issue, Hinton (1992) has an accessible overview of how learning is implemented in neural net models. Hinton discusses both the back propagation and competitive learning schemes. Squire is one of the most influential cognitive neuroscientists working in the area of the physiology of memory. Squire's (1987) *Memory and Brain* is an excellent and readable introduction to the topic, and his (1992) *Psychological Review* article summarizes well the research on the role of the hippocampus in the consolidation of memories. For you science fiction buffs, you might rent the films *The Terminator* and *Terminator 2: Judgment Day*, both directed by James Cameron. The former is one of my all-time favorite science fiction films. Look for the scenes in which it is established that the "bad guy" cyborg in *The Terminator* is programmed by conventional artificial intelligence techniques and the "good guy" cyborg in *Terminator 2* is programmed by neural net techniques. And then ask yourself which cyborg (both played by Arnold Schwarzenegger) wins the day.

7 *Reasoning and Rationality*

In a participatory society in which most people must make important decisions or pass judgments on the validity of ideas, it is especially critical to understand how—and how well—people reason. Can we trust the judgments of the ordinary person, or must people be schooled in the art of reasoning before their judgments become reliably sound? Consider the task of jurors. Can we trust that the ordinary people who serve on juries are capable of impartially weighing all the relevant evidence in order to come to a sound decision about whether a defendant accused of a crime is guilty beyond a reasonable doubt? Or might jurors routinely ignore some of the crucial evidence or be easily swayed by irrelevant issues and emotions that undermine the integrity of their verdict?

The main contribution of cognitive psychology to the topic of reasoning is the study of how ordinary people reason. **Reasoning** refers to the ability to form judgments and to draw inferences from known facts. One issue about reasoning that has historically dominated the topic, and will act as an integrating theme for this chapter, is whether the reasoning of the ordinary person is fundamentally **rational** or **irrational** (Henle, 1962; Gardner, 1985; Stich, 1990). By rational, I mean that reasoning is based on a systematic way to distinguish valid from invalid inferences using logical procedures that are consistent, sensible, and dispassionate. By irrational, I mean that reasoning fails to distinguish reliably valid from invalid inferences; it is based instead on procedures that are frequently contradictory, unsound, and emotional.

PERSPECTIVES ON REASONING: ARE PEOPLE RATIONAL OR IRRATIONAL ANIMALS?

One point of view, associated with Western philosophical, political, and economical traditions, maintains that humans are fundamentally rational. The judgments and decisions of the ordinary person are sound.

Aristotle defined humans as rational animals, and explicated the rules of logic. Plato divided the human mind into rational, emotional, and appetitive components, but believed that rationality was the morally superior and immortal component of mind. Thomas Hobbes (1588–1679), an early proponent of materialism, claimed that all reasoning is but reckoning, by which he meant that logic underlies reasoning. John Stuart Mill (1806–1873), one of the British Empiricists famous for the idea that simple thoughts and sensations underlie more complex thought, also believed that ordinary people reasoned according to the formal rules of logic. More recently, Jean Piaget, arguably the most influential developmental psychologist of this century, claimed that cognitive development may be viewed as the natural maturing of rational skills, analogous to the emergence of walking as a locomotive skill (Inhelder & Piaget, 1958).

The economic and political systems of the West reinforce the Aristotelian claim that humans are fundamentally rational. These systems assume that ordinary people are capable of making sound political decisions that serve the public good, and sound economic decisions that maximize gain and minimize loss. The American jury system is a good example of the implicit belief in human rationality. Juries are composed of ordinary citizens who receive no formal training in rendering verdicts. Yet juries are entrusted with the responsibility of determining whether the accused should be imprisoned, executed, or set free.

Advocates of the view that humans are fundamentally rational are certainly aware that many people routinely fail to apply logical principles to their reasoning. But deviations from rationality are thought to reflect performance errors caused by attention and memory lapses, anxiety, or incomplete cognitive development. An analogy might be made to walking as a form of locomotion. Walking is intrinsic to our nature. Virtually everyone in every culture learns to walk, a skill that is used routinely in almost all situations requiring movement. Yet sometimes we stumble and fall. So despite the intrinsic nature of walking, we do not always walk properly. A similar analogy is sometimes made to language acquisition. Virtually all children acquire their language's grammar (the rules for combining sounds and words to make sentences), yet adults will sometimes make a grammatical mistake or misuse a particular grammatical rule. The Aristotelian claim is that rationality is intrinsic to human nature in much the same sense that walking and talking are intrinsic. Errors in logic reflect occasional slips, performance execution errors, the influence of anxiety, or the occasional failure to properly apply a particular rule of logic (L. J. Cohen, 1981).

In contrast to these philosophical pronouncements, many cognitive psychologists and some philosophers claim that ordinary adults, even well-educated adults, routinely reason in ways that suggest that the reasoning process is fundamentally irrational, that the ordinary person's judgments are often unsound (see Nisbett & Ross, 1980; Kahneman, Slovic, & Tversky, 1982; Nickerson, 1986; Stich, 1985). It seems that errors of logic persist in many situations, even when memory and attention are not taxed, when participants in reasoning experiments are offered rewards for using logic to solve problems, and when the participants have been trained in logical reasoning.

Cognitive psychologists and philosophers who dispute the Aristotelian tradition do not claim that human reasoning is unprincipled or utterly ineffective. Instead, their claim is that cognitive mechanisms and limitations intrinsic to the cognitive system often result in reasoning processes and strategies that are less efficient or logical than the reasoning of a perfectly rational being. From this perspective, rationality is not intrinsic to our nature, but is a cultural invention. It is analogous to learning to drive a car for transportation or to program a computer to communicate. Certainly people can be taught to reason in a rational manner. And some people may, for any of a number of reasons, acquire better reasoning skills from their education in rationality. But such an education does not reflect an attempt to complete a naturally ongoing developmental process in the sense that correcting a child's walking techniques or grammatical mistakes serves to enhance the natural acquisition of walking and talking. Instead, rationality is a prescription for how people ought to reason. That there are some people who routinely reason in a rational way is due to the specialized education such people receive and benefit from.

Rationality may also characterize the collective efforts of groups of people who, through their interactions and use of artifacts (e.g., computer programs), may acquire the means for achieving rational procedures that no one person possesses (see Dawes, Faust, & Meehl, 1989, or Dawes, 1993, for a discussion of how information received from a variety of sources leads to making better decisions than can be made by individuals acting alone). Rather than draw an analogy to language learning, the notion of irrationality might draw an analogy to rote memorization. Most people find it difficult to memorize lists of information verbatim. Yet the collective rote memory of a group of people may be much better than the memory of any one person, especially if the group has access to artifacts, such as videotapes and libraries.

In this chapter I will review some of the experimental evidence relevant to the issue of whether the reasoning of the ordinary person is fundamentally rational or irrational. I will discuss reasoning as it manifests itself in a variety of reasoning paradigms, including deducing conclusions from premises, making judgments about the likelihood of uncertain events, evaluating the soundness of ideas, and making decisions when given choices. Much of the research on each of these paradigms would seem to suggest that humans are irrational animals (Stich, 1985, 1990). I will conclude a discussion of each paradigm by suggesting that reasoning is neither rational nor irrational, but is, instead, **adaptive**. An adaptive approach claims that human reasoning permits successful and efficient prediction of future events in the kinds of environments typically encountered by the ordinary person.

SECTION 1: REASONING FROM PREMISES: ARE PEOPLE INTUITIVE LOGICIANS?

One kind of reasoning paradigm—**deductive reasoning**—entails deriving conclusions from premises. Examples of deductive reasoning include the familiar categorical syllogisms supposedly invented by Aristotle (e.g., "All cancers are caused by viruses and no viruses respond to antibiotics, therefore no cancers respond to antibiotics"), linear reasoning problems (e.g., "Ringo makes less money than Paul but more money than George, so Paul is the richest"), simple conditional reasoning problems (e.g., "If the death penalty is instituted, then violent crimes will be deterred. Nevada has recently instituted the death penalty. Therefore the violent crime rate in Nevada should be reduced"), and complex conditional reasoning problems (e.g., "If a student has completed at least 32 courses and has passed a computer literacy exam or has taken a computer science course, then the student may graduate. Jacob has taken 33 courses but has not taken a computer science course or passed the computer literacy exam. Therefore Jacob does not graduate").

Deductive reasoning may be contrasted with inductive reasoning. In **deductive reasoning**, one goes from the general (e.g., the universe began in a hot dense state) to the specific (e.g., it therefore follows that there should be a blackbody radiation permeating the modern universe). In **inductive reasoning**, one goes from the particular to the general. That is, inductive reasoning uses observations (e.g., distant galaxies are red-shifted, the universe is permeated by a blackbody radiation) to derive generalizations (e.g., the universe began in a hot dense state).

In the context of deductive reasoning, the issue of whether the ordinary person reasons in a sound and rational manner takes the form of asking whether the ordinary person is an **intuitive logician**. Is it the case that people usually manage to reason in a manner consistent with the formal rules of logic? Or is it the case that people typically violate the rules of logic?

CONDITIONAL REASONING PROBLEMS

I have chosen to focus on simple conditional reasoning problems to explore the issue of whether the ordinary person is an intuitive logician. The simplest kind of conditional reasoning problem has three parts. First, there is the conditional premise, usually symbolized "If p then q." An example of a conditional premise is "If a student correctly answers 90% or more of the questions on the final exam, the student will automatically get a grade of A in the course." Second, there is an observation, symbolized by "p" (e.g., "Betty correctly answered 95% of the questions on the final"), "not p" (e.g., "Veronica correctly answered 81% of the questions on the final"), "q" (e.g., "Archie got an A in the course"), or "not q" (e.g., "Jughead got a C in the course"). The final part of the conditional problem is the conclusion, which may or may not follow from the premise and the observation. Conclusions are symbolically represented as "therefore p" (e.g., "therefore, Reggie correctly answered at least 90% of the questions on the final"), "therefore not p" ("therefore, Reggie correctly answered fewer than 90% of the questions on the final"), "therefore q" (e.g., "therefore, Reggie got an A in the course"), or "therefore not q" (e.g., "therefore, Reggie did not get an A in the course").

To see if people are intuitive logicians, we first need to specify what conclusions to conditional premises are justified and what conclusions are not justified, according to formal logic. Logicians tell us that conditionals admit of two valid conclusions and two invalid conclusions. A valid conclusion to a conditional premise is a statement that must be true if the original conditional premise is true. An invalid conclusion to a conditional premise is one that is only sometimes true when the conditional premise is true. "Invalid" does not mean that the conclusion is inevitably false.

Again, let's say that the premise is that if a student correctly answers 90% or more of the questions on the final exam, the student will automatically get a grade of A in the course. Suppose that Betty scores 93% on the final exam. It therefore follows that Betty received an A in the course. This type of argument is formally called **modus ponens**, and may be symbolized as "If p then q, observe p, therefore q." Now suppose that Betty received a B (or any grade lower than A) in the course. It therefore follows that Betty scored lower than 90% on the final. This type of argument is formally called **modus tollens**, and may be symbolized as "If p then q, observe not q, therefore not p." Modus ponens and modus tollens describe the two valid conclusions to all conditional problems.

Suppose, instead, Betty received an A in the class. What follows? It would be a mistake to assume that Betty must have scored 90% or better on the final exam. She may have, or she might have earned her A by doing well on the other assignments in the course. The premise does not specify all of the ways in which students might obtain As. In general, it is a fallacy to conclude that observing the consequent means that the antecedent must have occurred. This fallacy, formally known as the **affirmation of the consequent**, may be represented symbolically as "If p then q, observe q, mistakenly conclude: therefore p."

Finally, suppose that Betty scored 81% (or any score below 90%) on the final exam. What follows? It would be a mistake to conclude that Betty must have gotten a grade lower than A. Again, she may have, or she might have earned her A by doing well on the other assignments in the course. In general, it is a fallacy to conclude that observing that the antecedent does not occur means that the consequent will not occur. This fallacy, formally known as **denial of the antecedent**, may be symbolically represented as "If p then q, observe not p, mistakenly conclude: therefore not q." A summary of conditional reasoning problems is provided in Figure 7-1.

I describe conditional reasoning problems in some detail because they seem to represent an elementary form of deductive reasoning whose logical conclusions are explicated by formal logic. The question cognitive psychologists have asked is whether ordinary people, when confronted with conditional premises, draw the valid conclusions and avoid the invalid conclusions. Now in the example I just discussed, many people are already familiar with the grading practices of schools. So it would not be a particularly revealing test of reasoning skill to observe that people deduce only logically valid conclusions in such familiar situations, because people may just be remembering what they know about that situation. A fairer test of whether ordinary people are intuitive logicians requires examining performance on conditional reasoning problems for which the situations are unfamiliar and the valid conclusions are not known in advance.

Conditional Reasoning

Symbolic form	Formal label	Example
if *p* then *q* observe *p* therefore *q*	**modus ponens**	If student obtains 90% or better on final, then student receives A. Betty obtained 93 on final. Therefore Betty gets an A.
if *p* then *q* observe not *q* therefore not *p*	**modus tollens**	If student obtains 90% or better on final, then student receives A. Betty got a B. Therefore Betty scored less than 90% on final.
if *p* then *q* observe *q* no one conclusion follows	**invalid** (to conclude *p* is to make error called **affirmation of consequent**)	If student obtains 90% or better on final, then student receives A. Betty got an A. Therefore we don't know for sure whether Betty scored 90% or better on final.
if *p* then *q* observe not *p* no one conclusion follows	**invalid** (to conclude not *q* is to make error called **denial of antecedent**)	If student obtains 90% or better on final, then student receives A. Betty scored 81% on final. Therefore, we don't know for sure whether Betty got a grade lower than A.

FIGURE 7–1   Summary of conditional reasoning problems.

EXPERIMENTS INVESTIGATING CONDITIONAL REASONING

Cognitive psychologists have made use of at least two experimental paradigms to study conditional reasoning. In one paradigm, subjects are presented with an unfamiliar premise and an observation and must produce a conclusion or indicate whether some potential conclusion is valid. In this paradigm, subjects are told to assume that the premise is true. In the second paradigm, subjects are given an unfamiliar premise that may or may not be true. Subjects are then given four observations, and must indicate which observations provide evidence as to whether the premise is true or false.

Evaluating Conclusions Given Premises

Consider the first experimental paradigm, in which subjects are presented the premise and an observation and must draw the conclusions. In this experimental paradigm, the premise is assumed to be true; it is the conclusion that is in doubt.

An example of the paradigm is an experiment by Johnson-Laird, Byrne, and Schaeken (1992). In one of the conditions of their experiment, they provided subjects with premises such as "If Mary is in Dublin, then Joe is in Limerick" and an observation such as "Joe is in Cambridge." Subjects then had to deduce whatever conclusions they believed followed from the premise and the observation. The subjects made the correct deductions 97% of the time for the modus ponens problems (e.g., "If Mary is in Dublin, then Joe is in Limerick. Mary is in Dublin. What follows?"—Joe must be in Limerick) but made the correct deductions only 38% of the time for the modus tollens problems (e.g., "If Mary is in Dublin, then Joe is in Limerick. Joe is in Cambridge. What follows?"—Mary must not be in Dublin). Note that the subjects in the Johnson-Laird et al. experiment had trouble making the modus tollens argument. Other research has also found that subjects have trouble recognizing that the modus tollens conclusion is valid (Rips & Marcus,1977; Standenmayer, 1975; Rips, 1983: Braine, Reiser, & Rumain, 1984).

Deciding Which Observations Determine Whether a Premise Is True

The other experimental paradigm places in doubt whether the conditional premise is true. Instead, subjects indicate which observations would tell them if the conditional premise is true or false, and which observations are irrelevant to the truth value of the conditional premise. Subjects might be asked something like, "What observations tell you whether it is true or false that students who score at or above 90% on the final exam automatically get an A in the course?"

The pioneering version of an experiment that requires subjects to decide what evidence supports or refutes a conditional premise was developed by Wason and Johnson-Laird (Wason, 1966; Wason & Johnson-Laird, 1972). They invented what has come to be called the **card selection task**. The task presented college-educated subjects four cards whose faces displayed letters and numbers, such as an *E*, a *K*, a *4*, and a *7*. The task is illustrated in Figure 7-2. The subjects were told that the cards had letters on one side and numbers on the other side. The subjects were then told that they were supposed to determine whether the following conditional premise was true: "If a card has a vowel on one side, it has an even number on the other side." Subjects were asked which cards they should turn over to see if the premise was true or false, and which cards they should not bother turning over because the information so obtained would be irrelevant to determining the truth value of the premise. You might try solving this problem on your own before you read the next paragraph.

Formal logic tells us that the card with the E on it should be turned over because the conditional premise says that an even number should appear on

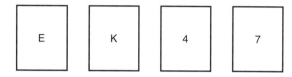

FIGURE 7–2   An example of cards used in the card selection task.

the other side (modus ponens). If the number is instead odd, then we know for sure that the premise is false. Turning over the card with the 7 on it would also be useful, because the premise requires that a consonant and not a vowel be on the other side of an odd number. Vowels have to have even numbers; if the card with the 7 has a vowel on the other side then we know for sure that the premise is false (modus tollens). Note that examining the card with the E corresponds to making the observation symbolized by "observe *p*," and examining the card with the 7 on it corresponds to making the observation symbolized by "observe not *q*."

Formal logic tells us that turning over the card with the K on it is useless, because the premise does not tell us whether odd or even numbers appear on the other side of consonants (the fallacy that is therefore avoided is denial of the antecedent). Turning over the card with the 4 on it is also useless, because even if that card had a consonant on the other side, the premise could still be true (the fallacy that is avoided is affirmation of the consequent). Again, the premise does not tell us what kind of number is on the other side of a consonant.

Wason and Johnson-Laird found that only about 4% of their subjects picked the card with the E ("observe *p*") and the card with the 7 ("observe not *q*"), while avoiding the card with the K ("observe not *p*") and the card with the 4 ("observe *q*"). Instead, the way many subjects responded was to say that they would turn over the card with the E on it and turn over the card with the 4 on it, and that there was no need to turn over the other two cards. Put formally, subjects made two kinds of mistakes: they committed the fallacy called affirmation of the consequent (by turning over the card with the 4 on it) and they failed to make the modus tollens argument (by not turning over the card with the 7 on it). The failure to make the modus tollens argument was the more frequent error.

Most subjects, then, do not seem to base their responses in the card selection task on the formal rules of logic. Yet the experimental situation does not seem to tax the subjects' memory or attention span. Even when the subjects are given explanations about how to reason in the card selection task, or are allowed to turn over many cards to see if their decisions are accurate, about half or more of the subjects still make errors (Wason & Johnson-Laird, 1970). Furthermore, professional mathematicians, experts in logic if anyone is, have trouble with the card selection problem (Dawes, 1975), as do college students who have just taken a semester course in logic (Cheng, Holyoak, Nisbett, & Oliver, 1986).

In short, people make a lot of mistakes on conditional reasoning problems, especially on problems requiring the modus tollens argument. The difficulty people have with conditionals would seem to have troubling implications for the ordinary person's reasoning when confronted with important issues whose resolution requires making logical deductions. Consider, again, a juror contemplating the guilt or innocence of the accused. Does the apparent unsoundness of the ordinary person's conditional reasoning mean that juries often render irrational verdicts? Indeed, research does suggest that many jurors have trouble deducing that certain kinds of evidence refute their own particular story of what happened in a criminal case (Kuhn, Weinstock, & Flaton, 1994)—a kind of failure to apply the modus tollens argument.

WHAT UNDERLIES THE DEVIATIONS FROM LOGIC IN CONDITIONAL REASONING PROBLEMS?

What causes people to deviate from formal logic when confronted with conditional reasoning problems? What is it about human cognition that disables logical reasoning and introduces biases into the reasoning process? In trying to answer this question, I will focus especially on the difficulty people have with conditional reasoning problems that are instances of modus tollens (if p then q, observe not q, therefore not p).

The Availability Hypothesis: Irrationality as Availability

One explanation for illogical performance on reasoning tasks is known as the **availability hypothesis** (Tversky & Kahneman, 1973; Pollard, 1982). The gist of the hypothesis is that subjects are prone to use whatever information is made salient, or available, by the premise to draw a conclusion. One underlying basis for availability may be the limited capacity of the brain for simultaneously activating information. If attention is captured by some piece of information, it is likely to "crowd out," as it were, other pertinent information that may be necessary to derive a logical conclusion. Implicit in the availability hypothesis is that people are radically irrational. Certainly there is nothing in formal logic that says that one should draw as a conclusion any information that happens to be made readily available by the premise.

A modification of the availability hypothesis is that reasoning makes use of similarity and contiguity. Should a premise seem similar to a conclusion or be closely connected to a conclusion in personal experience, people will tend to reflexively generate that conclusion (see Sloman, 1996).

The availability hypothesis claims that people are good at cases of modus ponens (if p then q, observe p, deduce q), because the correct conclusion (q) is contained directly in the premise. But people have difficulty with cases of modus tollens (if p then q, observe not q, deduce not p), because the correct conclusion (not *p*) is not contained directly in the premise. The salience of the premise, which does not contain the conclusion, crowds out the thought processes necessary to contemplate other propositions, such as the "not *p*" proposition.

An idea associated with the availability hypothesis and other models of human irrationality is that apparent instances of rationality are attributable to formal education and not to mental processes intrinsic to human nature. If logical reasoning depends on formal education, then it follows that people who do not receive a formal education should have even more difficulty with reasoning problems than do formally educated students.

Research on how nonliterate people solve reasoning problems suggests that they tend to treat problems as descriptions of real experiences and so have trouble accepting premises that either contradict or are outside their own experience (Luria, 1976; Cole & Scribner, 1974; see Galotti, 1994). For instance, Cole and Scribner (1974) gave nonliterate Kpelle farmers from Liberia conditional problems such as "Spider and black deer always eat together. Spider is eating. Is the black deer eating?" In the typical case, the Kpelle farmer initially protested that without seeing the events in question, the problem couldn't be solved. If pressed, the Kpelle farmer usually managed to reach a conclusion, but the conclusion was based on an idiosyncratic interpretation of the premises. For example, one Kpelle farmer agreed that black deer is eating. The reason: "Black deer always walks about all day eating leaves in the bush. Then he rests for a while and gets up to eat." Kpelle people educated in Western schools confront such problems in a manner similar to the way educated Westerners confront them (Scribner, 1975).

An Adaptive Approach to Conditional Reasoning

An alternative to a rational model of reasoning, which claims that people follow logical rules, and an alternative to an irrational model, such as that embodied by the availability hypothesis, is an approach to human cognition known as an **adaptive approach**. In biology, adaptation refers to reproductive success. A trait like upright walking is said to be adaptive if individuals who possess it or possess more of it are likely to reproduce and pass on the genetic basis of the trait to their offspring. Most biological adaptations have costs as well as benefits. For example, upright walking has resulted in lower-back problems and birthing difficulties in humans, even while freeing the hands for tool use and permitting better locomotion than the knuckle-walking mode used by apes. As long as the benefits of a trait outweigh the costs, though, the trait is adaptive.

A number of cognitive psychologists have argued for an analogous form of adaptation for human reasoning and cognition (Anderson, 1990, 1991; Arkes, 1991; Cosmides, 1989; Bjorklund & Green, 1992). In the context of deductive reasoning, an adaptive approach suggests that the manner in which people make deductions results in the successful prediction of future outcomes, given that those outcomes are potentially predictable and not random (Anderson, 1990, 1991). For example, to conclude that the evidence supports the premise that watching violent TV shows causes children to behave aggressively amounts to predicting that when Jacob watches the Power Rangers beat up evil space aliens on TV, he will become aggressive in his play. The adaptive approach stresses that people will use any and all relevant knowledge in order to maximize the likelihood of making accurate predictions. The adaptive approach also stresses that the bringing to bear on reasoning problems of all relevant knowledge incurs a cost. The cost is that the extra knowledge may contradict the logically correct solution.

Why has the cognitive system not evolved so as to make use of logical rules in all situations? What is adaptive about bringing to a reasoning problem extra knowledge that might undermine a rational analysis? A possibility is that deductions drawn from conditional premises must not contradict other knowledge. Prediction of future events in the real world often depends on drawing on knowledge from several sources. Ignoring those sources would undermine prediction.

Cummins (1995; see also Cummins, Lubart, Alksnis, & Rist, 1991) provides a nice experimental demonstration that real-world knowledge may undermine a logical but not adaptive analysis of conditional reasoning problems. Cummins compared reasoning on two types of problems. In one problem, world knowledge suggests that a premise might not always be true. An example is "If the brake is depressed, the car will slow down." Here it is possible that the brake might not function properly, and therefore depressing it would not invariably slow down the car. In the other problem, world knowledge suggests that the premise is almost always true. An example is "If Larry's fingerprints were on the glass, then he grasped it with his bare hands." Here it is hard to see any way for Larry's fingerprints to get on the glass other than his grasping it with his bare hands. Cummins found that the subjects' reasoning reflected this kind of knowledge. For instance, subjects were more likely to conclude—modus ponens—that finding Larry's prints on the glass meant that he grasped it with his bare hands than they were to conclude that observing a driver depressing the brakes meant that the car would slow down. From the perspective of the formal rules of logic, the subjects at times behaved irrationally. But from the perspective that reasoning services prediction, the subjects increased the likelihood of accurately predicting events, by taking into account the probabilistic nature of some causal relationships in drawing conclusions from premises. Similar results have been found in other deductive reasoning experiments (e.g., Markovits & Nantel, 1989; Lefford, 1946).

The idea that reasoning is well served by taking into account knowledge that lies outside the premises is also consistent with a proposal put forth by Oaksford and Chater (1994; for a dissenting opinion, see Evans & Over, 1996). In their deconstruction of the Wason card selection task, Oaksford and Chater claim that subjects can ordinarily expect to gain more useful information by turning over the "*p*" and "*q*"cards than by turning over the "*p*" and "*not q*" cards. The reason is that subjects assume that the causal relationships implicit in most versions of the Wason section task are rare in the real environment.

To see their argument, suppose you are asked to evaluate the claim that eating tripe makes people sick, in the context of the Wason card selection task. The cards you would be presented with would say: "eating tripe," "not eating tripe," "sick," and "healthy." Certainly it is worth asking someone who has just eaten tripe whether they are sick (i.e., turning over the card with the "p" observation). If the tripe eater is sick, the rule is verified. If the tripe eater is healthy, the rule is falsified. What about examining people who are sick to see if they have eaten tripe (i.e., turning over the card with the "q" observation)? If a sick person has eaten tripe, the rule is verified, but if the sick person has not eaten tripe, no conclusion can be drawn. It is also worth examining people who are not sick (i.e., turning over the card with the "not q" observation). If a healthy person has eaten tripe, then the rule is falsified. According to Oaksford and Chater, given that it is rare to encounter people who have eaten tripe and who are sick, it is actually more informative to see if a person who is sick has recently eaten tripe (i.e., select the "q" card) than to see if a person who is not sick has recently eaten tripe (i.e., select the "not q" card). In the real world, the odds of finding tripe eaters from among all the healthy people are much smaller than the odds of finding a tripe eater from among sick people. Consequently, the illogical choice to turn over the "q" card more often than the "not q" card, as subjects routinely do in the Wason card selection task (Oaksford & Chater, 1994), is actually rational in the adaptive sense that reasoning entails making predictions based on real-world knowledge.

Social Reasoning

Predicting future events is especially critical in the context of human social interactions. Human societies invariably devise a number of social rules in order to regulate, in various ways, how people ought to interact with one another. Predicting human behavior entails reasoning about the social rules that supposedly regulate behavior, and, especially, reasoning about whether people are actually following the social rules. If the adaptive approach to reasoning has merit, then it ought to be the case that people are especially good at reasoning about whether people are following social rules.

One kind of social rule regulates exchange, in which people agree to pay a cost in order to receive a benefit (e.g., A teacher agrees to give a student an A if the student writes an original paper on black holes). Social exchanges are important to successful cooperation and division of labor. Cosmides (1989) claims that humans have been shaped by evolution to reason logically about whether people follow the rules of social exchanges. Especially critical to social exchange is the detection of cheaters, who are defined as people who take the benefits without paying the costs (e.g., the student who plagiarizes a paper on black holes in order to get the A grade). Any individual who engaged in social exchange, but lacked the ability to detect cheaters, would end up paying too much cost for too little gain (e.g., the teacher who gives away the grade of A to the plagiarizer who has not provided an original paper on black holes). The interesting observation is that a procedure by which one detects cheaters is analogous to the rules of formal logic. For example, the modus tollens argument (if p then q, observe not q, deduce not p) is analogous to denying benefits to one who has not paid the costs (e.g., the student plagiarized a paper on black holes, therefore the teacher will not give the student an A). In a sense, the claim is that an understanding of how to detect cheaters of social exchanges is functionally identical in form to an understanding of the logical rules underlying conditional reasoning.

Cosmides tested these claims by showing that subjects do well on the Wason card selection task if the task reminds them of detecting cheaters. She presented her subjects with unfamiliar conditional premises such as "If a man eats cassava root, then he has a tattoo on his face." These rules were presented with either of two cover stories. One cover story was that the rule was supposed to be a description of the cultural practices of an obscure tribal people. The other cover story was that the rule was supposed to be a description of a social contract used by the tribe. In particular, the cassava root was a potent aphrodisiac, so eating it was highly desirable, but only married men were allowed to eat the root. According to the story, a facial tattoo meant that a man was married. So the men had to be married in order to receive the benefit of the root.

The subjects were given one or the other cover story, along with four cards labeled "eats cassava root", "eats molo nuts," "tattoo," and "no tattoo." The subjects were told that the cards represented individual members of the tribe. One side of a card told which food the man was eating, while the other side of a card told whether the man had a tattoo on his face. Subjects had to select which cards to turn over to see if the men were breaking the rule. When the cover story was that the rule was merely a description of a cultural practice, only about 20–25% of the subjects correctly selected the cards labeled "eats cassava root" ("p") and "no tattoo" ("not q"). But when the cover story was that the rule represented a social exchange, then about 70–75% of the subjects made the logically correct selections. When they understood that the rule was about exchange, subjects were prompted to think about cheaters, and so focused on people who had not paid the cost of having their face tattooed to see whether they got the benefit of eating cassava root. Subjects reasoned logically about this rule (and several other social exchange rules invented by Cosmides), even though it was unfamiliar to them.

It is sometimes claimed that people do better on conditional reasoning problems when the problem is concrete, as in the cassava root–tattoo example, than when the problem is abstract, as in the vowel–even number example discussed earlier (Griggs & Cox, 1982; see Mayer, 1992). Certainly, abstract conditional problems tend to present difficulties (Mayer, 1992). However, the Cosmides (1989; see also Kirby, 1994) study makes clear that it is not the concreteness per se that matters to successful reasoning but the kind of causal relationships evoked by the problem's elements. In the Cosmides study, both problem types were concrete, but the one that evoked social exchange was the easier problem for subjects to solve.

The ability to determine whether other people are following social rules is not limited to social exchanges. People also readily apply the rules of formal logic in the context of social permission (Cheng & Holyoak, 1985; Griggs & Cox,

1982). For instance, Griggs and Cox (1982) asked their subjects to evaluate the following familiar conditional premise: "If a person is drinking beer, then the person must be over 19 years of age." The subjects were asked to turn over cards that were labeled "drinking beer," "drinking Coke," "16 years of age," and "22 years of age." It was explained to the subjects that one side of each card provided a person's age while the other side described what the person was drinking. Subjects were told to turn over just those cards necessary to determine if these people were violating the rule. In contrast to the original unfamiliar Wason card selection task, a majority (about 74%) of the subjects made the logically correct responses. They correctly selected the cards corresponding to "drinking beer" ("observe *p*") and "16 years of age" ("observe not *q*").

However, Kirby (1994) showed that the frequency with which the "not *q*" card was selected depended on how the "not *q*" was instantiated. Subjects were less likely to choose a card with "12 years of age" or a card with "4 years of age" than they were a card with "19 years of age." (Since the early 1980s, when Griggs and Cox did their study, the minimum drinking age has been raised from 19 to 21 years of age.) That is, subjects selected the cards dictated by standard logic less often when it seemed implausible that the hypothetical people would ever drink beer. Kirby's results demonstrate that any putative social permission schema is influenced by general knowledge and that merely making logical problems concrete does not make them easy to solve.

In brief, the adaptive approach to deductive reasoning focuses on the long-term gains and costs of reasoning. The adaptive approach stands in contrast to the availability model, which claims that people are irrational, and in contrast to the Aristotelian model, which claims that people are rational in the sense of invariably following the formal rules of logic. Instead, people are rational in the sense that they seek to maximize prediction of future events, even though that entails the cost of sometimes drawing absurd conclusions to certain premises.

SECTION 2: PREDICTING UNCERTAIN EVENTS: ARE PEOPLE INTUITIVE STATISTICIANS?

To predict with some reasonable degree of accuracy an uncertain future, people must make use of the concept of probability. If people are the rational animals claimed by Aristotle, then their concept of probability ought to reflect what statisticians have learned about probability. That is, people ought to be **intuitive statisticians**. That is not to say that ordinary people will be able to calculate exactly the odds in complex situations like finding the probability of getting three or more heads in seven tosses of a fair coin. But it is to say that ordinary people will have a sense of the relative probabilities of events, so that their intuitions will bias them toward predicting the statistically more probable event. For example, if people are intuitive statisticians, then they ought to have the intuition that the probability of correctly guessing whether a fair coin will come up heads or tails is greater than the probability of correctly guessing the number that will come up after the roll of a fair six-sided die.

The classical statisticians of the Enlightenment, including Poisson and Laplace, believed that ordinary people are intuitive statisticians (Gigerenzer & Hoffrage, 1995). Laplace (1814/1951), for example, thought that the theory of probability was in essence a manifestation of a kind of human instinct.

Contradicting the notion that people are intuitive statisticians is the theoretical and empirical work of Amos Tversky and Daniel Kahneman, among the best-known researchers in the area of reasoning about uncertainty. Their work suggests that ordinary people do not make consistent use of principles of probability when predicting uncertain events. And the cause, it is alleged, is not merely performance lapses, or lack of interest, or ignorance. Rather, the cause is an intrinsically limited form of information processing whereby people are doomed to compute probability inaccurately. The concept of probability most people have seems to be characterized by a rather startling ignorance of statistical principles.

STATISTICAL FALLACIES

The Conjunctive Fallacy

One kind of statistical fallacy that seems to characterize the ordinary person's concept of probability is called the **conjunctive fallacy**. This fallacy is based on a simple statistical principle that says that the probability of two independent events' occurring at the same time (in conjunction) can never be more than the probability of the less probable event's occurring by itself. To think otherwise is a fallacy. For example, the probability that it will snow during a lunar eclipse cannot be greater than the probability that there will be a lunar eclipse. The occasions on which there is an eclipse of the moon include the times when it snows and the times when it does not snow.

Surprisingly, there are situations when people's judgments about the probability of uncertain events seems to violate the conjunctive principle (Tversky & Kahneman, 1983). Tversky and Kahneman demonstrated the conjunctive fallacy in a well-known experiment in which subjects were told about a hypothetical person named Linda, who is 31 years old, single, bright, and outspoken. She majored in philosophy in college, where she was deeply concerned with issues of discrimination and social justice and participated in antinuclear demonstrations. Subjects were then asked to rank order the likelihood that Linda is a teacher in elementary school, a bank teller, a bank teller and active in the feminist movement, among other selections. In general, subjects, even doctoral students majoring in decision making, ranked as more likely that Linda is a bank teller and active in the feminist movement than that Linda is a bank teller. Yet logically it must be true that it is more probable that Linda is a bank teller than that she is both a bank teller and a feminist. After all, the set of people who are bank tellers includes those people who are feminists as well as those who are not feminists, and so must be a larger set than the set of bank tellers who are also feminists. Even if every bank teller in the world is a feminist, it cannot be more probable that Linda is a bank teller and feminist than that she is a bank teller. So the subjects committed the conjunctive fallacy. They responded as if they believed that the probability of the conjunction of two events is greater than the probability of one of the events.

Tversky and Kahneman have demonstrated the conjunctive fallacy in many situations, and have shown that it is made even by people who are experts on the types of problem posed to them (see Tversky & Kahneman, 1983). For example, physicians were told that a 55-year-old female had pulmonary embolism (blood clots in the lung) documented angiographically 10 days after a cholecystectomy. The physicians were then asked to judge the probability that the patient would experience various symptoms. The physicians estimated that the patient was more likely to experience both dyspnea (shortness of breath) and hemiparesis (partial paralysis) than to experience only hemiparesis. Dyspnea is a typical symptom of pulmonary embolism whereas hemiparesis is an atypical symptom. Note that this problem is formally the same as the Linda-bank teller problem. The physicians, like the college students, committed the conjunctive fallacy. They mistakenly rated the probability of dyspnea and hemiparesis as greater than the probability of hemiparesis alone.

Neglect of Base Rate

Another example of a statistical fallacy that seems to characterize the ordinary person's concept of probability is called the **neglect of base rates**. The principle of base rates can be illustrated with a simple example. Suppose everyone who suffers from AIDS feels fatigued. Of course, there are many more people who feel fatigued for other reasons. Now suppose you are a physician who encounters a patient who complains of fatigue. Is it more likely that your patient has AIDS, still a relatively rare disease, or is it more likely that your patient is not suffering from AIDS? The answer is that it is more likely that your patient is not suffering from AIDS. After all, among all people who feel fatigued at any given moment, only a tiny percentage actually have AIDS. To properly estimate the probability of suffering from AIDS given fatigue, one must take into account the base rate of the disease in the population.

Tversky and Kahneman, as well as other researchers (e.g., Doherty, Schiavo, Tweney, & Mynatt, 1981), have demonstrated that subjects often ignore base rate information when they estimate the probability of uncertain events. One of their best-known demonstrations of a failure to use base rates (Kahneman & Tversky, 1973; see, also, Tversky and Kahneman, 1980) comes from an experiment in which subjects were presented the following cover story:

> A panel of psychologists have interviewed and administered personality tests to 30 engineers and 70 lawyers, all successful in their respective fields. On the basis of this information, thumbnail descriptions of the 30 engineers and 70 lawyers have been written. You will find on your forms five descriptions, chosen at random from

the 100 available descriptions. For each description, please indicate your probability that the person described is an engineer, on a scale from 0 to 100. The same task has been performed by a panel of experts, who were highly accurate in assigning probabilities to the various estimates. You will be paid a bonus to the extent that your estimates come close to those of the expert panel.

The subjects were then given descriptions of five hypothetical people, an example of which is:

Jack is a 45-year-old man. He is married and has four children. He is generally conservative, careful, and ambitious. He shows no interest in political and social issues and spends most of his free time on his many hobbies, which include home carpentry, sailing, and mathematical puzzles. The probability that Jack is one of the 30 engineers is ___%.

For another group of subjects the same cover story was provided except that they were told that the descriptions were drawn from a set of 30 lawyers and 70 engineers. Note that the description of Jack fits the stereotype most people have for engineers. Remember that the descriptions that the subjects read were supposed to have been sampled at random from 100 descriptions. So the probability that Jack is in fact an engineer must surely be much lower if there are only 30 engineers out of 100 people interviewed than if there are 70 engineers out of 100.

But the subjects did not seem to use the prior information about the frequency of engineers in the sample when estimating the probability that Jack is an engineer. Subjects who were told that there were only 30 engineers out of 100 produced a probability estimate of about 90% for the description of Jack. Subjects who were told that there were 70 engineers out of 100 also produced a probability estimate of about 90%. If subjects had taken into account the proportion of engineers in the sample, then the probability that Jack is an engineer would have been lower when there were only 30 engineers than when there were 70 engineers in the sample from which Jack's description was selected. In this example, the subjects' intuitions about the probability of uncertain events did not seem to reflect the prior frequencies of engineers in the sample at large. That is, the subjects neglected to use the base rate information. Instead, the subjects seemed to base their responses almost entirely on the stereotype that engineers are usually conservative, apolitical, mathematical, and so on. Note, by the way, that subjects were promised monetary rewards for correct answers.

EXPLAINING THE STATISTICAL FALLACIES

It seems, then, that the ordinary person is not an intuitive statistician. It seems, instead, that the ordinary person has a concept of probability riddled with fallacies. Furthermore, it seems that the adaptive approach to reasoning, developed in the previous section, is seriously undermined by the evidence of widespread statistical fallacies. After all, the adaptive approach claims that the reasoning system is good at predicting the future (given a basis for the prediction). But how can a person with an error-ridden model of probability be expected to predict future events accurately?

Representativeness and Availability

Tversky and Kahneman claim that the statistical fallacies displayed by the ordinary person are due to the widespread use of a misguided strategy that they call **representativeness**. The idea of representativeness is that there is a reflexive tendency to estimate the probability of an event based on the similarity between that event and some other conceptual category. So people think that it is more probable that Linda is a feminist than that she is a bank teller and a feminist, because the description of Linda is more similar to the stereotype of a feminist than it is to a stereotype of a bank teller. That is how representativeness accounts for the conjunctive fallacy. And people think that Jack is likely to be an engineer, regardless of the base rate of engineers in the population, because the description of Jack more closely matches the stereotype of an engineer than the stereotype of a lawyer. That is how representativeness accounts for the neglect of base rates.

The representativeness strategy, at least as it is articulated by Tversky and Kahneman, would seem to be a fundamentally irrational process. After all, it leads to making predictions that contradict simple and verifiable statistical principles, such as the principle that a conjunctive event cannot be more probable than the probability of either of its component events. Representativeness is another way of saying that people think in a rather shallow and foolish way about probabilities.

Note, by the way, that the representativeness strategy may be regarded as an example of availability. The similarity between the event and a category (e.g., between the description of Linda and the category of feminist) is what makes the association between the event and category seem strong. That association is therefore readily available, and so comes to dominate the probability judgment.

An Adaptive Approach to Statistical Fallacies

The adaptive approach assumes that reasoning strategies efficiently and effectively enable people to predict future events. But for prediction of future events to be reasonably accurate, people need to make use of statistical principles, and to avoid relying on the vividness of events as an indicator of their relative frequency. The failure of the ordinary person to embody rational probability assessment strategies undermines the adaptive approach to reasoning that I sketched out at the end of the section on conditional reasoning.

Or so it would seem. It may be, though, that the the neglect in base rates and the conjunctive fallacy, observed in experiments on probability judgments, reflect the problem of ecological validity. The notion of probability as it applies to everyday life refers to frequency of occurrence. Subjects may be somewhat unclear about what the word "probability" is supposed to mean, especially in hypothetical situations, or in situations that occur only once. To put it another way, the intuitions people have about probability may take the form of an algorithm that makes use of frequency data, rather than one that uses numeric representations of probability (Gigerenzer & Hoffrage, 1995). While numeric and frequency representations of probability may be mathematically equivalent (e.g., a 72% probability is the same as 72 times out of 100), the two formats are not necessarily psychologically equivalent.

Consistent with the adaptive analysis, subjects are more likely to use base rate information and to avoid the conjunctive fallacy if the frequency of occurrence notion of probability is made clear to the subjects. For instance, Gigerenzer and Hoffrage (1995) presented subjects base-rate problems in one of two formats. In one case, the numeric representation of probability was used and subjects had to estimate the probability of a hypothesis. An example was:

> The probability of breast cancer is 1% for women at age 40 who participate in routine screening. If a woman has breast cancer, the probability is 80% that she will also get a positive mammography. If a woman does not have breast cancer, the probability is 9.6% that she will also get a positive mammography. A woman in this age group had a positive mammography in a routine screening. What is the probability that she actually has breast cancer?

Most subjects given this scenario produced a probability estimate that was far too high (estimates of 70%–80% were typical). In fact, the correct answer is 7.8%. The reason is that of every 1,000 women, 990 do not have breast cancer, but 9.6% of those 990, or about 95, will still test positive. Of the 10 who do have breast cancer, 80%, or 8, will test positive. So only 8 out of the 103 (or 7.8%) of women who test positive actually would have breast cancer. Even physicians estimate that the percentage is near 80% (Eddy, 1982).

Now see what happens when subjects were given the following scenario in which probability was represented in terms of frequency of occurrence:

> Ten out of every 1,000 women at age 40 who participate in routine screening have breast cancer. Eight of every 10 women with breast cancer will get a positive mammography. Ninety-five out of every 990 women without breast cancer will also get a positive mammography. Here is a new representative sample of women at age 40 who got a positive mammography. How many of these women do you expect to actually have breast cancer?

Now Gigerenzer and Hoffrage (1995) found that many more subjects produced an estimate that was close to the correct percentage of 7.8%. When the format of the problem fit the ecologically useful sense of probability as frequency of occurrence, the subjects were much more likely to reason as intuitive statisticians.

In the case of the experiment about whether Jack is a lawyer or an engineer, Gigerenzer, Hell, and Blank (1988; see also Cosmides & Tooby, 1990) found that subjects did take into account base rate information if the subjects themselves were allowed to draw descriptions from an urn containing 100 descriptions of lawyers and engineers. When subjects could see that the description was truly randomly selected from the sample, they estimated that the description of

Jack was more likely of an engineer when there were 70 engineers out of 100 cases than when there were only 30 engineers out of 100.

Recent research suggests that the conjunctive fallacy may, like the neglect of base rates fallacy, also reflect a misunderstanding about what the experimenters mean by the concept of probability. If the conjunctive problem is worded so that the frequency notion of probability is made salient, subjects do not commit the conjunctive fallacy. For example, if subjects are asked to consider that there are 100 cases like Linda's and are asked to estimate the number out of 100 who are bank tellers, or are bank tellers and feminists, then subjects correctly estimate that there are more bank tellers than bank tellers who are also feminists (Fiedler, 1988; Jones, Jones, & Frisch, 1995).

It is also possible that subjects in conjunctive reasoning experiments interpret statements like "Linda is a bank teller" as meaning that Linda is a bank teller and not a feminist. Otherwise, why would the researcher also ask subjects to judge whether Linda is a bank teller and a feminist? Tversky and Kahneman (1983) acknowledged this possibility and accordingly asked subjects to judge the probability of statements like "Linda is a bank teller whether or not she is active in the feminist movement." Tversky and Kahneman found that subjects still committed the conjunctive fallacy. However, their phrasing is still ambiguous, as it could mean "Linda is a bank teller even if she is active in the feminist movement" (Hilton, 1995). When Dulany and Hilton (1991) used less ambiguous versions of conjunctive reasoning problems like the "Linda" problem, they found that subjects were much less likely to commit the conjunctive fallacy.

SECTION 3: CRITICALLY EVALUATING BELIEFS: ARE PEOPLE INTUITIVE SCIENTISTS?

From our personal experiences we acquire ideas. Some of these ideas we believe in. Most of us believe that certain bacteria cause certain diseases, that all children deserve a good education, and that the earth is a sphere. Other ideas we do not believe in. Most of us do not believe that the moon is made of green cheese, or that Elvis Presley is still alive, or that professional wrestling is a legitimate sport. How well do ordinary people judge the validity of ideas presented to them by others, or extracted from experience? In this context, a belief may be regarded as a sense that an idea is true.

Let me begin by explicating a rational model by which ideas are turned into beliefs. The rational model is based on a scientific approach to validation; in effect, it claims that people are **intuitive scientists**. The scientist is a skeptic. Ideas are not true just because we happen to think about them or just because other people claim they are true. From the perspective of a scientist, an idea ought to be judged as true (and therefore believed) only when it is based on evidence that is consistent with the idea. An idea ought to be judged as false (and therefore disbelieved) when the evidence is inconsistent with the idea. In the absence of any evidence, an idea ought to be held *in aequilibrio*; that is, considered as neither true nor false. In general, then, thinking like a scientist means believing in an idea when and only when it is justified by evidence (Kuhn, 1989).

Descartes, among others, thought that people were intuitive scientists, in the sense that I have developed that notion here (Gilbert, 1991). Descartes claimed that people first comprehend an idea, and then engage in rational procedures designed to determine whether the idea is true or false. To illustrate, consider an example used by Gilbert (1991). Suppose you read that armadillos make good appetizers. According to Descartes, you initially do not know whether to believe this proposition. Should you subsequently learn that armadillo meat is gamey and tough, you would probably decide that the proposition is false. Should you subsequently learn that many of the finest restaurants in San Antonio serve armadillo fritters, you would probably decide that the proposition is true. If you never learned anything more about armadillos, you would remain uncommitted as to their potential as appetizers.

Not everyone has agreed with Descartes's analysis of assessing the validity of ideas. Baruch Spinoza (1632–1677), the Dutch philosopher famous for his notion that God does not intervene directly in people's lives, developed an alternative to the Cartesian analysis (Gilbert, 1991). Spinoza thought that understanding an idea is tantamount to believing in the idea. Rejection of an idea may occur later, if information is uncovered that is inconsistent with it. So, according to Spinoza, if you read that armadillos make good appetizers, you initially understand and believe the proposition, even in the absence of supporting evidence. Should you later learn that armadillo meat is gamey and tough, you may then reject the proposition. Rejecting an idea is therefore a more effortful process than accepting an idea, which occurs automatically on comprehension of the idea. Note that the uncritical acceptance of ideas that lack any supporting evidence is essentially irrational, and it is inconsistent with the idea that people are intuitive scientists.

The question I wish to answer in this section is whether ordinary people defer judgment as to the validity of an idea until they obtain relevant evidence that is either consistent or inconsistent with the idea, as Descartes claimed. Or do they automatically believe ideas as they comprehend them, and only later and with much effort falsify them, as Spinoza claimed? As you will see, a variety of evidence suggests that Descartes was wrong. It seems, instead, that people are Spinozians (Gilbert, 1991).

HUMANS AS SPINOZIANS

Degrading the Judgment Process

Consider, again, Descartes's claim that people first understand and then assess an idea, and Spinoza's claim that people simultaneously understand and believe an idea, and only later possibly falsify the idea. Given sufficient effort and time, both models yield the same outcome. People will hold that some ideas are true and some are false, and base their beliefs on the evidence. Sometimes, though, people do not have the cognitive resources or the time to evaluate properly an idea that they have comprehended. That is, sometimes the reasoning process is degraded. In such situations, the Cartesian intuitive scientist would regard the idea as neither true nor false, while the Spinozian would regard the idea as true (Gilbert, 1991).

The evidence suggests that the ordinary person is a Spinozian: When the process of evaluating ideas is degraded, people are likely to believe in any idea, even rather implausible ideas, that they have been told. The Spinozian principle is sometimes exploited by totalitarian governments that deprive political prisoners of sleep, in order to degrade their reasoning process and consequently indoctrinate them with the political ideology of the state.

Festinger and Maccoby (1964) did not deprive their subjects of sleep, but did require them to listen to propositions they would normally find doubtful, while simultaneously watching an unrelated film. An example of a doubtful proposition was that fraternities encourage cheating and dishonesty (the subjects were fraternity men). The dual task paradigm was designed to overburden the cognitive system, and so degrade the validation process. Subjects performing the two tasks simultaneously were unable to make a full effort to assess the propositions. Consistent with the Spinozian hypothesis, such subjects were more likely to accept the doubtful propositions as true than were control subjects who only listened to the propositions but did not have to attend to the film (see Petty & Cacioppo, 1986, for a review of similar studies). The overburdened intuitive scientist would have been uncommitted to the doubtful propositions.

Another way to degrade the validation process is to limit the time people have to reflect on ideas. In an experiment by Gilbert, Krull, and Malone (1990), subjects were first required to study facts about an imaginary animal called a *glark* (e.g., "Glarks are covered with long white fur"). Subjects then entered a practice phase in which they were given one of two types of trials. On one type of practice trial, subjects were asked to decide whether various propositions were true (e.g., "Glarks have white fur") or false (e.g., "Glarks have brown fur"). Subjects were to base their answers on the facts they learned in the study phase of the experiment. On the other type of practice trial, subjects were required to read the propositions as rapidly as possible. The speed-reading requirement was designed to allow subjects only enough time to comprehend the propositions, but not enough time to assess the validity of the propositions. Finally, subjects entered a testing phase of the experiment in which they were again asked to judge whether the propositions were true or false.

The main results from the testing phase were these: (1) For true propositions (e.g., "Glarks have white fur"), a subject was as likely to judge them true when the subject had merely comprehended them during the practice phase as when the subject had assessed them during the practice phase. (2) But for false propositions (e.g., "Glarks have brown fur") a subject was less likely to judge them as false when the subject had merely comprehended them during the practice phase than when the subject had assessed them during the practice phase. The Spinozian hypothesis explains the results. When not given enough time to assess propositions, subjects regarded those "merely comprehended" propositions as true. Consequently, when those propositions were true, the subjects were accurate. But when those propositions were false, the subjects were not as accurate.

Failure to Examine Potentially Disconfirming Data

The intuitive scientist ought to be good at recognizing and even seeking potentially disconfirming evidence for any idea that is comprehended. That is because the intuitive scientist is a skeptic who finds it easy to withhold judgment about ideas until evidence is obtained. Because ideas may be true or false, recognizing or seeking evidence that an idea is false ought to be as easy as recognizing or seeking evidence that the idea is true. But the Spinozian is prone to consider any idea that is understood as a true idea. There is no particular need to seek falsifying evidence. At the same time, any evidence that the idea is true ought to be more readily noticed than comparable evidence that the idea is false. Experiments suggest, again, that the ordinary person is not an intuitive scientist, but a Spinozian (see Mynatt, Doherty, & Tweney, 1977, 1978).

An example of research that shows that people more readily notice confirming than disconfirming evidence comes from Arkes and Harkness (1983), who asked subjects to determine if a set of data justified the idea that seeding clouds causes rain. The subjects were given a series of descriptions of days on which it rained or did not rain and days on which the clouds were seeded or not seeded. Among the descriptions, there were more rainy days than dry days when the clouds were seeded. Consequently, subjects were prone to believe that the data justified the idea that seeding causes rain. Contradicting the idea, however, was the data that there were more rainy days than dry days when the clouds were not seeded. In other words, there were simply more rainy than dry days, regardless of whether the clouds were seeded. Seeding had nothing to do with raining. But the subjects ignored or did not make use of the evidence that disconfirmed the seeding hypothesis; they focused only on the evidence that confirmed the seeding hypothesis.

Another example of the tendency to hold tenaciously to beliefs despite contradictory evidence comes from an experiment by Wegner, Coulton, and Wenzlaff (1985), which was based on a paradigm originally developed by Ross, Lepper, and Hubbard (1975). In one of the Wegner et al. experiments, subjects were given the task of discriminating between authentic and unauthentic suicide notes. The subjects were told that they would get feedback on how well they were able to make the discriminations. The feedback was either that they were more accurate than most people, less accurate than most people, or about average on the task. As it turned out, the feedback was bogus; subjects were randomly assigned to the feedback conditions. The subjects were told about the bogus nature of the feedback before they started the task. That is, it was made clear to the subjects that the feedback they were about to receive would not be based on their behavior, but would only reflect the group to which they had been randomly assigned. (In some other experiments, such as the original Ross et al. 1975 experiment, the information that the feedback was bogus was provided after the discrimination task was finished). Then all subjects were given a series of suicide notes and required to judge for each if the note was authentic or unauthentic. The judgment task was followed by the bogus feedback. Later, subjects predicted their probable future success at tasks like the suicide task, and rated their ability to perform the suicide task.

The rather startling result was that the subjects who had been randomly assigned to the "above-average" feedback condition judged that they were better on the task and would do better in the future on such tasks than did the subjects in the "average" condition. Similarly, the subjects in the "below-average" condition thought that they would perform worse than did the subjects in the "average" condition. The subjects virtually ignored the information that the feedback was bogus. The feedback may be regarded as communicating an idea to the subjects, who, as Spinozians, therefore believed in the feedback (e.g., I really am good at discriminating between authentic and unauthentic suicide notes). With such a belief already established, it became difficult for the subjects to falsify the idea, and so come to disbelieve it.

The problem most people have with Wason's card selection task (described in a previous section) may be regarded as an instance of disconformation difficulty. In that and many other unfamiliar conditional reasoning tasks, subjects have trouble recognizing that the "not q" observation implies that the premise ("if p, then q") must be false. Wason (1960) provided another well-known demonstration of the reluctance of the ordinary person to examine potentially disconfirming data. He presented subjects with numeric sequences, such as "2, 4, and 6," and asked them to uncover the rule for generating the numbers. The subjects were allowed to generate their own numbers, and the experimenter would then say if the subject-generated numbers fit the rule. For example, a subject who was first presented the numbers 2, 4, and 6 might hypothesize that the rule is "add 2 to make the next number." In fact, the experimenters used the sequence of "2, 4, 6" deliberately to encourage subjects to generate this hypothesis. According to Spinoza, the subject who is induced to consider such a hypothesis is also inclined to believe that it must be true.

Consistent with the Spinozian model, subjects were prone to seek only confirming evidence, and not disconfirming evidence, for their belief. A typical subject asked if numbers like 8, 10, 12 fit the rule, to which the experimenter would respond that the new numbers did indeed fit the rule. Note that the typical subject sought only data that, if observed, would be consistent with the subject's initial hypothesis. The problem was that most subjects never thought to test their hypothesized rule by generating a sequence of numbers that did not fit the rule, but fit a rival rule also consistent with the originally presented numbers. They never looked for disconfirming data (a result confirmed in many similar experiments—see Klayman & Ha, 1987, 1989). In fact, the rule the experimenter had in mind (in one case) was that the next number in the sequence had to be larger than the previous number. An intuitive scientist would have been able to entertain a hypothesis, such as "add 2," without necessarily believing in the hypothesis. The intuitive scientist would have been as likely to seek disconfirming as confirming evidence for a hypothesis *in aequilibrio*.

Interestingly enough, real scientists seem to make the same sorts of mistakes that laypeople do. Most seem to have trouble considering alternative hypotheses and seeking data that if observed would disconfirm their hypothesis and confirm the rival hypothesis (see Mitroff, 1974; Rousseau, 1992). Even real scientists may not be intuitive scientists! They seem to be Spinozians, just like the rest of us. That scientists eventually come to consider rival hypotheses and perform the experiments that might disconfirm one hypothesis while confirming another probably happens because scientists share their ideas and perform extensive critiques of prevailing ideas. It may be that it is the shared nature of scientific reasoning, and not the natural propensities of individual scientists, that enables the scientific enterprise to approximate the scientific methodological ideal.

Quantity Versus Quality of Arguments

Descartes thought that the ordinary person, acting as an intuitive scientist, not only suspends belief in ideas until relevant data is acquired, but uses rational means for evaluating the data. A rational evaluation of the data means that a person ought to be able to tell whether the data are predicted by the idea, and whether the data distinguish between the idea and its antithesis.

Consider, again, the idea that armadillos make good appetizers. A prediction that follows from the idea is that armadillo meat tastes good. The observation that fine restaurants in San Antonio frequently serve armadillo fritters would be consistent with the prediction that armadillo meat tastes good, but inconsistent with the antithesis that armadillo meat is wretched. So the observation ought to be regarded as relevant to assessing the idea. On the other hand, the observation that the armadillo is the mascot for 20 high schools in Texas does not follow from the idea that armadillos make good appetizers, and so ought to be regarded as irrelevant to assessing the validity of the idea.

The Spinozian hypothesis suggests that ordinary people may have trouble rationally assessing evidence as to whether an idea ought to be believed. The problem is that the ordinary person has a bias toward regarding ideas as true, even in the absence of any evidence. It would therefore follow that Spinozians would be prone to regard any evidence that reminds them of the idea as reinforcing the validity of the idea.

Consistent with the Spinozian model, it seems that the ordinary person is easily persuaded by the number of arguments made for an idea (Wolf & Latane, 1983), and not by the quality of the arguments. Weak arguments are typically based on irrelevant observations, while strong arguments are based on observations predicted by the idea.

Consider an experiment by Petty and Cacioppo (1984; see also Petty, Cacioppo, & Goldman, 1981). They asked undergraduate subjects whether students should be required to pass a comprehensive exam in their major in order to graduate. The subjects first read either three or nine arguments that were either weak (e.g., "The Educational Testing Service would not market the exam unless it had great educational value") or strong (e.g., "The quality of under-graduate teaching has improved at schools with the exam"). Among subjects who understood that the new graduation requirement did not apply to them, they were more likely to agree with the requirement if they read nine rather than three arguments. But it did not matter to these subjects whether the arguments were well reasoned or poorly reasoned (the results are summarized in the left sides of Figure 7-3). Surely the intuitive scientist would be more persuaded by the reasonableness of the arguments than by the number of arguments. But the Spinozian would be more persuaded by the quantity of arguments, without regard to their reasonableness. Whether reasonable or unreasonable, arguments at least evoke the original idea. And the more often an idea is evoked, the stronger ought to be the Spinozian's belief in the idea. Among Spinozians, to be reminded of an idea is to believe in the idea.

The research outlined in this section would seem to have especially trou-bling implications for the soundness of human reasoning. It seems that the ordi-

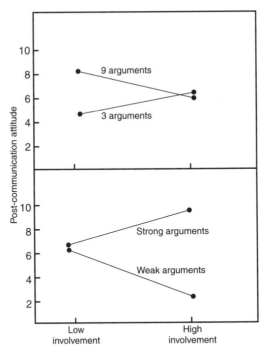

Top panel: Interactive effect of involvement and number of arguments on postcommunication attitudes. Bottom panel: Interactive effect of involvement and quality of arguments on postcommunication attitudes.

FIGURE 7–3   Degree of positive attitude towards a new graduation requirement. Based on Petty and Cacioppo (1984).

nary person can form strongly held beliefs merely by entertaining an idea, is especially prone to believing an idea when there is not time nor effort devoted to assessing the idea, is unlikely to challenge a belief by examining data that might contradict the belief, and can sustain a belief on the basis of irrelevant evidence. The ordinary person does not seem to be the intuitive scientist of Cartesian philosophy. More generally, the ordinary person does not seem to be the paragon of rationality implied by Aristotle's claim that humans are rational animals. Assuming that the findings from the cognitive psychology lab generalize to real-world situations, it would seem that the assessments of ideas required by ordinary people in a participatory society such as ours are frequently unsound. People's beliefs about minorities, about the actions of foreign governments, or about economic policies may not be based on any reasonable evidence, and may persist despite contradictory evidence.

WHY ARE PEOPLE SPINOZIANS?

Why has nature not arranged it so that people are intuitive scientists? Why are we instead Spinozians? Why can't we see that armadillos do not necessarily make good appetizers, just because someone said so?

Availability, Yet Again

The Spinozian model may be regarded as an example of the availability hypothesis. According to the availability hypothesis, reasoning is largely based on what the reasoning situation brings to mind, or makes salient. In situations in which people must assess the validity of ideas, the mere act of making an idea available is tantamount to believing the idea true. The more often or more readily an idea is brought to mind, the stronger is the belief in it.

Why should the mere availability of an idea mean that the idea is perceived as true? What is it about human cognition that turns people into Spinozians? A possibility, discussed by Gilbert (1991), is that ideas are regarded in the same way as perceptions. Ideas are conceptions of reality, perceptions describe the sensory data imparted by reality. That is, just as perceptions reflect the sensory information available to the perceptual systems, so, too, do beliefs reflect the ideas available to the reasoning system.

Consider that if you were to see an armadillo crawling along the highway, you would certainly believe that an armadillo is crawling along the highway. This is the case because perceptions are usually accurate, and because rapid responses to perceptions are critical to survival. Our ancestors would have become extinct had they spent much time trying to verify whether the charging lion was real or only an illusion. The Spinozian assessment procedure might have evolved from the perceptual system, and so retained the bias to believe what it comprehends. The new feature added to the cognitive system by evolution would have been the capability to falsify beliefs, given time and effort. Furthermore, it would have been biologically "costly" to evolve a Cartesian assessment procedure that requires suspending belief, and then engaging in procedures that either verify or falsify ideas.

This analysis of the availability hypothesis suggests that Hominids evolved into irrational Spinozians, albeit capable of inventing rational procedures that may be acquired, to varying degrees, given suitable education. The analysis suggests that human nature is decidedly inferior to the rational ideal conceived by Western philosophy. Perhaps this is why it is common in science fiction for robots and extraterrestrials to be depicted as super-rational entities capable of extraordinary feats of reasoning. Perhaps these fictional entities reflect our awareness of the discrepancy between the Aristotelian ideal and the Spinozian reality.

An Adaptive Analysis of the Spinozian Model

But, as I have suggested in previous sections of this chapter, the availability hypothesis may be an overly harsh depiction of human nature. Recall the discussion of an adaptive model of conditional reasoning. I suggested that conditional reasoning may trade an occasional failure to solve certain types of reasoning problems logically for the capability to make accurate predictions about the future. Consequently, the reasoning system makes use of knowledge that lies outside the formal conditional problem, in order to maximize predictive success.

An adaptive approach may be taken toward the assessment of ideas, as well. An important characteristic of any adaptive system is that it is **efficient**. If a system has to engage in a great deal of work for a minuscule gain, then that system is not adaptive. You would not work hundreds of hours just to get a taste of armadillo meat. Similarly, it may not pay off for a cognitive system to hold all comprehended ideas *in aequilibrio*, and then engage in "expensive" operations designed to uncover whether the idea is true or false. The adaptive approach claims that a Spinozian idea assessment model is actually a consequence of cognitive efficiency.

It is the case that the source of many of our ideas is the communications received from other people. And it is true that the vast majority of communications are sincerely made; that is, the sender believes them to be true (Grice, 1975). Communication among people would not be useful if most of the ideas communicated among people were false. Presumably, then, it is efficient for the cognitive system that assesses ideas to assume that the ideas it acquires from other people are likely to be true, until proven otherwise (Swann, 1984; see Gilbert, 1991). If I tell you that armadillos make good appetizers, you may figure that I have some good reasons to make that assertion and so choose to believe me, rather than to fly to Texas, hunt down an armadillo, and taste its meat. Of course, the cognitive system will sometimes be wrong, especially when ideas for which there is no evidence are communicated in a seemingly sincere way. And it is just that sort of situation that is often employed by experimenters studying the assessment of beliefs.

The efficiency analysis of why people usually act like Spinozians when assessing ideas can be tested. The analysis predicts that people will be more likely to hold ideas *in aequilibrio*, and engage in rational procedures to assess ideas, when (a) they have some good reason to believe that an idea has an uncertain status, and (b) the benefits for being right about the truth value of the idea outweigh the costs of examining the evidence.

This prediction was confirmed in the previously discussed experiment by Petty and Cacioppo (1984). Recall that they asked subjects to read three or nine arguments for a requirement to take a comprehensive examination in one's major. The arguments were either weak or strong. The subjects were persuaded by the number of arguments, and not by the quality of the arguments. But those results were observed only in subjects who understood that the graduation requirement did not apply to them. The experimenters also gave the task to a group of subjects who were led to believe that the graduation requirement did apply to them. These subjects were motivated to assess accurately the comprehensive examination requirement. Consistent with the adaptive analysis, the motivated subjects were more persuaded by the quality of the arguments than by the quantity (the results are summarized in the right sides of Figure 7-3).

Recall that subjects tend to ignore disconfirming evidence and focus only on confirming evidence in situations that supply both. Presumably this happens because people, following the Spinozian model, are predisposed to regard ideas as true. But with suitable motivation, subjects become influenced by disconfirming data. Evidence is provided by Harkness, DeBono, and Borgida (1985). They asked female undergraduates to read descriptions of other women whom a fellow named Tom either wanted to date or did not want to date. An example of information provided to the subjects was that of 12 women who were described as having a sense of humor, Tom wanted to date 8 of them and did not want to date 4 of them. Of 12 women who did not have a good sense of humor, Tom wanted to date 8 of them and did not want to date 4 of them. Some of the female subjects deduced that Tom liked women with a sense of humor. Acting as Spinozians, they paid attention to the confirming evidence but ignored the disconfirming evidence. But other female subjects expected to spend the next 3 to 5 weeks going out with Tom. These motivated subjects, acting like Cartesians, were much more likely to pay attention to both the confirming and the disconfirming evidence, and to correctly conclude that sense of humor was not critical to Tom. He was as likely to want to date a woman with a sense of humor as a woman without a sense of humor.

Another way to reduce the mental costs of evaluating ideas is to provide possible sets of positive evidence for an idea and let people choose which set of evidence is the most compelling. In this paradigm, subjects are not burdened with trying to determine whether an idea is true or whether evidence is relevant.

To illustrate the paradigm, consider an example from Lopez (1995): Suppose you are told that hippopotamuses have an ulnar artery. Which additional mammal would you study to see if all mammals have an ulnar artery—a rhinoceros or a hamster? One of the principles of science is the **diversity principle**, which says that a hypothesis is more strongly confirmed when supported by a diverse rather than a similar set of data (Hempel, 1966; Lopez, 1995). The diversity principle says to study the hamster. Research suggests that people use the diversity principle in assessing the value of evidence (Osherson, Smith, Wilkie, Lopez, & Shafir, 1990; Lopez, 1995).

For example, Lopez (1995) presented subjects short scenarios in which they were told that a particular exemplar of a natural category had a particular property with which subjects were unfamiliar. The subjects were then asked which additional listed exemplars of the category they would examine to see if all members of the category have the property. For example, subjects were told that oranges produce a germination agent called coumarin and were asked which one from a list of other fruit they would study to see whether all fruit produce the germination agent coumarin. Consistent with the diversity principle, subjects typically chose the exemplar that was most dissimilar to the original one. In the example, subjects were more likely to choose fruit dissimilar to oranges, such as dates, than fruit similar to oranges, such as grapefruit.

From the perspective of an adaptive analysis, then, evolution has turned us into rational Spinozians (the oxymoron notwithstanding). We seek to maximize the gain of successful predictions based on beliefs we hold, while minimizing the effortful processes required to adequately assess ideas before believing in them (see Arkes, 1991). The next section of this chapter builds on the point that human cognition is adaptive in the sense that it seeks to maximize gain and minimize cost.

SECTION 4: DECISION MAKING: ARE PEOPLE INTUITIVE ECONOMISTS?

People routinely make decisions, such as whether to rent or buy a home, vote for one presidential candidate or another, and go to a movie or a play on a Saturday night. How sound is the decision-making process of the ordinary person? A rational (and adaptive) analysis for decision making makes the fundamental assumption that people seek to maximize gain while minimizing loss (Coombs, Dawes, & Tversky, 1970; Edwards, 1954; see Fischhoff, 1988). For example, if you are offered two jobs that are identical except that one pays $10,000 a year more than the other, and if you are a rational decision maker, you should choose the higher paying job, because it maximizes the gain. For most people, money, security, affection, convenience, and so on, are all potential gains that one might seek to maximize. Cost refers to anything that takes away from gains, or is punishing. Costs might include loss of money, loss of security, effort, injury, and so on.

The question I pursue in this section is whether the ordinary person, when confronted with a choice, is an **intuitive economist**, rationally seeking to maximize gain and minimize loss. Again, a variety of experiments conducted by cognitive psychologists call into question the rationality of decision making. It seems that the decision making of the ordinary person is frequently affected by factors that have little to do with maximizing gain while minimizing loss. People do not always make decisions like rational economists.

LACK OF INVARIANCE IN DECISION MAKING

An important implication of the rational analysis of decision making is the **principle of invariance** (Kahneman & Tversky, 1984; Slovic, 1990). If decisions are made rationally—that is, based on maximizing gain and minimizing loss—then people should make the same decision in two similar situations as long as the gains and losses remain demonstrably constant. What actually happens, as Kahneman and Tversky (1984) have documented, is that people routinely violate the invariance principle. Their choices seem to be based instead on irrelevant factors.

Framing

One example of a violation of the invariance principle is that decisions are often affected by whether descriptions of the choices draw attention to positive or to negative outcomes. Unlike what we might expect of an intuitive economist, ordinary people may make very different decisions depending on how the choices are **framed** (e.g., Kahneman & Tversky, 1984; Tversky & Kahneman, 1981; Mellers & Cooke, 1996).

To illustrate, suppose you have lung cancer and are asked whether you want surgery or radiation to attempt a cure. You are told that among patients who choose surgery, 68% are alive after one year and 34% are alive after five years. But among patients who choose radiation, 77% are alive after one year and 22% are alive after five years. Do you choose surgery or radiation? The vast majority of people say they would choose the surgery option. Now suppose that you are told that among patients who choose surgery, 32% are dead after one year and 66% are dead after five years. But among patients who choose radiation, 23% are dead after one year and 78% are dead after five years. Again, do you choose surgery or radiation? Now only a slight majority of people select the surgery option (McNeil, Pauker, Sox, & Tversky, 1982). Clearly the choice is formally identical when framed in terms of living as when framed in terms of dying, but the way the decision was framed had a big effect on the alternative people preferred.

Another demonstration of the effect of framing on decision making comes from a well-known experiment by Tversky and Kahneman (1981). They first asked subjects to imagine that the United States is preparing for the outbreak of an unusual Asian flu that is expected to kill 600 people. Two alternative programs to combat the disease have been proposed. They asked subjects to choose which program should be followed. One group of subjects was presented this information:

> If program A is adopted, 200 people will be saved. If program B is adopted, there is a one-third probability that 600 people will be saved and a two-thirds probability that no people will be saved.

Based on this scenario, framed in terms of saving lives, 72% of the subjects chose program A, the sure thing, and only 28% choose program B, the risky choice. However, Tversky and Kahneman presented another group of subjects a scenario in which the choices were identical but were framed in terms of dying:

> If program A is adopted, 400 people will die. If program B is adopted, there is a one-third probability that nobody will die and a two-thirds probability that 600 people will die.

Now 22% favored program A, the sure thing, and 78% favored program B, the risky choice. When framed in terms of lives lost, the subjects preferred the risky alternative. Again, the decision did not remain invariant when the costs and benefits were invariant, as would be expected if people were intuitive economists.

One more example of a violation of the invariance principle comes from Irwin, Slovic, Lichtenstein, and McClelland (1993). They asked subjects to choose between improved air quality and an upgraded computer. Most subjects chose improved air quality as more valuable. Yet when subjects were asked how much money they would be willing to spend for improved air quality or for an upgraded computer, subjects typically were willing to spend more on the computer upgrade. Framing a choice in terms of its intrinsic value produced one preference, while framing the choice in terms of spending money produced a different preference.

Anchoring

Another violation of the invariance principle is that decisions are often affected by irrelevant information that happens to be associated with (or anchored to) the choices. The effect of **anchoring** is illustrated by the following scenario: Would you drive across town to purchase a $10 calculator that otherwise costs $15 at a nearby store? Perhaps the drive seems worth it. But would you drive across town to purchase a $120 calculator that otherwise costs $125 at a nearby store? Perhaps now the drive does not seem worth it. Yet in both situations, the benefits (save $5) and costs (drive across town) are the same. In this choice, the irrelevant information is the total cost of the calculator.

An experimental verification of the effect of anchoring on decision making comes from Tversky and Kahneman (1981; also Kahneman & Tversky, 1984). They gave their subjects the following choice:

> Imagine you are on your way to a play and discover that you lost the tickets. Would you be willing to pay another $40 to buy new tickets?

Only about 46% of the subjects said that they would purchase new tickets. Tversky and Kahneman gave another group of subjects this choice:

> Imagine that you are on your way to the theater to buy the tickets. Upon arrival you discover that you lost $40 in cash. Would you still buy the tickets to the play?

Now most subjects (about 88%) said that they would purchase the tickets. Yet the gains and losses are the same in these two situations; the gain is the tickets, the loss is the $40. It is as if the first group of subjects associated the loss of the tickets with the attending-the-theater scenario, and so become loath to pay another $40 to attend the play. Strictly speaking, however, the loss of the tickets is irrelevant to the choice.

WHAT ACCOUNTS FOR APPARENTLY IRRATIONAL DECISION MAKING?

Many economists are troubled by the finding that the decisions of ordinary people are perturbed by framing and anchoring—that the decision-making process violates the invariance principle (see Slovic, 1995). Why is it that people do not seem to be intuitive economists? Again, I will first develop an availability approach to decision making, and then counter with the adaptive approach.

Once Again, Availability

Throughout this chapter I have used variations of the concept of availability as a model that embodies the idea that humans are fundamentally irrational. In this section I will use availability to explain why people do not seem to be intuitive economists.

The essential characteristic of the availability model is that people's reasoning is dominated by whatever information is made salient or memorable by a situation. The lack of invariance in decision making, as revealed in the effects of framing and anchoring, seems consistent with availability. For example, if a decision about whether to choose surgery or radiation is framed in terms of dying, then the decision process is dominated by the strategy of avoiding the risk. The threat of immediate death is made salient and therefore encourages the avoidance of the more immediately risky alternative (surgery). When framed in terms of living, the risk of immediate death is not made as salient and so the tendency to avoid that risk is not as pronounced.

An Adaptive Approach to Decision Making

Certainly the research suggests that cost–benefit analyses of choices do not reliably predict the choices people make. The availability hypothesis accounts for such deviations from rationality. To counter the rather bleak and pessimistic assessment of human nature implied by the availability hypothesis, I have offered the adaptive approach to human reasoning.

Recall that two principles of the adaptive model of human reasoning are that (1) prediction is maximized if the reasoning process draws on a variety of information, including information that may lie outside the domain of the reasoning problem, and that (2) contemplative processes must be efficient—that is, worth the cognitive effort.

Now consider how the adaptive model might explain framing and anchoring effects in decision making. Information that may seem irrelevant to a decision may actually be legitimately interpreted as relevant by the decision maker. Grice (1975) discusses a variety of conversational maxims that characterize ordinary communication. These include the expectation that communications are informative and relevant. Many seemingly inconsistent responses can be explained as making appropriate use of Grice's communication maxims (Hilton, 1995).

To see how Grice's maxims might explain the framing and anchoring effects, consider the example of a patient given a choice between surgery and radiation. Framed in terms of dying, the choice is based on the fact that among patients who have the surgery, 32% are dead after one year and 66% are dead after five years, whereas among patients who have radiation treatment, 23% are dead after one year and 78% are dead after five years. Fewer patients choose surgery in this situation than in the situation where the facts are expressed in terms of percentages of patients who are alive. The implication is that people are irrational; the percentage of patients selecting each treatment should be impervious to the way the information is framed. From the perspective of the patient, however, the fact that the choice is expressed in terms of dying may be interpreted as an indication that the immediate risk of death for this patient is quite high; otherwise, why is the choice framed in terms of dying? Again, from the patient's perspective, the percentages of people alive or dead tells the patient very little about what will happen to him or her when one of the treatment options is selected. If a physician frames a choice by focusing on dying, and the immediate threat of dying is greater after surgery, it may be reasonable to assume that the physician believes that this particular patient will respond badly to the surgery, and so is especially likely to die.

Decisions are also likely to be based on a variety of kinds of knowledge triggered by the choice as it is presented. What appears to be irrational variance in choice selection may reflect the accessing of different knowledge bases. Recall that people prefer better air quality to an upgraded computer but are willing to spend more money on the computer. In the context of comparison between clean air and speedy computers, people may access their knowledge of what is good for humankind in general. But when asked about spending money, they may access what they know about economics. Maybe people figure that no one person can foot the bill to pay for clean air, but a little bit of money from a lot of people might be enough to improve air quality. On the other hand, one person might be able to afford the upgraded computer and certainly other people are not likely to contribute to the person's own computer fund. So people are willing to spend more on upgrading the computer than on improved air quality. My point here is simply that the lack of invariance seen in decision making may not mean that people are irrational (as the availability model would have it) but that people richly and sensibly interpret all the information contained in the decision-making environment, in order to make an informed choice (as the adaptive model would have it).

The idea that subjects perceive differences between two versions of the same decision problem finds support in research done by Frisch (1993). She presented subjects many of the standard decision problems (e.g., the Asian flu problem) used to demonstrate the framing effect. She found that subjects often provided sensible justifications for why the two ways in which a problem was framed should be interpreted differently. If two versions of a decision problem are really perceived as different, then it is hardly irrational to make a different decision depending on how the problem is framed.

A related point is that decisions made in everyday life typically have actual consequences. Assessing whether decision making is rational depends on how the consequences of decisions are perceived by the decision maker (Frisch & Clemen, 1994). Again, in this regard, the framing and anchoring effects may not be as irrational as they seem. For instance, it would seem to be irrational to choose ground beef that is described as 75% lean over ground beef that is described as 25% fat. Yet people who have in fact eaten ground beef described as 75% lean report a more favorable eating experience than do people who have eaten ground beef described as 25% fat (Levin & Gaeth, 1988). Maybe this is so because varying the description varies which aspect of the eating experience one focuses on. Whatever the reason, it certainly makes sense that people choose the ground beef more often when it is described as 75% lean. Similarly, the experience of merely being alive may be all the sweeter if one is confronted with the prospect of death. When a choice about surgery is framed in terms of dying, then, avoiding the risky surgery may have a more beneficial consequence than in the case when the surgery option is framed in terms of survival.

Summary and Conclusions

I began this chapter with the question of whether the reasoning of the ordinary person is rational or irrational. In the first section, I examined how people reason from premises, focusing on conditional reasoning (If p then q). In this context, the notion that people are rational means that people are intuitive logicians whose deductions to conditional premises are the same as those explicated by formal logic. Refuting the idea that humans are intuitive logicians is the finding that people have trouble following or making valid, and only valid, deductions. Most people find the modus tollens argument (i.e., if p then q, observe not q, deduce not p) to be especially difficult.

Throughout the chapter I developed a model of irrationality, labeled the availability hypothesis, which says that human reasoning is dominated by whatever information is salient. One possible reason that salience may be critical is that human cognition is inherently limited in its capacity. Modus tollens arguments (i.e., If p then q, observe not q, deduce not p) are difficult, according to the availability hypothesis, because a conditional reasoning problem does not supply within it the "not p" conclusion. The act of drawing a conclusion and examining the conditional premise uses up so much of the limited capacity that it becomes unlikely that the reasoner will be able to engage in the thought processes necessary to draw the "not p" conclusion.

In contrast to the availability hypothesis, I developed an approach to human reasoning labeled the adaptive approach. The adaptive approach claims that reasoning functions primarily to anticipate future events in order to prepare for them. Adaptation is a kind of rationality, but not one based on the formal application of logical, statistical, scientific, or economic principles, as espoused by Western culture and philosophy. Rather, the rationality of adaptation is based on success at predicting the future, in ecologically realistic environments, without paying too much "cognitive" cost.

In the context of conditional reasoning, the adaptive approach emphasizes the importance of making use of all relevant sources of knowledge when making deductions based on premises. Sometimes, the need to predict undermines the requirement to perform logically, as when people resist drawing logically valid conclusions that contradict other knowledge.

In the second section, I examined how well people are able to predict uncertain events. Research on predicting uncertain events usually asks people to judge the probability of various outcomes or observations. In the context of probability judgments, rationality means that people are intuitive statisticians, capable of making judgments that reflect simple laws of statistics. Refuting the idea that humans are intuitive statisticians are the findings that people are prone to make the conjunctive fallacy (believing that in some cases the conjunction of two events is more probable than one of the events) and are prone to neglect base rate information.

According to the availability hypothesis, the reason that people make such statistical errors is that their probability judgments are undermined by representativeness (e.g., the description of Jack resembles that of a typical engineer). The similarity between an instance (e.g., the description of Jack) and a conceptual category (e.g., the engineer) dominates the judgment about the probability that the instance is a member of the category.

In contrast to the availability hypothesis, the adaptive approach to human reasoning emphasizes that humans do make sound predictions about recurring real-world events. Many of the experiments that allegedly demonstrate ignorance of statistical principles actually require subjects to think about the probability of purely hypothetical events that may occur only once (e.g., the probability that a hypothetical person named Linda is a banker and a feminist). In fact, people successfully avoid the conjunctive fallacy and successfully make use of base rate information when the experiment makes clear that probability refers to frequency of occurrence; that is, when the experiment is more "ecologically valid." For example, subjects avoid the conjunctive fallacy if they are asked to predict the proportion of women they are likely to encounter who are both feminists and bankers.

In the third section, I discussed how well people critically evaluate beliefs. In the context of assessing beliefs, rationality means that people are intuitive scientists who initially regard ideas as neither true nor false until relevant data confirm or disconfirm the validity of the idea. Refuting the notion that people are intuitive scientists are the findings that people are prone to believe in ideas that they have merely contemplated, are unlikely to ponder or seek potentially disconfirming evidence for an idea, and are influenced more by the quantity than the quality of evidence used to assess an idea.

In the context of assessing the validity of ideas, the availability hypothesis takes the form of a Spinozian model of reasoning. According to Spinoza, understanding an idea is tantamount to believing in the idea. We are influenced more by the quantity than quality of ideas, because the more often an idea is presented to us, the more often our belief in the idea is reinforced.

The adaptive approach to reasoning emphasizes that the cognitive effort to assess an idea must be worth the gain of knowing whether the idea is valid or invalid. You may be willing to take my word for it that armadillos make good appetizers, because the effort to find out if I am right is not worth it to you. Consistent with the adaptive approach, people are more willing to seek potentially falsifying data, and are more willing to consider the quality rather than the quantity of ideas, when they are personally affected by the consequences of the analysis.

In the fourth section, I discussed decision making. In the context of decision making, rationality means that people are intuitive economists, seeking to maximize benefits while minimizing costs. Refuting the notion that people are intuitive economists is the finding that people's decisions do not remain invariant across situations, even when the costs and benefits are the same in each situation. People avoid risks when the choices are framed in a positive way, but embrace risks when the same choices are framed in a negative way.

Availability seems to explain the lack of invariance seen in decision making. If the risk is made salient, people try to avoid it. If, at times, a choice is anchored to irrelevant but salient information, the decision is perturbed by that information. For example, I may be willing to argue long and hard to save $500 on a new car purchase, but quietly accept an offer on my home that is $500 less than my asking price. Yet in both cases, the cost is the effort to make the argument, the gain is the $500. Again, it is as if the salient information burdens the limited capacity of the cognitive system, and so interferes with performing the calculations needed to make the rational decision.

In the context of decision making, the adaptive approach emphasizes that reasoning reflects the efficiency of the decision making process in the service of making sound predictions. From the perspective of the adaptive approach, the fact that the framing of choices influences the final decision need not be regarded as a manifestation of irrationality caused by the limited capacity of the cognitive system. Instead, the framing may reasonably be regarded as information pertinent to the unique situation of the decision maker. If a physician frames the choice between surgery and radiation in terms of when I am likely to die, and the surgery is the riskier choice, I may reasonably infer that the physician believes that I may be particularly susceptible to surgical stress. Otherwise, why would the physician frame the choice in terms of when I am likely to die?

In brief, the adaptive approach to reasoning seems consistent with most of the experimental findings. Human reasoning is practical. It serves well the necessity of anticipating the future. But it does so without necessarily or consistently embodying the principles of logic, statistics, science, and economics.

RECOMMENDED READINGS

Gardner's (1985) *"The Mind's New Science,"* that excellent book on the history and enduring controversies in cognitive science, has a chapter on the controversy over whether people are fundamentally rational or irrational. Arkes (1991) reviews some of the evidence for an adapted approach to human reasoning, as does Cosmides in her (1989) provocative research on reasoning in the context of social permission. You might read Wason's (1966) original paper in which he introduces the deceptively difficult card selection task. The idea that there seems to be a disturbingly irrational side to human reasoning is most associated with the work of Tversky and Kahneman. Their (1983) paper describes violations of the conjunctive principle, and their (1981) paper uses the Asian disease problem to describe violations of the invariant principle. Frisch and Clemen's (1994) paper provides a good example of research that seems to dispute the claim that decision making is irrational, in the Tversky and Kahneman sense. One of my favorite articles on human reasoning is a witty and scholarly review by Gilbert (1991) in which he introduces the Spinozian and Descartesian models of critical assessment of ideas.

8 *Problem Solving*

I recently purchased a special canvas to cover my brand-new and rather large outdoor central air conditioning unit, in order to protect the air conditioner from the winter elements. Unfortunately, the canvas was too small—it covered only the top and upper half of the air conditioning unit. I told my wife that there was absolutely no way to cover the lower half, because the hardware store only sold canvases of this one particular size. My wife pointed out that we could solve the problem by buying two canvases and cutting one canvas into a sleeve to wrap around the lower half of the unit.

My wife's insight is an example of **problem solving**, the subject matter of this chapter. Problem solving may be defined as an attempt to achieve a goal (e.g., protect the air conditioner) in a situation where there is a barrier (e.g., the only available canvas is too small) that seemingly prevents the goal from being achieved. Had the hardware store stocked canvases of many different sizes, including the size that fits my particular air conditioning unit, there would have been no barrier, and so no problem to solve. Problem solving presupposes that a situation is identified as a problem. Had it never occurred to me to protect my air conditioning unit from the winter elements, I would not have had the problem of an ill-fitting canvas. Much of the progress in science and technology, and even in the artistic fields, is made when people first discover that there is a problem to be solved. For example, progress in the field of cognitive psychology depended on asking questions such as "Why do people forget past experiences?" or "Why are people conscious?"

TYPES OF PROBLEMS

A variety of distinctions can be made among the many types of problems people encounter (see Mayer, 1989). One important distinction is between **well-defined** and **ill-defined problems**. A well-defined problem has three characteristics. It has a clearly specified solution state (e.g., protect the air conditioning unit with a canvas), a clearly specified beginning state (e.g., a naked air conditioning unit) and a clearly specified set of tools or techniques for finding the solution (e.g., look for canvases at the hardware store). Other examples of well-defined problems include finding the value of the unknown in the equation $24 = x/3.2$, rearranging the letters TULBRES to form an English word, getting an infant to stop crying, and, one of my favorites, figuring out how to get 27 pigs into 4 pens with an odd number of pigs in each pen. An ill-defined problem lacks a clear specification of at least one of these three characteristics. Writing a compelling novel, for example, is an ill-defined problem because the solution state is difficult to specify. When is a novel compelling and not merely pedestrian? Furthermore, the techniques for achieving the goal are underspecified: Should the novel be a romantic love story, a murder mystery, or an epic quest? Other examples of ill-defined problems are falling in love (What sorts of strategies induce romantic feelings? How can one be sure one is "in love"?), baking a delicious dessert for one's in-laws (When is a dessert considered delicious?), or improving the prestige of an academic institution (how can one measure prestige? What factors affect prestige?). Most of the research on problem solving investigates well-defined problems; however, many of the problems encountered in daily life are ill defined.

A second distinction can be drawn between **adversary** and **nonadversary problems**. Adversary problems involve a competition between two or more players, only some of whom can win the competition and therefore solve the problem. Winning at chess and obtaining admission to medical school are examples of adversary problems. Nonadversary problems do not involve competition. Examples are solving crossword puzzles, writing a compelling novel, and fixing a car. Cognitive psychologists have done appreciable amounts of research on both adversary and nonadversary problems. I will focus primarily on nonadversery problems in this chapter, although I will occasionally make use of adversary problems to illustrate a point.

A third distinction can be made between **potentially solvable problems** and problems that are impossible or virtually impossible to solve. Examples of unsolvable problems include traveling faster than the speed of light, making an English word out of the letters FLRX, and eliminating temper tantrums in an otherwise intelligent and healthy toddler (Penelope Leach notwithstanding!). Of course, we can be mistaken about which problems are and are not solvable. I thought that it was impossible to completely cover my air conditioning unit with a store-bought canvas; my wife found a simple solution after contemplating the problem for about 25 seconds. At any rate, I will primarily discuss problem solving in the context of solvable problems.

APPROACHES TO PROBLEM SOLVING: GENERIC, INFORMATION PROCESSING MODELS VERSUS DOMAIN-SPECIFIC MODELS

The primary issue that will serve as an integrating theme for this chapter contrasts two approaches to problem solving (see Mayer, 1989). One approach is usually labeled the *information processing model of problem solving*. The gist of the approach is that problem solving reflects the actions of an information processing system that is called into play whenever a problem is encountered. The problem-solving system is analogous in some respects to a visual perceptual system that functions to process any and all visual stimuli.

The information processing model makes three essential claims about problem solving. First, problem solving reflects the interaction of a set of cognitive components that efficiently solves problems. Efficiency is achieved by translating a problem into a useful form that lays bare the basis on which the problem will be solved, and by applying any of several strategies that reliably and in a timely fashion lead to a solution. Of course, people do not always solve problems successfully. A second claim of the information processing model is that the usual reason for failure to solve a problem is not the inefficiency of the problem-solving system per se, but the limitations of other cognitive systems, such as the limited capacity of short-term memory for holding in mind all of the procedures necessary to implement the solution strategy. As Shakespeare might have put it: The fault, dear Brutus, lies not in our problem-solving system but in our short-term memory. Third, the model claims that the same information processing system works to solve any and all types of problems. That is, the system is **generic**. All problems can be translated into a common representational form, usually consisting of descriptions of the dilemma posed by the problem, the initial state, the goal state, and a set of strategies. The judicious application of one of only a few strategy types is sufficient to enable us to reach a solution to nearly all problems. One implication of this claim is that students could become better problem solvers by taking a course in general problem solving, because all problems are thought to be solved in an essentially similar way.

In contrast to the information processing approach is an approach to problem solving I have chosen to label the **domain-specific model**. The gist of the domain-specific model is that problem solving makes use of a variety of skills, knowledge, and strategies that are different for every problem-solving domain. Examples of domains are literary analysis, cosmology, song writing, child rearing, motorcycle maintenance, and computer programming. Problem solving, according to the domain-specific approach, is really a loose collection of skills and strategies that have in common only that they pertain to problem solving. Problem solving is more analogous to memory, with its idiosyncratic set of specialized strategies for reconstructing past events, than to the visual system.

The domain-specific model makes two related claims about the nature of problem solving. First, the kinds of operations or strategies people use to work toward a solution will be different for each problem-solving domain. Problem-solving strategies are particularized. In many cases, a problem cannot be efficiently solved unless one learns a specialized strategy that is specific to only one domain of knowledge. An implication is that problem-solving skills learned in one domain will not readily transfer to other domains. Students may not profit all that much by taking a course that teaches generic problem-solving skills. Instead, problem-solving skill, like memory skill, tends to emerge as a natural consequence of becoming an expert in a domain. Second, the way people understand, or represent, a problem will reflect a construction process that is based on a variety of types of knowledge and information. In some cases the representations so constructed will function as a barrier to solving the problem, just as reconstructive memory strategies sometimes cause people to remember past events inaccurately. The fault, dear Brutus, may well lie in the various problem-solving skills and strategies. Short-term memory ought not be made the scapegoat.

In the next five sections I will develop the contrast between the information processing approach and the domain-specific approach to problem solving. In the first section I will discuss an influential information processing model of problem solving developed by Newell and Simon (1972).

In the second section I will dispute the information processing assumption that problems are translated into a set of elementary components that functionally lay bare the solutions to problems. Instead, difficulty in solving problems is not only, or primarily, due to a limited capacity for holding information in memory, but is due instead to the constructive nature of understanding problems.

In the third section I will dispute the information processing assumption that a few general strategies function to solve virtually all problems. Instead, solution strategies are idiosyncratic—they vary from problem to problem.

In the fourth section I will discuss research on the physiology of problem solving. The information processing approach suggests that there might be some system in the brain dedicated to solving problems. In fact, though, the evidence suggests that there is no single neural system for problem solving. Instead, and consistent with the domain-specific approach, different neural centers make different contributions to any given act of problem solving.

In the fifth and final section I will discuss some of the educational implications of the information processing and domain-specific approaches to problem solving. In particular, I will dispute the implicit claim of the information processing approach that students can greatly profit from taking a course in general problem solving. Instead, successful problem solving emerges primarily from developing expertise in some given domain.

SECTION 1: NEWELL AND SIMON'S GENERAL PROBLEM SOLVER

The historically most influential model of problem solving, and one that embodies the information processing approach to problem solving, was developed by Allen Newell and Herbert Simon (Newell & Simon, 1972). Their model is known as the **General Problem Solver**.

OVERVIEW OF THE GENERAL PROBLEM SOLVER MODEL

I'll begin the discussion of Newell and Simon's information processing approach to problem solving by introducing another example of a problem. Suppose a vacationer decides she wants to visit the obscure site of some ancient ruins that she has heard about and knows are somewhere in the general vicinity of her vacation lodging. However, the site is not marked on any of the maps she has nor known by any of the people she asks. How does she find the site? Newell and Simon propose that a person's understanding of a problem is composed of four elements: an understanding of the initial state (e.g., location of the ancient site is unknown), the goal state (e.g., find the ancient site), the set of possible actions that may be taken to remove the barrier (e.g., read a map, ask people who live in the vicinity about the location of the site), and the constraints on the possible solution (e.g., must find site within the next two days, must not spend more than $100 to find site). Collectively these four elements are called the **representation** of the problem. Newell and Simon's claim is that any problem can be represented by these four elements.

Newell and Simon propose that solutions to the problem entail using the representation to create a **problem space** (see Figure 8-1). The problem space is a description of all possible states that could be reached if the actions (e.g., drive a car) are applied to the initial state in accordance with the constraints (e.g., find the ruins within 48 hours). A solution is the sequence of actions that leads from the initial state to the goal state (e.g., the ruins are found on top of a mountain), and not to some other state (the valley between two mountains).

Newell and Simon claim that there are a few general strategies for searching problem spaces in order to find the set of actions that lead to the solution state. One strategy is **exhaustive search**, by which the problem solver examines all possible paths through the problem space, selecting the one that most efficiently leads to a solution. An exhaustive strategy is sometimes referred to as an **algorithm**, because it guarantees a solution to the problem. Exhaustive search is practical only if the problem space is small.

Consider the game of tick-tack-toe, for which the problem is to win the game. Suppose the situation is such that each player has played three times so

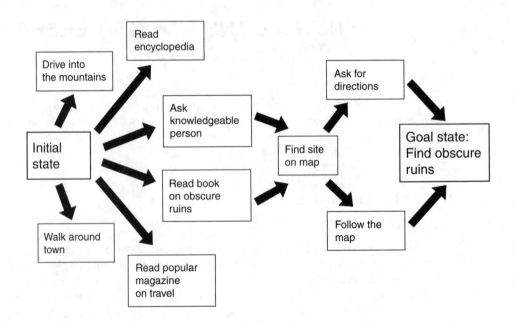

FIGURE 8-1   Depiction of problem space for finding obscure ruins.

that only three squares remain unplayed. At this point in the game a skilled player may be able to contemplate every remaining move he or she could make, every remaining countermove the opponent could make, and the final move. The player would have to contemplate six different sequences of moves in order to exhaustively search all possible sequences. Now consider the situation at the beginning of the game. Here the exhaustive search strategy is impractical, because there are hundreds of possible sequences of moves and countermoves. Once problem spaces become even moderately large, the number of possible pathways through the problem space is too large for it to be possible to examine every one.

Newell and Simon suggest that there are a few general strategies that function to reduce the number of searches through the problem space. Much of their work involves establishing the nature of such strategies, usually called **heuristics**. A heuristic does not guarantee that a pathway leading to a goal state will be found, but it increases the odds of doing so, compared with the odds of finding a solution by a random search through the problem space.

One general kind of heuristic is called the **hill climbing** heuristic. According to hill climbing, one seeks to make moves that reduce the distance between the current state and the goal state. For example, if your goal is to make a lot of money, you might first apply for a job in a large company, then work hard to be promoted to a higher paying job, then work hard to be promoted again to an even higher paying job, and so on, until you are paid the money required by your goal state. Each action applied to a state reduces the distance between the current state and the goal state. If your goal is to find the location of the ancient ruins, you might make use of the hill climbing heuristic by first driving to the general vicinity of the ruins and then asking people who live or work around there for more specific directions to the site.

Another general kind of heuristic is called the **backward search** heuristic. Backward search begins at the goal state and searches pathways backwards to see if any lead to the initial state. Backward search heuristics are more efficient than forward searches that begin with the initial state, if there are fewer pathways that connect to the goal state than connect to the initial state. In contemplating how to find the obscure site of ancient ruins not marked on any map, the problem solver might decide that there are only two paths that can lead directly to the goal state: a person knowledgeable about obscure ancient sites describes where the site is located, or a book about ancient ruins describes the location (see Figure 8-1). But there are lots of possible pathways that lead directly away from the initial state: for example, one path leads to finding a map, one leads to asking people at the lodging, one leads to driving to the library, one leads to driving to a known site of some other ancient ruins, and so on. This problem would therefore be a good candidate for the backward search heuristic.

A related heuristic, and one of the most powerful kinds of heuristics described by Newell and Simon, is called the **subgoal**, or **means–end**, heuristic. The idea of means–end is to determine an intermediate goal whose solution seems a prerequisite to solving the problem. Means–end makes use of both backward search and forward search strategies. Consider the problem of obtaining a job as a clinical psychologist. An intermediate goal may be to get into a graduate program in clinical psychology. That subgoal in turn has as the intermediate goal that of taking an undergraduate class in behavior disorders and obtaining a high grade in the class. As with other heuristics, means–end techniques reduce the number of pathways through the problem space that must be searched to solve the problem.

One difference between means–end and hill climbing is that the means–end strategies sometimes entail following pathways that temporarily take the problem solver farther away from the solution state. The person who wants to solve the problem of obtaining a lot of money may make use of a backward search heuristic whereby he or she notices that many physicians make a lot of money. However, the pathway that leads to becoming a physician requires attending medical school, where one is likely to make very little money, and even to have to borrow money. While in medical school, then, the problem solver is farther away from the goal state than he or she was initially. The person who wants to find the location of the ancient ruins might first have to travel to another site of ancient ruins where there is to be found a knowledgeable person. However, the knowledgeable person may be farther away from the target site than is the current location of the vacationer.

From the perspective provided by Newell and Simon, the rational solution to a problem would be one that entails finding the shortest possible pathway to the solution. This does not mean that rational solutions inevitably use hill climbing heuristics; the shortest pathway may in fact include a segment that temporarily increases the distance between the current and goal state. The only way to be sure of finding the shortest possible pathway to a solution is to use the exhaustive search strategy. Because human short-term memory and attention limitations make exhaustive search feasible only for problems that entail a few states, the rational goal has to be modified to finding a solution pathway that is reasonably short. According to Simon (1981), humans are good at finding reasonable if not optimal solutions to problems, a trait he labels **satisficing**. Simon emphasizes that errors in human problem solving generally reflect limitations to short-term memory, attention, and storage into and retrieval from long-term memory. Most problem-solving failures, claims Simon, are not attributable to deficiencies in the problem-solving system per se.

Newell and Simon investigated their information processing approach to problem solving in a rather interesting way. They developed a computer program that embodied the principles of problem solving just discussed and showed that the program was able to solve a range of problems. These problems included proving logical theorems, playing chess, and solving cryptarithmetic problems (e.g., "What number must A equal if $A/A = A$?"). Their program is called **GPS**, for General Problem Solver.

Newell and Simon's GPS was more than just a simulation of problem solving; GPS also helped establish the information processing paradigm in the field of cognitive psychology. In their view, human problem solving tends to work in a serial fashion in which people process one piece of information at a time. The kind of information humans use is symbolic; the ways in which symbols are processed resemble the actions of a program running on a computer. The capacity of short-term memory prevents the problem solver from being able to investigate every possible solution. When memory becomes overloaded, crucial information may drop out, leading to errors. For example, Newell and Simon found many instances in which novice subjects would forget which subgoal they were working on. Newell and Simon argue that the fundamental processes that underlie problem solving are rather simple—a few basic heuristics underlie nearly all problem-solving activity. The complexity of the thought processes that may accompany any act of problem solving reflects complexity in the problem, not in the cognitive system of the human solving the problem (a claim also made by Anderson, 1996).

REACTIONS TO GPS

Cognitive psychologists have had a number of reactions to Newell and Simon's GPS. Certainly much of the subsequent theoretical work (such as Anderson 1983; 1990) on problem solving has been strongly influenced by their model. And their elucidation of heuristics like means–end is a valuable contribution to our understanding of the nature of problem solving and to helping people become better problem solvers. Still, I think it fair to say that most cognitive psychologists regard GPS as incomplete, if not wrong in many important respects (Ashcraft, 1994; Mayer, 1989).

One kind of difficulty is that GPS sometimes performs too well. For example, it readily applies a means–end analysis that temporarily moves the program away from a solution but in the long run leads to a solution. Real humans are more reluctant to apply such means–end heuristics (Greeno, 1974). Another difficulty is that Newell and Simon rely too much on the verbal reports of subjects as evidence for the validity of their model. However, people may not always have introspective access to the underlying mechanisms involved in problem solving (Nisbett & Wilson, 1977; Metcalfe, 1986). But the main problem is that GPS is based on an information processing approach to problem solving (Mayer, 1989). Much of the rest of this chapter serves to elucidate the misleading implications of an information processing approach.

SECTION 2: UNDERSTANDING THE PROBLEM

Problem solving is customarily broken down into two broad stages. The first stage is understanding, or representing, the problem. The second stage is applying a strategy to remove the barriers to reaching the goal state. Presumably, one has to understand a problem (its initial conditions, constraints, and goals) before one can effectively select and apply solution strategies designed to overcome the barriers intrinsic to the problem.

In this section I will discuss how problems are represented. The main claim of the information processing model is that the representations are usually conducive to solving a problem. Failures to solve problems are usually attributed to the capacity limitations of short-term memory. In contrast, the domain-specific model suggests that there is no problem-solving system apart from the collective activities of a number of cognitive systems, including perceptual and linguistic systems responsible for constructing a representation of the problem. Failures in problem solving can be attributed to the actions of any of these various systems.

CONSTRUCTING PROBLEM REPRESENTATIONS

Difficulties in solving problems are sometimes a consequence of an inadequate understanding of the problem. Processes intrinsic to perception and interpretation can sometimes distort the representation of the problem in such a way that it becomes difficult to solve.

Historically, the connection between the perception of a problem and the problem-solving process was first studied by the Gestalt psychologists (e.g., Duncker, 1945; Maier, 1930, 1931; Kohler, 1925). Gestalt psychology claims that there are a number of organizing principles in perception (see chapter 3: Visual Perception); among these are the principle of proximity, the principle of similarity, and the principle of good continuation. These principles function to constrain how objects tend to be perceived.

The Connect-the-Nine-Dots Problem

Gestalt psychologists claim that the same organizing principles affect problem solving. My favorite example of the role of Gestalt organizing principles in problem solving is the oft-studied **connect-the-nine-dots** problem (Adams, 1974; Maier, 1930; Scheerer, 1963). In this problem you are to imagine a three-by-three matrix of dots that you must connect by no more than four straight lines (see the upper panel of Figure 8-2). The constraint is that the end of each line must connect to the beginning of the next line. In other words, you may not lift your writing implement from the paper while drawing the lines. You might try to solve this problem before reading any further.

The main reason people have trouble with this problem is that they perceive that the lines must be contained within the boundaries of the nine dots. The Gestalt principles of proximity and good continuation impose this perception on the problem. The boundaries are a salient feature of the dots. By focusing on that feature, people tend to ignore other possibilities for solving the problem. If the lines are allowed to extend beyond the boundaries of the nine dots, it becomes possible to connect the dots with four lines, as shown in the bottom panel of Figure 8-2. In fact, if the lines are drawn far enough outside the boundaries of the dots, it is possible to connect all nine dots with only three lines. Simply telling subjects to go outside the square defined by the nine dots

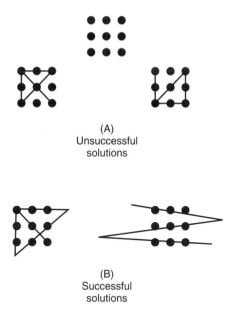

(A)
Unsuccessful
solutions

(B)
Successful
solutions

FIGURE 8–2   Successful and unsuccessful solutions to the connect-the-nine-dots problem.

improves performance (Lung & Dominowski, 1985), although many subjects supplied that hint still have difficulty solving the problem (Weisberg, 1986).

Changing Perceptions

Gestalt psychologists emphasize that the successful solving of a problem often involves changing the perception of the problem. Somehow the organizing principles of perception have to be deployed in a new way, have to be restructured, in order for a solution to become apparent to the problem solver.

Kohler (1925) was one of the first of the Gestalt psychologists to articulate this view of problem solving. He studied chimpanzees in cages in which bananas were hung out of reach from a ceiling and crates were strewn about the floor. The chimps solved the problem of getting the bananas by stacking the crates and climbing up them to reach the bananas. It seemed to Kohler that the solution came to the chimps as a sudden insight. He based this claim on his observation that the solution was usually preceded by a period of time in which the chimps stared quietly at the bananas and the crates. The chimps would then suddenly move in a purposeful manner by stacking the crates. Later, Birch (1945) showed that the only chimps who were able to solve this problem had prior experience with crates.

Experience can change how the organizing principles of perception are deployed. That is, people can learn to approach a particular problem with a different and more effective perceptual set. In the case of the connect-the-dots problem, people might be able to perceive that the problem space extends beyond the nine dots if they first have experience solving connect-the-dots problems that use fewer dots. With fewer dots, the organizing principles of proximity and continuation are not as powerful, so people are more likely to perceive the area outside the dots as part of the problem space. Consistent with this analysis are the results of Lung and Dominowski (1985). They allowed subjects to practice solving simpler connect-the-dots problems before tackling the nine dots problem. Such subjects were more likely to solve the nine dots problem than were control subjects who did not have the prior experience with simpler problems. The Gestalt explanation is that the practice on the simpler problems affected how the subjects perceived the relationship among the dots and surrounding space, permitting a perception of the nine dots problems that was more conducive to solving that problem.

Incidentally, there are other solutions to the connect-the-dots problem. Who says you cannot cut up the paper on which the dots are drawn? If you cut up the paper so as to rearrange the dots along a straight line, then you can connect all nine dots with only one line. Who says you cannot make the lines really thick? With a thick enough line, perhaps applied with a broad paintbrush, you can connect the original matrix of nine dots with one line. The tendency to infer constraints that are not really there misrepresents a problem, and so makes finding a solution difficult. The constraints derive from perceptual and conceptual interpretations biased by the salient features of the problem environment, but are not necessarily related to the requirements of the problem.

Note that the tendency to perceive nonexistent constraints is not due to the limited capacity of short-term memory nor to a failure to retrieve information from long-term memory, as the information processing model would have it. Instead, the tendency is an aspect of the way the problem is perceived and conceived in the first place, as the domain-specific model would have it.

Functional Fixation

Another way in which perceptions of stimuli affect problem solving goes by the name of **functional fixation**. People tend to perceive that the objects encountered in a problem are members of the same categories into which they have been placed in the past. Having made that categorical assignment, they tend to infer that the only way the objects can be used is as they have been used in the past. People fixate on the conventional function of objects. Sometimes, though, imaginative uses of common objects may enable a person to solve an otherwise difficult problem. For example, a person trying to repair a bike might think that the only tools available are tools in the toolbox, and so might overlook using a soda can. The soda can is perceived only as a container for soda. Yet the metal of the soda can could be used as solder.

The classic research on functional fixation was done by Duncker (1945). He required his subjects to figure out how to vertically mount a candle on a screen to serve as a lamp. Subjects were given a candle, a screen, matches, and thumbtacks. The candle was too thick for the thumbtacks to directly attach the candle to the screen. The solution is to mount one of the boxes containing the tacks or matches to the screen with the thumbtacks and then to melt wax off the candle onto the bottom of the box into which the candle is placed.

Subjects who were given the matches and tacks in their boxes took longer or were less likely to solve the problem than subjects who were supplied the matches and tacks outside the boxes. It seemed that if the objects were first encountered in their boxes, the boxes were perceived as containers and not as platforms. If the subjects first encountered the boxes empty of objects, then the boxes were less likely to be perceived as containers and more likely to be perceived as things that could be used to help solve the problem (see Adamson, 1952, for a replication). Subjects were also more likely to use the boxes to solve the problem if the experimenter explicitly mentioned the boxes as part of the experimental material than if the experimenter did not mention the boxes (Glucksberg and Danks, 1968; Weisberg and Suls, 1973).

Functional fixation has also been demonstrated in a problem originally developed by Maier (1930). The problem requires subjects to tie together two cords that are hanging from the ceiling. The cords are too far apart for the subjects to hold on to one end of one cord and reach the end of the other cord. The solution requires subjects to tie an object to one of the cords, swing that cord as if it were a pendulum, and wait for it to come close to the second cord, at which time it may be tied to the second cord. The problem is illustrated in Figure 8-3.

In one investigation of the two-cord problem, Birch and Rabinowitz (1951) placed two heavy objects, an electric switch and an electric relay, on the floor. All of the subjects eventually solved the problem by tying either the switch or the relay to one of the cords, although some subjects required an explicit hint (if the subject had not solved the problem after 9 minutes, the experimenter deliberately started swinging one of the cords). Prior to being presented the problem, the subjects had been divided into three groups. One group had first practiced using a switch to complete an electrical circuit on a "breadboard," a second group first practiced using a relay to complete the electrical circuit, and a third group received no prior practice. When presented the two-cord problem, the subjects who had used the switch in its ordinary capacity (as part of an electrical circuit) were more likely to use the relay to make the pendulum. On the

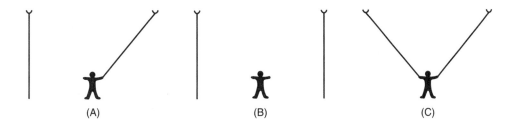

(A)   (B)   (C)

FIGURE 8–3   Maier's two-string problem.

other hand, the subjects who had used the relay in its ordinary capacity were more likely to use the switch to make the pendulum. The control subjects who had received no prior practice were as likely to use the switch as the relay to solve the problem. Using the object in its ordinary role as part of an electrical circuit made the object less likely to be perceived as relevant to solving the two-cord problem.

Making use of past experience to perceive objects does not inevitably distort the problem representation; frequently, past experiences have positive effects on the perceptual processes critical to successful problem solving (Mayer, 1992). Saugstad and Raaheim (1960, also Raaheim, 1965) investigated the possibility that if experiences help make appropriate functions salient to people, then they will readily be able to use the objects to solve problems. They presented their subjects with the following problem: Given newspapers, string, pliers, rubber bands, and a nail, figure out how to transfer a few steel balls from a glass jar on a wheeled platform to a bucket about 10 feet away, without crossing a chalk line separating the experimental subjects from the objects. (I know I have run into this problem more times than I care to remember.) The solution turns out to be to bend the nail with the pliers to make a hook, attach the hook to a string, throw the hook out to catch the moveable glass jar full of steel balls, pull the platform in, roll the newspapers into tubes that are held in shape with rubber bands, and drop the balls through the tubes into the bucket. But of course!

Before presenting this problem, Saugstad and Raaheim asked some of the subjects to give examples of how a bent nail could be used to catch things and how newspapers rolled into a tube could be used to conduct something through the tube. Subjects asked to give these examples had the new, problem-relevant functions of the objects made salient to them. When presented the problem about transporting the steel balls, 95 percent of the subjects who had been familiarized with the new functions for nails and newspapers were able to solve the problem, compared with only 22 percent of subjects who were not familiarized with the new functions.

SUDDEN INSIGHT AND INCUBATION

Insight Problems

An implicit claim of the information processing approach to problem solving is the idea that most solution strategies move the problem solver closer to the solution, or at least reduce the number of pathways connecting the initial state to the goal state. A claim of Gestalt psychology is that shifts in the perception of the problem underlie solving a problem. Again, the Gestalt approach is consistent with the domain-specific model of problem solving. The domain-specific model claims that problem solving is not an autonomous and inevitably efficient system, but reflects the actions of other cognitive systems, including the perceptual (and various conceptual) systems that create a representation of the problem.

One implication of the Gestalt approach is that the perceptual (and conceptual) shifts that underlie forming a new representation conducive to solving a problem are often sudden and unpredictable. It follows from this implication that people might sometimes lack any sense of how close they are to solving a problem. In particular, people might not necessarily know that they are on the verge of actually solving a problem.

In a fascinating research program, Janet Metcalfe and associates have shown that people are only able to judge whether they are getting close to a solution for problem types on which they already know an algorithm that reliably yields a solution. For problems on which subjects do not already know an algorithm, and indeed for which no algorithm even exists (Metcalfe calls these **insight problems**), subjects cannot tell how close they are to solving the problem (Metcalfe, 1986; Metcalfe & Wiebe, 1987). An example of an insight problem is "Describe how to put 27 pigs in 4 pens in such a way that there is an odd number of pigs in each pen." An example of what I will call an algorithmic problem is an algebra problem, such as "Solve for x in the equation $(x - 3)/2x - (x - 2)/(2x + 1) = 0$."

In one of Metcalfe's experiments (Metcalfe & Wiebe, 1987) subjects were presented either insight or algebra problems and had to indicate every 15 seconds how close they were to solving the problem (Metcalfe called this the "warmth rating"). The results are displayed in Figure 8-4. For algebra problems, the tendency was for the warmth ratings to increase over time as the subjects came closer to solving the problem. Warmth ratings were very high 15 seconds before a solution was found, for example. But for insight problems, the warmth ratings did not substantially change over time as the subjects came closer to solving the problem. Most subjects continued to provide very low warmth ratings for the insight problems even as little as 15 seconds before the solution came to them. In case you are wondering, a way to put 27 pigs in 4 pens with an odd number of pigs in every pen is to enclose 3 pens inside a fourth pen.

Time before solution

	45 seconds	30 seconds	15 seconds	0 seconds
Warmth ratings of noninsight problems	3.6	5.7	6.0	7.0
Warmth ratings of insight problems	3.0	2.75	3.0	7.0

FIGURE 8–4   Feelings of warmth ratings at 15 second intervals before solution. Warmth rating at time of solution is 7.

Nine pigs could be put into each of 3 pens which would all be placed inside the fourth pen.

What happens to make insight possible? The Gestalt claim is that some kind of perceptual or conceptual restructuring of the problem representation takes place prior to the sudden insight. It is difficult to study restructuring, because, as Metcalfe found, people are often unaware that they are getting close to a solution. In a nice example of problem solving about problem solving, Durso, Rea, and Dayton (1994) figured out a way to measure restructuring independently of insight. They presented their subjects the following insight problem: "A man walks into a bar and asks for a glass of water. The bartender points a shotgun at the man. The man says 'Thank you' and walks out." The subject was to induce some missing piece of information that made the story sensible and could ask yes–no questions (e.g., "Was the man thirsty?") of the experimenter to gain more information about the puzzle. Some subjects solved the puzzle (i.e., the man had hiccups) within a two-hour time period, some did not. All the subjects were then asked to rate the similarity of pairs of terms related to the problem. Examples of pairs were "man, bartender" and "surprise, shotgun." The pattern of similarity among pairs of terms was different between the group that solved the problem and the group that did not. For instance, the pair "surprise, remedy" was regarded as strongly related by the solvers but not by the nonsolvers.

In a follow-up experiment, subjects were asked to judge the similarity of terms while they were trying to solve the puzzle. Some of the terms were clearly related, like "bartender, bar," some were clearly unrelated, like "pretzel, shotgun," and some were related only in light of the solution, like "surprise, remedy." The main finding was that among subjects who solved the problem, their similarity rating of the solution-relevant pairs like "surprise, remedy" was low initially, but became gradually higher (more similar) the closer in time the subject got to solving the problem. So here is a case where the restructuring necessary to solve the problem was measured before the insight occurred. Apparently, people are unaware of the restructuring that is preparing them to have an insight, until they actually experience the insight.

Incubation

An implication of the Gestalt approach is that any activity that encourages a change in the perception of a problem should promote solving a problem for which no solution has yet been found. Consistent with this implication is the finding, called the **incubation effect**, that sometimes people do better at solving a problem if they put the problem aside for several days or weeks and then return to it (e.g., Goldman, Wolters, Nigel, & Winograd, 1992; Silveira, 1971; Houtz & Frankel, 1992). Poincaré, the great French mathematician, claimed that he discovered an important mathematical theorem (involving Fuchsian functions) by interrupting his work with a long break (Poincaré, 1913).

In a controlled experiment demonstrating incubation, Smith and Blankenship (1991) presented subjects problems from the Remote Associations

Test (known as the RAT). Each RAT problem consists of a stimulus set of three words for which subjects try to figure out what single word is associated with each word in the set. The associated word is only remotely related to each of the three stimulus words. An example is the stimulus set "family, apple, house" for which the correct answer is "tree." Smith and Blankenship made it difficult for some subjects to solve RAT problems by presenting along with the stimulus words some associated words that were likely to interfere with finding the common association. In the example of "family, apple, house" some subjects were given "mother, pie, home" as distracting associates. The presence of the distracting associates undermined performance, relative to the control group that was not given the distractors.

To test for incubation, subjects were given two presentations of each problem. For some subjects, virtually no time elapsed between the two presentations. So those subjects were given no opportunity to incubate. For the other subjects, 5 minutes elapsed before the second presentation of a problem, and the subjects spent the 5 minutes in reading an unrelated story. So these subjects had a chance to incubate on the RAT problems. The subjects who were given the chance to incubate solved more of the RAT problems than did the subjects not given the opportunity to incubate. This positive incubation effect was observed only when the RAT problems were made difficult by the distracting associate. No incubation effect was observed in subjects who were given the RAT problems without the distractors.

The Gestalt explanation of incubation is that the incubation period gives the subject a chance to extinguish the inappropriate perceptual or conceptual set initially used to represent the problem, thereby enabling the subject to employ a new and possibly more effective perceptual or conceptual set the next time the problem is encountered. Poincaré thought that the incubation effect reflected an unconscious process by which the "atoms" of the problem circulated freely, trying out new configurations, during the incubation period (Poincaré, 1913). Whatever the explanation, incubation probably works best for problems that depend on one key insight. For problems that involve algorithms, such as solving simultaneous equations, interruption is likely to have a detrimental effect on problem solving, because people will lose their place in the solution strategy (Anderson, 1990).

In brief, representations do not always lay bare the basis for a solution to a problem, as the information processing approach would seem to imply. Furthermore, the difficulties people sometimes have in constructing an adequate representation of the problem are often attributable to factors other than capacity limitations of memory. Factors such as Gestalt principles of organization and functional fixation can contribute to an inadequate representation of a problem. Conceptual and perceptual restructuring of a problem's representation can lead to the insight necessary to solve problems. For problems whose solution does not involve an algorithm (i.e., insight problems), the solutions often come without warning. The solving of such insight problems may sometimes be enhanced by taking a break.

SECTION 3: APPLYING STRATEGIES
TO SOLVE PROBLEMS

The second main stage of problem solving is applying a strategy designed to remove barriers to solutions. Implicit in information processing models, such as Newell and Simon's General Problem Solver, are two claims about the strategies people use. One claim is that the strategies that are selected are efficient; they are likely to lead to a solution. Errors in problem solving are attributable, not to the strategies per se, but to the limits of short-term memory for holding in mind all aspects of the strategy. The second claim is that the same sorts of strategies may be used across problem types. Examples of all-purpose strategies include hill climbing and means–end strategies.

In contrast, the domain-specific approach claims that people do not necessarily apply efficient strategies when confronted with problems. Instead, people construct a solution strategy out of information in the problem and information brought to mind by the problem. The strategies so constructed need not be efficient, however. The domain-specific model also claims that success at solving a problem is not usually due to the application of general strategies for removing barriers, but to specialized strategies that are unique to a given problem domain. To put it another way, the domain-specific model claims that describing successful strategies at an abstract level, such as "means-end," obscures the fact that any given successful strategy usually contains domain-specific features, without which the problem would not have been solved.

INEFFICIENT STRATEGIES

There are a number of reasons why the strategies people use to overcome barriers are not always efficient. I will discuss two reasons: problem solving set and failure to try to falsify hypotheses.

Problem Solving Set

The classic case of inefficiency in selecting a strategy is the phenomenon of **problem solving set**, also known as *einstellung* (Luchins, 1942). Problem solving set is similar to functional fixation. The most frequently cited example of problem solving set comes from experiments done by Luchins (Luchins, 1942; Luchins & Luchins, 1950). In his experiments, subjects were given a hypothetical situation in which there are three jars of varying volumes and unlimited water, and subjects must use the jars to obtain a target number of gallons of water. The only way to measure the volume of water is to use the three jars at hand. For example, subjects might be given jars that hold 21, 127, and 3 gallons and must obtain 100 gallons of water. The solution would be to fill the 127-gallon jar with water, empty 21 gallons into the first jar, and twice empty 3 gallons into the third jar. There would then be exactly 100 gallons of water remaining in the second jar.

Luchins found that if subjects were given about five problems that used the same solution strategy, the subjects continued to use that strategy on subsequent problems, even when there was a much simpler solution. For example, if subjects were given a series of problems in which the water in the second jar is emptied once into the first jar and twice into the third jar, they would be very likely to use that strategy to solve the relatively simple problem of obtaining 20 gallons given a 23-gallon jar, a 49-gallon jar, and a 3-gallon jar. The strategy works, but is much less efficient than the strategy of filling the 23-gallon jar and emptying 3 gallons into the 3-gallon jar. Control groups not given practice on the more complicated problems were easily able to see that the simpler problem could be solved in the more efficient manner.

Problem solving set may be especially common in children (Luchins & Luchins, 1950; see also Shore, Koller, & Dover, 1994). For example, children are sometimes taught the "keyword" system of arithmetic. In the keyword system, children are taught that numbers should be added when the problem contains the expression "altogether" and should be subtracted when the problem contains the expression "difference." Using the keyword system, children correctly solve problems such as "Jerry has 5 marbles and Sally has 3 marbles; how many marbles have they altogether?" The child using the keyword system would add 5 and 3 to get 8, the correct answer. However, the children will use the same procedure when confronting a problem such as "John has 5 marbles. Susan has 3 more marbles than John. How many marbles do they have altogether?" Again, the typical child using the keyword system will incorrectly conclude that the answer is $5 + 3 = 8$ (Briars & Larkin, 1984).

Falsification Strategies

Another way in which people tend to deploy inefficient strategies is reflected in the reluctance of many people to attempt to falsify their hypotheses. Instead, people tend to seek only the kinds of evidence that confirm their hypothesis. I discussed this tendency in chapter 7: Reasoning and Rationality. Here I wish to illustrate this tendency in the context of the problem of determining a classification rule. A classification rule is one that describes what objects that form a set have in common. Some real-life examples are determining what successful businesses have in common, differentiating those who are at risk for schizophrenia from those who are not, and describing the personality characteristics of effective leaders.

One way in which cognitive psychologists have studied the discovery of classification rules is by using a task called **concept learning**. In a typical concept learning experiment (e.g., Bruner, Goodnow, & Austin, 1956; Bower & Trabasso, 1963), a subject is given a series of stimuli, and must classify each stimulus as an instance of a concept or as a noninstance of the concept. Typically the stimuli vary along several dimensions, such as color of the object in a picture (e.g., black or white), the object's shape (e.g., round or square), and the object's size (e.g., large or small). The experimenter decides in advance the rule that determines whether the stimulus is an instance (e.g., all big objects) or a noninstance (e.g., all small objects). The experimenter, of course, does not tell the subjects the classification rule, but requires that they discover it on their own. The experimenter usually tells the subject on each trial whether the subject's classification of the stimulus as an instance or noninstance is correct. In some experiments the experimenter determines the order in which to present the stimuli, whereas in other experiments the subjects determine the order in which they wish to classify the stimuli, which are initially presented to them as one large set of stimuli.

There are a number of factors that influence how subjects go about trying to discover the classification rule (see Mayer, 1992). The main finding relevant here is that subjects tend to test their hypothesized rules by examining stimuli that would confirm their rule and avoiding stimuli that might disconfirm their rule (see Klayman & Ha, 1987, for a review). If subjects are allowed to select the order of stimuli to classify and from which to obtain feedback, they tend to pick a stimulus that would be an instance of the concept if their current hypothesis about the nature of the concept is true. For example, if subjects believe that the concept is "all black objects," they will select only black objects with which to test their hypothesis. Subjects tend to avoid picking a stimulus that would be a noninstance of the concept according to their currently held hypothesis. So the subjects who hypothesize that the rule is "black objects" would not select a white object with which to test their hypothesis. That is, the strategies subjects use to figure out the classification rule reflect a **confirmation bias**. Another way to say this is that problem-solving strategies reflect a bias against falsifying hypotheses.

In many cases, it is difficult to arrive at the correct classification rule unless one is willing to try to falsify a hypothesis. Suppose the classification rule is "any black object or any large object" (a disjunctive rule). If a subject hypothesizes that the rule is "any black object" and tests this hypothesis by selecting only black objects, the subject will always get positive feedback, yet never learn the disjunctive rule. Had the subject selected a large white object, in order to try to falsify the black object hypothesis, then the subject might have discovered the disjunctive rule ("black or large").

It is worth noting that confirmation biases are reduced in situations where there is a large payoff for making use of falsification strategies (see Friedrich, 1993, and chapter 7). Furthermore, people are likely to engage in falsification strategies in the context of evaluating whether people are following a rule or are cheating (Cosmides & Tooby, 1992).

In brief, the strategies selected by people to remove barriers to solutions are not necessarily efficient ones. People are prone to use strategies that have worked in the past, even when it is obvious that there are simpler and more effective strategies (problem solving set) and, outside of certain social contexts, they are reluctant to employ strategies that test hypotheses by trying to falsify them.

None of this is to say that people are miserably poor problem solvers. Indeed, I think it fair to say that most people are quite effective at solving most of the problems they confront in their day-to-day lives. Successful problem solving is likely when people have the time and incentive to solve problems, and when they can "pool" their ideas with other people working on the same problems. My point is that people do not inevitably select efficient and effective problem-solving strategies to remove barriers, stymied only by the limited capacity of short-term memory for keeping in mind all aspects of the strategies. Instead, people construct strategies from a variety of sources, such as the bias against falsification, and so sometimes construct an ineffective strategy.

EXPERTISE AND PROBLEM SOLVING

So far in this section I have focused on inefficient strategies for removing barriers to solutions. Now I will discuss how people learn efficient strategies. The main claim of the information processing approach to problem solving is that people make use of one or several of a small set of general strategies (e.g., means–end) that reliably solve problems. The same basic set of strategies works for virtually all problems. In contrast, the domain-specific approach emphasizes that problem solving is a matter of constructing a strategy based on a variety of knowledge and information, much of which is unique to any given problem-solving domain. In particular, the construction of such strategies is a manifestation of expertise in a domain, and is not a matter of drawing on some autonomous problem-solving mechanism evoked whenever barriers to solutions are encountered.

Conceptual Understanding of the Problem Domain

An expectation of the domain-specific model of problem solving is that as people acquire knowledge in a domain, they will become better problem solvers in that domain, even if they are not explicitly taught any problem-solving skills per se. The critical kind of domain knowledge that would enable people to become good problem solvers in that domain may be called **conceptual knowledge**. Conceptual knowledge refers to an understanding of the essential parts and cause-and-effect relationships that exist within a system. Because the conceptual underpinnings of systems are different from domain to domain, the knowledge needed to solve problems is also different from domain to domain.

A simple example illustrates how conceptual knowledge might be used to solve a problem. Bicycle pumps have a piston that moves up and down in a cylinder. As the pump's rod is pulled out, air passes through the piston and fills the area between the piston and a closed outlet valve, located at the bottom of the pump. As the rod is pushed back in, an inlet valve connected to the piston closes and the piston forces the air out through the outlet valve, which now has opened up (see Figure 8-5). Suppose pushing and pulling on the handle of a bicycle pump produces no air. What could be wrong?

An understanding of the bicycle pump system enables this trouble-shooting problem to be solved. Air first has to become trapped between the pis-

The Pump Passage (selected portion)

Bicycle tire pumps vary in the number and location of the valves they have and in the way air enters the cylinder. Some simple bicycle tire pumps have the inlet valve on the piston and the outlet valve at the closed end of the cylinder. A bicycle tire pump has a piston that moves up and down. Air enters the pump near the point where the connecting rod passes through the cylinder. *As the rod is pulled out, air passes through the piston and fills the areas between the piston and the outlet valve. As the rod is pushed in, the inlet valve closes and the piston forces air through the outlet valve.*

The Pump Model

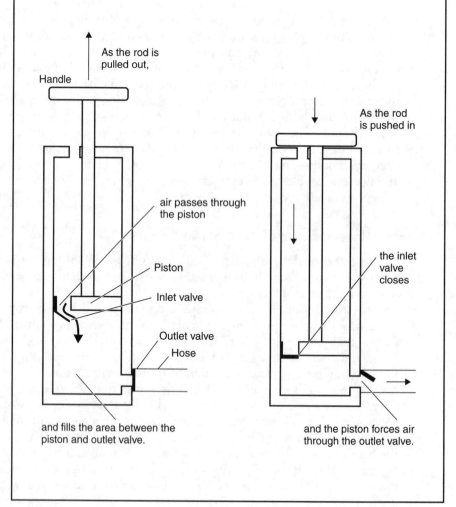

FIGURE 8–5   A model of a bicycle tire pump.

ton and outlet valve in order for the pump to be able to push air out through the outlet valve. If no air is coming out, then the air is not getting trapped. Therefore, possible solutions include a stuck valve or a hole in the cylinder. Such solutions are likely to occur to people who have the conceptual understanding of how a bicycle pump works, but are much less likely to occur to people who have no relevant conceptual knowledge.

Experimental evidence for the importance of conceptual knowledge for solving problems was obtained in a study by Mayer & Gallini (1990; also Mayer & Sims, 1994). They presented subjects with trouble-shooting problems involving bicycle pumps, and varied how much background conceptual knowledge they first provided the subjects. Some subjects were first provided with complete descriptions of the bicycle pump system, including an illustration of the system. Other subjects were provided with only an incomplete model of how the pump works. In addition, some subjects were highly experienced with mechanical systems such as the bicycle pump, while other subjects were mechanical novices.

The results of the Mayer and Gallini experiment were as follows. Among the mechanical experts, it did not matter whether they were first provided with complete models of the conceptual underpinnings of the pump system; the mechanical experts came up with as many trouble-shooting solutions when provided an incomplete model of the bicycle pump system as when provided a complete model. Presumably, the experts already possessed the conceptual knowledge, so providing it in the experiment was not helpful. Among novices, on the other hand, subjects provided with a complete model of the bicycle pump system came up with twice as many trouble-shooting solutions as did subjects provided only an incomplete model. Furthermore, the number of solutions reached by the novices given the complete model was about equal to the number of solutions provided by the experts. This experiment, then, nicely demonstrates that conceptual knowledge underlies success at solving a problem. Note that the novices who performed as well as the experts were not provided problem-solving strategies per se; rather, these novices were provided with the specialized conceptual knowledge that underlies this particular domain of problem. The problem-solving strategies emerged from the conceptual knowledge.

Other research makes a similar point. Gentner and Gentner (1983) found that subjects solved more problems involving batteries than problems involving resistors when presented with a model that likened an electrical circuit to water flow, but solved more problems involving resistors than batteries when presented with a model that likened an electrical circuit to a moving crowd. The water flow model of an electrical circuit evokes the idea that electricity can accumulate in a battery, as water accumulates in a reservoir. The crowd movement model of an electrical circuit evokes the idea that resistors function like gates impeding the movement of a crowd of people. Mayer (1989) found that subjects given a model that likened radar to a bouncing ball produced more solutions to radar problems than subjects not given the model. Bromage and Mayer (1981) showed that subjects provided with an explanation of how a camera works were better able to solve novel problems about cameras (e.g., "How might you make a camera out of a cigar box, a plate of film, lens, tape, glue, paper, razor, and a blade?") than were subjects not provided the explanation. Hong and O'Neil (1992) found that students provided with diagrams illustrating statistical concepts and the conceptual knowledge underlying those concepts solved more statistics problems than students who were not given the diagrams.

Experts Versus Novices

An emphasis on a domain-specific approach to problem solving has led researchers to examine differences between how experts in a domain, such as medicine, solve domain-relevant problems and how novices to that domain solve the same problems (see Mayer, 1992). In this context, experts often have many years of experience in their fields, whereas novices usually have less than two or three years of experience.

Experts, compared to novices, know more about their domain, are able to perceive domain-relevant information faster and more effortlessly, organize their knowledge in ways that make the information needed to solve problems more accessible, and make use of more complex strategies for solving domain-relevant problems (Anderson, 1990; Bedard & Chi, 1992; Mayer, 1992). The advantages experts have over novices come from years of experience that experts but not novices have at solving problems in the domain. The advantage is not due to experts' having larger-capacity memories, in the sense of memorizing new information, than novices (Chi, Glaser, & Rees, 1982). Indeed, an expert's skill is typically domain specific (Bedard & Chi, 1992).

Chase and Simon (1973) provided what has become a classic study illustrating the domain-specific nature of the skills of experts (this study was also discussed in chapter 2: Consciousness, and in chapter 4: Memory). They presented expert and novice chess players with a chessboard showing a configuration of chess pieces taken from real games of chess. Each board was presented for only 5 seconds and then covered. The subjects then had to reconstruct the locations of the appropriate pieces on a blank board. The novices remembered the location of about 4 pieces, whereas the experts remembered the location of about 16 pieces (out of 24 to 26 pieces). The same chess players were also presented chessboards with the pieces randomly arranged in ways that would never occur in a real game of chess. In the random case, both the experts and the novices were able to remember the location of about 4 pieces. The similarity of expert and novice memory for randomly arranged pieces rules out the possibility that expert chess players have better memories, in general, than novices. Chase and Simon suggested that experts have knowledge of thousands of configurations of chess pieces, and can apply that knowledge to their perception and memory of actual arrangements of chess pieces.

Similar results have been found in other domains. For example, McKeithen, Reitman, Rueter, and Hirtle (1981) found that computer programming experts recalled three times as many lines of programmming text as novices when presented with lines from actual programs for 3 minutes. But when the lines of the programs were randomly ordered, the recall performance of the experts was more similar to that of the novices.

Experts not only possess more knowledge about their domain of expertise, they also have the knowledge organized in more useful ways than do novices. In particular, experts have a better conceptual knowledge of the principles and models that underlie the relationships among facts and concepts, and organize this knowledge in a hierarchy of principles. Chi, Feltovich, and Glaser (1981) illustrated this difference in a study in which they asked experts in physics (students pursuing the PhD in physics) and novices (undergraduates) to sort 24 physics problems into categories based on similarity. The novices tended to sort on the basis of surface similarity—for example, placing together all problems that had to do with inclined planes. The experts tended to sort on the basis of principles of physics—for example, placing together all problems that had to do with the law of conservation of energy.

In another investigation of physicists, Larkin (1983) asked physics experts and novices to think out loud while they tried to solve physics problems. A typical problem asked subjects to determine the horizontal force that must be applied to a large cart so that two smaller carts, located on the top and on the front side of the large cart, and connected by a pulley, will not fall off the large cart. The novices focused on surface features (e.g., the problem involves carts and pulleys) whereas the experts focused on physics principles (e.g., the problem involves constant acceleration). That novices focus on surface features and experts on conceptual principles has been observed in other problem-solving domains as well, including computer programming (Adelson, 1981) and cardiology (Patel & Groen, 1986).

Another difference between experts and novices is that experts are more likely to use complex strategies that include contemplating a wide range of alternatives. To illustrate, Jeffries, Turner, Polson, and Atwood (1981) asked expert and novice software designers to think out loud as they designed a computerized system that would automatically create an index for to-be-published books. Although both the experts and the novices decomposed the problem into sub-problems, the experts produced many more sub-problems and produced them in a more systematic fashion. Furthermore, the experts were much more likely to think of alternatives and evaluate which alternative seemed superior. Novices seldom considered alternative ways to design the system. For similar results in the domain of medicine, see Johnson, Duran, et al. (1981).

The kinds of strategies used by experts depends critically on the domain. Expert computer programmers prefer to break problems down into many subgoals. Such a strategy is analogous to working backwards from the goal state to intermediate states (Anderson, 1990). As people acquire expertise in physics, on the other hand, their preferred problems-solving strategy shifts from backward to forward problem solving. Larkin, McDermott, Simon, and Simon (1980) studied the thinking-out-loud protocols of expert and novice physicists who were given simple physics problems such as "A car traveling 25 meters per second is brought to rest at a constant rate in 20 seconds by applying the brake. How far did it move after the brake was applied?" Subjects were also given four relevant equations (e.g., distance = average speed × time). Novices not only took four times longer to solve the problems, they usually worked backwards from the goal to an equation. For example, a novice would usually begin solving the car problem by studying the distance equation, because the goal is to find a distance. Unfortunately, the backward strategy, at least in this context, tends to result in a reliance on equations for which certain quantities are unknown. The distance equation cannot be used until average speed is known. Experts, on the other hand, tended to work forward from the givens to the unknown. An expert might begin by using the initial speed (25 meters per second) and the final speed (0 meters per second) to calculate average speed. By quickly focusing on using the given values to generate the values of the unknown quantities, the expert is more efficient at using the equations to yield a solution.

In summary, the acquisition of expertise, such as expertise in physics, enables people to solve problems in the domain of the expertise. Expertise means understanding the conceptual underpinnings of the models and systems that make up the domain. Novices supplied with such information can become relatively good problem solvers, even without any specific training on problem-solving techniques. From years of practice, experts acquire skills that enable them to efficiently and quickly represent problems, organize their knowledge in ways that are useful to solving problems, and learn the specialized strategies for eliminating barriers to solving problems. The skill with which experts solve problems does not appear to reflect the efficiency of a general problem-solving system, for then experts would readily transfer their problem-solving skills to other domains. In fact, though, experts must learn perceptual, conceptual, and strategic knowledge that is largely unique to their domain of expertise. Experts in chemistry, for example, are not necessarily able to solve problems on agricultural productivity (Voss, Greene, Post, & Penner, 1983; Voss, Tyler, & Yengo, 1983).

PRIOR PRACTICE ON SIMILAR PROBLEMS

One way experts can solve a novel problem is to use the same strategy that worked in the past to solve a similar problem. Indeed, even people who are not experts in a domain may be able to solve novel problems in that domain if the solution is similar to problems that they have had prior practice in solving. This section will review some of the research on the benefits of prior practice in solving new problems. One of the important findings from this research, and one that validates the domain-specific model of problem solving, is that for past exposure to problems to help solve new problems, the old and new problems must have features in common. When problems are dissimilar, transfer from one problem to another is not likely.

Analogies and Problem Solving

One way to illustrate the role of prior practice in solving new problems is with the use of analogies. It is sometimes claimed that many new discoveries are actually accomplished by drawing an analogy between a new problem and an already solved problem (Polya, 1957). For example, Gigerenzer (1991) has claimed that insights into theoretical explanations of cognitive phenomena often entail drawing an analogy between how methodological tools are used and how the mind works.

What does the research on problem solving tell us about how ordinary people use analogies to solve new problems? Consider the well-known "tumor problem" in the problem-solving literature (Duncker, 1945). The gist of the tumor problem is as follows: "Given a human being with an inoperable stomach tumor, and rays that destroy organic tissue at sufficient intensity, by what means can the rays be used to destroy the tumor without destroying the healthy tissue that surrounds the tumor?" One of the best solutions is the **dispersion solution**, which is to apply low-level rays from several different directions at once so that they simultaneously converge on the tumor. In this way, only the tumor absorbs the rays at tissue-destroying levels of intensity; the surrounding tissue is minimally damaged. Less elegant is the **operation solution**, which is to make an incision into the stomach to expose the tumor and then apply high-intensity rays directly to the tumor. In the operation solution, the healthy tissue in front of the tumor is damaged by the incision and the healthy tissue behind the tumor is damaged by the rays. How might people be encouraged to come up with the dispersion solution to the tumor problem?

Gick and Holyoak (1980) studied the use of analogies to solve the tumor problem. They initially presented subjects with a story about a general who wished to free his country of a ruthless dictator who ruled the country from a fortress. Unfortunately, the roads leading to the fortress were saturated with land mines that made it difficult for large armies to travel on the roads, although small bodies of soldiers could sneak between the mines. One group of subjects was told that the general divided his army into small groups, sent each group down a different road, and timed it in such a way that the groups converged on the fortress and so defeated the dictator. Note that this solution is analogous to the dispersion solution to the tumor problem. Another group was told that the general defeated the dictator by sending his entire army through an underground tunnel beneath the road and the land mines. Note that this solution is analogous to the operation solution to the tumor problem.

After reading about the general defeating the dictator, both groups tried to solve the tumor problem. The experimenters encouraged subjects to think of as many solutions as possible, and to use the information about the general defeating the dictator to help solve the tumor problem. The essential result was that the subjects were much more likely to propose the dispersion solution to the tumor problem if they had read about the general dispersing his troops than if they had read about the general using the tunnel. What's more, subjects in a control group given no story about a general never proposed the dispersion solution to the tumor problem, although some of them proposed the operation solution.

Difficulties in Making Use of Analogies

Although solving problems by analogy to related and previously solved problems seems a likely means by which new problems are solved, a lot of research suggests that it is surprisingly difficult to get subjects to recognize that two problem-solving situations are analogous (e.g., Reed, Ernst, & Banerji, 1974; Hayes & Simon, 1977; Reed, Dempster, & Ettinger, 1985; Perfetto, Bransford, & Franks, 1983; see Mayer, 1992). Instead, subjects routinely overlook the fact that an already-acquired solution to one problem can be applied with minor modifications to a new problem, unless the relationship between the problems is explicitly pointed out to them.

A study that reveals the importance of making explicit the relationship between analogous problems comes from Gick and Holyoak (1983), in some follow-up experiments to their 1980 experiment described above. They first required subjects to memorize three stories, including the story about a general defeating a dictator by dispersing his troops, and then required them to solve the tumor problem. Half of the subjects were not told that the stories they had memorized had anything to do with the tumor problem, while the other half were told that one of the memorized stories provided a useful hint for solving the tumor problem. The dispersion solution was generated by 92% of the subjects reminded of the utility of the memorized stories, but by only 20% of the subjects who were not reminded that the stories had something to do with the problem. The experiment makes the simple point that recognizing that useful analogies exist between already-solved problems and new problems does not invariably occur.

Under What Circumstances Do People Successfully Transfer Problem-Solving Knowledge?

A great deal of recent experimental work has investigated the circumstances under which practice in solving one problem helps people solve a new, analogous problem (e.g., Gholson, Morgan, Dattel, & Pierce, 1990; Catrambone, 1994; Novick & Hmelo, 1994; Gentner, 1989; see Singley & Anderson, 1989; Mayer, 1992; or Reeves & Weisberg, 1994, for reviews). One approach to understanding when analogical transfer is likely to take place focuses on when a new problem reminds people of the solution to the old problem (see Reeves & Weisberg, 1994). The idea is that people acquire several kinds of information as they solve problems; this information includes the surface content of the problem and the underlying relationships (structural content) of the problem. In the case of the analogous problems concerning the general dispersing his troops and the doctor destroying a tumor, the concept of a destructive force would be a surface similarity, while the concept of a destructive force not being allowed to harm something would be a structural similarity. Transfer is likely in a situation in which there is both surface and structural similarity between the two analogous problems, because in this situation the encounter with the new problem is most likely to remind a person of the old problem (Ross, 1984, 1987; Reed, 1987; see Reeves & Weisberg, 1994). Once reminded of the old problem, the person is likely to use knowledge of the relationships among objects—the structural knowledge—to solve the new problem (Gentner, Ratterman, & Forbus, 1993).

In one demonstration of the role of surface and structural similarity in transfer, Holyoak and Koh (1987; also Gentner et al., 1993) required subjects to summarize one of four stories about repairing a very expensive light bulb. The "light-bulb" stories described a solution that turned out to be analogous to the dispersion solution to the tumor problem. After summarizing one of the light-bulb stories, the subjects then had to solve the tumor problem. The descriptions of the light-bulb problems were such that one light-bulb problem was structurally similar to the tumor problem, one was superficially similar to the tumor problem, one was both structurally and superficially similar to the tumor problem, and one was neither structurally nor superficially similar to the tumor problem. The main result was that both structural and superficial similarity facilitated the spontaneous use of the dispersion solution to the tumor problem. In fact, when the light bulb story was structurally and superficially similar to the tumor problem, 69% of the subjects spontaneously provided the dispersion solution to the tumor problem. Only 13% provided the dispersion solution when the light bulb story was neither structurally nor superficially similar to the tumor problem. Similar results have been found in research on young, school-aged children (Chen, 1996).

The perspective that successful transfer requires that any new problem remind people of some old, previously solved problem suggests a focus on the content of the new problem to see when it activates the old problem. Another perspective on transfer suggests that people acquire transferable problem-solving skills when the problem-solving experience encourages the learning of the strategies and principles that are likely to be applicable to other problems (again, see Reeves & Weisberg, 1994). Here the focus is on the kinds of experiences people have when they are first learning how to solve a new type of problem.

One of the most helpful experiences consists of being given ample opportunity to learn the particularized heuristics that serve to solve problems within a domain of knowledge. The value of extended practice on old problems for transferring strategies to new problems is revealed in a lot of research (Bassok & Holyoak, 1989; Brown, Kane, & Echols, 1986; Cheng, Holyoak, Nisbett, & Oliver, 1986; Gick & Holyoak, 1983). To illustrate, Nisbett and his colleagues (Nisbett, Fong, Lehman, & Cheng, 1987; Fong & Nisbett, 1991) taught students various statistical principles, including the law of large numbers, which asserts that large samples are required to generalize about populations that are inherently variable. For example, the fact that a baseball player gets four hits in the first game of his major league career can hardly be used to predict that the player is destined to end up in the Hall of Fame. Nisbett and colleagues required subjects to learn such statistical principles by applying them to a variety of problems, in either the domain of sports or the domain of ability testing. So the subjects had extensive practice on statistical problems. Subjects were then given new problems in either the same or the other domain. The idea was to see whether subjects would transfer the strategies used in one domain to the other domain. Transfer occurred when subjects used principles, such as the law of large numbers, to solve problems. An example of a problem was to explain why the Rookie of the Year in baseball usually does not perform as well in his second year. An answer like "Some rookies are bound to have exceptional years—he may just have been lucky in his first year" would count as using the law of large numbers, whereas an answer like "slacking off" would not. When tested immediately after the training, subjects tested with problems from the other domain were as likely to use statistical principles as were subjects tested with problems from the same domain. That is, the subjects were able to transfer their problem-solving strategies to analogous domains. Still, when tested after two weeks, the subjects tested with problems from the other domain were no longer using the statistical principles as often as subjects tested with problems from the same domain (see also Reeves & Weisberg, 1993).

Some forms of practice may be more conducive to transfer than other forms. For example, it may be important that people be told why the strategies they are learning actually work to solve a problem. Catrambone (1994) taught subjects how to solve problems in probability and algebra. In the learning phase some subjects were given examples that emphasized a particular subgoal necessary to solve the problem. These subjects did better at solving novel but analogous problems than did subjects for whom the examples did not emphasize the subgoals.

Another helpful learning experience in which transfer from an old problem to a new, analogous problem is likely to occur is when people are given an opportunity to "explore" a variety of possible solutions to the old problem. Such exploration enables people to learn about the differences between strategies that work and strategies that do not work.

The importance of being allowed to explore the problem space was demonstrated in research by Ferguson and Hegarty (1995; see also Pierce, Duncan, Gholson, Ray, & Kamhi, 1993). They found that subjects given opportunities to actually manipulate a real pulley system did better on subsequent pulley problems than did subjects given only diagrams that illustrated how pulleys work. The importance of making mistakes in the facilitation of transfer was also demonstrated by Gick and McGarry (1992), who induced subjects to make errors while learning to solve a problem in determining whether dominoes could be used to cover a partially mutilated checkerboard. Those subjects were actually more likely to transfer the solution of the problem to an analogous problem than were subjects not induced to make errors.

GENERAL STRATEGIES

The research on analogical problems supports the domain-specific approach to problem solving. Transfer between even analogous problems is unlikely unless there is considerable surface and structural similarity between the problems. Transfer may occur with extensive and useful practice on problems, but what seems to transfer is a problem-solving strategy that works only in one domain.

Clearly, then, the basis of the transfer cannot be merely a matter of exercising the problem-solving system. Instead, the basis must be learning specialized knowledge and strategies that are useful for only a small class of problems. Still, it would be a gross exaggeration to claim that there are absolutely no general heuristics for solving problems in a variety of domains. In this section I will discuss two examples of general heuristics that might be usefully applied to many kinds of problems: adding structure to ill-defined problems and asking strategic questions during problem solving.

Adding Structure to Ill-Defined Problems

Cognitive psychologists have mostly studied how people solve problems in which people can agree on the initial conditions, the appropriate constraints, and the final goal. Obviously, to measure problem-solving success in a controlled situation, cognitive psychologists must make use of such well-defined problems. Yet many of the problems the ordinary person encounters in everyday life are of the ill-defined variety. Anderson (1990) asked members of a research seminar to "name a problem you tried to solve in the last 24 hours." Many of their problems, such as "planning a project with my advisor," "addressing a reviewer's comments," and "figuring a price to ask for my car," were of the ill-defined variety.

A number of educators and cognitive psychologists have suggested several general strategies for solving a wide variety of ill-defined problems (Hayes, 1981; Reitman, 1964). One strategy is to make the problem more clearly defined; that is, provide more conceptual structure to the problem. For example, if your problem is the ill-defined one of choosing a rewarding career, you might add structure by listing the goals you wish to accomplish from a career (e.g., make an above average salary) and the talents you actually possess (e.g., repairing machinery). In this way a potential solution (e.g., car mechanic) can be evaluated against the established structure.

Some evidence for the importance of adding conceptual structure to the problem representation comes from research comparing experts to novices in their approach to ill-defined problems. Voss and his coauthors (Voss, Greene, Post, & Penner, 1983; Voss, Tyler, & Yengo, 1983) studied people who were experts on the Soviet Union (now Russia) and compared their problem solving to novices, some of whom were chemistry professors. The problem was the ill-defined one of increasing crop productivity in the Soviet Union (ill-defined because it is not clear what means are permitted to effect change in crop productivity nor how much an increase in productivity is desirable). The thinking-out-loud protocols of the experts showed that they spent about 24% of their efforts on elaborating on the initial state of the problem, presumably to add structure to the problem. For example, the Soviet experts were likely to try to identify the amount of usable land. Novices, on the other hand, spent only about 1% of their efforts on establishing the initial state of the problem. The implication is that adding structure to the initial representation might be helpful to anyone confronting an ill-defined problem.

Question Asking

Another potentially useful general strategy for solving a wide range of problems is a systematic way of asking questions in order to obtain information and evaluate progress. King (1991) noted that children who spontaneously solved problems tended to be the ones who asked the most questions. Accordingly, she designed an experiment in which one group of fifth-grade children was taught a list of strategic questions to ask while trying to solve problems. Examples of the questions were "What is the problem?"; "What do we know about the problem so far?"; "Are we getting closer to the goal?"; "What worked?"; and "What didn't work?" Note that these kinds of questions could be used in virtually any problem-solving domain. Another group of children did not receive training in asking the questions, but did work on the same problems as the group that received the strategic-question training. The kinds of problems on which children practiced were mainly figural–spatial problems, such as finding out which of 25 squares hides a picture of an animal. After the practice, all the children were given a set of novel problems to solve. The novel problems were similar in type to the problems on which the children had practiced. The children given the training in asking questions solved more of the problems than did the children not given such training.

Applying General Strategies to Specific Domains

It is not clear, in the King (1991) study, whether the strategic-question training would have enabled the children to do better at solving problems that were quite dissimilar to those on which they practiced. It may be that general strategies, such as strategic question asking, need to be practiced within a domain before they effectively enhance problem solving in that domain. In particular, the training may need to specify precisely how the general heuristic can be applied in some specific domain (Singley & Anderson, 1989). What conditions call for using the heuristic? What actions should be taken?

The importance of learning how to apply general-purpose heuristics to specific domains is illustrated in a study by Schoenfeld (1985). In this study, one group of subjects was given five general heuristics to apply to a set of math problems. The control group worked on the same problems, but without the general heuristics. In a transfer test, novel problems were presented in such a way that only one of the heuristics was applicable to any one problem. The only heuristics that enhanced performance (relative to the control group) were the ones that specified the heuristic's conditions and actions. One of the useful subgoal heuristics told subjects to solve a complex problem with many variables by constructing a similar problem but with fewer variables, solving the simpler problem, and applying the solution method to the complex problem. One of the useless heuristics told subjects to establish subgoals by obtaining part of the answer or by decomposing the problem.

In summary, there are no doubt a number of general strategies, such as adding structure to ill-defined problems, that are useful in a wide range of domains. Nevertheless, people probably would not profit much from learning these heuristics unless it is made clear how the heuristics can be applied to a particular problem domain.

CREATIVITY

Creativity, a form of problem solving, usually refers to the production of conceptual or physical products that are **novel and valuable**. Other, more mundane forms of problem solving may not involve the production of a thing or idea that is both novel and valuable. Brain teasers, like the 27 pigs in 4 pens problem, already have known solutions, so any given person's solution is not especially novel. Solutions to brain teasers are not typically valuable or useful to anyone, either. Things that are more likely to be useful are conceptual or physical products of one kind or another, since they can be used or enjoyed by other people. So we regard beautiful works of art, inventions, and scientific discoveries as acts of creativity.

Creativity seems mysterious to some people. One mystery is how mental processes are sometimes able to produce highly unusual, individualistic, inherently unpredictable products. Where do creative ideas come from? That is, what is the origin of the problem-solving strategies underlying creativity, given that some acts of creativity seem to involve the use of completely novel strategies?

The mystery of how an individual person's mental processes create novel conceptual and physical products has resulted in a perspective that Weisberg (1986, 1988) calls a **romantic** view of creativity. In this view, creative products emerge from unique, mysterious, and unpredictable sources, such as muses. Shades of the supernatural perspective I discussed in the introductory chapter!

An alternative view, from cognitive science, is that creativity is merely the deployment of the same sorts of mental processes that are involved in noncreative cognitive acts (Weisberg, 1986, 1988; see Freyd, 1994, or Ward, 1994). The same mental processes that underlie perception, language, reasoning, categorizing, the use of previously acquired problem-solving heuristics, and so on, are also used to create something completely new. The distinctive aspect of many acts of creativity might be the **recursive deployment** of ordinary mental processes to generate a set of possible solutions from which a valuable solution is then selected. Recursive means that the same type of mental process is repeatedly activated until a solution emerges. Certainly a distinction between generating and selecting is a recurrent theme in the cognitive science literature on creativity (e.g., Finke, Ward, & Smith, 1992; see Freyd, 1994).

An illustration of the cognitive science approach to creativity comes from research described in Finke (1990). In a typical experiment on visual creativity, subjects were given a small set of simple forms (e.g., circles, squares) which they were instructed to combine mentally in order to invent novel objects. The main finding was that subjects were often able to do so, as when one subject, for example, invented a novel hamburger maker by mentally manipulating a sphere, half sphere, and cylinder. An important point is that the inventions were not obvious or even predictable from the forms. Rather, it was from the explicit attempt to manipulate and combine the forms that the inventions emerged. Note that the mental manipulation of visual forms is also a part of ordinary visual information processing, as, for example, when people imagine the motion of an object. The aspect unique to the visual creation was the recursive effort to construct a number of different combinations of forms, until a valuable combination emerged.

Another illustration of how ordinary cognitive processes underlie creative acts comes from research by Ward (1994) (also discussed in chapter 5: Implicit and Semantic Memory). In Ward's research, subjects were asked to imagine animals that might live on other planets elsewhere in the galaxy. Typically, subjects produced animals that had physical features (e.g., bilateral symmetry) similar to terrestrial animals. Moreover, an analysis of extraterrestrial animals in published works of science fiction revealed the same similarities. So when people create ideas for new kinds of animals, their mental processes are constrained by knowledge structures they already possess.

What about the claim of the domain-specific approach to problem solving—does it follow that creativity within a domain requires specialized, particularized strategies that do not necessarily generalize to other domains? At least some research suggests that tests designed to measure creativity do not predict creativity very well in any particular discipline (e.g., Blooberg, 1973; Mansfield & Busse, 1981; Mendelsohn, 1976). Creativity does seem domain specific. People who are judged as creative in a domain like architecture, for example, are not necessarily judged as creative in a domain like mathematics or music (Barron & Harrington, 1981). Other examples include the finding that students' scores on a test of verbal creativity correlated with their performance on an intelligence test while their scores on a test of figural creativity did not correlate with performance on the intelligence test (Yong, 1994) and that students whose original stories were judged as creative were not the same students whose original poems were judged as creative (Baer, 1994a, 1994b).

Still, there may be some heuristics that many acts of creativity have in common. At least, that is what some writers on the subject of creativity claim (e.g., Weber, 1993; Crovitz, 1970). Examples of generic creativity heuristics are the scale heuristic (changing the size of the components in an existing product), the dimensionality heuristic (changing the dimensionality of components of an existing product or idea), and a relational heuristic (varying the type of relationship between components of existing products or ideas). The invention of Velcro might be an example of the scale heuristic, the invention of the stereoscope might be an example of the dimensionality heuristic, and the creation of rap music might be an example of the relational heuristic.

There is another mystery surrounding creativity. Why are certain kinds of novel products perceived as valuable? Why, for example, do we regard as entertaining some paintings or musical compositions or fictional texts?

Securing food and shelter wouldn't seem to depend on an interest in and a capacity for art, music, and literature, yet these capacities have evolved in the human species.

A theme introduced in chapter 7: Reasoning and Rationality is that human cognitive processes are adaptive in the sense that they yield successful predictions about and control over events. Such an adaptation might provide (or have provided in our ancestral past) a reproductive advantage, especially if it is social behavior that we are adept at reasoning about. In what sense is creativity, especially artistic types of creativity, adaptive? Miller (cited in Freyd, 1994) has argued that human creativity evolved as a **protean courtship device**. Miller notes that in some other species individuals may favor mates who display physical qualities associated with survival or fertility ability, such as plumage quality in birds. Competition for mating opportunities within the species may produce runaway evolutionary growth in those display qualities, as in the case of the peacock's tail. Maybe our human ancestors favored mates who were more psychologically entertaining, rather than mates with certain physical properties. If so, then maybe competition for mates produced a kind of creativity arms race in which creative capacities, evolving over many generations, expanded to a point far beyond what was needed for survival purposes. Creativity, then, might be a human kind of peacock's tail. Of course, Miller's protean courtship device idea is currently only a speculative tale, entertaining though it might be.

SECTION 4: THE BRAIN AND PROBLEM SOLVING

The doctrine of materialism claims that problem solving, like any other cognitive activity, is a function provided by physical processes taking place in the brain. The information processing model's claim that there are general strategies that solve all problems suggests that there might be a system of neural tissue in the brain responsible for carrying out the implementation of those strategies. This neural system might be analogous to the neural system responsible for visual perception or for understanding the grammar of language. Evidence for such a neural system would be provided if brain damage sometimes resulted in difficulty in solving any of a wide range of problems, but left unaffected other aspects of cognition.

Alternatively, the domain-specific approach suggests that there ought not be any one neural system dedicated to solving problems. Rather, problem solving emerges from the actions of a variety of neural systems, much as does memory. Problem solving that involves verbal processing is likely to be impaired if the linguistic system is impaired, problem solving involving visual perception is likely to be impaired if the visual system is impaired, and so on. And, indeed, this is the case (see Ellis & Young, 1988). For example, damage to the right parietal lobe can undermine the ability to find a path through a maze (Ratcliff & Newcombe, 1973); damage to the posterior right cerebral cortex can undermine the ability to rotate upside-down stimuli to their normal orientation, in order to answer simple questions about the stimuli (Ratcliff, 1979); damage to Broca's area can undermine the ability of subjects to assign grammatical roles in complex sentences, such as "The man the woman is hugging is happy" (Caramazza & Zurif, 1976); and damage to the right hemisphere can undermine solving relational problems of the sort "If John is taller than Bill, who is shorter?" (Caramazza, Gordon, Zurif, & DeLuca, 1976).

Still, problem solving across a variety of domains does involve strategic planning in which one develops a strategy for organizing behavior (although different kinds of strategies are required in different domains). Frontal lobe damage is known to undermine the ability to implement and remain committed to strategic plans. As discussed in chapter 6: The Physiology of Learning and Remembering, frontal lobe damage can undermine the ability of people to implement a reconstruction strategy, such as a strategy that would allow a person to distinguish between past events that involved celebrities and past events that involved the self (Damasio, Graff-Radford, Eslinger, Damasio, & Kassell, 1985). Similarly, frontal lobe damage can undermine the capability of planning and executing complex problem-solving strategies (Stuss & Benson, 1986; Owen, Downes, Sahakian, Polkey, & Robbins, 1990; see Holyoak, 1990).

Illustrative is an experiment by Shallice (1982), who tested frontal lobe patients, along with other brain-damaged patients and people who were not brain-damaged, on a problem called the Tower of London puzzle. This puzzle requires subjects to move beads of various colors back and forth to three pegs of different lengths, in order to arrange the beads in a configuration established by the experimenter. The puzzle can be made easy or difficult by the minimum number of moves it takes to solve the problem. Shallice observed that patients with damage to the left frontal lobe had the most difficulty with the puzzle, especially on the more difficult versions of the puzzle. All the brain-damaged subjects, however, had more difficulty solving the puzzle than did the control subjects. The kinds of errors the left frontal lobe patients made reflected difficulty in establishing the appropriate order of subgoals. Interestingly, differences in the patients' short-term memory, as assessed by a digit span test, were unrelated to their problem-solving success.

Klouda and Cooper (1990) compared patients with frontal lobe damage to matched controls on their performance on the 20-questions game. This is the game where one person thinks of an object (e.g., elephant) and the other person, the problem solver, gets to ask up to 20 yes–no questions in order to identify the object. The frontal lobe patients were less likely to solve the problem, apparently because they were less likely to use the efficient strategy of first asking "constraint-seeking" questions (e.g., "Is it a zoo animal?") and were too quick to guess the object directly (e.g., "Is it a dog?").

SECTION 5: EDUCATION AND THE TRANSFER OF PROBLEM SOLVING

One of the essential goals of formal education is to prepare people to function effectively and ethically in everyday life. An important aspect of this goal is that formal education prepares people to solve problems that they might encounter outside of the school setting.

PROBLEM-SOLVING COURSES

An important implication of the information processing approach to problem solving is that students would benefit from a course that teaches general problem-solving skills (Simon, 1981). Having taken such a course, students ought to be able to solve problems from any of a number of domains with more efficiency than if they had not taken the general problem-solving course. A number of cognitive psychologists have proposed that schools ought to teach general problem-solving and critical thinking skills (e.g., Simon, 1981; Brown, Bransford, Ferrara, & Campione, 1983; Zohar, Weinberger, & Tamir, 1994). Some researchers have suggested that computer programming courses may function effectively to teach general problem-solving skills (e.g., Winston, 1984; Linn & Fisher, 1983).

Most of the courses in critical thinking, problem solving, and creativity that have been instituted in recent years have not been subjected to a critical analysis to see how well the skills transferred. Occasionally, though, researchers have undertaken a serious evaluation of such general problem-solving courses. The main conclusion from this research is that students do improve their problem-solving skills, but mainly on problems that are similar to the ones used in the course. For problems that are quite different from the ones used in the course, problem-solving efficiency is usually no better than for people who never took the course (Mansfield, Busse, & Krepelka, 1978; Torrance, 1972; Chance, 1986; see Mayer, 1992).

Illustrative is Chance (1986), who reports on the effectiveness of a problem-solving program called Odyssey. The Odyssey program teaches students various skills for solving a wide range of reasoning and creative-thinking problems. In the program, which consists of 99 45-minute lessons, a teacher leads a discussion on some sample problems, the students then work on their own on some similar problems, and then the students explain their solutions to the class. Students trained for a year in the Odyssey program solved twice as many novel problems as a comparable control group that did not receive the training, but only on problems similar to those covered in the program. The Odyssey students performed only slightly better than the controls on problems that were dissimilar to the ones given during Odyssey training.

Another example of research on a problem-solving course comes from Zohar (1994). College students participated in 20 sessions during which they studied how to solve problems such as determining what variables affect how children perform in school. Students were able to transfer what they had learned to new problems from within the same problem-solving domain. However, students were much less likely to transfer their problem-solving skill to problems within a different domain, such as figuring out which variables influence the speed of a race car, even when the new problems used solution strategies that were similar to those used in the original domain.

What of the claim that training in computer programming may function as an effective general problem-solving course? Most empirical studies show little benefit of courses in computer programming on solving problems in other domains (e.g., Gorman & Bourne, 1983; Pea, 1983; see Singley & Anderson, 1989). There is some evidence that people can transfer debugging skills learned in the context of computer programming to the debugging of other forms of instruction. Klahr and Carver (1988) taught children LOGO, a simple programming language, and in the process focused on how to find errors in programs. In a transfer test, these children did better at finding errors in instructions for such tasks as ordering food or arranging furniture than they did before they had been taught LOGO. In this case, though, the skill that transferred was the relatively specialized one of debugging written instructions (also see Lehrer & Littlefield, 1993).

TRANSFER OF PROBLEM SOLVING FROM SCHOOLS TO EVERYDAY LIFE

Much of the work on teaching problem solving has focused on the kinds of problems confronted by professionals, such as scientists and mathematicians. Consistent with the domain-specific approach to problem solving, the research suggests that problem-solving courses that teach general heuristics are not likely to be as helpful as courses that teach domain-specific knowledge and specialized strategies. In this section I will make this point in a different way, by focusing on the relationship between schooling and everyday problem solving. The research suggests that problem-solving skills developed in school do not always transfer to the kinds of problems most people confront in their day-to-day lives.

Consider a study by Carraher, Carraher, and Schliemann (1985). The experimenters posed as customers of Brazilian school-aged children who worked as street vendors. On the job, these children used rather sophisticated strategies for calculating the costs of orders, and could perform the calculations in their heads. The experimenters then invited the children to come to a laboratory where they were given written mathematical tests using the exact same numbers and operations the children had used successfully in the streets. For example, if a child had correctly calculated the total cost of 10 coconuts at 35 cruzeiros apiece on the street, the child was given the same problem written in a formal way; namely: "$10 \times 35 = ?$" Although the children solved 98% of the business transactions correctly, they solved only 37% of the same problems when those problems were presented in a formal way in the quasi-school setting.

Also telling was the finding that the number of years the vendors had spent in school was unrelated to their mathematical skill on the streets. Saxe (1988) found that street vendors with 5 to 7 years of schooling were no better at solving business transaction problems than street vendors with 0 to 2 years of schooling. Similar results were obtained by Ceci and Liker (1986). They found that among avid racetrack patrons, there was no difference in the amount of schooling between experts and nonexperts, where expertise was based on ability to predict post-time odds.

One would like to think that taking courses in some subject matter prepares the student to solve real-life problems in that domain. Unfortunately, some evidence suggests that school-acquired problem-solving skills within some domains, such as physics, do not readily transfer to real-life applications of the same domain. Voss, Blais, Means, Greene, and Ahwesh (1986) studied college-educated people, some of whom had taken courses in economics, and compared their performance on everyday economics problems with the performance of people without a college education. An example of an everyday economics problem was "If health care costs rise considerably, what effect, if any, do you think this would have on the size of the federal deficit, and why?" The college-educated subjects' responses were judged better than those of the subjects who were not college educated. However, among the college educated, it did not matter whether the subjects had any formal education in economics. The college-educated subjects who took courses in economics performed at the same level as those who took no courses.

McCloskey (1983) studied people trained in physics to see if they could apply the physics principles they learned in school to physical events outside the classroom. It turned out that the school-trained physicists often reverted to a kind of "pre-Newtonian" naive physics when confronted with real-world problems (see Figure 8-6). For example, if asked to trace the path of a ball once it leaves a circular tube through which it has been moving, many subjects erroneously thought that the ball would continue to move in a circumlinear path curving in the direction of the tube's curve, as if the ball somehow feels compelled to continue to move in the same direction it was forced to move by the sides of the tube even after it has left the tube. In fact, the ball would travel in a straight line way from the tube's opening once it left the tube. This error reflects a "curved impetus" belief. Another common error is reflected in the subjects' beliefs that an object dropped from a moving source would either drop straight down or move along a straight diagonal towards the ground. In fact, the object would take a curvilinear path towards the ground. This demonstration suggests that people have trouble transferring what they have learned in school settings to problems outside the classroom.

I do not wish to exaggerate the difficulty in transferring information learned in school to real-life settings. Certainly there is evidence that schooling can sometimes help people with problems confronted outside the school situa-

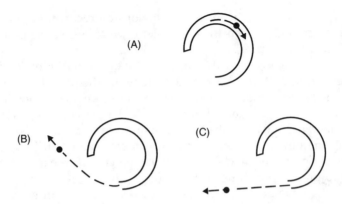

FIGURE 8–6   The "curved impetus" belief: In (A), a ball is moving through a curved tube. (B) shows one person's misconception of the path the ball travels as it leaves the tube. (C) shows the actual path the ball travels.

tion. Fong, Krantz, and Nisbett (1986; see also Kosonen & Winne, 1995) compared students who had just started taking a statistics course with students who had nearly completed the course in their ability to solve real-world statistics problems. The students who had nearly completed the course were more likely to apply statistical principles to the problems than were the beginning students. Indeed, Kosonen and Winne (1995) found that taking a course in statistics helped students solve everyday statistical problems that ranged over topics as varied as hiring people with particular qualifications, choosing restaurants with good food, and predicting a child's aptitude for sports. Similarly, Donley and Ashcraft (1992) showed that after taking two college-level physics courses, students were able to correct at least some of their naive beliefs about the physics of moving objects. In particular, the curved impetus belief was readily corrected. Misconceptions about falling objects, however, tended to persist even after the schooling.

Still, the fact that success at solving real-life problems is sometimes unaffected by classroom experiences reminds us of how difficult it can be to transfer problem-solving skills from one situation to another. Furthermore, such findings should warn us that schools need to make a concerted effort to discern the kinds of problems and the social contexts of problems people actually encounter in real life, if schools are serious about helping people prepare for real life. For example, mathematical problem-solving skills are usually used in real life to manage financial resources. Maybe, then, schools ought to teach math in the context of money management.

Admittedly, it would not always be easy for schools to accomplish this goal, given that the domains of problem solving actually encountered by ordinary people are going to vary quite a bit from person to person. Many of my real-life problems are not your real-life problems; furthermore, many of my current real-life problems are not the problems I had to confront years ago. It would seem that for schools to prepare people for real life, the school system itself would need to be radically restructured so as to accommodate each person's lifestyle, throughout each person's life span. Ivan Illich describes such a system in his revolutionary 1970 book *Deschooling Society*.

SUMMARY AND CONCLUSIONS

I began the chapter by contrasting two general points of view on problem solving, the information processing model and the domain-specific model. The information processing model claims that problem solving is accomplished by an efficient, all-purpose system that works to tackle any and all problems. Errors in problem solving are attributed mostly to memory failures. Newell and Simon's General Problem Solver, discussed in some detail in the first section, is a historically influential example of the information processing approach to problem solving. Alternatively, what I labeled the domain-specific model claims that problem solving typically depends on the use of specialized strategies that work in one domain (e.g., computer programming) but not in another domain (e.g., physics). Errors are mainly attributed to how problems are represented and how strategies are selected, and not to memory failures. The domain-specific approach represents, I think, the consensus view (see Mayer, 1989, 1992).

In section 2, I discussed how problems are represented (i.e., understood), with the intent of proving that, consistent with the domain-specific model, processes intrinsic to creating a problem representation may undermine solving the problem. The Gestalt psychologists were particularly influential in establishing how ordinary perceptual processes might undermine problem solving. One illustrative example of the Gestalt approach comes from the difficulty people have at solving the connect-the-nine-dots problem, the solution to which requires drawing the lines outside the confines of the dots. And therein lies the principle Gestalt metaphor for problem solving: Go outside the dots!

The Gestalt approach suggests that sudden and unpredictable changes in perception underlie solving problems whose solution depends on some key insight (e.g., "How might 27 pigs be put into 4 pens with an odd number of pigs in each pen?"). Consistent with the Gestalt approach, Metcalfe has shown that people are not ordinarily aware that they are about to solve an insight problem, even when the problem is solved only 15 seconds later.

In section 3 I focused on the strategies people use to remove barriers to solutions, with the intent of showing that such strategies are not necessarily efficient, and that efficient strategies are specific to a domain and not generic. Examples of inefficient strategies include the tendency for people to establish a problem solving set that is inappropriate for some particular problem and the failure to use falsification strategies to find a classification rule (e.g., "What distinguishes schizophrenics from the rest of the population?").

The particularized nature of effective strategies is revealed in the importance of expertise in a given domain for solving problems within that domain. Problem-solving skill tends to emerge as a natural consequence of becoming an expert. So, for example, if people are taught the underlying principles by which bicycle pumps work, they are able to trouble-shoot pump problems as well as mechanical experts can. In comparing experts to novices, the research suggests that experts perceive more relevant information; have more knowledge, and have it arranged by important principles; and tend to employ strategies that are tied to the conceptual principles that underlie the domain. But the problem-solving skills useful in one domain do not necessarily generalize to other domains. Expert computer programmers, for example, prefer subgoal strategies, while expert physicists prefer forward search strategies.

Also consistent with the domain-specific approach is the finding that practice at solving problems of a particular type enhances performance on new problems that are analogous to the type, but only when the new problems are also structurally similar to the practiced problems. Indeed, it is surprising how precarious is the successful transfer of solution strategy from one problem to an analogous problem. A number of experiments suggest that transfer is especially unlikely when nobody reminds the problem solver that he or she has recently solved an analogous problem. However, spontaneous transfer of strategies to new problems becomes more probable when people have had a lot of prior practice on old problems and are encouraged to explore both good and bad strategies when learning how to solve problems.

The domain-specific approach to problem solving is also consistent with research on creativity, which has to do with the production of ideas, artistic works, or devices that are novel and valuable. Consistent with the domain-specific approach, people who are creative in one domain (e.g., computer programming) are not necessarily creative in another domain (e.g., architectural design). In my discussion on creativity, I suggested that creativity need not be romanticized but may involve ordinary cognitive processes, used recursively. The intense interest many people have in music, art, and literature may reflect an evolutionary process in which ancestral humans with a capacity to be entertaining were more likely to be selected as mates.

In section 4, I discussed research on the neurological underpinnings of problem solving. Consistent with the domain-specific approach, problem solving seems to emerge from the actions of a variety of neural systems. For example, brain damage to visual areas undermines visual problem solving; brain damage to the language areas undermines solving problems about language. The frontal lobes seem to play a role in implementing the strategic aspects of problem solving. Some patients with frontal-lobe damage have trouble establishing the appropriate order of subgoals, for example.

In the fifth and final section I discussed some of the educational implications of the information processing and the domain-specific approach to problem solving. Consistent with the domain-specific approach, the classroom is effective at teaching people how to solve problems in the domain of problems formally covered in the class, if it is effective at all. Moreover, problem solving in the context of the classroom does not always generalize to same-domain problems in contexts outside of the classroom. Young Brazilian street vendors with 7 years of schooling, for example, were no better at conducting business transactions on the street than were vendors with only 2 years of schooling. As with the research on analogical transfer, the research on the impact of schooling on problem solving suggests that transfer is precarious.

Let me finish up by hedging a bit on some of my claims. First of all, most of the people working within the information processing tradition recognize the importance of particularized strategies in problem solving (Singley & Anderson, 1989, for example). In some respects, then, the information processing model I have sketched out in this chapter is a straw-person, designed mainly to serve as a basis for contrast. Second, there are heuristics that are quite general in their application. I discussed two examples of general heuristics (ones that could be usefully applied to a wide range of domains), namely, adding structure to ill-defined problems and employing strategic questions designed to elucidate progress toward solving a problem. Furthermore, extensive practice at solving problems in some domain, such as would happen in a college statistics course, does enable many students to solve a wide range of novel and practical problems from within that domain (Kosonen & Winne, 1995).

Still, I think it is fair to say that there are no tricks or shortcuts to becoming a good problem solver. You are not going to get a whole lot better at solving most of the problems you confront by taking a college class in problem solving or creativity. Problem solving emerges primarily from expertise in a domain of knowledge and skill, and only for that domain. And the level of expertise that it takes to become a good problem solver in a domain often takes years to acquire.

RECOMMENDED READINGS

Mayer's (1989) essay on problem solving was my inspiration for the contrast between the information processing approach and the domain-specific approach to problem solving. Mayer's (1992) *Thinking, Problem Solving, Cognition* is an excellent textbook reviewing a wide range of theories and experiments on problem solving. J. Anderson's rather challenging (1990) *The Adaptive Character of Thought* discusses how his ACT model solves problems; even more challenging is the classic on problem solving, *Human Problem Solving*, by Newell and Simon (1972). Some of the most creative studies on problem solving include Duncker's (1945) work on the tumor and the candle mounting problems, Metcalfe and Wiebe's (1987) study of warmth ratings while trying to solve insight problems, and Chase and Simon's (1973) well-known study comparing the memory of chess experts to that of novices. Larkin is one of the foremost experts on experts; check out her (1983) paper comparing physics experts to novices. Gick and Holyoak's (1983) study provides a good example of the precariousness of problem-solving transfer; Reeves and Weisberg (1994) review the major theories underlying the transfer (or lack of transfer) of problem-solving skill from one situation to another. Carraher et al.'s (1985) paper on young Brazilian street vendors is a sobering example of the difficulty in transferring academic knowledge to everyday settings. The very notion of institutionalizing education in schools is attacked in Illich's (1970) *Descabooling Society,* an engaging and radical treatise in which Illich argues that society would be better off without schools.

9 *Individual Differences in Cognition*

People differ with respect to their intellectual capabilities. Historically, the attempt to measure differences in intellectual ability has been the most conspicuous and influential branch of cognitive psychology.

Perspectives on Individual Differences in Intelligence: Hereditarian, Unitary Models versus Multifaceted, Domain-Specific Models of Intelligence

The assumptions historically made by researchers in the intelligence testing movement constitute a theory of intelligence that Steven Jay Gould calls the **hereditarian theory** (Gould, 1981; also Mackintosh, 1986). The hereditarian theory of intelligence makes two separate claims. First, it claims that intelligence is **unitary**—it is a reflection of an all-purpose system or process that permeates all intellectual activity. Another way of making this claim is to say that intelligence is **generic**. An implication of the generic notion is that intelligence is measurable using tests that are meaningfully converted into numbers that reflect the amount of intelligence a person possesses. The second claim, from which the hereditarian theory derives its name, is that the primary basis of intellectual differences among people is to be found in the genes they inherit; that is, intelligence is primarily **genetically determined**. Although these claims are logically distinct (intelligence could be unitary but differences among people could still be due primarily to environmental differences), historically they have been associated.

The main theme of this chapter will be a comparison between the unitary or generic view of individual cognitive differences, on the one hand, and a **domain-specific** or **multifaceted** view of individual cognitive differences, on the other (Gardner, 1983). The multifaceted view claims that people may display superior talent or skill in one intellectual domain without necessarily being superior in other domains. As I did in chapter 8: Problem Solving, I will champion here the domain-specific approach to individual intellectual differences. I will also discuss the evidence for a genetic basis for intellectual differences and try to make clear what are and are not reasonable implications of this evidence. Included in the section on the genetic basis of intelligence is a discussion of sex differences in cognitive skills.

SECTION 1: HISTORICAL BACKGROUND AND THE RISE OF THE HEREDITARIAN THEORY OF INTELLIGENCE

A confluence of several developments taking place in the 1800s led to an interest in the measurement of individual differences in cognition, culminating in the creation of **intelligence quotient (IQ)** tests around the turn of the 20th century. One development was the theory of evolution, which focuses on individual differences. For traits like abstract reasoning or language to evolve in a species, members of predecessor species must differ from one another on that trait. Only then can natural selection produce an increase in the number of individuals possessing the more adaptive trait. A second development was the growing acceptance of materialism—the view that what we label mental activity reflects only brain processes. In this view, any intellectual differences between people must also be reflected in differences in their brains. A third development was the rise of psychological experimentation and measurement. Sophisticated techniques for investigating and quantifying human behavior were being developed in the experimental laboratories of Europe and North America. Finally, the industrialized nations had become committed to universal education. But not everyone seemed to profit very much by formal education. Consequently, educators became interested in identifying students who might need special educational intervention.

THE RISE OF THE INTELLIGENCE TESTING MOVEMENT

Francis Galton

Francis Galton, Darwin's cousin and one of the founders of the intelligence testing movement, was a bright, independently wealthy man who had a passion for measuring things. He was the first to suggest that fingerprints be used for personal identification. He measured the degree of boredom at scientific lectures, and tried to find out which country had the most beautiful women.

Galton, along with his friend Karl Pearson (1867–1936), devised the concept and formula for **correlation** (see Boring, 1950; Gould, 1981; Hergenhahn, 1986). As it turns out, the concept of correlation is extremely important to the research on intelligence. Correlation is a measure of the degree to which two measurements are linearly related. Correlations range between +1 and −1. A positive correlation indicates that when scores on one measure increase, scores on the other measure tend to increase as well. A negative correlation indicates that when scores on one measure increase, scores on the other measure tend to decrease. A lack of correlation between two measures means that when scores on one measure increase, scores on the other measure tend neither to increase nor decrease. Height and weight are positively correlated—people who are tall also tend to be people who weigh more. Smoking and longevity are negatively correlated—people who smoke more tend to live fewer years. The last digit of one's social security number and one's annual income in dollars are not correlated—people with higher last digits are not likely to earn more money or less money.

It is important to note that just because two measures are correlated does not mean that there is a casual relationship between them. However, if there is a causal relationship, it is certain that the two measures will be correlated. There is a positive correlation between the speed with which a sprinter runs and the number of wins in a track meet. Here the faster speed is the cause of the winning. But there is also a positive correlation between the number of ice cream cones consumed in New York City on any given day and the number of deaths in Bombay, India on the same given day. Obviously, though, the eating of ice cream cones in New York does not cause people in Bombay to die; rather, both measures probably reflect global climate. When it is hot in the Northern Hemisphere, people in New York eat ice cream cones and people in Bombay endure heat and disease. Many correlations are simply coincidental. The gross national product of the United States in any given year is positively correlated to the distance between the North American continent and the European continent—both are increasing over time.

Based on his correlational and measuring techniques, Galton (1883) decided that intelligence is primarily a reflection of energy and the perceptual acuteness of the senses. Intelligent people, thought Galton, were especially good at perceptually discriminating between similar stimuli, such as between two similar colors differing only slightly in frequency. In 1884 he set up an anthropometric laboratory at the International Exposition where visitors, by paying a threepence, could have their skulls measured and have various tests taken of their perceptual functions. Some of the tests included judging the relative weight of a series of identical-looking objects, trying to detect very high frequency sounds, and reacting as quickly as possible to an auditory stimulus by punching a bag. This laboratory, later transferred to South Kensington Museum in London, constituted the first large-scale testing of individual differences.

Galton claimed that mentally retarded people did not discriminate heat, cold, and pain as well as "normal" people, and used this finding to bolster his argument that sensory discriminatory capacity underlies intelligence (Galton, 1883). Other research seemed to show that children classified by their teachers as "bright" tended to have faster reaction times than children classified as below average (Gilbert, 1894). Galton's procedures for measuring intelligence were adopted by James Cattell (1860–1944), who administered them to college students in the United States (Cattell, 1890).

Later research discredited some of Galton's ideas, when it was shown that an individual's performance on sensory and reaction time tests showed little relationship from test to test, and were unrelated to grades in school or to a teacher's estimates of intelligence (e.g., Wissler, 1901). More recent research (discussed below) suggests that there might be a modest relationship between performance on sensory or reaction-time tests and other measures of intellectual prowess.

Galton's interest in evolution led him to study the possibility that intelligence runs in families. Based on a study of families of people who were highly acclaimed scientists, artists, writers, and politicians, Galton found that children of illustrious people were more likely to be illustrious than children of ordinary folks (Galton, 1884). Galton concluded that the basis of high intelligence was favorable genes that the illustrious passed on to their offspring. Galton advocated a form of eugenics, in which the government would pay highly intelligent people to marry and bear children.

Alfred Binet

Alfred Binet (1857–1911), one of the founders of experimental psychology in France, conducted research on hypnotism, cognitive development, memory, and creativity. Some of his work with children was similar to that later conducted by Jean Piaget (see Boring, 1950; Gould, 1981; Hergenhahn, 1986).

In 1903 Binet and Theodore Simon (1878–1961) were commissioned by the French government to develop a test that could identify learning disabled or mentally retarded children, so that they could be given special education. At the time, tests based on Galton's theories were used, but, as discussed before, some research seemed to discredit Galton's ideas about the basis of individual differences. Besides, as Binet noted, children with vision and hearing impairments would be erroneously classified as retarded. Binet proposed instead that more complex tests of reasoning, motor performance, spatial thinking, and memory be used to assess a child's cognitive abilities. Binet and Simon's tests included reasoning problems, reflecting Binet's belief that the intelligent person was one who showed reasoned judgments when confronted with problems (Binet, 1911; Binet & Simon, 1916). Typical items on the test required children to define common words, name objects in pictures, tell how two objects are alike, draw designs from memory, repeat back a string of spoken digits, and answer abstract questions such as "When a person has offended you and comes to offer his apologies, what should you do?"

Binet ordered his hodgepodge of tests from simple ones, which most two-year-old children could answer, to difficult ones, which children could not answer but most adults could answer. The age associated with the most difficult tasks that the child could perform was designated the child's mental age, which was then compared with the child's chronological age. In 1911 William Stern (1871–1938) proposed that mental age be divided by chronological age and then multiplied by 100 to produce the familiar IQ score. Using this formula, if a 10-year-old child is able to answer most of the items that a typical 12-year-old could answer, then the 10-year-old child's IQ score would be $(12/10) \times 100 = 120$. More recently, IQ has been measured by looking at the average for the age group and determining how far above or below the average the test taker's score lies. Average is set as equal to 100; standard deviation (a measure of dispersion) is usually set as equal to 15. Using this formula, a person who scores two standard deviations above the average would be assigned an IQ score of 130.

Binet did not believe that an IQ score was a measure of intelligence, which he regarded as too complex to capture with a single number. He made it clear that IQ was not like weight or height, in that IQ does not represent a quality possessed by a person. Again, Binet believed that his test was good only as a guide to help identify children who needed special help. Furthermore, Binet did not believe that scores on IQ tests necessarily represented a genetically based intellectual potential. Rather, he was optimistic that, with special education, many children who scored low on the IQ test could greatly improve their reasoning, memory, and verbal skills. Binet recommended that special education be tailored to the individual's needs and aptitudes, that classrooms for special education be kept small, and that the initial focus be kept on motivation and work discipline.

CORRELATES OF IQ

Since the early 1900s, a large number of intelligence tests have been developed. These include the Stanford-Binet (a modification of Binet's original test), the Wechsler scales for children (WISC) and adults (WAIS), each of which computes a verbal IQ score and a performance IQ score; the Raven's Matrices, a nonverbal test of intelligence; and college entrance tests like the SAT.

Research on IQ tests demonstrates that various IQ test scores are positively correlated with one another; for example, the Wechsler IQ score correlates about .8 with the Stanford-Binet. IQ tests are also moderately correlated with grades in school (the correlation is usually about .5), number of years of formal education, occupational status, and, to a lesser extent, with success in an occupation (Kline, 1991; Neisser, Boodoo, et al., 1996). The correlation between success in an occupation (measured, for example, by supervisor ratings) and IQ scores is typically about .3. So people who get good grades, go to school for a long time, have professional jobs such as doctors and lawyers, and get higher ratings from supervisors evaluating their work tend to score higher on IQ tests than do people who get poor grades, drop out early, have jobs such as factory workers, and get lower evaluations from their supervisors.

Keep in mind that these correlations do not tell us much about the causes of the relationship between IQ scores and other measures, such as grades in school. It could be, for example, that the superior intellect some people possess causes them to score higher on IQ tests, do better in school, and get better jobs. But there are other possibilities. Perhaps motivation to succeed is the cause (or at least one of the causes) of the correlations—a generally motivated person will try harder to do well on IQ tests, stay in school longer, and work harder on the job. Or maybe health is a cause of the correlations—a generally healthy person is more likely than an unhealthy person to be alert in school, acquire the knowledge necessary to do well on IQ tests, and perform well on the job. It could also be that the economic advantage some people enjoy is what enables them to do better on IQ tests, do better in school, and get better jobs (McClelland, 1973).

It should be pointed out, however, that the relationship between IQ performance and educational and occupational success cannot be attributed entirely to socioeconomic factors (Barrett & Depinet, 1991). Parental background variables like parental income and education do not predict occupational achievement as well as do IQ test scores (Gottfredson & Brown, 1981). Grades in school are more strongly correlated with SAT scores than with parental income (Baird, 1984).

SECTION 2: IS INTELLIGENCE UNITARY?

As I suggested at the beginning of this chapter, much of the recent work on the nature of intellectual differences has taken the form of a reaction to the historically entrenched hereditarian theory of intelligence and the IQ enterprise it established. In this section I will discuss the evidence that intelligence is unitary, that it reflects a generic intellectual system. In the next major section I will develop the argument for a multifaceted model of intellectual differences.

EVIDENCE FOR THE UNITARY VIEW

Charles E. Spearman (1863–1945) was one of the first psychologists to demonstrate that people who do well on any one subtest of the IQ inventory tend to do well on any other subtest. That is, the various subtests that make up the IQ inventory are positively correlated (Kline, 1991). Spearman thought that the prevalence of positive correlations reflected a physical property of the brain, namely, a kind of mental energy that some brains happened to possess more of than other brains (Spearman, 1927). He labeled this idea "**g**," to stand for the **general factor** that underlies all intellectual activity. More recent but similar interpretations of g are that g reflects the capacity to pay attention to information (Hunt, 1980; Jensen, 1979), reflects nerve conduction velocity and rate of neural decay (Jensen, 1993), or reflects the ability of neurons to change connections (Larson & Saccuzzo, 1989).

Spearman, and many others since, have noted that subtests of the IQ inventory that are similar to one another are even more positively correlated than are dissimilar subtests. For example, two different subtests that measure spacial reasoning will be more highly correlated than a subtest that measures spacial reasoning and a subtest that measures vocabulary. This pattern of correlations, analyzed by a statistical technique called factor analysis, is sometimes interpreted as indicating that intelligence has a general (also known as **fluid**) component that reflects some genetically determined biological aspect of the

cognitive system, and a series of specialized (also called **crystallized**) components that reflect various learned skills (Kline, 1991).

There is other evidence for the unitary nature of intelligence. Correlations
among IQ tests are significant even when one IQ test is verbal and the other IQ
test is nonverbal. For example, the correlations between the Raven's Matrices (a
nonverbal IQ test) and conventional IQ tests range from about +.40 to +.75
(Anastasi, 1988). That IQ scores predict performance in very different situations,
such as school settings and job settings, also suggests that there is a unitary
aspect to intelligence.

WHAT UNDERLIES UNITARY INTELLIGENCE?: CONTRIBUTIONS OF INFORMATION PROCESSING

Recall from chapter 8: Problem Solving that I criticized an information processing
model that postulates that all problems are solved by the same, generic information processing system. A similar sort of information processing perspective has
been used as an account for why intelligence seemingly has a unitary character.

A generic information processing approach to intellectual differences has
all intellectual tasks performed by a single information processing system.
Individual differences in intellectual performance reflect differences in the speed
and efficiency with which the various components of the system are executed. I
do wish to note that information processing cognitive psychologists need not
postulate a generic information processing model of individual differences.
Perhaps human cognition is composed of many different, relatively autonomous
information processing systems. However, the idea of a generic information processing system is implicit in most information processing approaches to cognition (Lachman, Lachman, Butterfield, 1979), and so it is the generic form of it
that I will critique here.

The information processing approach, as I have discussed in several chapters of this text, rose to prominence in the 1950s, 1960s, and 1970s. An important
claim of information processing is that any given cognitive process can be broken down into a set of fundamental components, such as perceiving information, transforming information, storing information in memory, and retrieving
symbols from memory. Most information processing accounts claim that there is
a limited-capacity working memory—a place that holds the currently activated
information and the program for manipulating it. More discussion of information processing can be found in the introductory chapter.

The contribution of information processing to the study of intelligence is
its claim that any or all of these components of cognition could be the basic and
essential source of individual differences in intellectual activity (e.g., Carroll,
1983; Jensen, 1982; Vernon, 1983; Sternberg, 1985; Hunt, 1983; Pellegrino &
Glaser, 1979). Some people might be more intelligent than others because they
can more quickly and efficiently process stimulus input, retrieve information
from memory, or transform information from one form into another.

An Example of Research Based on Information Processing: Inspection Time

The information processing perspective has produced a variety of experimental paradigms for measuring the speed and efficiency with which people can carry out any component of cognitive processing. In the typical information processing experiment, researchers use established experimental paradigms to obtain from each subject an estimate of how quickly or efficiently the subject can execute one of the components, and then measure the correlation between that estimate and the subject's score on an IQ test.

One task that has been studied extensively is called the **inspection time task** (Deary & Stough, 1996). In a typical version of this task, subjects are given two parallel vertical lines joined at the top by a horizontal line. One of the vertical lines is longer than the other. An example of a stimulus used in the inspection time task is provided in Figure 9-1. Over a series of trials the longer line is presented on the left side about as often as it is presented on the right. Subjects must identify which is the longer line and can take as long as they want to make the decision. The task is made difficult by limiting the amount of time the stimulus is exposed to the subjects; that is, the inspection time is kept brief. The range of exposure durations is usually between 100 milliseconds to less than around 10 milliseconds. Any given subject's inspection time is usually expressed as the stimulus duration necessary for the subject to reach a given accuracy level, such as 75%. Be clear that inspection time does not refer to how long it takes a subject to make this simple discrimination; rather, it refers to how long the stimulus was exposed in order that the subject reach an acceptable level of performance.

The main finding of interest is that inspection times correlate with performance on standard tests of intelligence (e.g., Nettelbeck & 1976; Deary, 1993; see

FIGURE 9–1   A typical stimulus used in the inspection time task. From a very brief exposure to such a stimulus, subjects must decide whether the left or the right vertical line is longer. (See Deary and Stough, 1996.)

Deary & Stough, 1996). People whose inspection times are short tend to score higher on the intelligence tests. Across a variety of studies the correlation is usually around .5, a moderately strong correlation (Deary & Stough, 1996). One interpretation of the correlation is that inspection time measures a basic information processing component—namely, the speed with which information is taken in or initially perceived.

Other information processing measures have also been correlated to IQ. These include estimates of the span of working or short-term memory (Hunt, 1978; Schofield & Ashman, 1986; Daneman & Carpenter, 1980; Dark & Benbow, 1991; see Dempster, 1981), the speed with which subjects supposedly scan short term memory (Keating and Bobbit, 1978; Vernon, 1983), the speed with which people mentally rotate a visual stimulus (Mumaw Pellegrino, Kail, and Carter, 1984), the speed with which people access the name of a letter (Hunt, 1978, 1983; Hunt, Lunneborg and Lewis, 1975), and the speed with which subjects access the meaning of a word in memory (Goldberg, Schwartz, and Stewart, 1977; Vernon, 1983). Measures of the speed of information processing tasks correlate with scores on IQ tests even when the IQ test itself is not timed (Vernon and Kantor, 1986).

Problems with the Information Processing Perspective on Intellectual Differences

There are, however, problems with the information processing account of individual differences in cognition. One problem is that not every researcher finds a correlation between measures of the speed or efficiency of a component and IQ performance (e.g., Keating, 1982; Ruchalla, Scholt and Vogel, 1985; see Longstreth, 1984; Barrett, Eysenck, and Luching, 1989). Further, when a correlation is found, that correlation is often achieved by comparing college students to mentally retarded people. When the studies are done using subjects who were not mentally retarded, the correlation between any estimate of the speed with which a cognitive component is executed and IQ scores is usually quite modest, in the .3 to .4 range (see Kline, 1991; Mackintosh, 1986). The correlation between inspection time and IQ scores seems a bit more robust, however (Deary and Sough, 1996).

A more fundamental problem is that the information processing approach relies too much on establishing correlations between measures of information processing and IQ scores. What is generally lacking from this line of inquiry are demonstrations that measures of information processing can predict performance on real life tasks better than conventional IQ tests (Richardson, 1991).

Another difficulty with the information processing approach to individual differences is that of establishing cause and effect. Is the efficiency with which information is initially processed the cause of intelligence, or is speed of processing the effect of intelligence, whose cause is undetermined? Even if it is conceded that perception speed, as measured in tasks like the inspection time task, is a causal determinant of intelligence, what then causes there to be differences in perception speed (see Richardson, 1991)? What would be the biological basis for mental speed, or for any other component of cognition measured by information processing tasks?

Research on the Physiological Basis of Intelligence

Another way to get at the underlying nature of intelligence is to examine neurophysiological correlates of individual differences in cognition. Typically, research and theory studying the neurophysiological basis for intelligence has assumed, at least implicitly, that intelligence is a unitary phenomenon. For instance, researchers have speculated that the brain of a highly intelligent person has more synapses among neurons (Birren, Woods, & Williams, 1979), more efficiently metabolizes energy (Smith, 1984), or more efficiently reconfigures connections among neurons (Larson & Saccuzzo, 1989). Unfortunately, it is difficult to obtain clear-cut evidence for or against any of these conjectures, because the research on the physiological underpinnings of individual differences in cognition is meager and inconclusive. One of the main difficulties lies in measuring the critical physiological processes, which are likely to be dynamic phenomena reflected in the way neurons communicate with one another.

Are Smart Brains Metabolically Efficient?

Recently, brain imaging technology, such as positron emission tomography scanning (PET scans), has allowed researchers to study metabolic activity in various sections of the brain of an alive and awake person. Some studies suggest that people who do better on intelligence tests tend to display lower neural metabolic activity. Haier, Siegel, Nuechterlein, et al. (1988) found that performance on the Raven's Matrices was negatively correlated with overall cortical metabolic rate. Subjects who scored higher on the Raven's Matrices test (a nonverbal intelligence test) tended to have lower overall cortical metabolic rates than subjects who scored lower on the test. The authors speculated that people who are good at reasoning tasks have more efficient neural circuits which therefore use less energy than the neural circuits of people who have more trouble with the reasoning tasks.

Haier, Siegel, MacLachlan, et al. (1992) measured cortical metabolic activity during the initial stages of learning the complex computer game TETRIS, and again several weeks later after subjects practiced the game. They found that subjects who improved the most on the computer game displayed the largest drop in cortical metabolic activity while playing the game. Similar results have been found by Parks, et al., 1988.

In apparent contradiction to these studies, though, is research that has uncovered a positive correlation between metabolic rate and performance on IQ tests. This research, however, has usually used elderly subjects, some of whom have Alzheimer's disease and other forms of dementia (e.g., Butler, Dickinson, Katholi, & Halsey, 1983; Chase et al., 1984). Aging and disease may alter the normal functioning of the brain.

Even if the negative correlation between performance on intelligence tests and cortical metabolic activity proves reliable, interpretation problems remain. It is not clear what makes neural circuits more efficient. Is it the density of the neurons, the ease with which neurons affect the activity of other neurons, the number of glial cells that support the neurons, or any of a number of other possibilities? Furthermore, there may be other reasons for the slower cortical metabolic rate in people who score higher on the intelligence tests. Perhaps people who are able to remain calm while taking intelligence tests have lower cortical metabolic rates as a result, and thus do better on the tests. Both intelligence test performance and metabolic rate may be affected by control over anxiety. Haier et al. (1988) dismiss this possibility because their subjects did not appear to be anxious, and because other research suggests that anxiety increases metabolic rates primarily in the frontal lobes. The authors found that metabolic rate changes related to learning occurred primarily in the posterior regions. However, it is possible that anxiety responses interacting with the responses necessary to do cognitive tasks may produce a different pattern of cortical metabolic rate than observed in other situations.

Neural Conduction Rate and Smart Brains

Some recent research suggests that the rate at which neurons conduct electrical activity may be faster for people who score higher on intelligence tests. Reed and Jensen (1992) presented subjects with visual stimuli and measured the latency with which an evoked potential was detected in primary visual cortex. Shorter latencies imply faster neural conduction. They found a .37 correlation between scores on the Raven's Matrices test and conduction rates. Similar findings have been reported by Vernon and Mori (1992).

Again, though, the conduction latency results are not easy to interpret. What is different about the neural structure between people whose neurons conduct impulses faster and people whose neurons conduct impulses more slowly? Does the variation in conduction latency reflect intellectual efficiency, motivation, consistency of performance, or what?

Let me make one final comment on the studies of the physiological basis of individual intellectual differences. It is possible that certain physiological features on which people differ and which determine intelligence permeate much of the brain. There may be something about the development of neurons such that virtually all of them are more efficient in some people. In such a case, intelligence would have a unitary character, as much of the research on the neurophysiology of intelligence implicitly assumes. On the other hand, it is also possible that the relative efficiency of neurons varies across neural domains within any given brain. Such variability in efficiency within a single brain could be due to environmental experiences, genetic "programming," or some interaction between the two. At any rate, neural domain variability would give rise to a multifaceted form of intelligence. And it is to a multifaceted view of intelligence that I will now direct my discussion.

SECTION 3: BUILDING THE CASE FOR A MULTIFACETED APPROACH TO INTELLIGENCE

INTERPRETING THE EVIDENCE FOR UNITARY MODELS OF INTELLIGENCE

There have been a number of reactions to the unitary intelligence interpretation of the positive correlations observed among various measures of intelligence and information processing. One reaction is that the g factor has many possible interpretations besides the interpretation that it reflects the intrinsic efficiency of the cognitive system (Gould, 1981; Richardson, 1991). One possibility is that g reflects the encouragement people receive as they grow up. Children who are encouraged to learn and perform well, or are made to feel secure, may try harder and/or be less anxious when taking the various subtests of the IQ test. Such children would be expected to do well on the subtests of the IQ inventory and well in academic situations. Certainly it has been established that measures of a person's attitude and motivation tend to correlate with that person's performance on IQ tests (see Anastasi, 1988). For example, people who have positive attitudes toward learning and have a desire to succeed tend to do better in school and score higher on tests of intelligence (Anastasi, 1985; Dreger, 1968).

The connection between performance in information processing paradigms and performance on IQ tests may also be interpreted as a matter of attitude and motivation, and not necessarily a matter of the intrinsic efficiency of the cognitive system. Consider that from the perspective of the subject, tasks like the inspection time task are tedious. Subjects who try hard, especially by concentrating on every trial, will tend to have short inspection times. Subjects who occasionally let their attention wander, on the other hand, will get the occasional long inspection time that will increase their overall average (Mackintosh, 1986). If the subjects who try hard on the information processing tasks are also the ones who try hard on the IQ test, then there will be correlations between measures of the information processing task and IQ performance, as is observed.

EXPANDING THE CONCEPT OF INTELLIGENCE: CREATIVITY, SOCIABILITY, PRACTICALITY

To some extent, the issue of whether a given test of the intellect correlates with other tests depends on what sorts of tests one wishes to consider as revealing of intelligence. When people are given tests that are dissimilar in content to those found in conventional IQ inventories, researchers often find that performance on such tests (e.g., writing plots from descriptions of short stories) does not correlate with performance on the conventional tests (Guilford, 1964, 1967; Thurstone, 1938).

Creativity

One way to expand the concept of intelligence is to consider creativity as an aspect of intelligence. Recall that I first discussed creativity in chapter 8: Problem Solving. Most IQ tests have no measures of creativity, an admittedly difficult concept to define and measure objectively. Creativity usually refers to ideas or works that are novel and valuable to others. Einstein was creative when he declared that "$E = mc^2$," because the equation was novel and valuable, at least to physicists. Had he declared "$E = mc^3$" his equation would still have been novel, but not valuable.

A variety of research suggests that creativity, as measured by peer assessments, number of publications, and so on, bears little relationship to scores on IQ tests (Baird, 1982; Barron, 1969; MacKinnon, 1962; Wallach, 1976; see Perkins, 1988). For example, Yong (1994) studied Malaysian secondary students and found that a test of figural creativity was unrelated to scores on the Cattell Culture Fair test of intelligence.

Some disciplines requiring creativity tend to be populated by people who score high on IQ tests. For example, if one were to examine the general population, one would find a positive correlation between creative achievement in architecture and IQ performance. That is because nearly all of the creative efforts are accomplished by professional architects who, as a group, do well on IQ tests. But if one examines only professional architects, one does not find a strong relationship between degree of creative achievement (measured by peer ratings of creativity) and IQ performance (MacKinnon, 1962). Similarly, among psychology graduate students, Graduate Record Exam scores did not correlate significantly with faculty advisor ratings of the students' creative abilities (Sternberg and Williams, 1997). These results suggest that people who score very low on IQ tests tend to show less evidence of creative talent than people who score higher on IQ tests. But among people whose IQ performance is in the average-to-above-average range, IQ is at best only weakly related to performance on tests of creativity. Creativity, then, is a different aspect of the intellect or involves a different kind of motivation than the skills and motivations that enable people to do well on IQ tests (McDermid, 1965; Richards, Kinney, Benet, & Merzel, 1988).

Social Skill

One might also consider social skill as an aspect of intelligence, although IQ tests do not usually measure it. Again, social skill is a concept that is difficult to measure objectively. Research on social skill suggests that if social skill is measured using the same sorts of items that appear on IQ tests, then measures of social intelligence do correlate with IQ performance. An example of this is that memory for face–name associations and the tendency to correctly answer multiple choice questions about what to do in social situations are correlated with performance on IQ tests, especially IQ tests that measure verbal skills (Thorndike, 1936; Woodrow, 1939).

When social skill is assessed by directly observing people in social situations, however, there seems to be almost no relationship between it and IQ performance. Wong, Day, Maxwell, and Meara (1995) showed that people's performance on tests designed to measure cognitive aspects of social intelligence was only weakly related to their performance on tests of behavioral aspects of social intelligence. Frederiksen, Carlson, and Ward (1984) observed the interviewing skills of medical students who had to interact with "simulated" patients in several types of situations, including one in which the medical students had to inform the patient that she had breast cancer. Various aspects of the students' interviewing performance were rated by independent judges, in order to obtain a social skill score for each medical student. These scores were unrelated to the medical students' IQ scores and unrelated to their knowledge of science, as assessed by another test. Similarly, Rothstein, Paunonen, Rush, and King (1994) found that social–personality variables, especially self-confidence and a willingness to be the center of attention, predicted classroom performance (presenting convincing solutions, communicating clearly, and contributing to others' learning) in graduate school better than did standard measures of intellectual aptitude.

Practical Intelligence

Most people recognize a distinction between academic intelligence (book smarts) and practical intelligence (street smarts) (Sternberg, Wagner, Williams, & Horvath, 1995). Academic intelligence as measured by standard IQ tests is disembedded from an individual's ordinary experience. Practical intelligence, however, has to do with the actual attainment of goals that are valued. Sternberg and his colleagues (see Sternberg et al., 1995) have developed tests that supposedly measure **practical intelligence** (also known as **tacit knowledge**). Their tests typically present subjects with a set of work-related problems (e.g., how to achieve rapid promotion within a company) along with choices of strategies for solving the problem (e.g., write an article on productivity for the company newsletter, find ways to make sure that your supervisors are aware of your accomplishments). The subjects rank-order the strategies according to which is likely to achieve the goal. Their responses are then compared to those of acknowledged experts or to established rules of thumb used by experts. The greater the response overlap between subject and expert, the higher the subject's score on the test of practical intelligence.

A variety of studies suggest that scores on tests of practical intelligence correlate moderately with success on the job (see Sternberg et al., 1995). For instance, in one study, the correlation between practical intelligence test scores and performance ratings for the category "generating new business for the bank" was .56 (Wagner & Sternberg, 1985). However, scores on tests of practical intelligence are essentially unrelated to performance on standard IQ tests (Wagner & Sternberg, 1990). For instance, among Air Force recruits, the median correlation between scores on a test of practical intelligence and scores on various batteries of a standard IQ-type test was −.07 (Eddy, 1988, in Sternberg et al., 1995).

Similarly, Ceci and Liker (1986) found that, among avid racetrack patrons, the complexity of reasoning about handicapping horse races and success at predicting a horse's speed was unrelated to their IQ performance. Dorner and Kreuzig (1983) found that the sophistication of strategies used to solve city management problems was unrelated to a person's IQ. Yekovich, Walker, Ogle, and Thompson (1990) found that expertise in football, and not IQ, predicts who identifies the important facts in a passage about football, and who derives appropriate inferences about a football game. Lave (1988) showed that subjects who were easily able to perform algebraic calculations in the context of selecting which product is the best buy in a supermarket were unable to perform essentially the same calculations when the calculations were presented as math problems on a paper-and-pencil test.

The main point of the studies on creativity, social skill, and practicality is that if we expand our sense of the intellect, we find that people are not equally skilled in all areas. These observations suggest that the prevalence of g (the tendency for performance on the subtests of the IQ inventory to correlate) is largely an artifact of the restricted range of skills that the IQ inventory samples. It is probably true that the range of skills prized in academia tends to be limited to mathematical, reasoning, and verbal skills. Creativity, social skill, and practical skill, among other examples, are not usually emphasized in school.

GARDNER'S FRAMES OF MIND

Howard Gardner, a cognitive scientist from Harvard University, proposed an influential theory on intelligence in a book entitled *Frames of Mind* (Gardner, 1983). In contrast to unitary theorists, Gardner postulated six distinct, relatively autonomous categories of intelligence. These categories are **verbal intelligence**, exemplified by the poet; **logical intelligence**, exemplified by the mathematician; **musical intelligence**, exemplified by the composer; **spatial intelligence**, exemplified by the painter; **bodily-kinesthetic intelligence**, exemplified by the athlete or the dancer; and **social-emotional intelligence**, exemplified by the political leader or gifted parent. Gardner claimed that intellectual skill in one category is unrelated to intellectual skill in any other category. Similar claims have been made by Guilford (1964, 1967) and Thurstone (1938).

There are several remarkable features of Gardner's theory. First, he acknowledges the wide range of intellectual competencies that may be regarded as aspects of intelligence. Very few IQ tests examine the social-emotional realm, probably because, as I noted before, it is difficult to develop objective tests to see how well a person can motivate another person or understand his or her own feelings. Yet these sorts of skills are among the most prized in virtually all cultures. Very few IQ tests examine the musical or bodily-kinesthetic realm, because in our culture the intellect has historically been equated with verbal and logical intelligence. We have a hard time regarding a talented musician or dancer or athlete as unusually intelligent. Yet in many other cultures, these sorts of competencies are so regarded.

Evidence for Gardner's Frames

Gardner's theory is also remarkable for the kinds of evidence used to support it. Gardner has broken with the IQ tradition of examining patterns of correlations among subtests of the IQ inventory. Instead, he uses brain damage evidence, isolated talents, anthropological evidence, and the nature of mental operations to support his theory.

The brain damage evidence suggests that damage can interfere with one intellectual competency but leave the others intact. Damage to the left frontal and temporal regions of the brain can interfere with the use of language, but leave other skills, like logical or musical skill, intact. Damage to posterior portions of the right cerebral hemisphere can produce amusia—a difficulty in expressing and appreciating music. Yet spoken language, which also uses the auditory system, is unaffected. Similarly, damage to the anterior portions of the frontal lobes can interfere with certain aspects of emotional expression, yet language and all the other intellectual skills may remain intact.

The phenomenon of isolated talents also provides evidence for Gardner's theory. There are cases of people who are unusually talented in one realm, such as music or art, but are unremarkable and sometimes even retarded in other realms, such as logical reasoning. Similar support for Gardner's theory comes from the previously discussed findings that among people who score average or above on IQ tests, musical and social skill are unrelated to IQ performance, which tends to reflect language and reasoning skills (Shuter-Dyson, 1982; Frederiksen et al., 1984). Some research also suggests that logical reasoning skills are minimally correlated with language proficiency skills, especially when the logical reasoning task uses simple vocabulary (Boyle, 1987). Research also suggests that when memory span is measured using digits, it does not correlate with language proficiency, but when memory span is measured by words in a sentence, it does correlate with language proficiency (Daneman & Carpenter, 1980; King & Just, 1991; Perfetti & Lesgold, 1977). In my own research (Guenther, 1991), I found that the rate at which people could scan their memory of sentences that varied in word length (e.g., "Lions run quickly," "Lions jog") for a target word (e.g., "lions") was unrelated to the rate at which the same people could scan their memory of pictures of objects containing a variable number of properties (a house containing a door, window, and roof, a house containing a door and window) for some target property (e.g., a picture of a particular door).

Gardner notes that people in all cultures develop and appreciate his six proposed categories of intelligence. In all cultures virtually everyone learns something about music, movement skills such as those used in sports, spatial skills such as those used in drawing or navigating, social skills such as those used in soothing a troubled child, reasoning skills such as those underlying the exchange of goods and services, and language skills necessary to communicate. Although the IQ industry and academia implicitly claim that reasoning and language skills are of overwhelming importance, in most other cultures, including segments of our own culture outside of academia, skills such as musical and social skill are also prized.

Finally, Gardner notes that the mental operations are quite different in each category of intelligence. Language, for example, uses rules of grammar for combining symbols that bear an arbitrary relationship to ideas. Music uses rhythm and pitch to create aesthetically pleasing sounds. Logical reasoning entails comparing patterns or sequences and deriving implications, often from symbols that are quite abstract. Social intelligence involves understanding emotions and motivation. The dissimilarity among these mental operations suggests qualitative differences among categories of intellectual skill.

Criticisms of Gardner's Frames

Gardner's theory is not without its critics (see Sternberg, 1990; Richardson, 1991). One complaint is that it and any multifaceted theory of individual differences fails to explain the positive correlations among subtests of IQ inventories. For example, people who do well at explaining a proverb also tend to do well on spatial, nonverbal tests. A reasonable response to this complaint is the one already discussed, namely, that conventional IQ tests sample from a limited range of possibilities. There are few, if any, objective tests of musical, social, or kinesthetic skill, few measures of creativity, few tests measuring how well people learn new information, and few tests that confront people with problems like those actually encountered in real life.

Another complaint about Gardner's theory is that it seems to divide up the human intellect in a somewhat arbitrary way. Why, for example, is there no separate category for mechanical intelligence, which Gardner subsumes under bodily-kinesthetic? Is it not possible that a person could be a skilled mechanic but not a skilled dancer or athlete? Even Gardner admits, and others have found, that within a category like spatial intelligence, people who are good at one aspect of the skill are not necessarily good at other aspects of the skill. Kosslyn, Brunn, Cave, and Wallach (1984) found that people who are good at producing accurate visual images from verbal descriptions are not necessarily the same people who are able to make rapid rotational transformations of visual images. As another example, brain damage can interfere with the grammatical aspect of language but leave the semantic aspect more or less intact.

Gardner also seems to exclude categories that might be considered types of intelligence. Why is there not a category for religious intelligence? Have not virtually all cultures developed religion? Or for culinary intelligence? Is not food preparation essential to survival and is it not related to the brain mechanisms underlying olfactory and taste perceptions? Why not a category for practical intelligence? Are not measures of practical intelligence related to performance on the job (Sternberg, Wagner, Williams, & Horvath, 1995)?

It seems, then, that there may be an inherent arbitrariness to picking categories of intelligence. The concept of intelligence seems to reflect the values and ideology of a culture, or of an institution within a culture. Different value systems imply different notions of intelligence and different ways to measure intelligence. Advocates of this intelligence-as-ideology position include Garcia (1981), Berry (1974), Heath (1983), Helms (1992), and Keating (1982). From their perspective, the notion that one possesses a single kind of intelligence may be regarded as absurd. People possess skills of varying kinds that may be measured in many ways. Actually describing a skill and inventing a way to measure it reflects the values and goals of institutions, and not some essence of intelligence residing in a person. IQ tests tend to reflect the value the academic culture places on verbal and abstract reasoning skills, and on the objective measurement of people.

I think, then, that the unitary or generic view of intelligence is misleading. Instead, intelligence is multifaceted; it reflects performance on particularized, relatively autonomous skills. As I mentioned before, the multifaceted model of intelligence is reminiscent of the domain-specific nature of problem solving (discussed in the previous chapter). Just as there is no generic problem-solving system that kicks into action whenever a problem is encountered, there is no single unitary trait that permeates all of human cognition and gives rise to individual differences in intellectual performance. Chapter 11: Cognitive Development will also examine the generic versus domain-specific theme in human cognition.

SECTION 4: IS INTELLIGENCE DETERMINED PRIMARILY BY GENES?

Explicit in the hereditarian theory of intelligence is the idea that intelligence is a genetically determined intellectual potential. IQ is supposed to be an approximation of the amount of this potential. In this view, then, intellectual differences among people are largely attributable to their genetic differences. Most advocates of the genetic basis for intelligence concede that the environment can either nurture or thwart the acquisition of intellectual competency. But they contend that genes are the primary determinant of one's intellectual potential, and that in most cases IQ performance provides a rough index of this potential.

The hereditarian claim is often taken to imply that: (a) environmental intervention is not likely to help people who are "intellectually at risk" and that (b) ethnic or racial differences in IQ performance are caused primarily by genetic differences, and not by social or cultural factors. It is important to see that advocates of the hereditarian theory need not draw these implications, as I will discuss later. Indeed, my main purpose in this section is to demonstrate that the evidence for a genetic component to intellectual differences does not support these two claims.

EVIDENCE FOR A GENETIC BASIS FOR INTELLIGENCE

Familial IQ Correlations

Advocates of the hereditarian theory base the genetic hypothesis on the finding that intelligence (at least as measured by IQ tests) runs in families. For example, the correlation between parents' and children's performance on IQ tests is about .4 (see Bouchard & McCue, 1981, or Kline, 1991, for references on familial correlations in IQ scores). Especially compelling is the finding that the correlation between the IQ scores of children adopted at birth and the IQ scores of their biological parents is higher (about .32) than is the correlation between the children's IQ scores and the IQ scores of their adopted parents (about .15) (Horn, Loehlin, & Willerman, 1975). Figure 9-2 provides a table of familial correlations in IQ performance.

Evidence relevant to the genetic hypothesis comes from research on identical twins reared apart (e.g., Bouchard & McCue, 1981; Shields, 1962). In this situation, the individuals have virtually the same genes, but grow up in different environments. The usual finding is that the correlation between the IQ scores of twins reared apart is about .7, a high correlation. So despite a dissimilarity in environments, identical twins reared apart score about the same on IQ tests. This correlation is almost as high as the correlation in IQ between identical twins reared together (about .8) and much higher than the correlation between bio-

Relationship	Correlation
Identical twins reared together	.86
Identical twins reared apart	.72
Fraternal twins reared together	.60
Siblings reared together	.47
Siblings reared apart	.24
Biological parent and child, living together	.42
Biological parent and child, separated by adoption	.22
Unrelated children living together	.32
Adoptive parent and adopted child	.19

FIGURE 9–2 Familial correlations in IQ performance. The source of these correlations is Bouchard and McCue (1981).

logically unrelated siblings reared together (about .3). Biologically unrelated siblings reared together share family environments but not genes. So the inescapable conclusion seems to be that genes are a primary determinant of intelligence, at least as measured by IQ tests.

Problems with the Evidence Supporting a Genetic Basis for Intelligence

The interpretation that the familial IQ correlations support an overpowering influence of genes on intelligence is problematic, however. The pattern of familial correlations does not rule out a substantial influence of the environment on intellectual differences. After all, people learn child-rearing practices and other skills relevant to the cognitive development of the child from their parents. For example, children may acquire an interest in reading from their parents and pass this interest on to their own children. Children who become interested in reading are likely to read more, get better at reading, and so do well on IQ tests that are typically saturated with test items that depend on language skills.

The importance of the environment in accounting for familial IQ correlations is suggested by the fact that children and their parents are likely to grow up in similar cultural and economic circumstances. Even adopted children are likely to be placed in homes similar in educational and economic background to the homes of the biological parents. Furthermore, children adopted as infants may be more likely to have suffered from prenatal problems, which may undermine their intellectual development and reduce the correlation between their IQ scores and the IQ scores of the adopted parents.

Some of the familial correlations demonstrate an important effect of environment on intellectual differences. The IQ correlation between unrelated children living together is about .3, which is certainly much greater than zero. So there is at least some tendency for people who have dissimilar genes but similar family backgrounds to have similar IQ scores. Also, the correlation between IQ scores for ordinary biologically related siblings is about .4, which is much lower than the correlation for fraternal twins reared together (about .6), even though the genes of fraternal twins are no more similar than the genes of ordinary siblings. Presumably, though, the family environments of fraternal twins are more similar than the family environments of ordinary siblings, because twins share the same period of family history.

Turning to the twins-reared-apart paradigm, it is worth noting that the environments of twins reared apart are not necessarily all that different from those of siblings reared together. As I mentioned before, adoption agencies usually try to place adoptees in homes similar to the home of the biological parents. Furthermore, when twins are raised separately, one twin is often reared by another family member; twins are not usually separated until later childhood; and the twins often remain in contact with one another. In other words, there is a kind of environmental "contamination" that may make the environmental influences on the twins reared apart more similar than is commonly appreciated. Finally, twins are more susceptible to prenatal trauma, which can result in mental retardation, reflected in lowered IQ scores for both twins, even if reared apart. This inflates the IQ correlation between twins (see Anastasi, 1988).

Another kind of problem with the twins-reared-apart paradigm is that it does not identify which shared genes are the underlying cause of the similarity in IQ scores. One possibility is that the genes that produce the high correlations influence biological functions that are directly involved in many cognitive processes. But there are other possibilities.

Consider the following hypothetical scenario. Identical twins share facial and bodily features, the characteristics of which are established primarily by genes. How people are treated depends to some extent on their physical appearance. Consequently, people's social skills, confidence, and so on depend to some extent on their physical appearance. Social skills and confidence, in turn, may influence how one performs on IQ tests. The result would be that identical twins, even when reared apart, will tend to perform similarly on IQ tests, yet the similarity in performance has nothing to do with their intellectual potential. Instead, it has to do with their physical appearance. It could be that one twin, should she or he grow up in an environment that downplays physical appearance, might obtain a very different IQ score than the other twin.

There are other hypothetical examples I could work out. Maybe, for example, the similarity in IQ between twins reared apart is due to similarity of their metabolic rates, or to their resistance to diseases, or to any of a number of other factors that may be genetically inherited and indirectly affect performance on IQ tests. The point of these hypothetical examples is to show that establishing that twins reared apart perform similarly on IQ tests does not necessarily prove that there is a direct genetic basis for intellectual performance. Incidentally, the same argument can be made with respect to the higher IQ correlation between the biological parents and their children whom they do not raise than between the adoptive parents and those same children. Some of the genes the adopted children inherit from their biological parents influence their scores on IQ tests, but it remains unclear what aspect of biology those inherited genes control.

THE ROLE OF ENVIRONMENTAL FACTORS IN INTELLECTUAL DIFFERENCES

One of the unfortunate implications sometimes drawn from the hereditarian theory of intelligence is that environmental factors are likely to have a rather meager effect on intelligence. Consequently, it is not worth spending money and effort trying to improve substantially the intelligence of people who might seem "intellectually at risk." Now, strictly speaking, one need not draw this implication from hereditary theory, because hereditarians concede that the environment can have an impact on intellectual development. But the problem is that an emphasis on the genetic basis of intellectual differences can blind one to the possibility that environmental factors may have a rather potent effect on intelligence. Genetically based differences lead to the idea of inevitable differences (Gould, 1981). Yet a variety of studies have demonstrated that environmental intervention can substantially improve intellectual capabilities.

Family and School Environments

Some studies have looked at the behaviors of parents to see which are correlated with their children's intellectual competence. For example, the parents' use of language correlates with their children's performance on IQ tests (Hart & Risley, 1992). Child-rearing practices also correlate with the child's intellect. White (1978), for example, found that parents who reared intellectually competent children tended to do three things: first, they provided a structured, safe, and interesting physical environment for their children. Second, they spent a lot of time helping their children solve problems. Third, they established and enforced clear-cut rules, but in a loving and respectful manner.

Such studies suggest the importance of parenting styles in the acquisition of intellectual competence. The hereditarian could, however, still argue that is the favorable genes of the parents that lead them to use reasonable parenting techniques, and that the intellectual competence of their children is mainly a consequence of inheriting these favorable genes. A better way to show that parenting styles and other environmental variables have a causal effect on the acquisition of intelligence would be to rear one group of children under one set of environmental conditions and a comparable group under a different set of conditions. Ideally, the children should be randomly assigned to the two conditions, but random assignment is obviously socially and ethically impossible.

Still, some research comes close to performing the ideal experiment. Observations of children growing up in orphanages reveals that children who receive loving affection from the caretakers will tend to average higher on IQ tests than children who do not get the affection (Skeels, 1966). Other research has provided training to a group of low-income preschool children on the intellectual skills necessary to do well in school, and has shown that such children improve their IQ performance by an average of 10 to 15 points. Unfortunately, these sorts of studies typically reveal that the gains are temporary. By the fourth grade, the average IQ performance of the group that got the training declines to the level of comparable children who did not receive the training (Bronfenbrenner, 1974; Klaus & Gray, 1968; Ramey, Campbell, & Finkelstein, 1984). However, if the intervention program is extended into the school years, evidence suggests that the intervention has a beneficial effect on IQ performance that extends beyond the first few years of school (Lazar, Darlington, Murray, Royce, & Snipper, 1982; Miller & Bizzell, 1984).

A fairly dramatic environmental effect on IQ performance was accomplished by Garber (1988), who placed a group of children who were previously labeled to be at risk for mental retardation in an extensive home enrichment program. Garber found that, by age 6, the group scored 30 points higher on an IQ test than did a control group, and even by age 14 still scored about 10 points higher than the control group. Another dramatic case is the Carolina Abecedarian Project (Campbell & Ramey, 1994). In this project, infants from low-income families were placed into intellectually enriched environments until they began school. Compared with controls, the enriched children scored higher on tests of intelligence, even 7 years after the end of the intervention.

Generational Environmental Changes: IQ Scores Are Rising

One intriguing piece of evidence for an environmental influence on IQ performance is the finding that in this century there has been a steady worldwide rise in IQ scores (Flynn, 1984, 1987; see Neisser et al., 1996). The average gain has been about 3 IQ points per decade. The result is that most intelligence tests have to be periodically restandardized in order to keep the mean equal to a score of 100. So people who score 100 on an IQ test today (in 1997) would have averaged about 115 in 1947.

No one knows why IQ scores are rising. Among the proposed reasons (see Neisser et al., 1996) is the idea that the world's cultures are becoming informationally more complex, because of television, urbanization, prolonged schooling, and so on. Such complexity then produces improvements in the development of intellectual skill. Another idea is that the IQ increases are due to nutritional improvements, perhaps the same improvements that have also led to nutritionally based increases in height. Whatever the reason, it must be something in the environment that is producing the rising IQ scores. Certainly the gene pool of the humans species cannot be changing as rapidly as IQ scores are rising. Indeed, there is no evidence that people who score higher on IQ tests are reproducing at greater rates. If anything, the evidence suggests that people who score high on intelligence tests have lower fertility rates, at least within the last century (Van Court & Bean, 1985).

In general, then, the research is consistent with the notion that environmental factors can have a large effect on the development of intellectual competency, even as measured by conventional IQ tests. The fact that people inherit genes that somehow influence intelligence, however measured, does not mean that intelligence is immutable.

ETHNIC DIFFERENCES IN IQ PERFORMANCE

Another unfortunate implication sometimes drawn from the hereditarian theory of intelligence is based on the finding that people from minority groups, such as Native Americans and African Americans, tend to score lower on IQ tests than people from majority groups such as European Americans (Herrnstein & Murray, 1994; Neisser et al., 1996). Yet IQ tests predict academic performance among minority people, suggesting that the tests are not unreasonable measures of intelligence in minority populations (Scarr-Salapatek, 1971; Oakland, 1983). The unfortunate implication sometimes drawn from these findings is that European people possess a genetically determined intellectual potential that exceeds that possessed by peoples from other parts of the world (Jensen, 1969). Some hereditarians claim that Asian people possess the most favorable genes for intellectual potential (Rushton, 1988, 1991). Such claims have historically been used to justify racial segregation and racist social and economic policies. They have also been used to discourage the spending of economic resources on the education of people from minority cultures.

Again, the implication that ethnic differences in performance on IQ tests are genetic need not be drawn from a hereditarian theory of intelligence. It is perfectly consistent with the hereditarian view that individual differences in intelligence are primarily due to genes but ethnic differences in measured intelligence are primarily due to environmental factors. I think that the consensus position is that ethnic differences in IQ performance reflect differences in cultural environments. Specifically, the cultural environment of the typical European (and in some cases, Asian) is more conducive to learning the skills that enable a person to do well on IQ tests than is the cultural environment of the typical African American or Hispanic American or Native American.

Evidence Against a Genetic Basis for Ethnic IQ Differences

Several lines of evidence support the claim that ethnic differences in IQ performance are a consequence of environmental and cultural factors and not a matter of genetic differences.

First of all, when children from a minority group that typically scores lower on IQ tests are raised in the same environment as children from the majority culture, the IQ scores of those minority children are similar to the IQ scores of the majority children. Scarr and Weinberg (1976, 1983) examined the IQ scores of African-American children born of mostly lower income parents but adopted by European-American families from mostly the middle and upper middle economic brackets. The IQ scores of the adopted African Americans averaged about 20 points higher than the IQ scores of other African Americans living in lower income circumstances. Clearly, the family environment had a huge effect on the development of skills underlying the performance on IQ tests. Furthermore, these and other adoption studies indicate that when African-American children are adopted into European-American families, their average IQ performance typically comes to be nearly equal to that of the European Americans (Flynn, 1980; Eyferth, 1961; Tizard, Cooperman, Joseph, & Tizard, 1972; Scarr & Weinberg, 1976, 1983). Yet the IQ correlation between the African-American adopted children and their biological parents is greater than the correlation between the African-American children and their adopted parents. Again, that seemingly paradoxical result is because correlation reflects rank order. The IQ scores of the adopted African-American children may have been improved by their environment, but the environment did not affect their rank order on the IQ test. The rank order of the IQ scores of the adopted children continued to reflect the rank order of the IQ scores of their biological parents.

Other research that examines children in similar environments but with different racial backgrounds has also contradicted the hereditarian claim of a racial difference in intelligence. Loehlin, Lindzey, and Spuhler (1975) examined the IQ scores of children born to German mothers and American fathers stationed in Germany after World War II. One group of children was fathered by African Americans, while the other group was fathered by European Americans. Both groups were raised by German mothers in roughly similar economic circumstances. The averages of the IQ scores of the two groups of children were equal, even though one group received half of its genes from people of African descent. Furthermore, there is no correlation between degree of African ancestry of African Americans and their performance on IQ tests (Scarr, Pakstis, Katz, & Barker, 1977).

It is true that some Asian-American people, such as Japanese Americans, score higher on average on IQ tests than do European Americans. But cross-cultural studies that take into account cultural factors, such as the proportions of rural and urban dwellers, suggest no difference between Asians and Europeans in IQ test performance (Stevenson et al., 1985). Furthermore, some Asian groups that have immigrated to the West and subsequently endured poverty in the West score lower on IQ tests than do Europeans (see Mackintosh, 1986).

Sometimes people use the high correlations in IQ performance between twins reared apart as evidence that ethnic differences in IQ performance must be due to genetic differences. In fact, though, even if one overlooks the inter-pretation problems associated with this paradigm, the twin findings are per-fectly consistent with an environmental explanation for group differences in IQ performance.

To see why, consider the following hypothetical situation. Suppose we have three sets of twins (Jerry and Gerry, Robin and Robyn, and Sara and Seri) who are reared apart. On IQ tests, Jerry and Gerry both obtain 100, Robin and Robyn both obtain 110, and Sara and Seri both obtain 120. So the correlation between the IQ scores of the twins is 1.0. Now suppose the second member of each pair (Gerry, Robyn, and Seri) is each given extensive training so that each improves his or her IQ performance by 20 points. So now the IQ scores will be 100 and 120 for Jerry and Gerry respectively, 110 and 130 for Robin and Robyn respectively, and 120 and 140 for Sara and Seri respectively. Yet the correlation between the IQ scores of the twins will still be 1.0, because correlations reflect rank order, which remains the same. This hypothetical example makes clear that even when the correlation between twins reared apart is as high as it can be (1.0), the environment can still dramatically affect group differences in IQ performance.

Why Are There Ethnic Differences in IQ Performance?

If differences in IQ performance among ethnic groups are not due to genetics, what are they due to? Nobody knows for sure (Neisser et al., 1996). A clue comes from the finding that many politically and economically disadvantaged groups from all over the world tend to do less well in school and to score lower on IQ-type tests than do the more advantaged groups (Ogbu, 1978, 1994). The kinds of minority groups that score lower on IQ tests are those that became a minority group involuntarily or those that are regarded by the culture as caste-like (Ogbu, 1978, 1994). Immigrants who come to a country voluntarily may be optimistic that they can control and improve their conditions. These groups typ-ically do well on IQ tests. Groups that are involuntarily displaced, such as Native Americans, African Americans, and the Maori in New Zealand, or are excluded, like the "untouchables" of India or non-European Jews of Israel, may lack the conviction that hard schoolwork and serious commitment to the educational enterprise will be rewarded. It is these groups that tend to do poorly on IQ tests.

Furthermore, IQ tests take place in settings in which motivation and attitudes can affect performance (see Helms, 1992; Miller-Jones, 1989). Children from a minority culture that emphasizes the interpersonal nature of learning may be more likely to regard a lack of feedback from the tester as evidence that they are doing well on the test (Miller-Jones, 1989). These children may refrain from varying their strategies in the course of taking the test and consequently obtain a lower score. In some cultures, it is unusual for an adult who already knows the answer to a question to ask that question of a child, or for children to explain what they know (Heath, 1989; Rogoff & Morelli, 1989).

It is frequently observed that people from other cultures often misunderstand the instructions and fail to take seriously the test's requirements. Sinha (1983), for example, has provided an analysis of some of the cultural reasons why Asiatic Indians who have not been enculturated by the West have trouble with IQ tests. Asiatic Indians typically do not know that responses like "I don't know" or "I can't decide" will cause one to get lower scores on IQ tests. Also, Asiatic Indians are typically inhibited in responding, especially when the task seems pointless to them. In some cultures, such as the culture in which many African Americans are raised, a premium is placed on the creativity of responses. Sometimes African-American children are surprised to learn that they are expected to provide obvious answers on IQ tests (Heath, 1989; Helms, 1992). The creative answers they often do provide get them lower scores. Boykin (1994) argues that many African Americans are alienated from education and the accompanying psychometric enterprise because these institutions implicitly conflict with a heritage that emphasizes spirituality, harmony, expressive individualism, communalism, and orality, and not talent sorting and talent assessment. A consequence of that alienation may be a poorer average performance on IQ tests.

CULTURAL DIFFERENCES IN PRIZED INTELLECTUAL COMPETENCIES

In general, then, research shows that when the cultural and economic environments of ethnic groups are roughly equated, performance on IQ tests is roughly equated as well. But impoverished minority groups involuntarily displaced or shunned by the culture as a whole tend to do poorly on IQ tests. It would be a mistake, though, to conclude from the research that the poverty and cultural alienation endured by many minorities invariably suppresses intellectual development. Rather, people from different cultures place emphasis on different kinds of intellectual development (Garcia, 1981; Heath, 1983, 1989; Helms, 1992; Miller-Jones, 1989).

IQ tests were developed by middle- and upper-middle-class Europeans and people of European descent, so it is unsurprising that the intellectual skills relevant to IQ testing are emphasized more in their culture than in most other cultures. But the skills developed in other cultures in response to their environments, including impoverished environments, may be "invisible" to IQ tests. If care is taken to develop tests that reflect the intellectual competencies prized by a minority culture, but not necessarily by the majority culture, then the minority culture will do as well, and sometimes even better, on such tests.

Heath (1983) studied children from low-income African-American families, low-income European-American families, and middle-income European-American families. She noted that, on average, there were differences in the kinds of intellectual competencies with which these children began school. The African-American children from low-income families tended to be very skilled at responding to novel situations, defending themselves against a verbal insult, and telling creative stories. The European-American children from middle-income families were typically good at responding to requests, responding quickly when timed by a psychologist administering a test, and answering "why" questions. In general, then, this study makes the point that poverty or lack of formal education does not necessarily depress intellectual development; rather, it can lead to the development of intellectual skills different from those at which well-educated Europeans tend to excel and to measure with IQ tests.

Similar conclusions may be drawn from cross-cultural studies. Berry (1974) found that people from hunting cultures tend to do better on tests of perceptual discrimination and spacial processing than people from cultures in which hunting is less important. Rice farmers from Liberia are better than Americans at estimating quantities (Gay & Cole, 1967).

Children from Botswana, accustomed to storytelling, are better than American children at remembering stories (Dube, 1982). In one of my favorite examples, Cole, Gay, Glick, and Sharp (1971) asked adult Kpelle tribespeople to sort 20 familiar objects, such as knives, oranges, and so on, into groups of things that belong together. The Kpelle separated the objects into functional groups (e.g., knife with orange) and not taxonomic groups (e.g., knife with fork). Western adults, on the other hand, sort on the basis of taxonomy, as do children who receive higher IQ scores. But when the Kpelle adults were asked to sort the objects the way a "stupid" person would do it, the Kpelle sorted like the Western adults and high IQ children—that is, on the basis of taxonomy. At least with respect to those objects, the typical Kpelle adult regarded the functional grouping as more useful than the taxonomic grouping.

Sex Differences in Intellectual Competencies

Perhaps because people are fascinated by male–female differences, there have been many studies of sex differences in cognition. Many of these studies report that males tend to do better in tests of mathematical and spatial ability, and females tend to do better in tests of verbal ability (reviewed in Maccoby and Jacklin, 1974; Bjorklund, 1995; Kimura, 1992; Halpern, 1992). Examples of tasks that favor males and tasks that favor females are provided in figure 9-3. Men and women do not differ in IQ scores, vocabulary tests, or reasoning tasks.

TASKS FAVORING WOMEN

Perceptual Speed
Find the house that exactly matches the one on the left.

TASKS FAVORING MEN

Spatial Relations
A hole has been punched in the folded sheet. How will the sheet appear when unfolded?

 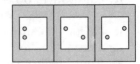

Verbal Fluency
Indicate another word that begins with the same letter, not included in the list.

Limp, Livery, Love, Laser, Liquid, Low, Like, Lag, Live, Lug, Light, Lift, Liver, Lime, Leg, Load, Lap, Lucid

Mathematical Reasoning
In the space at the left, write the answer to the following problem.

If only 60% of seedlings will survive, how many must be planted to obtain 660 trees?

Answers:
The house at the far right; Life or any other word beginning with L.

Answers:
The middle sheet; 1,100 seedlings.

FIGURE 9–3   Problem-solving tasks favoring women and problem-solving tasks favoring men. From *Psychology* by Fernald, Dodge, © 1994. Reprinted by permission of Prentice-Hall, Inc., Upper Saddle River, NJ.

The nature of the sex differences depends on how cognitive skills are measured. To illustrate, males do slightly better than females on spatial tests that measure the ability to orient oneself in relationship to objects or to mentally transform spatial information. But females do slightly better than males on spatial tests measuring ability to learn and remember spatial relationships (Silverman & Eals, 1992). Although males do better on most objective tests of mathematical ability, females get better grades in math courses than do males (Kimball, 1989).

It should be noted that there is considerable controversy surrounding sex differences in cognition. Some researchers claim that the average differences between males and females are usually small and often statistically insignificant (Hyde, 1981) whereas others claim that the differences are substantial (Eagly, 1995). Some researchers claim that the differences may have been declining in recent years (Feingold, 1988; Voyer, Voyer, & Bryden, 1995) but others claim that the differences have remained stable (Halpern, 1992). And, of course, the biggest controversy has to do with whether cognitive differences between the sexes are due to the different genes that the sexes inherit or to the different environments and cultures in which they grow up.

Genetic Basis of Sex Differences in Cognition

What is the cause of the sex differences in cognition? Obviously, boys and girls are treated differently and encouraged in different ways (Halpern, 1992). Boys are more likely to be encouraged to pursue careers in science, engineering, and mechanics, where mathematical and spatial skills are important. Girls are more likely to be encouraged to pursue careers in teaching and in child rearing, where communication skills are important.

Still, many researchers have proposed genetically based biological explanations for male–female differences in cognition (e.g., Kimura, 1992). Usually the ultimate cause of sex differences is attributed to the supposedly different selective pressures on males and females as humans evolved. Supposedly, males did the hunting, and so evolved better spatial skills for orienting to and transforming spatial information; and females did the gathering and child rearing, and so evolved better spatial memory and verbal skills.

What biological mechanism might be controlled by the genes that underlie sex differences in cognition? One example of a biological mechanism that may plausibly be coded for in the genes and that may give rise to sex differences in cognition is the production of sex hormones. Sex hormones, such as testosterone, are known to influence the organization of the mammalian brain during critical periods in prenatal development (Geschwind & Galabura, 1987; Halpern & Cass, 1994). A variety of research supports a correlation between sex hormones and performance on sex-differentiating cognitive tasks.

Women who were exposed to abnormally high levels of the male hormone androgen *in utero* score higher than do controls on tests of spatial ability (Resnick, Berenbaum, Gottesman, & Bouchard, 1986). Older males given testosterone improve on visual-spatial tasks (Janowsky, Oviatt, & Orwoll, 1994). Women do better on cognitive tasks that favor women over men, like verbal skills, and worse on cognitive tasks that favor men, like spatial rotation, when they are in the midluteal phase of the menstrual cycle than when they are in the late menstrual phase. Levels of estrogen and progesterone are higher during the midluteal phase (Hampson & Kimura, 1988; Hampson, 1990a, 1990b; see Kimura & Hampson, 1994). Men do better on tasks that favor men over women during the spring, when their testosterone levels are relatively low, than in the autumn, when their testosterone levels are relatively high (Kimura & Toussaint, 1991; see Kimura & Hampson, 1994). And it isn't just that men do better in the spring, when a young man's fancy supposedly turns to love—men's performance on tasks that do not favor men over women, such as reasoning, is the same in spring as in autumn. Apparently, average to below-average levels of testosterone are associated with optimal performance on visual-spatial tasks in men (Gouchie & Kimura, 1991).

What is it that sex hormones do to the brain that gives rise to differences in cognition? One possibility is that hormones affect how the cerebral hemispheres distribute their function. Recall that in most people the left hemisphere is more involved than the right in the control of language whereas the right hemisphere is more involved than the left in the control of spatial processing.

Perhaps the female advantage for some verbal skills reflects the involvement of more right-hemisphere neural tissue in language—neural tissue that at the same time encroaches on the neural tissue that would have been used for spatial processing. At least some evidence suggests that there is less tendency among women for their left hemisphere to control language more than their right hemisphere (e.g., Shaywitz et al., 1995), although not all studies find a sex difference in hemispheric specialization (Newcombe & Bandura, 1983; Waber, Mann, Merola, & Moylan, 1985).

Another possible neurological model of sex hormone differences in brain organization has been developed by Kimura (1992). Kimura suggests that the organization of functions within the left hemisphere differs between the sexes. For language functions, women may make more use of the anterior portions of the left hemisphere whereas men make more use of the posterior left hemisphere. Such a difference may give rise to the tendency for women to do better on tests of verbal fluency, because the grammatical aspect of language may be more anatomically connected to the planning and strategic components of information processing. The more intimate connection in males between language centers and the centers involved in visual perception may give rise to the male advantages on spatial reasoning tasks. One line of evidence consistent with this view is that aphasia (language disturbance) occurs more often in women when the damage is near the front of the left hemisphere, but more often in men when the damage is in the posterior area of the left hemisphere (Kimura, 1992).

It is important to point out that the supposed differences in the brains of men and women may not necessarily reflect the effects of sex hormones; those differences may be mediated by some other biological mechanism. Furthermore, the sex differences in relevant biological mechanisms need not be entirely or even at all due to genes. It may be that experiences, like playing with toys or studying mathematics, affect the production of hormones (and any other relevant biological mechanism) and thereby produce sex differences in certain cognitive skills.

Environmental Explanations of Sex Differences in Cognition

My own belief is that it remains a viable possibility that sex differences in cognition are due mostly to environmental factors (how is that for a hedge!). One line of evidence for an environmental explanation of sex differences is that parental attitudes and expectations are correlated with performance on math (Raymond & Benbow, 1986) and verbal tests (Roe, Drivas, Karagellis, & Roe, 1985). An especially compelling line of evidence is research that shows that, with practice and feedback, women improve as much as men do on spatial tasks (e.g., Law, Pellegrino, & Hunt, 1993; see Halpern, 1992 for a review). Some cross-cultural work shows that among Canadian Eskimos, a culture in which both males and females travel far from home and hunt, there are no differences in spatial abilities between males and females (Berry, 1966).

Indeed, at present in our culture, it is at least debatable whether there are any reliable male–female differences in verbal and math skills. Hyde and Linn

(1986, 1988) reviewed 165 studies of verbal ability representing over 1.4 million people and found no average difference between males and females. Moreover, Hyde, Fennema, and Lamon (1990) reviewed 100 studies of mathematical performance and found that sex differences were quite small, but tended to favor females in large samples that are taken from the general population. It is only in the population of mathematically gifted individuals that males outperform females, on the average.

Carol Tavris, in her splendid book *The Mismeasure of Woman* (Tavris, 1992), reviews evidence that suggests that male and female brains learn, reason, and process information in similar ways. Tavris also discusses the bias against publishing research that finds no sex differences in cognition, and the unfortunate consequences this bias has for women. For example, a belief that males have superior mathematical skills, sustained by a bias against publishing studies that show no sex differences in mathematical skill, provides a rationale for excluding women from the sciences and for denigrating the few women who do manage to become scientists.

CONCLUSIONS ABOUT THE GENETIC BASIS OF INTELLIGENCE

There seems to be no easy way to summarize the evidence relevant to the genetic basis for intelligence. Because we are unable to conduct controlled experiments that vary genes and environments, we remain ignorant of how to interpret correlations in the IQ scores of individuals who share genes. Individuals who share genes almost always share environments. With regard to sex differences in cognition, it is difficult to disentangle the influence of sex-linked genes and sex-linked environments. It is true that the twins-reared-apart studies, as well as other research on adoption, suggest that something that is genetically inherited causes differences in scores on IQ tests. However, it is not clear what genetically controlled biological mechanism is responsible for the similarity in IQ scores. Indeed, at this point we do not really know what biological mechanisms are the underlying basis for individual differences in any of the potentially limitless kinds of skills a person can acquire. All we can say with certainty is that the biological mechanisms underlying intellectual development are, especially in our species, designed to enable us to learn from the environment. Consequently, any act of the intellect will invariably reflect both biological and environmental factors. Genetic models of intellectual differences to date lack any clear explanation of what biological mechanisms underlie individual differences. Sex hormones may be a basis for male–female differences in cognition; however, it is possible that sex hormone production may be the effect of different environments and not necessarily the direct cause of cognitive differences.

Any useful model needs to explain how a genetically determined biological mechanism interacts with various aspects of the environment to produce intellectual development. It seems pointless to argue about whether intellectual development is primarily determined by the genes or by the environment, because either can dominate depending on the circumstances. If people are given no exposure to music, for example, they will not develop musical skill. If people are born deaf as a result of a genetic defect, they will not develop any musical skill.

And, of course, the role of genes and the biological mechanisms controlling intellectual differences is invariably complicated by the difficulty in defining and measuring intelligence. As I suggested in earlier sections of this chapter, a good case can be made that there are a potentially vast number of relatively autonomous skills that a person can acquire, any one of which could be assessed in many different ways. The effects of genetically controlled biological mechanisms and environmental variables could be quite different depending on what aspect of intelligence one cares to study.

My own sense is that the influence of genes and environmental variables is so complex and intertwined, the research limitations on the effects of genes so intractable, and the notion of intelligence so potentially multifaceted, that it is not possible to know exactly how genes and environmental variables interact to produce individual differences in cognition. This need not be a distressing state of affairs, however. Our goal as psychologists and educators should be to try to create the best possible environments for fostering the acquisition of intellectual competence in our children, regardless of their genetic makeup.

SUMMARY AND CONCLUSIONS

The integrating theme for this chapter was a contrast between a hereditarian approach to individual differences in intelligence and a multi-faceted approach. The hereditarian approach make two essential claims: intelligence is unitary and is determined primarily by the genes one inherits. The multi-faceted approach claims that there are many different and relatively autonomous domains of intelligence. Intellectual skill in one domain is typically unrelated to intellectual skill in other domains.

In the first section, I discussed the rise of the hereditarian approach to intelligence and the intelligence testing movement. Probably the most historically significant event in the history of intelligence testing was the development of IQ tests. IQ tests are known to be moderately correlated with grades in school, occupational status, and success in an occupation.

In section 2, I discussed the main evidence for a unitary view of intelligence, which is that performance on the subtests that make up the IQ inventory and between IQ scores and academic achievement are positively correlated. A generic information processing perspective proposes that intellectual tasks are performed by a common information processing system. Differences in intellectual capability are due to the speed and efficiency with which various stages of the system are executed. One line of evidence in support of the information processing perspective comes from research that shows that the shorter the stimulus exposure time at which people can accurately discriminate between the length of two lines, the higher the person's IQ score. In a sense, the rise of the information processing analysis of individual differences represents a reemergence of the ideas of Francis Galton, who espoused them about 100 years ago.

Recent physiological research has suggested correlations between performance on intelligence tests and physiological measures such as cortical metabolic rate or neural conduction speed. Usually, these neurophysiologically based models implicitly suppose that intelligence is unitary—that some aspect of neurophysiology that permeates all intellectual tasks is the factor that gives rise to individual differences in cognition. While intriguing, such research has not yet elucidated the underlying biological mechanisms or the causes of such correlations.

At any rate, correlations among IQ subtests or between IQ tests and academic success can be explained without supposing that all intellectual differences represent differences in a single underlying substrate of the various cognitive systems. In section 3 I discuss how the correlations could reflect motivation or the limited range of skills measured by IQ tests and taught in schools. Indeed, if one examines creativity, social skills, or practical skills used in everyday life, the correlations between such skills and IQ tests are essentially nonexistent.

One alternative to the unitary model is the claim that there are several distinct, relatively autonomous categories of intelligence. Howard Gardner (1983), for example, claims that there are six different categories of intelligence, and cites physiological and anthropological evidence to bolster his claim. Another alternative claims that there are potentially an unlimited number of categories of intelligence, any one of which may be measured in a potentially unlimited number of ways. The ways a culture defines and measures intelligence reflect the values and goals of the culture, and not something intrinsic to the biology of people.

In section 4 I discuss the hereditarian claim that intelligence is largely genetically determined. The claim is supported by familial correlations in IQ performance, and by the high correlation between the IQ scores of identical twins reared apart. However, the familial pattern of correlations is also consistent with a substantial impact of environmental factors on intelligence. The twins-reared-apart findings only show that some genetically determined biological mechanism underlies IQ performance. That mechanism might control intellectual processes, but it might also control physical appearance, metabolic rate, resistance to disease and/or any of a number of other traits.

One unfortunate implication sometimes drawn from a theory that emphasizes the genetic basis of intelligence is that environmental factors are likely to have minimal influence on intellectual development. In fact, though, a variety of studies demonstrate that appropriate environmental intervention can improve the intellectual performance of individuals who might otherwise be at "intellectual risk." Furthermore, performance on IQ tests is rising about 3 IQ points a decade all around the world.

Another unfortunate implication historically drawn by hereditarians is that ethnic differences in IQ performance reflect genetic differences among racial and other ethnic groups. However, adoption studies and other research convincingly makes the case that differences among the average IQ scores of ethnic groups reflect environmental and cultural differences among groups. If members from two different ethnic groups are raised in similar circumstances, their average IQ performances will be similar as well. Furthermore, some research suggests that different ethnic groups, in response to their respective environments, are likely to develop different skills, not all of which are measured by IQ tests.

Sex differences in cognition have been explored as well. Some hereditarian approaches have claimed that the superior performance of the average male on spacial and mathematical tests, and the superior performance of the average female on verbal tests, reflect sex-linked genetic differences between the sexes. Fluctuations in sex hormones are correlated with performance on just those tasks on which the sexes are different. However, once again, the sex differences may be largely attributable to environmental factors. I am personally impressed with the research that shows that, with practice and feedback, women improve as much as men do on spatial tasks. There is some admittedly controversial evidence that sex differences in cognition are shrinking over time, possibly because of cultural changes made in recent years whereby more women are encouraged to attend college and pursue careers in which mathematical and spatial skills are important.

Certainly both the biological mechanisms put into place by the genes and the environment invariably contribute to intellectual growth and individual differences. How could it be otherwise? A useful model of biology's role in intelligence must specify precisely how any given biological mechanism responds to the various aspects of the environment in the course of intellectual development. Given that controlled experiments are ethically and biologically impossible, we may never completely understand the precise contributions that genes and environmental factors make to individual intellectual differences.

RECOMMENDED READINGS

Gould's (1981) *The Mismeasure of Man* is a masterful and highly critical history of the rise of the intelligence testing movement. An equally masterful companion piece is Tavris's (1992) *The Mismeasure of Woman*, in which Tavris discusses her thesis that male–female differences in human emotions and cognition are greatly exaggerated. The case for important sex differences in human cognition is provided in an interesting *Scientific American* article by Kimura (1992). Gardner published his six categories of intelligence theory in his (1983) *Frames of Mind*, an exciting and wide-ranging book that has become highly influential in educational circles. Certainly people interested in intelligence testing should read Hernstein and Murray's (1994) best-seller *The Bell Curve*, but please read along with it reviews of *The Bell Curve* written by experts in the field; a collection of such reviews can be found in *The Bell Curve Wars*, edited by Fraser (1995). A summary of what psychologists know and don't know about intelligence and intelligence testing can be found in a recent *American Psychologist* review paper by Neisser et al. (1996).

10 *Language*

A stroke patient tries to describe a picture of a boy on a stool stealing cookies from a jar, with a woman on the right, washing dishes, distracted by water overflowing in the sink. The patient's description: "Cookie jar . . . fall over . . . chair . . . water . . . empty . . . ov . . . ov . . ." (Blumstein, 1982). This patient has suffered damage to **Broca's area**, located in the posterior frontal lobe of the left cerebral hemisphere, causing the patient to exhibit poorly articulated speech replete with grammatical errors. Tragic cases like this remind us of how precious language is to us.

Language is one of the most spectacular of human abilities, yet it is one we take for granted. Language enables us to communicate thoughts as diverse as our feelings of love for a child, the results of an exciting baseball game, and the nature of life in a prehistoric culture. Language allows us to learn from the experiences of others without having to have those experiences ourselves. Language enables groups of people to accomplish what no one person could ever accomplish alone. For example, no one person could build a computer from scratch. It takes some people to know how to extract raw materials from the earth, others to fashion these materials into tools and suitable parts, others to assemble parts into chips and keyboards, and so on. It is by sharing various bits of knowledge through language that humans are able to build complex machines like computers. In a sense, then, language amplifies our cognitive abilities. Indeed, most of what we regard as culture depends on language.

PERSPECTIVES ON LANGUAGE: A CULTURAL INVENTION OR A HUMAN COGNITIVE INSTINCT?

The thesis I will use to integrate the material on language is that language is a **biological specialization** unique to human communication. As Steven Pinker puts it, language is a **human instinct** (Pinker, 1994). Its acquisition and use are carried out by a specialized neural system that evolved as the human brain evolved. The idea of specialization (or instinct) means that language is a **module of cognition** with its own properties that distinguish it from other kinds of learning and reasoning. An important implication of the biological specialization theme is that all languages are fundamentally similar—that the nature of language does not depend on the culture in which it is acquired.

The notion that language is a specialized cognitive system may be contrasted with the view that language is a **cultural invention** accomplished by a *generic cognitive system*. The generic view implies that there is no specialized neural system dedicated specifically to language; rather, language learning and use are accomplished by the same neural mechanisms used to learn about cultural artifacts and other forms of general knowledge. According to the generic view, we learn and use language the way we learn animal husbandry, the Bill of Rights, or how to drive a car. The generic view implies that language was invented by human cultures in much the same way that human cultures have invented agriculture and democracy. The biological view, on the other hand, maintains that language is built into our biology—it is more analogous to knowing how to walk than to knowing how to farm or drive a car.

In section 1 of this chapter I outline the essential features of language, focusing on how the languages of the world are fundamentally similar and, as a whole, distinct from the communications of other animals and from other forms of human communication. That language is biological and not a cultural artifact is supported in the two sections that follow. In section 2 I discuss the evidence that the brain contains a language organ, and in section 3 I review the research that reveals how that organ accomplishes language comprehension. In section 4 I discuss the evolution of language. An important claim of the specialized, biological view of language is that differences in the world's languages are superficial and not fundamental, and that therefore there ought to be little effect of linguistic variation on thought. The evidence relevant to this claim is discussed in the fifth and final section. In the following chapter, on cognitive development, I discuss the evidence that children are born with a kind of preknowledge of language that gives them a leg up, so to speak, on the acquisition of language. The claim developed in that chapter is that language acquisition depends more on the instinct for language with which the child is born than it does on the specific teaching practices of the parents or other language users. I should point out that not all cognitive psychologists are enamored of the instinct theory of language and language acquisition (e.g., Bates & Snyder, 1985). In chapter 11 I will discuss theoretical and empirical work that challenges the instinct view and argues instead that language depends mostly on general learning mechanisms used to acquire a wide range of knowledge and skills.

SECTION 1: THE PROPERTIES OF LANGUAGE

Language is a communication system whereby people are able to transmit ideas by means of sounds (in this chapter I will focus mostly on spoken languages). The languages of the world are so diverse that speakers of one language cannot be understood by speakers of another language. The diversity may be misleading, however. There is a sense in which all languages are fundamentally similar and the differences superficial. As it turns out, the sense in which human languages are similar to one another is also the way in which they are fundamentally different from other forms of communication. Language is a communication system unlike the dance of bees, the calls and hoots of apes, the sounds of music, or the little visual icons used by computers.

So just what is this thing called language? In a nutshell, it is a communication system distinguished by three features. Language comprises a **vocabulary** made up of arbitrary associations between sounds and ideas. It contains a set of **grammar rules** for combining sounds to make words and sentences. And it is a system that can be implemented in any of a variety of mediums, including sounds, gestures, and pictures, although the **sound medium** is the only one used by all cultures throughout history, as far as we know. Much of what follows in this section comes from Steven Pinker's *The Language Instinct* (Pinker, 1994), a highly recommended treatise on the nature of language.

VOCABULARY

The vocabulary of any language is made up of a large number of words that constitute associations between sounds and concepts or ideas. The sounds stand for, or label, the concept. Words, then, derive their meaning from the association between sound and concept. The study of the meanings of words is called **semantics** (which may also include the study of the meaning of sentences). I discussed approaches to the nature of concepts underlying word meaning in chapter 5: Implicit and Semantic Memory. I will discuss some of the issues in how people comprehend the meaning of whole sentences later in this chapter.

One thing we can say about vocabulary is that we humans have words for virtually every thing and every idea that is relevant to the culture. We have words for ourselves, for all the animals and plants we encounter, for ideas about religion, for actions like pushing and eating, for mental states like happiness and hunger, and so on. Most adults have vocabularies on the order of tens of thousands of words (Seashore & Eckerson, 1940).

All languages have large numbers of words, but different cultures categorize at least some aspects of the world in different ways, and so devise different systems of words to refer to the categories. Consider the well-known example that English has many words for colors, while the language of the Dani Indians, a tribal people of New Guinea, has only two, one (*mola*) to refer to light colors and another (*mili*) to refer to the darker colors. Labeling of numbers is another way in which languages differ. Some preliterature cultures only have words for "one," "two," and "many" (Greenberg, 1978), whereas English has 13 primitive numbers (0–12), 7 "teen" numbers, 9 decade terms, a small number of special large-number terms like "million," and a few mathematical terms like "square root." Incidentally, and contrary to popular opinion, Eskimo people do not have a remarkable numbers of words for snow (Martin, 1986). It appears the Eskimo language has about as many words for snow (four or so) as English does.

The especially critical quality about the vocabulary of all of the world's languages is that the association between a word and its meaning is entirely arbitrary. The sound of a word tells us nothing about the meaning of the word. Another way of saying this is that words are symbols. Nothing in the sound of the word *cat* for instance, tells you that it is a feline thing that purrs, chases mice, becomes intoxicated from catnip, and arguably makes a nice pet. Instead, the sound "cat" is purely a symbol that stands for the concept or idea of a cat. And so it goes with virtually all other words. Even the very few words whose sounds supposedly have a nonarbitrary relationship with their meaning rarely in fact convey the meaning. Ducks don't really say "quack," a buzzing sound does not really sound like "buzz," and the dull crashing sound made by two pieces of metal striking one another does not really sound like "clang."

The arbitrariness of sound–concept associations is revealed in vocabulary differences among the world's languages. For instance, the word for cat is *chat* in French, *gorbeh* in Persian, and *mau* in Chinese. The word for the sound a duck makes is *gua gua* in Chinese and for the sound a pig makes is *boo boo* in Japanese. The word for "drank" as in "The boy drank the water" is *vypil* in Russian, *yasa* in Hausa (spoken in west Africa), and *upiarqan* in Quechua (spoken in western South America).

The arbitrariness of the sound–meaning association—the symbolic nature of language—gives to languages the capacity to express a wide range of ideas, including ideas that are abstract and so have no physical attributes. We have invented words for concepts as abstract as truth, justice, furniture, and God. Indeed, most words are abstract in the sense that the word refers to a class and not to a particular instantiation of the class. The word *cat*, for instance, refers to the class of cats, and not specifically to my friend Maggie's cat named Orson Welles. If words were limited to sounds that inherently contained their meaning, we would be unable to communicate the vast majority of concepts about which we think.

The symbolic quality of language does mean that language has to be transmitted by the culture. A child must learn the conventions of naming from its culture—that is, the child must memorize the meanings of words. The labels used by human languages cannot be encoded in the genes. But the propensity to make arbitrary associations between certain types of sounds and ideas can be genetically encoded. That is, we are biologically prepared to learn to connect symbols to ideas.

Because the associations between sound and meaning are arbitrary, different groups of humans are likely to invent different symbols for ideas, and as a consequence become unintelligible to other groups of humans. Indeed, much of the unintelligibility of another culture's language is due to differences in vocabulary caused by the arbitrariness of the sound–meaning association. The difficulty of cross-cultural communication, and the potential hostilities that result from this difficulty, are the price our species must pay for the flexibility to communicate a wide range of ideas.

GENERATIVE GRAMMAR

The second main distinctive feature of language is that it comprises a **generative grammar**. Generative grammar may be defined as a set of rules for combining linguistic sounds to produce words and sentences. The notion of rules as used here is to be understood as **descriptive**. The rules describe regularities in the speech of some groups of speakers. Descriptive grammar may be contrasted with **prescriptive grammar**, the kind you learn about in primary and secondary school. The notion that grammar rules are prescriptions for how we ought to talk and write is really a manifestation of the efforts of certain formally well-educated people to teach students one particular dialect of a language. Again, we are not concerned here with prescriptive grammar but only with descriptive grammar.

Descriptive grammar may also be contrasted with **mental grammar**, the linguistic rules and linguistic intuitions that may be in a person's head and may contribute to the comprehension and production of language. Strictly speaking, descriptive rules of grammar are only about the regularities observed when people use language. However, it seems likely that some kind of representation of the rules or regularities of language are stored in the brain and contribute to the comprehension and production of language. The way language is comprehended will be discussed in a subsequent section of this chapter.

There are three components of grammar: **phonology, morphology**, and **syntax**. Phonology refers to rules for combining sounds into natural-sounding words; morphology refers to rules for combining words or meaningful parts of words into new words; and syntax refers to rules for arranging words into phrases and sentences.

Grammar is said to be generative because a small number of rules make possible the creation and comprehension of an extraordinarily large number of words and utterances. A few rules of phonology enable us to generate hundreds of thousands of words from a few mostly meaningless sounds. A few rules of morphology allow us to derive many new words from a preexisting repertoire of words and word segments. A few rules of syntax enable us to generate an essentially infinite number of sentences from a vocabulary of tens of thousands of words.

Phonology

Phonological rules describe how people assemble basic linguistic sounds into words. All spoken languages are made up of a small number of discrete sounds called **phonemes**. A phoneme is the smallest unit of sound that makes a difference to the meaning of a word. For example, the word *home* contains three phonemes: the /h/ sound, the /o/ sound, and the /m/ sound. (The slashes are a linguistic convention used to indicate that the symbols inside stand for phonemes. However, I am not using the symbols usually used by linguists). If any one of these sounds is changed, then the meaning of the word changes. If the /h/ sound is replaced with /r/ then word becomes *roam*; if the /m/ sound is replaced with the /p/ sound then the word becomes *hope*; if the /o/ sound changes to /i/ then the word becomes *him*. Phonemes include both vowels and consonants. The difference is that for vowels the air flows freely through the vocal tract, whereas for consonants the vocal tract impedes the flow of air in some way.

All the world's phonemes make use of a restricted range of processes by which air may be forced through the oral cavity. Variation among phonemes is achieved by varying whether to vibrate the vocal folds (called voicing), whether to route some air through the nasal cavity, and the placement of the tongue and lips. Not all vocalizations can be phonemes. No language makes phonemes by varying the loudness of a sound, by grinding the teeth, or by squawking like Donald Duck (Pinker, 1994).

Still, there is considerable variation in the phonemes used by the languages of the world. First, languages differ in the number of phonemes they use to make words. The number of consonants in any given language ranges between 6 and 95 while the number of vowels ranges between 3 and 46 (Maddieson, 1984). The total number of phonemes used by all of the world's languages numbers in the hundreds, although any one language uses only some small subset of the world's total. A typical language uses about 23 consonants and 9 vowels. English uses about 24 consonants and 19 vowels.

Languages differ with respect to which phonemes are used. Phonemes like the /th/ sound in "these" or the click sound (usually symbolized as /!/) in some African languages are rare in the languages of the world. The relative pitch with which a combination of phonemes is spoken is a phonemic dimension in many African, Native American, and Asian languages, although not in Indo-European languages. For example, it makes no difference in English if you say the word *bat* in a higher or lower pitch than other words in the sentence—the meaning of *bat* stays the same. But in Nupe (spoken in Nigeria) if you say *ba* with a high pitch it means "to be sour" whereas if you say *ba* with a low pitch it means "to count."

Languages also differ with respect to the ways phonemes can be combined to form the tens of thousands of words that make up the lexicon of the typical language. An example of a varying phonological rule is one that has to do with the maximum number of consonants permitted at the beginning of a word. In English the maximum number of initial consonants is three (e.g., *strike*). But in Spanish the maximum number is two, in Russian the maximum number is four, and in Hebrew the maximum number is one. All languages, though, have a maximum number (Greenberg, 1977).

There are similarities among the world's languages in the rules for combining phonemes. The most fundamental similarity is that all languages have rules whereby meaningless phonemes are combined in a regular way to produce meaningful words. The meaning of words cannot be determined from the phonemes, however. Also, no language permits syllables made only of consonants.

There are restrictions on how one phoneme can be added to another phoneme. For instance, in English we make the past tense for regular verbs by adding an -*ed* ending to the verb. If the verb ends in a voiced consonant, as does *mug*, then the past tense is the voiced -*ed* ending, pronounced /mugd/. Again, voicing means that the vocal folds are vibrated. If the verb ends in a voiceless consonant, as does *muck*, then the past tense is the voiceless -*ed* ending, pronounced /mukt/. Such rules presumably make the transition between phonemes easier to accomplish in language production. While this particular past tense rule is unique to English, rules that make voicing a consonant contingent on whether some other consonant is voiced, and other such contingency rules, are found in other languages. The phonemic structure of languages makes learning how to produce and understand words considerably easier than if we had to make an entirely different kind of sound for each of the tens of thousands of words we use.

Morphology

A second component of grammar is morphology. Morphological rules describe how meaningful words and word parts may be combined to form new words whose meaning may be derived from the morphological rules. To understand morphological rules, it is helpful to understand the concept of a **morpheme**, which refers to the smallest part of a word that is meaningful. Some morphemes are analogous to atoms. They stand alone as whole words, like the morpheme *farm* and the morpheme *jump*. Other morphemes are analogous to quarks. They do not stand alone but must be part of a word to exert their meaning, like the *er* of *farmer* and the *ing* of *jumping*.

Morphological rules enable us to build words out of rules and morphemes. Even if you never heard of a wug, you know that *wugs* refers to more than one wug. In this way, morphological rules are quite different from phonological rules. One cannot guess the meaning of a new word from the phonemes that make it up—rather, the meaning must be rote-memorized. For instance, you would not know from the combination of the phonemes /m/, /u/, and /ng/ that *mung* means "to destroy." But now that you know that *mung* (a bit of computer hackerese) means to destroy, you can figure out from English morphological rules what *munged* and *unmungable* mean.

What the world's languages have in common is that they all permit words to be created by combining morphemes; and the rules for doing so generalize across morphemes with a wide range of meaning. For instance, in English we add an -*s* ending on regular nouns to make the plural. That morphological rule extends to nouns as different in meaning as *doors, gods, democracies,* and *flowers*. In English we can add *un* to the beginning of many words to mean to mean "the opposite of." That morphological rule extends to *unadjusted, unexciting, undigested,* and *unprogrammability*.

Still, there are variations in the use of morphological rules among the languages of the world. In particular, languages differ in how and how much burden they place on morphology for conveying meaning. To illustrate, consider that in English there are four forms for every regular verb. For example, ducks *quack*, a duck *quacks*, a duck *is quacking*, and a duck *quacked*. But there is much more we might want to say about an action expressed by the verb. For example, we might want to indicate that the quacking is hypothetical (the duck would have quacked) or that the quacking is ongoing (the duck continuously quacks). In English, such distinctions (technically called mood and aspect) require the use of syntactic rules—the rules for combining words to make sentences (discussed below). In some languages—Spanish, for example—morphological rules are used to make virtually all tense, mood, and aspect distinctions. Spanish has 50 different versions of any given regular verb. Kivunjo (a Bantu language) has about 500,000 possible forms for any verb (Pinker, 1994). Other languages, like Chinese, make little or no use of morphological rules to signal verb tense, mood, and aspect. In Chinese, past tense would ordinarily be made by saying something equivalent to "yesterday one duck quack."

While English has only a few inflectional rules like adding *-s* to nouns or adding *-s*, *-ed*, or *-ing* to verbs, it does permit, indeed encourage, the compounding of words to make new words. In English we have *counterprogramming*, *mousercise, disteach, indepthly*, and *Darwinism*, to name a few compound words I have encountered. Compounding rules like these are not unique to English, but in fact are common among the languages of the world.

Syntax

The third component of grammar is syntax—the rules describing how words are combined to make meaningful phrases and sentences. Syntax allows us to express relationships among concepts. With syntax we can express spatial relationships ("The dog is next to the cat"), temporal relationships ("The dog left before she ate her bone"), interactions ("The dog chased the cat"), properties of concepts ("Your dog is ugly"), and so on. Syntax enables us to make declarations ("The dog barks at night"), ask questions ("Is it your dog that keeps me awake with its incessant barking?"), and issue commands ("Get your dog to stop barking!").

As with morphology, syntax enables us to figure out the meanings of novel phrases and sentences from the meanings of words and the rules of syntax. Again, morphology and syntax stand in contrast to phonology, in that meaning cannot be determined from phonological rules. All languages have this **dual structure** as part of grammar. One rule system (phonology) enables us to create the sounds of words, but not their meanings, while the other rule system (morphology and syntax) enables us to determine the meanings of words, phrases, and sentences from their elementary parts.

Phrases

Let me begin by sketching out what the syntactic rule systems of the world's languages have in common. First, all languages have **syntactic categories** (parts of speech) that include **nouns** (e.g., *dog, truth*), **verbs** (e.g., *jump, love*), **adjectives** (e.g., *tall, nauseous*), **adverbs** (e.g., *slowly, soon*), **prepositions** (e.g., *in, before*), and **conjunctions** (e.g., *and, but*). Any given sentence is (usually) made up of words from more than one syntactic category. Most sentences minimally have a verb and a noun.

An important feature of any grammatical category, including syntactical categories, is that words from the category are all treated alike with respect to other grammar rules. For instance, all nouns can serve as subjects of a sentence, all adjectives modify nouns, and all conjunctions can combine two sentences. Furthermore, syntactical categories include words with a wide range of meanings. For instance, nouns can be as diverse in meaning as *dog, running, democracy,* and *love*.

Across the world's languages, syntactic categories are used to build *phrases*, which are parts of a sentence that behave as coherent, meaningful units within a sentence. The sentence "The frog kissed the witty princess," for instance, has two noun phrases ("the frog" and "the witty princess") and one verb phrase ("kissed the witty princess") that contains one of the noun phrases.

The coherence of phrases is revealed in two ways. First, phrases can be modified without affecting the rest of the sentence. Instead of "The frog kissed the witty princess" we could say "It kissed the witty princess." Here is a case where a pronoun can be used to replace a whole noun phrase without changing the meaning of the rest of the sentence. Or we could say "The handsome frog kissed the witty princess." Here, the insertion of an adjective into the initial noun phrase does not alter the meaning of the rest of the phrases of the sentence.

A second way the coherence of phrases is revealed is in ambiguity in the interpretation of sentences. Consider that "They are flying planes" can mean that some people are flying airplanes or that those things over there are the type of planes that fly. The ambiguity derives from the fact that sentences can sometimes be parsed in different ways. **Parsing** refers to the arranging of words into their phrases. In the "flying planes" sentence, "flying" can be the main verb of the verb phrase or can be an adjective in a noun phrase. A more comical example (quoted in Pinker, 1994) is "Dr. Ruth will discuss sex with Dick Cavett." This sentence's ambiguity derives from whether "with Dick Cavett" is a separate prepositional phrase and so describes with whom the discussion will take place, or whether "with Dick Cavett" is part of noun phrase headed by "sex," in which case what will be discussed is having sex with Dick Cavett. Cavett's wife, among others, may be quite concerned with how that sentence is parsed.

The idea that sentences are made of phrases is not just an idle piece of curiosity about language. The comprehension of a sentence depends on parsing—on establishing which words belong with which phrase. For instance, in "The frog who the cat chased kissed the princess" you know that it is the cat and not the frog doing the chasing because you understand that "who the cat chased" is a separate phrase (called a **clause**) modifying the noun phrase "the frog."

Phrases are important for another reason. As I mentioned before, most words, by themselves, are rather abstract in meaning. Consider that *duck* refers to a class of birds, while *quack* refers to a class of sounds made by ducks. Much of the time we use language to refer to more concrete senses of concepts than the words themselves supply. Phrases that contain words for the concepts allow us to make an abstract concept particular to some time and place. So I can say "My Aunt Martha's skinny little duck quacks loudly" or "The duck my pet boa constrictor tried to eat no longer quacks." Without phrases, we would be forced to invent new words for each and every instance of a concept—a virtual impossibility.

Some of the preceding examples revealed an important point about the phrases of sentences, namely, that phrases can contain phrases. Rules that permit the embedding of phrases within phrases are called **recursive rules**. A simple sentence like "The girl ran" has no embedding, but watch how recursive rules can expand on that simple sentence. We could have "The girl I used to love ran" or "The girl ran to the park next to the river I used to swim in as a young boy" or "The boy who claimed that the girl who was left at home last Saturday night ran away to the circus is mistaken." Recursive rules are a feature of all the world's languages and are a part of what makes syntax generative.

Another important universality in the syntactical systems of the world is that languages obey consistency in how they construct phrases. Some languages, like English, are said to be **head-first** languages. This means that in complex phrases, the focus of the phrase, its **syntactic head**, comes near the beginning of the phrase. So English has noun phrases such as "the warrior that she loved," where the main noun comes first; verb phrases such as "lost his mittens," where the main verb comes first; and prepositional phrases such as "in the park," where the preposition comes first. Other languages are **head-last** languages. This means that the head comes near the end of the complex phrase, and does so consistently across all types of phrases. Japanese is an example of a head-last language. In Japanese, speakers say the equivalent of "warrior his mittens park in lost" (Japanese also does not use articles like *the* and *a*). Any given language is either head-first or head-last, but not a mixture of both.

Verbs and Their Roles

Exactly how phrases might be combined to make sentences depends on the type of main verb around which the sentence is organized. Consider some sentences that sound ungrammatical: "My wife love me," "The boy killed," and "The lawyer dined the sandwich." What accounts for their ungrammatical quality?

Verbs provide the action or state that determines how a sentence conveys who does what to whom. The verb, in effect, assigns roles to the other phrases in the sentence. Examples of roles are **subject, object**, and **indirect object**. In a sentence such as "The teacher gave a book to the student" the teacher plays the role of subject, the book plays the role of object, and the student plays the role of indirect object. The verb *give* requires these roles, also known as **arguments of the predicate**. If the verb does not get its roles, the sentence is ungrammatical. The importance of role assignment of phrases is that the roles establish the relationships among the phrases in the sentence.

In the case of "My wife love me" the plural form of the verb *love* requires that the subject phrase be headed by a plural noun (so I could say "My wives love me" and be grammatical, though a bigamist). In the case of "The boy killed," the verb *kill* requires an object (as in "The boy killed the dragon") and in the case of "The lawyer dined the sandwich" the verb *dine* requires an indirect object (as in "The lawyer dined on the sandwich").

The requirement that phrases fulfill the roles dictated by verbs is true of all the world's languages. Exactly how a sentence can indicate the roles played by phrases varies among the world's languages, however. Basically, there are two ways that languages use to communicate the role of a phrase in a sentence. First, there is **word order**. In English, at least in the active-voice construction, the subject comes before the verb and the object and indirect object come after the verb. It is order that enables us English-speaking folks to distinguish between the mundane "Dog bites man" and the newsworthy "Man bites dog."

The other way languages have of assigning roles to phrases is by the use of **endings** (**inflections**) on the nouns to indicate the role played by the noun phrase. Examples of languages that use inflections are Russian, German, and Latin. In Latin, "Canem homo mordet" is news whereas "Canis hominem mordet" is mundane. In Quechua, ending a noun with a -*ta* means that it is the object of a sentence; without that inflection the noun is a subject. Centuries ago English used inflections to signal roles, and today a vestige of such an inflectional system remains in the personal pronouns. One can say "I bit the dog" or "The dog bit me" but not "Me bit the dog" nor "The dog bit I."

Transformations and Deep Structure

Many people know that Noam Chomsky, the great modern-day linguist, introduced the notion of **deep structure** into grammatical theory (Chomsky, 1957, 1965). What Chomsky was trying to show is that many sentences seem to have a similarity in the roles played by their phrases, yet the sentences have very different phrase structures.

To get a sense of deep structure, consider these sentences: "The girl hit the ball," "The ball was hit by the girl," "It was the girl who hit the ball," and "Who hit the ball?" While the placement of the phrases and the means of signaling the roles of the phrases is different in each of these sentences, the roles played by "the girl" and "the ball" in the action of hitting remain the same. The girl is doing the hitting and the ball is being hit. In the case of the "who" sentence we don't know who is doing the hitting but we do know that the interrogative pronoun *who* stands for the entity that is doing the hitting.

Chomsky would have said that these sentences have a similar deep structure. Deep structure may be defined as a description of a sentence in which all the roles associated with a verb are made explicit and put in their customary position. In the sentence "The lawyer sued the doctor" the deep structure would make explicit that the noun phrase preceding the verb is the subject and the noun phrase following the verb is the object. Any given deep structure can be expressed as several different surface structures, where surface structure is the grouping of phrases in the sentence itself.

Because there are several ways in which a deep structure may be expressed in a surface structure, one might talk of rules for converting deep into surface structures. Chomsky called these **transformational rules**, which again can be illustrated with the sentence "The lawyer sued the doctor." In a passive version of the sentence, one could say "The doctor was sued by the lawyer." Now the first noun phrase plays the role of the object and the second noun phrase plays the role of the subject. The transformations required to convert a deep structure into a passive surface structure involve the subject and object roles' swapping locations in the sentence and the insertion of the auxiliary verb (*was*) and the prepositional phrase ("by the lawyer") into the verb phrase. One could also say "The doctor was sued" and leave it at that. In this version of a passive sentence, the verb *to sue* is missing its subject role—it has been truncated. But that's okay; the verb permits the deletion of the subject role in a passive form of a surface structure. Such a deletion is another example of a transformational rule.

The reason that languages have transformational rules is to permit some flexibility in communications constrained by syntactical rule systems. Ordinarily, a sentence using the verb *to sue* requires a subject phrase and an object phrase. In English, at least, the subject phrase comes first. But what if the speaker wishes to place the emphasis on the object phrase? Or what if the speaker does not know the identity of the subject phrase? Transformations, such as rearranging and deleting phrases, give the speaker some options. The speaker might prefer to say "The doctor was sued by the lawyer" when the conversation is generally about the doctor, or to say "The doctor was sued" when the speaker does not know or wish to tell who is doing the suing.

The various aspects of generative grammar—phonology, morphology, and syntax—are summarized in Figure 10-1. Believe it or not, there is considerably more to grammar than I have sketched out here. Grammar includes qualifier rules that enable us to distinguish among sentences such as "All dogs make good pets," "No dogs make good pets," and "Some dogs do not make good pets." Other grammar rules handle time ("Dogs will make good pets"), negation ("Dogs do not make good pets"), necessity ("Dogs must make good pets"), and possibility ("Dogs might make good pets"). But I'll spare you any more grammar lessons.

Instead, let me finish this section on grammar by noting that the similarities among the grammar systems of the world have prompted some linguists to characterize them all as minor variants of a single universal grammar (Pinker, 1994). Certainly the world's grammars are more similar than they hypothetically could be. For instance, no grammar uses backward rules whereby one sentence is transformed into another by saying the words in backwards order. No grammar restricts sentences to one word or to any fixed number of words. No grammar puts markers of tense and aspect on nouns. All grammars use noun and verb phrases and permit embedding. The remarkable similarities and restrictions on the range of possibilities among the world's grammars is at least consistent with the idea that we are born with an instinct for language and that the instinct in some sense embodies the universal grammar that characterizes all human languages.

Generative Grammar

Phonology

Rules for combining sounds into meaningful words.

An English example is that a word can begin with no more than three consonants.

Morphology

Rules for combining words and word parts into new words.

An English example is adding the -s ending to nouns to make plural nouns.

Syntax

Rules for combining words into phrases and sentences. Includes syntactical rules for:

making phrases

An English example is that a noun phrase can include an article and a noun.

assigning roles to phrases

An English example is that the subject phrase comes before the verb phrase.

transforming sentences

An English example is that to convert an active sentence into a passive sentence, first reverse the locations of the subject and object phrases.

FIGURE 10–1   Summary of the major types of generative grammar rules.

LANGUAGE USES THE ORAL/AUDITORY SYSTEM

One final feature of language is important, although it does not distinguish human language from the communcation systems of some other animals. Language production uses the oral apparatus (mouth, tongue, larynx), whereas language reception uses the auditory apparatus (ears). Important advantages of using the **oral/aural system** over other plausible systems, such as hand gesture systems, are that sound waves can be transmitted in all directions, pass through many objects, and travel long distances. Furthermore, speaking frees the hands for other uses. More recently in human history, other forms of language have been invented to offset some of the disadvantages of spoken language. Written languages, first developed about 5 to 10 thousand years ago, enable a permanent record of a message to be made, and enable the message to travel great distances, without depending on a messenger's fallible memory. Sign languages, developed in communities of hearing-impaired people during the last few centuries, enable hearing-impaired people to communicate. Written and sign languages, then, are cultural inventions.

That humans have been able to invent new languages as the need arises demonstrates that the capacity to acquire and use language is not limited to one medium. In a sense, the biological capacity for language includes the capability to translate the vocabulary and grammar rules of spoken language into other mediums. Indeed, many of the neural mechanisms that underlie language serve the more abstract function of linguistic communication more than they do the more concrete function of perceiving speech and controlling the vocal apparatus. One line of evidence is that hearing-impaired children can acquire sign language as readily as hearing children acquire spoken language (I elaborate on this point in chapter 11: Cognitive Development). Moreover, brain damage in the frontal and temporal lobes that undermines spoken language (discussed later in this chapter) also undermines sign language (Poizner, Klima, & Bellugi, 1987).

HUMAN LANGUAGE AS A UNIQUE SYSTEM OF COMMUNICATION

How does human language compare with the communications of other animals? Certainly, all animals communicate with one another. Bees perform a kind of dance to communicate the location of pollen; simians (monkeys and apes) emit grunts and hoots, referred to as calls, that usually signal emotions like fear or anger; birds produce bird calls and songs that communicate reproductive readiness, territoriality, and other emotions; and cetaceans (dolphins and whales) are known to produce complex songs that seem to have rhythm and recurring themes, although the communicative intent of cetacean song is not entirely clear. In what way is human language different from the communication systems of other animals?

An important distinction between human language and the communications of other animals is that nonhuman animals lack grammar. Other animals, as far as we know, have no rules for combining their basic calls (or other meaningful units) to make new meaningful calls. Monkeys will not add a sound to their call for snake to indicate that there are lots of snakes nor combine their call for fear and their call for mating to yield a new call that might mean the kind of anxiety you feel about initiating an intimate relationship.

Similarly, there is no clear evidence that animals combine meaningful calls or songs into sentence-like constructions. Primates may repeat a call over and over, especially if the emotion they are expressing is intense. But they do not seem to combine several different calls in a rule-governed way to express a more complete and complex idea. Consequently, their communications systems are severely limited in the range of ideas about which they can communicate. A primate may know the difference between an acquaintance attacking a stranger and the stranger attacking the acquaintance, but without a syntactical system it has no way to communicate that distinction in its calls.

The communications of other animals also lack the **productivity** of human language—the human capacity for expressing an unlimited number of ideas. Productivity in human language is made possible by grammar. In this sense, grammar represents a uniquely human form of behavior and confers on human communication a power unprecedented in the communications systems of other forms of terrestrial life.

A particularly important kind of power that language confers is that of teaching people about ideas or events that they have never directly experienced. Apes may be able to reflect consciously on their past and anticipate some aspects of their future, but without a generative grammar they have no way of communicating such ideas. Consequently, their communications are tied to the here and now and so are limited in their value as a teaching device. When the ape calls out that it is ready to mate, it is not discussing its hopes for the day when it will become the alpha male, but only its state of mind here and now. Nor can an ape use its calls to teach its young to watch out for the leopard that lives across the river.

The generative nature of grammar is the main basis by which human communications can be displaced in space and time. Syntactic rules permit the expression of a virtually unlimited set of relationships among concepts. Consequently, it is easy to relate by means of language concepts that are not at the moment related in the environment. The important advantage of a communication system that communicates about displaced events is that the system can be used to teach. Through language a child can learn about the dangers lurking in the bush, the temperamental mood of an uncle when the subject of money comes up, and the linguistic evidence supporting the surface–deep distinction in grammatical theory.

The generative nature of human language has another consequence that sets it apart from other animals' communication systems. Grammar is autonomous from meaning. Consider Noam Chomsky's famous example: "Colorless green ideas sleep furiously." That sentence is grammatically impeccable, yet nonsensical. On the other hand "gimme eat," uttered by Major de Coverley when asked to sign a loyalty oath while waiting to be served dinner in Joseph Heller's *Catch-22*, makes sense but is ungrammatical. We can communicate grammatically without making sense, and communicate with sense without being grammatical. The value of the autonomy of grammar is that grammar rules can be applied to a wide range of words without regard to their meaning. In this way children need only learn a relatively few grammar rules in order to make use of an unlimited number of meaningful utterances.

Language is certainly not the only way people have of communicating ideas. Music serves as an example of another communicative system, as do facial expressions, gestures, drawings, and emotional cries and calls. Yet all of these human nonlinguistic modes of expression are severely limited in the range and precision of the ideas which they can communicate. A piece of music may move us to tears or a painting may evoke memories of a visit to the country, but neither can tell us that my uncle plans to serve my family pesto for an appetizer or that I am not standing next to a giraffe. A smile may indicate that we are happy, but not that we are happy that a rival's theory was refuted by the most recently published experiment. Language, with its huge set of arbitrary word–idea connections and its generative grammar replete with parts of speech, phrases, embeddings, role assignments, and transformational possibilities, confers on linguistic communication a unique capacity to express complex and displaced thoughts about an unlimited range of topics.

SECTION 2: THE BIOLOGY OF LANGUAGE

Section 1 described the nature of language, with an eye toward demonstrating that language is unique as a system of communication, representing a uniquely human biological specialization for solving the problem of communicating complex thoughts. The main theme of section 1 was that underlying the diversity of the world's languages are fundamental commonalities. It is the commonalities of language that the biological specialization provides.

In this section I discuss the evidence supporting the idea that there is a language organ in the brain. Evidence for a language organ reinforces the theme that language is a biological specialization and not merely the product of a general capacity for learning.

The study of the brain and the effects of brain damage have revealed two centers important in language comprehension and production (see Figure 10–2).

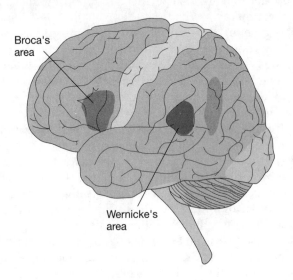

Broca's
area

Wernicke's
area

FIGURE 10–2   The locations of the primary language areas of the brain.

One center, located in and around **Broca's area**, functions to sequence the sounds of language in order to form words and to sequence the words of language in order to form sentences. The other center, located in and around **Wernicke's area**, functions to associate words (especially nouns) to their meaning. We might say, simplifying a bit, that Wernicke's area serves the semantic function while Broca's area serves the grammatical function.

BROCA'S AREA AND THE CONTROL OF GRAMMAR

The brain center for controlling grammar (phonology, morphology, and syntax) is called Broca's area, after Paul Broca (1824–1880), who first demonstrated its role in language. As shown in Figure 10–2, Broca's area is located in the posterior temporal region of the frontal lobe of the left cerebral hemisphere, at least among right-handed people. For perhaps 30% of left-handed people, Broca's area is located in either the right frontal lobe or in both frontal lobes (Springer & Deutsch, 1993). Broca's area is situated near the motor cortex that controls the speech apparatus and near the primary auditory cortex.

Most of what is known about Broca's area comes from patients who, as a result of stroke or injury, have experienced brain damage in Broca's area. Such damage produces a syndrome known as **Broca's aphasia** (Goodglass & Kaplan, 1972; Lecours, Lhermitte, & Bryans, 1983; Carlson, 1994). The full syndrome usually occurs when damage extends to the premotor cortex and the thalamus (Damasio & Geschwind, 1984). Evidence relevant to the neurophysiology of language also comes from brain imaging techniques such as positron emission tomography (PET) scans and magnetic resonance imaging (MRI).

Typically a Broca's aphasic has trouble producing fluent speech; speech tends to be slow, effortful, and poorly articulated. Broca's aphasics often report that they know what they want to say but have trouble expressing it. An example of the utterances typical of a Broca's aphasic is provided at the beginning of this chapter.

Because Broca's area is near the motor cortex, Broca's aphasia is often accompanied by motor paralysis on the right side of the body. However, the difficulties with articulation are not usually attributable to paralysis. Often the Broca's aphasic can use the articulatory apparatus to perform nonverbal tasks, like blowing out a match. Furthermore, the speech of the Broca's aphasic will often take the form of producing two or three well-articulated words, followed by a heightened difficulty in articulation.

Broca's aphasics would seem to have difficulty executing the motor program that combines phonemes. They tend to engage in what may be called simplifying strategies for combining phonemes. For example, phonemes may be dropped from consonant clusters (e.g., pronouncing *prince* as *pince*) or one phoneme will be substituted for another so as to make the transition between phonemes easier (e.g., pronouncing *book* as *gook*). In fact, young children display many of the same simplifying strategies in their articulation. An interpretation is that the Broca's aphasic is experiencing difficulties, not so much in articulating individual phonemes, as in executing phonological rules—the combining of phonemes to produce words and phrases.

Damage to Broca's area also interferes with the morphological and syntactical aspects of grammar. Just as the Broca's aphasic tends to simplify the process of combining phonemes, so too does the Broca's aphasic tend to adopt what might be called a simplified grammar for combining morphemes to make words and combining words to make sentences. For example, the sentences of the (English-speaking) Broca's aphasic's speech often lack morphological inflections such as the *-ed* ending to make a verb past tense, and lack auxiliary verbs and articles (e.g., *was* and *the*) necessary to establish syntactic phrases and the roles played by the phrases in sentences. Their sentences seem to have a telegraphic style, which is also typical of young children. (Unlike the young children's sentences, though, the sentences of the Broca's aphasic are usually longer than two or three words). Broca's aphasics might produce sentences such as "Me go P.T. nine o'cot." Verbs are more likely to be dropped from a sentence than are nouns. When verbs are used, they are often in the nominal form (e.g., *running*, *hitting*) even in sentences where nominal verbs are not appropriate. The fact that damage to frontal cortex can interfere with use of verbs and with the grammar of language reinforces the view that verbs provide the basis for assigning the roles played by phrases in a sentence (Damasio & Damaio, 1992).

It is sometimes asserted that the Broca's aphasic has normal comprehension skills, so that the function of Broca's area is to produce speech. It is true that comprehension usually seems normal in the Broca's aphasic. However, careful testing reveals that many Broca's aphasics have difficulty understanding sentences that are grammatically complex (Caramazza & Zurif, 1976; Heilman & Scholes, 1976; Schwartz, Saffran, & Marin, 1980). For example, in a sentence like "The boy who Bill thinks is smart kissed the girl," a Broca's aphasic is likely to think incorrectly that it is Bill who is smart and who kissed the girl. On the other hand, in a sentence like "The banana that Bill ate is ripe," the Broca's aphasic is likely to comprehend correctly that it is the banana and not Bill that is ripe. In the latter but not former sentence one does not need to know much about the grammar of the sentence to be able to assign the roles to the phrases expressed in the sentence. So it seems appropriate to characterize the function of Broca's area as regulating the use of grammar in both the comprehension and production of language.

It should be noted that the description just given of the language difficulties of Broca's aphasics is that of a typical Broca's aphasic. In many cases damage is not confined to Broca's area, and so other language difficulties may arise. Furthermore, the severity of the aphasia depends on the exact location and extent of the brain damage.

Why is it that the cortex in and around Broca's area, and not some other portion of the brain, has a grammatical function? It appears that Broca's area is involved in grammar because of its proximity to the auditory cortex important in speech recognition and to the motor cortex that controls the movements of the speech apparatus. Sequential processing tends to characterize all of the motor cortex, because all motor acts require a coordinated sequence of actions. Sequential processing also characterizes the way phonemes are combined and the way morphological and syntactical rules are implemented (Lieberman, 1984).

WERNICKE'S AREA AND THE ASSOCIATION BETWEEN IDEAS AND WORDS

As shown in Figure 10–2, the center important in associating ideas to words is found in and around the area of the cerebral cortex called Wernicke's area, located in the left temporal lobe posterior to Broca's area. Wernicke's area is named after Carl Wernicke (1848–1905), who first discovered it. Again, for perhaps about 30% of left-handed people, Wernicke's area is located in the right temporal lobe or is in both temporal lobes (Springer & Deutsch, 1993).

Damage to Wernicke's area produces a syndrome called **Wernicke's aphasia** (Goodglass & Kaplan, 1972; Lecours, Lhermitte, & Bryans, 1983). The typical Wernicke's aphasic produces effortless and rapid speech that seems grammatical. Unlike Broca's aphasics, the speech of English-speaking Wernicke's aphasics will contain endings like *-ed*; grammatical words like *the*, and verbs. But their speech seems nonsensical, and includes an inordinate number of *its*, *things*, and pronouns like *he* rather than more precise labels like *table*, *democracies*, or *Bill Smith*. For example, a Wernicke's aphasic shown the same picture as the one shown to the Broca's aphasic described at the beginning of the chapter produced: "Well this . . . mother is away her working out o'here to get her better, but when she's working the two boys looking in the other part. One their small tile into her time here . . ." (Blumstein, 1982).

Wernicke's aphasics usually have difficulty comprehending both spoken and written language. The kinds of words the Wernicke's aphasic usually has trouble with are those that refer to conceptual categories labeled by nouns (animals, proper names, body parts, and so on). Often such patients have no trouble retrieving verbs. A variety of evidence suggests that the mediation between word and abstract concepts, like "animal," takes place in the more posterior regions of the left temporal lobe, while mediation between word and more specific concepts, like "raccoon," takes place in the more anterior portions of the left temporal lobe (Damasio & Damasio, 1992).

Although their speech usually seems grammatical, Wernicke's aphasics sometimes seem to abandon one grammatical pattern for another right in the middle of a sentence. The incoherent nature of much of the speech of Wernicke's aphasics and their tendency to shift the grammar of sentences in midstream, as it were, may not necessarily reveal a problem in constructing a grammatical pattern. If the Wernicke's aphasic is having trouble associating words to ideas and ideas to words, then the feedback essential for keeping the sentence stream "on target" will be undermined. Consequently their speech will seem to ramble. But the rambling will still sound fluent and grammatical.

It seems, then, that Wernicke's aphasics are able to execute the linguistic programs necessary to speak grammatically, a function carried out by their intact Broca's area. They have trouble with accessing the meanings of words (especially nouns), given the word, and with retrieving the words, given an idea they have in mind.

As with Broca's aphasics, there is a great deal of symptom variability among Wernicke's aphasics depending on the exact location and extent of the brain damage. Furthermore, many brain-damaged patients show evidence of damage in several places and so have symptoms of both Broca's and Wernicke's aphasia.

Why is it that cortex in and around Wernicke's area, and not some other portion of the brain, is what accomplishes the function of making an association between a word and its idea? Again, the location of Wernicke's area seems critical. As shown in Figure 10-2, Wernicke's area is near the auditory and visual cortex important in perceiving words and it is close to other perceptual centers that detect and represent the physical characteristics of concepts, especially concepts denoted by nouns. Wernicke's area is directly connected to Broca's area, with which it must coordinate its function in order to comprehend and produce language that is both grammatical and meaningful.

A variety of techniques exist for developing images of the brains of alive and awake people. The results of studies using brain scanning technology, including PET and MRI, suggest that circuits of neural tissue involved in grammar and semantics (word–idea association) are more complex and widely distributed than is implicit in the model I have sketched out thus far (see Posner & Carr, 1992, for a review). Nevertheless, most of the brain imaging research, as well as the brain damage evidence, suggests that the brain separates the grammatical and semantic functions of language and that Broca's area and Wernicke's area play important and differentially specialized roles (Posner & Carr, 1992; Bock, 1990; Garrett, 1990).

That there is an area of the brain specifically dedicated to language reinforces the theme that language reflects a biological specialization and is not merely the product of a general capacity to learn and process information. Still, one might argue that the only reason that Broca's area and Wernicke's area end up playing a role in language is because Broca's area is located near the auditory perceptual system and the oral motor system. The presumed linguistic neural tissue itself may not be specialized for language; it just happens to be the most likely tissue used when language is encountered. Similarly, we do not need to postulate a specialized neural system for baseball batters processing pitched baseballs. But certainly the batter's visual system and the batter's motor system for moving the arms will inevitably be involved in hitting baseballs.

Supporting the language specialization theme, however, is sign language. Brain damage evidence (e.g., Poizner, Klima, & Bellugi, 1987) proves that sign language makes use of the same area of the brain as does spoken language, even though signing involves vision and the movement of fingers. Furthermore, language processing, especially the grammar of sentences and the semantics of words, takes place more in one cerebral hemisphere, usually the left, than in the other. Clearly, then, Broca's area and Wernicke's area are specialized for language, and are not merely an undifferentiated piece of cortical tissue used for general-purpose information processing.

SECTION 3: LANGUAGE COMPREHENSION

It is not enough to describe only where in the brain grammatical and semantic functions are performed or that the brain anatomically separates these functions. The question remains, how does the brain process grammar and associate words to ideas? Some neural simulation work, in the form of neural net models, offers an admittedly speculative approach to the ways and means of the brain's language organ (see Bock, 1990; McClelland & Rumelhart, 1981, 1986a; Forster, 1990; Kawamoto, 1993; MacWhinney, Leinbach, Taraban, & McDonald, 1989). Less speculative, but also less neural, are models of comprehension that focus on a purely functional characterization of how the brain accomplishes language comprehension.

In this section I will discuss the functional characteristics of language comprehension. I will cover the perception of linguistic sounds, the comprehension of words, the comprehension of sentences, and the comprehension of discourses, such as conversations and short stories. My review will necessarily be selective. I cannot, in a portion of a chapter, or even in several chapters, review all the issues involved in comprehending language. The interested reader is referred to Carroll (1994) for a more extensive discussion of language comprehension and for a discussion of how language is produced.

THE PERCEPTION OF SPEECH

The comprehension of spoken language requires that the comprehender identify from the sound waves the phonemes, syllables, and words in the speech signal. Speech perception is sometimes described as a biological miracle (Pinker, 1994). Part of its miraculous nature lies in the difference between what is objectively in the sound wave of speech and what is actually perceived by the listener. For instance, we hear speech as a stream of separate words. Yet in the sound wave produced by speakers there are no little silences between spoken words, as there are spaces between written words. You can be made aware of the lack of sound wave gaps in ordinary speech by listening to a conversation in an unfamiliar foreign language. It is difficult to tell where one word ends and another word begins.

Although spoken words are collections of phonemes, the phonemes cannot readily be perceived as meaningful in isolation. For instance, if you were to cut up a tape recording of someone saying "dog," you would not get pieces of sound waves that sounded anything like /d/, /o/, or /g/, as you would get individual letters if you were to cut up the printed word *dog*. The acoustical information corresponding to a single phoneme in a word is actually spread throughout most of the sound wave that corresponds to the whole word. Despite that spreading, the brain perceives the sound wave as a series of phonemes. To put it succinctly, the brain makes an analogical-to-digital conversion of the speech sound wave.

Speech perception is miraculous for other reasons. Speech is an extraordinarily fast way to get information into the brain through the ears. Good Morse code operators can recognize about 3 units per second. When a sound like a click is repeated at a rate greater than about 20 clicks per second, we hear not separate sounds but a low buzz. In contrast, we can hear distinct phonemes and the words they constitute when played as fast as 45 phonemes per second in artificially accelerated speech (ordinary speech transmits about 15 phonemes per second) (Liberman, Cooper, Shankweiler, & Studdert-Kennedy, 1967).

What is especially intriguing about speech perception is that the sound waves that correspond to a single phoneme change quite a bit depending on the other phonemes that come before and after the given phoneme. These changes occur even within an individual person's speech. The sound wave that corresponds to /d/, for instance, is different if the /d/ is followed by /a/, /i/, or /u/. Yet we perceive /d/ as identical in the spoken words *daft*, *dip*, and *dug*. Again, written letters are not that way. The printed *d* looks the same in the printed forms of *daft*, *dip*, and *dug*.

The reason that the sound of any given phoneme varies depending on its phonemic context has to do with **coarticulation**. As the mouth positions itself for a phoneme, it makes adjustments so as to make as easy as possible the production of the next phoneme. You can understand the adjustment if you pay close attention to where you place your tongue when you say "Cape Cod." Note that the tongue body is in different positions when it makes the two /k/ sounds, because the tongue is preparing for the vowel that follows the /k/ (Pinker, 1994). These minute adjustments alter the sound waves. Despite the alteration, the brain (of an English-speaking person) perceives the two /k/ sounds as identical.

Researchers studying speech perception have wondered whether speech is processed in the same way as are nonlinguistic sounds (e.g., the sound of a strummed guitar, the sound made by an accelerating sports car) or whether the speech signal activates a mechanism specifically designed to process only speech (Goldstein, 1996). Our ability to comprehend speech spoken at very rapid rates suggests that speech sounds are perceived in a different way than are nonlinguistic sounds. Perhaps one aspect of the language instinct is a **specialized speech perception mechanism**.

A model of speech perception that reflects its putative specialized nature is called the **motor theory of speech perception** (Liberman, Cooper, et al., 1967; for a discussion see Miller, 1990, or Goldstein, 1996). According to motor theory, the perception of speech is closely linked to the production of speech. A specialized module of neurons tries to recreate the activity of the vocal tract that produced the acoustic signals. That is, the module determines which phonetic features produced the acoustic signal. Phonetic features refer to whether a phoneme is voiced (accompanied by a vibration of the vocal folds) (e.g., /d/) or not voiced (e.g., /t/); the place of articulation, as when a stop consonant is made by placing the tongue at the lips (e.g., /p/) or at the roof of the mouth (e.g., /t/); and the manner of articulation, as when a consonant is oral (e.g., /b/) or nasal (e.g., /m/). The module involved in speech perception is activated only by speech, giving speech perception its special and distinct status. By the way, the motor theory does not claim that the perceivers literally have to talk to themselves in order to understand speech. Rather, the theory claims that some unconscious process figures out how the speech was produced, in order to perceive it.

One line of research initially taken as evidence for a specialized speech perception mechanism is referred to as **categorical perception**. Categorical perception is the phenomenon in which people have difficulty perceiving differences between linguistic sounds that are variants of the same phoneme. I will illustrate categorical perception of speech with the perception of the stop consonants /d/ and /t/. The main difference between the articulation of /d/ and the articulation of /t/ is that /d/ is produced with an accompanying vocal fold vibration within about 30 milliseconds after the tongue stops the flow of air. That is, /d/ is voiced. For /t/, the vibration occurs after a delay of at least about 30 milliseconds; that is, /t/ is unvoiced. The delay between stopping the flow of air and vibrating the vocal folds is called **voice-onset-time**.

People cannot easily vary their voice-onset-times with any degree of precision, but it is possible for voice synthesizers to vary quite precisely voice-onset-time. The interesting finding is that people have difficulty perceiving any difference between two sounds from the same phonemic set, but readily perceive a difference between two sounds from different sets (e.g., Liberman, Harris, et al., 1961; see Yeni-Komshian, 1993, for a review). For instance, a listener will not perceive any difference between a syllable with a voice-onset-time of 0 and a syllable with a voice onset time of 20 milliseconds (both are perceived as "di"), nor between a syllable with a voice-onset-time of 40 milliseconds and a syllable with a voice-onset-time of 60 milliseconds (both are perceived as "ti"). But the listener will easily perceive the difference between a syllable with a voice-onset-time of 20 milliseconds and one with a voice-onset-time of 40 milliseconds (the first will be perceived as "di," the second as "ti"). Yet the objective difference in all three cases is 20 milliseconds. But the contrast between 20 and 40 milliseconds of voice-onset-time is the only one that is readily perceived (based on Yeni-Komshian & LaFontaine, 1983).

It was at one time thought that categorical perception was unique to speech. However, categorical perception has been found for nonspeech sounds (Miller, Wier, Postore, Kelly, & Dooling, 1976) and in nonhuman animals including chinchillas (Kuhl, 1986) and monkeys (May, Moody, & Stebbins, 1989). Because nonhuman animals do not have speech, the argument that categorical perception reflects the specialized nature of speech perception was undermined.

Another line of evidence that has been offered as support specifically for the motor theory of speech perception is based on research that shows that watching a speaker's lips, mouth, and tongue influences the perception of the speaker's speech. This research is known as the **McGurk effect**, after the researcher who first demonstrated it. McGurk and MacDonald (1976; see also Dodd, 1977; Green, Kuhl, Meltzoff, & Stevens, 1991) presented to their subjects a film in which a person mouthed syllables, such as "ga," but the sound that simultaneously accompanied the vocalization was a different syllable, such as "ba." The remarkable result was that subjects seemed to combine both channels of information in their actual perception of the sound. In the case of seeing "ga" and hearing "ba," subjects actually perceived hearing "da." Notice that /g/ is made by stopping the flow of air near the back of the mouth, /b/ is made by stopping the flow at the lips, and /d/ is made by stopping the flow near the front of the mouth. So it was as if the speech perception process constructed a compromise interpretation of the conflicting information. The speech perception process functionally combined the information in the sound wave ("ba") with the information in the lip movements ("ga") to produce a perception of a phoneme ("da") that falls in between the actual stimuli.

But does the McGurk demonstration that observing speech production affects the perception of speech constitute evidence for a close link between speech production and perception? Probably not (Goldstein, 1996). Salsana and Rosenblum (1993) have created a similar effect with nonspeech stimuli. Their subjects saw a person pluck the string of a cello while listening to a tape recording of a person bowing the string. The subjects rated the perceived sound as sounding more pluck-like than did subjects who saw the person bowing the cello.

The Comprehension of Words

Obviously, language comprehension does not end with merely perceiving the phonemic content of a sound wave. The brain also has the semantic task of assigning meanings to words. Although there are a number of issues surrounding the comprehension of word meaning, the issue I will take up has to do with one aspect of the brain's semantic task—**ambiguity resolution**. Many words, indeed most words, have more than one meaning. Take the word *take*. It has at least 41 separate meanings. *Bug* has an insect meaning, a spy meaning, a defect meaning, and an annoy meaning. *Tire* has a wheel meaning and a fatigue meaning. How does the brain figure out which meaning is appropriate?

There seem to be at least two possible ways by which the brain's linguistic system might resolve ambiguity in the meaning of a word. One is that the system homes in on the intended meaning right from the get-go. Perhaps from contextual cues, the system builds some kind of model of a sentence's meaning that biases the system to pick one meaning and no other when it confronts the ambiguous word. The other possibility assumes a somewhat more mindless approach in which the brain's linguistic system initially selects all of the possible meanings and then lets contextual cues reinforce one of the meanings while the other meanings fade away. Introspection might seem to support the former, because we are usually aware of accessing only one of an ambiguous word's meanings. In fact, though, at least some research suggests the latter. The linguistic system first reflexively selects all the meanings, then discards the irrelevant ones.

The evidence that the linguistic system initially considers all meanings is based on an ingenious experimental paradigm in which subjects listen to sentences containing ambiguous words while simultaneously judging whether letter strings presented on a screen are words (Swinney, 1979; also see Seidenberg, Tanenhaus, Leiman, & Bienkowski, 1982). The paradigm is called the **cross-modal priming paradigm** (for a review of studies using the paradigm, see Simpson, 1984).

In the Swinney (1979) experiment, one of the passages to which subjects listened was the following:

> Rumor had it that, for years, the government building had been plagued with problems. The man was not surprised when he found several spiders, roaches, and other bugs in the corner of his room.

In this passage, *bugs* clearly refers to insects, not to surveillance devices used by spies. When the ambiguous word *bugs* was heard, subjects simultaneously saw a letter string on the screen and had to press one of two buttons to indicate whether the string was or was not a word (called a lexical decision task). Sometimes the letter strings weren't words. In the case when they were, the visual word could be related to the ambiguous spoken word in one of three ways. It could be related to the relevant meaning (as is the word *ant*), it could be related to the irrelevant meaning (as is *spy*), or it could be unrelated to any of the ambiguous word's meanings (as is *sew*).

It is well known that the reaction time to make lexical decisions is speeded up when a previously encountered word is related in meaning (Meyer & Schvaneveldt, 1971; Ehrlich & Rayner, 1981). For example, subjects will more quickly judge that the letter string *bear* is an English word if they have just read the word *lion* than if they have just read the word *loin*. In Swinney's cross-modal paradigm, subjects were similarly faster at recognizing that *ant* was a word than that *sew* was a word when they were listening to *bugs*. Surprisingly, the **priming effect**, as this effect is called, worked just as well with the irrelevant meaning of *bugs*. Subjects were also faster at recognizing that *spy* was a word than that *sew* was a word when they were listening to *bugs*, even though the prior context made it clear that only the insect meaning of *bugs* was intended. The implication is that the brain's linguistic system initially activates all of the meanings of an ambiguous word. If there was a delay of a few syllables between the ambiguous word and the letter string, then reaction time was speeded up only for the letter string related to the relevant meaning (e.g., only to *ant*). The implication is that after a few hundred milliseconds, the linguistic system manages to discard the irrelevant meanings of an ambiguous word.

Rarely do interpretations of influential experiments stand unchallenged. In a recent review, MacDonald, Pearlmutter, and Seidenberg (1994) pointed out that there are situations in which only one meaning of an ambiguous word is selected. Consider that for many words, some meanings are used much more often than other meanings. For instance, *port* can mean a harbor or the left side of a ship, among other possibilities. For most people, the harbor meaning is used more frequently than the left-side meaning. Research suggests that if the context favors the higher frequency meaning of a word, the tendency is for only that meaning to be accessed. If context favors a low-frequency meaning, the tendency is for both the higher and lower frequency meanings to be activated. If context favors a meaning that is about equal in frequency to another meaning, as in the case of the insect and surveillance equipment meanings of *bugs*, then again both meanings may be accessed.

THE COMPREHENSION OF SENTENCES

The comprehension of sentences is not merely a matter of stringing together the concepts activated by the semantic portion of the linguistic system. If that were all there were to sentence comprehension, we would be unable to tell "man bites dog" from "dog bites man." We wouldn't have a clue as to who did the slaying and who did the loving in "The warrior the minister loved slew the dragon." "Buffalo buffalo buffalo Buffalo buffalo" wouldn't be a meaningful sentence, and the retort "Purple people?" to the line "One eyed one horned flying purple people eater" wouldn't have been funny when Sheb Wooley and his chorus sang it back in 1958. In order to comprehend sentences, the brain's linguistic system needs to identify the phrases of a sentence and to assign the proper role to those phrases in the action or state expressed by the verb. I'm talking syntax.

Syntactic Ambiguity

In the previous section on the comprehension of words, I focused on ambiguity resolution. Similarly, here I will highlight some of the mechanisms involved in identifying phrases and assigning roles to phrases, by considering syntactic ambiguity. Phrases (e.g., "flying planes") and whole sentences (e.g., "The shooting of the hunters is disturbing") are frequently ambiguous. Consider this pair of sentences: "The judge believed the defendant and threw out the charges" and "The judge believed the defendant was lying." Initially, the noun phrase "the defendant" is ambiguous with respect to its role in the sentence. It is only determined later whether "the defendant" is the direct object of the verb "believed" or the subject of the "lying" clause.

How is such syntactic ambiguity resolved? One possibility is that the brain's linguistic system somehow computes several syntactic arrangements for any given string of words it encounters and then lets the context provided by the whole sentence or other sentences select one of the arrangements. Such a possibility would be analogous to what sometimes happens when accessing the meanings of ambiguous words. The idea that the linguistic system computes several syntactic interpretations for phrases and sentences seems unlikely, however. In particular, we wouldn't experience some sentences, such as "The prime number few" and "The fat people eat accumulates" as **garden path sentences** (Pinker, 1994). A garden path sentence is one in which an ambiguous phrase such as "the prime number" is initially given the wrong grammatical interpretation ("number" placed in noun phrase) that must later be corrected ("number" is the verb) to make sense of the sentence. The only way we could experience a sentence as a garden path is if the linguistic system committed itself to only one syntactic interpretation.

Minimal Attachment

How, then, does the brain's linguistic system resolve syntactic ambiguity? On what basis does it decide to which phrase structure and role assignment to commit? One of the likely ambiguity-resolving strategies is called **minimal attachment**, whereby the linguistic system attempts to parse a sentence so as to create the simplest syntactic structure.

The idea of a simple syntactic structure can again be illustrated with a sentence fragment: "The judge believed the defendant. . . ." When the brain's linguistic system first encounters the fragment, it prefers to assume that "the defendant" is the direct object of the verb "believed." This interpretation yields a structure that can be drawn like an upside-down tree (see the upper panel of Figure 10-3). The biggest branches constitute a potential sentence: One

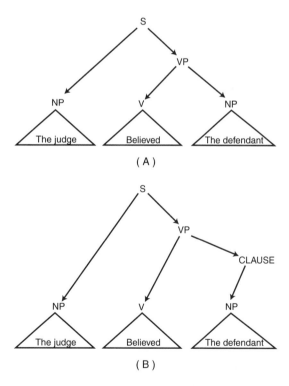

FIGURE 10–3   The upper panel depicts the simpler parse of the phrase "The judge believed the defendant." In the case where the whole sentence turns out to be "The judge believed the defendant was lying," that parse proves faulty and is replaced by the more complex parse in the lower panel.

branch holds the noun phrase ("the judge") and the other holds the verb phrase, from which two more branches sprout, one holding the verb ("believed") and the other holding the noun phrase "the defendant." I count four main branches in all.

But it is possible that "the defendant" is not believed at all, as in the case of the complete sentence: "The judge believed the defendant was lying." Why doesn't the brain's linguistic system initially assume that "the defendant" might be a subject of an entire complementary clause, as "the defendant was lying" is technically called? Too many branches. To describe the complementary interpretation, illustrated in the bottom panel of Figure 10-3, the sentence's structure would require the sentence to have a branch between the noun phrase ("the judge") and the verb phrase ("believed ..."), the verb phrase to have a branch between the verb ("believed") and the clause, and the clause to have a branch between the noun phrase ("the defendant") and the complement's verb phrase ("was lying"). I count five branches to describe this complementary interpretation of the sentence fragment "The judge believed the defendant. . . ." The brain prefers the simpler interpretation of the syntax, unless that interpretation later proves wrong.

That we initially assume the interpretation with the simpler syntactic structure suggest that simplification of structure is a bias built into the linguistic system used to parse sentences. At any rate, a variety of research supports the prediction that people prefer the minimally attached interpretation of syntactically ambiguous sentences (see Carroll, 1994). In a typical study, subjects have their eye movements monitored while reading sentences that are syntactically ambiguous. The usual result is that reading time is longer for phrases and sentences that end up violating the minimal attachment principle (e.g., "The judge believed the defendant was lying") than for sentences that follow the principle (e.g., "The judge believed the defendant and threw out the charges") (Frazier, 1987; Rayner, Carlson, & Frazier, 1983).

Traces of Roles

I mentioned before that verbs are not always given all the roles they want, although, as Mick Jagger might have put it, they get what they need. Recall that languages permit flexibility as to which roles associated with a verb must be filled in an actual sentence. So we can have "I made mistakes" or "Mistakes were made." In some cases such flexibility produces ambiguity. Consider the sentence "This is the rabbit I want to visit." In meaning #1 of the sentence, the self is doing the visiting and the rabbit is the object of the visit (I want to visit the rabbit). But in meaning #2, it is the rabbit doing the visiting and the self that is the object of the visit (I want the rabbit to visit me). The ambiguity is created by the syntactic device that allows speakers to highlight a noun phrase (the rabbit) by bringing it toward the front of the sentence. When "the rabbit" is brought forward, it vacates its usual position as a subject or object of "visit."

A currently popular theory of comprehension claims that the brain's linguistic system tends to compute the roles even when they are missing from, or

Meaning #1

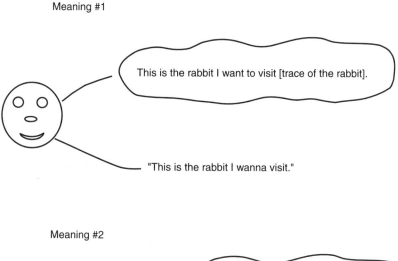

Meaning #2

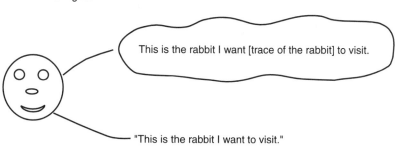

FIGURE 10–4   Traces of rabbits. The balloons depict the linguistic system's analysis of the intended sentence and the quotations depict the actual spoken version of the sentence. The inaudible and hypothetical trace of the rabbit in each intended sentence is indicated in parentheses. Note that when the trace of the rabbit is located between "want" and "to," the contraction of "want to" into "wanna" is blocked in the spoken sentence.

are misplaced in, the sentence (Pinker, 1994). Linguists describe this computation as **forming a trace** of the missing (or misplaced) role. The rabbit sentence illustrates the point. Suppose that the intention is that the self visits the rabbit. The speaker can contract "... want to ..." and say "This is the rabbit I wanna visit." But if the intention is that the rabbit visits the self, the speaker would resist the contraction and say "This is the rabbit I want to visit."

The explanation (L. White, 1989) is that the linguistic system computes a trace of the rabbit for the verb *to visit* (see Figure 10-4). In meaning #1, the trace is placed after "to visit" in order to indicate that the (missing) object of the visit is the rabbit. In meaning #2, the trace is placed just before "to visit" (between "want" and "to visit") in order to indicate that the (missing) subject of the visit is the rabbit. When the trace of the rabbit is placed between "want" and "to visit," the linguistic system resists contracting "want to" to "wanna." The trace of the missing rabbit blocks the contraction.

Other evidence that the brain's linguistic system computes traces comes from experiments measuring mental workload. In the relevant workload research (e.g., Garnsey, Tanenhaus, & Chapman, 1989; Kluender & Kutas, 1993; see Pinker, 1994), subjects are given sentences and must concurrently detect blips presented on a computer screen or must decide if letter strings presented on the screen are actual English words (the latter is the lexical decision task). As long as a verb is without a role, reaction time to detect the blip is slowed down, and EEG similarly shows evidence of mental strain. If an experimenter flashes the word associated with the trace (*rabbit*) at the time the trace is reached (just after "wanna visit"), lexical decision time to recognize the word is faster than for other words. It is as if at that point in the sentence the linguistic system inserts the noun phrase into its ordinary place in order to assign to it its proper role in the sentence.

A proper understanding of the relationships among words in a sentence, then, requires a linguistic system that must match phrases with the roles required of verbs. Presumably the trace operation reflects this matching process. Indeed, there is even a model of Broca's aphasia that claims that the main deficit associated with damage to Broca's area is an inability to match phrases to traces (Cornell, Fromkin, & Mauner, 1993).

DISCOURSES AND PRAGMATICS

Discourses and Causal Bridging

Sentences are rarely comprehended in isolation. Language comprehension depends not only on word and sentence comprehension but also on knowledge of the nature of **discourses**, such as stories, conversations, lectures, poems, and so on. To see how we use discourse knowledge in language comprehension, consider the following story fragment about Mary:

> "Mary heard the ice cream truck coming down the street. She remembered her birthday money. She ran into the house."

Let me ask you, where is Mary's birthday money? The answer is that it is in the house. Who does "she" refer to in the second and third sentences? The answer is "Mary." Why did Mary run into the house? The answer is that she was going to get money to buy ice cream. What is the expected outcome of the story? The answer is that Mary is going to eat an ice cream cone. How old is Mary? It seems that she is a young girl. These answers are not explicitly a part of the sentences of the story but are inferred from relationships among the sentences.

Knowledge of discourses enables the language comprehender to infer the conceptual relationships among the sentences necessary to understand the discourse. Note how different the inferences would be in the Mary story if the phrase "birthday money" were changed to "gun." Now why did Mary run into her house? Does she still plan to purchase an ice cream cone? Is she still the cute 9-year-old from the birthday money story? Changing the discourse topic radically alters the connections among the sentences.

How do people process discourses so as to understand the relationships among sentences of the discourse? As it turns out, there are a variety of kinds of relationships that connect sentences. To mention a few, integration of sentences sometimes requires determining the referents for pronouns (e.g., "She" refers to "Mary"), the temporal relationship among events depicted by sentences (e.g., "Mary heard the ice cream truck. She had been thinking about buying an ice cream cone"), and changes in topic (e.g., "Mary finished eating the ice cream cone. Now she was ready to begin her first day at school").

The kind of conceptual relationship, or bridge, that I will focus in this section is the **causal relationship** between two sentences. A causal bridge establishes that one sentence is the antecedent for which a second sentence is the consequent, as in the example where "She remembered her birthday money" provides the antecedent for "She ran into the house." Causal bridges might also establish the reasons or motives for events (e.g., "Mary was really hungry. No wonder the stale cookies tasted good to her."). I focus on causal bridges because they are among the most important in integrating the sentences of discourses (Singer, Halldorson, Lear, & Andrusiak, 1992).

How does a person infer the causal relationships among the sentences that make up a discourse? One reasonable possibility is that the ideas expressed in a discourse activate a variety of kinds of world knowledge, which are then used to build the causal bridge between sentences of a discourse. For example, in the story about Mary, the phrase "the ice cream truck" is likely to trigger a memory of the sequence of events that usually takes place when one encounters ice cream trucks on a warm summer evening. Such sequences of events are sometimes called **scripts** (Schank & Abelson, 1977). The script for the ice cream truck might include running inside to get money to buy an ice cream cone. The knowledge contained in that script can be used to infer that Mary is getting money in order to buy ice cream from the driver of the truck. Had Mary gone into the house to get her gun, then a very different knowledge structure—a different script—would have been activated and a very different set of causal relationships would have been established.

One implication of this analysis of causal bridges is that it should be more difficult to comprehend the relationship between sentences when it is difficult to obtain the prerequisite world knowledge on which to base the antecedent (Haviland & Clark, 1974; Just & Carpenter, 1978; Keenan, Baillet, & Brown, 1984; Singer et al., 1992). To illustrate, Singer et al. (1992) presented subjects with pairs of sentences such as "Mary poured the water on the bonfire. The fire went out." and "Mary placed the water by the bonfire. The fire went out." Subjects took longer to read the second sentence ("The fire went out.") when it was preceded by "Mary placed the water by the bonfire" than when it was preceded by "Mary poured the water on the bonfire." In the case where the first sentence explicitly supplied the antecedent ("poured") for the fire going out, it was easy for the subjects to obtain the prerequisite world knowledge necessary to construct the causal bridge. In the case where the first sentence did not explicitly provide the antecedent for the fire going out, then subjects had to infer the antecedent from their general knowledge of water and fires—a mental operation that takes additional time.

Other research establishes that people's memory for discourses improves as the number of causal relationships among sentences in a discourse increases (Graesser, Robertson, Lovelace, & Swinehart, 1980; Omanson, 1982; Millis, Graesser, and Haberlandt, 1993; Dooling & Lachman, 1971). When causal relationships are lacking or are obscure, memory for the discourse is typically poor.

One line of evidence for the importance of causal relationships in memory for discourse comes from studies of stories. Stories from Western cultures typically take place in some particular time and place where some main character tries to obtain some goal or resolve some dilemma. Usually there is some complication that impedes the main character's quest, and the character usually reacts to the complication in a series of episodes that finally result in a resolution. Other cultures have different story conventions. In some Alaskan Native American cultures, for example, a typical short story follows the principle of "fours"; it consists of four episodes, four main characters, four instruments, and so on.

Research has established that subjects find it easier to comprehend a story if it conforms to their culture's story conventions than if the story does not (e.g., Kintsch & van Dijk, 1978; Mandler, 1978; Mandel & Johnson, 1984). For example, Kintsch (1977) found that American college students were able to write better summaries of stories from Boccaccio's *Decameron*, which follow Western story structure conventions, than of Alaskan Native American stories translated into English. Yet the individual sentences that made up the Alaskan Native American stories were as easy to understand as the individual sentences that made up the *Decameron* stories. Presumably, knowledge of Western story structure helped the college students build the causal bridges (and bridges based on other types of relationships) among sentences of the *Decameron* stories and so write coherent summaries, whereas the lack of knowledge of Alaskan Native American story structure undermined the subjects' attempts to build causal bridges among sentences of the Alaskan stories.

Pragmatics and the Maxims of Conversation

Sentences and discourses are rarely comprehended in a social vacuum. Consider the following situation: Mary is an adult and is approached one evening by a stranger who asks, "Excuse me, but do you know the time?" Mary responds "It is six-thirty." Here, Mary has made a number of assumptions. First, and primarily, she understands that she is being asked to provide the time and not merely whether she knows the time. The stranger was trying to be polite by making the request in an indirect manner. It would be odd for Mary's best friend to make the request in the same manner; the friend is likely to make the request more directly (e.g., "Hey, what time is it?"). And Mary would be rude if she were to respond to the stranger's request with the literal "Yes, I do."

Mary is also making some more subtle evaluations in her interpretation of the stranger's request. She can presume that the stranger knows whether it is early morning or early evening, so she does not need to respond "It is six-thirty P.M." She can also presume that the stranger wants to know only the approximate time, so Mary does not respond with "It is six-twenty-nine and seventeen seconds," even though her digital watch permits that level of temporal precision. Mary is using her knowledge of the social situation to make inferences. Such knowledge is called **pragmatics** and is essential to understanding language.

What enables people to understand the pragmatics of language? Grice (1975) pointed out that conversation depends on the participants agreeing to cooperate with one another. Grice claimed that people follow four general rules, or maxims, when engaging in conversation. These are: (1) Be as informative as possible but not more informative than necessary. (2) Be truthful and so avoid falsehoods. (3) Be relevant. (4) Be clear and so avoid ambiguity, obscurity, and incoherency. And permit me to add a fifth rule: Be as polite as the social situation requires. Grice conceded that although people do not always follow these rules, they usually try to follow them most of the time. Furthermore, when rules are violated, the violation itself is usually expected to be understood by the listener as part of the message.

Rules such as Grice's maxims underlie both the production and comprehension of conversation—such rules constitute some of the pragmatic knowledge necessary to use language. Mary's response to the stranger's request makes use of all of the maxims. She recognizes that strangers should be polite to one another and so the request for the current time is made in an indirect manner. Her answer provides the right amount of information, is accurate (let's presume), is relevant to the question, and is clear.

You can get a good feel for the importance of conversational pragmatics by trying to make sense of conversation that clearly violates the maxims. Suppose Mary and Freddy are both enrolled in the same college class but Freddy missed yesterday's lecture and so asks Mary to summarize the lecture for him. Let's say that Mary finds this particular class to be duller than dishwater. Mary, wit that she is, might respond to Freddy's request with "it [the lecture] was on supply and demand." Mary doesn't give Freddy enough information, perhaps to signal that she found the lecture to be of no value. Or she might respond with "It was riveting, as usual." Here Mary seems to be lying; in fact, she is being ironic and expects Freddy to know that. Maybe Mary responds with "Well, at least I met a good-looking cognitive psychologist in the class." Her irrelevant remark might mean again that the lecture was of no importance. Finally, she might say, "Let's see—the prof made three points about supply and demand, or was it two points about buying low and selling high–no, wait—whatever you do, do not invest in junk bonds." Maybe Mary's incoherent description is meant to inform Freddy that the professor's lecture was incoherent as usual.

The Neurology of Discourse and Pragmatics

What parts of the brain play a role in using discourse and pragmatic knowledge to process language? Damage to the frontal lobes and to the right hemisphere outside of Broca's area can sometimes affect language. It is usually the discourse and pragmatic skills that are undermined the most; typically such damage leaves intact the capacity to process the meaning of words and isolated sentences. Of course, discourse and pragmatic deficits are also associated with Broca's and Wernicke's aphasia, because such aphasias disturb the comprehension of grammar and semantics.

The linguistic deficits associated with frontal lobe damage include disorganized speech, an inability to inhibit irrelevant or socially inappropriate speech, a tendency to leave sentences unfinished, a reliance on set expressions, an inability to make indirect request, and a tendency to mistakenly interpret as literal indirect conversation, such as sarcasm (for a review of the research, see Coelho, 1995, or McDonald, 1993). Similar deficits are associated with the nonfrontal areas of the right hemisphere, although right-hemisphere damage appears to be more unpredictable than frontal lobe damage (McDonald, 1993). Right-hemisphere damage seems especially associated with difficulties in drawing inferences from coherent discourses (Beeman, 1993), in organizing sentences to tell stories (Brownell, Potter, Birhrle, 1986), and in ascertaining the emotional content of discourse (Bloom, Borod, Obler, & Gerstman, 1992).

In the main, there are not localized areas within frontal and right-hemisphere brain tissue that when damaged are consistently associated with discourse and pragmatic deficits (McDonald, 1993). Presumably, the regulation/control function of the frontal lobes and the synthesizing functions of the right hemisphere involve integrating many disparate areas of the brain. Damage in any one of these areas may diminish the capacity to process relationships among sentences and to associate language with knowledge of socially appropriate behavior.

SECTION 4: THE EVOLUTION OF LANGUAGE

The main theme of this chapter is that language is a biological adaptation, and not a cultural invention. The essential similarities among the languages of the world provide a strong argument that language is biological. If its origins were cultural, we would expect greater variation in the communications systems invented by different cultures. That language is a biological adaptation is also revealed by the presence of a linguistic organ in the brain, situated in and around Broca's area and Wernicke's area.

Language, I have been claiming, is more analogous to the evolution of walking than to the invention of, say, agriculture. If language evolved, then we should find evidence for an emerging language skill on our predecessor species. And indeed we do, as I discuss in this section of the chapter.

OVERVIEW OF HUMAN EVOLUTION

Let me begin my discussion of the evolution of human language by summarizing what we believe to be true about the evolution of hominid species. For the most part I will skip the evidence on which the summary is based, but the interested reader may find discussions of the evidence in Campbell (1988) and Leakey (1994). I'll begin the story around 4 to 7 million years ago, when a line of primates with some distinctively human characteristics first appeared on the planet.

Australopithecus

Around 4 to 7 million years ago, a group of apelike animals first began to walk upright, rather than use the technique of knuckle walking. These primates are called *Australopithecus*, which means southern ape (the first fossils were found in southern Africa). *Australopithecus* lived in Africa. *Australopithecus* did not evolve from modern apes; rather, all the modern great apes (chimps, gorillas, and orangutans) and *Australopithecus*, evolved from a common and now extinct ancestral ape around 4 to 7 million years ago. Most species of *Australopithecus* had about the same body size and cranial capacity (around 500 cc) as modern apes.

The essential human trait of *Australopithecus* was its bipedal form of locomotion. In fact, all primates that walk upright, including humans, are called **hominids**. Presumably the advantage of upright walking over the knuckle-walking mode preferred by apes is that upright walking is more calorically efficient. It takes less energy to walk upright than to knuckle walk (although four-legged locomotion actually takes less energy than does two-legged locomotion). Apparently, *Australopithecus* evolved in a way that enabled it to move out of forested regions, where all modern apes live, and into more open country, where food and water sources are spread out over greater distances.

In all probability, the cognitive capabilities of *Australopithecus* were similar to those of modern chimps. Now, modern chimps certainly have impressive problem-solving skills and the capacity to make simple tools. But apes lack at least some of the cognitive capacity of modern humans. Modern apes do not use tools to make tools, they do not have anything resembling art or music, and they do not have a generative grammar. There is no evidence that *Australopithecus* made tools or created works of art. At least, we find no such evidence among their fossilized remains.

What about language? The evidence is meager, but what there is suggests that *Australopithecus* had no language. We have several main sources of evidence concerning language. First, we know that Broca's area leaves a distinguishing, albeit faint, impression on the inside of a skull. Based on examinations of fossilized *Australopithecine* skulls, the prominence of Broca's area in *Australopithecus* was not as great as in the hominid species that evolved later.

Second, we know that in modern humans the **larynx**, the tissue that contains the vocal folds, is located a few inches down into the throat. In humans, the larynx is descended. In all other mammals, including modern apes (and infant humans), the larynx is located in the back of the throat; that is, the larynx is not descended.

The descent of the larynx down into the throat provides both a blessing and a curse for humans. The blessing is that its location creates a larger and more curved cavity in the back and upper part of the throat, called the **pharynx**, which permits the production of a great range of phonemes. Apes literally cannot produce many of the phonemes of human languages, especially vowels like the /i/ sound in "bit." The reason is that apes lack the larger and more curved pharynx. Presumably, the addition of vowels to the articulatory system makes it easier to string together rapidly a series of consonants. The curse of a descended larynx is that the human larynx is not in a position to block the passage of food into the trachea, where it can cause death by choking. Other mammals don't have the problem of swallowing food into their tracheas.

It would seem, then, that a descended larynx would be a sign that *Australopithecus* had language. Unfortunately, soft tissue does not fossilize. Fortunately, we know from modern human and ape skulls that the presence of a descended larynx in humans is associated with a kind of flexion in the base of the skull. Older humans have a flexed basicranium; infant humans and all other primates have an essentially flat basicranium. The fossilized remains of the bases of *Australopithecine* skulls suggest that they had no flexion, therefore no descended larynx, and therefore no capacity for producing many of the vowels of modern languages (see Lieberman, 1984, and, for an alternative position, see Duchin, 1990).

A third line of evidence is based on the fact that, in modern humans, language is lateralized. Broca's area and Wernicke's area are almost always on the left side of the brain. Similarly, fine motor control is also lateralized. Most humans (about 90%) prefer to use their right hands for precise manual operations. We are a right-handed species. The motor control over the right hand is accomplished by the left hemisphere. There is no clear-cut evidence that modern apes have a hand preference. About half prefer to use their right hands, about half prefer to use their left hands.

Did *Australopithecus* show a right-handed tendency? We do not really know, because *Australopithecus* apparently did not make tools from which it might be possible to discern handedness. There is some evidence from the fractured remains of skulls of baboons dated 2 million years ago that the baboons had been clubbed to death by right-handed assailants (see Corballis, 1989). Maybe it was members of the species *Australopithecus africanus* that did the clubbing, because their remains were found in the same sites as the baboons.

A fourth, although perhaps less decisive, source of evidence comes from tool technology. It is possible that sophisticated tool manufacturing is aided by language. A parent or teacher can use language to explain and share toolmaking techniques. The linguistic transmission of information might enable more rapid progress in tool technology than would be possible without language. To the extent that this argument has merit, it would appear that, because *Australopithecus* lacked a sophisticated toolmaking technology, it also lacked language.

One other point about *Australopithecus*. Its cranial capacity was about the same as that of a modern ape. And modern apes don't have language, at least in the wild. Just about everybody knows that modern-day researchers have attempted to teach humanlike languages to chimps and other great apes. Washoe (Gardner & Gardner, 1969) and Nim Chimpsky (Terrace, Petitto, Sanders, & Bever, 1979), for example, were taught a kind of sloppy version of American Sign Language. As it turns out, there is some controversy about how much language such apes have actually acquired. Apes do seem to use a consistent word order when creating simple sentences and to respond differently, depending on word order, to sentences signed to them by people. For example, Washoe seemed to understand the difference between sentences like "Washoe tickle Roger" and "Roger tickle Washoe." However, the grammatical capacity of apes seems rather limited (see Pinker, 1994, or Terrace et al., 1979). For example, no ape has learned to expand simple phrases into longer phrases or to embed phrases into other phrases, as even rather young humans routinely do. Perhaps, then, a brain has to be big enough to accommodate the grammatical aspects of language, and the ape brain falls just short. If so, then so too did the brain of *Australopithecus*.

Homo habilis and Homo erectus

Australopithecus became extinct around 1½ to 2 million years ago, at about the same time that a larger-brained hominid emerged, possibly evolving from an australopithecine species. The larger-brained hominid had only a slightly bigger body than that of *Australopithecus* and modern chimpanzees, but had a significantly larger cranial capacity (about 600–750 cc) than either *Australopithecus* or modern chimpanzees. This hominid species is called **Homo habilis**, which means handy human. And handy they were. There is evidence that *habilis* made stone tools such as flakes, which may have been used to cut meat that they scavenged, and hammerstones, which may have been used to crush bone to release marrow. *Homo habilis* also may have been able to make shelters from animal skins.

Did *habilis* have language? Anthropologists have not yet found any intact fossilized *habilis* basicraniums, so have been unable to measure the flexion that would tell us whether *habilis's* larynx was descended. Examination of the inside of *habilis* skulls do suggest the presence of a Broca's area on the left side of the brain. Flakes made by the manufacture of stone tools found among *habilis* remains suggest that *habilis* was a right-handed species (see Corballis, 1989). We can presume, then, that *habilis* had the biological talents (lateralized brain, Broca's area, and 700 cc cranial capacity) for language. And maybe, just maybe, it was language that enabled *habilis* to develop and sustain a tool technology.

Around 1 to 1½ million years ago, *habilis* became extinct and **Homo erectus** emerged, also in Africa. *Homo erectus* means upright human, although *erectus* was certainly not the first hominid to walk upright. *Erectus* was bigger bodied (nearly as big as modern humans) and bigger brained (900 cc cranial capacity) than *habilis*, from whom they may have evolved. Indeed, some *erectus* individuals had cranial capacities larger than those of some modern humans, whose cranial capacity averages around 1,400 cc.

Erectrus was the first hominid to venture out of Africa. Their fossilized remains are found in Africa, Europe, and Asia. Some *erectus* people lived in cold places, suggesting that they built warm shelters, harnessed fire, and wore clothes. The stone tools, such as hand axes, associated with *erectus* are clearly more technologically sophisticated than the tools made by *habilis*. And they clearly hunted, not just scavenged, big game. *Erectus* people were probably no stronger in body and tooth, nor swifter in foot, than modern humans, so their ability to kill big game must have originated in their mental capacity.

Did *erectus* have language? We do find evidence, from *erectus* skulls, of a Broca's area on the left side of the skull, and evidence of right-handedness from the flakes of stone left by *erectus* tools (Corballis, 1989). The few *erectus* basicrania that have been found have only a partial flexion, implying that the *erectus* larynx was only partially descended. Perhaps, then, *erectus* had a somewhat less efficient language, one in which there were fewer vowel phonemes (Lieberman, 1984). While *erectus* tool technology was impressive by *habilis* and ape standards, it is worth noting that we see little evidence of technological progress in the roughly 1 million years *erectus* lived on the planet. The tool kits of the most recent *erectus* groups were only slightly more advanced than the tool kits of *erectus* groups that lived nearly a million years earlier. Maybe it was a lack of a full-blown language system that impeded technological progress in *erectus*.

Homo Sapiens

Homo erectus became extinct around 300,000 years ago, around the time an archaic form of **Homo sapiens** first emerged, possibly evolving from *erectus* or from a hominid species similar to *erectus* (Tattersall, 1997). *Homo sapiens* means wise human. The archaic version of *sapiens* had a slightly smaller brain than modern humans. Who knows if they were any less wise? Fully modern *Homo sapiens* (i.e., modern humans) were present in Africa by around 100,000 years ago. *Homo sapiens* were well established in Europe and Asia by around 50,000 years ago, in Australia by around 40,000 years ago, and in the Americas by around 10,000 years ago.

Homo sapiens not only developed a much more sophisticated tool technology than *erectus* or *habilis*, but exhibited an astonishingly rapid rate of progress in technology, especially in the last 50,000 years. We find evidence of large-scale improvements in tools when comparing *sapiens* tool kits from, say, 50,000 years ago with *sapiens* tool kits from 20,000 years ago. Beginning somewhere between 50,000 and 30,000 years ago, *sapiens* created breathtakingly beautiful works of art, made musical instruments, and practiced the burial of the dead. Presumably the rapid pace of cultural and technological advancements observed in *Homo sapiens* was a result of the evolution of an even larger brain. And, claim many scholars (see Corballis, 1992; Lieberman, 1994; Leakey, 1994), it was a result of the evolution of a brain with a fully modern linguistic capacity.

HOW DID LANGUAGE EVOLVE?

The big news in hominid evolution is the evolution of bigger brains. We see the progression from *habilis* through *erectus* to *sapiens* of a gradually increasing cranial capacity. One of the capacities that evolved out of the expanding brain was generative grammar. To speculate, it may have been that the tissue from which the generative function was fashioned was motor tissue involved in the sequencing of motor acts for the purpose of reaching a goal (Lieberman, 1984; Corballis, 1989). An example of a motor-sequencing behavior is the series of actions necessary to strip a twig of its leaves and then use the bare twig to fish for termites (chimpanzees do this). A portion of motor-sequencing tissue may have been recruited by adaptive pressures to serve the communication function of sequencing calls and the sounds that combine to make calls. The evolution of a generative grammar module would also have required the evolution of cerebral lateralization and of a descended larynx that allowed the production of vowel and consonant phonemes.

It is also possible that some neural tissue involved in representing relationships among concepts was recruited by evolution for a role in expressing and understanding phrases and sentences. Not all of human language had to have been fashioned out of the calls and gesture systems of apes. After all, modern humans retain many of the nonverbal forms of communication (e.g., smiles) seen in apes. Yet humans have, in addition, the linguistic system. Had human language evolved directly from primate communication, we might expect that language would have replaced nonverbal communication in humans, rather than merely supplementing nonverbal communication (Burling, 1993).

In brief, the evidence suggests that language evolved in hominid species over a period of several million years. There seems to be good evidence that *habilis* and *erectus* had linguistic capacities that were more advanced than those of *Australopithecus* and modern apes but not quite as advanced as those of modern people. The evolutionary story, as best it can be reconstructed from fossils, seems consistent with the theme that language is a unique human biological adaptation—a human instinct.

SECTION 5: LANGUAGE AND THOUGHT

Maybe I have convinced you that language is a sort of instinct. Even still, obviously not all groups of people speak the same language. (Nor does the instinct notion require that they do. The idea of a language instinct only requires that languages have certain general properties, such as phrases, in common. I discuss this point in a bit more detail in chapter 11: Cognitive Development.) Human cultural groups migrate; conquer one another; and change politically, economically, and technologically over time. The result is that the specific vocabulary and grammatical rules come to differ among cultural groups, even while the instinct for language, and for the universal grammar system underlying the instinct, remains the same for all groups.

Scholars have long been intrigued by the possibility that the vocabulary and grammatical differences among the world's languages give rise to differences in how people think, even when they are thinking nonverbally. Could it be that users of different languages perceive, reason about, and remember reality in fundamentally different ways because of the differences in their languages? This possibility is especially intriguing to cognitive scientists because they are concerned with the factors that determine mental processes. Indeed, a number of cognitive psychologists have recently called for a renewal of experimental interest in the study of the effect of language on thought (Hunt & Agnoli, 1991; Hardin & Banaji, 1993).

The main theme of this chapter is that language is a biological adaptation that evolved, and not a cultural invention. As such, language is a relatively autonomous system with properties unique to language. Similarities among the languages of the world and in the linguistic mechanisms by which languages are comprehended suggests that all humans use essentially the same language system. This theme would seem compatible with the hypothesis that linguistic differences ought not to lead to remarkable differences in thought processes. That is because the linguistic differences are superficial. Of course, it would still be possible, from the perspective that language is a biological adaptation, that even the superficial differences among languages are enough to have at least some influence on at least some aspects of thought processes.

LINGUISTIC RELATIVITY

There are several possible variants on the thesis that language influences thought. One variant is that language influences verbal modes of thought, as when people are judging whether letter strings are words. For example, subjects can identify *he* faster than *she* if they have recently been exposed to words like *fireman* and *father* but can identify *she* faster than *he* if they have recently been exposed to words like *waitress* and *mother* (Hardin & Banaji, 1993). A similar variant is that the use or choice of language, the particular words and sentences used in a situation, influences how people will perceive, remember, or solve a problem. For example, people who verbally describe a thief's face while watching a film of a bank robbery later recognize the face less well than people who did not (Schooler & Engstler-Schooler, 1990). As another example, people will remember different details about a film depicting a woman and a man at dinner depending on whether the woman is labeled a waitress or a librarian (C. E. Cohen, 1981).

The variant I wish to discuss is usually called the **linguistic relativity hypothesis**, made famous by Edward Sapir (1884–1939), an American linguist, and his student Benjamin Whorf (1897–1941). Linguistic relativity asserts that different languages differentially bias how people perceive, remember, and think about the world. According to linguistic relativity, the differences among languages, especially grammatical differences, cause speakers of different languages to think in fundamentally different ways even when (especially when) speakers are thinking in nonverbal modes.

To get a sense of how languages might differentially influence nonverbal thought, consider the concept of time. Presumably a perception of the passing of time is not in and of itself a verbal form of thought. But might grammar nevertheless influence how people perceive the passing of time? In Indo-European languages like English, words that stand for time are treated linguistically in much the same way as objects. For example, we pluralize temporal words in the same way we pluralize objects. We can say "two weeks" or "five hours" just as we say "two dogs" or "five houses."

In a Native American language like Hopi, on the other hand, words that refer to time are not pluralized like words that refer to objects (at least according to Whorf, 1956). A Hopi speaker would not say the equivalent of "five months" but would say instead the equivalent of "the fifth repetition of month." Whorf argues that, as a consequence of this sort of grammatical difference, the westerner is likely to perceive time as having spatial-like qualities, as being an object that one might possess, or as moving in one direction. The Hopi is more likely to perceive time as the repetition of events and as naturally occurring cycles. Perhaps a Hopi might find it odd to be expected to show up at a friend's house at a particular time like 9 o'clock in the evening. Rather, the Hopi might be more inclined to think of showing up after the dinner and evening rituals are completed, whenever that would be. A westerner, on the other hand, might be more inclined than the Hopi to think of time as lost, as when one gets older or when one is late for an appointment.

The alternative to the linguistic relativity hypothesis may be called the **linguistic universality hypothesis**. It claims that the grammatical and vocabulary differences among the languages of the world have no important differential impact on how people perceive, reason, or think about the world. Instead, people all around the world think in fundamentally the same ways. Or if there are important differences, the cause of the differences is not the properties of language but other cultural factors, such as differences in religious beliefs, economic systems, and the like.

Consider how the linguistic universality hypothesis would treat the time example discussed above. The hypothesis would claim either that westerners and Hopi people experience the passing of time in the same way, or, if there is a difference in their perceptions of time, the difference is due entirely to the economic and social differences between the cultures. The Western economic system requires elaborate and precise temporal coordination of events, whereas the Hopi culture is based more on an agricultural lifestyle that is attentive to the cycles of weather. The grammatical differences in temporal coding, then, would only accidentally parallel the cultural differences in perception of time. In most cases, in fact, grammatical differences do not correspond to cultural differences.

Most of the research on the relationship between language and nonverbal modes of thought has taken the form of a competition between the linguistic relativity and the linguistic universality hypotheses. Some experiments have focused on vocabulary differences between languages; other experiments have focused on grammatical differences. Because Sapir and Whorf stressed that it is the grammatical structure of a language that is an especially potent force in shaping thought, I will discuss only research on grammatical differences. For the reader curious about this issue, an interesting example of work investigating vocabulary differences and their relationship to perception of color and form is to be found in the research of Rosch, who used to publish under the name of Heider (Heider, 1972; Heider & Olivier, 1972; Rosch, 1973; Rosch, Mervis, Gray, Johnson, & Boyes-Braem, 1976).

RESEARCHING THE LINGUISTIC RELATIVITY HYPOTHESIS

How might a cognitive scientist go about researching the relationship between language and other mental processes, in order to see if there is convincing evidence for the linguistic relativity hypothesis? The ideal experiment must first find an interesting grammatical difference between two languages, then determine what sort of effect that particular difference is likely to have on nonverbal thought, and then devise some reasonable measure of that sort of thought process. The measure of thought should reflect the characteristic ways people interpret their experiences. The research should also rule out nonlinguistic cultural effects on the measured thought process. That is, it should be the case that any observed difference in thought processes be due only to the language difference and not to nonlinguistic cultural differences such as schooling practices, child-rearing practices, religious traditions, or economic systems (Takano, 1989).

Hypothetical Reasoning

One of the best examples of research testing the linguistic relativity hypothesis was conducted by Bloom (1981). Bloom compared Chinese to English subjects on their ability to reason about hypothetical situations. In English, the **subjunctive mood** is used to talk about hypothetical events that could have happened, but, in fact, did not happen. Consider this example of how English conveys a hypothetical idea: "Had Bill studied for his ecology exam he would have learned the reasons for the destruction of the Amazon rain forest." Note the use of "had" and "would have" (the grammatical indices of the subjunctive mood) to convey the hypothetical nature of the event of studying for the exam. Note, too, that the sentence implies that Bill did not study for his exam and therefore did not learn about reasons for the Amazon rain forest destruction. What the sentence asserts never really happened; therefore these sorts of constructions are called **counterfactuals**.

What about people who use languages, like Chinese, that have no subjunctive mood? Will they reason differently about counterfactuals than will English speakers? Chinese can only indicate the counterfactual nature of the passage in an indirect way. For example, one way Chinese speakers might express the hypothetical passage would be to say something equivalent to: "Bill

not study for ecology exam. If Bill study for ecology exam, he learn about reason for destruction of Amazon rain forest." The linguistic relativity hypothesis
would argue that because Chinese has no subjunctive, Chinese speakers do not
pay as much attention to or think as much about hypothetical situations as do
English speakers. Thus the linguistic relativity hypothesis predicts that English
speakers will do better than Chinese speakers on a task measuring counterfactual reasoning.

To test the linguistic relativity prediction, Bloom (1981) had Chinese and
American subjects read fairly complicated passages that included statements
grammatically similar to "If Bill had studied for his ecology exam, he would
have learned about the reasons for the destruction of the Amazon rain forest.
He would have been so distraught about the destruction that he would have
written a letter to the Brazilian government. . . ." Bloom prepared both Chinese
and English versions of the passages. After reading the passages in their own
language, the subjects were given a set of mostly false statements about the passage (again, in their own language) and had to say whether they were true or
false. An example of a false statement would be "Bill wrote a letter to the
Brazilian government."

Consistent with the linguistic relativity hypothesis, the English speakers
did much better on the task than did the Chinese speakers, who tended to
respond "true" to the counterfactual statements. Note that both the Chinese and
American subjects were college students and so were familiar with tests of reasoning. So there is some reason to believe that the nonlinguistic cultures of the
subjects were similar (But see Au, 1983).

Unfortunately for the linguistic relativity hypothesis, follow-up studies
did not find a difference between English and Chinese speakers on the counterfactual task. It turns out that Bloom's passages could be translated into
Chinese in several different ways, some of which make clearer the hypothetical
nature of the passages. For example, one way for a Chinese person to express
"If Bill had studied for his ecology exam, he would have learned the reasons
. . ." would be to say the equivalent of "If Bill study ecology exam, he certainly
learn reason . . ." whereas another way would be to say the equivalent of "If
Bill study for ecology exam, then he learn reason. . . ." It turns out that the sentence with the Chinese equivalent of "then" is more likely to be interpreted as
counterfactual by Chinese speakers. Au (1983) and Liu (1985) found that if at
least some of the passages were translated in a way more natural to the way
Chinese speakers would ordinarily discuss hypothetical situations, then the
Chinese subjects performed as well as the American subjects on the reasoning
task based on all the passages.

A variety of other research also implies no convincing evidence for linguistic relativity, either because no cultural differences in thought processes
were found (e.g., Politzer, 1991) or because cultural differences in thought
processes could be attributed to factors other than grammatical differences (e.g.,
Carroll & Casagrande, 1958). In fact, Lardiere (1992) found that native Arabic
speakers responded to counterfactuals more as Bloom's (1981) Chinese speakers
did than as his English speakers did, yet the Arabic language, like the English

language, contains explicit markers of counterfactuals. Most psycholinguists characterize the linguistic relativity hypothesis as provocative, but lacking convincing evidence (McNeil, 1987; Steinberg, 1982; Pinker, 1994; for a contrary view in favor of linguistic relativity, see Hardin & Banaji, 1993).

Math and Morphology

Some recent research on Asian–American differences in mathematical skill suggests that at least one form of linguistic relativity may be valid (e.g., Miura, Kim, Chang, & Okamoto, 1988). This research is based on the fact that in some Asian languages, Chinese for example, the morphological system for naming numbers makes clearer the base 10 nature of numbers than does the morphological system used in English.

The main difference between Chinese and English is the labels for the numbers 11 through 99. In English, the names for the number 11 (*eleven*) and 12 (*twelve*) are unrelated to the names for 1 and 2. In the case of the numbers 13 through 19, the English system places the morpheme for the unit value before the morpheme for the decade value (*teen*), as in the example of *eighteen*. But for numbers between 20 and 99, the decade value comes before the unit value, as *thirty-five*. In Chinese, the naming system is more regular for numbers in this range. For all numbers between 11 and 99, Chinese uses a rule in which the decade morpheme consistently comes before the unit morpheme (e.g., the literal translation of the Chinese word for 18 is ten-eight, and for 35 it is three-ten-five). Presumably such regularity in Chinese makes clearer the idea that the numbers between 11 and 99 represent units of 10 plus single units. For numbers between 1 and 10 and for numbers greater than 99, the Chinese and English naming conventions are essentially the same.

Miller, Smith, Zhu, & Zhang (1995) studied counting competence in preschool children living in university communities in Urbana, Illinois, and Beijing, China. The children were required to count from 1 to as high a number they could reach, to count the number of objects placed before them, and to produce a set of objects of a particular number from a larger set of objects. In general, the Chinese children did better than the English children, but only on numbers in the 11 to 99 range. For instance, there was no difference between the two groups in the percentage of children who were able to count to at least 10 or were able to count to more than 99. But more Chinese children were able to count to numbers between 11 and 99. It should be noted, though, that very few children from either culture were able to count to a number greater than 99. English children made more mistakes on the object counting and set production tasks, but only for numbers in the 11 to 19 range (the object counting and set production tasks did not require the children to work with amounts greater than 19).

Still, the Miller et al. (1995) experiment may not be entirely persuasive as evidence for linguistic relativity. For one thing, the tasks used in the experiment may reflect only counting, and not calculating or other higher level kinds of arithmetic thinking. Perhaps counting taps into an essentially linguistic mode of thinking and not into a nonverbal mathematical mode of thinking.

Furthermore, there are other reasons why the Chinese children may have done better than the Americans on these tests of counting competence. Perhaps arithmetic skill is more valued in China than in the United States, and so Chinese parents encourage their children's interest in numbers more than do American parents. Perhaps the Chinese use more effective educational techniques for teaching arithmetic skills. Still, the Miller et al. (1995) finding that the counting competence differences were limited to numbers in the 11 to 99 range, just where the Chinese and English-language morphological systems differ, does suggest that the morphology may be part of the reason for the superior performance of Chinese children in arithmetic. Language is used to teach, after all, and so maybe a consistent morphology across a wide range of numbers is easier for children to understand.

SUMMARY AND CONCLUSIONS

The main thesis of this chapter is that language is a distinct biological specialization, an instinct, that evolved in hominid species. Language is unlike the communication systems of nonhuman animals and the nonverbal communications of humans. Learning and using language draws on cognitive processes that are different in important ways from the processes that underlie general learning, such as the acquisition of the rules of baseball. The instinct thesis may be contrasted with the claim that language is a cultural invention and as such reflects the use of a general system of learning and thought. According to this alternative, learning and using language is essentially similar to learning and using one's knowledge of baseball.

In the first section I outlined the three major features of language. First, language includes a lexicon of sound–idea labels. In all languages, there are at least tens of thousands of words in the lexicon. Furthermore, and most critically, the sounds bear a completely arbitrary connection to the ideas that they stand for. In this way, words constitute a semantic system capable of representing virtually any idea.

Second, language includes generative grammar, the rules that generate an unlimited number of meaningful words and utterances from a few sounds. With generative grammar, language can communicate useful information about almost anything. The phonological component of grammar describes how sounds may be combined to form meaningful words. The morphological component of grammar describes how words may be combined with inflections and other words to form new words. The syntactic component of grammar describes how words may be combined to form meaningful phrases and sentences.

Third, language uses the oral–aural mode. In all the cultures of the world, virtually all children will acquire a spoken language, provided they are exposed to the sounds of the language (see chapter 11 on the development of cognition). Recently in human history, cultures have invented language systems that for the most part "obey" the rules of spoken language. Examples include written and sign languages.

Throughout this section I stressed two points. First, the differences among the world's languages, although striking enough to make translation between them difficult, are rather superficial. Second, animal and nonverbal human communications lack either a semantic system or a generative grammar. Music, for instance, is generative but lacks semantics; the calls of apes have a limited kind of semantics but lack a generative grammar. The similarities among the world's languages and the differences between language and nonlinguistic forms of communication are consistent with the idea that language is a unique and encapsulated biological specialization inherited by virtually every human.

In section 2, I bolstered the thesis that language is a human biological specialization by discussing the evidence for a linguistic organ, located in most people in the left cerebral hemisphere of the brain. In the posterior frontal lobe sits Broca's area, which provides the generative grammar function. In the temporal lobe sits Wernicke's area, which provides the semantic function of associating ideas to words. The main evidence for these two linguistic centers comes from brain damage and the resulting aphasias. A typical Broca's aphasic will produce halting and ungrammatical speech and have trouble understanding grammatically complex utterances. A typical Wernicke's aphasic will produce fluent and grammatical-sounding speech that is largely nonsensical, and will have trouble understanding the meanings of words.

Research has established where in the brain language is processed; it has not as clearly established how the neurons of the linguistic system accomplish the tasks of comprehending and using language. Some important clues are provided by behavioral research on language comprehension. I discussed in section 3 the functional characteristics of speech perception and of word, sentence, and discourse comprehension.

Spoken language perception requires that the sounds of speech be perceived, that is, identified. Some theorists maintain that speech is perceived by a different mechanism than is used to perceive other, nonlinguistic sounds. The motor theory of speech perception is the best-known example of a specialized speech mechanism. Research on categorical perception and on the effects of observing the production of speech on speech perception were initially taken as evidence for a specialized speech system. However, both of those effects are also observed in the perception of nonlinguistic sounds.

In my discussion of the comprehension of words, I focused on how people resolve ambiguities in the meanings of words. It appears that the brain's linguistic system first activates all of the commonly used meanings of a word and then discards all of those meanings save the one consistent with the context.

In the case of phrases and sentences, however, it appears that the brain's linguistic system commits quickly to a single interpretation of the relationships among words and discards it only after further processing reveals it to be nonsensical. One strategy the linguistic system has for doing so is the minimal attachment strategy, whereby the linguistic system guesses that the intended phrase structure of a sentence has a few branches as possible. The study of comprehension also reveals that the brain's linguistic system prefers to form a trace of a verb's role when that role is missing or misplaced in an actual sentence. The formation of traces may also help the linguistic system decide an utterance's meaning.

Sentences are rarely encountered in isolation. Discourses have to do with meaningfully connected sentences; examples include stories, lectures, and poems. I focused especially on causal connections among sentences in discourses. Knowledge of event scenarios and character motives is among the kinds of knowledge people draw on to construct the causal relationships among sentences and so make sense of the discourse. One kind of knowledge that aids the comprehension of a discourse is knowledge of the discourse structure, such as the structure of a short story. Comprehension of discourse structure seems to be undermined by brain damage in widely distributed right and frontal lobes of the brain.

Language is usually used in a social context. Pragmatics has to do with making use of knowledge about social situations in order to use and comprehend language. Grice's (1975) conversational maxims are an important example of the kind of social knowledge that helps people make sense of language.

Having established that the brain possesses an organ for language, and having discussed some of the ways that the brain comprehends language, I then discussed, in section 4, the evidence that language evolved in hominid species. Hominids made their appearance about 4 to 7 million years ago when an apelike hominid, called *Australopithecus*, began to walk upright. The small cranial capacity, the lack of evidence for tools, the lack of evidence for a Broca's area, and a flat flexion in the base of the skull all suggest that *Australopithecus* had no language. Around 2 million years ago *Homo habilis* evolved, with a somewhat bigger brain than that of *Australopithecus*. *Homo habilis* made tools and shelter and had a Broca's area. Later, the bigger brained *Homo erectus* evolved. *Homo erectus* had more sophisticated tools than *habilis*, possessed a Broca's area, and had a partial flexion of the skull. The presence of a Broca's area and sophisticated tool use as early as 2 million years ago in *habilis* suggest that language might have begun its evolution in *habilis*. The bigger brain and more sophisticated tools of *erectus* suggest that *erectus* may have had more linguistic capacity than *habilis*. Still, the partial flexion suggests that *erectus* might not have been able to produce some of the vowels of modern languages. Consistent with the idea that *erectus* had less linguistic capacity than that of modern humans is the observation that *erectus* displayed minimal progress in the manufacturing of tools. Finally, beginning around a few hundred thousand years ago, *Homo sapiens* evolved. Perhaps the rapid pace of technological change, as well as an interest in art and a fully flexed basicranium in *sapiens*, are indications that the full-blown linguistic system of modern humans only first emerged in *Homo sapiens*.

In the fifth and final section of the chapter, I briefly discussed the linguistic relativity hypothesis: that linguistic differences among the world's languages cause differences in the nonverbal thought processes underlying reasoning, perceiving, and remembering. The biological specialization thesis, while not exactly inconsistent with linguistic relativity, is more consistent with the linguistic universality hypothesis. After all, the biological specialization thesis claims that grammar differences among the world's languages are largely superficial. Whatever effect language has on thought, it ought to have the same effect regardless of the particular language of the thinker.

One example of research on linguistic relativity comes from Bloom (1981), who found that Chinese speakers had more trouble evaluating counterfactual statements than did English speakers, and attributed the difference to the lack of the subjunctive mood in Chinese. However, the real reason appears to be that Bloom's Chinese passages were translated awkwardly. A better translation of the experimental passages gave results in which there was no difference between Chinese and English-speaking people with respect to counterfactual reasoning.

On the other hand (and there always seems to be one), some research does suggest that Chinese-speaking children can count better than English-speaking children, at least in the 11-to-99 range of numbers. And that is the range in which the Chinese morphological system for numbers is more regular than is the English system. Still, the results could be due to nonlinguistic differences, such as a greater educational emphasis on arithmetic in Chinese culture. Even if the morphological basis for the difference holds up, it still could be that morphology affects the more verbal-like task of counting while having no effect on the more purely mathematical thought processes involved in quantitative reasoning.

One of the strongest lines of evidence for the thesis that language is a uniquely human biological specialization that is distinct from other modes of thought and communication comes from research on the acquisition of language. And it is in the next (and last) chapter of this book that I discuss language acquisition. See you there!

RECOMMENDED READINGS

If you read only one book on language, it has to be Pinker's (1994) *The Language Instinct*. The *New York Times* raved about this book, and I concur. Pinker is witty, engaging, and provocative in developing the thesis that language is a human instinct. *The Language Instinct* covers virtually all the major topics having to do with language, including language evolution, language comprehension, and language acquisition. Another well-written book making many of the same points as *The Language Instinct* is Jackendoff's (1994) *Patterns in the Mind*. Swinney (1979) describes his elegant experiment on how the brain resolves the meaning of ambiguous words like *bug*. Miller (1990) has a very nicely written chapter ("Speech Perception") summarizing the motor theory of speech perception. The chapter can be found in Osherson's and Lasniks's "Language." Hardin and Banaji (1993) review a wide range of studies relevant to the thesis that language influences thought. Contrary to Pinker's (1994) claims, Hardin and Banaji conclude that there is good experimental evidence in favor of Whorf's ideas. And for those of you interested in the work on teaching animals human language, you should know that this type of research is not confined to apes. Herman, Richards, and Wolz (1984) report success at teaching dolphins a gesture language and an acoustic language. Fa loves Pa!

11 *Cognitive Development*

A 4-year-old boy is asked "Do you have a brother?" and replies "Yes." The 4-year-old is then asked "What is your brother's name?" "Jim" replies the child. Finally, the boy is asked "Does Jim have a brother?" He replies "No" (from Phillips, 1969).

In this chapter I discuss the cognitive development of the child. The two essential questions I will try to answer are these: (1) What precisely is different about the cognitive capabilities of the developing child when compared with the cognitively competent adult? (2) What causes cognitive development to happen; that is, what mechanism(s) turns the cognitively immature infant into the cognitively competent adult? In the example above, why does the 4-year-old boy mistakenly believe that his brother has no brother? What enables him to learn that his brother must have a brother?

PERSPECTIVES ON COGNITIVE DEVELOPMENT: GENERIC OR DOMAIN SPECIFIC?

The main theme I will use to integrate this chapter is one introduced in chapter 8: Problem Solving and chapter 9: Individual Differences in Cognition. Is cognitive development based on generic learning and developmental processes? That is, are the mechanisms by which infants and children acquire knowledge essentially the same in all domains of knowledge, and, if so, what is the best way to characterize this **generic process** of development? Or, on the other hand, is cognitive development **domain specific**—that is, are the mechanisms by which infants and children acquire knowledge different depending on the domain? If cognitive development is domain specific, what are the relevant domains and in what sense are the various developmental mechanisms underlying each domain different from one another?

In the first two major sections, I will discuss two generic approaches to cognitive development. Section 1 examines the approach taken by Jean Piaget, who postulated four major stages of cognitive development, with the kinds of conceptualizations available to the child different in each stage. In section 2 I discuss a maturational approach, based mainly on information processing and Piagetian ideas, in which genetically determined changes to the brain are thought to give rise to cognitive development.

I discuss domain-specific cognitive development in section 3. Although there are several possible kinds of domain-specific approaches, I focus especially on a domain-specific approach usually called **nativism**, or sometimes **innatism**. Nativism postulates that children are born with cognitive instincts, such as a language instinct, that take the form of implicit domain-specific principles that give the child a leg up in acquiring knowledge in a domain. Instincts influence and constrain how infants and children extract and process information in a particular domain. A cognitive instinct for language, for example, would affect the acquisition of language, but not the acquisition of social skill, which would be affected by any cognitive instinct for human social relationships and values. Usually the domains postulated by nativism are those most directly relevant to survival and reproductive success, such as language, socialization, and knowledge of the biological world but not baseball, agriculture, or astronomy. I focus the discussion on the evidence for a cognitive instinct for language.

SECTION 1: PIAGET'S THEORY OF COGNITIVE DEVELOPMENT

Jean Piaget is usually regarded as the most influential cognitive developmental psychologist of the 20th century. Although a number of cognitive psychologists have regarded Piagetian theory as empirically wrong or epistemologically weak (e.g., Modgil & Modgil, 1982; Siegal, 1991), his work seems to be enjoying a renewed appreciation in the 1990s (Beilin, 1992; Lourenco & Machado, 1996; Flavell, 1996). Certainly an understanding of research and theory in the field of cognitive development requires an understanding of Piaget's work (Siegler & Ellis, 1996).

   Jean Piaget was born on August 9, 1896 in Neuchatel, Switzerland. He received his PhD in biology but later studied at the Alfred Binet Testing Laboratory in Paris, where he worked with Pierre Janet and helped standardize intelligence tests. While at the Binet Laboratory, Piaget developed an interest in the intellectual abilities of children—an interest that led him to develop his theory of cognitive development. The theory was based, in part, on the work of an American psychologist, James Mark Baldwin (1861–1934), who worked closely with Alfred Binet and Pierre Janet in Paris (Baldwin, 1894; see Case, 1985, and Cairns, 1992, for a discussion of Baldwin). Baldwin was a neo-Darwinian who believed that the cognitive development of the human child recapitulates the biological evolution of *Homo sapiens*.

   Piaget, in his reworking of Baldwin's theory, stressed that changes in how knowledge is represented and manipulated are not based on genetically programmed maturational changes in the brain. Instead, Piaget viewed children as young scientists who are driven to understand the world and to change their understanding in the face of mistaken predictions about what ought to happen in the world. As children develop, they acquire ever more sophisticated knowledge structures by which to interpret the world. Changes in knowledge structures cause changes in fundamental cognitive capabilities. According to Piaget, these cognitive capabilities undergo a series of improvements until they resemble the capabilities of the typical adult. The knowledge structures underlying cognitive capabilities are bound to emerge in an orderly way, as the kinds of knowledge the universe affords require that certain ways of thinking be mastered before other ways of thinking become possible.

Knowledge structures change over time, but the mechanism that underlies that change, according to Piaget, is the same in all knowledge domains. Understanding of number, space, self, biology, language, and so on, all follow the same orderly developmental process, driven by the same quasi-scientific mechanism by which children alter knowledge in the face of mispredictions.

Piaget continued to refine his theory throughout his long and remarkably productive professional life. In his later years, Piaget developed models of how children acquire the capacity for reflective thought and use that capacity to initiate actions. Jean Piaget died in 1980, after having published about 30 books and more than 200 articles (e.g., Piaget, 1926a, 1952, 1976; Piaget & Inhelder, 1958, 1964; see Howes, 1990, for a detailed discussion of Piaget that contrasts Piagetian theory with more mainstream traditions, and Beilin, 1992, or Flavell, 1996, for a discussion of Piaget's contributions to developmental psychology).

In this section I will first outline Piaget's stages of cognitive development and the evidence on which the claims for the stages are based. I will then outline how the generic learning mechanisms postulated by Piaget produce the orderly transitions in the cognitive capabilities of the child.

STAGES OF COGNITIVE DEVELOPMENT

Piaget claimed that there are four major stages of cognitive development. These are known as the **sensorimotor stage**, the **preoperational stage**, the **concrete operations stage**, and the **formal operations stage**. The stages are characterized by differences in how children understand their world and how they are able to manipulate or transform their knowledge. A summary of these stages is provided in Figure 11-1.

Sensorimotor Stage

According to Piaget, the human baby is born with only some rudimentary perceptual capacities for sensing the world and rudimentary reflexive motoric capabilities for manipulating the body and external objects. Babies soon learn to make nonrandom movements that constitute effective action. For example, the baby may learn to move its head and lips in such a way as to more effectively suck from the mother's nipple. Accordingly, the young infant understands the world in terms of coordinating its movements with its sensations; hence the name *sensorimotor* for this stage of development.

According to Piaget, the essential cognitive limitation of the young infant is that the infant lacks the ability to represent mentally an object or event in its absence. The young infant who sees another child playing with a

Piaget's stages and approximate age ranges	Characteristics of children in these stages
Sensorimotor Birth–2 years	Young infant understands only sensations and movements. Infant initially lacks mental representations.
Preoperational 2 years–5 years	Toddler has mental representations, but has difficulty mentally transforming representations.
Concrete operations 5 years–11 years	Child has capacity to mentally transform mental representations. Child lacks capacity to transform abstract ideas or understand relationships between relationships.
Formal operations 11 years–adulthood	Adolescent learns to think abstractly.

FIGURE 11–1   A summary of Piaget's major stages of cognitive development.

toy would not be able to imagine the toy, were it not in the infant's visual field. This lack of representational capacity is most clearly revealed in the young infant's interactions with objects. Young infants will grasp for objects within their visual field, but will make no effort at all to search for the very same objects if the objects are covered with a cloth in full view of the infants. If the hidden object should reappear, the infant acts surprised. That is to say, the infant seems to lack any sense that objects have permanency. Out of sight, out of mind!

Preoperational Stage

By the age of 2; the typical toddler has acquired the capacity to think about objects and events in their absence. The toddler has **representational thought**. According to Piaget, the essential cognitive limitation of young children is that they are unable to perform **mental transformations** of, or operations on, their ideas and mental images. Hence the young child's thinking is characterized as preoperational.

The preoperational nature of the young child's thought manifests itself in several ways. The child has difficulty imagining the movement of mental elements unless the child observes those movements in the perceptual world. The child has difficulty understanding the relationships among elements of thought, particularly if those elements represent movement or change. The child is prone to an unstructured flow of thought, primarily because the child has difficulty seeing that certain mental elements are contradictory or unrelated. The child's thinking is **egocentric**, in the sense that the child has difficulty imagining that other people may perceive the world differently than the child (recall from the beginning of this chapter the example of the 4-year-old boy who thought that his brother had no brother).

Much of the evidence that young children's thought is preoperational in nature comes from observations of how children solve, or fail to solve, simple problems in reasoning. The best-known of these problem-solving failures is with a problem in which the solution requires understanding the concept of **conservation**. Conservation involves the understanding that an element that moves in space does not thereby change its fundamental properties. Conservation of volume, for example, involves the understanding that a volume of water in a container does not change just because the water is moved to a new container with a different shape. The main mental operation that the child lacks, but needs in order to understand conservation, is that of reversibility. The child can observe A changing into B and so mentally represent that transformation, but the child has difficulty in imagining B going back into A (and therefore conserving the essential properties of A) in the absence of directly observing the reversible transformation.

Consider the following experiment (Piaget, 1952; see Flavell, 1985, for a discussion of studies investigating conservation in children) that demonstrates that young children lack an understanding of conservation. In the experiment, children are presented two identical containers of water, filled with the same amount of water, and a third empty container. Children recognize that the second container has the same amount of water as the first container. However, if the water from the second container is poured into a third container that is taller and thinner, the children will now respond that there is more water in the third container than in the first container. Children are struck by the fact that the column of water in the third container is higher, and conclude that there must therefore be more water in the third container. Some children may be struck by the fact that the column of water is narrower, and conclude that there is less water in the third container. Young children have trouble transforming the image of the volume of water in the third container back into an image of the volume of water in the second container. Young children also have trouble understanding conservation of number (e.g., a group of five pennies remain five in number even if they are spread out over a table), conservation of weight, conservation of length of bendable objects, and conservation of volume of solid objects.

The limitations of preoperational thinking are also revealed in the difficulty young children have with reasoning about simple **transitive relationships** (Piaget, 1926b; see Howes, 1990, for a discussion of experiments investigating transitive reasoning in young children). For instance, if young children are told that Mary is taller than Linda and Lisa is taller than Mary, they have difficulty deducing that Lisa is the tallest. In many cases, the young child will conclude that Mary is the tallest, presumably because she is described as taller and men-

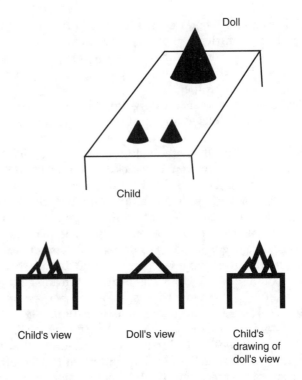

FIGURE 11–2   The three-mountain experiment illustrating egocentricity in young children.

tioned in both sentences. According to Piaget, the child has trouble with transitive reasoning because the task requires making a comparison among relational concepts, an operation unavailable to the young child.

Egocentric thought is a predictable consequence of preoperational thinking. Egocentricity does not mean that young children are selfish (although they certainly can be very possessive about their toys!); it means that young children lack the capability to take another person's perceptual perspective. Presumably, being able to take another's perspective requires being able to transform mentally the image of one's own perceptual field. An example of a child's egocentricity comes from the three-mountain problem used by Piaget (Piaget & Inhelder, 1956). In this problem, illustrated in Figure 11-2, children sit at a table on which are placed models of three mountains. A doll sits across from the child on the other side of the mountains. The child is asked to draw what the doll sees. Younger children (under the age of 5 or 6 years) are likely to draw what *they* see, even though such a drawing is more complex than a drawing made from the doll's perspective. Older children are able to make the mental transformations necessary to represent the doll's perspective, and so draw the scene from that perspective.

Concrete Operations Stage

By the age of 5 years or so, the typical child will begin to master the concept of conservation, to solve at least simple transitive reasoning problems, and to take other people's perspectives. In general, the older child's thinking seems characterized by an ability to perform operations on the elements of thought.

The primary cognitive difficulty of the older child, according to Piaget, is an inability to perform mental operations on purely abstract or hypothetical elements of thought. Instead, the older child is only able to perform mental transformations on concrete ideas and objects; that is, on elements that represent what is directly observed in the world. In particular, older children have difficulty understanding highly abstract concepts that represent a relationship among relationships. Hence, this stage of cognitive development is known as the concrete operations stage.

An example of the limitations of concrete operational thinking comes from a problem called the **balance-scale task** (Piaget & Inhelder, 1958). In this task, illustrated in Figure 11-3, children are given a balance scale on which can be placed varying numbers of weights positioned at various distances from a fulcrum. Children are asked to predict which side of the balance scale will go down, given some arrangement of weights on the balance scale. Children around the age of 5 usually predict that the side with the most weights will go down; they do not consider distance from the fulcrum. Children around the age of 10 begin to have some sense that both distance and weight are important to predicting accurately which side will go down, but they do not seem to have mastered the nature of the trade-off between weight and distance. Adolescents around the age of 15 typically reason quite accurately about balance-scale problems, often applying the correct mathematical formula (multiply weight and distance for each side and compare the products). The notion of the product of weight and distance is a concept that is not directly observed, but represents a relationship between two other relational concepts (the effect of distance on the movement of the balance scale and the effect of weight on the movement of the balance scale).

Formal Operations Stage

By the time of early adolescence, the typical child has entered the formal operations stage, which Piaget claims is the final stage of cognitive development. According to Piaget, formal operational thought emerges gradually throughout adolescence, and is more or less completed by around age 18. Further cognitive development reflects only the accumulation of knowledge and skills, and not the

FIGURE 11–3   The balance beam used to demonstrate an understanding of abstract concepts.

acquisition of new cognitive capabilities. In the formal operations stage the adolescent is able to understand and transform mentally even highly abstract concepts, such as those having to do with mathematical product (e.g., length times distance), hypothetical concepts (e.g., utopia), and concepts involving interaction (e.g., anxiety enhances performance of well-practiced skills but undermines performance of newly acquired skills). Some older adolescents may discard a personal moral system that is based on observable consequences of actions (e.g., what leads to a reward is good) and replace it with a moral system that is based on abstract principles of justice (e.g., what benefits the community and does not harm the individual is good) (Kohlberg, 1969). Adolescents are able to perform mathematical operations on abstract numbers, such as the infamous x of algebraic equations, that may be difficult for younger children.

PIAGETIAN MECHANISMS OF COGNITIVE DEVELOPMENT

An important aspect of Piagetian theory is the mechanism, or force, that makes it possible for the developing child to pass through the developmental stages and become a cognitively competent adult. Essentially, Piaget's claim is that a child's ways of thinking are constructed from what is called the **assimilation–accommodation** mechanism, a claim originally articulated by Baldwin. Assimilation refers to associating new information with what is already known, as when a child first learns that a polar bear is part of the bear family. Accommodation refers to changing what is known when the currently available knowledge is inadequate for solving some problem, as when a child expands the concept of bear to include the attribute of white fur. When information cannot be easily assimilated by some existing knowledge structure—when that structure is challenged—then the structure will change its form in order to try to assimilate the information.

Critical to understanding assimilation and accommodation is the notion that the kinds of assimilations and accommodations available to the developing child change over time, as new kinds of knowledge structures, also known as **schemas**, are acquired. Consider a pecuniary metaphor: Although earning money is the essential means by which one survives in our culture, the way money can be earned is quite different if one has a million dollars (and so can earn money from interest) than if one has no money (and so can earn money from labor) (Carey, 1990). Similarly, assimilation and accommodation are used throughout the life span. But the kinds of assimilations and accommodations available to the developing child change as the child accumulates knowledge.

Piaget's notion of an assimilation–accommodation mechanism makes him a **constructionist** (Howes, 1990; Flavell, 1996). If a knowledge structure is inadequate to understanding some situation, the state of disequilibrium into which the structure is consequently placed causes it to examine other knowledge structures in order to accomplish an effective accommodation. Accommodation may result in fusing together several schemas to form a more general schema; in fracturing a schema into several more specialized schemas; or in constructing hierarchies of schemas to represent relationships among ideas. It is because of the child's need to assimilate and accommodate experiences that cognitive capabilities change as the child develops. In this sense the developing child actively contributes to the development of its knowledge; the child is not merely a passive recipient of information.

An example, admittedly simplified, should make the nature of the assimilation–accommodation process clearer. Consider an infant who enjoys hugging a small brown teddy bear. According to Piaget, this knowledge structure or schema is merely an association between the sight of the teddy bear and the action of hugging. Suppose that the infant eventually encounters a small white teddy bear and a large brown teddy bear and discovers that they are also huggable. The simple sensorimotor schema that only associated hugging with the sight of the small brown teddy bear will be challenged by these new encounters. The teddy-bear-hugging schema will be placed into a state of disequilibrium. The disequilibrium causes the schema to use its capacity for "noticing" similarities among teddy bears to associate the different types of teddy bears with the hugging schema. At the same time, the developing infant will learn to respond in several ways to teddy bears. The infant will discover that teddy bears can be bitten, thrown, and dropped, for example. The teddy bear schema will restore the equilibrium disturbed by these surprising discoveries by associating to the schema a wider range of responses. Eventually, then, the teddy bear schema will have associated enough stimulus and response elements to it that it will be adequately prepared to understand virtually all new encounters with all types of teddy bears.

The evocation of this more complex teddy bear schema also enables the older infant to ponder stimulus and response elements that are not necessarily present in the current environment. For instance, the older infant who feels a need to hug can mentally evoke the attributes of the teddy bear. The older infant may even seek out the teddy bear to satisfy a hugging urge. The younger infant with the urge to hug would not be likely to seek out the teddy bear, because the infant would not have any mental representation of teddy bears to evoke.

Driven, then, by the failure of the initial sensorimotor schema to adequately assimilate new encounters with teddy bears, the similarity among teddy bear experiences provides a basis on which the schema can accommodate those experiences. With respect to teddy bears, our hypothetical infant has become preoperational. Over time this will happen across a wide range of objects and events; consequently, our hypothetical infant will have become fully preoperational.

Once the developing infant acquires a large enough number of mental representations, the infant will be able to use those mental representations to assimilate new experiences. For instance, a young child may encounter a variety of living creatures including dogs, spiders, and birds. These creatures do not resemble one another physically. Furthermore, each creature requires of the child a rather different kind of response. Still, the creatures do have some behavioral similarities; for example, they can all move on their own. Such a similarity enables the cognitive system of the young child to place schemas associated with the idea of a bear, spider, and bird into a hierarchical relationship with a more abstract schema, the idea of animal. This abstract schema can be used to assimilate new experiences, as when a child assimilates its first encounter with a kangaroo into the animal schema, and therefore correctly predicts that kangaroos can initiate movement.

Two important points are made by the animal schema example. First, the animal schema allows a deduction about the nature of reality (i.e., kangaroos can initiate movement) without the need for any direct experience with the aspect of reality that is correctly deduced. Second, the creation of relationships among schemas for animals is a kind of accommodation that is unavailable to the young infant who does not yet have mental representations for objects and events.

CRITICISMS OF PIAGET'S THEORY

One criticism often leveled against Piaget is that Piaget underestimated the competence of infants and young children (e.g., Siegal, 1991; see Lourenco & Machado, 1996). Consider transitive relationships. Certain modifications of the standard demonstration of lack of transitivity in young children seem to suggest that young children can make logical transitive inferences (e.g., Hooper, Toniolo, & Sipple, 1978; Trabasso, 1977; Brainerd, 1974). For example, in what I will call the modified procedure, sticks of decreasing length are arranged on a table, but separated so that children cannot perceive directly their differences in length. Let's say that stick A is the longest, stick B the next longest, and stick C the shortest. The sticks are then moved so that the child sees stick A next to stick B, then stick B next to stick C. The idea of the modified procedure is to minimize memory demands and to make the nature of the task clearer to the child. In the modified procedure the typical child is able to deduce that stick A is longer than stick C.

Now is this really evidence that, contrary to the predictions of Piagetian theory, young children are capable of transitive inference—that what Piaget attributed to a failure to reason transitively was really only a difficulty in remembering the relationships or in understanding that one is supposed to make use of a memory of the relationships to solve the problem? Perhaps not. Maybe in the modified procedure children merely notice that sticks are decreasing in size from left to right and use that knowledge to answer the question about which stick, A or C, is longest. But Piaget was interested in the way in which children solve problems, not merely in whether children could solve problems. In this case, children could solve the modified problem preoperationally (attending to the order of descent) or operationally (using logical operations). Indeed, when young children are asked to give reasons for their conclusions in the modified procedure, they typically say, or indicate by pointing, that stick A is longer than stick C because stick A is to the left of stick C. But when young children are able to solve the original transitive problem, where they are presented only pairs of sticks at a time, they typically say that A is longer than C because A is longer than B and B is longer than C (Chapman & Lindenberger, 1988; see Lourenco & Machado, 1996). Furthermore, how well children perform on a transitive reasoning task is independent of whether they remember the relationships on which deductions are based (Brainerd & Reyna, 1993).

Another standard criticism of Piaget's theory is that it seems to imply an evenness in cognitive development. An infant who acts as if the teddy bear ceases to exist when it is hidden behind a pillow should also act as if an uncle ceases to exist when he leaves the house. A young child who seems unable to take another person's perspective in one situation should have difficulty in reasoning about transitive relationships in another situation. In fact, though, unevenness in cognitive development is widespread (e.g., Flavell, 1982; Jackson, Campos, & Fischer, 1978; see Fischer & Silvern, 1985, for a discussion), as even Piaget acknowledged (Piaget, 1971). A child may be able to conserve volume but not number, for instance.

However, I am not sure that unevenness, also called **decalage**, really presents a threat to Piaget's theory (neither does Beilin, 1992, nor Lourenco & Machado, 1996). After all, Piaget emphasized that knowledge structures make accommodations when they fail to assimilate experiences adequately. There is no reason to expect that disequilibrium will occur in all knowledge structures at the same time. A child who has more experience observing water poured into glasses than counting objects whose spatial arrangements change would be expected to acquire conservation of volume before conservation of number. Indeed, one could argue that Piaget's theory predicts decalage.

Another one of the areas of controversy surrounding Piaget's theory is whether the typical person ever actually reaches the formal operational stage. Keating (1980) claimed that only about 50% to 60% of people in the 18–20 age range in our culture use formal operations at any time. There may even be entire cultures in which virtually nobody ever reaches the formal operations stage. Adults from non-Western cultures who do not attend formal schools tend to perform poorly on tests of formal operations, such as the balance-scale problem (Laurendeau-Bendavid, 1977; Shea, 1985).

Piaget thought that all normal adults in any culture typically achieve formal operational thinking in at least two areas. Usually such areas reflect a person's central concerns. According to Piaget, apparent failures to observe formal operational thinking in adults or entire cultures may be due to the fact that the observer uses tasks that are inappropriate for demonstrating formal operational thought. As evidence for Piaget's claims, Australian aborigines have difficulty with formal operations in the domain of school problems (e.g., the balance-scale problem), presumably because they do not attend schools. But the same aborigines are able to imagine a range of hypothetical possibilities in the domain of game-hunting, a domain in which many are experts (Tulkin & Konner, 1973). Hypothetical constructs are the hallmarks of formal operational thought.

SECTION 2: MATURATION
OF PROCESSING CAPACITY

Piaget's theory represents a generic approach to cognitive development. The stages of intellectual growth and the assimilation–accommodation mechanism apply to all domains of knowledge.

A different kind of generic approach suggests that cognitive growth is based on **maturational processes** intrinsic to the growth of the brain throughout infancy and young childhood. This biological maturation results in an **expanding processing capacity** (Baldwin, 1894; Case, 1985; van Geert, 1991; Kail, 1986; Kail & Park, 1992, 1994), reflected in an expansion in short- and long-term memory, attentional capacity, and network of excitatory and inhibitory relationships among concepts (Pascual-Leone, 1970; Dempster, 1981). As processing capacity increases, the child is able to incorporate more complex sets of rules and ideas into strategies and knowledge bases that can be used to solve problems, remember the past, and use language (Siegler, 1986; Klahr, 1984). Some theorists claim that an increase in processing speed leads to an increase in working or short-term memory capacity, which in turn leads to more effective reasoning and problem-solving skill (Kail & Park, 1994; Fry & Hale, 1996).

The theory that cognitive growth reflects increases in processing capacity inherent in the maturation of the brain is different from Piagetian theory in that the cause of cognitive growth is not attributed only to failures of assimilation but to improvements in the computational efficiency caused by a genetically based maturation of the brain. Most maturational theories, however, are similar to Piagetian theory in that both approaches are generic. That is, both postulate that the underlying basis of cognitive development is the same for all domains of knowledge (Gopnik, 1996).

DEMONSTRATIONS OF DEVELOPMENTAL INCREASES IN PROCESSING CAPACITY

A number of experiments show that short-term memory span in children tends to increase with age (e.g., Pascual-Leone, 1970; Case, 1972; Dempster, 1981; Crammond, 1992). Experiments also show that children's processing efficiency, usually measured by the speed with which they make basic discriminations, also increases with age (e.g., Hale, Fry, & Jessie, 1993; Fry & Hale, 1996; see Kail, 1991).

One experiment demonstrating the expansion of short-term memory in infants was done by Case (1985), who studied infants who ranged in age from 4 months to 18 months. The infants' short-term memory capacity was assessed by showing them an apparatus that contained four pegs which, when pulled, produced a chime. The experimenter demonstrated the apparatus to the infants, who were then invited to pull the pegs. The pegs were set far enough part so that the infant could look at only one peg at a time. Short-term memory capacity was estimated by the greatest number of pegs the infant pulled in all trials. At age 4–8 months the infants averaged 1.33 pegs, at age 8–12 months the infants averaged 2.29 pegs, and at age 12–18 months the infants averaged 3.27 pegs.

Short-term memory capacity continues to increase during childhood. Crammond (1992) asked children in the age range of 4 to about 11 years to inspect a 4 × 4 matrix and note which cells in the matrix had been shaded. On a blank 4 × 4 matrix the children had to indicate which cells had been shaded in the previously presented matrix. At the age of about 4½ children remembered only about 1 cell. By age 10½ children remembered about 3½ cells.

Long-term memory also improves as children age (e.g., Dirks & Neisser, 1977; see Bjorklund, 1995). An example of research comes from Brainerd and Reyna (1995). They studied memory in younger children (second-graders) and older children (sixth-graders). Children first learned to recall a list of words without error and then were tested again two weeks later. Even after taking into account how long it took children to originally learn the list, rates of forgetting the list were greater in the younger than in the older children.

CAPACITY AND THE DEVELOPMENT OF REASONING

Important to a theory that posits an expanding memory and attentional capacity is a demonstration that improvements in other cognitive domains, such as reasoning, are due to an increase in that capacity, and not due to some other developmental process (Kail & Park, 1994; Fry & Hale, 1996). One demonstration is based on correlations between reasoning capacity and memory capacity.

The notion that expanding capacity underlies improvements in reasoning suggests that estimates of memory capacity should correlate with success at solving reasoning problems. In one study, Case (1985) measured the short-term memory capacity of 6-year-old children and examined how well they could perform on a task designed to measure their understanding of volume. Ordinarily, 6-year-olds base their estimate of volume only on the height of liquid in a container—they ignore the width of the liquid in the container. The children selected for the experiment all focused only on height. This sample of 6-year-old children came from those who scored either low or high on a test of short-term memory capacity. The high score was the population average of all 8-year-olds, the low was the population average of all 6-year-olds.

In the experiment itself, the children were shown, on a series of trials, beakers with different volumes of water and had to judge which beaker had more water. After making their judgment, which was initially based only on height, some of the children were required to pour the water of each test flask into each of two identical reference flasks, in order to see for themselves which test flask had contained more water. A control group of children received no feedback.

The research question was: which group would be able to expand their strategy to include some consideration of width of the liquid? It turned out that some children in all the groups, including the control groups, learned to focus on both height and width. But by far the greatest improvement was seen in the group that had the larger memory span and was given the feedback. In fact, every child in this group learned to combine height and width when making volume judgments. Children with the smaller memory span given feedback performed only slightly better than the children not given the feedback. In short, this study, along with some others reported in Case (1985; see also Fry & Hale, 1996), suggests that in order for children to use feedback to expand their rule system, they must have an adequate working memory capacity. Children with a smallish memory capacity do not profit as much from the feedback.

PHYSIOLOGICAL BASIS OF INCREASED PROCESSING CAPACITY

The notion that processing capacity expands as the infant matures into the adult leads logically to the next question: What makes processing capacity expand? Given what we know about how neurons change when learning takes place (see chapter 6: The Physiology of Learning and Remembering) it is reasonable to assume that the physiological basis for cognitive development lies in changes in connections among neurons. Such changes could be genetically programmed to occur at certain ages, or could reflect the effects of experience and practice.

Synaptic Density

One explanation for the increase in working memory capacity is that neurons gradually acquire more, and more efficient, connections with other neurons. It is known that the number of connections among neurons (**synaptic density**) increases dramatically in the late prenatal and early postnatal periods, until the number actually exceeds the adult level of connection density. Beginning around age 2, children actually begin to lose many of these connections. The decrease in synaptic density continues to the age of 7 or so, at which time the typical child achieves the adult level of number of connections (see Siegler, 1989). As discussed in chapter 6, change in synaptic density underlies some forms of learning. Turner and Greenough (1985), for example, found that rats housed in visually stimulating environments formed about 25% more synaptic connections per neuron of visual cortex than did rats raised in visually impoverished environments.

Presumably an early increase in the supply of synaptic connections should make it easier for the developing infant to extract information from the world and to use that information to learn about objects in the world. A later judicious pruning of synaptic connections may underlie a greater capacity for focus in thought. Such focus may enable the developing child to discriminate more efficiently among objects and events and to select useful knowledge bases and courses of action.

One example of how changes in synaptic density may serve to drive cognitive development comes from research that correlates synaptic density with capacity to acquire object permanence. Goldman-Rakic (1987a, 1987b) studied object permanence in monkey and human infants. There comes a point at which infants are able to solve simple object permanence problems, such as finding a hidden object behind a screen. But the same infants have trouble on a slightly more difficult problem in which, after a few trials of hiding the object behind one screen, the object is then hidden behind a second screen. This problem is known as the **A-not-B object permanence problem**. The tendency on the A-not-B problem is for the infant to look for the object behind the first screen, despite the fact that it was hidden behind the second screen in full view of the infant. It turns out that the age at which the infant shows signs of beginning to solve the A-not-B problem corresponds to the age at which the synaptic density first exceeds adult levels, about age 2 months in monkeys and 6 months in humans.

Apparently it is the overproduction of synaptic connections in the prefrontal cortex that is critical to solving this and other visual-spatial tasks that require overcoming habitual performance. Surgically produced lesions in the prefrontal cortex of adult monkeys cause the adults to regress to the young infant level, with respect to the A-not-B problem. Goldman-Rakic (1987b) theorized that prefrontal cortex is critical for keeping some thoughts active in memory while suppressing others. That is, the prefrontal cortex plays an especially important role in short-term or working memory. Indeed, lesioned monkeys do not make many mistakes on the A-not-B problem if the delay between the placement of the object behind the screen and the opportunity to respond is under 2 seconds. At delays longer than 2 seconds, though, the lesioned monkeys' performance declines. Presumably, once the prefrontal synapses reach some critical density, the child acquires the capacity for sustaining thoughts and suppressing actions, such as the preservation response in the object permanence task. One consequence of this neural efficiency may be the emergence of object permanence.

One way that neurons may acquire more efficient connections with other neurons is through a process known as **myelinization**. Myelin sheath is a fatty substance that resembles a series of segmented tubes that surround and insulate the axons of many neurons. Myelin sheath increases the speed of neural function. There is evidence that spurts in the rate of increase of myelinization take place at around the same time as do important cognitive changes, and do so in children from diverse cultures (Bjorklund & Harnishfeger, 1990; Konner, 1991). Spurts of myelinization begin or end around age 1 month, 4 months, 1 to 2 years, 10 years, and 18 to 25 years (Yakovlev & Lecours, 1967). Moreover, these spurts take place in different parts of the brain. The earliest spurt of myelinization affects neurons that control isolated sensory and motor systems. The neurons that become myelinated around age 4 months to 1½ years control the coordination between sensory and motor systems. Neurons serving abstract functions become more myelinated between 1½ and 18 years of age.

Frontal Lobe Reorganization and the Development of Processing Capacity

Frontal lobe development may be especially critical to the acquisition of processing efficiency (Case, 1992). Recent work by Thatcher (1992) and others (see Case, 1992, and Nelson, 1995) suggests that the frontal lobe undergoes several waves of development between the ages of 18 months and 11 years. During these waves the frontal lobe effectively establishes greater control over and coordination with other cortical systems. The primary evidence for this reorganization comes from the study of brain damage evidence and from Thatcher's findings that the EEG of the frontal cortex becomes increasingly coordinated with the EEG of other cortical sites. Based on the EEG data, it appears that the initial coordination involves connections formed among groups of neurons that are anatomically close to one another. Later, connections seem to be made among groups of neurons that are anatomically more distant.

Changes in EEG coordination are correlated with important cognitive developmental changes (summarized in Case, 1992). To illustrate, consider some of the important developmental milestones that take place around 6 years of age, which is also the age at which the rate of increase in EEG coordination between frontal sites and other cortical sites is most pronounced. In Piagetian theory, age 6 years is the time of the transition from preoperational to concrete operational thought. There is also evidence that age 6 years is about the time when children acquire substantially more control over initiating novel behaviors and inhibiting old behaviors. Four-year-old children have trouble inhibiting expressions of anger and sadness in social situations in which our culture expects the inhibition of such emotions, but by age 8 most children are able to inhibit such emotions (Griffin, 1992). The rate of growth in memory span is also greatest around age 6 (Crammond, 1992).

As we learn more about how the brain matures in infants and young children, and as we learn more about how the brain controls memory and problem solving, we will have a better sense of the role of neural maturation in cognitive development. The research done to date (Nelson, 1995) certainly suggests that genetically programmed changes in neural myelinization, synaptic density, frontal lobe reorganization, and other neurological changes may be associated with developmental improvements in memory and processing capacity.

Increased Memory Capacity and Cognitive Development: Which Is the Cart and Which Is the Horse?

While the research certainly demonstrates that processing capacity correlates with age, it is not necessarily the case that an increase in processing capacity is the (sole) cause of cognitive developmental changes. Perhaps, instead, an increase in processing capacity is the result of developmental changes whose cause lies elsewhere.

In the first place, in certain cases, younger children have at least as good a memory as older children and adults (see Bjorklund, 1995; or Searleman & Herrmann, 1994, for reviews). Dempster (1985) found that age differences in

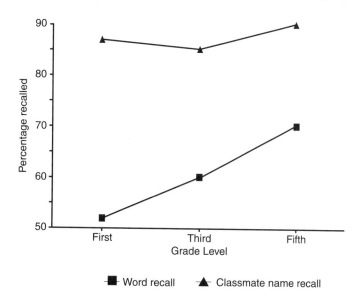

FIGURE 11–4   Recall of word list improves as children get older, but recall of classmates' names stays high across all ages. Based on Bjorklund and Zeman (1982).

memory span were greatly reduced if the items used to test memory were familiar and if the subjects were not given any opportunity to rehearse the items. Bjorklund and Zeman (1982) tested first-, third-, and fifth-grade children on their recall of a list of words that included animal names and the names of their classmates. As illustrated in Figure 11-4, the number of words recalled from the word list increased as grade level increased. However, the three grade levels were about equal in their recall of names of classmates. Presumably the three grades of children were all very familiar with their classmates. The older children, however, probably knew more about the concepts underlying the words and could use that knowledge to reconstruct the words presented on the list.

As children develop, they acquire knowledge in various domains and acquire various strategies, such as rehearsal and organization, for remembering new information. In other words, they acquire the ability to reconstruct the past.

Evidence demonstrating that reconstructive processes drive recollection in young children comes from research on the suggestibility of children's memory (see Doris, 1991). A typical example is an experiment by Leichtman and Ceci (1995; see, also, Lindberg, 1991). Preschool children (ages 3 to 6 years) were interviewed after observing a stranger named Sam Stone enter their classroom, interact briefly with the teacher, comment on a story the teacher was reading, and leave. One group of children was later given misleading questions about Sam's visit that implied that Sam ripped a book and soiled a teddy bear. A control group was given no misleading questions. Weeks later, all the children were given a standard forensics interview in which they were asked to recall what they could of Sam's visit and to say whether they saw Sam engage in some activity with a book and a teddy bear. Virtually no child in the control group erroneously recalled that Sam ripped a book or soiled a teddy bear. In the misleading question group, 21% of the younger children and 14% of the older children spontaneously recalled that Sam had damaged at least one of the items. In response to more direct questions, 53% of the younger and 38% of the older children indicated that Sam did one or the other of the misdeeds. Adults naive to the details of the experiment were later shown videotapes of some of the children's recall and found it difficult to judge which child's memory was accurate and which child's memory was false.

If improvements in memory capacity reflect the acquisition of learning and reconstruction strategies, then we would expect that young children explicitly taught a strategy for remembering new information should perform as well on memory tests as older children. Kobasigawa (1974) presented first-, third-, and sixth-grade children with a series of pictures to recall. The pictures were grouped by categories, such as the category of zoo animals. Older children recalled more word labels for the pictures than younger children. However, when the children were provided cues, such as a picture of a zoo, and were directed to use the cues to recall the word labels, then the performance of the younger children improved to the level of the older children (see Bjorklund, 1995, for a discussion of similar studies).

The idea that improvements in memory capacity reflect acquisition of skill and knowledge also suggests that children's memory for information in some domain should surpass that of adults if the children but not the adults are experts in the domain (see Bjorklund, 1995, for a discussion). Chi (1978) compared 10-year-old children with college-aged adults on their memory of lists of digits and on their memory for the positions of chess pieces on a chessboard. The children were expert chess players, and the adults were only novice players. The adults recalled more digits, but the children recalled more positions of chess pieces. Presumably the children were able to use their knowledge of chess to deduce the positions of the chess pieces.

An implication from such observations may be that what we identify as processing capacity is really the consequence of knowledge and strategies accumulated over time. As children acquire knowledge in enough domains, and acquire strategies for using that knowledge, they will do better on most tests of memory and other kinds of processing efficiency. That is to say, it may not be an increase in processing efficiency and capability, per se, that serves as the mechanism of cognitive development. Instead, cognitive development may be driven by the accumulation of experiences from which knowledge and strategies are extracted. The inherent processing capabilities of the child may not undergo any developmental change at all.

I would not want to end this section drawing such a radical conclusion from a few selected pieces of research, however. A more plausible view is that the developing child acquires new processing capabilities (Fry & Hale, 1996) and accumulates experiences from which to extract useful knowledge. Certainly what we have recently learned about developmental changes to the brain suggests that both mechanisms, changing capabilities and knowledge accumulation, underlie cognitive development.

SECTION 3: IMPLICIT THEORIES, LANGUAGE ACQUISITION, AND THE DOMAIN-SPECIFIC NATURE OF COGNITIVE DEVELOPMENT

Piagetian theory and most theories of biological maturational capacity stress that the main forces driving cognitive development are the same for all domains of knowledge. Indeed, one of the strongest criticisms of Piaget's theory is that it insists that cognitive development is similar in all domains of knowledge (Gopnik, 1996). In contrast to such generic approaches are domain-specific approaches, discussed in this section.

IMPLICIT THEORIES

One currently influential domain-specific approach to cognitive development is based on the idea that children acquire **implicit theories** in various domains (for a discussion of implicit theories, see Wellman and Gelman, 1992). A child's implicit theory is supposed to consist of a loose network of generalizations and explanations that describe the relationships among concepts within a domain of knowledge. Each domain has a different implicit theory. A child might have an implicit theory of the mind, of social relationships, of the physics of movement, and of the biology of plants and animals. While implicit theories are not easy for the child to articulate, they guide the child's thoughts, deductions, and behaviors. The essential relationships underlying an implicit theory are bound to be different in each domain and are likely to emerge at different times depending on the child's experiences.

The notion that cognitive development depends on the child's acquisition of implicit theories is an intriguing modification of Piaget's idea that the child is a quasi-scientist who actively constructs models of reality. Most researchers studying implicit theories do not consider themselves Piagetians in any sense, however. They prefer to emphasize differences between the standard Piagetian approach and the newer implicit theory approach. Piaget looked to developmental mechanisms that transcend domains; implicit memory theorists look to mechanisms that pertain to only one domain. In some cases, but by no means all, researchers taking the implicit theory approach have proposed inborn mechanisms that constrain the type of theory a child is likely to acquire in a domain. Piaget did not believe in domain-specific innate constraints on cognitive development.

Implicit Theories of the Mind

I will illustrate the implicit theory approach to cognitive development with a brief discussion of one kind of implicit theory, a **theory of the mind** (see Wellman & Gelman, 1992, and Flavell, 1993). One of the surprising results of research on the child's acquisition of a theory of mind is that even very young children seem to have adultlike ideas about the nature of mind. Children in the 2-to-three-year age range seem to use words like *want, hope,* and *remember* in the same way adults do (Shatz, Wellman, & Silber, 1983). Young children distinguish between real objects and mental representations of the object. They know, for example, that they can see a real cookie but not another child's idea of a cookie (Wellman & Estes, 1986). Children by the age of 3 to 4 years understand that another person's beliefs (e.g., a lost teddy bear is in the basement) can be used to predict that persons's behavior (e.g., going down to the basement to look for the teddy bear) (Wellman & Bartsch, 1988). Note that children aged 4 and younger would ordinarily be considered preoperational and therefore incapable of taking other people's perspective, under the Piagetian approach. Yet these young children seem to have a surprisingly adultlike notion of the nature of human mental life.

False Beliefs

Although very young children already have an adultlike theory of mind, they seem to have difficulty understanding **false beliefs** (Carey, 1990; Flavell, 1993; Wimmer & Perner, 1983). The young child may understand that other people believe that teddy bears are lovable, but not understand that other people believe that they can play with the child's own teddy bear, which would be, from the point of view of the child, a false belief. (Toddlers are very possessive of their teddy bears!)

In one study of false beliefs, Perner, Leekman, and Wimmer (1987) presented a crayon box to a group of 3-year-old children and asked the children to predict what was inside the box. The children guessed that the box contained crayons. They were then shown that the box in fact contained pencils. The children were then asked to predict what another child shown the box would guess that the box contained. The children predicted that the other child would say that the box contained pencils. The children had trouble attributing false beliefs to another child.

Indeed, young children seem to have trouble attributing false beliefs to themselves. Gopnik and Astington (1988) asked children who had been shown that a candy box contained pencils, and not the candy that they had first guessed, what they had thought the box contained when they first saw it. The children incorrectly recalled that they had guessed that the box contained pencils. By around age 4 most children do seem to be able to understand the notion of a false belief.

The difficulty very young children have with false beliefs is reminiscent of the Spinozian model of reasoning that I presented in chapter 7: Reasoning and Rationality. Recall that Spinoza claimed that people are prone to regard as true any idea that they comprehend (Gilbert, 1991). It is only with additional effort that people falsify beliefs. That is to say, to know is to believe. Apparently this tendency is there from the start, and is retained in adulthood in the form of a greater difficulty with falsifying ideas than with accepting them as true.

As it turns out, there is some dispute over whether the difficulty young children have with the false belief task really means that young children do not actually understand false beliefs (Fodor, 1992). For one thing, even 2-year-old children are capable of pretend play and of recognizing that other people are engaged in pretend play (Leslie, 1987). It is hard to see how a child who cannot understand the notion of an idea as false could at the same time understand the idea of pretend. Furthermore, some experimental evidence suggests that 3-year-old children will attribute false or different beliefs to the other (e.g., Bartsch & Wellman, 1989; Sullivan & Winner, 1993) and will, at the urging of an experimenter, try to deceive the other about the location of a reward (Chandler, Fritz, & Hala, 1989).

NATIVISM

Many advocates of implicit theories also claim that infants are born with implicit general principles and constraints that influence the acquisition of implicit theories (e.g., Wellman & Gelman, 1992). More generally, this claim is called nativism, or innatism.

Immanuel Kant (1724–1804), the great 18th-century German philosopher, established the modern form of nativism. He conceded that ideas of specific objects and actions in the physical world are not innate. Kant believed that people are not born with knowledge of apples or courage or running. In this respect Kant differed from Plato, who claimed that people are born with knowledge of specific things and actions, albeit in an idealized form. According to Plato, an infant might have knowledge of an idealized apple, or an idealized act of courage. Kant thought otherwise. Kant argued instead that the mind possesses a number of innate and distinctive modes of thinking, each of which interprets experiences in a different way. These modes construct the reality by which experiences are rendered meaningful.

Kant's analysis can be illustrated with one of his examples. Humans tend to perceive that objects exist someplace in space, even though one never actually makes sensory contact with space. If we relied only on sensations, argued Kant, we would never impose a three-dimensional spatial arrangement on the world around us. Kant claimed that space is an *a priori* thought—it is one that cannot be conceptualized by humans in any other form. Other *a priori* notions include time, causality, negation, and unity. However, the ideas that we have about objects are provided to us by experience, subject to the constraints of *a priori* ways of thinking. For example, the idea of a chair as an object on which one sits derives from experiences with actual chairs. The idea of a chair is an *a posteriori* thought. It is possible to have a world without chairs, or a world in which chairs have no legs. There is no Platonic ideal of a chair with which the child is innately endowed. However, not just any old kind of idea about chairs can be acquired; rather, whatever idea of chair we conceive, it will reflect the notion that chairs must exist in space (and exist in time, have unity, and so on).

The view of nativism as advocated by many late-20th-century developmental psychologists seems Kantian, and not Platonic. Innate intuitions about grammar are a 20th-century example of Kant's *a priori* thought, for instance. I will refer to Kantian *a priori* thought as **pre-knowledge**. In general, the modern nativist idea is that the infant comes into the world with various kinds of pre-knowledge that bias what information is extracted from the world and how inductions, deductions, and generalizations based on that information are made (Wellman & Gelman, 1992; Gardner, 1983; Carey, 1985; Spelke, 1988; Keil, 1989; Geary, 1995). The information processing biases associated with pre-knowledge are said to be primary or privileged in the sense that they make learning in the relevant domain easier and more rapid than would be possible if the biases were not built in from the start. Pre-knowledge may also be called cognitive **instinct**, to make the point that the pre-knowledge is innate, or may be called a **module** of learning, so as to make the point that each kind of pre-knowledge operates in a different domain. The putative instinct that guides language acquisition, for instance, represents a very different set of information processing biases than does the putative instinct that guides the development of an implicit theory of mind.

Usually the domains of knowledge that nativists posit as involving cognitive instincts are based on evolutionary importance (Flavell, 1992). Cognitive instincts should play some plausible role in enhancing survival and reproduction in the ancestral environment in which humans evolved. Evolutionarily relevant domains might include, but are not be limited to, spatial perception, social relationships and values, language, food consumption, human faces, simple arithmetic, mind, biology, and mechanics.

The idea that children are born with cognitive instincts—with pre-knowledge—stands in contrast to the long-standing generic **social learning model** of human nature that says that people are born only with a general capacity for learning, so that culture, and not biology, completely determines what knowledge one acquires. The social learning model is more generally referred to as **empiricism**. Empiricism is usually identified with Aristotle, John Locke (1632–1704), James Mill (1775–1836), and B. F. Skinner, among others.

Be clear that nativists do not insist that all of cognitive development is based on cognitive instincts. Many forms of knowledge and skill make simultaneous use of several cognitive instincts and typically originate in only some cultures (Geary, 1995). Examples of culturally dependent domains include higher mathematics, abstract logical reasoning, reading, political history, tick-tack-toe, baseball, and agriculture. Such domains may be nonprivileged, secondary domains that are learned later in childhood, often only with considerable effort, and involve learning mechanisms that are generic.

Note, by the way, that I have conceptualized the standard **nature–nurture controversy** in a different, and, I hope, more useful way. It is a bit vague to say that cognitive development is either due to nurture, the environment one experiences, or nature, the instincts one inherits. First of all, something innate must be in place for any kind of learning to take place. "Generic" captures the idea that the "nurture" perspective postulates the minimum innate machinery necessary to account for cognitive development in all of the various domains in which people acquire knowledge. Minimally, we must be born with a generic capacity to learn that is used to acquire knowledge in domains as diverse as language and face recognition. The "nature" perspective really postulates more innate learning mechanisms than merely some generic capacity to learn. These additional mechanisms are the cognitive instincts, the domain-specific modules, postulated by nativism.

I hope, too, that this conceptualization of the nature–nurture issue will clear up a bit of confusion some people have about the role of genetically inherited cognitive processes in individual differences. Recall from chapter 9: Individual Differences in Cognition that differences in performance on standard intelligence tests probably reflect, to some extent, genetic differences. At the same time, the genes one inherits can account for cognitive similarities among people. The cognitive instincts discussed in this chapter are the basis of human cognitive similarities, not individual differences. Perhaps an analogy will help you understand why. Virtually all humans inherit bipedalism, which presumably reflects a kind of instinct contained in the genes. Yet some people, such as those with the potential to win an Olympic gold medal in the 20,000 meter walk event, walk more efficiently than others. Presumably, slight differences in the exact genetic makeup of the genes responsible for bipedalism give rise, in part, to such individual differences.

One of the main battlegrounds in the war between nativist and generic approaches to cognitive development is the domain of language acquisition. Language is intriguing because it is unique to humans and underlies human social interactions and most of human culture. Language allows us to learn without directly experiencing what we learn. Through language we store, accumulate, and use knowledge that no one person can possess. Language is also of interest because on the surface it seems that language cannot possibly be innate; after all, we learn the language of our culture, and that language is typically unintelligible to people from another culture.

Indeed, generic approaches to language acquisition claim that language is acquired the way any other domain is acquired, using generic developmental mechanisms. Language is not privileged. Infants have no advanced knowledge about the nature of language. A nativist approach to language acquisition, on the other hand, claims that children are born with a kind of Kantian preknowledge of language, the form of which includes a predisposition to pay more attention to speech than to other auditory information, to infer readily the grammatical structure of language, and to prefer some generalizations about language more than others. Be clear, though, that no modern-day nativist claims that children are born with knowledge of specific words or specific grammar rules. Furthermore, children are not expected to be conscious of their linguistic pre-knowledge.

The idea that children are born with a tacit understanding of language was introduced in chapter 10: Language. In that chapter I made the case that language is a biological specialization, an instinct, and not a cultural invention (Pinker, 1994). All cultures, without exception, have language; furthermore, and despite their apparent diversity, the world's languages are strikingly similar with respect to their grammatical properties. The putative language instinct consists of tacit knowledge of what the languages of the world have in common. Evidence for a language-specific organ-like system in the brain, centered in and around Broca's area and Wernicke's area, also supports the notion of a language instinct. In this section I will focus on the developmental evidence for a language instinct—for the claim that the way language is acquired is different from other forms of cognitive development, because language acquisition is controlled and constrained by the pre-knowledge of language.

OVERVIEW OF LANGUAGE DEVELOPMENT

Recall that language is composed of a vocabulary of word–idea relationships and a grammar for combining simple sounds into words and sentences. Grammar consists of phonology, morphology, and syntax. Children learn about vocabulary, phonology, morphology, and syntax simultaneously, but researchers sometimes find it useful to separate them. Much of the following is based on discussions in Ingram (1989), Reich (1986), Pinker (1990), and Carroll (1994).

The Acquisition of Vocabulary

Usually around the age of 6 months children begin to babble the fundamental sounds—the phonemes—of language (Reich, 1986). Because even deaf children babble (Locke, 1983), we can assume that babbling is a genetically programmed behavior. The babblings of the young infant do not seem to be correlated with objects and events, so we can presume that they lack any semantic content. By around age 1 year, hearing children will typically begin to produce meaningful words. (So will deaf children, if they are taught sign language.) Words that are among the first that children produce include *encyclopedia*, *ramrod*, and *nuance*.

Just kidding! The first words usually refer to the parents (e.g., *mommy* and *daddy*), objects with which the infant interacts (e.g., *ball* and *truck*), simple actions and gestures (e.g., *up* and *bye-bye*), and simple desires (e.g., *no* and *eat*). Less common are words that refer to objects with which the infant does not interact (e.g., *sofa* or *wall*), words that refer to the self (e.g., the infant's own name or *I*), or words that have purely grammatical functions (e.g., *the* or *and*). Although the words that infants use are usually spoken frequently in the infant's presence, most of the frequently heard words are not part of the infant's early vocabulary. Consider that words like *I*, *the*, and *wall* are likely to be spoken relatively frequently by the infant's caretakers, yet an infant rarely produces these words (Ingram, 1989; Reich, 1986). Also noteworthy is the observation that infants will behave as if they understand words before they can produce them. In general, comprehension seems to precede production throughout the language acquisition process. For example, the typical child reaches the milestone of comprehending 50 words at around age 1 year, which is about 8 months before reaching the milestone of producing 50 words (Benedict, 1979).

Between ages 1½ and 3, vocabulary size grows exponentially (Smith, 1926; see Reich, 1986). By age 3, children will typically have vocabularies on the order of about 900 words. After age 3, the rate of vocabulary growth tapers off to a level of about 500 to maybe 2,000 new words a year throughout the remainder of the preschool years. Incidentally, these estimates of vocabulary size and rates of growth should be viewed with caution. It is, in fact, quite difficult to determine the size of a child's vocabulary. Children may use certain words for a brief period of time and then stop using them. Some words may be used only rarely. Furthermore, it is not always clear what a child means when it uses a word or what it understands when it hears a word. And, of course, there are large individual differences in the timing and rate of vocabulary acquisition. Still, it is rather remarkable that children are able to acquire an average of several new words a day throughout childhood.

The meaning a child attaches to a word may not necessarily reflect what an adult means by the same word. In chapter 5: Implicit and Semantic Memory I discussed several approaches to the meaning of concepts associated with words, and described some of the experimental studies on the child's acquisition of word meaning. One of the approaches to the meaning of words is called the **semantic feature approach** (Brown, 1958; Clark, 1973), which claims that children gradually associate primitive semantic features (e.g., living) with a word label (e.g., *bird*) until the bundle of features resembles the adult version. It is possible that children acquire some of the semantic features associated with words before they acquire all of them (Clark, 1973), which may account for why children frequently overextend words—using *doggie* to refer to dogs, cats, and horses, for instance.

Another approach to the meaning of words is called the **implicit theory approach** (e.g., Keil, 1989), which claims that children acquire a complex network of various types of relationships among concepts that serve to organize, explain, and predict. An adult implicit theory of the meaning of *bird* might include relationships among the concepts of DNA, biological growth, and biological form, for example. Younger children may have implicit theories that are initially rather abstract and vague (e.g., animals have blood inside them) but over time become more concrete and precise (e.g., animals have two lungs for breathing inside them) (Simons & Keil, 1995). I refer the reader to chapter 5 for a discussion of semantic features and implicit theories. The implicit theory idea was also discussed earlier in this chapter.

The Acquisition of Grammar

Children encounter most words in the context of sentences. At the same time, they must learn how to combine words to make meaningful sentences. The meaning of an utterance is captured not only by the meanings of words, but also by the relationships among the words. Critical to language acquisition, then, is the acquisition of the rules of grammar.

Children typically begin to put two words together around the age of 17½ months. By around age 22 months, two-word sentencelike combinations (e.g., "Daddy coming") are about as common as single-word utterances (e.g., "daddy"), which in turn are about as common as word sequences that seem to be a string of single-word utterances and not sentencelike sequences (e.g., "daddy, mommy"). The first multiword utterances usually have a **telegraphic style**. Most of the words are content words, and not words with a purely grammatical function. So instead of saying "mommy's sock" the child says "mommy sock"; instead of saying "I will go to the store" the child says "I go store" (Bloom, Lightbown, & Hood, 1975; see Brown, 1973; and Bloom, 1973, for major observational studies of children's language).

As children's vocabulary expands, so too does the length and grammatical complexity of their utterances. One way to estimate the child's utterance length is with the statistic of **mean length of utterance (MLU)** (Brown, 1973). For this statistic, one computes the average number of morphemes per utterance, where a morpheme is a meaningful unit. A sentence such as "Dinosaurs are scary" has four morphemes, one of which is the plural ending. Children typically have an MLU of 1.75 at around age 22 months, 2.75 at age 32 months, and 4.00 at age 45 months. Of course, there is wide variability in the rates at which children expand the length of their sentences.

As children's vocabulary expands, they also begin to acquire an expanding set of words for the syntactic categories they are learning. For example, the set of words that can serve as adjectives (e.g., *big*) will expand over time. In this way, these categories become truly grammatical as they contain a semantically diverse set of words (e.g., *big, red, funny, bad*).

As the MLU increases, young children begin to acquire **grammatical morphemes**, which are morphemes and inflections that have minimal meaning except in the context of a sentence. These include the possessive (*'s*), past-tense markers (*-ed*), and contractions. One of the more fascinating trends observed in the acquisition of grammatical morphemes is the tendency for children to overgeneralize the rules underlying the use of the grammatical morphemes (Cazden, 1968; Ervin, 1964; Marcus, 1996). The classic example is that of past tense. In English, about 180 verbs (e.g., *hit, go, eat*) are irregular; that is, the past-tense form is made in an idiosyncratic way. Other verbs (e.g., *jump, laugh, clean*) are regular—the past tense follows the *-ed* rule. In the linguistic environment of the child, irregular verbs are more frequently encountered than are regular verbs. Consequently, children sometimes use irregular forms correctly, at first. After encountering many regular verbs, however, the child catches on to the rule and begins to overgeneralize it. The child starts to say things like "I goed home."

Eventually, and it may take a number of years, the child manages to sort out the regular and irregular verbs, applying the -*ed* rule only to the regular forms. The tendency to overgeneralize grammatical rules occurs in other cases, as well. English-speaking children also tend to overgeneralize the plural, for which there are regular forms (*boys*) and irregular forms (*men*). Overgeneralization is observed in all languages in which the grammar admits both regular and irregular forms (see Slobin, 1979).

For a child to have truly mastered a particular grammar rule, the child ought to be able to use the rule on new words. In a well-known study, Berko (1958) taught preschoolers novel words by showing them pictures illustrating the meaning of the words. The children were encouraged to display their understanding of grammar rules by prompts associated with the pictures. For example, the children were shown a picture of a fictional birdlike creature. The children were then presented with a question such as: "This is a wug. Now there are two of them. There are two ____." Although the children had never encountered *wug*, because the experimenter made it up, most were able to provide spontaneously the correct plural form, namely *wugs*.

DEVELOPMENTAL EVIDENCE FOR A LANGUAGE INSTINCT

What enables infants and children to acquire language, particularly the grammar of language? As I discussed before, the nativist position is that children are born with a form of linguistic pre-knowledge which they use to induce the properties of the language(s) they encounter (Chomsky, 1981; Hyams, 1986; Pinker, 1990, 1994). The result is that language is acquired in a different way than other intellectual skills are acquired, such as logical reasoning. It is important to see that the nativist does not claim that experiences have no effect on language acquisition. It is obvious that they do. The child growing up in a French-speaking environment learns French, the child growing up in a Chinese-speaking environment learns Chinese. Again, the kinds of pre-knowledge that all children are supposedly born with reflect properties that all languages have in common. The idea is that the child's processing of linguistic input is constrained by the linguistic pre-knowledge.

It is also important to see that the notion of a human language instinct does not imply that all people will acquire the same language. Consider bird song. In many species of birds the basics of song production and the capacity to learn the song are instinctive. Yet in some of these species, such as sparrows, young birds must hear their species' song in order to acquire it. Furthermore, different groups of birds of the same species sing in strikingly different "dialects" of the song, depending on their geographic location (Marler, 1991). Of course, bird song is not language (bird song lacks grammar) nor did human language evolve from bird song. The point is that the bird song example makes it clear that instincts may require that members of a species have certain experiences before the instinct is properly activated and that some group variation within a species for an instinctive behavior is possible.

Pre-knowledge of Semantics

An example of the kind of pre-knowledge with which a child might be born is knowledge about how word–idea relationships are constrained. One characteristic of the semantics of the world's languages is that different words refer to different concepts. Although there are some exceptions to this generalization (e.g., *car* and *automobile*), it seems to hold in most cases.

Markman (1992) has proposed that infants are born with this knowledge, called the **mutual exclusivity constraint**, which they can use to figure out which sounds in the sound stream are to be associated with objects and events in the environment. So if Daddy uses the word *tractor* while driving down the street, and the child sees a car and a tractor from the car window and knows only the word *car*, then the child would assume that the other object is the tractor. If Mommy shows the child a picture of a house, refers to a chimney on the house, and the child knows only the word *house*, then the child would be motivated to look for some part of the house to which the word *chimney* refers.

One line of evidence for pre-knowledge of the mutual exclusivity constraint comes from an experiment that presented to 3-year-old children pictures that contained both a familiar object (e.g., spoon) and an unfamiliar object (e.g., tongs) (Markman & Wachtel, 1988). If the experimenter merely asked the child to point to an object, the child was as likely to point to the familiar as to the unfamiliar object. But if the experimenter asked the child to point to the object the experimenter labeled with a nonsense word, then the child was likely to point to the unfamiliar object.

Poverty of the Linguistic Stimulus

Notice that if children are born with pre-knowledge in the form of the mutual exclusivity constraint, then parents do not always need to teach them to which aspect of the environment a word label is associated. Indeed, it is often observed that parents do not supply adequate information with which to teach children about language. Children hear only some examples of grammatically correct utterances, yet are able to generalize grammar rules to many sentences they have never encountered. Children produce and even hear lots of ungrammatical sentences, yet parents do not provide much information about when and why sentences are ungrammatical. In short, information is either missing from the parent's own utterances or from the teaching methods they use. Yet children manage to learn language, and learn it with surprising ease, despite the **poverty of the linguistic stimulus**. If the input is impoverished, goes the argument, then it must be the case that children use pre-knowledge of language to deduce, from whatever input they receive, the rules of language.

An implication of the poverty of stimulus argument is that children have tendencies to deduce grammar and vocabulary rules even in the absence of any stimulus model. The overgeneralization of grammatical rules provides a nice illustration of how children use pre-knowledge of grammar to infer the specific grammatical rules of their language. The ratio of irregular to regular verbs remains constant in the linguistic environment of the child throughout the period in which overgeneralizations appear (Pinker, 1990). Yet at one point the child uses the irregular forms correctly (e.g., "I went"), but then shifts to using the irregular forms incorrectly (e.g., "I goed"). The impetus to make this shift must come from inside the child; certainly adults do not encourage overgeneralizations or provide models of overgeneralization. The idea is that the child is born with pre-knowledge of syntactic classes, such as verbs, and so is prepared to generalize any regularity it observes of words in the class, such as the -*ed* rule for English verbs. Another way to make this critically important point is that children do not learn language by imitating the language they hear. Instead, they learn language by extracting the rules of language based on their pre-knowledge of language and on the linguistic examples they encounter.

Linguistic pre-knowledge may be used, not only to make some linguistic generalizations, but to block other linguistic generalizations. Consider this example (from Corballis, 1991). Language permits embedding of phrases into a main sentence, as in "The man who is here is tall." In learning to ask yes–no questions (in English), children will see that a sentence like "The man is tall" can be converted into a question by bringing the to-be verb to the front of the sentence (i.e., "Is the man tall?"). How will children generalize from such common examples to make a question out of an embedded sentence such as "The man who is here is tall"?

One generalization children could make, but never do, is to bring the first to-be verb to the front of the sentence. Children do not produce questions such as "Is the man who here is tall?" In this example, the first to-be verb is in the embedded phrase. Instead, it is as if children readily recognize embedding and treat embedded phrases as units that are distinct from the main sentence. Consequently, they are reluctant to move the embedded to-be verb to the front. This generalization is blocked, despite its similarity to the acceptable generalizations that children do make (Crain & Nakayama, 1987). Yet parents never teach these facts to children or supply them with many examples of this pattern of acceptable and unacceptable generalizations. The nativist claims that this pattern of generalizations is one that children are predisposed to make because they have pre-knowledge of embedding. The pre-knowledge drives the process by which children deduce which grammatical forms may be extended to new sentences and what restrictions apply to these extensions.

Another implication of the poverty of stimulus argument is that feedback and deliberate attempts to correct a child's speech errors will have minimal impact on the course of language acquisition. The reason for this implication is that nativist theory claims that the child's innate knowledge makes a substantial contribution to language acquisition. The child merely needs to hear (or, in the case of sign language, see) language and have the opportunity to use it in order to acquire language.

Consistent with the poverty of stimulus argument is the well-known finding that parents rarely correct their children's ungrammatical utterances and rarely praise their children's grammatical utterances (Brown & Hanlon, 1970; Hirsh-Pasek, Treiman, & Schneiderman, 1984). Instead, most of the parent's corrections seem to pertain to the truth or falsity of utterances, irrespective of their grammaticality. Furthermore, parents do not understand their children's grammatical utterances any better than their children's ungrammatical utterances. Despite this sort of feedback, children manage to learn grammar and even become grammatical liars!

Of course, parents do make an effort to simplify their children's utterances to their children, presumably to make it easier for the children to acquire vocabulary and grammar. In general, speech to children is shorter, more concrete, more intonationally exaggerated, and more grammatical than adult-to-adult speech (see Carroll, 1994). Surprisingly, this kind of instruction is neither necessary nor especially helpful to the child. At least some studies suggest that the speech of children is, for the most part, unrelated to the characteristics of the parents' speech (Newport, Gleitman, & Gleitman, 1977; Furrow, Nelson, & Benedict, 1979). In some cultures, parents do not even make any effort to simplify their speech to young children, and, in fact, often avoid speaking directly to young children. Nevertheless, children in these cultures grow up to be fluent speakers of their language (Schieffelin & Einsenberg, 1981).

Home Signs

One rather remarkable finding is that deaf children who are not exposed to sign language will sometimes invent their own idiosyncratic signs (**home signs**) and a simple grammatical system for the home signs (Goldin-Meadow & Mylander, 1990). An example of a home sign invented by one child was using a twisting motion to refer to opening a jar. By around age 2 these children begin to combine home signs into longer utterances. The grammatical nature of the longer utterances reveals itself in several ways. The children tended to sign in a consistent order—for example, placing the home sign for "give" after the home sign for the person benefiting from the giving. In some cases children developed a kind of inflection system for home signs indicating action. One boy displaced his home signs for action in the direction of the object affected by the action. The sign language deaf children invent also includes noun and verb classes, distinguished by using a different set of gestures for each syntactic class (Goldin-Meadow, Butcher, Mylander, & Dodge, 1994).

What is especially remarkable about home signing is that the deaf children managed to develop grammatically structured utterances without much help from their parents, who would begin to use the home signs of their children only after the children first started using them. The home sign phenomenon is consistent with the idea that children are born with pre-knowledge of semantics and grammar, and will impose it on their own gestures in the absence of parental models.

An especially compelling example of home sign is that of a child who was born hearing-impaired. His normal-hearing parents then learned American Sign Language (ASL) in order to communicate with him (Singleton & Newport, 1993, as reported in Pinker, 1994). His parents never learned ASL well, however, making frequent grammatical mistakes and failing to use properly certain ASL grammatical devices, such as raising the eyebrows and lifting the chin to indicate that a noun is the topic of a sentence. With only his parents' signing as a model, the child learned a form of sign that was in fact more grammatical (it approximated the full grammar of ASL) than that used by the parents. For example, he reliably used the eyebrow and chin "inflection" to indicate topic. It is as if his parents' signing awakened in the child the pre-knowledge of grammar that was then used to fill in the missing portions of the adults' model. Presumably the parents were unable to fill in what was missing from their own sign because they had lost much of their capacity to acquire language, a point on which I will elaborate below.

Developmental Independence

An important claim of a nativist approach to language is that language acquisition follows a developmental trajectory that is independent, at least in some respects, of the developmental trajectories observed in other domains, such as logical reasoning. It seems that language is acquired much more rapidly than other cognitive skills. The preschool child already has mastered most of the rules of grammar, despite the complexity of grammar. Yet other intellectual domains, such as abstract reasoning, take a child many more years to master.

The independence of language from other cognitive skills seems especially well established by cases of individuals who are severely mentally retarded in most intellectual domains but can nevertheless acquire the vocabulary and grammar of their language (Curtiss, 1982; Yamada, 1990). Laura, a retarded girl with an IQ of 41, has remarkable spoken language skills. She spoke this sentence, for example: "He was saying that I lost my battery-powered watch that I loved." Yet Laura cannot read, write, tell time, tell you her age or the country in which she lives (Yamada, 1990).

That language acquisition is independent of other kinds of cognitive development is also supported by the phenomenon of **Specific Language Impairment (SLI)** (Gopnik, 1990; Gopnik & Crago, 1991). People with SLI have trouble acquiring the rules of grammar. They produce, as adults, utterances such as "Carol is cry in the church" and "The boys eat four cookie." Furthermore, adults with SLI have trouble passing Berko's test of generalizing grammatical rules to new words (*wug* → *wugs*). Yet in most cases individuals with SLI perform normally on general tests of intelligence. What's more, children with SLI are able to learn nonverbal rules in a discrimination task as well as do children with normal language (Kiernan, Snow, Swisher, and Vance, 1997). SLI apparently runs in families—the pattern of affliction suggests that the cause is a defect on one gene.

Critical Period in Language Acquisition

One sense in which language acquisition may be independent of other domains of cognitive development is based on the possibility that language acquisition is characterized by a sensitive or **critical period** that is not observed in other domains (Lenneberg, 1967). A critical period is a time early in life when an infant or child has an enhanced capability of acquiring language. As children grow up, they gradually lose some of their capacity for acquiring a first language, although adults who acquired a first language in childhood still retain a residual capacity for learning additional languages (the amount of residual capacity for learning additional languages in adulthood is debated, however; see Bialystok & Hakuta, 1994). A possible evolutionary advantage of a critical age for language acquisition is that an enhanced capacity in the young helps ensure that the young will quickly acquire the ability to communicate with adults (see Hurford, 1991).

One line of evidence for a critical period in language acquisition comes from the observation that young children whose language has been undermined by brain injury are likely to recover most of their language skill and go on to become competent users of language, although they may have more difficulty than most people in comprehending grammatically complex sentences. However, when adults suffer brain damage that undermines language, they usually recover very little of their language skill (Lenneberg, 1967).

Other evidence for a critical period in language acquisition comes from a few very tragic cases in which children grew up isolated from human interaction, and therefore were denied opportunities to hear or use language. One of the best-known of these cases is that of Genie (not her real name) (Curtiss, 1977; Rymer, 1993). Genie's abusive father confined her almost all of the time to a small room where she rarely heard language. Genie was occasionally beaten by her father and suffered from emotional neglect. Genie's horrifying predicament was discovered by authorities when she was 13 years old, at which time she had no appreciable language skills. With the help of various caretakers and psychologists, Genie did manage to acquire a rather extensive vocabulary, but had much more trouble mastering the rules of grammar, her use of which never reached the level of the typical older child. For instance, about 7 years after she began to learn language, she produced this sentence: "Think about Mama love Genie." Although Genie is right-handed, her language is atypically controlled by her right hemisphere, as determined by dichotic listening measures (Fromkin, Krashen, Curtiss, Rigler, & Rigler, 1974). Yet Genie does not appear to be mentally retarded. In fact, she did quite well on nonverbal visual-spatial tests of cognitive development, on one test scoring higher than anyone ever has! Clearly the impact of extreme social isolation was to undermine her grammar and not her visual-spatial skills. It should be noted, though, that the social isolation did undermine the development of her social skills. Her case is doubly tragic, as she is now institutionalized and has apparently regressed in her use of language.

Another case is that of a woman known as Chelsea (not her real name) who was misdiagnosed as retarded but was raised in a normal family with normal social interactions (Curtiss, 1994). In fact, Chelsea is hearing impaired. After she was finally fitted with hearing aids at the age of 31, she began to learn spoken language. After 9 years of language training, she has acquired a vocabulary of around 2,000 words, but her grammar remains at the level of a young child. She tends to leave out of her utterances inflections (e.g., the -ed ending), function words (e.g., the), and even the subjects of sentences.

Actually, a disturbingly large percentage of congenitally deaf children have little contact with human language until they become adolescents or adults. Usually this happens because they are born to hearing parents who do not know or learn to use sign language. If taught sign language, deaf children will acquire it as readily and in the same manner as hearing children acquire spoken language. For instance, young deaf children taught sign language will initially sign in a telegraphic fashion, using two signs without the hand movements that indicate grammatical distinctions like plurality (Newport & Ashbrook, 1977). As with spoken language, the left hemisphere provides most of the control over the grammatical aspects of sign language (Poizner, Klima, & Bellugi, 1987).

Consistent with the idea of a critical period is the finding that deaf people who are never exposed to sign language until they are adolescents or adults tend not to become very proficient at grammar, even after decades of exposure and practice (Newport, 1990). What seems to be important is that people get exposure to some kind of language as children. There are cases of adults who had normal hearing as children but became deaf after the onset of adolescence, at which time they learned ASL as a second language. They will perform better on tests of ASL grammar than will congenitally deaf adults who also learned ASL after the onset of adolescence, but who were never exposed to language as children (Mayberry, 1993).

Presumably, many other categories of intellectual development are not characterized by a critical period. People at any age can acquire proficiency in any of a number of intellectual skills, including logical, problem solving, and perceptual–motor skills. Indeed, there are certain skills, such as hypothetical reasoning, that adolescents and adults seem better prepared to acquire than are young children. For example, Siegler (1978) found that children near the age of adolescence benefited more than younger children from training on the balance scale problem used by Piaget to test for abstract reasoning.

An intriguing implication raised by nativist approaches to cognition is that cognitive development is not always characterized by an improvement in cognitive capabilities. In fact, the capacity to acquire language actually declines with age, even while knowledge of language increases. The notion of declining capabilities undermines generic developmental approaches, such as Piagetian theory, where the assumption is that cognitive capabilities always show improvement until they reach the adult ideal. Perhaps adulthood brings with it cognitive losses as well as cognitive gains.

HOW INSTINCTS INFLUENCE LANGUAGE ACQUISITION

How might an instinct for language be realized in the biology and behavior of a child? The instinct would have to be represented in the DNA the child inherits. Let me offer a speculative and highly simplified account of the connection between DNA and language acquisition (based on Pinker, 1984, 1994).

As the brain develops, proteins prescribed by DNA guide the growth of axons that seek out particular receptor sites, based on the concentrations of chemicals on the synaptic membranes of neurons in the growing brain. It is estimated that it takes about 30,000 genes, the majority of the human genome, to build the brain. It is possible that certain banks of neurons, in and around the language centers of the brain, form connections that function to encode some of the universal features of grammar and vocabulary. For example, neurons that connect to those parts of the auditory system that detect sounds associated with phonemes might in turn connect to neurons that represent longer segments of phonemes. Such neurons might be destined to represent noun phrases and verb phrases. In turn, some of these phrase-representing neurons might be connected to neurons that detect features of meaning, such as whether something is an object or an action.

Now consider what happens to a young child with such a brain. The child will have a tendency to associate objects with one phrase and actions with another phrase. A child who hears a sentence such as "The dog is barking" may notice that *the* and *dog* are grouped together, in part because there is likely to be a slightly longer pause between *dog* and *is* than between *the* and *dog*. The child may also notice that there is an actual dog present, or already know what *dog* means. Because the dog is an object, the phrase containing *dog* will become associated with the neurons that represent the phrase connected to object. In this way, the child assigns *the dog* to a noun-like phrase. Similarly, the phrase that denotes action, *is barking*, will become associated with the neurons that represent the phrase connected to action. Now the child assigns *is barking* to a verb-like phrase.

Certain phonemic features will be reliably associated with noun-like phrases and with verb-like phrases, and these features will teach the child the ways noun and verb phrases are expressed in the particular language the child encounters. The child acquiring English, for instance, will learn that *-ed* endings on verbs signal tense and *-s* endings on nouns signals plurality. The child will also then associate to noun phrases those words that possess such features even when the words do not have to do with objects. In this way, noun-like phrases are expanded into the more adult form. In adult language, noun phrases are about both objects (. . . the dogs of war . . .) and nonobjects (. . . the loves of Dobie Gillis . . .). Similarly, verb-like phrases will be expanded to include both actions (. . . is barking . . .) and nonactions (. . . is feeling . . .).

This approach, called **bootstrapping**, is one of several proposed schemes that detail how the putative language instinct might guide the language acquisition process. Often people associate instincts with inflexibility in behavior. The bird that has an instinct to fly south in the winter hasn't the luxury of choosing to winter up north. The language instinct, however, enhances flexibility. Not only would pre-knowledge of phrases speed up learning of language (and children do learn language relatively quickly), but such knowledge would also give the child the ability to construct and understand an unlimited number of sentences. Suppose for the sake of argument that phrases come in only two types, noun and verb phrases. Then the child who encounters the phrase "the dog that the cat . . ." will understand that one noun phrase is embedded in another and not that there is a new kind of phrase to learn. The recognition of the embedded structure of phrases allows children to insert virtually any noun phrase into any other noun phrase and so increase the generative capacity of their language. As Pinker (1994) points out, general-purpose learning, relying on people and culture, constrains the child; instincts set the child free.

GENERIC DEVELOPMENTAL MODELS OF LANGUAGE ACQUISITION

Not everyone buys the nativist argument for language. In contrast to the nativist approach is the generic approach to cognitive development, which takes as its main claim that all domains of knowledge are acquired in fundamentally the same way. According to the generic approach, children are not born with pre-knowledge of certain domains but only with general cognitive capacities that drive development in all domains (see Gleason & Ratner, 1993; or Reich, 1986, for reviews of generic approaches).

One example of a generic approach to language acquisition is cognitive theory. According to cognitive theory, language is merely one subordinate part of cognitive development. Children are not born with implicit knowledge of language but learn to attach language symbols to concepts and to acquire all the rules of grammar entirely from their linguistic experiences (Piaget, 1926b; Sinclair-De-Zwart, 1973; Bates & Snyder, 1985; Macnamara, 1972). A related proposal focuses on social interactions and the need for children to communicate with other people. According to these views, children receive considerable help acquiring language from their caretakers (Snow, 1981; Bruner, 1983; Gleason, Hay, & Cain, 1989; Vygotsky, 1978).

Much of the evidence for environmental influences on language acquisition is obvious. Children learn the language to which they are exposed. Dialect differences in vocabulary, accent, and grammar among children reflect the speech of their caretakers.

Some studies have attempted to control the linguistic input children receive in order to see whether the input affects the acquisition of certain grammatical forms. The input can, in some cases, have an influence on language acquisition (see Carroll, 1994, for a review). An example comes from a study by Nelson, Carskaddon, and Bonvillian (1973). They assigned children between 30 and 40 months of age to one of three groups. In one group the parents regularly recasted the sentences of their children by expanding them into longer and more grammatical utterances. In the second group the parents regularly followed up their children's sentences with short grammatical sentences that excluded words used by the children. In the third group, the control group, the parents made no special effort to alter their linguistic interactions with their children. On a variety of measures of linguistic advancement, the recast group of children outperformed the control group. The recast group also marginally outperformed the new sentence group, but only on verb development.

Generic approaches to language acquisition can also point to parallels between the acquisition of language and the acquisition of other cognitive skills (see Gleason & Ratner, 1993, for a review). To illustrate, Kelly and Dale (1989) demonstrated that infants tend to produce their first words at about the same time as they enter Piaget's fourth or fifth stage of sensorimotor development. Presumably the use of words to refer to objects requires an understanding of object permanence. They also found that a toddler's first use of multiword utterances typically emerged just after the child showed signs of entering the final stage of sensorimotor development. Despite such correlations, though, there are some striking dissociations between language development and other kinds of cognitive development, such as the cases of individuals with very low IQ scores who nevertheless display sophisticated language skill (Yamada, 1990).

Generic approaches also discount the evidence supposedly favoring a nativist approach to language acquisition. Some of the striking aspects of language development may not be unique to language. Who is to say that a young child denied all opportunities to reason would still be able to learn more complex forms of reasoning? Maybe critical periods are essential to all areas of cognitive development. It is well known, for example, that if a human infant born with strabismus (imbalance of the muscles of the eyeballs) does not have the problem corrected at a young age, the child will have permanent visual impairment. Still, it is worth pointing out that the existence of critical periods in several different areas of development is hardly inconsistent with nativist theory. After all, the kind of input required in a critical period of development is different for each domain. The language domain needs language input, although any sensory modality for the language will do. It does not matter for language acquisition if the child hears spoken language or sees sign. The visual perceptual system, on the other hand, must have specifically visual information in order to develop properly.

What of the poverty of the stimulus argument? Recall that this argument claims that parents do not supply enough feedback about grammaticality to account for their children's learning of grammar. However, the claim that parents do not supply helpful feedback has been disputed (e.g., Snow, 1986). While the nature of parental feedback does not necessarily take the form of explicit corrections of grammatical mistakes, it appears that at times parents do provide expansions, recasts, and clarifications of their children's ungrammatical sentences that can serve as cues to help their children learn grammar. Bohannon and Stanowicz (1988) demonstrated that parents were more likely to modify or request clarification from their children's grammatically ill-formed sentences than from their well-formed ones. What is lacking, however, is clear-cut evidence that such feedback is actually used by children to acquire language, although Farrar (1992) showed that children respond to such feedback by imitating the correct grammatical form contained in the parent's corrective recasts. However, Morgan, Bonamo, and Travis (1995) found little evidence that parental recasts of their children's syntactic errors actually helped the children to recover from the errors. Furthermore, and contrary to the generic approach, there remains the amazing example of hearing-impaired children denied an adequate model of sign language who nevertheless manage to acquire a sign language that is considerably more sophisticated than that used by their parents.

THE BOTTOM LINE?

So which kind of theory, nativist or generic, is the superior account of language acquisition? I lean toward nativist theory, as do most psycholinguists (e.g., Jackendoff, 1994; Pinker, 1994). There does seem to be good evidence for critical periods in language development. There are children who develop competency in language but not in other domains and children who fail to develop competency in language but are competent in other intellectual domains. Most remarkably of all, there are children who acquire grammar in the absence of adequate models. And all children seem to be able to generalize rules correctly, for instance producing "Is the man who is here tall?" and not "Is the man who here is tall?" Furthermore, the languages of the world are strikingly similar at the level of abstract grammatical and semantic properties, and there is a specific portion of the brain dedicated to language. All cultures, without exception, have language.

Still, there may be a way of accounting for these observations without the need to postulate an innate pre-knowledge of general vocabulary and grammatical principles. Braine (1992), for example, argues that the bootstrapping account of noun and verb phrase acquisition discussed previously does not require postulating any innate pre-knowledge of grammar. And even if one concedes the need for some form of language instinct, it remains an open question how much and what kind of pre-knowledge actually underlies language acquisition.

OTHER COGNITIVE INSTINCTS?

As I have pointed out, language is not the only proposed instinct or privileged cognitive domain in which infants may be born with pre-knowledge. Some developmental psychologists (see Wellman & Gelman, 1992) have proposed that infants are born with pre-knowledge of arithmetic (Wynn, 1995), biology (Keil, 1989), and social values (see Wright, 1994), just to name a few domains. Again, such pre-knowledge is thought to constrain learning in particular ways unique to the domain.

Numerical Infants

Consider arithmetic (the following is from Wynn, 1995; see also Starkey, 1992; Starkey, Spelke, & Gelman, 1990; Geary, 1995). Infants as young as 5 months can distinguish between stimulus sets that vary only with respect to the number of items in the set. An infant can distinguish between two puppets and three puppets, between a puppet jumping twice or three times, and between a drum beating two or three times. The infant seems to have an abstract sense of small numbers (and only of positive integers from about 1 to 4, and not, for example, of fractions).

Five-month-old infants can also engage in simple addition and subtraction (Wynn, 1995). The proof comes from what is called the **preferential looking paradigm**. To illustrate, suppose an infant is shown two dolls. A screen comes up and occludes the dolls. An empty hand reaches behind the screen and removes one doll. The screen is dropped and the infant sees either one or two dolls. The result is that the infant looks longer at the two-doll display than at the one-doll display, even though the two-doll display is the same stimulus the infant just saw (infants prefer to look at novel or unexpected displays). The conclusion seems to be that the infant, having seen one doll subtracted from two dolls, expects to see one doll, and is surprised if there are two dolls. That is, the infant performs subtraction. Chimpanzees are also capable of addition and subtraction of simple integers (Boysen & Berntson, 1989).

Wynn (1995) suggests that human infants (and infants of some other species) are born with an accumulator that is sensitive to the number of stimuli, but not to the stimulus modality of the stimuli, and that contains procedures for operating on (i.e., adding and subtracting) numbers. Such a counting capability might help animals count their offspring or their enemies. In humans, an instinct for counting might be a precursor of more advanced arithmetic skills, such as those involved in negative numbers, fractions, and algebra.

Infants as Biologists

Research similar to that which suggests an instinct for counting also suggests that infants are born with or readily acquire intuitions about the biological world. In one line of research (Spelke, Phillips, & Woodward, 1995), infants were presented a ball rolling behind a screen and another ball emerging from the other side. After infants habituated, the screen was removed and the infants saw one ball striking another ball, setting the second ball in motion. Or they saw one ball stop just short of the second ball, yet the second ball moved anyway. The infant looked longer at the display of the ball moving on its own, as if the infant expected that it was only through a collision that the second ball could receive the impetus to move (see also Bailargeon, 1994).

The same experiment was done with people moving behind the screen. Now the infant was more surprised if shown the display of one person colliding into the other than if shown the display in which the second person moved on his/her own. The experiment suggests that infants have knowledge of movement and expect that movement is different for animate things, which can initiate movement on their own, than for inanimate things, which ordinarily cannot initiate movement.

Furthermore, and consistent with the idea that some intuitions about biology are innate, all cultures have similar folk biological systems of knowledge (Berlin, Breedlove, & Raven, 1973; see Pinker, 1994). In all cultures, people group plants and animals into *genus* level categories that are strictly hierarchical. If a thing is a kangaroo, for example, it can be an animal but not a plant, and a kangaroo cannot be a koala. On the other hand, strict hierarchies do not usually characterize inanimate objects. A piano can be a piece of furniture or a musical instrument; a rock can be a tool or a weapon.

Be clear that the research on infants does not mean that infants are necessarily born with substantive beliefs about numbers or objects. Infants may be born with highly constrained developmental mechanisms that affect development in one area differently than in other areas. For example, the infant may be predisposed to notice reactive impetus in inanimate things and to notice volition in animate things. However, the infant would still need exposure to actual events to form beliefs and intuitions about movement that distinguish the animate from the inanimate. That is, what is innate may be Kantian, not Platonic.

BEYOND INSTINCTS

As I pointed out before, a commitment to nativism in cognitive development does not mean that one completely rejects any role for more generic mechanisms of development that draw on information supplied by the physical and social environment. Among the putative innate abilities (also called **primary abilities**) might be an especially important innate ability to draw on and integrate other innate abilities in the service of culturally dependent goals. The co-option of innate cognitive abilities might lead to the development of **secondary cognitive abilities** (Geary, 1995). Examples of secondary cognitive abilities might include reading, higher mathematics, tick-tack-toe, abstract logical reasoning, and so on. Secondary abilities are the kind that are found in some cultures but not in others, and are dependent on the extent to which formal institutions, such as schools, emphasize the development of the skill. Usually, secondary skills take longer to acquire or are acquired later in childhood than are the supposed innate, primary skills. The integrative skill on which the acquisition of secondary skills largely depends may mature later, as the child's processing capacity and frontal lobe circuitry mature (Nelson, 1995). A capacity for co-opting primary abilities in the service of secondary abilities is, arguably, one of the most important differences between humans and other animals (Gould & Vrba, 1982; Hall, 1992). It may be that the integrative skill is what allows humans to acquire such a wide range of skills and knowledge.

The integrative skill can be illustrated with language. The evidence that language is an instinct, and therefore a primary ability, has already been discussed at length. Reading, however, is certainly a secondary ability. Many cultures never developed reading. Even in literate cultures, children learn to read only years after they have already acquired considerable skill in the spoken language. Reading seems to integrate language and visual scanning skills, among other skills (see Geary, 1995). Children need to integrate the perceptual skills necessary to identify letters and words with the spoken language skills underlying vocabulary and grammar. Children's initial success at learning to read seems to be strongly predicted by their skill at phonological processing (e.g., knowing to say "up" when asked to pronounce "cup" without the /k/ sound) assessed before they learn to read (Wagner, Torgesen, & Rashotte, 1994).

The development of arithmetic also reinforces the idea that innate, primary abilities are co-opted in the service of a culturally dependent goal. As I discussed in the previous section, there is some evidence that human infants are born with a capacity to count and to do a kind of simple addition and subtraction for positive integers in the range of about 1 to 4 items. Because chimpanzees also have this skill, arithmetic is not a human-specific instinct, as is language. Counting and simple arithmetic are found in all of the world's cultures (Geary, 1995). However, the use of negative numbers, zero, fractions, algebra, calculus, and so on, are found in only some cultures. Usually it takes children years to master such culturally dependent forms of mathematical skill, and much of that mastery depends on schooling. Mathematical problem solving, for instance, seems to require an integration of primary counting abilities with skills such as spatially representing numbers and translating words into numbers and equations (Geary, 1995).

Many of the Piagetian tasks, such as conservation, transitive inference, and balance scales, might require the development of secondary skills. Conservation of number, for example, might require the integration of the primary counting skill with the primary spacial processing skill. The integration of primary skills to create secondary skills may be an important reason why conservation skills take years to emerge and why such skills have a more generic character.

In short, the primary skill of integrating other cognitive skills may correspond with a generic learning mechanism. Cognitive development, then, involves both the emergence of cognitive instincts and the deployment of generic learning mechanisms.

SUMMARY AND CONCLUSIONS

The main theme of this chapter is a contrast between generic approaches to cognitive development, which claim that all domains of knowledge are acquired in the same way, and domain-specific approaches, which claim that there are fundamental differences in the way knowledge is acquired, depending on the domain. The version of a domain-specific approach discussed at length was nativism, which claims that for certain biologically important domains infants are born with pre-knowledge specific to that domain.

In section 1, I discussed Jean Piaget's influential theory of cognitive development. Piagetian theory assumes that experience drives cognitive development and that all domains of knowledge are acquired in essentially the same way. However, Piagetian theory claims that the developing child's cognitive capabilities undergo a series of changes. The emergence of new cognitive capabilities comes about because the child is driven to change its knowledge structures (to accommodate) when those structures fail to provide an adequate understanding of experience (fail to assimilate). As new knowledge structures are created, the child gains new ways of processing and reasoning about information. Furthermore, some of the knowledge the child acquires is deduced, and not experienced, as the child is driven to restore equilibrium that is perturbed when a particular knowledge structure fails to comprehend new information.

Evidence for Piagetian theory comes from experiments in which infants or children are given various kinds of simple problems to solve. The nature of their mistakes is used to infer the underlying capabilities. Infants readily seem to give up on searching for an object that is hidden and seem surprised if the object reappears. Presumably, then, infants lack the concept of object permanence; more generally, they lack the capability to represent objects mentally. Young children have difficulty seeing that objects conserve essential properties, such as volume, when the object undergoes movement. Presumably, young children lack the capability to reverse an image of movement; more generally, they lack the capability to mentally transform representations of objects and events. Older children have difficulty solving the balance scale problem. Presumably, they lack the capability to transform hypothetical ideas or to contemplate relationships among relationships.

Among the criticisms of Piaget's theory are that it underestimates the capabilities of the infant and young child and that it seems to imply an evenness in cognitive development. I did my best to defend Piaget. For instance, I suggested that one interpretation of Piagetian theory is that it does, in fact, predict *decalage* (unevenness in development). Piaget claimed that cognitive development is driven by failures to assimilate experience. Because a child is not likely to have the same amount of experience in every domain, new knowledge structures are bound to emerge in one area before they emerge in another area.

Piaget eschewed maturation as the mechanism of cognitive development. In section 2, I discussed biological maturational theories, based especially on information processing psychology, that propose that the child's basic attention and processing capacity increases throughout childhood. The expanding capacity theory often attributes the expansion to genetically programmed changes in the growing brain. Myelinization, increases in synaptic density, and coordination between frontal lobes and other cortical areas all have been proposed as examples of biological changes that enable processing capacity to expand.

The main evidence for expanding capacity comes from measures of basic processing, such as memory span, which clearly do improve throughout childhood. Furthermore, some of the developmental spurts in processing capacity seem to be correlated with important changes in the brain, such as the formation of functional connections between frontal lobes and other cortical sites. Still, some of the apparent increase in processing capacity may not represent changes in basic capability per se, but increases in factual and skill knowledge. Indeed, if children of two different age levels are compared, their memories for information may be equal if their knowledge about that information is also equal.

Piagetian theory and biological maturation theory drawing on information processing concepts are examples of generic approaches to cognitive development. In section 3 I introduced domain-specific approaches, beginning with implicit theories. The idea behind implicit theories is that the child is acquiring in each major domain of knowledge a sort of theory that provides an underlying explanation for phenomena and a basis for predicting future behavior. These theories are implicit, but resemble the explicit theories created by scientists.

The example of an implicit theory I discussed was the child's understanding of the mind. One of the interesting, although somewhat controversial, findings from this research is that it seems that children initially acquire a theory of mind in which the mind is not capable of entertaining false ideas. Yet it does seem that even 1-year-old children have a sense that the ideas are different from the objects they represent and that behavior can be based on ideas.

Some advocates of implicit theories claim that children are born with cognitive instincts (also known as mental modules, primary abilities, or privileged capacities) for acquiring implicit theories in particular domains. Such a claim reflects the philosophy of nativism. The proposed cognitive instincts are associated with domains of evolutionary importance and take the form of preknowledge that constrains how children perceive and reason about information within a domain.

Nativist models of cognitive development have often focused on language acquisition. I first summarized some of the data on vocabulary and grammar acquisition and then outlined the evidence for the nativist position. Nativists point out that the information and feedback children get from the environment is too impoverished to explain language acquisition; consequently, children must be relying on inborn knowledge to accomplish the task of learning grammar. For example, parents rarely comment on the grammaticality of their children's utterances but more frequently comment on the truth value of the utterance, irrespective of its grammaticality. Yet children manage to learn to speak grammatically.

Consistent with nativism is a critical, or sensitive, period during which the young child has a heightened capacity for acquiring language that is gradually reduced as the child grows up. Evidence for a critical period for language acquisition comes from several sources. The most compelling lines of evidence are the finding that deaf people achieve more fluency in sign language if they learn it while they are young and the finding that young children are more likely to recover language after brain damage than are adults. Furthermore, language seems dissociated from other areas of cognitive development. We know of a few cases of individuals who are severely retarded yet are remarkably fluent, and of individuals who are intellectually normal except that they have difficulty acquiring grammar.

Perhaps the most persuasive evidence for a nativist approach to language acquisition is that children who are provided meager models of language nevertheless acquire grammar systems that are more sophisticated and adultlike than the models. It is as if the child's pre-knowledge of grammar fills in the pieces that are missing from the linguistic examples the child actually experiences.

Advocates of a generic approach to language acquisition are not persuaded by the evidence. Certainly it is true that environmental experiences have an impact on language acquisition, so it is not clear that one has to resort to innate knowledge of grammar to explain language acquisition. At the same time, the arguments having to do with the poverty of the stimulus or having to do with sensitive periods have not clearly demonstrated that these phenomena are unique to the domain of language. Still, I think it fair to say that most developmental psychologists favor some form of nativist theory.

I concluded the chapter with a short discussion of two other proposed cognitive instincts—namely, an instinct for counting and simple arithmetic and an instinct for extracting the properties of the biological world that distinguish biological entities from inanimate objects. I also provided a kind of synthesis of the generic and nativist positions, following a thesis developed by Geary (1995). Some capabilities, such as language, numbers, and biology, may, in some sense, be inborn and so learned relatively early and quickly. These inborn primary abilities may be integrated into secondary abilities in the service of culturally dependent goals. Language and visual processing may be integrated to form a reading skill, for example. Secondary abilities take longer to learn and often depend on formal institutions for their development. Integrative abilities may be the generic, Piagetian mechanisms of cognitive development that initially make use of primary cognitive abilities whose origins may be traced to biological evolution.

RECOMMENDED READINGS

Bjorklund's excellent *Children's Thinking* (1995) is a recommended textbook on cognitive development that covers a wide range of research and theory. Howe's (1990) *The Psychology of Human Cognition* compares and contrasts Piaget's approaches with those she labels "mainstream" approaches to cognitive development. Those of you who are serious about studying human development should read something actually written by Piaget, and a good place to start might be Piaget's (1952) *The Origins of Intelligence in Children*. Case's (1985) *Intellectual Development* provides a good introduction to the information processing/brain maturation approach to cognitive development. Case (1992) discusses the thesis that the maturation of the frontal lobes is especially critical to cognitive development. Wellman and Gelman (1992) review the research pertinent to the implicit theories approach to cognitive development. And, of course, Pinker's (1994) *The Language Instinct*, which earned my praise in the previous chapter's recommended readings, is must reading for those interested in how children acquire language. Pinker also includes a discussion of other possible human instincts, including an instinct for counting and an instinct for biology. Geary (1995) develops the thesis that cognitive development is two-tiered: primary abilities, like the language instinct, are integrated by culture to create secondary abilities, like reading. Rymer's (1993) *Genie* is an absorbing and compulsively readable account of the tragic case of Genie, the young girl deprived of a childhood by her cruel and deranged father. Rymer uses the case to discuss the critical period hypothesis, the instinct hypothesis, and the troubling ethical issues surrounding the scientific investigation of Genie. Auster's fictional "City of Glass," the first story in his highly praised *New York Trilogy* (1990), brilliantly weaves the hypothesis of a critical period for language into a deconstruction of the conventional mystery novel. Carkeet's (1980) witty and delightful *Double Negative* is a more conventional mystery novel in which the hero is a linguist interested in child language.

12   *Epilogue*

Way back in the preface I promised you themes, in the form of the fundamental and enduring debates within the field of cognitive science. And such themes you got. Here I will briefly summarize what I think are the essential contrasting perspectives in the field of human cognition, and where I think the field as a whole stands or seems to be leaning with respect to these perspectives.

1. Is the mind a spiritual entity? Descartes argued for dualism—for the idea that mind is a nonmaterial spiritual substance that interacts with the brain but is not itself physical. Modern cognitive science takes as its working premise the doctrine of materialism—that mind is the label we give to the functions provided by brain processes. A useful analogy to this might be that the mind is to the brain as digestion is to the stomach. The numerous examples of dissociations between consciousness and cognitive processes caused by brain damage suggests that even consciousness reflects brain processes, and nothing more.

2. Given materialism, is the mind a computerlike machine? Materialism suggests that physical mechanisms underlie mental phenomena—that is, that there is a machinelike quality to the mind. The conventional digital computer has been used as a metaphor for the nature of the mechanisms underlying mental processes. However, a growing consensus is that the mind is not computerlike at all. Instead, it is a connectionist machine, a parallel processing machine, a machine we might characterize as a neural net. Neural nets simulate what we believe to be the essential properties of neurons that give rise to cognitive phenomena. In a sense, neural net models are plausibility studies of materialist accounts of cognition.

3. Is the mind necessary? Behaviorists claim that models of the mind are unnecessary to an account of how the stimulus world influences observable behavior. The premise of cognitive psychology, on the other hand, is that models of mental phenomena increase the power of explanations to account for what people say and do. An external stimulus's influence depends on the nature of the internal processes. For instance, the child who has internalized a model of a secure world will respond to stressful situations differently than will a child who has internalized a model of an insecure world.

4. Is the mind's perception of the outside world direct? The claim of direct perception is that the perceptual systems directly and accurately pick up infor-

mation from the world; no internal mental process is required to account for perception. Most cognitive scientists, however, claim that perception is a constructed process whereby the perceptual system combines information from the external stimulus with other, extrasensory information in order to infer the interpretation of the stimulus. Even visual imagination reflects an influence of nonvisual knowledge.

5. Is the mind's memory of past experiences direct? Historically, record-keeping models of memory have dominated the study of memory. Record keeping says that remembering is like finding a memory record, like reexperiencing the past. That is, the past is directly represented in the memory. There is a growing consensus, however, that memory is like perception in that both are constructed. In particular, memory is a process whereby a plausible rendition of the past is reconstructed from the current state of various cognitive systems, such as the perceptual and language systems. For example, a person's memory for an event can be perturbed by other knowledge, as when an eyewitness sees a car drive through a yield sign, then reads about a stop sign, and later remembers that the car drove through a stop sign. According to constructionist theory, there are no memory records or memory systems as such; rather, memory is a byproduct of reconstructive processes. Models of memory based on constructionist principles clarify the distinction between conscious (explicit) and unconscious (implicit) memory and more accurately reflect what is known about the physiology of learning and memory.

6. Is the mind rational or irrational? Philosophical, political, and economical traditions of Western culture presuppose that humans are, as Aristotle claimed, rational animals. Recent research on human reasoning seems to suggest that humans are irrational, in the sense that ordinary people, even well-educated people, make regular and predictable errors in their reasoning. For instance, people frequently fail to deduce the *modus tollens* conclusion of a conditional reasoning problem and often estimate probabilities of events without taking into account the base rate probability. Many cognitive psychologists have claimed that reasoning is neither rational nor irrational; rather, it is adaptive. By adaptive reasoning they mean reasoning effectively so as to anticipate and predict events in ecologically realistic environments where such predictions are put to use and when the effort to reason does not exceed the potential gain. People use common sense and knowledge from many sources, especially knowledge of social relationships, to make deductions, calculate probabilities, critically assess ideas, and make decisions.

7. Does the mind solve problems by using all-purpose, generic strategies? The information processing tradition in psychology suggests that problem solving is a matter of using a generic problem-solving system designed by nature to solve all problems in fundamentally the same way. Most cognitive psychologists argue instead that problem solving is domain specific. A different set of strategies and skills is required for each problem-solving

domain (examples of domains include computer programming, song writing, and parenting). An implication of the domain-specific approach is that problem solving emerges as a consequence of domain expertise—it is not a general skill one might learn or hone in a college course on problem solving.

8. Are differences among minds a result of differences in generic mental process whose efficiency depends on genes? Implicit in the intelligence-testing enterprise is the idea that one's degree of intelligence reflects unitary, generic processes. Hereditarian models of intelligence reinforce the generic approach, and claim moreover that one's degree of intelligence is genetically inherited. Many cognitive psychologists claim, instead, that a broader perspective on the nature of intelligence leads to the conclusion that intelligence is domain specific. People who excel in one area—social reasoning, for example—do not necessarily excel in another area—logical reasoning, for example. Differences in skill level within any domain almost always reflect both environmental influences and genes; how could it be otherwise? The likelihood that genes do play a role in cognitive differences among people does not mean that race or culture or sex differences in skill are due to genetic differences.

9. Is the language the mind uses to communicate with other minds a cultural invention, acquired by children in the same manner as are other cultural artifacts? The 20th century has seen the rise of the social-learning model, which claims that virtually everything a child learns reflects the child's experiences and culture. Many cognitive scientists are now disputing the generality of the social-learning model. Language, in particular, seems a specialized module of cognition, a kind of human cognitive instinct. Language evolved, it was not invented. In fact, despite their apparent diversity, the languages of the world have surprisingly similar features, such as phonemes, syntactic phrases, and embedded phrases. The brain has an organ dedicated to semantics and to generative grammar. This organ apparently evolved gradually as hominid brains became larger. A child's acquisition of language depends as much on the language instinct as it does on the linguistic environment. For example, children who are provided only meager bits and pieces of language will infer the fuller grammatical system of the language. The cognitive autonomy of language is revealed by the observation that some children are born mentally retarded, yet linguistically quite competent. Others are born with good general smarts, but are incapable of mastering the basics of grammar.

10. Is the mind's development the same in all domains? Piaget, the most influential developmental psychologist of the 20th century, claimed that all domains of cognitive development proceed through the same stages and are driven by the same assimilation/accommodation mechanism. A growing consensus, though, is that cognitive development is different in each of several domains. The language instinct is one example. Inborn intuitions about

language guide its acquisition, but those instinctive linguistic intuitions are unrelated to the acquisition of reasoning or arithmetic. There may be other domain-specific mechanisms—cognitive instincts—that guide cognitive development. Among the proposed instincts are an instinct for counting and an instinct for biology.

Human children may be especially talented, compared with other animals, at integrating instincts into more complex skills that serve culturally determined goals. Such an integrative instinct represents a kind of generic learning process, and the one that allows us to learn a potentially wide range of skills. Learning to read, for example, requires an integration of perceptual instincts and language instincts. Indeed, the integrative instinct may be our species' most valuable cognitive capability, the capability that really does make us infinite in faculty and the paragon of animals.

References

ABRAHAM, W. C., CORBALLIS, M. C., & WHITE, K. G. (1991). *Memory mechanisms: A tribute to G. V. Goddard.* Hillsdale, NJ: Erlbaum.

ABRAHAM, W. C., & GODDARD, G. V. (1983). Asymmetric relationships between homosynaptic long-term potentiation and heterosynaptic long-term depression. *Nature, 305,* 717–719.

ACORN, D. A., HAMILTON, D. L., & SHERMAN, S. J. (1988). Generalization of biased perceptions of groups based on illusory correlations. *Social Cognition, 6,* 345–372.

ADAMS, J. L. (1974). *Conceptual blockbusting.* New York: Freeman.

ADAMS, L. T., KASSERMAN, J. E., YEARWOOD, A. A., PERFETTO, G. A., BRANSFORD, J. D., & FRANKS, J. J. (1988). Memory access: The effects of fact-oriented versus problem-oriented acquisition. *Memory and Cognition, 16,* 167–175.

ADAMSON, R. E. (1952). Functional fixation as related to problem solving: A repetition of three experiments. *Journal of Experimental Psychology, 44,* 288–291.

ADELSON, B. (1981). Problem solving and the development of abstract categories in programming language. *Memory and Cognition, 9,* 422–433.

AGNEW, H. W., JR., WEBB, W. B., & WILLIAMS, R. L. (1967). Comparison of stage 4 and 1-REM sleep deprivation. *Perceptual and Motor Skills, 24,* 851–858.

ANASTASI, A. (1985). Reciprocal relations between cognitive and affective development: With implications for sex differences. In T. B. Sonderegger (Ed.), *Psychology and gender (Nebraska Symposium on Motivation, Vol. 32, pp. 1–35).* Lincoln: University of Nebraska Press.

ANASTASI, A. (1988). *Psychological testing.* New York: Macmillan.

ANCH, A. M., BROWMAN, C. P., MITLER, M. M., & WALSH, J. K. (1988). *Sleep: A scientific perspective.* Englewood Cliffs, NJ: Prentice-Hall.

ANDERSON, J. R. (1974). Retrieval of propositional information from long-term memory. *Cognitive Psychology, 5,* 451–474.

ANDERSON, J. R. (1976). *Language, memory and thought.* Hillsdale, N. J.: Erlbaum.

ANDERSON, J. R. (1983). *The architecture of cognition.* Cambridge, Mass.: Harvard University Press.

ANDERSON, J. R. (1990). *The adaptive character of thought.* Hillsdale, NJ: Erlbaum.

ANDERSON, J. R. (1991). The adaptive character of human categorization. *Psychological Review, 98,* 409–429.

ANDERSON, J. R. (1995). *Cognitive psychology and its implications.* New York: Freeman.

ANDERSON, J. R. (1996). ACT: A simple theory of complex cognition. *American Psychologist, 51,* 355–365.

ANDERSON, J. R., & BOWER, G. H. (1973). *Human associative memory.* Washington, DC: Winston.

ANDERSON, J. R., & MILSON, R. (1989). Human memory: An adaptive perspective. *Psychological Review, 96,* 703–719.

ANDERSON, J. R., & SCHOOLER, L. J., (1991). Reflection of the environment in memory. *Psychological Science, 2,* 396–408.

ANGLIN, J. (1977). *Word, object, and conceptual development.* New York: Norton.

ANISFELD, M., & KLENBORT, I. (1973). On the functions of structured paraphrase: The view from the passive voice. *Psychological Bulletin, 79,* 117–126.

ANTROBUS, J. (1991). Dreaming: Cognitive processes during cortical activation and high afferent thresholds. *Psychological Review, 98,* 96–121.

ANTROBUS, J. (1993). Dreaming: Could we do without it? In A. Moffitt, M. Kramer, & R. Hoffman (Eds.), *The functions of dreaming,* (pp. 549–558). Albany, NY: State University of New York Press.

ARKES, H. R. (1991). Costs and benefits of judgment errors: Implications for debiasing. *Psychological Bulletin, 110*, 486–498.

ARKES, H. R. & HARKNESS, A. R. (1983). Estimate of contingency between two dichotomous variables. *Journal of Experimental Psychology: General, 112*, 117–135.

ARKIN, A. M., & ANTROBUS, J. S. (1978). The effects of external stimuli applied prior to and during sleep on sleep experience. In A. M. Arkin, J. S. Antrobus, & S. J. Ellman (Eds.), *The mind in sleep psychology and psychophysiology* (pp. 35–391). Hillsdale, NJ: Erlbaum.

ARONIADOU, V. A., & TEYLER, T. J. (1991). The role of NMDA receptors in long-term potentiation (LTP) and depression (LTD) in rat visual cortex. *Brain Research, 562*, 136–143.

ASHBY, F. G., PRINZMETAL, W., IVRY, R., & MADDOX, W. T. (1996). A formal theory of feature binding in object perception. *Psychological Review, 103*, 165–192.

ASHCRAFT, M. H. (1994). *Human memory and cognition*. New York: HarperCollins College.

ATKINSON, R. C., & RAUGH, M. R. (1975). An application of the mnemonic keyword method to the acquisition of a Russian vocabulary. *Journal of Experimental Psychology: Human Learning and Memory, 104*, 126–133.

ATKINSON, R. C., & SHIFFRIN, R. M. (1968). Human memory: A proposed system and its control processes. In K. W. Spence & J. T. Spence (Eds.), *The psychology of learning and motivation: Advances in research and theory* (Vol. 2). New York: Academic Press.

AU, T. K.-F. (1983). Chinese and English counterfactuals: The Sapir-Whorf hypothesis revisited. *Cognition, 15*, 155–187.

AUSTER, P. (1990). *The New York trilogy*. New York: Penguin.

BADDELEY, A. D. (1982). Domains of recollection. *Psychological Review, 22*, 88–104.

BADDELEY, A. D. (1986). *Working memory*. Oxford, England: Oxford University Press.

BADDELEY, A. D. (1992). Working memory. *Science, 255*, 556–559.

BADDELEY, A. D., & ECOB, J. R. (1973). Reaction-time and short-term memory: Implications of repetition for the high speed exhaustive scan hypothesis. *Quarterly Journal of Experimental Psychology, 25*, 229–240.

BADDELEY, A. D., & HITCH, G. (1974). Working memory. In G. A. Bower (Ed.), *Recent advances in learning and motivation* (Vol. 8). New York: Academic Press.

BADDELEY, A. D., THOMSON, N., & BUCHANAN, M. (1975). Word length and the structure of short-term memory. *Journal of Verbal Learning and Verbal Behavior, 14*, 575–589.

BAER, J. (1994a). Divergent thinking is not a general trait: A multidomain training experiment. *Creativity Research Journal, 7*, 35–46.

BAER, J. (1994b). Generality of creativity across performance domains: A replication. *Perceptual and Motor Skills, 79*, 1217–1218.

BAHRICK, H. P. (1984). Replicative, constructive, and reconstructive aspects of memory: Implications for human and animal research. *Physiological Psychology, 12*, 53–58.

BAHRICK, H. P., BAHRICK, P. C., & WITTLINGER, R. P. (1975). Fifty years of memories for names and faces: A cross-sectional approach. *Journal of Experimental Psychology, 104*, 54–75.

BAILARGEON, R. (1994). How do infants learn about the physical world? *Current Directions in Psychological Science, 3*, 133–140.

BAIRD, L. L. (1982). *The role of academic ability in high-level accomplishment and general success* (College Board Rep. No. 82–6). New York: College Entrance Examination Board.

BAIRD, L. L. (1984). Relationships between ability, college attendance and family income. *Research in Higher Education, 21*, 373–395.

BALDWIN, J. M. (1894). *The development of the child and of the race*. New York: MacMillan.

BANAJI, M. R., & CROWDER, R. G. (1989). The bankruptcy of everyday memory. *American Psychologist, 44*, 1185–1193.

BARCLAY, C. R., & WELLMAN, H. M. (1986). Accuracies and inaccuracies in autobiographical memories. *Journal of Memory and Language, 25*, 93–106.

BARNES, J. M., & UNDERWOOD, B. J. (1959). "Fate" of first-list associations in transfer theory. *Journal of Experimental Psychology, 58*, 97–105.

BARRETT, G. V., & DEPINET, R. L. (1991). A reconsideration of testing for competence rather than for intelligence. *American Psychologist, 46*, 1012–1024.

BARRETT, P., EYSENCK, H. J., & LUCHING, S. (1989). Reaction time and intelligence: A replicated study. *Intelligence, 10*, 9–40.

BARRON, F. (1969). *Creative person and creative process.* New York: Holt, Rinehart and Winston.

BARRON, F., & HARRINGTON, D. M. (1981). Creativity, intelligence, and personality. *Annual Review of Psychology, 32*, 439–476.

BARRON, R. W., & BARON, J. (1977). How children get meaning from printed words. *Child Development, 48*, 587–594.

BARSALOU, L. W. (1989). Intra-concept similarity and its impliction for inter-concept similarity. In S. Vosneadou & A. Ortony (Eds.), *Similarity and analogical reasoning* (pp. 76–121). New York: Cambridge University Press.

BARTLETT, F. C. (1932). *Remembering: A study in experimental and social psychology.* Cambridge, England: Cambridge University Press.

BARTSCH, K., & WELLMAN, H. M. (1989). Young children's attribution of action to beliefs and desires. *Child Development, 60*, 945–964.

BASS, E., & DAVIS, L. (1988). *The courage to heal.* New York: Harper & Row.

BASSOK, M., & HOLYOAK, K. J. (1989). Interdomain transfer between isomorphic topics in algebra and physics. *Journal of Experimental Psychology: Learning, Memory, and Cognition, 15*, 153–166.

BATES, E., & SNYDER, L. (1985). The cognitive hypothesis in language development. In I. Uzgeres & J. M. Hunt (Eds.), *Research with scales of psychological development in infancy.* Champaign-Urbana: University of Illinois Press.

BAUM, W. M., & HEATH, J. L. (1992). Behavioral explanations and intentional explanations in psychology. *American Psychologist, 47*, 1312–1317.

BEACH, K. D. (1988). The role of external mnemonic symbols in acquiring an occupation. In M. M. Grueneberg, P. E. Morris, & R. N. Sykes (Eds.), *Practical aspects of memory: Current research and issues* (Vol. 1, pp. 342–346). Chichester, England: Wiley.

BEAUVOIS, M. F., & SAILLANT, B. (1985). Optic aphasia for colours and colour aphasia. A distinction between visual and visio-verbal impairment in the processes of colours. *Cognitive Neuropsychology, 2*, 1–48.

BECHTEL, W., & ABRAHAMSEN, A. (1991). *Connectionism and the mind.* Cambridge, MA: Basil Blackwell.

BEDARD, J., & CHI, M. T. (1992). Expertise. *Current Directions in Psychological Science, 1*, 135–139.

BEEMAN, M. (1993). Semantic processing in the right hemisphere may contribute to drawing inferences from discourse. *Brain and Language, 44*, 80–120.

BEGG, I., & WHITE, P. (1985). Encoding specificity in interpersonal communication. *Canadian Journal of Psychology, 39*, 70–87.

BEILIN, H. (1992). Piaget's enduring contribution to developmental psychology. *Developmental Psychology, 28*, 191–204.

BELLEZA, F. S., & BUCK, D. K. (1988). Expert knowledge as mnemonic cues. *Applied Cognitive Psychology, 2*, 147–162.

BELSKY, J., & CASSIDY, J. (1994). Attachment: Theory and evidence. In M. Rutter & D. Hay (Eds.), *Development through life: A handbook for clinicians* (pp. 373–402). Oxford, England: Blackwell.

BELSKY, J., SPRITZ, B., & CRNIC, K. (1996). Infant attachment security and affective-cognitive information processing at age 3. *Psychological Science, 7*, 111–114.

BENEDICT, H. (1979). Early lexical development: Comprehension and production. *Journal of Child Language, 6*, 183–200.

BERGER, T. W. (1984). Neural representation of associative learning in the hippocampus. In M. Butters & L. R. Squire (Eds.), *The neuropsychology of memory.* New York: Guilford Press.

BERGSON, H. (1911). *Matter and memory.* New York: Macmillan.

BERKO, J. (1958). The child's learning of English morphology. *Word, 14,* 150–177.

BERLIN, B., BREEDLOVE, D., & RAVEN, P. (1973). General principles of classification and nomenclature in folk biology. *American Anthropologist, 75,* 214–242.

BERRY, J. W. (1966). Temne and Eskimo perceptual skill. *International Journal of Psychology, 1,* 207–229.

BERRY, J. W. (1974). Radical cultural relativism and the concept of intelligence. In J. W. Berry & P. R. Dasen (Eds.), *Culture and cognition: Readings in cross-cultural psychology* (pp. 225–229). London: Methuen.

BEST, J. B. (1995). *Cognitive psychology.* Minneapolis/St. Paul: West.

BIALYSTOK, E., & HAKUTA, K. (1994). *In other words.* New York: Basic Books.

BIEDERMAN, I. (1995). Visual object recognition. In S. M. Kosslyn & D. N. Oskerson (Eds.), *Visual cognition* (Vol. 2, pp. 121–165). Cambridge, MA: MIT Press.

BIEDERMAN, I. (1987). Recognition by components: A theory of human image understanding. *Psychological Review, 94,* 115–147.

BIEDERMAN, I. (1990). Higher level vision. In D. N. Oskerson, S. M. Kosslyn, & J. M. Hollerbach (Eds.), *Visual cognition and action* (pp. 41–72). Cambridge, MA: MIT Press.

BIEDERMAN, I., RABINOWITZ, J. C., GLASS, A. L., & STACY, W. E., JR. (1974). On the information extracted at a glance from a scene. *Journal of Experimental Psychology, 103,* 597–600.

BINET, A. (1911). *Les indees modernes sur les enfants.* Paris: Flamarion.

BINET, A., & SIMON, T. (1916). *The intelligence of the feeble-minded.* Baltimore: Williams and Wilkins.

BIRCH, H. G. (1945). The relation of previous experience to insightful problem solving. *Journal of Comparative Psychology, 38,* 367–383.

BIRCH, H. G., & RABINOWITZ, H. S. (1951). The negative effect of previous experience on productive thinking. *Journal of Experiemental Psychology, 41,* 121–125.

BIRREN, J. E., WOODS, A. M., & WILLIAMS, M. V. (1979). Speed of behavior as an indicator of age changes and the integrity of the nervous system. In F. Hoffmeister & C. Muller (Eds.), *Brain function in old age.* New York: Springer-Verlag.

BISIACH, E. Z., LUZZATTI, C., & PERANI, D. (1979). Unilateral neglect, representational schema, and consciousness. *Brain, 102,* 609–618.

BJORK, R. A. (1975). Short-term storage: The ordered output of a central processor. In F. Restle, R. M. Shiffrin, N. J. Castellan, H. R. Lindeman, & D. B. Pisoni (Eds.), *Cognitive theory* (Vol. 1). Hillsdale, N. J.: Erlbaum.

BJORKLUND, D. F. (1995). *Children's thinking: Developmental function and individual differences.* Pacific Grove, CA: Brooks/Cole.

BJORKLUND, D. F., & GREEN, B. L. (1992). The adaptive nature of cognitive immaturity. *American Psychologist, 47,* 46–54.

BJORKLUND, D. F., & HARNISHFEGER, K. K. (1990). The resources construct in cognitive development. Diverse sources of evidence and a theory of inefficient inhibition. *Developmental Review, 10,* 48–71.

BJORKLUND, D. F., & ZEMAN, B. R. (1982). Children's organization and metameric awareness in their recall of familiar information. *Child Development, 53,* 799–810.

BLANEY, P. H. (1986). Affect and memory: A review. *Psychological Bulletin, 99,* 229–246.

BLAXTON, T. A. (1989). Investigating dissociations among memory measures: Support for a transfer-appropriate processing framework. *Journal of Experimental Psychology: Learning, Memory and Cognition, 15,* 657–668.

BLISS, T. V. P., & LOMO, T. (1973). Long-lasting potentiation of synaptic transmission in the dentate area of the anaesthetized rabbit following stimulation of the perforant path. *Journal of Physiology (London), 232,* 331–356.

BLOOBERG, M. (1973). Introduction: Approaches to creativity. In M. Blooberg (Ed.), *Creativity: Theory and research.* New Haven, CT: College and University Press.

BLOOM, A. H. (1981). *The linguistic shaping of thought: A study in the impact of thinking in China and the West.* Hillsdale, NJ: Erlbaum.

BLOOM, L. (1973). *One word at a time.* The Hague, Netherlands: Mouton.

BLOOM, L., LIGHTBOWN P, & HOOD, L. (1975). Structure and variation in child language. *Monograph of the Society for Research in Child Development, 40* (2, Serial No. 160).

BLOOM, R. L., BOROD, J. C., OBLER, L. K., & GERSTMAN, L. J. (1992). Impact of emotional content on discourse production in patients with unilateral brain damage. *Brain and Language, 42,* 153–164.

BLUM, G. S., & BARBOUR, J. S. (1979). Selective inattention to anxiety-linked stimuli. *Journal of Experimental Psychology: General, 108,* 182–224.

BLUMSTEIN, S. E. (1982). Language dissolution in aphasia: Evidence from linguistic theory. In L. Obler & L. Menn (Eds.), *Exceptional language and linguistics* (pp. 203–215). New York: Academic Press.

BOBROW, S., & BOWER, G. H. (1969). Comprehension and recall of sentences. *Journal of Experimental Psychology, 80,* 455–461.

BOCK, K. (1990). Structure in language: Creating form in talk. *American Psychologist, 45,* 1221–1236.

BOGEN, J. E., DEZARE, R., TENHOUTEN, W. D., & MARSH, J. F. (1972). The other side of the brain. IV: The A/P ratio. *Bulletin of the Los Angeles Neurological Societies, 37,* 49–61.

BOHANNON, J. N. III, & STANOWICZ, L. (1988). The issue of negative evidence: Adult responses to children's language error. *Developmental Psychology, 24,* 684–689.

BOLLES, E. B. (1988). *Remembering and forgetting.* New York: Walker.

BONANNO, G. A. (1990). Repression, accessibility, and the translation of private experience. *Psychoanalytic Psychology, 7,* 453–473.

BORING, E. G. (1950). *A history of experimental psychology.* New York: Appleton-Century-Crofts.

BOUCHARD, T. J., & McCUE, M. (1981). Familial studies of intelligence: A review. *Science, 212,* 1055–1059.

BOWER, G. H. (1974). Selective facilitation and interference in retention of prose. *Journal of Educational Psychology, 66,* 1–8.

BOWER, G. H., CLARK, M. C., LESGOLD, A. M., & WINZENZ, D. (1969). Hierarchical retrieval schemes in recall of categorical word lists. *Journal of Verbal Learning and Verbal Behavior, 8,* 303–343.

BOWER, G. H., & TRABASSO, T. R. (1963). Reversals prior to solution in concept identification. *Journal of Experimental Psychology, 66,* 409–418.

BOWER, G. H., & WINZENZ, D. (1970). Comparison of associative learning strategies. *Psychonomic Science, 20,* 119–120.

BOWERS, K. S., & FARVOLDEN, P. (1996). Revisiting a century-old Freudian slip—from suggestion disavowed to the truth repressed. *Psychological Bulletin, 119,* 355–380.

BOYKIN, A. W. (1994). Harvesting talent and culture: African-American children and educational reform. In R. Rossi (Ed.), *Schools and students at risk,* (pp. 116–138). New York: Teachers College Press.

BOYLE, J. P. (1987). Intelligence, reasoning, and language proficiency. *The Modern Language Journal, 71,* 277–288.

BOYSEN, S. T., & BERNTSON, G. G. (1989). Numerical competence in a chimpanzee (Pan Troglodyte). *Journal of Comparative Psychology, 103,* 23–31.

BRAINE, M. D. S. (1992). What sort of innate structure is needed to "bootstrap" into syntax? *Cognition, 45,* 77–100.

BRAINE, M. D. S., REISER, B. J., & RUMAIN, B. (1984). Some empirical justification for a theory of natural propositional logic. *The psychology of learning and motivation* (Vol. 18). San Diego, CA: Academic Press.

BRAINERD, C. J. (1974). Training and transfer of transitivity, conservation, and class inclusion of length. *Child Development, 45,* 324–334.

BRAINERD, C. J., & REYNA, V. F. (1993). Memory independence and memory interference in cognitive development. *Psychological Review, 100,* 142–167.

BRAINERD, C. J., & REYNA, V. F. (1995). Learning rate, learning opportunities, and the development of forgetting. *Developmental Psychology, 31,* 251–262.

BRANSFORD, J. D., BARCLAY, J. R., & FRANKS, J. J. (1972). Sentence memory: A constructive versus interpretive approach. *Cognitive Psychology, 3,* 193–209.

BRANSFORD, J. D., & FRANKS, J. J. (1971). The abstraction of linguistic ideas. *Cognitive Psychology, 2,* 331–350.

BRANSFORD, J. D., & JOHNSON, M. K. (1972). Contextual prerequisite for understanding: Some investigations of comprehension and recall. *Journal of Verbal Learning and Verbal Behavior, 11,* 717–726.

BRANSFORD, J. D., McCARRELL, N. S., FRANKS, J. J., & NITSCH, K. E. (1977). Toward unexplaining memory. IN R. S. Shaw & J. D. Bransford (Eds.), *Perceiving, acting and knowing: Toward an ecological psychology.* Hillsdale, NJ: Erlbaum.

BRAUN, C. (1976). Teacher expectations: Sociopsychological dynamics. *Review of Educational Research, 46,* 185–213.

BREGER, L., HUNTER, L., & LANE, R. W. (1971). The effects of stress on dreams. *Physiological Issues Monograph Number 27.* New York: International University Press.

BRENNER, C. (1957). The nature and development of the concept of repression in Freud's writings. *Psychoanalytic Study of the Child, 12,* 19–46.

BREWER, W. F. (1984). The nature and function of schema. In J. Strachey & T. K. Srult (Eds.), *Handbook of social cognition* (Vol. 1, pp. 119–160). Hillsdale, NJ: Erlbaum.

BREWIN, C. R. (1988). *Cognitive foundations of clinical psychology.* London: Erlbaum.

BRIARS, D. J., & LARKIN, J. H. (1984). An integrated model of skill in solving elementary word problems. *Cognition and Instruction, 1,* 245–296.

BRITT, M. A., PERFETTI, C. A., GARROD, S., & RAYNER, K. (1992). Parsing in discourse: Context effects and their limits. *Journal of Memory and Language, 31,* 293–314.

BROADBENT, D. E. (1958). *Perception and communication.* New York: Pergamon.

BROADBENT, D. E. (1971). *Decision and stress.* New York: Academic Press.

BROMAGE, B., & MAYER, R. E. (1981). Relationships between what is remembered and creative problem solving performance in science learning. *Journal of Educational Psychology, 43,* 451–461.

BRONFENBRENNER, U. (1974). *Is early intervention effective? A report on longitudinal evaluations of preschool programs* (Vol. 2). Washington, DC: Department of Health, Education, and Welfare, Office of Child Development.

BROOKS, L. (1978). Nonanalytic concept formation and memory for instances. In E. Rosch & B. B. Lloyd (Eds.), *Cognition and categorization.* Hillsdale, NJ: Erlbaum.

BROOKS, L. W., & DANSEREAU, D. F. (1983). Effects of structural schema training and text organization on expository prose processing. *Journal of Educational Psychology, 75,* 811–820.

BROWN, A. L., BRANSFORD, J. D., FERRARA, R. A., & CAMPIONE, J. C. (1983). Learning, remembering, understanding. In J. H. Flavell & E. M. Markman (Eds.), *Handbook of child psychology, Vol. 4, cognitive development.* New York: Wiley.

BROWN, A. L., KANE, M. J., & ECHOLS, K. (1986). Young children's mental models determine transfer across problems with a common goal structure. *Cognitive Development, 1,* 103–122.

BROWN, A. S., & MITCHELL, D. B. (1994). A reevaluation of semantic versus nonsemantic processing in implicit memory. *Memory and Cognition, 22,* 533–541.

BROWN, E., DEFFENBACHER, K., & STURGILL, W. (1977). Memory for faces and the circumstances of encounter. *Journal of Applied Psychology, 62,* 311–318.

BROWN, N. R., RIPS, L. J., & SHEVELL, S. K. (1985). The subjective dates of natural events in very-long-term memory. *Cognitive Psychology, 17,* 139–177.

BROWN, R. (1958). How shall a thing be called? *Psychological Review, 65,* 14–21.

BROWN, R. (1973). *A first language: the early stages.* Cambridge, MA: Harvard University Press.

BROWN, R., & HANLON, C. (1970). Derivational complexity and order of acquisition in child speech. In J. R. Hayes (Ed.), *Cognition and the development of language.* New York: Wiley.

BROWN, R., & KULIK, J. (1977). Flashbulb memories. *Cognition, 5,* 73–99.

BROWN, R., & McNEILL, D. (1966). The "tip of the tongue" phenomenon. *Journal of Verbal Learning and Verbal Behavior, 5,* 325–337.

BROWN, T. H., GANONG, A. H., KAIRISS, E. W., KEENAN, C. L., & KELSO, S. R. (1989). Long-term potentiation in two synaptic systems of the hippocampal brain slice. In J. H. Byrne & W. O. Berry (Eds.), *Neural models of plasticity: Experimental and theoretical approaches.* San Diego, CA: Academic Press.

BROWNELL, H. H., POTTER, H. H., & BIHRLE, A. (1986). Inference deficits in right brain–damaged patients. *Brain and Language, 27,* 310–321.

BRUER, J. T. (1993). *Schools for thought: A science of learning in the classroom.* Cambridge, MA: MIT Press.

BRUNER, J. S. (1983). *Child's talk: Learning to use language.* New York: Norton.

BRUNER, J. S., GOODNOW, J. J., & AUSTIN, G. A. (1956). *A study of thinking.* New York: Wiley.

BUCKHOUT, R., EUGENIO, P., LICITIA, T., OLIVER, L., & KRAMER, T. H. (1981). Memory, hypnosis, and evidence: Research or eyewitnesses. *Social Action and the Law, 7,* 67–72.

BUELL, S. J., & COLEMAN, P. D. (1978). Dendritic growth in the aged human brain and failure of growth in senile dementia. *Science, 206,* 854–856.

BULMER, R. (1967). Why is the cassowary not a bird? A problem of zoological taxonomy among the Karam of the New Guinea highlands. *Man, 2,* 5–25.

BURGARD, E. C., & SARVEY, J. M. (1990). Muscarinic receptor activity facilitates the induction of long-term potentiation (LTP) in the rat dentate gyrus. *Neuroscience Letters, 116,* 34–39.

BURLING, R. (1993). Primate calls, human language, and nonverbal communication. *Current Anthropology, 34,* 25–53.

BUSS, D. M., & CRAIK, K. H. (1983). The act frequency approach to personality. *Psychological Review, 90,* 105–126.

BUTLER, M. S., DICKINSON, W. A., KATHOLI, C., & HALSEY, J. H. (1983). The comparative effects of organic brain disease on cerebral blood flow and measured intelligence. *Annals of Neurology, 13,* 155–159.

BUTTERS, N., HEINDEL, W. C., & SALMON, D. P. (1990). Dissociation of implicit memory in dementia: Neurological implications. *Bulletin of the Psychonomic Society, 28,* 359–366.

CAIRNS, R. B. (1992). The making of a developmental science: The contributions and intellectual heritage of James Mark Baldwin. *Developmental Psychology, 28,* 17–24.

CAMPBELL, B. G. (1988). *Humankind emerging.* Glenview, IL: Scott, Foresman.

CAMPBELL, F. A., & RAMEY, C. T. (1994). Effects of early intervention on intellectual and academic achievement: A follow-up study on children from low-income families. *Child Development, 65,* 684–698.

CANAS, J. J. & NELSON, D. C. (1986). Recognition and environmental context: The effects of testing by phone. *Bulletin of the Psychonomic Society, 24,* 407–409.

CANTOR, N., & MISCHEL, W. (1977). Traits as prototypes: Effects on recognition memory. *Journal of Personality and Social Psychology, 35,* 38–48.

CARAMAZZA, A., GORDON, J., ZURIF, E. B., & DELUCA, D. (1976). Right-hemispheric damage and verbal problem solving behavior. *Brain and Language, 3,* 41–46.

CARAMAZZA, A., & ZURIF, E. B. (1976). Dissociation of algorithmic and heuristic processes in language comprehension: Evidence from aphasia. *Brain and Language, 3,* 572–582.

CAREY, S. (1985). *Conceptual change in childhood.* Cambridge, MA: MIT Press.

CAREY, S. (1990). Cognitive development. In D. N. Oskerson & E. E. Smith (Eds.), *Thinking.* Cambridge, MA: MIT Press.

CARKEET, D. (1980). *Double negative.* New York: Washington Square Press.

CARLSON, N. R. (1994). *Physiology of behavior.* Boston: Allyn and Bacon.

CARRAHER, T. N., CARRAHER, D., & SCHLIEMANN, A. D. (1985). Mathematics in the streets and in schools. *British Journal of Developmental Psychology, 3,* 21–29.

CARROLL, D. W. (1994). *Psychology of language.* Pacific Grove, CA: Brooks/Cole.

CARROLL, J. B. (1983). Individual differences in cognitive abilities. In S. H. Irvine & J. W. Berry (Eds.), *Human assessment and cultural factors.* New York: Plenum.

CARROLL, J. B., & CASAGRANDE, J. B. (1958). The function of language classification. In E. E. Maccoby, T. M. Newcomb, & E. L. Hartley (Eds.), *Readings in social psychology (3rd ed.),* 18–31. New York: Holt, Rinehart and Winston.

CARTWRIGHT, R. D. (1977). *Nightlife: Explorations in dreaming.* Englewood Cliffs, NJ: Prentice-Hall.

CARTWRIGHT, R. D., & LAMBERG, L. (1992) *Crisis dreaming.* New York: HarperCollins.

CASE, R. (1972). Validation of a neo-Piagetian mental capacity construct. *Journal of Experimental Child Psychology, 14,* 287–302.

CASE, R. (1985). *Intellectual development: From birth to adulthood.* Orlando, FL: Academic Press.

CASE, R. (1992). The role of the frontal lobes in the regulation of cognitive development. *Brain and Cognition, 20,* 51–73.

CASTALDO, V., KRYNICKI, V., & GOLDSTEIN, J. (1974). Sleep stages and verbal memory. *Perceptual and Motor Skills, 39,* 1023–1030.

CATRAMBONE, R. (1994). Improving examples to improve transfer to novel problems. *Memory and Cognition, 22,* 606–615.

CATTELL, J. M. (1890). Mental tests and measurements. *Mind, 15,* 373–380.

CAZDEN, C. B. (1968). The acquisition of noun and verb inflections. *Child Development, 39,* 433–448.

CECI, S. J., & LIKER, J. K. (1986). A day at the races: A study of IQ, expertise, and cognitive complexity. *Journal of Experimental Psychology: General, 115,* 255–266.

CERMAK, L. S., & MOREINES, J. (1976). Verbal retention deficits in aphasic and amnesic patients. *Brain and Language, 3,* 16–27.

CERMAK, L. S., & TARLOW, S. (1978). Aphasic and amnesic patients' verbal vs. nonverbal retentive abilities. *Cortex, 14,* 32–40.

CHALMERS, D. J. (1995, December). The puzzle of consciousness. *Scientific American,* 80–86.

CHANCE, P. (1986). *Thinking in the classroom: A survey of programs.* New York: Teachers College Press.

CHANDLER, C. C. (1994). Studying related pictures can reduce accuracy, but increase confidence, in a modified recognition test. *Memory and Cognition, 22,* 273–280.

CHANDLER, M. J., FRITZ, A. S., & HALA, S. M. (1989). Small scale deceit: Deception as a marker of 2-, 3-, and 4-year olds' early theories of mind. *Child Development, 60,* 1263–1277.

CHANG, F. F., & GREENOUGH, W. T. (1982). Lateralized effects of monocular training on dendritic branching in adult split-brain rats. *Brain Research, 232,* 283–292.

CHANG, T. M. (1986). Semantic memory: Facts and models. *Psychological Bulletin, 99,* 199–220.

CHAPMAN, M., & LINDENBERGER, U. (1988). Functions, operations, and decalage in the development of transitivity. *Developmental Psychology, 24,* 542–551.

CHASE, T. N., FEDIO, P., FOSTER, N. L., BROOKS, R., DICHIRO, G., & MANSI, L. (1984). Wechsler Adult Intelligence Scale performance. Cortical location by fluorodeoxyglucose F 18-positron emission tomography. *Archives of Neurology, 41,* 1244–1247.

CHASE, W. G., & SIMON, H. A. (1973). Perception in chess. *Cognitive Psychology, 4,* 55–81.

CHEN, Z. (1996). Children's analogical problem solving: The effects of superficial, structural, and procedural similarity. *Journal of Experimental Child Psychology, 62,* 410–431.

CHENG, P. W., & HOLYOAK, K. J. (1985). Pragmatic reasoning schemas. *Cognitive Psychology, 17,* 391–416.

CHENG, P. W., HOLYOAK, K. J., NISBETT, R. E., & OLIVER, L. M. (1986). Pragmatic versus syntactic approaches to training deductive reasoning. *Cognitive Psychology, 18,* 293–328.

CHERNIK, D. A. (1972). Effect of REM sleep deprivation on learning and recall by humans. *Perceptual and Motor Skills, 34,* 283–294.

CHERRY, E. C. (1953). Some experiments on the recognition of speech with one and with two ears. *Journal of the Acoustical Society, 25,* 975–979.

CHI, M. T. H. (1978). Knowledge structure and memory development. In R. Siegler (Ed.), *Children's thinking: What develops?* Hillsdale, NJ: Erlbaum.

CHI, M. T. H., FELTOVICH, P. J., & GLASER, R. (1981). Categorization and representation of physics problems by experts and novices. *Cognitive Science, 5,* 121–152.

CHI, M. T. H., GLASER, R., & REES, E. (1982). Expertise in problem solving. In R. J. Sternberg (Ed.), *Advances in the psychology of human intelligence* (Vol. 1). Hillsdale, NJ: Erlbaum.

CHIESA, M. (1992). Radical behaviorism and scientific frameworks: From mechanistic to relational accounts. *American Psychologist, 47,* 1287–1299.

CHIESI, H., SPILICH, G., & VOSS, J. F. (1979). Acquisition of domain related information in relation to high and low domain knowledge. *Journal of Verbal Learning and Verbal Behavior, 18,* 257–273.

CHOMSKY, N. (1957). *Syntactic structures.* Paris: Mouton.

CHOMSKY, N. (1959). Review of Skinner's *Verbal behavior. Language, 35,* 26–58.

CHOMSKY, N. (1965). *Aspects of the theory of syntax.* Cambridge, MA: MIT Press.

CHOMSKY, N. (1981). *Lectures on government and binding.* Dordrecht, Netherlands: Foris.

CHRISTIAANSEN, R. T., & OCHALEK, K. (1983). Editing misleading information from memory. Evidence for the coexistence of original and post-event information. *Memory and Cognition, 11,* 467–478.

CHRISTIANSON, S., & NILSSON, L. (1984). Functional amnesia as induced by a psychological trauma. *Memory and Cognition, 12,* 142–155.

CHRISTIANSON, S. A. (1992). Emotional stress and eyewitness memory: A critical review. *Psychological Bulletin, 112,* 284–309.

CHRISTIANSON, S. A., & HUBINETTE, B. (1993). Hands up! A study of witnesses' emotional reactions and memories associated with bank robberies. *Applied Cognitive Psychology, 7,* 365–379.

CHRISTIANSON, S. A., & LOFTUS, E. F. (1991). Remembering emotional events: The fate of detailed information. *Cognition and Emotion, 5,* 81–108.

CHURCHLAND, P. M. (1988). *Matter and consciousness.* Cambridge, MA: MIT Press.

CHURCHLAND, P. S., & SEJNOWSKI, T. J. (1992). *The Computational brain.* Cambridge, MA: MIT Press.

CIPOLLI, C., BARONCINI, P., FAGIOLI, I., & FUMAI, A. (1987). The thematic continuity of mental sleep experience in the same night. *Sleep, 10,* 473–479.

CLARK, E. V. (1973). What's in a word? On the child's acquisition of semantics in his first language. In T. E. Moore (Ed.), *Cognitive development and the acquisition of language* (pp. 65–110). New York: Academic Press.

CLIFFORD, B. R., AND & BULL, R. (1978). *The psychology of person identification.* London: Routledge and Kegan Paul.

COELHO, C. A. (1995). Discourse production deficits following traumatic brain injury: A critical review of the recent literature. *Aphasiology, 9,* 409–429.

COHEN, C. E. (1981). Person categories and social perception: Testing some boundaries of the processing effects of prior knowledge. *Journal of Pesonality and Social Psychology, 40,* 441–152.

COHEN, L. J. (1981). Can human irrationality be experimentally demonstrated? *The Behavioral and Brain Sciences, 4,* 317–370.

COHEN, L. J. (1982). Are people programmed to commit fallacies? Farther thoughts about the interpretation of experimental data on probability judgement. *Journal for the Theory of Social Behavior, 12,* 251–274.

COHEN, M. E., & CARR, W. J. (1975). Facial recognition and the VonRestorff effect. *Bulletin of the Psychonomic Society, 6,* 383–384.

COHEN, N. J. (1984). Preserved learning capacity in amnesia: Evidence for multiple memory systems. In L. R. Squire & N. Butters (Eds.), *Neuropsychology of memory.* New York: Guilford Press.

COHEN, N. J., & CORKIN, S. (1981). The amnesic patient H.M.: Learning and retention of a cognitive skill. *Society for Neuroscience Abstracts, 7,* 235.

COHEN, N. J., EICHENBAUM, H., DEACEDO, B. D., & CORKIN, S. (1985). Different memory systems underlying acquisition of procedural and declarative knowledge. *Annals of the New York Academy of Sciences, 444,* 55–71.

COLE, M., GAY, J., GLICK, J., & SHARP, D. W. (1971). *The cultural context of learning and thinking.* New York: Basic Books.

COLE, M., & SCRIBNER, S. (1974). *Culture and thought*. New York: Wiley.

COLLINS, A. F., & HAY, D. C. (1994). Connectionism and memory. In P. E. Morris & M. Gruneberg (Eds.), *Theoretical aspects of memory* (pp. 196–237). New York: Routledge.

COLLINS, A. M., & LOFTUS, E. F. (1975). A spreading activation theory of semantic processing. *Psychological Review, 82*, 407–428.

COLLINS, A. M., & QUILLIAN, M. R. (1969). Retrieval time from semantic memory. *Journal of Verbal Learning and Verbal Behavior, 8*, 240–248.

COLLINS, A. M., & QUILLIAN, M. R. (1970). Does category size affect categorization time? *Journal of Verbal Learning and Verbal Behavior, 9*, 432–438.

COLLINS, A. M., & QUILLIAN, M. R. (1972). Experiments on semantic memory and language comprehension. In L. W. Gregg (Ed.), *Cognition in learning and memory* (pp. 117–137). New York: Wiley.

COOMBS, C. H., DAWES, R. M., & TVERSKY, A. (1970). *Mathematical psychology*. Englewood Cliffs, NJ: Prentice-Hall.

COOPER, L. A., & SHEPARD, R. N. (1973). Chronometric studies of the rotation of mental images. In W. G. Chase (Ed.), *Visual information processing*. New York: Academic Press.

CORBALLIS, M. C. (1989). Laterality and human evolution. *Psychological Review, 96*, 492–505.

CORBALLIS, M. C. (1991). *The lopsided ape*. Oxford, England: Oxford University Press.

CORBALLIS, M. C. (1992). On the evolution of language and generativity. *Cognition, 44*, 197–226.

CORBETTA, M., MIEZIN, F. M., DOOBMEYER, S., SHULMAN, G. L., & PETERSEN, S. E. (1991). Selective and divided attention during visual discrimination of shapes, color, and speed: Functional anatomy by positron emission tomography. *Journal of Neuroscience, 11*, 2383–2402.

COREN, S., & GIRGUS, J. S. (1978). Visual illusions. In R. Held, H. W. Leibowitz, & H. L. Teuber (Eds.), *Handbook of sensory physiology* (Vol. 8, pp. 551–568). Berlin: Springer-Verlag.

CORKIN, S. (1968). Acquisition of motor skill after bilateral medial temporal-lobe excision. *Neuropsychologia, 6*, 255–265.

CORNELL, T. L., FROMKIN, V. A., & MAUNER, G. (1993). A linguistic approach to language processing in Broca's aphasia: A paradox resolved. *Current Directions in Psychological Science, 2*, 47–52.

CORTER, J. E., & GLUCK, M. A. (1992). Explaining basic categories: Feature predictability and information. *Psychological Bulletin, 111*, 291–303.

COSMIDES, L. (1989). The logic of social exchange: Has natural selection shaped how humans reason? *Cognition, 31*, 187–276.

COSMIDES, L., & TOOBY, J. (1990). In the mind a frequentist? Paper presented at the annual meeting of the Psychonomic Society, New Orleans, LA.

COSMIDES, L., & TOOBY, J. (1992). Cognitive adaptations for social exchange. In J. H. Barkow, L. Cosmides, & J. Tooby (Eds.), *The adapted mind* (pp. 163–228). Oxford, England: Oxford University Press.

COTMAN, C. W., MONAGHAN, D. T., & GANONG, A. H. (1988). Excitatory amino acid neurotransmission: NMDA receptors and Hebb-type synoptic plasticity. *Annual Review of Neuroscience, 11*, 61–80.

COWAN, N. (1994). Mechanisms of verbal short-term memory. *Current Directions in Psychological Science, 3*, 185–189.

CRAIK, F. I. M., & LOCKHART, R. S. (1972). Levels of processing: A framework for memory research. *Journal of Verbal Learning and Verbal Behavior, 11*, 671–684.

CRAIK, F. I. M., & LOCKHART, R. S. (1986). CHARM is not enough: Comments on Eich's model of event recall. *Psychological Review, 93*, 360–364.

CRAIK, F. I. M., MOSCOVITCH, M., & MCDOWD, J. M. (1994). Contributions of surface and conceptual information to performance on implicit and explicit memory tasks. *Journal of Experimental Psychology: Learning, Memory, and Cognition, 20*, 864–875.

CRAIK, F. I. M., & TULVING, E. (1975). Depth of processing and the retention of words in episodic memory. *Journal of Experimental Psychology: General, 104*, 268–294.

CRAIK, K. J. W. (1943). *The nature of explanation*. Cambridge, England: Cambridge University Press.

CRAIN, S., & NAKAYAMA, M. (1987). Structure dependence in grammar function. *Language, 63*, 522–543.

CRAMMOND, J. (1992). Analyzing the basic cognitive development processes of children with specific types of learning disabilities. In R. Case (Ed.), *The mind's staircase: Exploring the conceptual underpinnings of human thought and knowledge*, (pp. 285–303). Hillsdale, NJ: Erlbaum.

CRICK, F., & KOCH, C. (1990). Toward a neurobiological theory of consciousness. *Seminars in the Neurosciences, 2*, 263–275.

CROVITZ, H. F. (1970). *Galton's walk*. New York: Harper & Row.

CUMMINS, D. D. (1995). Naive theories and causal deduction. *Memory and Cognition, 23*, 646–658.

CUMMINS, D. D., LUBART, T., ALKSNIS, O., & RIST, R. (1991). Conditional reasoning and causation. *Memory and Cognition, 19*, 274–282.

CURTISS, S. (1977). *Genie: A psycholinguistic study of a modern-day "wild child."* New York: Academic Press.

CURTISS, S. (1982). Developmental dissociation of language and cognition. In L. Obler & L. Menn (Eds.), *Exceptional language and linguistics*. New York: Academic Press.

CURTISS, S. (1994). Language as a cognitive system: Its independence and selective vulnerability. In C. Otero (Ed.), *Noam Chomsky: Critical assessments* (Vol. 4). London: Routledge.

CUTLER, B. L., & PENROD, S. D. (1988). Context reinstatement and eyewitness identification. In G. M. Davies & D. M. Thomson (Eds.), *Memory in context: Context in memory*. Chichester, England: Wiley.

DAHL, D., & SARVEY, J. M. (1989). Norepenephrine induces pathway specific long-lasting potentiation and depression in the hippocampal dentate gyrus. *Proceedings of the National Academy of Sciences, USA, 86*, 4776–4780.

DALE, H. C. A., & BADDELEY, A. D. (1962). On the nature of alternatives used in testing recognition memory. *Nature, 196*, 93–94.

DAMASIO, A. R., & DAMASIO, H. (1992). Brain and language. *Scientific American, 267*, 88–95.

DAMASIO, A. R., & GESCHWIND, N. (1984). The neural basis of language. *Annual Review of Neuroscience, 7*, 127–147.

DAMASIO, A. R., GRAFF-RADFORD, N. R., ESLINGER, P. J., DAMASIO, H., KASSELL, N. (1985). Amnesia following basal forebrain lesions. *Archives of Neurology, 42*, 263–271.

DAMASIO, A. R., YAMADA, T., DAMASIO, H., CORBETT, J., & MCKEE, J. (1980). Central achromatopsia: Behavioral, anatomic, and physiologic aspects. *Neurology, 30*, 1064–1071.

DANEMAN, M., & CARPENTER, P. A. (1980). Individual differences in working memory and reading. *Journal of Verbal Learning and Verbal Behavior, 9*, 450–466.

DARK, V. J., & BENBOW, C. P. (1991). Differential enhancement of working memory with mathematical versus verbal precocity. *Journal of Educational Psychology, 83*, 48–60.

DARWIN, C. J., TURVEY, M. T., & CROWDER, R. G. (1972). An auditory analogue of the Sperling partial report procedure and evidence for brief auditory storage. *Cognitive Psychology, 3*, 255–267.

DAUM, I., CHANNON, S., & CANAVAR, A. (1989). Classical conditioning in patients with severe memory problems. *Journal of Neurology and Neurosurgery Psychiatry, 52*, 47–51.

DAVIS, J., & SCHIFFMAN, H. R. (1985). The influence of the wording of interrogatives on the accuracy of eyewitness recollection. *Bulletin of the Psychonomic Society, 23*, 394–396.

DAVIS, K. L., MOHS, R. C., TINKLENBERG, J. R., PFEFFERBAU, A., HOLLISTER, L. E., & KOPELL, B. S. (1978). Physostigmine: Improvement of long-term memory processes in normal humans. *Science, 201*, 272–274.

DAVIS, M. (1986). Pharmacological and anatomical analysis of fear conditioning using the fear-potential startle paradigm. *Behavioral Neuroscience, 100*, 814–824.

DAVIS, P. J. (1987). Repression and the inaccessibility of affective memories. *Journal of Personality and Social Psychology, 53*, 585–593.

DAVIS, S., BUTCHER, S. P., & MORRIS, R. G. M. (1992). The NMDA receptor antagonist D-2-amino-S-phosphoropentan-oate (D-AP5) impairs spatial learning and LTP *in vivo* at intracellular concentrations comparable to those that block LTP *in vitro*. *Journal of Neuroscience, 12*, 21–34.

DAVIS, S. E., & PALLADINO, J. J. (1997). *Psychology 2*, Upper Saddle River, NJ: Prentice Hall.

DAWES, R. M. (1975). The mind, the model, and the task. In F. Restle, R. M. Shuffring, N. J. Costellan, H. R. Lindman, and D. B. Pisoni (Eds.), *Cognitive theory* (Vol. 1, pp. 119–129). Hillsdale, NJ: Erlbaum.

DAWES, R. M. (1993). Prediction of the future versus an understanding of the past: A base asymmetry. *American Journal of Psychology, 106*, 1–24.

DAWES, R. M., FAUST, D., & MEEHL, P. E. (1989). Clinical versus actuarial judgment. *Science, 243*, 1668–1674.

DAWSON, M. E., & SCHELL, A. M. (1983). Lateral asymmetries in electro-dermal responses to unattended stimuli: A reply to Walker and Ceci. *Journal of Experimental Psychology: Human Perception and Performance, 9*, 148–150.

DEAN, R. S., & KULHAVY, R. W. (1981). Influence of spatial organization in prose learning. *Journal of Educational Psychology, 73*, 97–64.

DEANGELIS, T. (1988). Dietary recall is poor: Recall study suggests. *APA Monitor, 19*, 14.

DEARY, I. J. (1993). Inspection time and WAIS-R IQ subtypes: A confirmatory factor analysis study. *Intelligence, 17*, 223–236.

DEARY, I. J., & STOUGH, C. (1996). Intelligence and inspection time: Achievements, prospects, problems. *American Psychologist, 51*, 599–608.

DEESE, J. (1959). On the prediction of occurrence of particular verbal intrusions in immediate recall. *Journal of Experimental Psychology, 58*, 17–22.

DE GROOT, A. D. (1965). *Thought and choice in chess*. The Hague, Netherlands: Mouton.

DE GROOT, A. D. (1966). Perception and memory versus thought. In B. Kleinmuntry (Ed.), *Problem-solving*. New York: Wiley.

DE KONOICK, J., LORRAIN, D., CHRIST, G., & PROULX, G. (1989). Intensive language learning and increases in rapid eye movement sleep: Evidence of a performance factor. *International Journal of Psychophysiology, 8*, 43–47.

DEMARIE-DREBLOW, D. (1991). Relation between knowledge and memory: A reminder that correlation does not imply causation. *Child Development, 62*, 484–498.

DEMENT, W. C. (1960). The effect of dream deprivation. *Science, 131*, 1705–1707.

DEMPSTER, F. N. (1981). Memory span: Sources of individual and developmental differences. *Psychological Bulletin, 89*, 63–100.

DEMPSTER, F. N. (1985). Short-term memory development in childhood and adolescence. In C. Brainerd & M. Pressley (Eds.), *Basic processes in memory development: Progress in cognitive development research* (pp. 209–248). New York: Springer-Verlag.

DENIS, M. & CARFANTAN, M. (1985). People's knowledge about images. *Cognition, 20*, 49–60.

DENKLA, M. B., & RUDEL, R. G. (1976). Rapid automatized naming (R. A. N.): Dyslexia differentiated from other learning disabilities. *Neuropsychologia, 14*, 471–479.

DENNETT, D. C. (1991). *Consciousness explained*. Boston: Little, Brown.

DEREGOWSKI, J. B. (1972). Pictorial perception and culture. *Scientific American, 227*(5), 82–88.

DERENZI, E., & NICHELLI, P. (1975). Verbal and nonverbal short-term memory impairment following hemispheric damage. *Cortex, 11*, 341–354.

DESMOND, N. L., & LEVY, W. B. (1988). Anatomy of associative long-term synaptic modification. In P. W. Landfield & S. Deadwyler (Eds.), *Long-term potentiation: From biophysics to behavior*. New York: A. R. Liss.

DESROCHER, M. E., SMITH, M. L., & TAYLOR, M. J. (1995). Stimulus and sex differences in performance of mental rotation: Evidence from event-related potentials. *Brain and Cognition, 28*, 14–38.

DEVINE, P. G. (1989). Stereotypes and prejudice: Their automatic and controlled components. *Journal of Personality and Social Psychology, 56*, 680–690.

DI LOLLO, V., & HOGBEN, J. H. (1987). Suppression of visible persistence as a function of spatial separation between inducing stimuli. *Perception and Psychophysics, 41*, 345–354.

DIRKS, J., & NEISSER, U. (1977). Memory for object in real scenes: The development of recognition and recall. *Journal of Experimental Child Psychology, 23,* 315–328.

DOBSON, M., & MARKAM, R. (1993). Imagery ability and source monitoring: Implications for eyewitness memory. *British Journal of Psychology, 84,* 111–118.

DODD, B. (1977). The role of vision in the perception of speech. *Perception, 6,* 31–40.

DOHERTY, M. E., SCHIAVO, M. B., TWENEY, R. D., & MYNATT, C. R. (1981). The influence of feedback and diagnostic data on pseudodiagnosticity. *Bulletin of the Psychonomic Society, 18,* 191–194.

DOLPHIN, A. C., ERRINGTON, M. L., & BLISS, T. V. P. (1982). Long-term potentiation of the perforant path in vivo is associated with increased glutamate release. *Nature, 297,* 496–498.

DONDERS, F. C. (1868). On the speed of mental processes. Reprinted in *Acta Psychologica, 30*(1969), 412–431.

DONDERS, K., SCHOOLER, J. W., & LOFTUS, E. F. (1987, November). *Troubles with memory.* Paper presented at the annual meeting of the Psychonomic Society, Seattle, WA.

DONLEY, R. D., & ASHCRAFT, M. H. (1992). The methodology of testing naive beliefs in the physics classroom. *Memory and Cognition, 20,* 381–391.

DOOLING, D. J., & CHRISTIAANSEN, R. E. (1977). Episodic and semantic aspects of memory for prose. *Journal of Experimental Psychology: Human Learning and Memory, 3,* 428–436.

DOOLING, D. J., & LACHMAN, R. (1971). Effects of comprehension on retention of prose. *Journal of Experimental Psychology, 88,* 216–222.

DORIS, J. (1991). *The suggestibility of children's recollections.* Washington, DC: American Psychological Association.

DORNER, D., & KREUZIG, H. (1983). Problemlosefahigkeit und intelligenz. *Psychologische Rundhaus, 34,* 185–192.

DOUGLAS, M. (1966). *Priority and danger.* London: Routledge and Kegan Paul.

DRACHMAN, D. A. (1978). Central cholinergic system and memory. In M. A. Lipton, A. DiMascio, & K. F. Killman (Eds.), *Psychopharmacology: A generation of progress.* New York: Raven.

DREGER, R. M. (1968). General temperament and personality factors related to intellectual performances. *Journal of Genetic Psychology, 113,* 275–293.

DRETSKE, F. (1995). Meaningful perception. In S. M. Kosslyn & D.N. Oskerson (Eds.), *Visual cognition* (Vol. 2, pp. 331–352). Cambridge, MA: MIT Press.

DUBE, E. F. (1982). Literacy, cultural familiarity, and "intelligence" as determinants of story recall. In U. Neisser (Ed.), *Memory observed: Remembering in natural contexts* (pp. 274–292). New York: Freeman.

DUCHIN L. E. (1990). The evolution of articulate speech: comparative anatomy of the oral cavity in *Pan* and *Homo. Journal of Human Evolution, 19,* 687–697.

DUDEK, S. M., & BEAR, M. F. (1992). Homosynoptic long-term depression in area CAI of hippocampus and effects of N-methyl-o-osportate receptor blockade. *Proceedings of the National Academy of Sciences, 89,* 4363–4367.

DULANY, D. L., & HILTON, D. J. (1991). Conversational implicature, conscious representation, and the conjunction fallacy. *Social Cognition, 9,* 85–100.

DUNCKER, K. (1945). On problem solving. *Psychological Monographs, 58* (5) (Whole No. 270).

DURSO, F. T., REA, C. B., & DAYTON, T. (1994). Graph theoretic confirmation of restructuring during insight. *Psychological Science, 5,* 94–98.

D'ZURILLA, T. (1965). Recall efficiency and mediating cognitive events in "experimental repression." *Journal of Personality and Social Psychology, 3,* 253–256.

EAGLY, A. H. (1995). The science and politics of comparing women and men. *American Psychologist, 50,* 145–158.

EBBINGHAUS, H. (1885). *Uber das Gedachtnis.* Leipzig: Dunker and Humblot.

EDDY, D. M. (1982). Probabilistic reasoning in clinical medicine: Problems and opportunities. In D. Kahneman, P. Slovic, & A. Tversky (Eds.), *Judgment under uncertainty: Heuristics and biases* (pp. 249–267). Cambridge, England: Cambridge University Press.

EDELMAN, G. M. (1992). *Bright air, brilliant fire.* New York: Basic Books.

EDELMAN, S. (1995). Representation of similarity in three-dimensional object discrimination. *Neural Computation, 7*, 408–423.

EDWARDS, W. (1954). The theory of decision making. *Psychological Bulletin, 51*, 380–417.

EHRLICH, S. F., & RAYNER, K. (1981). Contextual effects on word perception and eye movements during reading. *Journal of Verbal Learning and Verbal Behavior, 20*, 641–655.

EICH, E. (1995). Mood as mediator of place dependent memory. *Journal of Experimental Psychology: General, 124*, 293–308.

EICH, E., & BIRNBAUM, L. M. (1982). Repetition, cuing, and state-dependent memory. *Memory and Cognition, 10*, 103–114.

EICHENBAUM, H., & BUNSEY, M. (1995). On the binding of associations in memory: Clues from studies on the role of hippocampus region in paired-associate learning. *Current Directions in Psychological Science, 4*, 19–23.

EINSTEIN, G. O., McDANIEL, M. A., & LACKEY, S. (1989). Bizzare imagery, interference, and distinctiveness. *Journal of Experimental Psychology: Learning, Memory, and Cognition, 15*, 137–146.

EISELEY, L. (1972). *The firmament of time.* New York: Atheneum.

ELLIS. A. W., & YOUNG, A. W. (1988). *Human cognitive neuropsychology,* London: Erlbaum.

ELLIS, B. (1992). Satanic ritual abuse and legend ostension. *Journal of Psychology and Theology, 20*, 274–277.

EMPSON, J. (1993). *Sleep and dreaming.* New York: Harvester Wheatsheaf.

EMPSON, J. A. C., & CLARKE, P. R. F. (1970). Rapid eye movement and remembering. *Nature, 227*, 287–288.

ENGLE, R. W., CONWAY, A. R. A., TUHOLSKI, S. W., & SHISLER, R. J. (1995). A resource account of inhibition. *Psychological Science, 6*, 122–125.

ERDELYI, M. H. (1990). Repression, reconstruction, and defense: History and integration of the psychoanalytical and experimental frameworks. In J. L. Singer (Ed.), *Repression and dissociation* (pp. 1–31). Chicago: University of Chicago Press.

ERDELYI, M. H. & GOLDBERG, B. (1979). "Let's not sweep repression under the rug." Toward a cognitive psychology of repression. In J. F. Kihlstrom & F. U. Evans (Eds.), *Functional disorders of memory* (pp. 355–402). Hillsdale, NJ: Erlbaum.

ERICKSON, J. R., & JEMISON, C. R. (1991). Relations among measures of autobiographical memory. *Bulletin of the Psychonomic Society, 29*, 233–236.

ERICSSON, K. A., CHASE, W. G., & FALOON, S. (1980). Acquisition of a memory skill. *Science, 208*, 1181–1182.

ERICSSON, K. A., & POLSON, P. G. (1988). An experimental analysis of the mechanisms of a memory skill. *Journal of Experimental Psychology: Learning, Memory and Cognition, 14*, 305–316.

ERVIN, S. M. (1964). Imitation and structural change in children's language. In E. H. Lenneberg (Ed.), *New directions in the study of language* (pp. 163–189). Cambridge, MA: MIT Press.

EVANS, J. ST. B. T., & OVER, D. E. (1996). Rationality in the selection task: Epistemic utility versus uncertainty reduction. *Psychological Review, 103*, 356–363.

EYFERTH, K. (1961). Leistungen verschiedener Gruppen von Besatzungskindern in Hamburg-Wechsler Intelligenztest fur Kinder (HAWIK). *Archiv fur die gesamte Psychologie, 113*, 223–241.

FAGERSTROM, K. (1980). Reliving a forgotten rape. *Scandinavian Journal of Behaviour Therapy, 9*, 45–50.

FANSELOW, M. S. (1993). Associations and memories: The role of NMDA receptors and long-term potentiation. *Current Directions in Psychological Science, 2*, 152–156.

FARAH, M. J. (1988). Is visual imagery really visual? Overlooked evidence from neuropsychology. *Psychological Review, 95*, 307–317.

FARAH, M. J., & McCLELLAND, J. L. (1991). A computational model of semantic memory impairment: Modality specificity and emergent category specificity. *Journal of Experimental Psychology: General, 120*, 339–357.

FARAH, M. J., SOSO, M. J., & DASHEIFF, R. M. (1992). Visual angle of the mind's eye before and after unilateral occipital lobectomy. *Journal of Experimental Psychology: Human Perception and Performance, 8,* 241–246.

FARRAR, M. J. (1992). Negative evidence and grammatical morpheme acquisition. *Developmental Psychology, 28,* 90–98.

FARTHING, G. W. (1992). *The psychology of consciousness.* Upper Saddle River, NJ: Prentice Hall.

FEINGOLD, A. (1988). Cognitive gender differences are disappearing. *American Psychologist, 43,* 95–103.

FERGUSON, E. L., & HEGARTY, M. (1995). Learning with real machines or diagrams: Application of knowledge to real-world problems. *Cognition and Instruction, 13,* 129–160.

FERNALD, D. (1997). *Psychology.* Upper Saddle River, NJ: Prentice Hall.

FERNANDEZ, A., & GLENBERG, A. M. (1985). Changing environmental context does not reliably affect memory. *Memory and Cognition, 13,* 333–366.

FESTINGER, L., & MACCOBY, N. (1964). On resistance to persuasive communications. *Journal of Abnormal and Social Psychology, 68,* 359–366.

FIEDLER, K. (1988). The dependence of the conjunctive following on subtle linguistic factors. *Psychological Research, 50,* 123–129.

FINKE, R. A. (1990). *Creative imagery: Discoveries and inventions in visualization.* Hillsdale, NJ: Erlbaum.

FINKE, R. A., WARD, T. B., & SMITH, S. M. (1992). *Creative cognition: Theory, research, and application.* Cambridge, MA: MIT Press.

FISCHER, K. W., & SILVERN, L. (1985). Stages and individual difference in cognitive development. *Annual Review of Psychology, 36,* 613–648.

FISCHHOFF, B. (1988). Judgment and decision making. In R. J. Sternberg & E. E. Smith (Eds.), *The psychology of human thought.* Cambridge, England: Cambridge University Press.

FLAVELL, J. (1955). Repression and the "return of the repressed." *Journal of Consulting Psychology, 19,* 441–443.

FLAVELL, J. H. (1982). On cognitive development. *Child Development, 53,* 1–10.

FLAVELL, J. H. (1985). *Cognitive development.* Englewood Cliffs, NJ: Prentice-Hall.

FLAVELL, J. H. (1992). Cognitive development: Past, present, and future. *Developmental Psychology, 28,* 998–1005.

FLAVELL, J. H. (1993). Understanding children's understanding of thinking and consciousness. *Current Directions in Psychological Science, 2,* 40–43.

FLAVELL, J. H. (1996). Piaget's legacy. *Psychological Science, 7,* 200–203.

FLEW, A. (1964). *Body, mind, and death.* New York: Macmillan.

FLYNN, J. R. (1980). *Race, IQ and Jensen.* London: Routledge & Kegan Paul.

FLYNN, J. R. (1984). The mean IQ of Americans: Massive gains 1932 to 1978. *Psychological Bulletin, 95,* 29–51.

FLYNN, J. R. (1987). Massive IQ gains in 14 nations: What IQ tests really measure. *Psychological Bulletin, 101,* 171–191.

FODOR, J. A. (1992). A theory of the child's theory of mind. *Cognition, 44,* 283–296.

FODOR, J. A., & PYLYSHYN, Z. W. (1981). How direct is visual perception: Some reflections on Gibson's ecological approach. *Cognition, 9,* 139–196.

FODOR, J. A., & PYLYSHYN, Z. W. (1988). Connectionism and cognitive architecture: A critical analysis. *Cognition, 28,* 3–71.

FONG, G. T., KRANTZ, D. H., & NISBETT, R. E. (1986). The effects of statistical training on thinking about everyday problems. *Cognitive Psychology, 18,* 253–292.

FONG, G. T., & NISBETT, R. E. (1991). Immediate and delayed transfer of training effect in statistical reasoning. *Journal of Experimental Psychology: General, 120,* 34–45.

FORSTER, K. I. (1990). Lexical processing. In D. N. Osherson & H. Lasnik (Eds.), *Language* (pp. 95–131). Cambridge, MA: MIT Press.

FORSTER, K. I., & OLBREI, I. (1973). Semantic heuristics and syntactic analysis. *Cognition, 2,* 319–347.

FRANKS, J. J., & BRANSFORD, J. D. (1971). Abstraction of visual patterns. *Journal of Experimental Psychology, 90,* 65–74.

FRASER, S. (ED.). (1995). *The bell curve wars.* New York: Basic Books.

FRAZIER, L. (1987). Sentence processing: A tutorial review. In M. Coltheart (Ed.), *Attention and performance: Vol. XII. The psychology of today* (pp. 559–586). Hillsdale, NJ: Erlbaum.

FREDERIKSEN, N., CARLSON, S., & WARD, W. C. (1984). The place of social intelligence in a taxonomy of cognitive abilities. *Intelligence, 8,* 315–337.

FREEMAN, L. C., ROMNEY, A. K., & FREEMAN, S. C. (1987). Cognitive structure and informant accuracy. *American Anthropologist, 89,* 310–325.

FREUD, S. (1953). *The interpretation of dreams.* Vols. 4 and 5 of *The standard edition.* London: Hogarth. (Originally published in 1900.)

FREUD, S. (1957). Repression. *The complete psychological works of Sigmund Freud* (Vol. 14). London: Hogarth. (Originally published in 1915.)

FREUD, S. (1962). *Screen memories* (J. Strachey, Trans.). In the standard edition of *The complete psychological works of Sigmund Freud* (Vol. 3). London: Hogarth. (Originally published in 1899.)

FREYD, J. J. (1994). Circling creativity. *Psychological Science, 5,* 122–126.

FRIEDRICH, J. (1993). Primary error detection and minimization (PEDMIN) strategies in social cognition: A reinterpretation of confirmation bias phenomenon. *Psychological Review, 100,* 298–319.

FRIES, E., GREEN, P., & BOWEN, D. J. (1995). What did I eat yesterday? Determinants of accuracy in 24-hour food memories. *Applied Cognitive Psychology, 9,* 143–155.

FRISCH, D. (1993). Reasons for framing effects. *Organizational Behavior and Human Decision Processes, 54,* 399–429.

FRISCH, D., & CLEMEN, R. T. (1994). Beyond expected utility: Rethinking behavioral decision research. *Psychological Bulletin, 116,* 46–54.

FROMKIN, V., KRASHEN, S., CURTISS, S., RIGLER, D., & RIGLER, M. (1974). The development of language in Genie: A case of coverage beyond the "critical period." *Brain and Language, 1,* 81–107.

FRY, A., & HALE, S. (1996). Processing speed, working memory, and fluid intelligence: Evidence for a developmental cascade. *Psychological Science, 7,* 237–241.

FUNAHASHI, S., BRUCE, C. J., & GOLDMAN-RAKIC, P. S. (1989). Mnemonic coding of visual space in the monkey's dorsolateral prefrontal cortex. *Journal of Neurophysiology, 61,* 331–349.

FURROW, D., NELSON, K., & BENEDICT, H. (1979). Mothers' speech to children and syntactic development: Some single relationships. *Journal of Child Language, 6,* 423–442.

GABRIELI, J. D. E., FLEISCHMAN, D. A., KEANE, M. M., REMINGER, S. L., & MORRELL, F. (1995). Double dissociation between memory systems underlying explicit and implicit memory in the human brain. *Psychological Science, 6,* 76–82.

GAERTNER, S. L., & MCLAUGHLIN, J. P. (1983). Racial stereotypes: Associations and ascriptions of positive and negative characteristics. *Social Psychology Quarterly, 46,* 23–30.

GALOTTI, K. M. (1994). *Cognitive psychology in and out of the laboratory.* Pacific Grove, CA: Brooks/Cole.

GALOTTI, K. M. (1995). Memories of a "decision-map": Recall of real-life decision. *Applied Cognitive Psychology, 9,* 307–319.

GALTON, F. (1883). *Inquiries into human faculty and its development.* London: Macmillan.

GALTON, F. (1884). *Hereditary genius.* New York: D. Appleton.

GANAWAY, G. K. (1989). Historical versus narrative truth: Clarifying the role of exogenous trauma in the etiology of MPD and its variants. *Dissociation, 2,* 205–220.

GARBER, H. L. (1988). *The Milwaukee Project: Preventing mental retardation in children at risk.* Washington, DC: American Association of Mental Retardation.

GARCIA, J. (1981). The logic and limits of mental aptitude testing. *American Psychologist, 36,* 1172–1180.

GARDNER, H. (1975). *The shattered mind: The person after brain damage.* New York: Knopf.

GARDNER, H. (1983). *Frames of mind.* New York: Basic Books.

GARDNER, H. (1985). *The mind's new science: A history of the cognitive revolution.* New York: Basic Books.

GARDNER, R. A., & GARDNER, B. T. (1969). Teaching sign language to a chimpanzee. *Science, 165,* 664–672.

GARNSEY, S. M., TANENHAUS, M. D., & CHAPMAN, R. M. (1989). Evoked potentials and the study of sentence comprehension. *Journal of Psycholinguistic Research, 18,* 51–60.

GARRETT, M. F. (1990). Sentence processing. In D. N. Oskerson & H. Lasnik (Eds.), *Language.* Cambridge, MA: MIT Press.

GAY, J., & COLE, M. (1967). *The new mathematics and old culture: A study of learning among the Kpelle of Liberia.* New York: Holt, Rinehart & Winston.

GAZZANIGA, M. S. (1970). *The bisected brain.* New York: Appleton-Century-Crofts.

GAZZANIGA, M. S. (1985). *The social brain.* New York: Basic Books.

GAZZANIGA, M. S. (1988). *Mind matter: How mind and brain interact to create our conscious lives.* Boston: Houghton Mifflin.

GEARY, D. C. (1995). Reflections of evolution and culture in children's cognition. *American Psychologist, 50,* 24–37.

GEINISMAN, Y., DE TOLEDO-MORRELL, L., & MORRELL, F. (1991). Induction of long-term potentiation is associated with an increase in the number of axospinous synapses with segmented postsynaptic densities. *Brain Research, 566,* 77–78.

GEISELMAN, R. E. (1988). Improving eyewitness memory through mental reinstatement of context. In G. M. Davies & D. M. Thomson (Eds.), *Memory in context: Context in memory* (pp. 231–244). Chichester, England: Wiley.

GEISELMAN, R. E., FISHER, R. P., MACKINNON, D. P., & HOLLAND, H. L. (1985). Eyewitness memory enhancement in the police interview: Cognitive retrieval mnemonics versus hypnosis. *Journal of Applied Psychology, 70,* 401–412.

GEISLER, C. (1986). The use of subliminal psychodynamic activation in the study of repression. *Journal of Personality and Social Psychology, 51,* 844–851.

GENTNER, D. (1989). The mechanisms of analogical learning. In S. Vosniadout & A. Ortony (Eds.), *Similarity and analogical reasoning.* Cambridge, England: Cambridge University Press.

GENTNER, D., & GENTNER, D. R. (1983). Flowing waters or teeming crowds: Mental models of electricity. In D. Gentner & A. L. Stevens (Eds.), *Mental models.* Hillsdale, NJ: Erlbaum.

GENTNER, D., RATTERMAN, M. J., & FORBUS, K. (1993). The role of similarity in transfer: Separating retrievability from inferential soundness. *Cognitive Psychology, 25,* 524–575.

GERNSBACHER, M. A. (1985). Surface information loss in comprehension. *Cognitive Psychology, 17,* 324–363.

GERSHUNY, B. S., & BURROWS, D. (1990). The use of rationalization and denial to reduce accident related and illness related death anxiety. *Bulletin of the Psychonomic Society, 28,* 161–163.

GERTZMAN, A., & KOLODNER, J. L. (1996). A case study of problem-based learning in a middle school classroom: Lessons learned. In E. Domeshek & D. Edelman (Eds.), *Proceedings of the 1996 International Conference of the Learning Sciences* (pp. 91–98). Charlottesville, VA: American Association for Computers in Education.

GESCHWIND, N., & GALABURDA, A. M. (1987). *Cerebral lateralization: Biological mechanisms, associations, and pathology.* Cambridge, MA: MIT Press.

GHOLSON, B., MORGAN, D., DATTEL, A. R., & PIERCE, K. A. (1990). The development of analogical problem solving: Strategic processes in scheme acquisition and transfer. In D. F. Bjorklund (Ed.), *Children's strategies: Contemporary view of cognitive development* (pp. 269–308). Hillsdale, NJ: Erlbaum.

GIBSON, E. J. (1969). *Principles of perceptive learning and development.* New York: Prentice-Hall.

GIBSON, J. J. (1950). *The perception of the visual world.* Boston: Houghton Mifflin.

GIBSON, J. J. (1966). *The senses considered as perceptual systems.* Boston: Houghton Mifflin.

GIBSON, J. J. (1979). *The ecological approach to visual perception.* Boston: Houghton Mifflin.

GICK, M. L., & HOLYOAK, K. J. (1980). Analogical problem solving. *Cognitive Psychology, 12,* 306–355.

GICK, M. L., & HOLYOAK, K. J. (1983). Scheme induction and analogical transfer. *Cognitive Psychology, 15,* 1–38.

GICK, M. L., & McGARRY, S. J. (1992). Learning from mistakes: Inducing analogous solution failures to a source problem produces later successes in analogical transfer. *Journal of Experimental Psychology: Learning, Memory, and Cognition, 18,* 623–639.

GIGERENZER, G. (1991). From tools to theories: A heuristic of discovery in cognitive psychology. *Psychological Review, 98,* 254–267.

GIGERENZER, G., HELL, W., & BLANK, H. (1988). Presentation and content: The use of base rates as a continuous variable. *Journal of Experimental Psychology: Human Perception and Performance, 14,* 513–525.

GIGERENZER, G., & HOFFRAGE, U. (1995). How to improve Bayesian reasoning without instruction: Frequency formats. *Psychological Review, 102,* 684–704.

GILBERT, D. T. (1991). How mental systems behave. *American Psychologist, 46,* 107–119.

GILBERT, D. T., KRULL, D. S., & MALONE, P. S. (1990). Unbelieving the unbelievable: Some problems in the rejection of false information. *Journal of Personality and Social Psychology, 59,* 601–613.

GILBERT, J. A. (1894). Researches on the mental and physical development of school children. *Studies from the Yale Psychological Laboratory, 2,* 40–100.

GLASER, R. (1984). Education and thinking. *American Psychologist, 39,* 93–104.

GLASER, R., & BASSOK, M. (1989). Learning theory and the study of instruction. *Annual Review of Psychology, 40,* 631–666.

GLASS, A. L., KREJCI, J., & GOLDMAN, J. (1989). The necessary and sufficient conditions for motor learning, recognition, and recall. *Journal of Memory and Language, 28,* 189–199.

GLEASON, J. B., HAY, D., & CAIN, L. (1989). The social and affective determinants of language development. In M. Rice & R. Schiefelbursch (Eds.), *The teachability of language* (pp. 171–186). Baltimore: Paul Brookes.

GLEASON, J. B., & RATNER, N. B. (1993). Language development in children. In J. B. Gleason & N. B. Ratner (Eds.), *Psycholinguistics* (pp. 301–350). Fort Worth, TX: Harcourt Brace Jovanovich.

GLENBERG, A., SMITH, F. M., & GREEN, C. (1977). Type 1 rehearsal: Maintenance and more. *Journal of Verbal Learning and Verbal Behavior, 16,* 339–352.

GLENBERG, A. M., & SWANSON, N. C. (1986). A temporal distinctiveness theory of recency and modality effects. *Journal of Experimental Psychology: Learning, Memory, and Cognition, 12,* 3–15.

GLUCK, M. A., & MYERS, C. E. (1995). Representation and association in memory: A neurocomputational view of hippocampal function. *Current Directions in Psychological Science, 4,* 23–29.

GLUCKSBERG, S., & DANKS, J. (1968). Effects of discriminative labels and of nonsense labels upon availability of novel function. *Journal of Verbal Learning and Verbal Behavior, 7,* 72–76.

GODDEN, N. N., & BADDELEY, A. D. (1975). Context-dependent memory in two natural environments: On land and underwater. *British Journal of Psychology, 66,* 325–332.

GOETHALS, G. R., & RECKMAN, R. F. (1973). The perception of consistency in attitudes. *Journal of Experimental Psychology, 9,* 491–501.

GOLDBERG, R. A., SCHWARTZ, S., & STEWART, M. (1977). Individual differences in cognitive processes. *Journal of Educational Psychology, 699*–14.

GOLDENBERG, G., PODREKA, I., STEINER, M., SUESS, E., DEEKE, L., & WILLMES, K. (1988). Pattern of cerebral bloodflow related to visual and motor imagery, results of emission computerized tomography. In M. Denis, J. Engelkamp, & J. T. E. Richardson (Eds.), *Cognitive and neuropsychological approaches to mental energy* (pp. 363–373). Dordrecht, Netherlands: Martinus Nijhoff.

GOLDIN-MEADOW, S., BUTCHER, C., MYLANDER, C., & DODGE, M. (1994). Nouns and verbs in a self-styled gesture system: What's in a name? *Cognitive Psychology, 27,* 259–319.

GOLDIN-MEADOW, S., & MYLANDER, C. (1990). Beyond the input given: the child's role in the acquisition of language. *Language, 66,* 323–355.

GOLDMAN, W. P., & NIGEL, N. C., & WINOGRAD, E. (1992). A demonstration of incubation in anagram problem solving. *Bulletin of Psychonomic Society, 30,* 36–38.

GOLDMAN-RAKIC, P. S. (1987). Circuitry of primate prefrontal cortex and regulation of behavior by representational memory. In F. Plum & V. Mountcastle (Eds.), *Handbook of physiology (Vol. 5,* 373–417), Bethesda, MD: American Physiological Society.

GOLDMAN-RAKIC, P. S. (1987b). Development of circuity and cognitive function. *Child Development, 58,* 601–622.

GOLDMAN-RAKIC, P. S. (1992). Working memory and the mind. *Scientific American, 267(3),* 88–95.

GOLDSTEIN, A. G., & CHANCE, J. (1970). Visual recognition memory for complex configurations. *Perception and Psychophysics, 9,* 237–241.

GOLDSTEIN, D. B., HINRICHS, J. V., & RICHMAN, C. L. (1985). Subjects' expectations, individual variability, and the scanning of visual images. *Memory and Cognition, 13,* 365–370.

GOLDSTEIN, E. B. (1996). *Sensation and perception.* Pacific Grove, CA: Brooks/Cole.

GOLINKOFF, R. M., HARDING, C. G., CARLSON, V., & SEXTON, M. E. (1984). The infant's perception of causal events: The distinction between animate and inanimate objects. In L. Lipsitt & C. Rovee-Colber (Eds.), *Advances in infancy research* (Vol. 3, pp. 146–165). Norwood, NJ: Ablex.

GOODGLASS, H., & KAPLAN, E. (1972). *The assessment of aphasia and related disorders.* Philadelphia: Lea and Febiger.

GOPNIK, A. (1996). The post-Piaget era. *Psychological Science, 7,* 221–225.

GOPNIK, A., & ASTINGTON, J. W. (1988). Children's understanding of representational change and its relation to the understanding of false belief and the appearance–reality distinction. *Child Development, 59,* 26–37.

GOPNIK, M. (1990). Dysphasia in an extended family. *Nature, 344,* 715.

GOPNIK, M. & CARGO, M. (1991). Familial aggregation of a developmental language disorder. *Cognition, 39,* 1–50.

GORMAN, H., & BOURNE, L. G. (1983). Learning to think by learning LOGO: Rule learning in third grade computer programmers. *Bulletin of the Psychonomic Society, 21,* 165–167.

GOTTFREDSON, L. S., & BROWN, V. C. (1981). Occupational differentiation among white men in the first decade after high school. *Journal of Vocational Behavior, 19,* 251–289.

GOUCHIE, C., & KIMURA, D. (1991). The relationship between testosterone levels and cognitive ability patterns. *Psychoneuroendocrinology, 16,* 323–344.

GOULD, S. J. (1981). *The mismeasure of man.* New York: Norton.

GOULD, S. J., & VRBA, E. S. (1982). Exaptation—a missing term in the science of form. *Paleobiology, 8,* 4–15.

GRAESSER, A. C., ROBERTSON, S. P., LOVELACE, E. R., & SWINEHART, D. M. (1980). Answers to why-questions expose the organization of story plot and predict recall of actions. *Journal of Verbal Learning and Verbal Behavior, 19,* 110–119.

GRAF, P. (1990). Life-span changes in implicit and explicit memory. *Bulletin of the Psychonomic Society, 28,* 353–358.

GRAF, P., & MANDLER, G. (1984). Activation makes words more accessible, but not necessarily more retrievable. *Journal of Verbal Learning and Verbal Behavior, 23,* 553–568.

GRAF, P., SQUIRE, L. R., & MANDLER, G. (1984). The information that amnesic patients do not forget. *Journal of Experimental Psychology: Learning, Memory, and Cognition, 10,* 164–178.

GRAHAM, R. B. (1990). *Physiological psychology.* Belmont, CA: Wadsworth.

GRAUBARD, S. R. (1988). *The artificial intelligence debate: False starts, real foundations.* Cambridge, MA: MIT Press.

GRAY, C. M., & SINGER, W. (1989). Stimulus-specific neuronal oscillations in orientation column of cat visual cortex. *Proceedings of the National Academy of Sciences of the United States of America, 86,* 1698–1702.

GREEN, K. P., KUHL, P. K., MELTZOFF, A. N., & STEVENS, E. B. (1991). Interpreting speech information and sensory modality: Female faces and male voices in the McGurk effect. *Perception and Psychophysics, 50,* 524–536.

GREENBERG, J. H. (1977). *A new invitation to linguistics.* Garden City, NY: Anchor Press.

GREENBERG, R., PILLARD, R., & PEARLMAN, C. (1972). The effect of dream (stage REM) deprivation on adaptation to stress. *Psychosomatic Medicine, 34,* 257–262.

GREENE, R. L. (1986). Sources of recency effects in free recall. *Psychological Bulletin, 99,* 221–228.

GREENO, J. G. (1964). Paired-associate learning with massed and distributed repetition of items. *Journal of Experimental Psychology, 67,* 286–295.

GREENO, J. G. (1974). Hobbits and orcs: Acquisition of a sequential concept. *Cognitive Psychology, 6,* 270–292.

GREENOUGH, W. T. (1975). Experimental modification of the developing brain. *American Scientist, 63,* 37–46.

GREENOUGH, W. T. Possible structural substrates of plastic neural phenomena. In G. Lynch, J. L. McGaugh, N. M. Weinberger (Eds.), *Neurobiology of learning and memory.* New York: Guilford Press.

GREENOUGH, W. T., & BAILEY, C. H. (1988). The anatomy of memory: Convergence of results across a diversity of tests. *Trends in Neuroscience, 11,* 142–147.

GREENWALD, A. G., & BANAJI, M. R. (1995). Implicit social cognition: Attitudes, self-esteem, and stereotypes. *Psychological Review, 102,* 4–27.

GREGORY, R. L. (1970). *The intelligent eye.* New York: McGraw-Hill.

GRICE, H. P. (1975). Logic and conversation. In P. Cole & J. L. Morgan (Eds.), *Syntax and semantics: Vol. 3. Speech acts* (pp. 41–58). New York: Seminar Press.

GRIFFIN, S. A. (1992). Young children's awareness of their inner world: A neo-structured analysis of the development of intrapersonal intelligence. In R. Case (Ed.), *The mind's staircase: Exploring the conceptual underpinnings of children's thoughts and knowledge* (pp. 189–206). Hillsdale, NJ: Erlbaum.

GRIGGS, R. A., & COX, J. R. (1982). The elusive thematic-materials effect in Wason's selection task. *British Journal of Psychology, 73,* 407–420.

GRONINGER, L. D. (1971). Mnemonic imagery and forgetting. *Psychonomic Science, 23,* 161–163.

GROSSBERG, S. (1978). Behavioral contrast in short-term memory: Serial binary models or parallel continuous memory models? *Journal of Mathematical Psychology, 17,* 199–219.

GROSSBERG, S. (1980). How does the brain build a cognitive code? *Psychological Review, 87,* 1–51.

GROSSBERG, S. & STONE, G. (1986). Neural dynamics of word recognition and recall: Attentional priming, learning, and resonance. *Psychological Review, 93,* 46–74.

GUENTHER, R. K. (1991). Generic versus specialized information processing. *American Journal of Psychology, 104,* 193–209.

GUENTHER, R. K., KLATZKY, R. L., & PUTNAM, W. (1980). Commonalities and differences in semantic decisions about pictures and words. *Journal of Verbal Learning and Verbal Behavior, 19,* 54–74.

GUILFORD, J. P. (1964). Zero correlations among tests of intellectual abilities. *Psychological Bulletin, 61,* 401–404.

GUILFORD, J. P. (1967). *The nature of human intelligence.* New York: McGraw-Hill.

GUTHRIE, E. R. (1959). Association by contiguity. In S. Koch (Ed.), *Psychology: A study of science* (Vol. 2). New York: McGraw-Hill.

HABER, R. N. (1983). The impending demise of the icon: A critique of the concept of iconic storage in visual information processing. *The Behavioral and Brain Sciences, 6,* pp. 1–11 and 51–54.

HABER, R. N., & HABER, L. R. (1988). The characteristics of eidetic imagery. In L. K. Obler & D. Fein (Eds.), *The exceptional brain: Neuropsychology of talent and special abilities* (pp. 218–241). New York: Guilford Press.

HAIER, R. J., SIEGEL, B. V., MACLACHLAN, A., SODERLING, E., LOTTENBERG, S., & BUCHSBAUM, M. S. (1992). Regional glucose metabolic changes after learning a complex visio-spatial-motor task: A positron emission tomography study. *Brain Research, 570*, 134–143.

HAIER, R. J., SIEGEL, B. V., NUECHTERLEIN, K. H., HAZLETT, E., WU, J. C., PAEK, J., BROWNING, H. L., & BUCHSBAUM, M. S. (1988). Cortical glucose metabolic rate correlates of abstract reasoning and attention studies with positron emission tomography. *Intelligence, 12*, 199–217.

HALDANE, E., & ROSS, G. R. T. (1931). *The philosophical works of Descartes.* Cambridge, England: Cambridge University Press.

HALE, S., FRY, A. F., & JESSIE, K. A. (1993). Effects of practice on speed of information processing in children and adults: Age sensitivity and age invariance. *Developmental Psychology, 29*, 880–892.

HALEY, J. E., WILCOX, G. L., & CHAPMAN, P. F. (1992). The role of nitric oxide in hippocampal long-term polentiation. *Neuron, 8*, 211–216.

HALGREN, E. (1984). Human hippocampal and amygdala recording and stimulation: Evidence for a neural model of recent memory. In L. R. Squire & N. Butters (Eds.), *The neuropsychology of memory* (pp. 165–182). New York: Guilford Press.

HALL, B. K. (1992). *Evolutionary developmental biology.* London: Chapman & Hall.

HALL, C. S. (1984). A ubiquitous sex difference in dreams revisited. *Journal of Personality and Social Psychology, 46*, 1109–1117.

HALL, C. S., DOMHOFF, G. W., BLICK, K. A., & WESNER, K. E. (1982). The dreams of college men and women in 1950 and 1980: A comparison of dream content and sex differences. *Sleep, 5*, 188–194.

HALL, J. F. (1990). Reconstructive and reproductive models of memory. *Bulletins of the Psychonomic Society, 28*, 191–194.

HALPERN, D. F. (1992). *Sex differences in cognitive abilities* (2nd ed.). Hillsdale, NJ: Erlbaum.

HALPERN, D. F. & CASS, M. (1994). Laterality, sexual orientation, and immune system functioning: Is there a relationship? *International Journal of Neuroscience, 77*, 167–180.

HAMANN, S. B. (1996). Implicit memory in the tactile modality: Evidence from Braille stem completion in the blind. *Psychological Science, 7*, 284–288.

HAMPSON, E. (1990b). Estrogen-related variations in human spatial and articulatory motor skills. *Psychoneuroendocrinology, 15*, 97–111.

HAMPSON, E. (1990a). Variations in sex-related cognitive abilities across the menstrual cycle. *Brain and Cognition, 14*, 26–43.

HAMPSON, E., & KIMURA, D. (1988). Reciprocal effects of hormonal fluctuations on human motor and perceptual-spatial skills. *Behavioral Neuroscience, 102*, 456–459.

HANAWALT, N. G., & DEMAREST, I. H. (1939). The effect of verbal suggestion in the recall period upon the reproduction of visually perceived forms. *Journal of Experimental Psychology, 25*, 151–174.

HARDIN, C., & BANAJI, M. R. (1993). The influence of language on thought. *Social Cognition, 11*, 277–308.

HARKNESS, A. R., DEBONO, K. G., & BORGIDA, E. (1985). Personal involvement and strategies for making contingency judgments: A stake in the dating game makes a difference. *Journal of Personality and Social Psychology, 49*, 22–32.

HARRIS, R. O., & MONACO, G. E. (1978). Psychology of pragmatic implication: Information processing between the lines. *Journal of Experimental Psychology: General, 107*, 1–22.

HART, B., & RISLEY, T. R. (1992). American parenting of language-learning children: Persisting differences in family–child interaction observed in natural home environments. *Developmental Psychology, 28*, 1096–1105.

HART, J. T. (1967). Memory and the memory-monitoring process. *Journal of Verbal Learning and Verbal Behavior, 76*, 685–691.

HARTLEY, J., & HOMA, D. (1981). Abstraction of stylistic concepts. *Journal of Experimental Psychology: Human Learning and Memory, 7*, 33–46.

HASHER, L., & ZACKS, R. T. (1979). Automatic processing of fundamental information: The case of frequency occurrence. *American Psychologist, 39*, 1372–1388.

HAURI, P. (1970). Evening activity, sleep mentation, and subjective sleep quality. *Journal of Abnormal Psychology, 76,* 270–275.

HAVILAND, S. E., & CLARK, H. H. (1974). What's new? Acquiring new information as a process in comprehension. *Journal of Verbal Learning and Verbal Behavior, 13,* 512–521.

HAYES, J. R. (1981). *The complete problem solver.* Philadelphia: Franklin Institute Press.

HAYES, J. R., & SIMON, H. A. (1974). Understanding written instructions. In L. W. Gregg (Ed.), *Knowledge and cognition.* Hillsdale, NJ: Erlbaum.

HAYES, J. R., & SIMON, H. A. (1977). Psychological differences among problem isomorphs. In N. J. Costellar, D. B. Pisoni, G. R. Potts (Eds.), *Cognitive theory* (Vol. 2). Hillsdale, NJ: Erlbaum.

HEATH, S. B. (1983). *Ways with words.* Cambridge, England: Cambridge University Press.

HEATH, S. B. (1989). Oral and literate traditions among Black Americans living in poverty. *American Psychologist, 44,* 367–373.

HEBB, D. (1949). *The organization of behavior.* New York: Wiley.

HEIDER, E. R. (1972). Universals in color naming and memory. *Journal of Experimental Psychology, 93,* 10–20.

HEIDER, E. R., & OLIVIER, D. C. (1972). The structure of the color space in naming and memory for two languages. *Cognitive Psychology, 3,* 337–354.

HEILMAN, K. M., & SCHOLES, R. J. (1976). The nature of comprehension errors in Broca's conduction and Wernicke's aphasics. *Cortex, 17,* 258–265.

HEINDEL, W. C., BUTTERS, N., & SALMON, D. P. (1988). Impaired learning of a motor skill in patients with Huntington's disease. *Behavioral Neuroscience, 102,* 141–147.

HELLIGE, J. B. (1990). Hemispheric asymmetry. *Annual Review of Psychology, 41,* 55–80.

HELMHOLTZ, H. VON. (1962). Vol. 3, Section 26. In *A treatise on physiological optics* (J. P. C. Southall, Ed. & Trans.). New York: Dover (original work published 1866).

HELMS, J. E. (1992). Why is there no study of cultural equivalence in standardized cognitive ability testing? *American Psychologist, 47,* 1083–1101.

HEMPEL, C. G. (1966). *Philosophy of natural science.* Upper Saddle River, NJ: Prentice-Hall.

HENLE, M. (1962). The relationship between logic and thinking. *Psychological Review, 69,* 366–378.

HERGENHAHN, B. R. (1986). *An introduction to the history of psychology.* Belmont, CA: Wadsworth.

HERMAN, J. L., & SCHATZOW, E. (1987). Recovery and verification of memories of childhood sexual trauma. *Psychoanalytic Psychology, 4,* 1–14.

HERMAN, L. M., RICHARDS, D. G., & WOLZ, J. P. (1984). Comprehension of sentences by bottlenosed dolphins. *Cognition, 16,* 129–219.

HERRNSTEIN, R., & MURRAY, C. (1994). *The bell curve.* New York: Free Press.

HILTON, D. J. (1995). The social context of reasoning conversational inference and rational judgment. *Psychological Bulletin, 118,* 248–271.

HILTON, S. M. & ZBROZYNA, A. W. (1963). Amygdaloid region for defense reaction and its efferent pathway to the brain stem. *Journal of Physiology (London), 165,* 160–173.

HINTON, G. E. (1992). How neural networks learn from experience. *Scientific American, 267,* 144–151.

HINTON, G. E., & SHALLICE, T. (1991). Lesioning an attraction network: Investigations of acquired dyslexia. *Psychological Review, 98,* 74–95.

HIRSH-PASEK, K., TREIMAN, R., & SCHNEIDERMAN, M. (1984). Brown and Hanlon revisited: Mothers' sensitivity to ungrammatical forms. *Journal of Child Language, 11,* 81–88.

HIRST, W. (1986). The psychology of attention. In J. E. LeDoux & W. Hirst (Eds.), *Mind and brain: Dialogues in cognitive neuroscience.* Cambridge, England: Cambridge University Press.

HIRST, W., SPELKE, E. S., REAVES, C. C., CAHARACK, G., & NEISSER, U. (1980). Dividing attention without alternation or automaticity. *Journal of Experimental Psychology: General, 109,* 98–117.

HOBSON, J. A. (1988). *The dreaming brain.* New York: Basic Books.

HOFFMAN, R. R., BRINGMANN, W., BAMBERG, M., & KLEIN, R. (1986). Some historical observations on Ebbinghaus. In D. Gorfein & R. Hoffman (Eds.), *Memory and learning: The Ebbinghaus centennial conference*. Hillsdale , NJ: Erlbaum.

HOLMES, D. (1990). The evidence for repression: An examination of sixty years of research. In J. Singer (Ed.), *Repression and dissociation: Implications for personality theory, psychopathology, and health* (pp. 85–102). Chicago: University of Chicago Press.

HOLMES, D. S. (1972). Repression or interference: A further investigation. *Journal of Personality and Social Psychology, 22,* 163–170.

HOLMES, D. S. (1974). Investigation of repression: Differential recall of material experimentally or naturally associated with ego threat. *Psychological Bulletin, 81,* 632–653.

HOLTGRAVES, T., & HALL, R. (1995). Repressors: What do they repress and how do they repress it? *Journal of Research in Personality, 29,* 306–317.

HOLYOAK, K. J. (1990). Problem solving. In D. N. Osherson & E. E. Smith (Eds.), *Thinking: An invitation to cognitive science*. Cambridge, MA: MIT Press.

HOLYOAK, K. J., & GLASS, A. L. (1975). The role of contradictions and counterexamples in the rejection of false sentences. *Journal of Verbal Learning and Verbal Behavior, 14,* 215–239.

HOLYOAK, K. J., & KOH, K. (1987). Surface and structural similarity in analogical transfer. *Memory and Cognition, 15,* 332–340.

HOMA, D. (1978). The abstraction of ill-defined form. *Journal of Experimental Psychology: Human Learning and Memory, 4,* 407–416.

HONG, E., & O'NEIL, H. F. (1992). Instructional strategies to help learners build relevant mental models in inferential statistics. *Journal of Educational Psychology, 84,* 150–159.

HOOPER, F., TONIOLO, T., & SIPPLE, T. (1978). A longitudinal analysis of logical reasoning relationships: Conservation and transitive inference. *Developmental Psychology, 14,* 674–682.

HORN, G. (1985). *Memory, imprinting and the brain*. Oxford, England: Oxford University Press.

HORN, J. L., LOEHLIN, J., & WILLERMAN, L. (1975). Preliminary report of Texas adoption project. In Munsinger, H., The adopted child's IQ: A critical review. *Psychological Bulletin, 82,* 623–659.

HORNE, J., & MCGRATH, M. (1984). The consolidation hypothesis for REM sleep function: Stress and other confounding factors—a review. *Biological Psychology, 18,* 165–184.

HOUSE, W. C. (1975). Repression-sensitization and response to the implicit cue requirements of a social situation. *Journal of Clinical Psychology, 31,* 505–509.

HOUTZ, J. C., & FRANKEL, A. D. (1992). Effects of incubation and imagery training on creativity. *Creativity Research Journal, 5,* 183–189.

HOWARD, D. V., FRY, A. F., & BRUNE, C. M. (1991). Aging and memory for new associations: Direct versus indirect measures. *Journal of Experimental Psychology: Learning, Memory, and Cognition, 17,* 779–792.

HOWES, M. B. (1990). *The psychology of human cognition: Mainstream and Genevan traditions*. New York: Pergamon Press.

HUBEL, D. H., & WIESEL, T. N. (1977). Functional architecture of macaque monkey visual cortex. *Proceedings of the Royal Society of London, 198,* 1–59.

HUBEL, D. H., & WIESEL, T. N. (1979). Brain mechanisms of vision. *Scientific American, 241,* 150–162.

HUNT, E. (1980). Intelligence as an information-processing concept. *British Journal of Psychology, 71,* 449–474.

HUNT, E. (1983). On the nature of intelligence. *Science, 219,* 141–146.

HUNT, E., & LOVE, T. (1972). How good can memory be? In A. W. Melton & E. Martin (Eds.), *Coding processes in human memory*. Washington, DC: Winston.

HUNT, E., LUNNEBORG, C., & LEWIS, J. (1975). What does it mean to be high verbal? *Cognitive Psychology, 7,* 194–227.

HUNT, E. B. (1978). Mechanisms of verbal ability. *Psychological Review, 85,* 199–230.

HUNT, E. B., & AGNOLI, F. (1991). The Whorfian hypothesis: A cognitive psychology perspective. *Psychological Review, 98,* 377–389.

HURFORD, J. R. (1991). The evolution of the critical period for language acquisition. *Cognition, 40*, 159–201.

HYAMS, N. M. (1986). *Language acquisition and the theory of parameters.* Dordrecht, Netherlands: Reidel.

HYDE, J. S. (1981). How large are cognitive gender differences? A meta-analysis using w2 and d. *American Psychologist, 36*, 892–901.

HYDE, J. S., FENNEMA, E., & LAMON, S. J. (1990). Gender differences in mathematics performance: A meta-analysis. *Psychological Bulletin, 107*, 139–155.

HYDE J. S., & JENKINS, J. J. (1975). Recall for words as a function of semantic, graphic, and syntactic orienting tasks. *Journal of Verbal Learning and Verbal Behavior, 12*, 471–480.

HYDE, J. S., & LINN, M. C. (EDS.). (1986). *The psychology of gender advances through meta-analysis.* Baltimore: Johns Hopkins University Press.

HYDE, J. S., & LINN, M. C. (1988). Gender differences in verbal ability: A meta-analysis. *Psychological Bulletin, 104*, 53–69.

ILLICH, I. (1970). *Deschooling society.* New York: Harper & Row.

INGRAM, D. (1989). *First language acquisition: Method, description, and explanation.* Cambridge, England: Cambridge University Press.

INHELDER, B., & PIAGET, J. (1958). *The growth of logical thinking from childhood to adolescence* (A. Parsons & S. Milgram, Trans.). New York: Basic Books.

INTONS-PETERSON, M. J. (1983). Imagery paradigms: How vulnerable are they to experimenters' expectations? *Journal of Experimental Psychology: Human Perception and Performance, 9*, 394–412.

INTRAUB, H. (1981). Identifying and naming of briefly glimpsed visual scenes. In D. F. Fisher, R. A. Marty, & J. W. Senders (Eds.), *Eye movements: Cognitive and visual perception.* Hillsdale, NJ: Erlbaum.

IRIKI, A., PAVLIDES, C., KELLER, A., & ASANUMA, H. (1989). Long-term potentiation in the motor cortex. *Science, 245*, 1385–1387.

IRWIN, D. E., ZACKS, J. L., & BROWN, J. S. (1990). Visual memory and the perception of a stable visual environment. *Perception and Psychophysics, 47*, 35–46.

IRWIN, J., SLOVIC, P., LICHTENSTEIN, S., & MCCLELLAND, G. (1993). Preference reversals and the measurement of environmental values. *Journal of Risk and Uncertainty, 6*, 5–18.

ISINGRINI, M., VAZOU, F., & LEROY, P. (1995). Dissociation of implicit and explicit memory tests: Effect of age and divided attention on category exemplar generation and cued recall. *Memory and Cognition, 23*, 462–467.

ITTELSON, W. H., & CANTRIL, H. (1954). *Perception: A transactional approach.* New York: Doubleday.

JACKENDOFF, R. (1994). *Patterns in the mind.* New York: Basic Books.

JACKSON, E., CAMPOS, T. T., & FISCHER, K. W. (1978). The question of decaloge between object permanence and person permanence. *Developmental Psychology, 14*, 1–10.

JACOBY, L. L. (1978). On interpreting the effects of repetition: Solving a problem versus remembering a solution. *Journal of Verbal Learning and Verbal Behavior, 17*, 649–667.

JACOBY, L. L. (1983). Remembering the data: Analyzing the interactive processes in reading. *Journal of Verbal Learning and Verbal Behavior, 22*, 485–508.

JACOBY, L. L., & DALLAS, M. (1981). On the relationship between autobiographical memory and perceptual learning. *Journal of Experimental Psychology: General, 110*, 306–340.

JACOBY, L. L., LINDSAY, S., & TOTH, J. P. (1992). Unconscious influences revealed: Attention, awareness, and control. *American Psychologist, 47*, 802–809.

JACOBY, L. L., & WITHERSPOON, D. (1982). Remembering without awareness. *Canadian Journal of Psychology, 36*, 300–324.

JACOBY, L. L., WOLOSHYN, V. T., & KELLEY, C. (1989). Becoming famous without being recognized: Unconscious influences of memory produced by dividing attention. *Journal of Experimental Psychology: General, 118*, 115–125.

JANOWSKY, J. S., OVIATT, S. K., & ORWOLL, E. S. (1994). Testosterone influences spatial cognition in older men. *Behavioral Neuroscience, 108*, 325–332.

JANOWSKY, J. S., SHIMAMURA, A. P., & SQUIRE, L. R. (1989). Memory and metamemory: Comparisons between patients with frontal lobe lesions and amnesic patients. *Psychobiology, 17,* 3–11.

JEANNARET, P., & WEBB, W. (1963). Strength grip on arousal from full night's sleep. *Perceptual and Motor Skills, 17,* 759–761.

JEFFRIES, R., TURNER, A., POLSON, P., & ATWOOD, M. (1981). The process involved in designing software. In M. T. Anderson (Ed.), *Cognitive skills and their acquisition.* Hillsdale, NJ: Erlbaum.

JENKINS, J. G., & DALLENBACH, K. M. (1924). Oblivescence during sleep and working. *American Journal of Psychology, 35,* 605–612.

JENKINS, J. J., STRANGE, W., & EDMAN, T. R. (1983). Identification of vowels in "vowelless" syllables. *Perception and Psychophysics, 34,* 441–450.

JENSEN, A. R. (1969). How much can we boost IQ and scholastic achievement? *Harvard Educational Review, 39,* 1–123.

JENSEN, A. R. (1979). g: Outmoded theory or unconquered frontier? *Creative Science Technology, 2,* 16–29.

JENSEN, A. R. (1982). Reaction time and psychometric g. In H. J. Eysenck (Ed.), *A model for intelligence* (pp. 93–132). Berlin: Springer-Verlag.

JENSEN, A. R. (1986). Methodological and statistical techniques for the chronometric study of mental abilities. In C. R. Reynolds & V. L. Willson (Eds.), *Methodological and statistical advances in the study of individual differences.* New York: Plenum.

JENSEN, A. R. (1993). Why is reaction time correlated with psychometric g? *Current Directions in Psychological Science, 2,* 53–56.

JOHANSSON, G. (1973). Visual perceptions of biological motion and a model for its analysis. *Perception and Psychophysics, 14,* 201–211.

JOHNSON, M. H., & MORTON, J. (1991). *Biology and cognitive development: The case of face recognition.* Oxford, England: Blackwell.

JOHNSON, M. K., KIM, J. K., & RISSE, G. (1985). Do alcoholic Korsakoff's syndrome patients acquire affective reactions? *Journal of Experimental Psychology: Learning, Memory, and Cognition, 11,* 22–36.

JOHNSON, P. E., DURAN, A. S., HASSELBROK, F., MOLLER, J., PRIETULA, M., FELTOVICH, P. J., & SWANSON, D. B. (1981). Expertise and error in diagnostic reasoning. *Cognitive Science, 5,* 235–283.

JOHNSON-LAIRD, P. N., BYRNE, R. M. J., & SCHAEKEN, W. (1992). Propositional reasoning by model. *Psychological Review, 99,* 418–439.

JOHNSTON, J. C., & MCCLELLAND, J. L. (1973). Visual factors in word perception. *Perception and Psychophysics, 14,* 365–370.

JONES, E. G., & POWELL, T. P. S. (1970). An anatomical study of converging sensory pathways within the cerebral cortex of the monkey. *Brain, 93,* 793–820.

JONES, G. V. (1983). Identifying basic categories. *Psychological Bulletin, 94,* 423–428.

JONES, S. K., JONES, K., & FRISCH, D. (1995). Biases of probability assessment: A comparison of frequency and single-case judgments. *Organizational Behavior and Human Decision Processes, 61,* 109–122.

JONES, W. P., & ANDERSON, J. R. (1987). Short- and long-term memory retrieval: A comparison of the effects of information load and relatedness. *Journal of Experimental Psychology: General, 116,* 137–153.

JORDAN, K., & HUNTSMAN, L. A. (1990). Image rotation of misoriented letter strings: Effects of orientation cuing and repetition. *Perception and Psychophysics, 48,* 363–374.

JUST, M. A., & CARPENTER, P. A. (1978). Inference processes during reading: Reflections from eye fixations. In J. W. Senders, D. F. Fisher, & R. A. Monty (Eds.), *Eye movements and the higher psychological functions.* Hillsdale, NJ: Erlbaum.

KAHL, R. (1971). *Selected writings of Hermann von Helmholtz.* Middletown, CT: Wesleyan University Press.

KAHNEMAN, D. (1973). *Attention and effort.* Englewood Cliffs, NJ: Prentice-Hall.

KAHNEMAN, D., SLOVIC, P., & TVERSKY, A. (EDS.). (1982). *Judgment under uncertainty: Heuristics and biases.* Cambridge, England: Cambridge University Press.

KAHNEMAN, D., & TVERSKY, A. (1973). On the psychology of prediction. *Psychological Review, 80,* 237–251.

KAHNEMAN, D., & TVERSKY, A. (1984). Choices, values and power. *American Psychologist, 39,* 341–350.

KAIL, R. (1986). Sources of age differences in speed of processing. *Child Development, 57,* 969–987.

KAIL, R. (1991). Developmental change in speed of processing during childhood and adolescence. *Psychological Bulletin, 109,* 490–501.

KAIL, R., & PARK, Y.-S. (1992). Global developmental change in processing time. *Merril-Palmer Quarterly, 38,* 525–541.

KAIL, R., & PARK, Y.-S. (1994). Processing time, articulation time, and memory span. *Journal of Experimental Child Psychology, 57,* 281–291.

KALAT, J. W. (1992). *Biological psychology.* Belmont, CA: Wadsworth.

KALBAUGH, G. L., & WALLS, R. T. (1973). Retroactive and proactive interference in prose learning of biographical and science materials. *Journal of Educational Psychology, 65,* 244–251.

KANDEL, E. R., & HAWKINS, R. D. (1992). The biological basis of learning and individuality. *Scientific American, 267,* 78–86.

KARNI, A., TANNE, D., RUBENSTEIN, B. S., BARTON, S., ASKENASY, J. J. M., & SAGI, D. (1994). Dependence on REM sleep of overnight improvement of a perceptual skill. *Science, 265,* 679–682.

KASPER, L. F., & GLASS, A. L. (1988). An extension of the keyword method facilitates the acquisition of simple Spanish sentences. *Applied Cognitive Psychology, 2,* 137–146.

KAWAMOTO, A. (1993). Nonlinear dynamics in the resolution of lexical ambiguity: A parallel distributed processing account. *Journal of Memory and Language, 32,* 474–516.

KEATING, D. P. (1980). Thinking processes in adolescence. In J. Adelson (Ed.), *Handbook of adolescent psychology.* New York: Wiley.

KEATING, D. P. (1982). The emperor's new clothes: The "new look" in intelligence research. In R. Sternberg (Ed.), *Advances in the psychology of human intelligence* (Vol. 2, pp. 1–45). Hillsdale, NJ: Erlbaum.

KEATING, D. P., & BOBBIT, B. L. (1978). Individual and developmental differences in cognitive-processing components of mental ability. *Child Development, 49,* 155–167.

KEENAN, J. M., BAILLET, S. D., & BROWN, P. (1984). The effects of causal cohesion on comprehension and memory. *Journal of Verbal Learning and Verbal Behavior, 23,* 115–126.

KEIL, F. C. (1989). *Concepts, kinds, and cognitive development.* Cambridge, MA: MIT Press.

KEITH, J. R., & RUDY, J. W. (1990). Why NMDA-receptor-dependent long-term potentiation may not be a mechanism of learning and memory: Reappraisal of the NMDA-receptor blockade strategy. *Psychology, 18,* 251–257.

KELLY, C., & DALE, P. (1989). Cognitive skills associated with the onset of multicultural utterances. *Journal of Speech and Hearing Research, 32,* 645–656.

KIERNAN, B., SNOW, D., SWISHER, L., & VANCE, R. (1997). Another look at nonverbal rule induction in children with SLI: Testing a flexible reconceptualization hypothesis. *Journal of Speech, Language, and Hearing Research, 40,* 75–82.

KIM, J. J., FANSELOW, M. S., DECOLA, J. P., & LANDEIRA-FERNANDEZ, J. (1992). Selective impairment of long-term but not short-term conditional fear by the NMDA antagonist APV. *Behavioral Neuroscience, 106,* 591–596.

KIMBALL, M. M. (1989). A new perspective on women's math achievement. *Psychological Bulletin, 105,* 198–214.

KIMURA, D. (1992). Sex differences in the brain. *Scientific American, 267* (3), 118–125.

KIMURA, D., CARIA, M. A., MELIS, F., & ASANUMA, H. (1994). Long-term potentiation within the cat motor cortex. *Neuroreport: An International Journal for the Rapid Communication of Research in Neuroscience, 5,* 2372–2376.

KIMURA, D., & HAMPSON, E. (1994). Cognitive pattern in men and women is influenced by fluctuation in sex hormones. *Current Directions in Psychological Science, 3,* 57–61.

KIMURA, D., & TOUSSAINT, C. (1991). Sex differences in cognitive function vary with the season. *Society for Neuroscience Abstracts, 17,* 868.

KING, A. (1991). Effects of training in strategic questioning on children's problem-solving performance. *Journal of Educational Psychology, 83,* 307–317.

KING, J., & JUST, M. A. (1991). Individual differences in syntactic processing: The role of working memory. *Journal of Memory and Languages, 30,* 580–602.

KINNEY, G. C., MARSETTA, M., & SHOWMAN, D. J. (1966). *Studies in display symbol legibility, part XXI. The legibility of alphanumeric symbols for digitized television.* (ESD-TR-66-117). Bedford, MA: Mitre Corporation.

KINTSCH, W. (1977). On comprehending stories. In M. A. Carpenter and P. A. Just (Eds.), *Cognitive processes in comprehension.* Hillsdale, NJ: Erlbaum.

KINTSCH, W., & GREENE, E. (1978). The role of culture-specific schemata in the comprehension and recall of stories. *Discourse Processes, 1,* 1–13.

KINTSCH, W., & VAN DIJK, T. A. (1978). Toward a model of text comprehension and production. *Psychological Review, 85,* 363–394.

KIRBY, K. N. (1994). Probabilities and utilities of fictional outcomes in Wason's four-card selection task. *Cognition, 51,* 1–28.

KLAHR, D. (1984). Transition processes in quantitative development. In R. S. Sternberg (Ed.), *Mechanism of cognitive development.* New York: Freeman.

KLAHR, D., & CARVER, S. (1988). Cognitive objectives in a LOGO debugging curriculum: Instruction, learning, and transfer. *Cognitive Psychology, 20,* 362–404.

KLATZKY, R. L. (1980). *Human memory: Structure and processes.* San Francisco: Freeman.

KLAUS, R. A., & GRAY, S. (1968). The early training project for disadvantaged children: A report after five years. *Monographs of the Society for Research in Child Development, 33* (Serial No. 120).

KLAYMAN, J., & HA, Y. W. (1987). Confirmation, disconfirmation, and information in hypothesis testing. *Psychological Review, 94,* 211–228.

KLAYMAN, J., & HA, Y. (1989). Hypothesis testing in rule discovery: Strategy, structure, and content. *Journal of Experimental Psychology: Learning, Memory, and Cognition, 15,* 596–604.

KLINE, P. (1991). *Intelligence: The psychometric view.* New York: Routledge.

KLINGER, M. R., & GREENWALD, A. G. (1995). Unconscious memory of association judgments. *Journal of Experimental Psychology: Learning, Memory, and Cognition, 21,* 569–581.

KLOUDA, G. V., & COOPER, W. G. (1990). Information search following damage to the frontal lobes. *Psychological Report, 67,* 411–416.

KLUENDER, R., & KUTAS, M. (1993). Bridging the gap: Evidence from ERPs on the processing of unbounded dependencies. *Journal of Cognitive Neuroscience, 5,* 196–214.

KOBASIGAWA, A. (1974). Utilization of retrieval cues by children in recall. *Child Development, 45,* 127–134.

KOHLBERG, L. (1969). Stage and sequence: The cognitive developmental approach to socialization. In D. A. Goslin (Ed.), *Handbook of socialization theory of research* (pp. 347–480). Chicago: Rand McNally.

KOHLER, W. (1925). *The mentality of apes.* New York: Harcourt, Brace, and World.

KOLODNER, J. L. (1997). Educational implications of analogy: A view from case-based reasoning. *American Psychologist, 52,* 57–66.

KONDO, T., ANTROBUS, J., & FEIN, G. (1989). Later REM activation and sleep mentation. *Sleep Research, 18,* 147.

KONNER, M. (1991). Universal of behavioral development in relation to brain myelinization. In K. R. Gibson & A. C. Petersen (Eds.), *Brain maturation and cognitive development: Comparative and cross-Cultural Perspectives* (pp. 181–223). New York: Aldine de Gruyter.

KORIAT, A., & MELKMAN, R. (1987). Depth of processing and memory organization. *Psychological Records, 49,* 183–187.

KORSAKOFF, S. S. (1889). Etude medico-psychologique sur une forme des maladies de la memoire. *Revue Philosophique, 28,* 501–530.

KOSLOWSKI, L. T., & CUTTING, J. E. (1977). Recognizing the sex of a walker from a dynamic point-light display. *Perception of Psychophysics, 21,* 575–580.

KOSONEN P., & WINNE, P. H. (1995). Effects of teaching statistical laws on reasoning about everyday problems. *Journal of Educational Psychology, 87,* 33–46.

KOSSYLN, S. M. (1975). Information representation in visual language. *Cognitive Psychology, 7,* 341–370.

KOSSYLN, S. M. (1983). *Ghosts in the mind's machine: Creating and using images in the brain.* New York: Norton.

KOSSYLN, S. M. (1994). *Imagery and brain.* Cambridge, MA: MIT Press.

KOSSYLN, S. M., BALL, T. M., & REISER, B. J. (1978). Visual images preserve metric spatial information: Evidence from studies of image scanning. *Journal of Experimental Psychology: Human Perception and Performance, 4,* 47–60.

KOSSYLN, S. M., BRUNN, J., CAVE, K. R., & WALLACH, R. W. (1984). Individual differences in mental imagery ability: A computational analysis. *Cognition, 18,* 195–243.

KRASS, J., KINOSHITA, S., & McCONKEY, K. M. (1989). Hypnotic memory and confidence reporting. *Applied Cognitive Psychology, 3,* 35–51.

KUHARA-KOJIMA, K., & HATANO, G. (1991). Contribution of content knowledge and learning ability to the learning of facts. *Journal of Educational Psychology, 83,* 253–263.

KUHL, P. K. (1986). Theoretical contributions of tests on animals to the special-mechanisms debate in speech. *Experimental Biology, 53,* 31–39.

KUHN, D. (1989). Children and adults as intuitive scientists. *Psychological Review, 96,* 674–689.

KUHN D., WEINSTOCK, M., & FLATON, R. (1994). How well do jurors reason? Competence dimensions of individual variation in a juror reasoning task. *Psychological Science, 5,* 289–296.

KUNZENDORF, R. G., & MORGAN, C. (1994). Repression: Active censorship of stressful memories vs. source amnesia for self-consciously dissociated memories. *Imagination, Cognition, and Personality, 13,* 291–302.

LABERGE, D., & SAMUELS, S. J. (1974). Toward a theory of automatic information processing in reading. *Cognitive Psychology, 6,* 293–323.

LABERGE, S. (1985). *Lucid dreaming.* Los Angeles: Tarcher.

LACHMAN, R., LACHMAN, J. L., & BUTTERFIELD, E. C. (1979). *Cognitive psychology and information processing: An introduction.* Hillsdale, NJ: Erlbaum.

LAKOFF, G. (1987). *Women, fire, and dangerous things: What categories reveal about the human mind.* Chicago: University of Chicago Press.

LAMM, J. B. (1991). Easing access to the courts for incest victims: Toward an equitable application of the delayed discovery rule. *The Yale Law Journal, 100,* 2189–2208.

LANGLOIS, J. H., & ROGGMAN, L. A. (1990). Attractive faces are only average. *Psychological Science, 1,* 115–121.

LANGLOIS, J. H., ROGGMAN, L. A., CASEY, R. J., RITTER, J. M., RIESER-DANNER, L. A., & JENKINS, V. Y. (1987). Infant preferences for attractive faces: Rudiments of a stereotype? *Developmental Psychology, 23,* 363–369.

LANGLOIS, J. H., ROGGMAN, L. A., & MUSSELMAN, L. (1994). What is average and what is not average about attractive faces? *Psychological Science, 5,* 214–220.

LAPLACE, P. S. (1814/1951). *A philosophical essay on probabilities* (F. W. Truscott & F. L. Emory, Trans.). New York: Dover. (Original work published in 1814.)

LARDIERE, D. (1992). On the linguistic shaping of thought: Another response to Alfred Bloom. *Language in Society, 21,* 231–251.

LARKIN, J. H. (1983). The role of problem representation in physics. In D. Gentner & A. L. Stevens (Eds.), *Mental models.* Hillsdale, NJ: Erlbaum.

LARKIN, J. H., McDERMOTT, J., SIMON, D. P., & SIMON, H. A. (1980). Expert and novice performance in solving physics problems. *Science, 208,* 1335–1342.

LARSON, G. E., & SACCUZZO, D. P. (1989). Cognitive correlates of general intelligence: Toward a process theory of g. *Intelligence, 13,* 5–31.

LARSON, J., & LYNCH, G. (1986). Induction of synaptic potentiation in hippocampus by patterned stimulation involves two events. *Science, 232,* 985–988.

LAURENDEAU-BENDAVID, M. (1977). Culture, schools and cognitive development: A comparative study of children in French-Canada and Rwanda. In P. R. Dasen (Ed.), *Piagetian psychology: Cross-cultural contributions* (pp. 123–168). New York: Gardner/ Wiley.

LAVE, J. (1988). *Cognition in practice.* Cambridge, England: Cambridge University Press.

LAW, D. J., PELLEGRINO, J. W., & HUNT, E. B. (1993). Comparing the tortoise and the hare. Gender differences and experience in dynamic spatial reasoning tasks. *Psychological Science, 4,* 35–40.

LAZAR, I., DARLINGTON, R., MURRAY, H., ROYCE, J., & SNIPPER, A. (1982). Lasting effects of early education: A report from the Consortium for Longitudinal Studies. *Monographs of the Society for Research in Child Development, 47* (Serial No. 195).

LEAKEY, R. (1994). *The origin of humankind.* New York: Basic Books.

LEAKEY, R. E., & LEWIN, R. (1977). *Origins.* New York: Dutton.

LECOURS, A. R., LHERMITTE, F., & BRYANS, B. (1983). *Aphasiology.* London: Bailliere Tindall.

LEDOUX, J. E. (1987). Emotion. In J. M. Brookshort & V. B. Mountcastle (Eds.), *Handbook of physiology: The nervous system v. higher function of the nervous system* (F. Plum Vol. Ed. pp. 419–460). Bethesda, MD: American Physiological Society.

LEEPER, R. W. (1935). A study of a neglected portion of the field of learning—the development of sensory organization. *Journal of Genetic Psychology, 46,* 41–75.

LEFFORD, A. (1946). The influence of emotional subject matter on logical reasoning. *Journal of General Psychology, 34,* 127–151.

LEHKY, S., & SEJNOWSKI, T. J. (1988). Computing shape from shadowing with a neural network model. In E. Shwarz (Ed.), *Computational neuroscience.* Cambridge, MA: MIT Press.

LEHRER, R., & LITTLEFIELD, J. (1993). Relationships among cognitive components in logo learning and transfer. *Journal of Educational Psychology, 85,* 317–330.

LEIBNIZ, G. W. (1704/1916). *New essays concerning human understanding.* Chicago: Open Court.

LEICHTMAN, M. D., & CECI, S. J. (1995). The effects of stereotypes and suggestions on preschoolers' reports. *Developmental Psychology, 31,* 568–578.

LENNEBERG, E. H. (1967). *Biological foundation of language.* New York: Wiley.

LESLIE, A. M. (1987). Pretense and representation. The origin of theory of mind. *Psychological Review, 94,* 412–426.

LEVIN, I. P., & GAETH, G. J. (1988). How consumers are affected by the framing of attribute information before and after consuming the product. *The Journal of Consumer Research, 15,* 374–378.

LEVY, J., TREVARTHEN, C., & SPERRY, R. W. (1972). Perception of bilateral chimeric figure following hemispheric disconnection. *Brain, 95,* 61–78.

LEVY, W. B., & STEWARD, O. (1979). Synapses as associative memory elements in the hippocampal formation. *Brain Research, 175,* 233–245.

LEWIN, L., & GOMBOSH, D. (1973). Increase in REM time as a function of the need for divergent thinking. In W. P. Koella & P. Levin (Eds.), *Sleep: Physiology, biochemistry, psychology, pharmacology, clinical implications.* Basel, Switzerland: Karger.

LEWONTIN, R. C., ROSE, S., & KAMIN, L. (1984). *Not in our genes.* New York: Pantheon.

LIBERMAN, A. M., COOPER, F. S., SHANKWEILER, D. P., & STUDDERT-KENNEDY, M. (1967). Perception of the speech code. *Psychological Review, 74,* 431–461.

LIBERMAN, A. M., HARRIS, K. S., KINNEY, J. A., & LANE, H. (1961). The discrimination of relative onset time of the components of certain speed and nonspeed patterns. *Journal of Experimental Psychology, 61,* 379–388.

LIEBERMAN, D. A. (1990). *Learning behavior and cognition.* Belmont, CA: Wadsworth.

LIEBERMAN, P. (1984). *The biology and evolution of language*. Cambridge, MA: Harvard University Press.

LIEBERMAN, P. (1994). Human language and human uniqueness. *Language and Communication, 14*, 87–95.

LIGHT, L. L., & LAVOIE, D. (1993). Direct and indirect measures of memory in old age. In P. Graf and M. E. U. Masson (Eds.), *Implicit memory: New directions in cognition, development and neuropsychology* (pp. 207–230). Hillsdale, NJ: Erlbaum.

LINDBERG, M. (1991). An interactive approach to assessing the suggestibility and testimony of eyewitnesses. In J. Doris (Ed.), *The suggestibility of children's recollections* (pp. 47–55). Washington, DC: American Psychological Association.

LINDSAY, D. S. (1990). Misleading questions can impair eyewitnesses' ability to remember details. *Journal of Experimental Psychology: Learning, Memory, and Cognition, 16*, 1077–1083.

LINDSAY, D. S. (1993). Eyewitness suggestibility. *Current Directions in Psychological Science, 3*, 86–89.

LINN, M. C., & FISHER, C. W. (1983). The gap between promise and reality in computer education: Planning a response. In *Making our schools more effective: A conference for California educators*. San Francisco: ACCCEL.

LINTON, M. (1978). Real world memory after six years: An in vivo study of very long term memory. In M. M. Gruneberg, P. E. Morris, & R. N. Sykes (Eds.), *Practical aspects of memory*. Orlando, FL/London: Academic Press.

LIU, L. G. (1985). Reasoning counterfactually in Chinese: Are there any obstacles? *Cognition, 21*, 239–270.

LOCKE, J. L. (1983). *Phonological acquisition and change*. New York: Academic Press.

LOCKHART, R. S., LAMON, M., & GLICK, M. L. (1988). Conceptual transfer in simple insight-problems. *Memory and Cognition, 16*, 36–44.

LOEHLIN, J. C., LINDZEY, G., & SPUHLER, J. N. (1975). *Race differences in intelligence*. San Francisco: Freeman.

LOFTUS, E., & KETCHAM, K. (1994). *The myth of repressed memory*. New York: St. Martin's Press.

LOFTUS, E. F. (1979). *Eyewitness testimony*. Cambridge, MA: Harvard University Press.

LOFTUS, E. F. (1980). *Memory*. Menlo Park, CA: Addison-Wesley.

LOFTUS, E. F. (1982). Remembering recent experiences. In L. S. Cermak (Ed.), *Human memory and amnesia*. Hillsdale, NJ: Erlbaum.

LOFTUS, E. F. (1986). Two years in the life of an expert witness. *Law and Human Behavior, 10*, 241–263.

LOFTUS, E. F. (1993). The reality of repressed memories. *American Psychologist, 48*, 518–537.

LOFTUS, E. F., & HOFFMAN, H. G. (1989). Misinformation and memory: The creation of new memories. *Journal of Experimental Psychology: General, 118*, 100–104.

LOFTUS, E. F., & KLINGER, M. R. (1992). Is the unconscious smart or dumb? *American Psychologist, 47*, 761–765.

LOFTUS, G. R., & LOFTUS, E. F. (1974). The influence of one memory retrieval on a subsequent memory retrieval. *Memory and Cognition, 2*, 467–471.

LOFTUS, E. F., & LOFTUS, G. R. (1980). On the permanence of stored information in the human brain. *American Psychologist, 35*, 49–72.

LOFTUS, E. F., MILLER, D. G., & BURNS, H. J. (1978). Semantic integration of verbal information into visual memory. *Journal of Experimental Psychology: Human Learning and Memory, 4*, 19–31.

LOFTUS, E. F., & PALMER, J. C. (1974). Reconstruction of automobile destruction: An example of the interaction between language and memory. *Journal of Verbal Learning and Verbal Behavior, 13*, 585–589.

LOMO, T. (1966). Frequency potentiation of excitatory synaptic activity in the dentate area of the hippocampal formation. *Acta Physiologica Scandinavica, 68*(Suppl. 227), 128.

LOMO, T. (1971). Patterns of activation in a monosynaptic cortical pathway: The perforant path input to the dentate area of the hippocampal formation. *Experimental Brain Research, 12*, 18–45.

LONGSTRETH, L. E. (1984). Jensen's reaction-time investigations of intelligence: A critique. *Intelligence, 8*, 139–160.

LOPEZ, A. (1995). The diversity principle in the testing of arguments. *Memory and Cognition, 23*, 374–382.

LORAYNE, H., & LUCAS, J. (1974). *The memory book*. New York: Ballantine.

LORCH, R. F. (1978). The role of two types of semantic information in the processing of false sentences. *Journal of Verbal Learning and Verbal Behavior, 17*, 523–537.

LORCH, R. F., & LORCH, E. P. (1985). Topic structure representation and text recall. *Journal of Educational Psychology, 77*, 137–148.

LOURENCO, O., & MACHADO, A. (1996). In defense of Piaget's theory: A reply to 10 common criticisms. *Psychological Review, 103*, 143–164.

LU, S. T., HAMALAINEN, M. S., HARI, R., ILMONIEMI, R. J., LOUMASMAA, O. V., SAMS, M., & VILKMAN, V. (1991). Seeing faces activates three separate areas outside the occipital visual cortex in man. *Neuroscience, 43*, 287–290.

LUCHINS, A. S. (1942). Mechanization in problem solving. *Psychological Monographs, 54* (6, Whole No. 248).

LUCHINS, A. S., & LUCHINS, E. H. (1950). New experimental attempts at preventing mechanization in problem solving. *Journal of General Psychology, 42*, 279–297.

LUNG, C., & DOMINOWSKI, R. L. (1985). Effects of strategy instructions and practice time on nine dot problem solving. *Journal of Experimental Psychology: Learning, Memory, and Cognition, 11*, 804–811.

LURIA, A. R. (1968). *The mind of mnemonist*. New York: Basic Books.

LURIA, A. R. (1973). *The working brain: An introduction to neuropsychology*. New York: Basic Books.

LURIA, A. R. (1976). *Cognitive development: Its cultural and social foundations* (M. Cole, Ed., M. Lopez-Morillas & L. Solotaroff, Trans.). Cambridge, MA: Harvard University Press.

LYNCH, G., & BAUDRY, M. (1991). Reevaluating the constraints on hypotheses regarding LTP expression. *Hippocampus, 1*, 9–14.

LYNCH, G., LARSON, J., KELSO, S., BARRIONEUEVO, G., & SCHOTTLER, F. (1984). Intracellular injections of EGTA block induction of long-term potentiation. *Nature, 305*, 719–721.

LYNCH, G., MULLER, D., SEUBERT, P., & LARSON, J. (1988). Long-term potentiation: Persisting problems and recent results. *Brain Research Bulletin, 21*, 363–372.

MACCOBY, E. E., & JACKLIN, C. N. (1974). *The psychology of sex differences*. Stanford, CA: Stanford University Press.

MACDONALD, M. C., PEARLMUTTER, N. J., & SEIDENBERG, M. S. (1994). Lexical nature of syntactic ambiguity resolution. *Psychological Review, 101*, 676–703.

MACKINNON, D. W. (1962). The nature and nurture of creative talent. *American Psychologist, 17*, 484–495.

MACKINTOSH, J. J. (1986). The biology of intelligence? *British Journal of Psychology, 77*, 1–18.

MACKINTOSH, N. J., & MASCIE-TAYLOR, C. G. N. (1985). The IQ question in *Report of Committee of Inquiry into the Education of Children from Ethnic Minority Groups*, pp. 126–163. London: Her Majesty's Stationery Office.

MACLEOD, C. M., & BASSILI, J. N. (1989). Are implicit and explicit tests differentially sensitive to item-specific vs. relational information? In S. Lewandowsky, J. C. Dunn, & K. Kirsner (Eds.), *Implicit memory: Theoretical issues* (pp. 159–172). Hillsdale, NJ: Erlbaum.

MACNAMARA, J. (1972). Cognitive basis of language learning in infants. *Psychological Review, 79*, 1–13.

MACWHINNEY, B., LEINBACH, J., TARABAN, R., & McDONALD J. (1989). Language learning: Cues or rules? *Journal of Memory and Language, 28*, 255–277.

MADDIESON, I. (1984). *Patterns of sounds*. New York: Cambridge University Press.

MADIGAN, S., & ROUSE, M. (1974). Picture memory and the visual-generation process. *American Journal of Psychology, 87*, 151–158.

MAIER, N. R. F. (1930). Reasoning in humans I: On direction. *Journal of Comparative Psychology, 10*, 115–143.

MAIER, N. R. F. (1931). Reasoning in humans II: The solution of a problem and its appearance in consciousness. *Journal of Comparative Psychology, 12*, 181–194.

MAINE DE BIRAN. (1929). *The influence of habit on the faculty of thinking*. Baltimore: Williams and Wilkins.

MAKI, R. (1989). Recognition of added and deleted details in scripts. *Memory and Cognition, 17*, 274–282.

MANDEL, R. G., & JOHNSON, N. S. (1984). A developmental analysis of story recall and comprehension. *Journal of Verbal Learning and Verbal Behavior, 23*, 643–659.

MANDLER, G. (1979). Organization and repetition: Organizational principle with special reference to rote learning. In L. G. Nelson (Ed.), *Perspectives on memory research: Essays in honor of Uppsala University's 500th Anniversary*. Hillsdale, NJ: Earlbaum.

MANDLER, J. M. (1978). A code in the node: The use of a story schema in retrieval. *Discourse Processes, 1*, 14–35.

MANGELSDORF, S., GUNNAR, M., KESTENBAUM, R., LANG, S., & ANDREAS, D. (1990). Infant proneness to distress temperament, maternal personality, and mother–infant attachment, association and goodness of fit. *Child Development, 61*, 820–831.

MANSFIELD, R. S., & BUSSE, T. V. (1981). *The psychology of creativity and discovery*. Chicago: Nelson-Hall.

MANSFIELD, R. S., BUSSE, T. V., & KREPELKA, E. J. (1978). The effectiveness of creativity training. *Review of Educational Research, 48*, 517–536.

MARCUS, G. F. (1996). Why do children say "breaked"? *Current Directions in Psychological Science, 5*, 81–85.

MARKMAN, E. M. (1992). Constraints on word learning: Speculation about their nature, origins and domain specificity. In M. R. Gunnar & M. P. Moratsos (Eds.), *Minnesota Symposia on Child Psychology*, (Vol. 25). Hillsdale, NJ: Erlbaum.

MARKMAN, E. M., & WACHTEL, G. R. (1988). Children's use of mutual exclusivity to constrain the memory of words. *Cognitive Psychology, 20*, 121–157.

MARKOVITS, H., & NANTEL, G. (1989). The belief-bias in the production and evaluation of logical conclusions. *Memory and Cognition, 17*, 11–17.

MARKRAM, H., & SEGAL, M. (1990). Acetylcholine potentiates responses to V-methyl-D-ospartate in the rate hippocampus. *Neuroscience Letters, 113*, 62–65.

MARKUS, G. B. (1986). Stability and change in political attitudes: Observe, recall, and "explain." *Political Behavior, 8*, 21–44.

MARLER, P. (1991). The instinct to learn. In S. Carey & R. Gelman (Eds.), *The epigenesis of mind: Essays on biological cognition*. Hillsdale, NJ: Erlbaum.

MARR, D. (1982). *Vision: A computational investigation into the human representation and processing of visual information*. San Francisco: Freeman.

MARSHALL, J. C., & HALLIGAN, P. W. (1988). Blindsight and insight in visio-spatial neglect. *Nature, 336*, 766–767.

MARTIN, L. (1986). Eskimo words for snow: A case study on the genesis and decay of an anthropological example. *American Anthropologist, 88*, 418–423.

MARTINDALE, C. (1991). *Cognitive psychology: A neural network approach*. Pacific Grove, CA: Brooks/Cole.

MASSON, M. E. J. (1989). Fluent reprocessing as an implicit expression of memory for experience. In S. Lewandowsky, J. C. Dunn, & K. Kirsner (Eds.), *Implicit memory: Theoretical issues* (pp. 123–138). Hillsdale, NJ: Erlbaum.

MASSON, M. E. J. (1995). A distributed model of semantic priming. *Journal of Experimental Psychology: Learning, Memory, and Cognition, 21*, 3–23.

MATLIN, M. W. (1994). *Cognition*. Orlando, FL: Holt, Rinehart and Winston.

MAY, B., MOODY, D. B., & STEBBINS, W. C. (1989). Categorical perception of unspecific communication sounds by Japanese macaques, *Macaca Juscata. Journal of the Acoustical Society of America, 85*, 837–846.

MAYBERRY, R. I. (1993). First-language acquisition after childhood differs from second-language acquisition: The case of American sign language. *Journal of Speech and Hearing Research, 36*, 1258–1270.

MAYER, R. E. (1980). Elaboration techniques that increase the meaningfulness of technical text: An experimental test of the learning strategy hypothesis. *Journal of Educational Psychology, 72*, 770–784.

MAYER, R. E. (1987). *Educational psychology: A cognitive approach*. Boston: Little, Brown.

MAYER, R. E. (1989). Human nonadversary problem solving. In K. J. Gilhooly (Ed.), *Human and machine problem solving*. New York: Plenum.

MAYER, R. E. (1992). *Thinking, problem solving, cognition*. New York: Freeman.

MAYER, R. E., & BROMAGE, B. D. (1980). Different recall protocols for technical tests due to advance organizers. *Journal of Educational Psychology, 72*, 209–225.

MAYER, R. E., & GALLINI, J. (1990). When is an illustration worth ten thousand words? *Journal of Educational Psychology, 82*, 715–726.

MAYER, R. E., & SIMS, V. K. (1994). For whom is a picture worth a thousand words? Extensions of a dual-code theory of multimedia learning. *Journal of Educational Psychology, 86*, 389–401.

MCARTHUR, L. Z., & BERRY, D. S. (1987). Cross-cultural agreement in perceptions of baby-faced adults. *Journal of Cross-cultural Research, 18*, 165–192.

MCCLELLAND, D. C. (1973). Testing for competence rather than for "intelligence." *American Psychologist, 28*, 1–14.

MCCLELLAND, J. L., & RUMELHART, D. E. (1981). An interactive activation model of context effects in letter perception, part 1: An account of basic findings. *Psychological Review, 88*, 375–407.

MCCLELLAND, J. L., & RUMELHART, D. E. (1985). Distributed memory and the representation of general and specific information. *Journal of Experimental Psychology: General, 114*, 159–188.

MCCLELLAND, J. L., & RUMELHART, D. E. (1986b). Amnesia and distributed memory. In J. L. McClelland & D. E. Rumelhart (Eds.), *Parallel distributed processing* (Vol. 2). Cambridge, MA: Bradford/MIT Press.

MCCLELLAND, J. L., & RUMELHART, D. E. (1986a). *Parallel distributed processing: Exploration in the microstructure of cognition, Vol. 2. Psychological and biological models*. Cambridge, MA: Bradford/MIT press.

MCCLOSKEY, M. (1983). Naive theories of motion. In D. Gentner & A. L. Stevens (Eds.), *Mental models*. Hillsdale, NJ: Erlbaum.

MCCLOSKEY, M., & GLUCKSBERG, S. (1979). Decision processes in verifying category membership statements: Implications for models of semantic memory. *Cognitive Psychology, 11*, 1–37.

MCCLOSKEY, M., WIBLE, C. G., & COHEN, N. J. (1988). Is there a special flashbulb-memory mechanism? *Journal of Experimental Psychology: General, 117*, 171–181.

MCCLOSKEY, M., & ZARAGOZA, M. (1985). Misleading postevent information and memory for events: Arguments and evidence against memory impairment hypotheses. *Journal of Experimental Psychology: General, 114*, 1–16.

MCDERMID, C. D. (1965). Some correlates of creativity in engineering personnel. *Journal of Applied Psychology, 49*, 14–19.

MCDONALD, S. (1993). Viewing the brain sideways? Frontal versus hemisphere explanations of monophasic language disorders. *Aphasiology, 7*, 535–549.

MCDONOUGH, L., & MANDLER, J. M. (1989). Immediate and deferred imitations with 11-month-olds. A comparison between familiar and novel action. Poster presented at the meeting of the Society for Research in Child Development, Kansas City, MO.

MCDOUGALL, R. (1904). Recognition and recall. *Journal of Philosophical and Scientific Methods, 1*, 229–233.

McGeoch, J. A. (1942). *The psychology of human learning.* New York: Longmans, Green.

McGrath, M. J., & Cohen, D. B. (1978). REM sleep facilitation of adaptive working behavior: A review of the literature. *Psychological Bulletin, 85,* 24–57.

McGurk H., & MacDonald, J. (1976). Hearing lips and seeing voices. *Nature, 264,* 746–748.

McKeithen, K. B., Reitman, J. S., Rueter, H. H., & Hirtle, S. C. (1981). Knowledge organization and skill differences in computer programmers. *Cognitive Psychology, 13,* 307–325.

McNaughton, B. L. (1989). Neural mechanisms for spatial computation and information storage. In L. Nadel, L. Cooper, P. Culicover, & R. M. Harnish (Eds.), *Neural connections, mental computation.* Cambridge, MA: MIT Press.

McNaughton, B. L., & Nadel, L. (1990). Hebb-Marr networks and the neurobiological representation of action in space. In M. Gluck & D. Rumelhart (Eds.), *Neuroscience and connectionist theory* (pp. 1–63). Hillsdale, NJ: Erlbaum.

McNeil, B. J., Pauker, S. J., Sox, H. C., Jr., & Tversky, A. (1982). On the elicitation of references for alternative therapies. *New England Journal of Medicine, 306,* 1259–1262.

McNeill, D. (1987). *Psycholinguistics: A new approach.* New York: Harper & Row.

Mednick, S. A. (1962). The associative basis of the creative process. *Psychological Review, 69,* 220–232.

Medin, D. L., Goldstone, R. L., & Gentner, D. (1993). Respects for similarity. *Psychological Review, 100,* 254–278.

Medin, D. L., & Schaffer, M. M. (1978). Context theory of classification learning. *Psychological Review, 85,* 207–238.

Medin, D. L., & Shoben, E. J. (1988). Context and structure in conceptual combination. *Cognitive Psychology, 20,* 158–190.

Mellers, B. A., & Cooke, A. D. J. (1996). The role of task and context in preference measurement. *Psychological Science, 7,* 76–82.

Melton, A. W., & Irwin, J. M. (1940). The influence of degree of interpolated learning on retroactive inhibitions and the overt transfer of specific responses. *Journal of Experimental Psychology, 53,* 173–203.

Mendelsohn, G. A. (1976). Associative and attentional processes in creative performance. *Journal of Personality, 44,* 341–369.

Menzies, R. (1936). The comparative memory value of pleasant, unpleasant, and indifferent experiences. *Journal of Experimental Psychology, 18,* 267–297.

Merrill, R. (1954). The effect of pre-experimental and experimental anxiety on recall efficiency. *Journal of Experimental Psychology, 48,* 167–172.

Mervis, C. B., Catlin, J., and Rosch, E. (1976). Relationships among goodness-of-example, category norms, and word frequency. *Bulletin of the Psychonomic Society, 7,* 283–284.

Metcalfe, J. (1986). Premonitions of insight predict impending error. *Journal of Experimental Psychology: Learning, Memory, and Cognition, 12,* 623–634.

Metcalfe, J., & Wiebe, D. (1987). Intuition in insight and noninsight problem solving. *Memory and Cognition, 15,* 238–246.

Meyer, D. E., & Schvaneveldt, R. W. (1971). Facilitation in recognizing pairs of words: Evidence of a dependence between retrieval operations. *Journal of Experimental Psychology, 90,* 227–235.

Miller, G. A. (1956). The magical number seven, plus or minus two: Some limits on our capacity to process information. *Psychological Review, 63,* 81–97.

Miller, J. D., Wier, C. C., Postore, R., Kelly, W. J., & Dooling, R. J. (1976). Discrimination and labeling of noise-buzz sequences with varying noise-lead times: An example of categorical perception. *Journal of the Acoustical Society of America, 60,* 410–417.

Miller, J. L. (1990). Speech perception. In D. N. Osherson & H. Lasnik (Eds.), *Language* (pp. 69–93). Cambridge, MA: MIT Press.

MILLER, K. F., SMITH, C. M., ZHU, J., & ZHANG, H. (1995). Preschool origins of cross-national differences in mathematical competence: The role of number-naming systems. *Psychological Science, 6,* 56–60.

MILLER, L. B., & BIZZELL, R. P. (1984). Long-term effects of four preschool programs: Ninth- and tenth-grade results. *Child Development, 55,* 1570–1587.

MILLER-JONES, D. (1989). Culture and testing. *American Psychologist, 44,* 360–366.

MILLIS, K. K., GRAESSER, A. C., & HABERLANDT, K. (1993). The impact of connectives on the memory for expository text. *Applied Cognitive Psychology, 7,* 317–339.

MILNER, B. (1962). Les troubles de la memoire accompagnant des lesions hippocampiques bilaterales. In *Physiologie de l'hippocamper* (pp. 257–272). Paris: Centre National de la Recherche Scientifique.

MILNER, B. (1970). Memory and the temporal regions of the brain. In K. H. Pribram & D. E. Broadbent (Eds.), *Biology of memory.* New York: Academic Press.

MILNER, B., CORKIN, S., & TEUBER, H. L. (1968). Further analysis of the hippocampal amnesic syndrome: 14-year follow-up study of H. M. *Neuropsychologia, 6,* 215–234.

MISHKIN, M., & APPENZELLER, T. (1987, June). The anatomy of memory. *Scientific American,* 80–89.

MITCHELL, D. B. (1989). How many memory systems: Evidence from aging. *Journal of Experimental Psychology: Learning, Memory, and Cognition, 15,* 31–49.

MITROFF, I. I. (1974). *The subjective side of science.* Amsterdam: Elsevier.

MIURA, I. T., KIM, C. C., CHANG, C. M., & OKAMOTO, Y. (1988). Effects of language characteristics on children's cognitive representation of number: Cross-national comparisons. *Child Development, 59,* 1445–1450.

MOAR, I., & BOWER, G. H. (1983). Inconsistency in spatial knowledge. *Memory and Cognition, 11,* 107–113.

MODGIL, S., & MODGIL, C. (1982). *Jean Piaget: Consensus and controversy.* London: Holt, Rinehart and Winston.

MOFFITT, A., KRAMER, M., & HOFFMAN, R. (1993). *The functions of dreaming.* Albany, NY: State University of New York Press.

MORAY, N. (1959). Attention in dichotic listening: Affective cues and the influence of instructions. *Quarterly Journal of Experimental Psychology, 11,* 56–60.

MORGAN, J. L., BONAMO, K. M., & TRAVIS, L. L. (1995). Negative evidence on negative evidence. *Developmental Psychology, 31,* 180–197.

MORRIS, C. D., BRANSFORD, J. D., & FRANKS, J. J. (1977). Levels of processing versus transfer appropriate processing. *Journal of Verbal Learning and Verbal Behavior, 16,* 519–534.

MORRIS, P. (1988). Memory research: past mistakes and future prospects. In G. Claxton (Ed.), *Growth points in cognition.* London: Routledge.

MORRIS, R. G. M., ANDERSON, E., LYNCH, G., & BAUDRY, M. (1986). Selective impairment of learning and blockade of long-term potentiation by N-methyl-D-aspartate receptor antagonist, AP5. *Nature, 319,* 774–776.

MOSS, H. E., OSTRIN, R. K., TYLER, L. K., & MARSLEN-WILSON, W. D. (1995). Accessing different types of lexical semantic information: Evidence from priming. *Journal of Experimental Psychology: Learning, Memory and Cognition, 21,* 863–883.

MUKHAMETOV, L. (1988). The absence of paradoxical sleep in dolphins. In W. P. Koella, F. Obal, H. Schulz, & P. I. Visser (Eds.), *Sleep '86* (pp. 154–156). Stuttgart and New York: Gustav Fischer Verlag.

MUMAW, R. J., PELLEGRINO, J. W., KAIL, R. V., & CARTER, P. (1984). Different slopes for different folks: Process analysis of spatial aptitude. *Memory and Cognition, 12,* 515–521.

MURDOCK, B. B., JR. (1962). The serial position effect of free recall. *Journal of Experimental Psychology, 64,* 482–488.

MURPHY, G. L., & MEDIN, D. L. (1985). The role of theories in conceptual coherence. *Psychological Review, 92,* 289–316.

MUSEN, G., & TREISMAN, A. (1990). Implicit and explicit memory for visual patterns. *Journal of Experimental Psychology: Learning, Memory, and Cognition, 16,* 127–137.

MYERS, L. B., & BREWIN, C. R. (1995). Repressive coping and the recall of emotional material. *Cognition and Emotion, 9*, 637–642.

MYNOTT, C. R., DOHERTY, M. E., & TWENEY, R. D. (1977). Confirmation bias in a simulated research environment: An experimental study of scientific inference. *Quarterly Journal of Experimental Psychology, 29*, 89–95.

MYNOTT, C. R., DOHERTY, M. E., & TWENEY, R. D. (1978). Consequences of confirmation and disconfirmation in simulated research environment. *Quarterly Journal of Experimental Psychology, 30*, 395–406.

NAGEL, T. (1974). What is it like to be a bat? *Philosophical Review, 83*, 435–450.

NASH, M. (1987). What, if anything, is regressed about hypnotic age regression? A review of the literature. *Psychological Bulletin, 102*, 42–52.

NATHAN, D. (1992, October). Cry incest. *Playboy* (pp. 84–88, 162–164).

NEALE, M. A., & NORTHCRAFT, G. B. (1986). Experts, amateurs and refrigerators: Comparing expert and amateur negotiators in a novel task. *Organizational Behavior and Human Decision Processes, 38*, 305–317.

NEEDHAM, D. R., & BEGG, I. M. (1991). Problem-oriented training promotes spontaneous analogical transfer: Memory-oriented training promotes memory for training. *Memory and Cognition, 19*, 557–543.

NEELY, J. H. (1977). Semantic priming and retrieval from lexical memory: Roles of inhibitiveless spreading activation and limited capacity attention. *Journal of Experimental Psychology: General, 106*, 1226–1254.

NEISER, U. (1984). Interpreting Harry Bahrick's discovery: What confers immunity against forgetting? *Journal of Experimental Psychology: General, 113*, 32–35.

NEISSER, U. (1964). Visual search. *Scientific American, 210*, 94–102.

NEISSER, U. (1967). *Cognitive psychology.* New York: Appleton-Century-Crofts.

NEISSER, U. (1978). Memory: What are the important questions? In M. M. Gruneberg, P. E. Morris, & R. N. Sykes (Eds.), *Practical aspects of memory* (pp. 3–24). London: Academic Press.

NEISSER, U. (1981). John Dean's memory: A case study. *Cognition, 9*, 1–22.

NEISSER, U., BOODOO, G., BOUCHARD, T. J., BOYKEN, A. W., BRODY, N., CECI, S. J., HALPERN, D. F., LOEHLIN, J. C., PERLOFF, R., STERNBERG, R. J., & URBIVA, S. (1996). Intelligence: Knowns and unknowns. *American Psychologist, 51*, 77–101.

NEISSER, U., & HARSCH, N. (1991). Phantom flashbulbs: False recognition of hearing the news about the *Challenger*. In E. Winnograd & U. Neisser (Eds.), *Flashbulb memories: Recalling the Challenger explosion and other disasters.* New York: Cambridge University Press.

NELSON, C. A. (1995). The ontogeny of human memory: A cognitive neuroscience perspective. *Developmental Psychology, 31*, 723–738.

NELSON, K. E., CARSKADDON, G., & BONVILLIAN, J. D. (1973). Syntax acquisition: Input of experimental variation in adult verbal interaction with the child. *Child Development, 44*, 497–504.

NELSON, T. O. (1988). Predictive accuracy of feeling of knowing across different criterion tasks and across different subject populations and individuals. In M. M. Gruneberg, P. E. Morris, & R. N. Sykes (Eds.), *Practical aspects of memory: Current research and issues* (Vol. 1, pp. 190–196). Chichester, England: Wiley.

NETTLEBECK, T., & LALLY, M. (1976). Inspection time and measured intelligence. *British Journal of Psychology, 67*, 17–22.

NEWCOMBE, N., & BANDURA, M. M. (1983). Effects of age at puberty on spatial ability in girls: A question of mechanism. *Developmental Psychology, 19*, 215–244.

NEWELL, A., & SIMON, H. A. (1972). *Human problem solving.* Upper Saddle River, NJ: Prentice-Hall.

NEWPORT, E. L. (1990). Maturational constraints on language learning. *Cognitive Science, 14*, 147–172.

NEWPORT, E. L., & ASHBROOK, E. F. (1977). The emergence of semantic relations in ASL. *Papers and Reports on Child Language Development, 13*, 16–21.

NEWPORT, E. L., GLEITMAN, H., & GLEITMAN, L. R. (1977). Mother, I'd rather do it myself: Some effects and non-effects of maternal speech style. In C. E. Snow & C. A. Ferguson (Eds.), *Talking to children: Language input and language acquisition* (pp. 109–149). Cambridge, England: Cambridge University Press.

NICKERSON, R. S. (1986). *Reflections on reasoning*. Hillsdale, NJ: Erlbaum.

NICKERSON, R. S., & ADAMS, M. J. (1979). Long-term memory for a common object. *Cognitive Psychology, 11,* 287–307.

NILSSON, L. G., LAW, J., & TULVING, E. (1988). Recognition failure of recallable unique names: Evidence for an empirical law of memory and learning. *Journal of Experimental Psychology: Learning, Memory, and Cognition, 14,* 266–277.

NISBETT, R. E., & BORGIDA, E. (1975). Attribution and the psychology of medication. *Journal of Personality and Social Psychology, 32,* 932–943.

NISBETT, R. E., & ROSS, L. (1980). *Human inference: Strategies and shortcomings of social judgment*. Englewood Cliffs, NJ: Prentice-Hall.

NISBETT, R. E., & WILSON, T. D. (1977). Telling more than we know: Verbal report on mental processes. *Psychological Review, 84,* 231–259.

NISBETT, R. E., FONG, G. T., LEHMAN, D. R., & CHENG, P. W. (1987). Teaching reasoning. *Science, 238,* 629–631.

NORMAN, D. A., RUMELHART, D. E., & the LNR Research Group (1975). *Explorations in cognition*. San Francisco: Freeman.

NORTHCRAFT, G. B., & NEALE, M. A. (1986). Opportunity costs and the framing of resource allocation decisions. *Organizational Behavior and Human Decision Processes, 37,* 348–356.

NOSOFSKY, R. M. (1991). Tests of an exemplar model for relating perceptual classification and recognition memory. *Journal of Experimental Psychology: Human Perception and Performance, 17,* 3–27.

NOVICK, L. R., & HMELO, C. E. (1994). Transferring symbolic representations across non-isomorphic problems. *Journal of Experimental Psychology: Learning, Memory, and Cognition, 20,* 1296–1321.

OAKLAND, T. (1983). Joint use of adaptive behavior and IQ to predict achievement. *Journal of Consulting and Clinical Psychology, 51,* 298–301.

OAKSFORD, M., & CHATER, N. (1994). A rational analysis of the selection task as optimal data selection. *Psychological Review, 101,* 608–631.

OGBU, J. U. (1978). *Minority education and caste: The American system in cross-cultural perspective*. New York: Academic Press.

OGBU, J. U. (1994). From cultural differences to differences in cultural frames of reference. In P. M. Creenfield & R. R. Cocking (Eds.), *Cross-cultural roots of minority child development* (pp. 365–391). Hillsdale, NJ: Erlbaum.

OLIO, K. A. (1989). Memory retrieval in the treatment of adult survivors of sexual abuse. *Transactional Analysis Journal, 19,* 93–94.

OLTON, D. S., & SAMUELSON, R. J. (1976). Remembrance of places past: Spatial memory in rats. *Journal of Experimental Psychology: Animal Behavior Process, 2,* 97–116.

OMANSON, R. C. (1982). The relation between centrality and story category variation. *Journal of Verbal Learning and Verbal Behavior, 21,* 326–337.

OSHERSON, D. N., SMITH, E. E., WILKIE, O., LOPEZ, A., & SHAFIR, E. (1990). Category-based induction. *Psychological Review, 97,* 185–200.

OWENS, A. M., DOWNES, J. J., SAHAKIAN, B. U., POLKEY, C. E., & ROBBINS, T. W. (1990). Planning and spatial working memory following frontal lobe lesions in man. *Neuropsychologia, 28,* 1021–1034.

PAIVIO, A. (1971). *Imagery and verbal processes*. New York: Holt, Rinehart and Winston.

PALMER, C. F., JONES, R. K., HENNESSY, B. L., UNZE, M. G., & PICK, A. D. (1989). How is a trumpet known? The "basic object level" concept and the perception of musical instruments. *American Journal of Psychology, 102,* 17–37.

PALMER, S. E. (1975). The effects of contextual scenes on the identification of objects. *Memory and Cognition, 3,* 519–526.

PARKIN, A. J. (1984). Levels of processing, context, and facilitation of pronunciation. *Acta Psychologica, 55,* 19–29.

PARKS, R. W., LOEWENSTEIN, D. A., DODRILL, K. L., BARKER, W. W., YOSHI, F., CHANG, J. Y., EMRAN, A., APICELLA, A., SHERAMATA, W. A., & DUARA, R. (1988). Cerebral metabolic effects of a verbal fluency test: A PET scan study. *Journal of Clinical and Experimental Neuropsychology, 10,* 565–575.

PARRY, H., & CROSSLEY, H. (1950). Validity of responses to survey questions. *Public Opinion Quarterly, 14,* 61–80.

PASCUAL-LEONE, J. (1970). A mathematical model for the transition rule in Piaget's developmental stage. *Acta Psychologica, 32,* 301–345.

PATEL, V., & GROEN, G. J. (1986). Knowledge based solution strategies in medical reasoning. *Cognitive Science, 10,* 91–116.

PAUL, K., & DITTRICHORIA, J. (1975). Sleep patterns following learning in infants. In P. Levin & W. D. Koella (Eds.), *Sleep, 1974.* Basel, Switzerland: Kager.

PAVLIDES, C., & WINSON, J. (1989). Influences of hippocampal place cell firing in the awake state on the activity of these cells during subsequent sleep episodes. *Journal of Neuroscience, 9,* 2907–2918.

PAVLOV, I. (1927). *Conditioned reflexes.* Oxford, England: Oxford University Press.

PEA, R. D. (1983). LOGO programming and problem solving. In *Proceedings of the American Educational Research Association Conference.* Montreal.

PELLEGRINO, J. W., & GLASER, R. (1979). Cognitive correlates and components in the analysis of individual differences. *Intelligence, 3,* 187–214.

PENFIELD, W. W. (1969). Consciousness, memory, and man's conditioned reflexes. In K. Pribram. (Ed.), *On the biology of learning.* New York: Harcourt, Brace and World.

PENFIELD, W. W., & JASPER, H. (1954). *Epilepsy and the functional anatomy of the human brain.* Boston: Little, Brown.

PENFIELD, W. W. & PEROT, P. (1963). The brain's record of auditory and visual experience. *Brain, 86,* 595–696.

PENN, N. (1964). Experimental improvements on an analogue of repression paradigm. *Psychological Record, 14,* 185–196.

PERFECT, T. J., WATSON, E. L., & WAGSTAFF, G. F. (1993). Accuracy of confidence ratings associated with general knowledge and eyewitness memory. *Journal of Applied Psychology, 78,* 144–147.

PERFETTO, G. A. (1983). Individual differences in verbal processes. In R. Dillon & R. Schmeck (Eds.), *Individual differences in cognition.* New York: Academic Press.

PERFETTO, G. A., BRANSFORD, J. D., & FRANKS, J. J. (1983). Constraints on access in a problem-solving context. *Memory and Cognition, 11,* 24–31.

PERFETTO, G. A., & LESGOLD, A. M. (1977). Discourse comprehension and sources of individual differences. In M. A. Just & P. A. Carpenter (Eds.), *Cognitive processes in comprehension* (pp. 141–183). Hillsdale, NJ: Erlbaum.

PERKINS, D. N. (1988). Creativity and the quest for mechanism. In R. J. Sternberg & E. E. Smith (Eds.), *The psychology of human thought.* Cambridge, England: Cambridge University Press.

PERNER, J. J., LEEKMAN, R., & WIMMER, H. (1987). Three-year-olds' difficulty with false belief: The case for a conceptual shift. *British Journal of Developmental Psychology, 5,* 125–137.

PETERSON, L. R., & PETERSON, M. J. (1959). Short-term retention of individual verbal items. *Journal of Experimental Psychology, 58,* 193–198.

PETTY, R. E., CACIOPPO, J. T., & GOLDMAN, R. (1981). Personal involvement as a determinant of argument-based persuasion. *Journal of Personality and Social Psychology, 41,* 847–855.

PETTY, R. E., & CACIOPPO, J. T. (1984). The effects of involvement or response to argument quantity and quality: Central and peripheral routes to persuasion. *Journal of Personality and Social Psychology, 46,* 69–81.

PETTY, R. E., & CACIOPPO, J. T. (1986). The elaboration likelihood model of persuasion. In L. Berkowitz (Ed.), *Advances in experimental social psychology* (Vol. 19, pp. 123–205). San Diego, CA: Academic Press.

PEZDEK, K., MAKI, R., VALENCEA-LOVER, D., WHETSTONE, T., STOECKERT, J., & DOUGHERTY, T. (1988). Picture memory: Recognizing added and deleted details. *Journal of Experimental Psychology: Learning, Memory and Cognition, 14,* 468–476.

PHILLIPS, J. L. (1969). *The origins of the intellect: Piaget's theory.* San Francisco: Freeman.

PIAGET, J. (1926a). *Judgment and recovery in the child* (M. Warden, Trans.). New York: Harcourt, Brace and World.

PIAGET, J. (1926b). *The language and thought of the child.* New York: Harcourt, Brace, Jovanovich.

PIAGET, J. (1952). *The origins of intelligence in children* (M. Cook, Trans.). New York: International University Press.

PIAGET, J. (1962). *Play, dreams, and imitation in childhood.* New York: Norton.

PIAGET, J. (1970). Piaget's theory. In Vol. 1 of P. H. Mussen (Ed.), *Carmichael's manual of child psychology.* New York: Wiley.

PIAGET, J. (1971). The theory of stages in cognitive development. In D. R. Green, M. P. Ford, & G. B. Flower (Eds.), *Measurement and Piaget* (pp. 1–11). New York: McGraw-Hill.

PIAGET, J. (1972). Intellectual evolution from adolescence to adulthood. *Human Development, 15,* 1–12.

PIAGET, J. (1976). *The grasp of consciousness.* Cambridge, MA: Harvard University Press.

PIAGET, J., & INHELDER, B. (1956). *The child's concept of space* (F. J. Langdon & J. L. Lanzer, Trans.). London: Routledge-Kegan Paul.

PIAGET, J., & INHELDER, B. (1958). *The growth of cognitive thinking from childhood to adolescence* (A. Parsons & S. Seagren, Trans.). New York: Basic Books.

PIAGET, J., & INHELDER, B. (1964). *The early arousal of logic in the child.* (E. A. Lunzer & D. Papert, Trans.). London: Routledge-Kegan Paul.

PIERCE, K. A., DUNCAN, M. K., GHOLSON, B., RAY, G. E., & KAMHI A. G. (1993). Cognitive load, schema acquisition and procedural adaptation in nonisomorphic analogical transfer. *Journal of Educational Psychology, 85,* 66–74.

PILLEMER, D. B. (1984). Flashbulb memories of the assassination attempt on President Reagan. *Cognition, 16,* 63–80.

PINKER, S. (1984). *Language learnability and language development.* Cambridge, MA: Harvard University Press.

PINKER, S. (1990). Language acquisition. In D. N. Osherson & H. Tasnik (Eds.), *Language.* Cambridge, MA: MIT Press.

PINKER, S. (1994). *The language instinct.* New York: Morrow.

PINKER, S., & PRINCE, A. (1988). On language and connectionism: Analysis of a parallel distributed processing model of language acquisition. *Cognition, 28,* 73–193.

PITTENGER, J. B., & SHAW, R. E. (1975). Aging faces as viscal-elastic events: Implications for a theory of nonrigid shape perception. *Journal of Experimental Psychology: Human Perception and Performance, 1,* 374–382.

POINCARÉ, H. (1913). Mathematical creation. In *The foundations of science* (G. H. Halstead, Trans.). New York: Science Press.

POIZNER, H., KLIMA, E. S., & BELLUGI, U. (1987). *What the hands reveal about the brain.* Cambridge, MA: MIT Press.

POLITZER, G. (1991). Comparison of deductive abilities across language. *Journal of Cross-Cultural Psychology, 22,* 389–402.

POLLACK, I., & PICKETT, J. M. (1963). The intelligibility of excerpts from conversation. *Language and Speech, 6,* 165–171.

POLLARD, P. (1982). Human reasoning: Some possible effects of availability. *Cognition, 12,* 65–96.

POLYA, G. (1957). *How to solve it.* Garden City, NY: Doubleday/Anchor.

POMERANTZ, J. R., & KUBOVY, M. (1986). Theoretical approaches to perceptive organization. In K. R. Boff, L. Kaufman, & J. P. Thomas (Eds.), *Handbook of perception and human performance* (pp. 36.1–34.36). New York: Wiley.

POPPER, K., & ECCLES, J. C. (1977). *The self and its brain.* New York: Springer-Verlag.

PORTELL, I. G., MARTI, N., SEGURA, I. P., & MORGADO, B. T. (1989). Correlations between paradoxical sleep and shuttle box conditioning in rats. *Behavioral Neuroscience, 103,* 984–990.

POSNER, M. I., & CARR, T. H. (1992). Lexical access and the brain: Anatomical constraints on cognitive models of word recognition. *American Journal of Psychology, 105,* 1–26.

POSNER, M. I., & KEELE, S. W. (1968). On the genesis of abstract ideas. *Journal of Experimental Psychology, 77,* 353–363.

POSNER, M. I., & KEELE, S. W. (1970). Retention of abstract ideas. *Journal of Experimental of Psychology, 83,* 304–308.

POSNER, M. I., & SNYDER, C. R. R. (1975). Facilitation and inhibition in the processing of signals. In P. M. A. Rabitt & S. Dormec (Eds.), *Attention and performance* (Vol. 5). New York: Academic Press.

POSNER, M. I., & WARREN, R. E. (1972). Traces, concepts, and conscious constructions. In A. W. Melton & T. E. Martin (Eds.), *Coding processes in human memory.* Washington, DC: Winston.

POSTMAN, L., & PHILLIPS, L. (1965). Short-term temporal changes in free recall. *Quarterly Journal of Experimental Psychology, 17,* 132–138.

POSTMAN, L., STARK, K., & FRASER, J. (1968). Temporal changes in interference. *Journal of Verbal Learning and Verbal Behavior, 7,* 672–694.

PREDEBON, J., & DOCKER, S. B. (1992). Free-throw shooting performance as a function of preshot routines. *Perceptual and Motor Skills, 75,* 167–171.

PRESSLEY, M., & BREWSTER, M. E. (1990). Cognitive elaboration of illustrations to facilitate acquisition of facts: Memories of Prince Edward School. *Applied Cognitive Psychology, 4,* 359–369.

PRESSLEY, M., & VAN METER, P. (1994). What is memory development the development of? In P. E. Morris & M. Cruneberg (Eds.), *Theoretical aspects of memory* (pp. 79–129). London: Routledge.

PRINZ, W. (1992). Why don't we perceive our brain states? *European Journal of Cognitive Psychology, 4,* 1–20.

PRINZMETAL, W. (1995). Visual feature integration in a world of objects. *Current Directions in Psychological Science, 4,* 90–94.

PUTNAM, B. (1979). Hypnosis and distortions in eyewitness memory. *International Journal of Clinical and Experimental Hypnosis, 27,* 437–448.

PUTNAM, H. (1975). The meaning of "meaning." In H. Putnam (Ed.), *Mind, language, and reality: Philosophical papers* (Vol. 2, pp. 215–271). New York: Cambridge University Press.

PYLYSHYN, Z. W. (1973). What the mind's eye tells the mind's brain: A critique of mental imaging. *Psychological Bulletin, 8,* 1–14.

PYNOOS, R. S., & NADER, K. (1989). Children's memory and proximity to violence. *Journal of the American Academy of Child Adolescent Psychiatry, 28,* 236–241.

QUINE, W. V. O. (1977). Natural kinds. In S. P. Schwartz (Ed.), *Naming, necessity, and natural kinds* (pp. 155–175). Ithca, NY: Cornell University Press.

RAAHEIM, K. C. (1965). Problem solving and past experience. In P. H. Mussen (Ed.), *European research in cognitive development. Monograph Supplement of the Society for Research on Child Development, 30,* No. 2.

RAAIJMAKERS, J. G. W., & SHIFFRIN, R. M. (1981). Search of associative memory. *Psychological Review, 88,* 93–134.

RAAIJMAKERS, J. G. W., & SHIFFRIN, R. M. (1992). Models for recall and recognition. *Annual Review of Psychology, 43,* 205–234.

RADVANSKY, G. A., & ZACKS, R. T. (1991). Mental models and the fan effect. *Journal of Experimental Psychology: Learning, Memory, and Cognition, 17,* 940–953.

RAMEY, C. T., CAMPBELL, F. A., & FINKELSTEIN, N. W. (1984). Course and structure of intellectual development in children at risk for developmental retardation. In P. H. Brooks, R. Sperber, & C. McCauley (Eds.), *Learning and cognition in the mentally retarded.* Hillsdale, NJ: Erlbaum.

RATCLIFF, G. (1979). Spatial thought, mental rotation and the right cerebral hemisphere. *Neuropsychologia, 17,* 49–54.

RATCLIFF, G., & NEWCOMBE, F. (1973). Spatial orientation in man: Effects of left, right, and bilateral posterior cerebral lessions. *Journal of Neurology, Neurosurgery, and Psychiatry, 36,* 448–454.

RAYMOND, C. L., & BENBOW, C. P. (1986). Gender differences in mathematics: A function of parental support and student sex typing? *Developmental Psychology, 22,* 808–819.

RAYNER, K., CARLSON, M., & FRAZIER, L. (1983). The interaction of syntax and semantics during sentence processing: Eye movement in the analysis of semantically biased sentences. *Journal of Verbal Learning and Verbal Behavior, 22,* 358–374.

READ, J. D., TOLLESTRUP, P., HAMMERSLEY, R., McFADZEN, E., & CHRISTENSEN, A. (1990). The unconscious transference effect: Are innocent bystanders ever misidentified? *Applied Cognitive Psychology, 4,* 3–31.

REDER, L. M., & ROSS, B. H. (1983). Integrated knowledge in different tasks: The role of retrieval strategy on fan effects. *Journal of Experimental Psychology: Learning, Memory, and Cognition 9,* 55–72.

REED, S. F. (1987). A structural–swapping model for word problems. *Journal of Experimental Psychology: Learning, Memory, and Cognition, 13,* 124–139.

REED, S. F., DEMPSTER, A., & ETTINGER, M. (1985). Usefulness of analogous solutions for solving algebra word problems. *Journal of Experimental Psychology: Learning, Memory, and Cognition, 11,* 106–125.

REED, S. K. (1972). Pattern recognition and categorization. *Cognitive Psychology, 3,* 382–407.

REED, S. K., ERNST, G. W., & BANERJI, R. (1974). The role of analogy in transfer between similar problem states. *Cognitive Psychology, 6,* 436–450.

REED, T. E., & JENSEN, A. R. (1992). Conduction velocity in a brain nerve pathway of normal adults correlates with intelligence level. *Intelligence, 16,* 259–272.

REEVES, L. M., & WEISBERG, R. W. (1993). Abstract versus concrete information as the basis for transfer in problem solving. Comment on Fong and Nisbitt (1991). *Journal of Experimental Psychology: General, 122,* 125–128.

REEVES, L. M., & WEISBERG, R. W. (1994). The role of content and abstract information in analogical transfer. *Psychological Bulletin, 115,* 381–400.

REICH, P. A. (1986). *Language development.* Englewood Cliffs, NJ: Prentice-Hall.

REICHER, G. M. (1969). Perceptual recognition as a function of meaningfulness of stimulus material. *Journal of Experimental Psychology, 81,* 275–280.

REITMAN, W. (1964). Heuristic decision procedures, open constraints, and the structure of ill-defined problems. In W. Shelly & G. L. Bryan (Eds.), *Human Judgements and Optimality.* New York: Wiley.

RESNICK, S. M., BERENBAUM, S. A., GOTTESMAN, I. F., & BOUCHARD, T. J., JR. (1986). Early hormonal influence on cognitive functioning in congenital adrenal hyperplasia. *Developmental Psychology, 22,* 191–198.

RHODES, G., & TREMEWAN, T. (1996). Averageness, exaggeration, and facial attractiveness. *Psychological Science, 7,* 105–110.

RICHARDS, R., KINNEY, D. K., BENET, M., & MERZEL, A. P. C. (1988). Assessing everyday creativity characteristics of the lifetime creativity scales and validation with three large samples. *Journal of Personality and Social Psychology, 54,* 476–485.

RICHARDSON, K. (1991). *Understanding intelligence.* Philadelphia: Open University Press.

RICHARDSON-KLAVEHN, A., & BJORK, R. A. (1988). Measures of memory. *Annual Review of Psychology, 39,* 475–543.

RIEKER, P. P., & CARMEN, E. H. (1986). The victim-to-patient process: The disconfirmation and transportation of abuse. *American Journal of Orthopsychiatry, 56,* 360–370.

RIPS, L. J. (1983). Cognitive processes in propositional reasoning. *Psychological Review, 90,* 38–71.

RIPS, L. J. (1989). Similarity, typicality, and categorization. In S. Vosniadow & A. Ortony (Eds.), *Similarity and analogical reasoning* (pp. 21–59). Cambridge, England: Cambridge University Press.

RIPS, L. J., & MARCUS, S. L. (1977). Suppositions and the analysis of conditional sentences. In M. A. Just & D. A. Carpenter (Eds.), *Cognitive processes in comprehension*. Hillsdale, NJ: Erlbaum.

RIPS, L. J., SHOBEN, E. J., & SMITH, E. E. (1973). Semantic distance and the verification of semantic relationships. *Journal of Verbal Learning and Verbal Behavior, 12*, 1–20.

RIVERS, W. H. R. (1905). Observation on the senses of the Todas. *British Journal of Psychology, 1*, 321–396.

RIZZO, M., NAUROT, M., BLAKE, R., & DAMASIO, A. (1992). A human visual disorder resembling area V4 dysfunction in the monkey. *Neurology, 42*, 1175–1180.

ROBBINS, L. C. (1963). The accuracy of parental recall of aspects of child development and of child rearing practices. *Journal of Abnormal and Social Psychology, 66*, 261–270.

ROBERTS, R. J., HAGER, L. D., & HERON, C. (1994). Prefrontal cognitive processes: Working memory and inhibition in the antisaccade task. *Journal of Experimental Psychology: General, 123*, 374–393.

ROBERTSON, L. C. (1994). The multivariate nature of unilateral neglect. *Neuropsychological Rehabilitation, 4*, 199–202.

ROBINSON, G. S., JR., CROOKS, G. B., SHINKMAN, P. G., & GALLAGHER, M. (1989). Behavioral effects of MK-801 mimic deficits associated with hippocampal damage. *Psychobiology, 17*, 156–164.

ROBINSON, K. J. & ROEDIGER, H. L. (1997). Associative processes in false recall and false recognition. *Psychological Science, 8*, 231–237.

ROCK, I., HALL, S., & DAVIS, J. (1994). Why do ambiguous figures reverse? *Acta Psychologica, 87*, 33–57.

ROCK, I., & MITCHENER, K. (1992). Further evidence of failure of reversal of ambiguous figure by uninformed subjects. *Perception, 21*, 39–45.

ROCKEL, A. J. HIORNS, R. W., & POWELL, T. P. S. (1980). The basic uniformity in structure of the neocortex. *Brain, 103*, 221–244.

ROE, K. V., DRIVAS, A., KARAGELLIS, A., & ROE, A. (1985). Sex differences in vocal interaction with mother and stranger in Greek infants: Some cognitive implications. *Developmental Psychology, 21*, 372–377.

ROEDIGER, H. L. (1980). Memory metaphors in cognitive psychology. *Memory and Cognition, 8*, 231–246.

ROEDIGER, H. L., & McDERMOTT, K. B. (1995). Creating false memories: Remembering words not presented in lists. *Journal of Experimental Psychology: Learning, Memory, and Cognition, 21*, 803–814.

ROEDIGER, H. L., SRINIVAS, K., & WELDON, M. S. (1989). Dissociations between implicit measures of retention. In S. Lewandowsky, J. C. Dunn, & K. Kirsner (Eds.), *Implicit memory: Theoretical issues* (pp. 67–84). Hillsdale, NJ: Erlbaum.

ROGOFF, B., & MORELLI, G. (1989). Perspectives on children's development from cultural psychology. *American Psychologist, 44*, 343–348.

ROSCH, E. (1973). Natural categories. *Cognitive Psychology, 4*, 328–350.

ROSCH, E. (1975). Cognitive representations of natural categories. *Journal of Experimental Psychology: General, 104*, 192–233.

ROSCH, E. (1978). Principles of categorization. In E. Rosch & B. B. Lloyd (Eds.), *Cognition and categorization*. Hillsdale, NJ: Erlbaum.

ROSCH, E., & MERVIS, C. B. (1975). Family resemblances: Studies in the internal structure of categories. *Cognitive Psychology, 7*, 573–605.

ROSCH, E., MERVIS, C. B., GRAY, W. D., JOHNSON, D. M., & BOYES-BRAEM, P. (1976). Basic objects in natural categories. *Cognitive Psychology, 8*, 382–439.

ROSENBERG, C. R., & SEJNOWSKI, T. J. (1987). Parallel networks that learn to pronounce English text. *Complex Systems, 1*.

ROSENFIELD, I. (1988). *The invention of memory*. New York: Basic Books.

ROSS, B. H. (1984). Remindings and their effects on learning a cognitive skill. *Cognitive Psychology, 16*, 371–416.

Ross, B. H. (1987). This is like that: The use of earlier problems and the separation of similarity effects. *Journal of Experimental Psychology: Learning, Memory, and Cognition, 13,* 629–639.

Ross, D. F., Ceci, S. J., Dunning, D., & Toglia, M. P. (1994). Unconscious transference and mistaken identity: When a witness misidentifies a familiar but innocent person. *Journal of Applied Psychology, 79,* 918–930.

Ross, L., Lepper, M. R., & Hubbard, M. (1975). Perseverance in self perception and social perception: Biased attributional processes in the debriefing paradigm. *Journal of Personality and Social Psychology, 32,* 880–892.

Ross, M. (1989). Relation of implicit theories to the construction of personal histories. *Psychological Review, 96,* 341–357.

Rothbart, M., & Lewis, S. (1988). Inferring category attributes from exemplar attributes: Geometric shapes and social categories. *Journal of Personality and Social Psychology, 55,* 861–872.

Rothstein, M. G., Paunonen, S. V., Rush, J. C., & King, G. A. (1994). Personality and cognitive ability indicators of performance in graduate business school. *Journal of Educational Psychology, 86,* 516–530.

Rousseau, D. L. (1992). Case studies in pathological science. *American Scientist, 80,* 54–63.

Ruchalla, E., Schalt, E., & Vogel, F. (1985). Relations between mental performance and reaction time: New aspects of an old problem. *Intelligence, 9,* 189–205.

Rumelhart, D. E., Hinton, G. E., & Williams, R. J. (1986). Learning internal representation by error propagation. In D. E. Rumelhart & J. L. McClelland (Eds.), *Parallel distributed processing: Explorations in the microstructure of cognition* (Vol. 1, pp. 216–271). Cambridge, MA: MIT Press.

Rumelhart, D. E., & McClelland, J. L. (1986). *Parallel distributed processing: Explorations in the microstructure of cognition: Vol. 1. Foundations.* Cambridge, MA: MIT Press.

Rushton, J. P. (1988). Race differences in behaviour: A review and evolutionary analysis. *Personality and Individual Differences, 9,* 1009–1024.

Rushton, J. P. (1991). Do r-K strategies underlie human race differences? *Canadian Psychology, 32,* 29–42.

Ryan, R. H., & Geiselman, R. E. (1991). Effects of biased information on the relationship between eyewitness confidence and accuracy. *Bulletin of the Psychonomic Society, 29,* 7–9.

Rymer, R. (1993). *Genie: A scientific tragedy.* New York: Harper Perennial Scientific.

Sachs, J. D. S. (1967). Recognition memory for syntactic and semantic aspects of connected discourse. *Perception and Psychophysics, 2,* 437–442.

Sakitt, B. (1975). Laws of short-term visual storage. *Science, 190,* 395–403.

Saldana, H. M., & Rosenblum, L. D. (1993). Visual influences on auditory pluck and bow judgments. *Perception and Psychophysics, 54,* 406–416.

Samuel, A. G. (1981). Phonemic restorations: Insights from a new methodology. *Journal of Experimental Psychology: General, 10,* 474–494.

Samuel, A. G. (1987). Lexical uniqueness effects on phonemic restoration. *Journal of Memory and Language, 26,* 36–56.

Samuel, A. G. (1990). Using perceptual restoration to explore the architecture of perception. In G. T. M. Altman (Ed.), *Cognitive models of speed processing* (pp. 295–314). Cambridge: MIT Press.

Sanders, B., & Soares, M. P. (1986). Sexual maturation and spatial ability in college students. *Developmental Psychology, 22,* 199–203.

Saufley, W. H., Otaka, S. R., & Bavaresco, J. L. (1985). Context effects: Classroom tests and context independence. *Memory and Cognition, 13,* 522–528.

Saugstad, P., & Raaheim, K. (1960). Problem solving, past experience and availability of functions. *British Journal of Psychology, 51,* 97–104.

Saxe, G. B. (1988). Candy selling and math learning. *Educational Researcher, 17*(6), 14–21.

Scarr, S., Pakstis, A. J., Katz, S. H., & Barker, B. (1977). Absence of a relationship between degree of white ancestry and intellectual skills within a Black population. *Human Genetics, 39,* 69–86.

SCARR, S., & WEINBERG, R. A. (1976). IQ test performance of black children adopted by white families. *American Psychologist, 31*, 726–739.

SCARR, S., & WEINBERG, R. A. (1983). The Minnesota adoption studies: Genetic differences and malleability. *Child Development, 54*, 260–267.

SCARR-SALAPATEK, S. (1971). Race, social class, and IQ. *Science, 174*, 1285–1295.

SCHACTER, D. L. (1987). Implicit memory: History and current status. *Journal of Experimental Psychology: Learning, Memory, and Cognition, 13*, 501–518.

SCHACTER, D. L. (1990). Introduction to implicit memory: Multiple perspectives. *Bulletin of the Psychonomic Society, 28*, 338–340.

SCHACTER, D. L. (1996). *Searching for memory*. New York: Basic Books.

SCHACTER, D. L., CHURCH, B., & TREADWELL, J. (1994). Implicit memory in amnesic patients: Evidence for spared auditory priming. *Psychological Science, 5*, 20–25.

SCHACTER, D. L., & GRAF, P. (1986). Effects of elaborative processing on implicit and explicit memory for new associations. *Journal of Experimental Psychology: Learning, Memory, and Cognition, 12*, 432–444.

SCHACTER, D. L., & GRAF, P. (1989). Modality specificity of implicit memory for new associations. *Journal of Experimental Psychology: Learning, Memory, and Cognition, 15*, 3–12.

SCHACTER, D. L., McANDREWS, M. P., & MOSCOVITCH, M. (1988). Access to consciousness: Dissociations between implicit and explicit knowledge in neuropsychological syndromes. In L. Weishrantz (Ed.), *Thought without language* (pp. 242–278). Oxford, England: Oxford University Press.

SCHANK, R. C., & ABELSON, R. (1977). *Scripts, plans, goals, and understanding*. Hillsdale, NJ: Erlbaum.

SCHEERER, M. (1963). Problem solving. *Scientific American, 208*, 118–128.

SCHIEFFELIN, B., & EISENBERG, A. R. (1981). Cultural variation in children's conversation. In R. L. Shiefelbusch & D. D. Bricker (Eds.), *Early language: Acquisition and intervention*. Baltimore: University Park Press.

SCHMIDT, S. R. (1985). Encoding and retrieval processes in the memory for conceptually distinctive events. *Journal of Experimental Psychology: Learning, Memory, and Cognition, 11*, 565–578.

SCHMIDT, S. R. (1991). Can we have a distinctive theory of memory? *Memory and Cognition, 19*, 523–542.

SCHNEIDER, W. (1993). Varieties of working memory as seen in biology and in connections/control architectures. *Memory and Cognition, 21*, 184–192.

SCHNEIDER, W., KORKEL, J., & WEINERT, F. E. (1987, April). *The knowledge base and memory performance: A comparison of academically successful and unsuccessful learners*. Paper presented at the meeting of the American Educational Research Association, Washington, DC.

SCHNEIDER, W., & SHIFFRIN, R. M. (1977). Controlled and automatic human information processes: I. Detection, search, and attention. *Psychological Review, 84*, 1–66.

SCHOENFELD, A. H. (1985). *Mathematical problem solving*. Orlando, FL: Academic Press.

SCHOFIELD, N. J., & ASHMAN, A. F. (1986). The relationship between digit span and cognitive processing across ability groups. *Intelligence, 10*, 59–73.

SCHOOLER, J. W., & ENGSTLER-SCHOOLER, T. Y. (1990). Verbal overshadowing of visual memories: Some things are better left unsaid. *Cognitive Psychology, 22*, 36–71.

SCHWARTZ, M. F., SAFFRAN, E. M. & MARIN, O. S. M. (1980). The word order problem in agrammatism. *Brain and Language, 10*, 249–262.

SCOTT, J. (1969). Performance after abrupt arousal from sleep: Comparison of a simple motor task, a visual/perceptual task, and a cognitive task. *Proceedings, 77th Annual Convention, APA*, 225–226.

SCRIBNER, S. (1975). Recall of classical syllogisms: A cross-cultural investigation of error on logical problems. In R. J. Falmagne (Ed.), *Recovery: Representation and process* (pp. 153–174). Hillsdale, NJ: Erlbaum.

SCRIBNER, S. (1984). Studying working intelligence. In B. Rogoff & J. Lave (Eds.), *Everyday cognition: Its development in social context*. Cambridge, MA: Harvard University Press.

SEARLE, J. R. (1980). Minds, brains, and programs. *The Behavioral and Brain Sciences, 3,* 417–457.

SEARLE, J. R. (1990, January). Is the brain's mind a computer program? *Scientific American,* 26–31.

SEARLEMAN, A. & HERRMANN, D. (1994). *Memory from a broader perspective.* New York: McGraw-Hill.

SEASHORE, R. H., & ECKERSON, L. D. (1940). The measurement of individual differences in general English vocabularies. *Journal of Educational Psychology, 31,* 14–38.

SEGALL, M. H., CAMPBELL, D. T., & HERSKOVITS, J. (1966). *The influence of culture on visual perception.* Indianapolis: Bobbs Merrill.

SEIDENBERG, M. S., TANENHAUS, M. K., LEIMAN, J. L., & BIENKOWSKI, M. (1982). Automatic access of meanings of ambiguous words in context: Some limitations of knowledge-based processing. *Cognitive Psychology, 14,* 489–537.

SEKULER, R., & BLAKE, R. (1994). *Perception.* New York: McGraw-Hill.

SHALLICE, T. (1982). Specific impairment of planning. In D. E. Broadbent & L. Weiskrantz (Eds.), *The neuropsychology of cognitive function.* London: Royal Society.

SHARKEY, A. T. C., & SHARKEY, N. E. (1992). Weak contextual constraints in text and word priming. *Journal of Memory and Language, 31,* 543–572.

SHARKEY, N. E. (1990). A connectionist model of text comprehension. In G. M. Olson & E. E. Smith (Eds.), *Proceedings of the 11th Annual Conference of the Cognitive Science Society* (pp. 860–867). Hillsdale, NJ: Erlbaum.

SHATZ, M., WELLMAN, H. M., & SILBER, S. (1983). The acquisition of mental verbs: A systematic investigation of the first reference to mental state. *Cognitive Psychology, 14,* 301–321.

SHAW, R., & PITTENGER, J. (1977). Perceiving the face of change. In R. Shaw & J. Bransford (Eds.), *Perceiving, acting and knowing* (pp. 103–132). Hillsdale, NJ: Erlbaum.

SHAYWITZ, B. A., SHAYWITZ, S. E., PUGH, K. R., CONSTABLE, R. T., SKUDLARSKI, P., FULBRIGHT, R. K., BRONEN, R. A., FLETCHER, J. M., SHANKWELLER, D. P., KATZ, L., & GORE, J. C. (1995). Sex differences in the functional organization of the brain for language. *Nature, 373,* 607–609.

SHEA, J. D. (1985). Studies of cognitive development in Papua, New Guinea. *International Journal of Psychology, 20,* 33–51.

SHEPARD, R. N. (1967). Recognition memory for words, sentences and pictures. *Journal of Verbal Learning and Verbal Behavior, 6,* 156–163.

SHEPARD, R. N. (1984). Ecological constraints on internal representation: Resonant kinematics of perceiving, imagining, and dreaming. *Psychological Review, 91,* 417–447.

SHEPARD, R. N., & METZLER, J. (1971). Mental rotation of three-dimensional objects. *Science, 171,* 701–703.

SHIELDS, J. (1962). *Monoygotic twins brought up apart and brought up together.* London: Oxford University Press.

SHIFFRIN, R. M., & SCHNEIDER, W. (1977). Controlled and automatic human information processing II: Perceptual learning, automatic attending and general theory. *Psychological Review, 84,* 127–190.

SHIMAMURA, A. P., JANOWSKY, J. S., & SQUIRE, L. R. (1990). Memory for the temporal order of events with frontal lobe lesions and amnesic patients. *Neuropsychologia, 28,* 803–814.

SHIMAMURA, A. P., & SQUIRE, L. R. (1991). The relationship between fact and source memory: Findings from amnesic patients and normal subjects. *Psychobiology, 19,* 1–10.

SHORE, B. M., KOLLER, M., & DOVER, A. (1994). More from the water jars: A reanalysis of problem solving performance among gifted and nongifted children. *Gifted Child Quarterly, 38,* 179–183.

SHUTER-DYSON, R. (1982). Musical ability. In D. Deutsch (Ed.), *The psychology of music.* New York: Academic Press.

SIEGAL, M. (1991). *Knowing children.* Hillsdale, NJ: Erlbaum.

SIEGELBAUM, S. A., & KANDEL, E. R. (1991). Learning-related synoptic plasticity: LTP and LTD. *Current Opinion in Neurobiology, 1,* 113–120.

SIEGLER, R. S. (1978). The origins of scientific reason. In R. S. Siegler (Ed.), *Children thinking: What develops?* Hillsdale, NJ: Erlbaum.

SIEGLER, R. S. (1986). *Children's thinking*. Upper Saddle River, NJ: Prentice-Hall.

SIEGLER, R. S. (1989). Mechanism of cognitive development. *Annual Review of Psychology, 40*, 353–379.

SIEGLER, R. S., & ELLIS, S. (1996). Piaget on childhood. *Psychological Science, 7*, 211–215.

SIL'KIS, I. G., RAPOPORT, S. SH., VEBER, N. V., & GUSHCHIN, A. M. (1994). Neurobiology of the integrative activity in the brain: Some properties of long-term posttetanic heterosynaptic depression in the motor cortex of the cat. *Neuroscience and Behavioral Physiology, 24*, 500–506.

SILVEIRA, J. (1971). *Incubation: The effect of interruption timing and length on problem solving and quality of problem solving.* Doctoral dissertation, University of Oregon. Eugene, OR.

SILVERMAN, I., & EALS, M. (1992). Sex difference in spatial abilities. Evolutionary theory and data. In J. Barkow, L. Cosmides, & J. Tooby (Eds.), *The adapted mind: Evolutionary psychology and the generation of culture* (pp. 539–549). New York: Oxford University Press.

SIMON, H. A. (1981). *Sciences of the artificial*. Cambridge, MA: MIT Press.

SIMONS, D. J., & KEIL, F. C. (1995). An abstract to concrete shift in the development of biological thought: The inside story. *Cognition, 56*, 129–163.

SIMPSON, G. B. (1984). Lexical ambiguity and its role in models of word recognition. *Psychological Bulletin, 96*, 316–340.

SINCLAIR-DE-ZWART, H. (1973). Language acquisition and cognitive development. In T. Moore (Ed.), *Cognitive development and the acquisition of language*. New York: Academic Press.

SINGER, M., HALLDORSON, M., LEAR, J. C., & ANDRUSIAK, P. (1992). Validation of casual bridging inferences in discourse understanding. *Journal of Memory and Language, 31*, 507–524.

SINGLEY, M. K., & ANDERSON, J. R. (1989). *The transfer of cognitive skill*. Cambridge, MA: Harvard University Press.

SINHA, D. (1983). Human assessment in Indian context. In S. H. Irvine & J. W. Berry (Eds.), *Human assessment and cultural factors* (pp. 17–34). New York: Plenum.

SIREVAAG, A. M., & GREENOUGH, W. T. (1987). Differential rearing effects on rat visual cortex synapses. III. Neuronal and glial nuclei, boutons, dendrites, and capillaries. *Brain Research, 424*, 320–332.

SKEELS, H. M. (1966). Adult status of children with contrasting early life experiences. *Monographs of the Society for Research in Chikd Development, 31* (Serial No. 105).

SKINNER, B. F. (1957). *Verbal behavior*. New York: Appleton-Century-Crofts.

SKINNER, B. F. (1990). Can psychology be a science of mind? *American Psychologist, 45*, 1206–1210.

SLOBIN, D. I. (1979). *Psycholinguistics*. Glenview, IL: Scott, Foresman.

SLOMAN, S. A. (1996). The empirical case for two systems of reasoning. *Psychological Bulletin, 119*, 3–22.

SLOVIC, P. (1990). Choice. In D. N. Oskerson & E. E. Smith (Eds.), *Thinking: An invitation to cognitive science*. Cambridge, MA: MIT Press.

SLOVIC, P. (1995). The construction of reference. *American Psychologist, 50*, 364–371.

SMITH, A. D., & WINOGRAD, E. (1978). Adult age differences in remembering faces. *Developmental Psychology, 14*, 443–444.

SMITH, A. F., JOBE, J. B., & MINGAY, D. J. (1991). Retrieval from memory of dietary information. *Applied Cognitive Psychology, 5*, 269–296.

SMITH, C. (1993). REM sleep learning: Some recent findings. In A. Moffitt, M. Kramer, & R. Hoffman (Eds.), *The functions of dreaming* (pp. 341–362). Albany, NY: State University of New York Press.

SMITH, C. (1996). Sleep states, memory processes and synaptic plasticity. *Behavioural Brain Research, 78*, 49–56.

SMITH, C. B. (1984). Aging and changes in cerebral energy metabolism. *Trends in Neurosciences, 7,* 203–208.

SMITH, E. E. (1988). Concepts and thought. In R. J. S. Sternberg & E. E. Smith (Eds.), *The psychology of human thought.* Cambridge, England: Cambridge University Press.

SMITH, E. E., ADAMS, N., & SCHORR, D. (1978). Fact retrieval and the paradox of interference. *Cognitive Psychology, 10,* 438–464.

SMITH, E. E., BALZANO, G. J., & WALKER, J. H. (1978). Nominal, perceptual, and semantic codes in picture categorization. In J. W. Cotton & R. L. Klatzky (Eds.), *Semantic factors in cognition* (pp. 137–168). Hillsdale, NJ: Erlbaum.

SMITH, E. E., SHOBEN, E. J., & RIPS, L. J. (1974). Structure and process in semantic memory: A featural model for semantic decisions. *Psychological Review, 81,* 214–241.

SMITH, E. E., & SLOMAN, S. A. (1994). Similarity-versus rule-based categorization. *Memory and Cognition, 22,* 377–386.

SMITH, M. C., MACLEOD, C. M., BAIN, J. D., & HOPPE, R. B. (1989). Lexical decision as an indirect test of memory. *Journal of Experimental Psychology: Learning, Memory, and Cognition, 15,* 1109–1118.

SMITH, M. E. (1926). An investigation of the development of the sentence and the extent of vocabulary in young children. *University of Iowa Studies in Child Welfare, 3,* 5.

SMITH, S. (1988). Environmental context-dependent memory. In G. M. Davies & D. M. Thomson (Eds.), *Memory in context: Context in memory.* London: Wiley.

SMITH, S. M., & BLANKENSHIP, S. E. (1991). Incubation and the persistence of fixation in problem solving. *American Journal of Psychology, 104,* 61–87.

SMITH, V. L., KASSIN, S. M., & ELLSWORTH, P. C. (1989). Eyewitness accuracy and confidence: Within versus between-subjects correlations. *Journal of Applied Psychology, 74,* 356–359.

SNOW, C. E. (1981). Social interaction and language acquisition. In P. Dale & D. Ingram (Eds.), *Child language: An international perspective.* Baltimore: University Park Press.

SNOW, C. E. (1986). Conversation with children. In P. Fletcher & M. Garman (Eds.), *Language acquisition* (pp. 69–89). Cambridge, England: Cambridge University Press.

SNYDER, F. (1966). Toward an evolutionary theory of dreaming. *American Journal of Psychiatry, 123,* 121–136.

SNYDER, M., & URANOWITZ, S. W. (1978). Reconstructing the past: Some cognitive consequences of person perception. *Journal of Personality and Social Psychology, 36,* 941–950.

SNYDER, M., & WHITE, P. (1982). Moods and memories: Elation, depression and the remembering of the events of one's life. *Journal of Personality, 50,* 142–167.

SOLOMON, P., SOLOMON, S., VAN DE SCHAAF, E., & PERRY, H. (1983). Altered activity in the hippocampus is more detrimental to classical conditioning than removing the structure. *Science, 220,* 329–331.

SPANOS, N. P., MENARY, E., GABORA, N. J., DEBREUIL, S. C., & DEWHIRST, B. (1991). Secondary identity enactments during hypnotic post-life regression: A sociocognitive perspective. *Journal of Personality and Social Psychology, 61,* 308–320.

SPEARMAN, C. (1927). *The abilities of man.* New York: Macmillan.

SPELKE, E. (1988). Where perceiving ends and thinking begins: The apprehension of objects in infancy. In A. Yonos (Ed.), *Perceptual development in infancy: Minnesota Symposium in Child Psychology* (pp. 197–234). Hillsdale, NJ: Erlbaum.

SPELKE, E. S., PHILLIPS, A., & WOODWARD, A. L. (1995). Infants' knowledge of object motion and human action. In D. Sperber, D. Premack, & A. J. Premack (Eds.), *Causal cognition: A multidisciplinary debate.* Oxford, England: Oxford University Press.

SPERLING, G. (1960). The information available in brief visual presentations. *Psychological Monographs, 74,* 1–29.

SPERRY, R. W., ZAIDEL, E., & ZAIDEL, D. (1979). Self-recognition and social awareness in the disconnected minor hemisphere. *Neuropsychologist, 17,* 153–166.

SPIRO, R. J. (1977). Remembering information from text: The state of the schema approach. In R. C. Anderson, R. J. Spiro, & W. E. Monague (Eds.), *Schooling and the acquisition of knowledge.* Hillsdale, NJ: Erlbaum.

SPORER, S. L. (1991). Deep-deeper-deepest? Encoding strategies and the recognition of human faces. *Journal of Experimental Psychology: Learning, Memory, and Cognition, 17*, 323–333.

SPRINGER, S. P., & DEUTSCH, G. (1993). *Left brain, right brain*. New York: Freeman.

SQUIRE, L. R. (1987). *Memory and brain*. New York: Oxford University Press.

SQUIRE, L. R. (1992). Memory and the hippocampus: A synthesis from findings with rats, monkeys, and humans. *Psychological Review, 99*, 195–231.

SQUIRE, L. R., HAIST, F., & SHIMAMURA, A. P. (1989). The neurology of memory: Quantitative assessment of retrograde amnesia in two groups of amnesic patients. *Journal of Neuroscience, 9*, 828–839.

SQUIRE, L. R., SLATER, P. C., & CHACE, P. M. (1975). Retrograde amnesia: Temporal gradient in very long-term memory following electroconvulsive therapy. *Science, 187*, 77–79.

STANDENMAYER, H. (1975). Understanding conditional reasoning with meaningful propositions. In R. J. Falmagne (Ed.), *Reasoning: Representation and process in children and adults*. Hillsdale, NJ: Erlbaum.

STANDING, L. (1973). Learning 10,000 pictures. *Quarterly Journal of Experimental Psychology, 25*, 207–222.

STANDING, L., CONEZIO, J., & HABER, R. N. (1970). Perception and memory for pictures. Single trial learning of 2560 visual stimuli. *Psychonomic Science, 19*, 73–74.

STANTON, P. K., & SEJNOWSKI, T. J. (1989). Associative long-term depression in the hippocampus induced by Hebbian covariance. *Nature, 339*, 215–218.

STARKEY, P. (1992). The early development of mathematical reasoning. *Cognition, 43*, 93–126.

STARKEY, P., SPELKE, E. S., & GELMAN, R. (1990). Numerical abstraction by human infants. *Cognition, 36*, 97–127.

STAUBLI, U., THIBAULT, O., DiLORENZO, M., & LYNCH, G. (1989). Antagonism of NMDA receptors impairs acquisition but not retention of olfactory memory. *Behavioral Neuroscience, 103*, 54–60.

STEIN, B. S., & BRANSFORD, J. D. (1979). Constraints on effective elaboration: Effects of precision and subject generation. *Journal of Verbal Learning and Verbal Behavior, 18*, 769–777.

STEIN, B. S., LITTLEFIELD, J., BRANSFORD, J. D., & PERSAMPIERI, M. (1984). Elaboration and knowledge acquisition. *Memory and Cognition, 12*, 522–529.

STEINBERG, D. D. (1982). *Psycholinguistics: Language, mind and world*. New York: Longman.

STEPHENSON, G. M. (1984). Accuracy and confidence in testimony: A critical review and some fresh evidence. In D. J. Muller, D. E. Blackman, & A. J. Chapman (Eds.), *Psychology and law: topics from an international conference* (pp. 229–249). Chichester, England: Wiley.

STEPHENSON, G. M., CLARK, N. K., & WADE, G. S. (1986). Meetings make evidence? An experimental study of collaborative and individual recall of a simulated police interrogation. *Journal of Personality and Social Psychology, 50*, 1113–1122.

STERN, J. (1988). Pet attachment as a delayed mourning process. *Anthrozoos, 2*, 18–21.

STERN, L. (1985). *The structures and strategies of human memory*. Homewood, IL: Dorsey Press.

STERNBERG, R. J. (1985). *Beyond IQ: A triarchic theory of human intelligence*. Cambridge, MA: Cambridge University Press.

STERNBERG, R. J. (1990). *Metaphors of mind: Conceptions of the nature of intelligence*. Cambridge, England: Cambridge University Press.

STERNBERG, R. J., WAGNER, R. K., WILLIAMS, W. M., & HORVATH, J. A. (1995). Testing common sense. *American Psychologist, 50*, 912–927.

STERNBERG, R. J., AND WILLIAMS, W. M. (1997). Does the Graduate Record Exam predict meaningful success in the graduate training of psychologists? *American Psychologist, 52*, 630–641.

STERNBERG, S. (1966). High-speed scanning in human memory. *Science, 153*, 652–654.

STERNBERG, S. (1969). Memory scanning: Mental process revealed by reaction-time experiments. *American Scientist, 57*, 421–457.

STEVENS, A. & COUPE, P. (1978). Distortions: Unjudged spatial relations. *Cognitive Psychology, 10,* 422–437.

STEVENSON, H. W., STIGLER, J. W., LEE, S., LUCKER, G. W., KITAMURA, S., & HSU, C. (1985). Cognitive performance and academic achievement of Japanese, Chinese, and American children. *Child Development, 56,* 718–734.

STEWART, K. R. (1951). Dream theory in Malaya. *Complex, 6,* 21–33.

STEWART, V. (1973). Tests of the "carpentered world" by hypothesis of race and environment in America and Zambia. *International Journal of Psychology, 8,* 83–94.

STICH, S. P. (1985). Could man be an irrational animal? *Synthese, 64,* 115–135.

STICH, S. P. (1990). Rationality. In D. N. Osherson & E. E. Smith (Eds.), *Thinking* (pp. 173–196). Cambridge, MA: MIT Press.

STROMEYER, C. F. III, PSOTKA, J. (1970). The detailed texture of eidetic images. *Nature, 225,* 346–349.

STROUFE, L. A. (1979). The coherence of individual development. *American Psychologist, 34,* 834–841.

STROUFE, L. A. (1983). Infant caregiving attachment and patterns of adaptation in preschool: The roots of maladaptation and competence. In M. Perlmutter (Ed.), *Minnesota Symposium in Child Psychology, Vol. 16.*

STUSS, D. T., & BENSON, D. F. (1986). *The frontal lobes.* New York: Raven Press.

SULIN, R. A., & DOOLING, D. J. (1974). Intrusion of a thematic idea in retention of prose. *Journal of Experimental Psychology, 103,* 255–262.

SULLIVAN, K., & WINNER T. (1993). Three-year-olds' understanding of mental states: The influence of trickery. *Journal of Experimental Child Psychology, 56,* 135–148.

SUSULOWSKA, M. (1983). Interpretation of dreams of former prisoners of concentration camps. *Psychiatria Fennica, 1985 Supplement,* 149–154.

SVENKO, B., JERNEIC, A., & KULENOVIC, A. (1983). A contribution to the investigation of time-sharing ability. *Ergonomics, 26,* 151–160.

SWANN, W. B., JR. (1984). Quest for accuracy in person perception: A matter of pragmatics. *Psychological Review, 91,* 457–477.

SWINNEY, D. A. (1979). Lexical access during sentence comprehension: (Re)consideration of context effects. *Journal of Verbal Learning and Verbal Behavior, 18,* 645–659.

TAKANO, Y. (1989). Methodological problems in cross-cultural studies of linguistic relativity. *Cognition, 31,* 141–162.

TANAKA, J. W., & TAYLOR M. (1991). Object categories and expertise: Is the basic level in the eye of the beholder? *Cognitive Psychology, 23,* 457–482.

TANAKA, K. (1992). Inferotemporal cortex and high visual functions. *Current Opinion in Neurobiology, 2,* 502–505.

TATTERSALL, I. (1997, April). Out of Africa again . . . and again. *Scientific American, 276,* 60–67.

TAVRIS, C. (1992). *The mismeasure of woman: Why women are not the better sex, the inferior sex, or the opposite sex.* New York: Simon & Schuster.

TEASDALE, J. D., & FOGARTY, S. J. (1979). Differential effects of induced mood on retrieval of pleasant and unpleasant events from episodic memory. *Journal of Abnormal Psychology, 188,* 248–257.

TERRACE, H. S., PETITTO, L. A., SANDERS, R. J., & BEVER, T. G. (1979). Can an eye create a sentence? *Science, 206,* 891–902.

THATCHER, R. W. (1992). Cyclic cortical reorganization during early childhood. *Brain and Cognition, 20,* 24–50.

THOMPSON, C. P. (1985). Memory for unique personal events: Effects of pleasantness. *Motivation and Emotion, 9,* 277–289.

THOMPSON, C. P., COWAN, T., FREIMAN, J., MAHADEVAN, R. S., & VOGL, R. J. (1991). Rajan: A study of a memorist. *Journal of Memory and Language, 30,* 702–724.

THORNDIKE, E. L. (1924). Mental discipline in high schools. *Journal of Educational Psychology, 15,* 1–22.

THORNDIKE, E. L. (1936). Factor analysis of social and abstract intelligence. *Journal of Educational Psychology, 27,* 231–233.

THORNDYKE, P., & HAYES-ROTH, B. (1979). The use of schemata in the acquisition and transfer of knowledge. *Cognitive Psychology, 11*, 82–106.

THORNDYKE, P. W. (1976). The role of inferences in discourse comprehension. *Journal of Verbal Learning and Verbal Behavior, 15*, 437–446.

THURSTONE, L. L. (1938). *Primary mental abilities.* Chicago: University of Chicago Press, Psychometric Monographs, No. 1.

TILLEY, S. J., & EMPSON, J. A. C. (1978). REM sleep and memory consolidation. *Biological Psychology, 6*, 293–300.

TIZARD, B., COOPERMAN, O., JOSEPH, A., & TIZARD, J. (1972). Environmental effects on language development: A study of young children in long-stay residential nurseries. *Child Development, 43*, 337–358.

TORRANCE, E. P. (1972). Can we teach children to think creatively? *Journal of Creative Behavior, 6*, 114–143.

TRABASSO, T. R. (1977). The role of memory as a system in making transitive inferences. In R. Kail & J. Hagen (Eds.), *Perspectives on the development of memory and cognition* (pp. 333–366). Hillsdale, NJ: Erlbaum.

TREISMAN, A., & SCHMIDT, H. (1982). Illusory conjunctions in the perception of objects. *Cognitive Psychology, 14*, 107–141.

TREISMAN, A. M. (1988). Features and objects: The fourteenth Bartlett Memorial Lecture. *Quarterly Journal of Experimental Psychology, 40A*, 201–237.

TREISMAN, A. M., & GELADE, G. (1980). A feature-integration theory of attention. *Cognitive Psychology, 12*, 97–136.

TREISMAN, A. M., VIEIRA, A., & HAYES, A. (1992). Automaticity and preattentive processing. *American Journal of Psychology, 105*, 341–362.

TRICKETT, P. K., & PUTNAM, F. W. (1993). Impact of child sexual abuse on females: Toward a developmental, psychobiological integration. *Psychological Science, 4*, 81–87.

TULKIN, S. R., & KONNER, M. U. (1973). Alternative conceptions of intellectual functioning. *Human Development, 16*, 33–52.

TULVING, E. (1983). *Elements of episodic memory.* New York: Oxford University Press.

TULVING, E., SCHACTER, D. L., & STARK, H. A. (1982). Priming effects in word-fragment completion are independent of recognition memory. *Journal of Experimental Psychology: Learning, Memory, and Cognition, 8*, 336–342.

TULVING, E., & THOMSON, D. M. (1973). Encoding specificity and retrieval processes in episodic memory. *Psychological Review, 80*, 352–373.

TURNER, A. M., & GREENOUGH, W. T. (1985). Differential rearing effects on rat visual cortex synapses I. Synaptic and neural density and synapses per neuron. *Brain Research, 329*, 195–203.

TURVEY, M. T., SHAW, R. E., REED, E. S., & MACE, W. M. (1981). Ecological laws of perceiving and activity. In reply to Fodor and Pylyshyn (1981). *Cognition, 9*, 237–304.

TVERSKY, A., & KAHNEMAN, D. (1973). Availability: a heuristic for judging frequency and probability. *Cognitive Psychology, 5*, 207–232.

TVERSKY, A., & KAHNEMAN, D. (1980). Causal scheme in judgment under uncertainty. In M. Fishbein (Ed.), *Progress in social psychology* (Vol. 1, pp. 49–72). Hillsdale, NJ: Erlbaum.

TVERSKY, A., & KAHNEMAN, D. (1981). The framing of decisions and the psychology of choice. *Science, 211*, 453–458.

TVERSKY, A., & KAHNEMAN, D. (1983). Extensional versus intuitive reasoning: The conjunction fallacy in probability judgment. *Psychological Review, 90*, 292–315.

TVERSKY, B., & TUCHIN, M. (1989). A reconciliation of the evidence on eyewitness testimony: Comments on McCloskey and Zaragoza. *Journal of Experimental Psychology: General, 118*, 86–91.

ULLMAN, S. (1980). Against direct perception. *Behavioral and Brain Sciences, 3*, 373–415.

VANCOURT, M., & BEAN, F. D. (1985). Intelligence and fertility in the United States: 1912–1982. *Intelligence, 9*, 23–32.

VAN DE CASTLE, R. L. (1971). *The psychology of dreaming.* New York: General Learning Corporation.

VAN DER HEIJDEN, A. H. C. (1981). *Short-term visual forgetting.* London: Routledge and Kegan Paul.

VAN DER KOLK, B. A., BLITZ, R., BURR, W., SHERRY, S., & HARTMANN, E. (1984). Nighttime and trauma. A comparison of nightmares after combat with lifelong nightmares in veterans. *American Journal of Psychiatry, 141,* 187–190.

VAN GEERT, P. (1991). A dynamic systems model of cognitive and language growth. *Psychological Review, 98,* 3–53.

VERNON, P. A. (1983). Speed of information processing and general intelligence. *Intelligence, 7,* 53–70.

VERNON, P. A., & KANTOR, L. (1986). Reaction time correlates with intelligence test scores obtained under either timed and untimed conditions. *Intelligence, 10,* 315–330.

VERNON, P. A., & MORI, M. (1992). Intelligence, reaction times, and peripheral nerve conductor velocity. *Intelligence, 16,* 273–288.

VERTES, R. P. (1986). A life sustaining function for REM sleep: A theory. *Neuroscience and Biobehavioral Reviews, 10,* 371–376.

VON RESTORFF, H. (1933). Uber die Wirkung von Bereichsbildungen in Spurenfeld. *Psychologisch Forschung, 18,* 299–342.

VOSS, J. F., BLAIS, J., MEANS, M. L., GREENE, T. R., & AHWESH (1986). Informal reasoning and subject matter knowledge in the solving of economics problems by naive and novice individuals. *Cognition and Instruction, 3,* 269–302.

VOSS, J. F., GREENE, T. R., POST, T. A., & PENNER, B. C. (1983). Problem solving in the social sciences. In G. H. Bower (Ed.), *The psychology of learning and motivation: Advances in research theory* (Vol. 17, pp. 165–213). New York: Academic Press.

VOSS, J. F., TYLER, S. W., & YENGO, L. A. (1983). Individual differences in the solving of social science problems. In R. F. Dillon & R. R. Schmeck (Eds.), *Individual differences in cognition* (pp. 205–232). New York: Academic Press.

VOYER, D., VOYER, S., & BRYDEN, M. F. (1995). Magnitude of sex difference in spatial abilities: A meta-analysis and consideration of critical variables. *Psychological Bulletin, 117,* 250–270.

VYGOTSKY, L. S. (1978). *Mind in society: The development of higher psychological processes.* Cambridge, MA: Harvard University Press.

WABER, D. P., MANN, M. B., MEROLA, J., & MOYLAN, P. (1985). Physical maturation rate and cognitive performance in early adolescence: A longitudinal examination. *Developmental Psychology, 21,* 666–681.

WAGENAAR, W. A. (1986). My memory: A study of autobiographical memory over six years. *Cognitive Psychology, 18,* 225–252.

WAGNER, D. A. (1977). Ontogeny of the Ponzo illusion. Effects of age, schooling and environment. *International Journal of Psychology, 12,* 161–176.

WAGNER, R. K., & STERNBERG, R. J. (1985). Practical intelligence in real-world pursuits: The role of tacit knowledge. *Journal of Personality and Social Psychology, 49,* 436–458.

WAGNER, R. K., & STERNBERG, R. J. (1990). Streetsmarts. In K. E. Clark & M. B. Clark (Eds.), *Measures of leadership* (pp. 493–504). West Orange, NJ: Leadership Library of America.

WAGNER, R. K., TORGESEN, J. K., & RASHOTTE, C. A. (1994). Development of reading-related phonological processing abilities: New evidence of bidirectional causality from a latent variable longitudinal study. *Developmental Psychology, 30,* 73–87.

WAKEFIELD, H., & UNDERWAGER, R. (1992). Recovered memories of alleged sexual abuse: Lawsuits against parents. *Behavioral Sciences and the Law, 10,* 483–507.

WALKER, C. H. (1987). Relative importance of domain knowledge and overall aptitude on acquisition of domain-related information. *Cognition and Instruction, 4,* 25–42.

WALLACE, C. S., KILMAN, V. L., WITHERS, G. S., & GREENOUGH, W. T. (1992). Increases in dendritic length in occipital cortex after 4 days of differential housing in weanling rats. *Behavioral and Neural Biology, 58,* 64–68.

WALLACH, M. A. (1976). Tests tell us little about talent. *American Scientist, 64,* 57–63.

WANG, J., AIGNER, T., & MISHKIN, M. (1990). Effects of neostriatal lesions on visual habit formation in rhesus monkeys. *Society for Neuroscience Abstracts, 16,* 617.

WARD, T. B. (1994). Structured imagination: The role of category structure in exemplar generation. *Cognitive Psychology, 27*, 1–40.

WARREN, R. M. (1970). Perceptual restoration of missing speech sounds. *Science, 167*, 392–393.

WARRINGTON, E. F., & JAMES, M. (1988). Visual apperceptive agnosia: A clinico-anatomical study of three cases. *Cortex, 24*, 1–32.

WARRINGTON, E. K., & WEISKRANTZ, L. (1973). In J. A. Deutsch (Ed.), *The physiological basis of memory*. London: Academic Press.

WASON, P. C. (1960). On the failure to eliminate hypotheses in a conceptual task. *Quarterly Journal of Experimental Psychology, 12*, 129–140.

WASON, P., & JOHNSON-LAIRD, P. (1970). A conflict between selecting and evaluating information. *British Journal of Psychology, 61*, 509–515.

WASON, P. C. (1966). Reasoning. In B. M. Foss (Ed.), *New horizons in psychology* (pp. 135–151). Harmondsworth, England: Penguin.

WASON, P. C., & JOHNSON-LAIRD, P. N. (1972). *Psychology of reasoning*. Cambridge, MA: Harvard University Press.

WATERS, R., & LEEPER, R. (1936). The relation of affective tone to the retention of experience in everyday life. *Journal of Experimental Psychology, 19*, 203–215.

WATKINS, M. J. (1979). Engrams as cuegrams and forgetting as cue overload: A cueing approach to the structure of memory. In C. R. Puff (Ed.), *Memory organization and structure*. New York: Academic Press.

WATKINS, M. J., & TULVING, E. (1975). When recognition fails. *Journal of Experimental Psychology: General, 104*, 5–29.

WEBB, W. (1975). *Sleep: The gentle tyrant*. Upper Saddle River, NJ: Prentice-Hall.

WEBBER, S. M., & MARSHALL, P. H. (1978). Bizarreness effects in imagery as a function of processing level and delay. *Journal of Mental Imagery, 2*, 291–300.

WEBER, E. U., & MURDOCK, B. B. (1989). Priming in a distributed memory system. Implications for models of implicit memory. In S. Lewandowsky, J. C. Dunn, & K. Kirsner (Eds.), *Implicit memory: Theoretical issues* (pp. 87–98). Hillsdale, NJ: Erlbaum.

WEBER, R. J. (1993). *Forks, phonographs, and hot-air balloons: A field guide to inventive thinking*. New York: Oxford University Press.

WEGNER, D. M. (1994). Ironic processes of mental control. *Psychological Review, 101*, 34–52.

WEGNER, D. M., COULTON, G., & WENZLAFF, R. (1985). The transparency of denial: Briefing in the debriefing paradigm. *Journal of Personality and Social Psychology, 49*, 338–346.

WEILER, I. J., HAWRYLAK, N., & GREENOUGH, W. T. (1995). Morphogenesis in memory formation: Synaptic and cellular mechanisms. 69th Titisee Conference: The Neurobiology of Memory Formation in Vertebrates: Neuronal Plasticity and Brain Function. *Behavioral Brain Research, 66*, 1–6.

WEINBERGER, D. A., SCHWARTZ, G. E., & DAVIDSON R. L. (1979). Low-anxious, high-anxious, and repressive coping strategies: Psychometric patterns and behavioral and physiological responses to stress. *Journal of Abnormal Psychology, 88*, 369–380.

WEINER, L. J. (1988). Issues in sex therapy with survivors of intrafamily sexual abuse. *Women and Therapy, 7*, 253–264.

WEINGARDT, K. R., LOFTUS, E. F., & LINDSAY, D. S. (1995). Misinformation revisited: New evidence on the suggestibility of memory. *Memory and Cognition, 23*, 72–82.

WEISBERG, R. (1988). Problem solving and creativity. In R. J. Sternberg (Ed.), *The nature of creativity: Contemporary psychological perspectives* (pp. 220–238). Cambridge, England: Cambridge University Press.

WEISBERG, R., DICAMILLO, M., & PHILLIPS, D. (1978). Transferring old associations to new problems: A nonautomatic process. *Journal of Verbal Learning and Verbal Behavior, 17*, 219–228.

WEISBERG, R., & SULS, J. (1973). An information processing model of Duncker's candle problem. *Cognitive Psychology, 4*, 255–276.

WEISBERG, R. W. (1986). *Creativity: Genius and other myths*. New York: Freeman.

WEISKRANTZ, L. (1980). Varieties of residual experience. *Quarterly Journal of Experimental Psychology, 32,* 365–386.

WEISKRANTZ, L. (1986). *Blindsight: A case study and implications.* Oxford College Series, 12. Oxford, England: Oxford University Press.

WEISKRANTZ, L. (1990). Outlooks for blindsight: Explicit methodologies for complicit processes. *Proceedings of the Royal Society of London, 239,* 247–278.

WEISKRANTZ, L. (1995). Blindsight: Not an island unto itself. *Current Directions in Psychological Science, 4,* 146–151.

WELLMAN, H. M., & BARTSCH, K. (1988). Young children's reasoning about beliefs. *Cognition, 30,* 239–277.

WELLMAN, H. M., & ESTES, D. (1986). Early understanding of entities: A re-examination of childhood realism. *Child Development, 57,* 910–923.

WELLMAN, H. M., & GELMAN, S. A. (1992). Cognitive development: Foundational theories of core domains. *Annual Review of Psychology, 43,* 337–375.

WELLS, G. L., & MURRAY, D. M. (1984). Eyewitness confidence. In G. L. Wells & E. F. Loftus (Eds.), *Eyewitness testimony: Psychological perspectives* (pp. 155–170). New York: Cambridge University Press.

WERTHEIMER, M. (1923/1958). Principle of perceptual organization. In D. C. Beardslee & M. Wertheimer (Eds.), *Readings in perception* (pp. 115–135). Princeton, NJ: Von Nostrand.

WHALEY, C. P. (1978). Word–nonword classification time. *Journal of Verbal Learning and Verbal Behavior, 17,* 143–154.

WHEELER, D. D. (1970). Processes in word recognition. *Cognitive Psychology, 1,* 59–85.

WHITE, B. L. (1978). *Experience and environment: Major influences on the development of the young child* (Vol. 2). Englewood Cliffs, NJ: Prentice Hall.

WHITE, L. (1989). *Universal grammar and second language acquisition.* Philadelphia: Benjamins.

WHITE, R. T. (1982). Memory for personal events. *Human Learning, 1,* 171–183.

WHITE, R. T. (1989). Recall of autobiographical events. *Applied Cognitive Psychology, 3,* 127–135.

WHORF, B. L. (1956). *Language, thought, and reality.* Cambridge, MA: MIT Press.

WICKELGREN, W. A. (1972). Trace resistance and the decay of long-term memory. *Journal of Mathematical Psychology, 9,* 418–455.

WICKELGREN, W. A. (1975). Alcoholic intoxication and memory storage dynamics. *Memory and Cognition, 3,* 385–389.

WICKELGREN, W. A. (1977). *Learning and memory.* Englewood Cliffs, NJ: Prentice-Hall.

WICKENS, C. D. (1984). Processing resources in attention. In R. Parasurania & D. R. Davies (Eds.), *Varieties of attention.* Orlando, FL: Academic Press.

WILLIAMS, M. (1987). Reconstruction of an early seduction and its aftereffects. *Journal of the American Psychoanalytic Association, 15,* 145–163.

WIMMER, H., & PERNER, J. (1983). Beliefs about beliefs: Representation and constraint functions of wrong beliefs in young children's understanding of deception. *Cognition, 13,* 103–128.

WINNOGRAD, E. (1981). Elaboration and distinctiveness in memory for face. *Journal of Experimental Psychology: Human Learning and Memory, 7,* 181–190.

WINNOGRAD, T. (1976). Computer memories: A metaphor for memory organization. In C. N. Cofer (Ed.), *The structure of human memory.* San Francisco: Freeman.

WINSON, J. (1990). The meaning of dreams. *Scientific American, 263,* 86–96.

WINSTON, P. H. (1984). *Artificial intelligence.* Reading, MA: Addison-Wesley.

WISSLER, C. (1901). The correlation of mental and physical tests. *Psychological Review Monograph Supplements, 3*(6), Whole No. 16.

WITTGENSTEIN, L. (1953). *Philosophical investigations* (G. E. M. Anscombe, Trans.). New York: Macmillan.

WIXTED, J. T., & EBBESEN, E. B. (1991). On the form of forgetting. *Psychological Science, 2,* 409–415.

WOLF, S., & LATANE, B. (1983). Majority and minority influence on restaurant preference. *Journal of Personality and Social Psychology, 45*, 282–292.

WONG, G. M. T., DAY, J. D., MAXWELL, S. E., & MEARA, N. M. (1995). A multitrait-multimethod study of academic and social intelligence in college students. *Journal of Educational Psychology, 87*, 117–133.

WOOD, N., & COWAN, N. (1995). The cocktail party phenomenon revisited: How frequent are attention shifts to one's name in an irrelevant auditory channel? *Journal of Experimental Psychology: Learning, Memory, and Cognition, 21*, 255–260.

WOODROW, H. (1939). The common factors in fifty-two mental tests. *Psychometrika, 4*, 99–108.

WRIGHT, L. (1994). *Remembering Satan*. New York: Knopf.

WYNN, K. (1995). Infants possess a system of numerical knowledge. *Current Directions in Psychological Science, 6*, 172–177.

YAKOVLEV, P. I., & LECOURS, A. R. (1967). The myelenogentic cycle of regional maturation of the brain. In A. Minkowski (Ed.), *Regional development of the brain in early life*. Oxford, England: Blackwell.

YAMADA, J. (1990). *Laura: A case for the modularity of language*. Cambridge, MA: MIT Press.

YEKOVICH, F. R., WALKER, C. H., OGLE, L. T., & THOMPSON, M. A. (1990). The influence of domain knowledge on inferencing in low-aptitude individuals. *The Psychology of Learning and Motivation, 25*, 259–278.

YENI-KOMSHIAN, G. H. (1993). Speech perception. In J. B. Gleason & N. B. Ratner (Eds.), *Psycholinguistics* (pp. 89–131). New York: Harcourt Brace Jovanovich.

YENI-KOMSHIAN, G. H., & LAFONTAINE, L. (1983). Discrimination and identification of voicing and close contrast in aphasic patients. *Canadian Journal of Psychology, 37*, 107–131.

YONG, L. M. S. (1994). Relations between creativity and intelligence among Malaysian pupils. *Perceptual and Motor Skills, 79*, 739–742.

YOUNG, S. L., FANSELOW, M. S., & BOHENEK, D. L. (1992). The dorsal hippocampus and contextual fear conditioning. *Society for Neuroscience Abstract, 18*, 1564.

YUILLE, J. C., & CUTSHALL, J. C. (1986). A case study of eyewitness memory of a crime. *Journal of Applied Psychology, 71*, 291–301.

ZARAGOZA, M. S., & LANE, S. M. (1994). Source misattributions and the suggestibility of eyewitness memory. *Journal of Experimental Psychology: Learning, Memory, and Cognition, 20*, 934–945.

ZARAGOZA, M. S., & MITCHELL, K. J. (1996). Repeated exposure to suggestion and the creation of false memories. *Psychological Science, 7*, 294–300.

ZEKI, S., WATSON, J. D. G., LUECK, C. J., FRISTON, K., KENNARD, C., & FRACKOWIAK, R. S. J. (1991). A direct demonstration of functional specialization in human visual cortex. *Journal of Neuroscience, 11*, 641–649.

ZELLER, A. (1950). An experimental analogue of repression: 11. The effect of individual failure and success on memory measured by relearning. *Journal of Experimental Psychology, 40*, 411–422.

ZIEGLER, S. G. (1987). Comparison of imagery styles and past experience in skills performance. *Perceptual and Motion Skills, 64*, 579–586.

ZIHL, J., TRETTER, F., & SINGER, W. (1980). Phasic electrodermal responses after visual stimulation in the cortically blind hemifield. *Behavioral Brain Research, 1*, 197–203.

ZIHL, J., VON CRAMON, D., & MAI, N. (1983). Selective disturbance of movement vision after bilateral brain damage. *Brain, 106*, 313–340.

ZOHAR, A. (1994). Teaching a thinking strategy: Transfer across domains and self-learning versus class-like setting. *Applied Cognitive Psychology, 8*, 549–563.

ZOHAR, A., WEINBERGER, Y., & TAMIR, P. (1994). Developing critical thinking: A useful and promising instructional strategy for promoting in depth science learning. *Journal of Research in Science Teaching, 3*, 183–196.

ZUBIN, J., & BARRERA, S. E. (1941). Effect of electric convulsive therapy on memory. *Proceedings of Society for Experimental Biology and Medicine, 48*, 596–597.

Author Index

Subject Index